Michele Dillon

INTRODUCTION TO SOCIOLOGICAL THEORY

Theorists, Concepts, and their
Applicability to the Twenty-First Century

WILEY-BLACKWELL
A John Wiley & Sons, Ltd., Publication

This edition first published 2010
© 2010 Michele Dillon

Blackwell Publishing was acquired by John Wiley & Sons in February 2007. Blackwell's publishing program has been merged with Wiley's global Scientific, Technical, and Medical business to form Wiley-Blackwell.

Registered Office
John Wiley & Sons Ltd, The Atrium, Southern Gate, Chichester, West Sussex, PO19 8SQ, United Kingdom

Editorial Offices
350 Main Street, Malden, MA 02148-5020, USA
9600 Garsington Road, Oxford, OX4 2DQ, UK
The Atrium, Southern Gate, Chichester, West Sussex, PO19 8SQ, UK

For details of our global editorial offices, for customer services, and for information about how to apply for permission to reuse the copyright material in this book please see our website at www.wiley.com/wiley-blackwell.

The right of Michele Dillon to be identified as the author of this work has been asserted in accordance with the Copyright, Designs and Patents Act 1988.

Wiley also publishes its books in a variety of electronic formats. Some content that appears in print may not be available in electronic books.

Designations used by companies to distinguish their products are often claimed as trademarks. All brand names and product names used in this book are trade names, service marks, trademarks or registered trademarks of their respective owners. The publisher is not associated with any product or vendor mentioned in this book. This publication is designed to provide accurate and authoritative information in regard to the subject matter covered. It is sold on the understanding that the publisher is not engaged in rendering professional services. If professional advice or other expert assistance is required, the services of a competent professional should be sought.

Library of Congress Cataloging-in-Publication Data

Dillon, Michele, 1960–
    Introduction to sociological theory : theorists, concepts, and their applicability to the twenty-first century / Michele Dillon.
        p.   cm.
    Includes bibliographical references and index.
    ISBN 978-1-4051-7002-4 (pbk. : alk. paper)
    1. Sociology. 2. Sociology–History. I. Title.
    HM585.D55 2010
    301–dc22
                                                                            2009004217

A catalogue record for this book is available from the British Library.

Set in 10/13pt Sabon by SPi Publisher Services, Pondicherry, India
Printed and bound in Singapore by Markono Print Media Pte Ltd

05   2012

Dedicated to the memory of my parents
Peg (O'Farrell) Dillon, 1920–2009, and Michael Dillon, 1917–2003

Remembering the past inspires confidence in the future

CONTENTS

BOXED FEATURES

ACKNOWLEDGMENTS

I am very grateful to Justin Vaughan at Wiley-Blackwell for persuading me to write this book and for his support throughout the process. I also appreciate the editorial production assistance of Barbara Duke and Ben Thatcher, and Fiona Sewell's careful copyediting. Claire Cameron was very helpful, especially her editorial suggestions and her efficient organization and collation of chapter reviews. I greatly appreciate the efforts of several reviewers whose close reading of various chapters provided detailed comments that helped make the book stronger. I am especially appreciative of the hard work of those reviewers who read a full draft of the book. I also benefited from the assistance of graduate assistants at the University of New Hampshire, including Diana Dumais, Catherine Seabury, Megan Henly, Michelle Stransky, Karen Schreiner, Jennifer Esala, and Genevieve Cox.

translated by W. D. Halls. Edited with an introduction by Steven Lukes. Copyright © 1982 by Steven Lukes. Copyright © 1982 by Macmillan Press, Ltd. All rights reserved. Emile Durkheim, *The Rules of Sociological Method*, translated by W. D. Halls. Edited with an introduction by Steven Lukes. Copyright © 1982 by Steven Lukes. Copyright © 1982 by Macmillan Press, Ltd. Reproduced with permission of Palgrave Macmillan.

Quotations in chapter 3 from: WEBER, MAX, PROTESTANT ETHIC & THE SPIRIT OF CAPITALISM, 1st Edition, ©1977, Pgs. 35, 53–54, 107, 115, 117, 119, 154, 158–159, 166–167, 181. Reprinted by permission of Pearson Education, Inc., Upper Saddle River, NJ. Max Weber, *Economy and Society*, 1978. By permission of the University of California Press. "From Max Weber: Essays in Sociology" by Max Weber edited by H. H. Gerth and C. W. Mills (1946). By permission of Oxford University Press, Inc.

Quotations in chapter 4 reprinted with the permission of The Free Press, a Division of Simon & Schuster, Inc., from ESSAYS IN SOCIOLOGICAL THEORY by Talcott Parsons. Copyright © 1949, 1954 by The Free Press. Copyright © renewed 1977 by Talcott Parsons and 1982 by Helen W. Parsons. All rights reserved.

Quotations in chapter 5 from: Max Horkheiner and Theodor Adorno/Gunzelin Schmid Noerr. *Dialectic of Enlightenment* translated by Edmun Jephcott. Copyright © 1944 by Social Studies Association, NY. New edition: © S. Fisher Verlag GmbH, Frankfurt am Main, 1969; English trans. © 2002 Board of Trustees of Leland Stanford Jr. University. All rights reserved. Used with the permission of Stanford University Press, www.sup.org. *One-Dimensional Man* by Herbert Marcuse. Copyright 1964 by Herbert Marcuse. Reprinted by permission of Beacon Press, Boston.

Quotations in chapter 9 from GARFINKEL, STUDIES IN ETHNOMETHODO-LOGY, 1st Edition, © 1967, Pgs. vii–viii, 105–106, 119–121, 167, 285. Reprinted by permission of Pearson Education, Inc., Upper Saddle River, NJ.

Quotations in chapter 10 from: Patricia Hill Collins, *Black Feminist Thought: Knowledge, Consciousness, and the Politics of Empowerment*. 1990. Copyright 1991 by Routledge, Chapman and Hall, Inc. By permission of the rightsholder. Arlie Hochschild, *The Managed Heart: Commercialization of Human Feeling*. Twentieth Anniversary Edition, With a New Afterword. By permission of the University of California Press. Dorothy Smith, *The Conceptual Practices of Power: A Feminist Sociology of Knowledge*, 1990. Northeastern University Press. Copyright 1990 by Dorothy E. Smith. © University Press of New England, Hanover, NH. Reprinted with permission. Dorothy Smith, *The Conceptual Practices of Power: A Feminist Sociology of Knowledge*, 1990. Northeastern University Press. Copyright 1990 by Dorothy E. Smith. University of Toronto Press Inc. Reprinted with permission of the publisher.

Quotations in chapter 11 from *The History of Sexuality* by Michel Foucault. Originally published in French as *La Volonté du Savoir*. Copyright © 1976 by Editions Gallimard. Reprinted by permission of Georges Borchardt, Inc., for Editions Gallimard.

Quotations in chapter 13 from DISTINCTION: A SOCIAL CRITIQUE OF THE JUDGMENT OF TASTE by Pierre Bourdieu, translated by Richard Nice, pp. 12, 23, 53–57, 77, 81, 105, 114, 133, 190–196, 202, 241, 250, 373–375, Cambridge, Mass: Harvard University Press, Copyright © 1984 by the President and Fellow of Harvard College and Routledge and Kegan Paul, Ltd; and *Distinction: A Social Critique of the Judgment of Taste*, Pierre Bourdieu, Copyright © 1984 Harvard University Press. Reproduced by permission of Taylor and Francis Books UK.

Quotations in chapter 15 reprinted from *The Modern World System I*, Immanuel Wallerstein, Copyright © 1974. By permission of Immanuel Wallerstein, and Elsevier.

The information in the timelines is derived from various sources including: Colin McEvedy (1985), *The Macmillan World History Factfinder*, New York: Macmillan; H. E. L. Mellersh (1999), *Chronology of World History*, Volumes 1–4, Santa Barbara, CA: BC-CLIO; Derrick Mercer, ed. (1996), *Chronicle of the World*, London: Dorling Kindersley; Hans-Albrecht Schraepler (1997), *Directory of International Economic Organizations*, Washington, DC: Georgetown University Press; and Caroline Zilborg and Susan Gall, eds. (1997), *Women's Firsts*, Detroit, MI: Gale.

Photo on chapter openings © Lise Gagne/istockphoto.

HOW TO USE THIS BOOK

As you read through the individual chapters in this book, you will find the following features designed to help you to develop a clear understanding of sociological theory and to apply it to everyday life.

Key Concepts   Each chapter opens with a list of its key concepts, presented in the order in which they appear in the chapter. They are printed in **blue** when they first appear in the text, and are defined in the glossaries at the end of each chapter and at the end of the book (pp. 493–511).

Chapter Menu   A menu gives you the main headings of the chapter that follows.

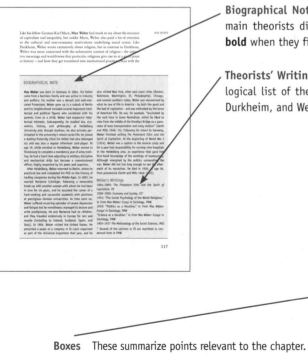

Biographical Note   These provide background information on the main theorists discussed in the chapter. Their names are given in **bold** when they first appear in the chapter.

Theorists' Writings   Each of the first three chapters has a chronological list of the major writings of the theorists discussed: Marx, Durkheim, and Weber.

Boxes   These summarize points relevant to the chapter.

Timelines Where a historical framework will aid your understanding of the chapter, timelines list major events with their dates.

Web Supplements You will also see in the margins references such as 'WEB 1.1'. The numbers refer to the list of web supplements at the end of each chapter. These are short summaries of particular topics that are relevant as background or context to some of the themes discussed in the book, and they are included in the content of the website designed specifically for this book, available at www.wiley.com/go/dillon. The website includes supplements, for example, on the Industrial Revolution, the Reformation, World Wars I and II, the Holocaust, slavery, the National Association for the Advancement of Colored People (NAACP), US and international suicide data, labor unions, the civil rights movement, the disability movement, the public relations industry, patterns of mass media ownership, and Census data on workers employed in service and emotion-intensive occupations. The website will be updated to include new news articles that bring up to date or bear on any of the news stories and themes discussed in the text.

Topics These features draw on information reported in the news about an event or issue that has particular salience for the concepts being discussed in the chapter. The stories highlight how particular everyday events can be used to illustrate or probe larger social processes. The icon in the margin indicates the source, listed at the end of the chapter with other Relevant Newspaper Stories.

Relevant Newspaper Stories Throughout the text you will see in the margins references such as 'NEWS 1.1'. The numbers refer to the list of relevant newspaper stories at the end of each chapter, where I give the article's title and the date of its publication. Most of these stories come from the *New York Times* (*NYT*); if the article is not from the *NYT*, I give the name of its source. You can access these articles via the website for this book at www.wiley.com/go/dillon (see below) or by searching online yourself. The *NYT* has made all its content available for free on the web. Instructors could ask their students to download and read a particular news article from the chapter list either for a homework assignment or for classroom group discussion, asking them to discuss how some of the information reported in the news article can be understood from the perspective of a particular theorist and/or of particular concepts.

cont'd

Summary   The text of the chapter is summarized in a final paragraph or two.

Points to Remember   These list in note form the main learning points of the chapter.

Glossary   At the end of each chapter its key concepts are listed again, this time in alphabetical order, and defined. The glossary at the end of the book combines the end-of-chapter glossaries to define all the key concepts covered in the book.

SUMMARY

Across his prolific writings, Bourdieu's overarching focus was on social inequality – on stratification in schools, art, clothes, food, etc. – and on how inequality gets reproduced across varied institutional and cultural domains. He outlines the details of individual choices in the micro contexts of everyday life, but his analysis overall is more concerned with macro structures and processes than with micro relations. Of particular note, his conceptualization of the habitus shows how micro practices are conditioned by and reproduce macro structures (e.g., of class inequality), and how objective macro structures (e.g., the educational system, the social class system) get internalized into individuals' everyday habits and dispositions. His approach thus exemplifies how sociologists must necessarily attend to the interplay of micro and macro processes.

Finally, although Bourdieu discusses the strategic choices made by individuals and the fact that, for example, there are economic efficiencies in working-class tastes (dictated by necessity), he does not regard individual choices as motivated by the same individual self-interested, utilitarian motives elaborated by rational choice theorists such as James Coleman (cf. chapter 7). For Bourdieu, individual choices are invariably located within a class-conditioned cultural habitus and thus are structured by a particular social, economic, and cultural context.

POINTS TO REMEMBER

Pierre Bourdieu (France, 1930–2002)
- Focus on the reproduction of inequality in society
- Inequality due to class-conditioned differences in volume of capital (economic, social, cultural capital)
- Special attention to the links between economic and cultural capital
- School is a major transmitter and reproducer of cultural and economic capital
- Everyday taste is socially conditioned by the class habitus
- Different social classes construe the body, food, and eating differently
- Different social classes have a taste for different cultures, different everyday habits
- Taste reproduces social hierarchies; we distinguish ourselves by the distinctions we make
- Different institutional fields (e.g., education, art, etc.) have their own respective logics of symbolic differentiation and inequality

424

- The transformation of sexual desire and behavior into discourse was first accomplished by the Catholic confession and subsequently extended by the state (e.g., the Census) for political and economic purposes
- Discourses of sex/the body are imbued with, and add to the circulation of, power
- Debates about homosexuality contrast essentialist biological and social constructionist perspectives

Queer theory:
- Another standpoint from which to analyze social relations
- Rejects the binary, homosexual/heterosexual categories we use to think about and organize sexuality, instead emphasizing the fluidity of sexuality
- Focuses attention beyond sexual categories onto how sexuality and assumptions about sexuality are embedded in and constituted by institutional and everyday practices

GLOSSARY

bio-power the institutional use of bodies and body practices for purposes of political, administrative, and economic control.

confession production of discourse as a result of the interrogation of the self (by the self or others, real and imagined), typically with regard to body practices.

constructionist view of sexuality the idea that homosexuality and what it means to be gay has varied across history and social context; contrasts with an essentialist view.

disciplinary practices institutional practices (through schools, churches, clinics, prisons, etc.) used to control, regulate, and subjugate individuals, groups, and society as a whole.

discourse categorizations, talk, and silences pertaining to social practices.

docile bodies produced as a result of the various institutional techniques and procedures used to discipline, subjugate, use, and improve individual (and population) bodies.

essentialist view of sexuality the idea that being gay, and the social characteristics associated with being gay, are a natural and essential part of the gay individual's biology.

genealogy (of knowledge/power) interconnected social, political, and historical antecedents to, and context for, the emergence of particular ideas/social categories.

heterosexist presumption that heterosexuality is normative (and normal) and that other sexual feelings and practices are socially deviant.

Panopticon model (invoked by Foucault) to highlight how disciplinary power works by keeping the individual a constant object of unceasing surveillance/control.

power an ongoing circulatory process with no fixed location or fixed points of origin and resistance.

queer theory rejects the heterosexual/homosexual binary in intellectual thought, culture, and institutional practices; shifts attention from the unequal status of gays and lesbians in (heterosexist) society to instead focus intellectual and political agendas on the fluidity of all sexuality.

regime of truth institutional system whereby the state and other institutions (government agencies, the military, medical and cultural industries) and knowledge producers (e.g., scientists, professors) affirm certain ideas and practices as true and delegitimate or silence alternative practices and interpretations.

ritual of discourse society's orderly, routinized ways (e.g., confession) of producing subjects talking about socially repressed secrets and practices.

368

INTRODUCTION
WELCOME TO SOCIOLOGICAL THEORY

KEY CONCEPTS

sociological theory
concepts
conceptual frameworks
pluralistic
macro
social structures
micro
culture
agency
classical theory
canon
contemporary theory
Enlightenment
democracy
reason
rationality
inalienable rights
utilitarianism
scientific reasoning
empiricism
positivist
objectivity
interpretive understanding
emancipatory knowledge

Timeline I.1 Major pre-Enlightenment influences, and events from the Enlightenment to the establishment of sociology

500 BC–AD 999 The Classical World
1000–1490 The Feudal Age
1490–1664 The Age of Discovery

1599	Francis Bacon, *Essays*
1620	English Pilgrims arrive at Plymouth Rock, Massachusetts
1633	Galileo summoned by the Inquisition to defend his theory that the earth moves around the sun
1636	Harvard College founded
1637	Rene Descartes, "I think, therefore, I am"

1665–1774 The Enlightenment

1670	Blaise Pascal, "Man is only a reed, the weakest thing in nature; but he is a thinking reed"
1687	Isaac Newton explains laws of motivation and theories of gravitation
1689	John Locke, *On Civil Government*
1702	Cambridge University establishes faculty chairs in the sciences
1733	Voltaire praises British liberalism
1752	Benjamin Franklin invents a lightning conductor; demonstrates the identity of lightning and electricity
1762	Jean-Jacques Rousseau, *The Social Contract*
1771	The right to report parliamentary debates established in Britain

1775–1814 The Age of Revolution

1775	American War of Independence; battles of Lexington and Concord (Massachusetts)
1776	British troops evacuate Boston; Declaration of Independence
1776	Adam Smith, *The Wealth of Nations*
1788	Bread riots in France
1789	Fall of the Bastille; beginning of the French Revolution; New French Constituent Assembly abolishes feudal rights and privileges
1791	Bill of Rights in America; first 10 amendments to the US Constitution
1792	Mary Wollstonecraft, *Vindication of the Rights of Woman*
1796	Freedom of the press established in France

1805	First factory to be lit by gaslight (in Manchester, England)
1807	Air pump developed for use in mines
1813	Jane Austen, *Pride and Prejudice*
1823	Jeremy Bentham, Utilitarianism
1831	John Stuart Mill, *The Spirit of the Age*
1835–1840	Alexis de Tocqueville, *Democracy in America*
1837	Harriet Martineau, *Society in America*
1839	Comte gives sociology its name
1855	Harriet Martineau translates Comte's *Positive Philosophy*
1859	Charles Darwin, *The Origin of Species* (modern evolutionary theory)
1861–1865	American Civil War, the South (Confederates) versus the North (Union)
1865	US president Abraham Lincoln assassinated
1865	Thirteenth amendment to the US Constitution, abolishing slavery

---

Topic I.1 Hotel rooms get plusher, adding to maids' injuries

Some call it the "amenities arms race," some "the battle of the beds." It is a competition in which the nation's premier hotels are trying to have their accommodations resemble royal bedrooms. Superthick mattresses, plush duvets and decorative bed skirts have been added, and five pillows rather than the pedestrian three now rest on a king-size bed. Hilton markets these rooms as Suite Dreams, while Westin boasts of its heavenly beds. The beds may mean sweet dreams to hotel guests, but they mean pain to many of the nation's 350,000 hotel housekeepers. Several new studies [by unions and health scientists] have found that thousands of housekeepers are suffering arm, shoulder, and lower-back injuries ... it is so strenuous a job that [housekeepers have] a higher risk of back disorders than autoworkers who assemble car doors ... The problem, housekeepers say, is not just a heavier mattress, but having to rush because they are assigned the same number of rooms as before while being required to deal with far more per room: more pillows, more sheets, more amenities like bathrobes to hang up and coffee pots to wash. Ms. Reyes [a hotel housekeeper] complained that some days she must make 25 double beds, a task that entails taking off, and putting on, 100 pillowcases ... Housekeepers who earn $17,300 a year on average, invariably stoop over to lift mattresses, some of which are only 14 inches off the floor. They frequently twist their backs as they tuck in the sheets, often three of them rather than the two of yesteryear. Since it can take 10 to 12 minutes a bed, a house-keeper who makes 25 beds a day frequently spends four to five hours on the task, lifting mattresses 150 to 200 times ... [A Hilton spokesman] said the company had increased training to try to minimize harm to housekeepers ... [and to ease] workloads ... [and said that the unions are] pushing the injury issue as a smoke screen, largely to pressure hotel companies to agree to procedures making it easier to unionize workers.

NEWS I.1

Welcome to sociological theory. It might seem unusual to begin a theory book with an excerpt about hotel bedrooms and the burdens plush mattresses impose on housekeepers. But it is precisely this sort of daily occurrence that sociological theory, with its breadth of concepts or analytical ideas, is well suited to illuminating. Although theory, by definition, is abstract, this book illustrates the richness of sociological theory by emphasizing its practical application and explanatory relevance to daily life. I will introduce you to the major theorists whose writings and conceptual frameworks inform sociological thinking. The book will equip you with the theoretical vocabulary and understanding that will enable you to appreciate the plurality of perspectives within sociological theory. It will give you confidence to apply these ideas to the many sociological topics you study (e.g., inequality, crime, medical sociology, race, political sociology, family, gender, sexuality, culture, religion, community, globalization, etc.), and help you to think analytically about the many occurrences in daily life far beyond the classroom.

ANALYZING SOCIAL LIFE

The short excerpt on housekeepers and hotel mattresses provides a single snapshot of contemporary society, but its elements can be used to highlight the different ways that sociological theorists approach the study of society. For example, Karl Marx (1818–1883), a towering figure in the analysis of modern capitalism (see chapter 1), would focus on the relations of economic inequality and exploitation that underlie hotel maids' injuries. His theory highlights the extent to which the capitalist pursuit of profit structures the service production process in hotels (and in factories, corporations, etc.) – e.g., the number of hotel rooms that have to be cleaned every day by each worker – and determines the low wages paid to workers, as well as consolidating the economic or class inequality that is part and parcel of capitalism. You might suggest that if the maids are unhappy, they should just leave the Westin. But if they leave, what are their options? Very limited, Marx would respond. Because hotel maids (and other workers) have to live, they need money in order to survive (especially in a "welfare-to-work" society in which there is very little government economic support available to those who are unemployed long-term). Therefore, while the maids are free to leave the Westin they are not free to withhold labor from every hotel – they must work someplace. Hence wage-workers must sell their labor on the job market, even if what they receive in exchange for their labor will always be significantly less than the profit the capitalist will make from their work. Although hotel owners have to pay the many costs associated with the upkeep and running of a hotel, there still remains a large gap between the minimum wage paid to hotel maids (and waitresses, etc.; approx. $7 an hour) and the price paid by hotel guests for a one-night stay in the luxury hotel room ($399 and upwards) that the maids clean.

Further, the competitive nature of capitalism and the economic competition between hotels (as noted in the excerpt) mean that the profit-driven working conditions in one luxury hotel will not vary much from those in another. If a hotel company were to lose in "the battle of the beds," in the battle for affluent customers, profit decline spells that particular owner's likely demise too. Low wages and occupational injuries, therefore, are what maids can expect, regardless of the particular hotel (whether the Westin or the Hilton). Moreover, if hotel maids are unable to work as a result of their injuries, there will always be others waiting to take their place; one of the effects of globalization (the topic discussed in chapter 15) is to increase the competition between low-wage-workers whose pool is expanded by the increasing numbers of immigrant and migrant workers available to the low-paying service industries (e.g., Ehrenreich and Hochschild 2002; Sassen 2007).

In focusing on the profit and economic relations within capitalist societies, Marx also alerts us to how ideology, i.e., a society's taken-for-granted ideas about work, achievement, freedom, consumption, etc., determines how we explain and justify all sorts of social phenomena, whether social inequality, the Olympic Games, or the latest consumer fad. Marx – and more recent theorists influenced partly by Marx, such as members of the Frankfurt School (see chapter 5) – would argue that the ideology of freedom – typically used to denote political freedom and democracy – has in today's world become the freedom to shop. We all (more or less) want the plush consumer lifestyle that we associate with luxury hotels, a pursuit promoted by the (globalizing) capitalist class, and especially by advertising, mass media, and pop culture industries. Thus, for example, MTV's Jam of the Week for June 6, 2008, was "Louie," a Blood Raw/Young Jeezy song celebrating Louis Vuitton merchandise; similarly Kanye West's "Flashing Lights" reminds us that consumption trumps everything else. Indeed, Marx would argue that it is largely because hotel housekeepers (and their families and neighbors) buy into the allure of consumption that they consent to work as hard as they do, despite their injuries, and without fully realizing or acknowledging the inequality of the capitalist system with its ever-growing gap between the rich and the poor. In fact, in the US, many maids would consider themselves middle-class, a "self-definition" that takes the sting out of class inequality (and dampens any spark of class warfare).

Max Weber (1864–1920) (his surname is pronounced *vayber*), also offers an analysis of modern capitalism. But unlike Marx, he orients us to the various subjective motivations and meanings that lead social actors – either individually, or collectively as workers, hotel companies, unions – to behave as they do (see chapter 3). Among the many engines driving behavior, Weber, somewhat like Marx, highlights the centrality of strategic or instrumental motivations underlying social behavior, including the maids' actions. In particular, hotel owners and unions pursue their own economic and political interests by making cost–benefit assessments of which courses of action are the most expedient given the respective objectives of each group. Hotel companies, for example, are suspicious of the union's objectives beyond the specific issue of housekeeper injuries; the companies are concerned that their strategic interests (in making money, hiring particular workers, and competing with other hotel chains) will be undermined if their work force is unionized. And union leaders, too, are concerned if they think that workers can garner a good deal without the union's intervention. Not surprisingly, as some contemporary theorists highlight (e.g., Ralph Dahrendorf; see chapter 6), inter-group conflict is common in democratic societies as various economic and other interest groups compete for greater recognition of their specific agendas.

Life, however, is not all about economic and strategic interests. One of the theo-retical achievements of Weber was to demonstrate that values and beliefs also matter; they orient social action (something subsequently emphasized by Talcott Parsons, an American theorist who was highly influential for several decades (1940s–1970s) in shaping sociological thinking and research; see chapter 4). Individuals, groups, organizations, and whole countries are motivated by values, by commitments to particular understandings of friendship, family, patriotism, envi-ronmental sustainability, education, religious faith, etc. Subjective values, such as commitment to their family, to providing for their children, may explain why hotel housekeepers work as hard as they do; and indeed why many immigrant women leave their children and families in their home country while they work abroad earn-ing money to send home (e.g., England 2005b; Sassen 2007). The strong cultural value of individualism in the US, for example, also helps to explain why labor unions have a much harder time gaining members and wielding influence in the US than in Western European countries such as the UK, Ireland, and France. The his-torical-cultural influence of Protestantism and its emphasis on self-reliance and individual responsibility in the US means that Americans tend to believe that being poor is largely an individual's own responsibility (and a sign of moral weakness), beliefs that impede the expansion of state-funded social welfare programs.

As recognized by both Marx and Weber, differences in economic resources are a major source of inequality (or of stratification) in society, determining individuals' and groups' rankings relative to one another; e.g., upper-class, middle-class, lower-class strata. Additionally, Weber, unlike Marx, argues that social inequality is not only based on differences in income but also associated with differences in lifestyle or social status. Weber, and contemporary theorists influenced by his conceptualization of the multiple sources of inequality – such as Pierre Bourdieu – argue that individuals (and groups) pursue distinct lifestyles that demonstrate and solidify social class dif-ferences. Such differences are evident not only between the upper and lower classes, but also between those who are closely aligned economically. This helps to explain why affluent people stay in premier rather than economy hotels and why some afflu-ents prefer the Ritz Carlton to the Westin. For similar status reasons, some women will spend hundreds of dollars on a Louis Vuitton handbag rather than buy a cheaper, though equally functional one by Coach (see especially Bourdieu; chapter 13).

The cultural goals (e.g., consumption, economic success) affirmed in society are not always readily attainable. Children who grow up in poor neighborhoods with under-funded schools are disadvantaged by their limited access to the social insti-tutions (e.g., school) that provide the culturally approved means or path toward academic, occupational, and economic success (e.g., MacLeod 1995). Thus as the American sociologist Robert Merton (see chapter 4) shows, society creates devi-ance (e.g., stealing) as a result of the mismatch between cultural goals (e.g., con-sumer lifestyle) and blocked access to the acceptable institutional means to attain those goals.

Although deviance is a social creation and is "normal" – as classical theorist Emile Durkheim (1858–1917) emphasizes, because it comes from society and exists in all societies (e.g., as indicated by crime rates) – "too much" deviance (or crime) ultimately threatens the social order. Social order and cohesion are Durkheim's core theoretical preoccupation (see chapter 2). He is basically interested in what knits society together; what binds and ties individuals into society. Therefore, rather than focusing on what Marx, for example, would see as exploitation, Durkheim would highlight the social interdependence suggested in our story of the hotel maids. For Durkheim, hotel owners, workers, guests, unions, and occupational health scientists are all part of the social collectivity, a collectivity whose effective functioning is dependent on all doing their part in the social order. In like manner, Talcott Parsons sees social institutions such as the economy, the family, and the political and legal systems as working separately but also interdependently to produce an effectively functioning society (see chapter 4).

Social interdependence for Durkheim is underscored by the fact that without guests, for example, there would be no hotel maids and no hotel owners (this is well understood by people living in seaside towns; business is seasonal and with hotels/restaurants closed for the winter, there are fewer work opportunities). Durkheim is not interested in analyzing the (unequal) economic relations in the hotel industry or the historical origins of tourism. What is relevant to him is how, for example, occupations, hotels, tourism, and consumption patterns (and all other social things) have a determining force on individual-social behavior; all of these for Durkheim are collective, social forces that shape, constrain and regulate social behavior, and in the process, tie individuals and groups into social relationships with one another.

Tipping hotel maids and restaurant waitresses is not required by law. But we are constrained into doing so – even though no one other than the maid can tell whether or not you left money for her in the hotel room – by the (equally strong) collective force of social convention. As Durkheim would stress, all social conventions (and laws) both come from society and function to affirm and bolster the interdependence of individuals within society. Moreover, as contemporary network theorists demonstrate, even *weak* ties among individuals, among acquaintances who chat (share information) when they occasionally run into one another on the street, are socially beneficial to individuals (in finding jobs, etc.) and to enhancing community well-being (e.g., in mobilizing people to participate in neighborhood projects; see chapter 7).

In contrast to Durkheim, exchange theorists emphasize that we tip and give gifts and invite friends to dinner with the expectation that this will yield some specific return to us; in this view of self-interested action, all social exchange has use-value: one never gets or gives something for nothing (e.g., George Homans; Peter Blau; chapter 7). Therefore, when I tip the hotel maid even though I don't expect to return to that hotel (and with the tip-related expectation of better service), I must be getting something in return, such as the validation of my own superior status relative to the maid – perhaps found in the slight nod of the head or smile when passing the maid and her cart in the corridor. For exchange theorists, exchange relationships are not just those based on money (as for Marx), but those based on the exchange of status (see also Bourdieu, chapter 13), information, friendship, advice, housework, political influence, etc., and the power imbalances in relationships (e.g., between friends, spouses, governments, etc.) that they reflect and perpetuate. In all relationships, rational choice theorists contend, we assess what we get and what to give on the basis of its probable use-value to us as (resource maximization) individuals (see chapter 7).

So far I have not commented on the fact that the hotel worker quoted in our excerpt is a woman. Indeed, the very word "maid" is a gendered word, i.e., used to denote a woman and "women's work" (male domestic servants, by contrast, are referred to in more elegant language as "butlers"). Today, despite the advances in women's equality, women comprise a disproportionate share of low-wage service workers. Feminist standpoint theorists (e.g., Dorothy Smith; Patricia Hill Collins; see chapter 10), coming out of a tradition that focuses on women's inequality in society, have much to say about these matters. In particular, they highlight the day-in/day-out routines and experiences of women who make 25 beds a day, and who, after the paid work-day ends, make the beds and cook dinner and do many other chores for their families. Feminist theorists also underscore that women's chores, experiences, and opportunities are typically different than men's, and when similar, women's work is rewarded very differently than men's work (at work and at home); women continue, for example, to remain on the margins of the decision-making power elites in society (cf. C. Wright Mills; see chapter 6).

The phenomenological tradition (see chapter 9) emphasizes the significance of ordinary everyday knowledge in defining individuals' concrete "here-and-now" social reality. Partly influenced by phenomenology, feminist standpoint theorists (e.g., Smith) underscore how the knowledge that derives from women's everyday experiences is very different to the knowledge that is recognized as the legitimate, objective knowledge in society. Whether in Congress, in corporate offices, in law courts, or even among sociologists, the knowledge that comes from women's experiences – as mothers and homemakers, and from the challenges they face as, increasingly, they simultaneously move within the "man-made" world of work and public life – tends to be demeaned. It does not fit well with the male-centered (see chapter 10) and indeed heterosexist bias (see chapter 11) that characterizes sociology and other established sources of knowledge.

Feminist theorists (e.g., Collins), along with race theorists (see chapter 12) and globalization scholars (see chapter 15), would also highlight that it is not just women but particular types of women who tend to be employed in the low-wage service sector, namely, women of minority racial and ethnic background, many of whom are immigrants. Many feminist scholars, therefore, focus on exploring how the multiple intersecting experiences of inequality – of gender, race, class, immigration, sexuality, etc. – shape the life-chances and experiences of women (e.g., Collins). Feminist and race theorists (e.g., Paul Gilroy; see chapter 12) further attend to how advertising and mass media promote particular cultures of femininity and masculinity that invariably entwine contradictory (gender- and race-based) messages that perpetuate social inequality.

Feminist scholars also draw attention to the fact that a lot of women's work is not just physical body work (e.g., lifting heavy mattresses), but emotion work, whether in mothering (e.g., Nancy Chodorow), or as work for pay (e.g., Arlie Hochschild; see chapter 10). Hotel housekeepers do mostly "back-stage" work – e.g., cleaning toilets, making beds, etc. – preparing bedrooms whose presentation will impress guests as well as the maids' supervisors (as elaborated by Erving Goffman; see chapter 8). Hotel housekeepers have fewer opportunities than receptionists and waitresses to smile at guests. But it is women far more than men who are expected to smile – at home, and at, and as, work – irrespective of body-pain or of how they are actually feeling (e.g., Hochschild; see chapter 10). Thus, when I smile (or pick up the trash left behind on the seminar table), I am engaged in "doing gender" – as ethnomethodologists would argue (see chapter 9). I am following the everyday procedures or methods that women use on an ongoing basis to establish their credibility as women (as mothers, wives, teachers, colleagues, friends, etc.) in a society where a particular gender order is the norm. Ours is a society characterized by particular gender-specific roles and role expectations (cf. Parsons; chapter 4), a point underscored by women's predominance in care-giving occupations (e.g., England 2005b) and the fact that working wives do more housework than their husbands (e.g., Bittman et al. 2003). And there are gender-subordinated ways of self-presentation – e.g., typically in advertisements, women smile up at men, and men smile down at women, thus reaffirming the gender-role hierarchy (cf. Goffman; chapter 8). This is a social order that, if disrupted (by me withholding smiles, or the politician's wife refusing to stand behind him in a show of support despite his affair), can cause a great deal of bewilderment all round, an effect which helps illustrate the relative fragility of the order that underlies all social life (cf. Harold Garfinkel; see chapter 9).

Although the self-presentation of bodies is a core part of everyday social behavior (underscored by the rising prevalence of cosmetic surgery and dermatology; see chapter 11), Michel Foucault sees the body more generally as a targeted object of social control. For Foucault, all social institutions – the church, the prison, the school, the clinic, the government – have made control of the body, what bodies do, and what bodies are allowed to do with other bodies (e.g., sexual practices) a core objective, the results of which inform what we think of as "normal" sexuality (see chapter 11). Just think, for example, of the controversies on several college campuses about shared gender-neutral bathrooms; these debates largely revolve around body practices and what particular bodies do and can do in the presence of other bodies.

Finally, our hotel excerpt also points to something that many sociologists emphasize: facts – data – do not speak for themselves. Rather, the presentation and interpretation of facts will invariably depend on the context of those who are using the facts for a particular purpose – whether these users are media reporters, business leaders, unions, scientists, academics, etc. Thus, the occupational injury data referenced in our hotel excerpt are contested by those (unions and hotel companies) who have a particular interest in the meaning and implications of those facts. While some see the maids' annual income of $17,300 as clear evidence of exploitation (e.g., Marx), others construe it as a sign of great job opportunities in the US compared, let's say, to Guatemala, where an average woman's wage might be $2,000 a year. Yet other researchers might consider the issue of wages as largely irrelevant given that it is not money but an individual's social ties and community support that, for example, buffer against despair and suicide (e.g., Durkheim; chapter 2).[1]

Facts, therefore, are interpreted differently depending on the political context in which they are being discussed. Importantly too, the interpretation of facts depends on the theoretical lens used. Different theorists make different assumptions and lead us to focus on some things and not others. Going far beyond this contextual point, postmodern theorists, most of whom are located outside of sociology, but whose writings have implications for sociological analysis, provocatively contest the existence of any coherent reality, emphasizing instead its illusionary character (as we discuss in chapter 14). Thus some postmodernists (e.g., Jean Baudrillard) would argue that luxury hotels, for example, comprise not a "real" or authentic reality but an artificial and glossy "hyperreality" in which ordinary, everyday routines (e.g., eating a hot-dog) are made into lavish, Disney-like fantasies and spectacles (see chapter 14).

IMMERSION IN THEORY

By getting to know the array of theorists and ideas that comprises sociological theory, you will develop the competence to thoughtfully analyze the complexity of social life. Theoretical immersion will enable you to adopt an analytical attitude – to see beyond your own experiences and impressions in ways that expose and help you recognize the patterns and social forces underlying the wide range of social phenomena that characterize the world we live in. One of the advantages of knowing sociological theory is that it allows us to try to make sense of virtually any aspect of social behavior we might be interested in. Although different theorists, as evident from our brief discussion of the hotel workers, tend to emphasize different aspects of society and of social behavior, there is also conceptual overlap in their ideas and in the subject matter they address (e.g., economic inequality). Overall, as a body of interrelated analytical ideas, sociological theory provides a pluralistic and varied, though comprehensive resource by which we can understand and explain social life.

Sociological theory focuses on how macro, or large-scale, social structures – such as capitalism (e.g., the economic structure of the hotel industry); bureaucracy; occupational, gender, and racial structures; migration – shape the organization of the social environment; how these structures constrain the choices and opportunities available to any individual, family, or larger collectivity (e.g., a particular social class or gender or geographically located group); and thus how they shape the patterns of social action and interaction that occur. But it also attends to the micro-dynamics of individual experience (e.g., of particular hotel workers in particular hotels) and interpersonal interaction in and across the many varied contexts of everyday life. And while sociological theorists emphasize the determining and constraining force exerted by social structures on individual and collective behavior, as well as on the culture(s) – the strategies of action and the ways of thinking and feeling – in any particular society (or among any particular group, region, or class in society), they are also attentive to the impact of culture (e.g., ideas and beliefs) in shaping social structures and institutions (e.g., the economy, law, education, government, religion, family, mass media). Sociological theorists affirm, moreover, the agency that individuals exert personally and collectively (e.g., through social movements) in responding to, reworking, creatively resisting, and transforming (highly stable) structures and processes; though as sociologists we are also highly cognizant of the tension that invariably exists between agency and structural and cultural constraints.

CLASSICAL AND CONTEMPORARY THEORY

It is customary in sociology to talk about classical theory and contemporary theory. The term classical theory is used, as noted above, to refer primarily to the writings of Karl Marx (1818–1883), Emile Durkheim (1858–1917), and Max Weber (1864–1920). Their writings produced what sociologists generally acknowledge as the classic or foundational texts in sociology; their ideas constitute the canon or body of conceptual knowledge that all sociologists are expected to know. Hence, this book begins with Marx, Durkheim, and Weber, and I give their ideas greater elaboration than contemporary successors. Other late nineteenth-century sociologists such as Georg Simmel (1858–1918) also made important contributions (see Frisby 1994), which I acknowledge throughout the text. Similarly, previously overlooked early theorists, such as **Harriet Martineau** (1802–1876) and Charlotte Perkins Gilman (1860–1935), and the black sociologist William E. B. Du Bois (1868–1963), are now increasingly recognized for their ground-breaking sociological analyses, especially of gender and racial inequality. I discuss their respective contributions (see this chapter, pp. 20–27, and chapters 10 and 12, respectively).

What comprises contemporary theory is more open-ended. Although called *contemporary*, the theorists that are customarily referred to in this way include

BIOGRAPHICAL NOTE

Harriet Martineau (1802–1876) was born in England into a relatively prosperous Unitarian family, which suffered a great economic loss upon the death of her father. Under pressure to support herself, but constrained by her own weak health – she was deaf by age 20 – Harriet worked as a dressmaker before succeeding as a writer. As well as translating Comte and writing sociology she also wrote non-fiction. Martineau was popular in London's intellectual and literary circles; she was close, for example, to Charles Darwin (founder of biological evolutionism) and his brother (see Hoecker-Drysdale 1992).

sociologists such as Talcott Parsons, Max Horkheimer, C. Wright Mills, George Homans, and Erving Goffman, who wrote in the decades around the mid-twentieth century (1940s–1970s), as well as those, like Dorothy Smith, Patricia Hill Collins, Michel Foucault, Pierre Bourdieu, and Immanuel Wallerstein, whose ideas came to prominence in the mid-1970s and subsequently. Many of these contemporary theorists are, in fact, dead. But, like those of the classical theorists, their ideas are still relevant in helping us understand contemporary society. A survey of current sociology professors asking whom they would categorize and how they would rank the importance of contemporary theorists would undoubtedly produce some variation. Nonetheless, there would be a fairly strong consensus that sociology students should have familiarity with the ideas of all or at least almost all of the theorists included in this book – though depending on a given sociologist's particular areas of interest, some might give greater prominence to the ideas of some theorists over others.

My criteria for choosing which contemporary theorists to include is the extent to which a given theorist's ideas build on and extend some of the ideas found in classical theory; and, in line with the practical, pluralistic, and analytical intent underlying this book, the extent to which exposure to particular theorists/ theoretical perspectives is useful. The more we are knowledgeable of, and open to, the wide range of ideas that comprises sociological theory, the better we will be able to productively draw on and critique different analytical concepts and selectively use them to tackle the multilayered realities of social life. The relevance of particular theorists or of a particular concept will necessarily vary depending on the issue you are interested in understanding/explaining. This book aims to provide you with sufficient grounding in sociological theory so that you will be confident in evaluating which theorists/constructs offer the stronger explanatory framework for the specific empirical questions of interest to you.

SOCIETAL TRANSFORMATION AND THE ORIGINS OF SOCIOLOGY

Sociology is a relatively recent discipline. Unlike philosophy, theology, astronomy, and mathematics, for example, all of which have their origins in medieval times, sociology had its birth in the nineteenth century. Why is this the case? For a scientific discipline to emerge as an independent field of study, certain conditions have to be met. If you think for a moment about what sociology does, you will begin to see that it could not really have emerged any earlier than it did. Sociology is about analyzing (and evaluating and critiquing) social structures. For this to happen, social structures have to be seen as having a *social* existence – they have to be seen as human-social creations, and thus amenable to criticism and change – rather than as natural or divinely ordained structures. This may seem to you like an obvious point, but from a historical perspective it is not so obvious. For many centuries, in both the East and the West, monarchs and emperors, for example, were seen as deriving their authority from divine sources. Can you imagine a budding sociologist trying to analyze the legitimacy or the foundation of such authority?

Just think of the current situations in North Korea and in Myanmar, where political leaders go to such lengths to suppress any challenge to their authority that they even refuse to allow foreign aid workers to bring in food supplies to their famine-threatened people. Or think even of China. Although a major player in the global economy, it routinely represses individuals' basic rights, even stifling the public protests of parents whose children were killed in the devastating earthquake in its Sichuan Province in May 2008; deaths apparently due to the schools' shoddy construction. Thus, one school employee was sent to labor camp for a year for simply taking photos of a collapsed school. In some societies today, therefore, the freedom to probe social reality, and to identify the social forces that underlie economic and social inequalities, is severely constrained. You can imagine, then, how even more preposterous it would have seemed in earlier eras, when the divine right of kings was accepted as an obvious truth, to suggest that it is social rather than divine or natural forces that structure the order and organization of things.

It is not accidental, therefore, that the seeds allowing sociology to emerge as a discipline were sown during the era of the Enlightenment, culminating in the French Revolution and the American Declaration of Independence. Whereas the eighteenth century was still characterized by a power structure consolidated among relatively few wealthy landowners and members of the nobility, the nineteenth century witnessed a radical shift of power associated with the Industrial Revolution. The emergence of large factories and the rapid expansion of trade meant an increase in the middle class and a large migration of people from the country to the city. These shifts in socio-economic arrangements resulted in a power struggle regarding voting rights and the status of the monarchy.

Most notably, the French Revolution and the storming of the Bastille (July 14, 1789) marked the revolt of the non-privileged masses of ordinary people against the feudal privileges and rights long enjoyed by the monarchy and the aristocracy in France. The French Revolution overturned the inherited privileges of the few in favor of equality and freedom for all. It rejected the long-standing practice whereby what family you were born into determined once and for all time your life-long status, whether among the monarchy, nobles, and aristocrats; or among the peasants. The French Revolution also marked the beginning of the decline of the power of the established Catholic church in France and its alliance with the monarchy (and ushered in the political belief, so important in American law, that church and state should be kept separate).

A similar rejection of the inherited authority of kings and queens, and the affirmation instead of political equality, underlay the War of Independence in America (1775–1783), and the Americans' bold step in proclaiming independence from Britain, with the Declaration of Independence in 1776 (July 4). These were radical political events. Up until the American and French revolutions, individuals were accustomed to thinking that it was normal and right that they should be subject to a ruling power that was external to themselves. And for most people, this ruling power was represented by kings and queens. Instead, the revolutionaries

NEWS I.2

NEWS I.3

argued that the authority of government leaders should derive from the will of the people; hence the opening line in the US Constitution: "We the People …"

THE ENLIGHTENMENT: THE ELEVATION OF REASON

The ideas that American and French revolutionaries had about the will of the people, and the authority of democracy over monarchy, came from Enlightenment thought (Ham 1999: 856). Although Enlightenment thinkers (e.g., Jean-Jacques Rousseau, Immanuel Kant, David Hume, Thomas Jefferson) came from different countries and different family backgrounds, and wrote about different things, they all affirmed the importance of reason *and* rationality. Enlightenment writers argued that reason was the individual's naturally endowed gift; that each of us, by virtue of being human, possesses the innate ability to think or to reason about things and about ourselves. Reason gives the individual inalienable rights (human rights) that no external authority can strip away; individuals, therefore, should use reason to determine their destiny and to achieve the political freedom and social progress worthy of their humanity. For Enlightenment philosophers, reason not only allows but *requires* humankind to move away from reliance on the dark forces, the non-rational explanations represented by religion, myth, and tradition.

THE INDIVIDUAL AND SOCIETY

Given humans' innate ability to reflect on and reason about things, Enlightenment thinkers argued that humans should be able to use reason to govern themselves as individuals and in their relations with others. In this view, collective life – society and its governance – should be based on principles of reason rather than defer-ence to non-rational forces such as those represented by the monarchy, for exam-ple. Although this principle may seem obvious – it is, after all, the core principle underlying democratic societies – it is not at all self-evident how society should protect and support individual freedom while simultaneously bolstering the well-being of the society as a whole. The relation of the individual to society is a core underlying theme informing classical and contemporary sociological theorizing: sociologists variously probe the autonomy of the individual vis-à-vis social insti-tutions (e.g., the economy, education, law), social relationships (e.g., in marriage, at work), and other social forces (e.g., immigration, racism, globalization).

Individual rights

Prior to the establishment of sociology, early political theorists debated the issue of individual rights vis-à-vis the state and society.[2] For example, the seventeenth-century English philosopher Thomas Hobbes (1588–1679) believed that individ-uals are necessarily selfish and, if left to their own devices, would produce social chaos and disorder. The Hobbesian view is well depicted in William Golding's novel *The Lord of the Flies*, where a group of adolescents, shipwrecked on a desert island, create a society full of viciousness and mayhem. Hobbes used his view of human nature as brutish to argue in favor of a strong monarch who would have very few limits on his power to rein in individuals; a view that sat well with monarchical feudal Europe.

We can contrast Hobbes's view with that of John Locke (1632–1704), another English philosopher, and writing less than 100 years after Hobbes. According to Locke, humans are born basically good and, therefore, they should not have to surrender their rights to a strong monarch in order to survive. Rather, Locke argued, individuals give over certain rights to, or make a contract with, a government that is responsible to them and which performs functions that maintain social order (e.g., regulating crimes against private property). This view of the role of the state fitted well with the growing wealth and power of the English middle classes resulting from the Industrial Revolution (cf. Smelser 1959).

Utilitarianism

Another important strand in Locke's philosophy was **utilitarianism**. This thesis argues that rational, self-determining individuals act on their own rational self-interests, and by doing so, simultaneously ensure their own individual well-being and that of society as a whole. If individuals can be trusted to make decisions that are useful to advancing their own self-interests, then by extension, the government does not need to intervene and regulate human-social behavior. These ideas, often referred to as Liberal Enlightenment Thought, were also variously articulated by Adam Smith (1723–1790), the eighteenth-century Scottish economist who emphasized the self-interested nature of individual economic exchange (1776/1925). Similarly, too, the English philosophers, John Stuart Mill (1806–1873), and Harriet Taylor Mill (1807–1858) – early proponents of women's equality – advocated an understanding of society based on self-interested action. Both Mills believed, for example, that women should have the right to vote not only as a way to maximize their own particular self-interests but also simultaneously in order to constrain men's self-interests. (Self-interest is a prominent theme in many political and economic debates today, and in sociological theorizing emphasizing exchange and resource maximization behavior; see chapter 7.)

Social contract

Focusing on the larger community rather than individual self-interests, the French philosopher Jean-Jacques Rousseau (1712–1778) argued that the best way to regulate individuals' different interests was through the voluntary coming together of individuals as citizens committed to the common good. He envisaged individuals adhering to a social contract – principles about the collective political life of society as a civic community – that prioritized the good of the whole community rather than advancing particular self-interests. Of course, what constitutes the common good is itself something that is highly contested today. On any issue, questions regarding what rights and whose rights to favor are necessarily complicated, but ones which human reason is, in principle, capable of reconciling. Reasonable solutions tend to be those that aim for some sort of balance among competing interests, and which work in practice to produce some form of societal consensus. For example, on the complicated issue of abortion, where there is a clash between the right to life and the right to liberty (fetal life versus women's freedom), most western societies have legalized abortion, but with restrictions imposed on the circumstances in which abortions can occur. In the US, this working solution is broadly acceptable to the public at large, as consistently indicated by opinion polls (Pew Forum 2006), and it maintains social order (e.g., as suggested by the infrequency of violent protest over abortion), even though the consensus does not completely satisfy the demands of activist groups on either side of the issue.

Socially situating the individual

Sociological theory fully affirms the Enlightenment view of individual rationality and the related supposition that political and social structures emerge from society rather than being divinely prescribed. But sociologists also depart from the Enlightenment emphasis, especially prevalent in classical economics, that the self-determining, rational individual is largely responsible for his or her destiny. Sociologists emphasize that while individuals have free will, their behavior in society is not freely determined by them alone; rather it is shaped and constrained by social structures, including culture, and by how particular norms and ideas get structured into everyday ways of thinking about and doing things. In other words, the sociological lens frames the individual within his or her social context, the social environment that necessarily surrounds and envelops and is acted on by the individual. Sociologists thus highlight how particular social circumstances and forms of social organization produce particular social outcomes.

SCIENTIFIC REASONING

While Enlightenment thinking drew attention to the human-social origins of political structures, another corollary of its emphasis on human rationality was the elevation of science, of scientific reasoning, as the canon of truth, i.e., as the only valid explanatory logic in a modern society. As with the idea of democracy, the Enlightenment affirmation of scientific reason was also grounded in the work of earlier philosophers. One particularly crucial influence was the emphasis by Francis Bacon (1561–1626) and other British philosophers (including Locke, and David Hume, 1711–1776), on empiricism. This approach gives primacy to observation and experience rather than abstract reasoning per se. It maintains that knowledge based on scientific methods rather than derived from non-rational and non-scientific authority is the only knowledge that matters, the only way to truth. In this view, scientific principles and scientific explanations have a necessary superiority over the use of any other type of argument including appeals, for example, to non-rational arguments based on tradition, religious faith, or some superstition. Scientific reasoning requires visible, demonstrated evidence or proof that x causes y, or that x offers a reasonable explanation as to why y occurred or is likely to happen.

Again, these principles of scientific reasoning may seem somewhat obvious. But, only 400 years ago Giordano Bruno (1548–1600), an Italian priest and philosopher, was sentenced to death, in part for expressing the belief that it is the sun rather than the earth that is the center of our planetary system. Both Copernicus (1473–1543) and Galileo (1564–1642) had to recant similar views in order to escape the censure of the Catholic church. It was not that Galileo was led astray by being a bad scientist or a poor empiricist. He was, after all, the inventor of the telescope; and by pointing it at the moon and showing the moon's craters, he was able to disprove the erroneous belief – held since the time of Socrates and the ancient Greeks – that heavenly bodies (planets, moons) were simply well-polished crystal balls (Feyerabend 1979). What got Galileo into trouble was that he dared to challenge beliefs that were held as core truths grounded in a religiously based worldview that was accepted as being beyond empirical refutation. The conflict between religion and science did not end with the Enlightenment; the controversies in the US today between proponents of evolution and those of creationism attest to lingering tensions. In any event, our contemporary view of science as being able 🔖 NEWS I.4 to refute non-empirically grounded beliefs is a relatively new development.

In sum, the Enlightenment was of critical importance for sociology. Its emphasis on reason meant that reason could be applied not only to reflect about the self but also to reflect about (and study) the self in society, and about social structures in general. Further, by emphasizing the acquisition of knowledge through scientific empirical reasoning, it opened up a unique place for what would come to be defined as sociology. Sociology was envisaged as being able to provide a reasoned, scientific analysis of social life, which, by doing so, would illuminate the impact of social forces on societal processes, thus displacing the pre-Enlightenment view of society ordered by divine hand.

THE ESTABLISHMENT OF SOCIOLOGY

The Enlightenment's affirmation of scientific rationality, and the notion of social authority derived from a social contract among individuals in society rather than from divine prescription, paved the way for the emergence of sociology as an intellectual discipline. **Auguste Comte** (1798–1857), the figure most associated with the initial establishment of sociology, embraced the Enlightenment's scientific approach and adapted it to the study of human society. Comte was a French philosopher, and truly a child of the Enlightenment. He believed that a science of society was not only possible but necessary to social progress.

EVOLUTIONARY PROGRESS AND AUGUSTE COMTE'S VISION OF SOCIOLOGY

Comte had a highly ambitious vision for sociology. In this he was influenced by his intellectual collaborator, Claude Henri de Saint-Simon (1760–1825), a French aristocrat who renounced his privileges during the French Revolution, and who fought as a soldier with the French army against the British in the American War of Independence (Taylor 1975: 14–15). Saint-Simon was driven by "the desire to do what is of most use to the progress of the *science of man*" (Saint-Simon 1813/1975: 111, italics in original); toward this endeavor, he argued for a science of society, one whose knowledge would provide a blueprint, a map, for implementing progressive forms of social organization.

BIOGRAPHICAL NOTE

Auguste Comte (1798–1857) was born into an aristocratic Catholic family in France; he studied science and for many years was the private secretary and collaborator of Claude Henri de Saint-Simon (1760–1825), who emphasized an observation-based, positivist social scientific method. Comte elaborated a "Positive Philosophy" for the study of humanity, and won renown for coining the term "sociology," a word designed to capture his belief that a social physics, a science that would emulate the natural sciences, could discover laws explaining society (see Blumberg 1974).

In the spirit of the Enlightenment, Saint-Simon argued for the superiority of science and empiricism – positive science, i.e., "a doctrine based on observation" (1810/1975: 107) – over non-rational religion. He argued:

> It was [the English philosopher/essayist, Francis] Bacon [1561–1621] who founded general positive science, just as Moses founded sacred and superstitious science. Bacon's superiority over Moses has been proved by experience: the two peoples which have adopted his doctrine have risen above the rest of humanity. The English and the French, through the force of arms and the accuracy of their political and military calculations, have subjected all the inhabitants of the universe, so that today there are virtually only two national powers on the globe, the French and the English. (1810/1975: 106)

Building on Saint-Simon's trust in the power of science to produce calculated order and social progress, Comte believed that sociology could be the science of humanity. Comte envisaged a positivist sociology – paralleling Saint-Simon's emphasis on the superiority of an observation-based "positive science." In Comte's view, sociology would focus only on *observable* data, and approach its subject matter with the same objectivity and impartiality, and the same systematic attention to processes and causes, that physical scientists use; what, for example, biologists do in studying plants. We don't expect the biologist's observations of plant life to be impacted by his or her values or social background; and so too, Comte believed that social life could be similarly studied, i.e., objectively, by sociologists who would approach their subject matter with the same detachment that a biologist or physicist brings to laboratory experiments. Sociology would be what

Comte called the "positive philosophy" – a field whose knowledge of humanity would be determined by science, not speculation, and by the affirmation only of that which is discoverable and objectively evident in society.

Comte explained:

> All good intellects have repeated, since Bacon's time, that there can be no real knowledge but that which is based on observed facts. This is incontestable, in our present advanced age ... the first characteristic of the Positive Philosophy is that it regards all phenomena as subjected to invariable natural *Laws*. Our business is ... to pursue an accurate discovery of these Laws, with a view to reducing them to the smallest possible number ... Our real business is to analyze accurately the circumstances of phenomena, and to connect them by the natural relations of succession and resemblance ... Theologians and metaphysicians may imagine and refine about such questions [about the nature of life]; but positive philosophy rejects them ... Now that the human mind has grasped celestial [astronomy] and terrestrial physics [physics, chemistry, and physiological] ... there remains one science, to fill up the series of sciences of observation – Social physics. This is what men have now most need of. (1855/1974: 28–30)

In Comte's view, sociology – social physics – would represent a progressive advance on all other disciplines. Just as each new generation tends to think of themselves as being more advanced, more liberated, more sophisticated than their parents' generation, this view of a constantly evolving progress was very much part and parcel of how Enlightenment thinkers thought about humanity. It was also present (in different ways) in how Marx and Durkheim thought about society and its forms of social organization. There is thus a deep-seated presumption in intellectual and scientific thought (across all disciplines) that progress invariably occurs along with the march of time. This perspective is often referred to as a progressive, evolutionary view of social change: in this understanding, changes that occur in society are not simply changes, but are changes that are better than what existed previously.

This evolutionary-progressive view got expressed in Comte's vision of sociology. For Comte, sociology would be the superior science; its later evolution meant that it could mimic and improve on the observational-scientific methods of existing scientific disciplines. Comte emphasized, moreover, that sociology's focus on observable behavior across all aspects of society rather than in specialized domains of physical-biological activity (e.g., studied by physicists, chemists, biologists etc.), or compartmentalized social activity (as studied by economics, political science, anthropology, psychology, etc.), also added to its superiority. Therefore, Comte believed that sociology could offer a highly elaborated synthesis of the human-social condition. In short, sociology would be *the* science of humanity, of society. It would elaborate "the most systematic theory of the human order" (Comte 1891/1973: 1).

Thus Comte saw himself as "the founder of the religion of humanity" (1891/1973: 26), of a scientific sociology whose knowledge would guide society. He believed that once sociology, "social physics," discovered the scientific laws of humanity/society and thus demonstrated how society works, how it functions, humans could then move society progressively forward and impose some order on its organization and development. Humans could then rightfully, in his view, turn their backs on all the inferior and speculative knowledge that had preceded their era.

Although you may not find the idea of sociology-as-social-physics problematic, Comte's positivism was, and still is, a hotly debated issue. This is the case because most social phenomena cannot be observed in the way that scientists observe phenomena in the realm of physics or chemistry. You can see, for example, a culture grow in a biology experiment, but you cannot see social cohesion no matter how hard you try. Consequently, in order to study social phenomena you have to first operationalize them – you have to devise a working definition of what indicators of the particular social phenomenon you will observe and measure, i.e., count. The positivist tradition is exemplified in the work of one of sociology's founding theorists, Emile Durkheim (cf. chapter 2), and is most apparent today in the quantitative methodology of sociologists who use large data sets and sophisticated statistical techniques to measure particular social phenomena and the relations between them. For example, one way sociologists measure social cohesion is by counting the number of

With social progress comes a preoccupation with social order

friends individuals see during the week. Sociologists devise similar indicators of other social phenomena; e.g., one index of gender inequality is to measure the difference in women's and men's wages in a particular occupation. As we will see, however, many sociological theorists (e.g., Max Weber, chapter 3; Dorothy Smith, chapter 10) have misgivings about such measurement; their concern is that we miss out on much of the real social significance of important phenomena by reducing them to a set of objective indicators.

HARRIET MARTINEAU: SOCIOLOGY AS THE SCIENCE OF MORALS AND MANNERS

Comte's vision of scientific sociology was translated into English by the prolific English writer and feminist Harriet Martineau, the "first woman sociologist" (Hoecker-Drysdale 1992). Seeing Comte's *Positive Philosophy* as "one of the chief honors of the [nineteenth] century" (1855/1974: 3), Martineau regarded its dissemination as crucial to the march of social progress. She wrote: "The law of progress is conspicuously at work throughout human history. The only field of progress is now that of Positive Philosophy ... whose repression would be incompatible with progress" (ibid.: 11).

Not only did Martineau translate Comte, she also wrote a detailed instructional booklet explaining the systematic way in which "morals and manners" – her definition of the subject matter of sociology – should be scientifically observed. In *How to Observe Morals and Manners* (1838), she emphasized that "The powers of observation must be trained, and habits of method in arranging the materials presented to the eye must be acquired before the student possesses the requisites for understanding what he contemplates" (1838: 13). Paralleling the scientific methodology of the natural scientist, Martineau advised:

> The traveler must not generalize on the spot ... Natural philosophers do not dream of generalizing with any such speed as that used by the observers of men ... The geologist and the chemist make a large collection of particular appearances before they commit themselves to propound a principle drawn from them though their subject matter is far less diversified than the human subject, and nothing of so much importance as human emotions, – love and dislike, reverence and contempt, depends upon their judgment. (1838: 18–19)

Martineau's perception of the breadth of sociology's subject matter was underscored by the range of topics in her research manual (and in her other writings). She included social class, religion, suicide, health, family, crime, newspapers, popular idols, and the arts – topics that would variously receive extensive elaboration by sociology's core classical theorists (Marx, Durkheim, Weber) and their contemporary successors. Moreover, long before it was fashionable for sociologists to discuss the relevance of the researcher's own social context and personal biases for the research conducted (e.g., Pierce 1995), Martineau warned researchers not to be judgmental regarding people's habits and not to evaluate the observed behavior in terms of their own or their society's values (1838: 25–26). She cautioned that "Every prejudice, every moral perversion dims or distorts whatever the eye looks upon" (1838: 51).

Martineau was committed to sociology as an observation-based science. At the same time, however, she recognized, unlike Comte, that the subject matter of sociology – with its inclusion of human emotions and values – is different to what is studied by natural scientists, and therefore presents different challenges than that encountered by biologists, physicists, etc. Given the specific relevance of the human-emotional element in the study of social life, Martineau emphasized the need for sociologists to adopt an attitude of empathy and understanding toward those they were observing. She stated:

> The observer must have sympathy; and his sympathy must be untrammeled and unreserved. If a traveler be a geological inquirer he may have a heart as hard as the rocks he shivers, and yet succeed in his immediate objects ... if he be a statistical investigator he may be as abstract as a column of figures, and yet learn what he wants to know: but an observer of morals and manners will be liable to deception at every turn, if he does not find his way to hearts and minds. (1838: 52)

INTERPRETIVE UNDERSTANDING

With this approach, Martineau anticipated the second strand of research methodology in sociology: the emphasis on interpretive understanding (or hermeneutics) elaborated by the German philosopher Wilhelm Dilthey (1833–1911). Unlike Comte, who argued for the unity of all sciences, namely, the idea that sociology is a science methodologically similar to the natural sciences, Dilthey maintained that there is, in fact, a distinction between the natural and the human sciences (Outhwaite 1975: 24–30). In Dilthey's view, sociology as a human science is different to physics (and to other natural sciences), as a result not of its logic but of its *content* – its concern with social life and the lived experience of individuals. Unlike atoms, humans engage in mental activity; they experience everyday reality, and mentally and emotionally internalize this reality.

Therefore, Dilthey argued, the study of social life, of lived experience, requires a different methodology than that applied to the study of natural phenomena. Studying society, Dilthey argued, requires a method of empathic understanding (or *Verstehen*, the German word for understanding). This requires us to enter with empathy into the lived experiences, the everyday reality of those whom we are studying and to seek to understand those individuals' interpretation of their reality (Outhwaite 1975: 24–26). This interpretive methodological tradition was consolidated in sociology by Dilthey's fellow-German Max Weber (cf. chapter 3). It is the method embraced by sociologists when they conduct historically grounded research (using diaries, letters, sermons, archival materials, etc.), or when they conduct ethnographic studies and in-depth interviews. Its influence is most apparent today in the research of those who conduct ethnographic studies of particular groups, communities, neighborhoods, workplaces, etc. They wish to acquire a deep understanding of a particular group's practices, their way of life and their worldviews – whether of hotel workers (Sherman 2007) and maids (Romero 1992), boxers (Wacquant 2004), street culture (Anderson 1999a), homeless people (Duneier 1992), or adolescents in a low-income neighborhood (MacLeod 1995). To do so, they typically combine detailed observation of the group's diverse everyday practices over a relatively long period of time (e.g., 2–3 years) with in-depth interviews with some of the group/community members as a way to further understand the underlying motivation in some of the everyday habits and attitudes they have observed.

Sociology, therefore, is characterized by two dominant methodological approaches to the study of society: a positivist tradition which focuses on the explanation of social reality using various measures as indicators of particular social phenomena and demonstrating the statistical relations between social phenomena (e.g., education and income); and an interpretive tradition that focuses on explaining social phenomena through understanding the everyday reality of individuals in a particular social context. Thus, for example, sociologists explain economic inequality in the US by showing the statistical links (in a large aggregate population) between an individual's family background – using such measures as parental income, parental education, number of siblings, etc. – and the individual's subsequent social status in adulthood, measured by his or her level of education, employment status, income, etc. But sociologists also expand the explanation of social processes by providing an understanding of what it means to be poor (or rich), and of how growing up in a poor family and neighborhood hinders an individual's success in school (and subsequent income), by entering into the lives and life-contexts of individuals in these particular situations. Importantly, while there is some tension between these two research traditions, they are not mutually exclusive. Both methodologies are necessary in order to provide a comprehensive picture of a particular social phenomenon (e.g., inequality).

Moreover, whether using statistical or interpretive research methods, sociologists can pursue research topics that have the additional purpose of contributing to the empowerment of individuals and groups. Sociological inquiry can be used to advance emancipatory knowledge, that is, to liberate people from the various historical and social structural barriers that hinder their full participation in society (Habermas 1968/1971: 301–317). Research in this tradition (such as documenting the over-representation of migrant women in low-wage service jobs; e.g., Ehrenreich and Hochschild 2002) provides knowledge which in turn can be used by workers, activists, and policy-makers to change some of the conditions underlying particular patterns of inequality. Irrespective of the specific research methodology used, we come to appreciate the emancipatory power of sociological inquiry when, for example, we enter into the everyday lives of welfare-mothers (Hays 2003), or see an in-depth analysis of statistical trend data demonstrating the determining impact of family socio-economic background and access to educational opportunities, as opposed to innate intelligence or other genetic traits, on income and racial inequality (Fischer et al. 1996).

Whatever the research topics we pursue, all sociological theorizing prompts us to ask questions (though the questions asked and the assumptions informing them vary). The very act of asking questions about the social and cultural forces that structure individual behavior, social relations, and the organization of society invariably prompts us to rethink our existing assumptions about the world and how it works. As such, sociological theory provides intellectual and analytical resources for critical thinking. Theory directs us to ask certain questions and to look for certain patterns in certain societal contexts, and at the same time, the data sociologists gather and the empirical patterns they find help to challenge and refine sociological theory. There is thus an ongoing conversation between theory and data. And, as I noted at the outset of this chapter, good sociological theory is theory whose constructs are relevant in helping us make sense of the social reality that surrounds us.

THE SOCIOLOGICAL CRAFT IN THE NINETEENTH CENTURY

In this last part of this introductory chapter, I invite you to briefly consider early examples of the sociological craft as practiced by two quite different observers. Alexis de Tocqueville and Harriet Martineau visited the US in the mid-nineteenth century and both provided perceptive accounts of American life. Both explored how Americans negotiated issues of individual freedom while simultaneously participating in the robust social institutions and cultural practices that would come to define American society. Additionally, their writings sensitize us to the importance of the observer's contextual background (or standpoint; e.g., Smith 1987; see chapter 10) in what is reported and how it is interpreted. Notably, the contrasts that emerge in de Tocqueville's and Martineau's accounts of American life revolve primarily around issues of social inequality, contrasts that help to highlight the significance of gender, social background, and intellectual orientation in differentiating how an apparently similar social reality is observed and assessed.

ALEXIS DE TOCQUEVILLE: CULTURE AND SOCIAL INSTITUTIONS

De Tocqueville (1805–1859), a French aristocrat, was among the first social observers to highlight the dynamic relation between cultural ideas and individual and institutional practices. De Tocqueville traveled extensively across the eastern part of America in the 1830s, and he made extensive notes in his journals based on what he observed about everyday habits and learned from conversations with ordinary Americans, an account that resulted in his two volumes of *Democracy in America* (1835–1840/2004). Coming from a country with a long history of non-democratic, hierarchical power (e.g., the monarchy and the church), de Tocqueville was especially interested in the way in which democracy, and its ideals of freedom, took hold and got expressed in American social structures and everyday life.

De Tocqueville's account has become highly influential among successive generations of sociologists because it draws attention to how cultural norms and the routines put in place by social institutions create a particular tempo for everyday life, a mix of habits that shape how individuals engage in the life of their community/society while simultaneously realizing their own individual aspirations (e.g., Bellah et al. 1985). De Tocqueville showed that family, religion, and politics – the social institutions to which he gave most attention – are strong in America and provide the backbone of its community-civic activities precisely because these institutions allow individuals a great degree of freedom and autonomy; and individuals use this freedom not to abandon but to participate in community. De Tocqueville (1835–1840/2004) was impressed, for example, with the way in which religious institutions and individual freedom intertwined in American society rather than, as was the French experience, being opposed to one another – the French idea being that in a modern (Enlightened) democratic society, freedom should mean freedom *from* the controlling power of religion. But in America, de Tocqueville found, individual freedom and church participation went hand in hand.

By contrast with post-Revolutionary France (and its anti-religious ethos), the everyday habits and norms that American democracy established provided opportunities for religious as well as political and economic fulfillment. De Tocqueville argued that these freedoms and opportunities produced an order in America that simultaneously allowed for both individual fulfillment and strong institutions amidst the turmoil of economic transformation and social change. In this view, Americans could realize their new political and economic ambitions while also maintaining their (traditional) religious and family commitments.

HARRIET MARTINEAU: CULTURAL IDEALS AND SOCIAL CONTRADICTIONS

Harriet Martineau visited America around the same time as de Tocqueville, 1834–1836. She similarly traveled through the eastern, southern and mid-western states (Martineau 1837/1981: 50–52), and with a similar intent – out of a "strong curiosity to witness the actual working of republican institutions … [and] with a strong disposition to admire democratic institutions" (ibid.: 50). Martineau marveled at the hospitality she received from a broad swath of people, including the president, members of Congress and the Supreme Court, and slave-owners, clergy, lawyers, merchants, and farmers (ibid.: 53). She was also impressed with what she saw at the many institutions (factories, hospitals, prisons, schools, etc.) and families she visited, and with her interactions with women and children in kitchens, nurseries and boudoirs – "all excellent schools in which to learn the morals and manners of a people" (ibid.).

Martineau commented approvingly on the honesty and kindness of Americans, but unlike de Tocqueville, she was also very critical of many of the things she observed, taking particular note of the contradictions she witnessed between American ideals of democratic equality and everyday practices. She identified several contradictions: long an abolitionist, she wrote at length about slavery – the division of society "into two classes, the servile and the imperious" (Martineau 1837/1981: 220), and criticized the oppression and degradating subjugation to which slaves were subjected (ibid.: 223). She also noted the prejudices against "people of colour" in the North, evident for example in families "being locked out of their own hired pew in a church, because their white brethren will not worship by their side" (ibid.: 122–123). Beyond racial issues, she commented on the mass conformity, apathy, and timidity in political opinion (ibid.: 106–108, 250–253); the mass disapproval of religious skepticism and atheism (ibid.: 333–338); the many social status hierarchies and cliques that existed, even among children (ibid.: 259–261); and the inequalities in wealth and luxury (e.g., ibid.: 268–269), arguing that "enormous private wealth is inconsistent with the spirit of republicanism" (ibid.: 263).

De Tocqueville too commented at length on racial inequality in America and the degraded and oppressed status of both the Negro and the Indian (e.g., 1835–1840/2004: 365–476). He argued that slavery "can not endure in an age of democratic liberty and enlightenment" (ibid.: 419), but he found it hard, nonetheless, to imagine an American society in which blacks and whites would be equal. He believed that the consequences of slavery (even after abolition) would continue to foster servility among blacks and lead them to abuse freedom (ibid.: 367, 419), with the overarching consequence that blacks and whites would invariably be in conflict. He commented:

Plunged into this abyss of woe, the Negro scarcely feels his affliction. Violence made him a slave but habituation to servitude has given him the thoughts and ambitions of one. He admires his tyrants even more than he hates them and finds his joy and his pride in servile imitation of his oppressors ... Should he become free, independence will often strike him as a chain heavier to bear than slavery itself ... You can make the Negro free, but you cannot make him anything other than alien vis-à-vis the European ... those who believe that the Negroes will one day blend in with the Europeans are nursing a chimera [an illusion]. (ibid.: 367, 394, 395)

De Tocqueville took a similarly passive, though a far more praising (but highly idealized) view of the status of women in America. He commented approvingly that Americans believe in a democratic equality which recognized the complementary "natural differences" between men and women (1835–1840/2004: 705), something that accounted for women's comportment. Thus, "American women, who often display a manly intelligence and an energy that is nothing less than virile, generally maintain a very delicate appearance and always remain women in manners, although they sometimes reveal themselves to be men in mind and heart" (ibid.: 706). American women, de Tocqueville further observed, did not "topple the husband from power and confuse lines of authority within the family" (ibid.); instead, they "prided themselves on the voluntary sacrifice of their will and demonstrated their greatness by freely accepting the yoke rather than seeking to avoid it. That, at any rate, was the sentiment expressed by the most virtuous among them" (ibid.). Indeed, so admiring was de Tocqueville of American women that he concluded the "superiority of their women," most of whom "seldom venture outside the domestic sphere," was what was "primarily responsible for the singular prosperity and growing power of this people [in the US]" (ibid.: 708).

In stark contrast to de Tocqueville's assessment, Martineau was especially critical of the contradictions between democratic ideals of equality and women's inequality. In particular, she underscored the "political non-existence of women" (1837/1981: 125–128) due to their lack of voting rights. She also commented on the narrowness of women's interests, a narrowness forced by their general exclusion from the public sphere of economics and politics: "Wifely and motherly occupation may be called the sole business of woman there [in America]. If she has not that, she has nothing" (ibid.: 301).

Anticipating an argument elaborated by Karl Marx with regard to economic class inequality (see chapter 1), Martineau exhorted women collectively as a group to take responsibility for their own emancipation, a freedom, she argued, which was necessary to the realization of American ideals of equality. She stated:

The progression or emancipation of any class usually, if not always, takes place through the efforts of individuals of that class: and so it must be here. All women should inform themselves of the condition of their sex and of their own position. It must necessarily follow that the noblest of them will, sooner or later, put forth a moral power which shall [expose hypocrisy], and burst asunder the bonds (silken to some, but cold iron to others,) of feudal prejudices and usages. In the meantime, is it to be understood that the principles of the Declaration of Independence bear no relation to half of the human race? ... how is the restricted and dependent state of women to be reconciled with the proclamation that "all are endowed by their Creator with certain inalienable rights; that among these are life, liberty, and the pursuit of happiness?" (ibid.: 307–308)

THE INTERPRETIVE-SOCIAL CONTEXT OF KNOWLEDGE

In sum, the contrasting observations and interpretations that two equally keen visitors could offer of the same social reality – America in the 1830s – alert us to the importance of recognizing that all observations and interpretations are shaped by the social-theoretical context of the observer. De Tocqueville's primary interest was in documenting the "laws of democracy in America," and this would seem to have contributed to his taking a rose-colored view of gender inequality. On the other hand, Martineau, a woman and a feminist sensitized to inequality, readily saw and highlighted the various ways in which women were excluded from full democratic participation in society (denied access to voting/the public sphere). Accordingly, what for de Tocqueville might be seen as an "adaptation" to democratic equality – complementary male–female differences – was for Martineau a clear contradiction.

SUMMARY

The intent of this book is to provide you with a thorough grounding in sociological theory. It discusses the conceptual frameworks elaborated by sociology's core founding theorists – Marx, Durkheim, and Weber – as well as the broader range of ideas and concepts that comprise contemporary theory. My approach is to demonstrate the applicability of sociological theory and its relevance in helping us make sense of the complexity of the social world in which we live. This chapter highlighted the historical background to the emergence of sociology as an intellectual discipline, giving particular note to the influence of Enlightenment thought, and especially to Auguste Comte, in envisaging sociology as a scientific field of social inquiry.

POINTS TO REMEMBER

- Sociological theory:
  - Concern with explaining empirical social phenomena
  - Focus on social structures, including culture, and institutional practices
  - Macro- and micro-level approaches to the study of society
  - Interplay between individual/collective agency and structural forces
  - Critical analytical thinking skills

- Sociology is a relatively new discipline – its origins date to the mid-nineteenth century
- The Enlightenment (eighteenth century) set the scene for the emergence of sociology
  - Emphasis on reason and progress
  - Move away from the dark forces of the past (myth, tradition, despotism)
  - Reason in politics; equality
  - US Declaration of Independence, 1776
  - French Revolution, 1789
  - Scientific reasoning
  - Emphasis on observable, empirical phenomena
- Auguste Comte: sociology as the positive science of society
  - Positive sociology: scientifically discoverable laws of society
- Harriet Martineau: sociology as the scientific study of morals and manners
  - Subject matter of sociology different to that of natural science
  - A positive scientific method that includes sympathetic understanding of individuals
- Wilhelm Dilthey: sociology as interpretive understanding
- Early observers of American society include Harriet Martineau and Alexis de Tocqueville
  - Martineau's and de Tocqueville's contrasting interpretations highlight the importance of recognizing the interrelation between an observer's social background and theoretical questions on that which is observed/critiqued

GLOSSARY

agency individuals, groups, and other collectivities exerting autonomy in the face of social institutions, social structures, and cultural expectations.

canon established body of core knowledge/ideas in a given field of study.

classical theory the ideas, concepts, and intellectual framework outlined by the founders of sociology (Marx, Durkheim, Weber, Martineau).

concepts specifically defined ideas about the social world elaborated by a given theorist/school of thought.

conceptual framework the relatively coherent set of ideas or concepts that a given theorist or a given school of thought uses to elaborate a particular perspective on things; a particular way of looking at, theorizing about, social life.

contemporary theory the successor theories/ideas elaborated to extend and engage with the classical theorizing of Marx, Durkheim, Weber, and Martineau.

culture beliefs, rituals, ideas, worldviews, and ways of doing things. Culture is socially structured, i.e., individuals are socialized into a given culture and how to use it in everyday social action.

democracy political structure derived from the ethos that because all individuals are endowed with reason and created equal they are entitled (and required) to participate in the political governance of their collective life in society.

emancipatory knowledge the use of sociological knowledge to advance social equality.

empiricism use of evidence or data in describing and analyzing society.

Enlightenment eighteenth-century philosophical movement emphasizing the centrality of individual reason and scientific rationality over against non-rational beliefs and forms of social organization (e.g., monarchy).

inalienable rights Enlightenment belief that all individuals by virtue of their humanity and their naturally endowed reason are entitled to fully participate in society in ways that reflect and enrich their humanity (e.g., freedom of speech, of assembly, to vote, etc.).

interpretive understanding *Verstehen;* task of the sociologist in making sense of the varied motivations that underlie meaningful action; because sociology studies human lived experience (as opposed to physical phenomena), sociologists need a methodology enabling them to empathically understand human-social behavior.

macro analytical focus on large-scale social structures (e.g., capitalism) and processes (e.g., class inequality).

micro analytical focus on small-scale, individual, face-to-face, and small group interaction.

objectivity positivist idea (elaborated by Comte) that sociology can provide an unbiased (objective) analysis of a directly observable and measurable, objective social reality. This approach presumes that facts stand alone and have an objective reality independent of social and historical context and independent of any theories/ideas informing how we frame, look at, and interpret facts.

pluralistic simultaneous co-existence of many diverse strands (of thought, of research, of people).

positivist the idea that sociology as a science is able to employ the same scientific method of explanation used in the natural sciences, focusing only on observable data and studying society with the same objectivity used to study physical/biological phenomena.

rationality emphasis on the authority of reason in deliberating about, and evaluating explanations of, the nature of reality/social phenomena.

reason human ability to think about things; to create, apply, and evaluate knowledge; and as a consequence, to be able to evaluate one's own and others' lived experiences and the socio-historical context which shapes those experiences.

scientific reasoning emphasis on the discovery of explanatory knowledge through the use of empirical data and their systematic analysis rather than relying on philosophical assumptions and faith/religious beliefs.

social structures forms of social organization (e.g., capitalism, democracy, bureaucracy, education, gender) in a given society which structure or constrain social behavior across all spheres of social life, including the cultural expectations and norms (e.g., individualism) which underpin and legitimate social institutional arrangements.

sociological theory the body of concepts and conceptual frameworks used to make sense of the multilayered, empirical patterns and underlying processes in society.

utilitarianism idea from classical economics that individuals are rational, self-interested actors who evaluate alternative courses of action on the basis of their usefulness (utility) or resource value to them.

RELEVANT NEWSPAPER STORIES

All news stories are from the *New York Times* unless otherwise noted, and can be accessed via www.wiley.com/go/dillon. See NEWS icons in the margins above.

NEWS I.1 "Hotel rooms get plusher, adding to maids' injuries," April 21, 2006.

NEWS I.2 North Korea to widen access for aid workers; US ship arrives," July 1, 2008.

NEWS I.3 "Chinese stifle grieving parents' protest of shoddy school construction," June 4, 2008.
"Penalty for China quake photos reported," July 31, 2008.

"Chinese security agents block meeting of rights lawyers and U.S. lawmakers," July 2, 2008.

NEWS I.4   "Finding creation and evolution in Grand Canyon," October 6, 2005.

"Teaching of Creationism endorsed in new survey," August 31, 2005.

NOTES

1   The social context of facts and knowledge is also something we should be aware of regarding journalism and the news. Although journalism as a profession embraces ideals of objectivity rather than partisanship, the organizational and logistical constraints on news-gathering and production mean that some things get in the news and other things don't. The *New York Times*, for example, has a short sentence printed every day at the top left corner of its front page stating: "All the news that's fit to print" (and now too, more fashionably for the electronic age, it also claims "All the news that's fit to *click*"). What is fit to print or click, however, does not appear as some objective reality that the *NYT* simply transmits; these decisions are made by *NYT* (and other news organizations') journalists, editors, and executives working within a specific socio-cultural and news media context which defines what news is (e.g., Gitlin 1980). I mention this constraint on journalistic objectivity because throughout this book I draw on news stories from the *NYT* (as near the beginning of this chapter) for examples of social events and everyday social processes. These stories help me to illustrate the relevance of the various theories I discuss. I want you to be aware, however, that these news stories do not have a life independent of the social, economic, cultural, and organizational context in which news occurs (and is defined).

2   A helpful introduction to the various philosophers and other thinkers associated with the Enlightenment can be found in the *Cambridge Dictionary of Philosophy*, edited by Robert Audi (1999).

CHAPTER ONE
KARL MARX (1818–1883)

KEY CONCEPTS

capitalism
bourgeoisie
inequality
mode of production
means of production
proletariat
private property
historical materialism
class relations
class consciousness
exploitation
dialectical materialism
communism
subsistence
species being
capital
profit
use-value
commodification of labor
false consciousness
surplus value
exchange-value
division of labor
alienated labor
alienation from products
objectification
alienation in the
production
   process
alienation from our species
   being
alienation of individuals
   from one another
standpoint of the
   proletariat
ideology
fetishism of commodities
superstructure
economic base
ruling class
ruling ideas

CHAPTER MENU

Timeline 1.1 Major events in Marx's lifetime (1818–1883)

1818	First steamship (the *Savannah*) to cross the Atlantic Ocean, taking 26 days
1819	British Factory Act prohibiting employment of children under 9 in the cotton industry; and 12-hour days for those ages 10–16.
1821	US population: 9.6 million
1830	Revolution in France, fall of Charles X and Bourbons
1833	Britain abolishes slavery in its empire
1837	US Congress passes a "gag" law to suppress debate on slavery
1840	Railway-building boom in Europe
1841	First university degrees granted to women in America
1842	Depression and poverty in England
1842	British Mines Act forbids underground employment for women and girls and sets up inspectorate to supervise boy labor
1843	Skiing becomes a sport
1845	Engels, *The Condition of the Working Class in England*
1845	Florida and Texas gain statehood
1846	Height of potato famine in Ireland
1848	Revolutions against monarchy/aristocracy in Europe (Paris, Berlin, Prague, Budapest)
1848	Marx and Engels, *The Communist Manifesto*
1848	California Gold Rush
1850	Sydney University established
1854	Charles Dickens, *Hard Times*
1859	Peaceful picketing during a strike legalized in Britain
1862	Abraham Lincoln issues Emancipation Proclamation declaring slaves free
1862	Lincoln issues the first legal US paper money
1862	Victor Hugo, *Les Miserables*
1866	National Labor Union (crafts union) established in the US
1867	Marx, *Capital (Das Kapital)*
1867	Trade Unions declared illegal in Britain
1871	Trade Union Act in Britain secures legal status for trade unions, but picketing illegal

1872	Penny-farthing bicycle in general use
1876	Alexander Graham Bell invents the telephone
1877	US railroad strike; first major industrial dispute in US
1879	Thomas Edison produces incandescent electric light
1882	Standard Oil Company controls 95 percent of US oil-refining capacity

EXPANSION OF CAPITALISM

When you hear the name **Karl Marx** it is tempting to wonder why you should be studying him. Not only has Marx been dead for over one hundred years, but communism, the political system with which his theoretical vision is associated, has all but disappeared around the world. The dominant communist power of the twentieth century, the Soviet Union, collapsed – an event captured literally by the fall of the Berlin Wall on November 9, 1989. Today, the largest ex-Soviet republic, Russia, is in the throes of adopting capitalism, crystallized by the development of shopping malls in Siberia, and its expanding global economic reach; Russian millionaire Roman A. Abramovich recently became the owner of the world-famous Chelsea (England) Football (soccer) Club. Such developments would have been unimaginable 10 years ago. Capitalist markets are steadily expanding too in China; its role in the global economy is such that the next bouquet of flowers you buy is as likely to come from China as from within the US.

📖 NEWS 1.1

📖 NEWS 1.2

Lest you think that this capitalist expansion is all the more reason not to study Marx, you might be surprised to know that Marx, in fact, predicted it:

> The need of a constantly expanding market for its products chases the **bourgeoisie** [the capitalist ownership class] over the whole surface of the globe. It must nestle everywhere, settle everywhere, establish connections everywhere ... The bourgeoisie, by the rapid improvement of all instruments of production, by the immensely facilitated means of communication, draws all, even the most barbarian, nations into civilization. The cheap prices of its commodities are the heavy artillery with which it batters down all Chinese walls, with which it forces the barbarians' intensely obstinate hatred of foreigners to capitulate. It compels all nations, on pain of extinction, to adopt the bourgeois mode of production; it compels them to introduce what it calls civilization into their midst, i.e., to become bourgeois themselves. In one word, it creates a world after its own image. (CM 83–84)[1]

Clearly a prophecy of today's global economy! The expansion of capitalism and its need to have ever-larger global markets for its commodities create capitalist societies whose progress or civilization is defined by the extent of their bourgeois, capitalist culture, i.e., their adaptability to meeting the demands of capitalism by producing commodities for global consumption. Western capitalism has expanded to create a globalizing capitalist world in which consumerism – commodity production and exchange – is the common currency. This is a theme we will discuss in chapter 15.

But while many people enjoy the wide range of consumer goods available, what Marx emphasizes is the inequality that inheres in capitalism. Capitalism is one way of organizing production – meeting the needs of our existence; it is the mode of production that characterizes our organization of society. From a long historical perspective, capitalism is not the only mode of production known to society; medieval Europe (for approximately five hundred years, from 1000 to 1490), for example, was characterized by a feudal mode of production whereby serfs worked and cultivated the land of medieval lords, who, in turn, were responsible for the everyday welfare of the serfs and their families.

BIOGRAPHICAL NOTE

Karl Marx was born in Germany (in Prussia, in 1818) into a middle-class family and completed several years of university education studying law, history, languages, and philosophy. Rather than pursuing an academic career, he turned to journalism and devoted his attention to business and economics, writing about labor conditions during this era of rapid industrialization. The year 1848 was the "Year of Revolutions" in Europe, as workers and ordinary people rose up against the ruling monarchies in Germany, Italy, Austria, Hungary, and France. Marx himself had participated in the German revolutionary movement, and that same year he and Friedrich Engels published their famous treatise *The Communist Manifesto*. Marx was expelled from Germany and subsequently too from France because of his revolutionary views. He eventually settled in England in 1849, with his German wife, Jenny von Westphalen. For many years subsequently, they and their six children suffered abject poverty, relying on money from Engels

and small fees from Marx's political articles for the American radical newspaper the *New York Daily Tribune*. He died in 1883, predeceased by his wife and three of their children (Tucker 1978: xvii; Kimmel 2007: 170).

Marx's Writings
1844a: "Alienation and Social Classes," ASC
1844b: *Economic and Philosophical Manuscripts of 1844*, EPM
1846 [1932]: *The German Ideology* (with Engels), GI
1847: *Wage Labour and Capital*, WLC
1848: *The Communist Manifesto* (with Engels), CM
1852: "The Eighteenth Brumaire of Napoleon Bonaparte,", Bru
1858: *The Grundrisse: Foundations of the Critique of Political Economy*, Gru
1859: "Preface to 'A Contribution to the Critique of Political Economy,'" Preface
1867: *Capital (Das Kapital)*, Cap

Capitalism is a mode of production based on unequal private ownership of the means of production (in contrast, for example, to state ownership in socialist societies, e.g., the Soviet Union, North Korea). Under capitalism, a minority of capitalists, the bourgeoisie, who own and monopolize the means of production, i.e., property – land, oil wells, railroads, factories, corporations – accumulate profit based on the labor of the many – the wage-workers, the proletariat, who must work hard to meet production demands in factories, farms, mines, corporate offices, and hotels (cf. Introduction), and who through their work convert raw materials into commodities (and services) that are sold by the capitalists for profit. In turn, capitalists use this profit to expand their ownership of private property while the property-less workers – like hotel housekeepers (cf. Introduction, Topic I.1) – continue to toil for minimal wages, thus maintaining, as Marx argued, the ever-growing economic and social gap between capitalists and workers.

Thus Ronald Perelman, the billionaire chairman of Revlon cosmetics, can buy an emerald necklace for his wife (the actress Ellen Barkin, now his ex-wife) that is estimated to be worth between $250,000 and $350,000; a diamond ring worth at least $1 million; and upward of 100 pieces worth $15 million. By contrast, many wage-workers make great personal sacrifices, often working at two low-paying jobs, simply to buy the food for their family's dinner (e.g., Hays 2003). This inequality, according to Marx, is inherent in capitalism; it is both necessary to, and a consequence of, capitalism.

NEWS 1.3

MARX'S THEORY OF HISTORY

Marx understands history as the progressive expansion in the material or economic forces in society, i.e., in the advances made by societies in organizing their material production (e.g., agriculture, manufacturing). Marx's theory is often referred to as historical materialism because he focuses on the material (economic) conditions in society and how these determine social structures and social relations. As elaborated by Marx's intellectual collaborator, Friedrich Engels,

> The materialist conception of history starts from the proposition that the production of the means to support human life and, next to production, the exchange of things produced, is the basis of all social structure; that in every society that has happened in history, the manner in which wealth is distributed and society divided into classes or orders is dependent upon what is produced, how it is produced, and how the products are exchanged. (1878: 700–701)

History, Marx emphasizes, does not simply evolve independent of individuals and of the objective social relations (e.g., unequal class relations) which condition their lives. Rather, Marx argues that historical change, i.e., change in the material conditions of society and in how economic-social relations are organized, emerges out of the *contradictions* perceived in the existing economic and social arrangements. Thus, in Revolutionary France, the bourgeoisie overthrew the despotism of feudal monarchs and the aristocracy to create progressive economic and social institutions grounded in democratic principles (see Introduction).

As part of a similar historical logic, Marx predicted that the expansion of capitalism with its endless pursuit of profit would lead to its downfall. Capitalism produces crises that threaten its very foundations; these crises include recessions; the collapse of stock markets; severe capital losses for companies and households;

high levels of unemployment; worker unrest; and the depletion of natural resources. Marx argued that under the cumulative impact of these ongoing crises and the polarized class antagonisms he predicted they would create (between the bourgeoisie and the proletariat), the working class would develop a class consciousness, i.e., individual wage-workers would come to recognize that their exploitation is part of the mass exploitation of all wage-workers, and recognize that this exploitation is inherent in the structural organization of capitalism. Class consciousness would propel the working class to revolt against capitalism. Thus, in Marx's construal, the downfall of capitalism is contingent on both the bourgeoisie and the proletariat. The bourgeoisie, through their constant efforts to expand capitalist markets, sow the seeds of their own and of capitalism's downfall; they are its "grave-diggers" (CM 94). And the proletariat is the "revolutionary class" – the "special and essential product" of modern industrial society (CM 91), the class that would overthrow capitalism and usher in a new society. We saw a glimmer of this revolutionary potential in the US in the 1920s with the rise of the anti-establishment Anarchist Party, and a surge in labor union protests against factory owners. This disruption was relatively short lived, however, dampened in part by the social-democratic New Deal policies of the Roosevelt government which provided economic benefits to those hardest hit by the Depression.

Despite the ongoing crises that capitalism produces, Marx's failed prediction of its downfall (so far) can be understood in terms of the assumptions he made about its likely development. One, Marx assumed that the expansion of capital (and profit accumulation) would also require the expansion of the proletariat (i.e., that more laborers are needed to produce more commodities), and lead to an increase in workers' mass association and consolidation (unionization; CM 89–90). Two, he envisaged that the expanding proletariat would remain poor (CM 87–88), and thus would be further motivated by their pauperism to revolt against the capitalists. These conditions did not occur. Technological advances have made commodity production less contingent on manual labor than Marx anticipated, and while there is poverty and substantial class inequality in capitalist societies, the working class is today relatively well-off compared to in Marx's times, and partakes of many of the economic and consumer opportunities in a capitalist society – the mall has become an equalizer of sorts; we can all (more or less) go shopping. Thus the working class, like the capitalist class, has a major stake in the ongoing success of capitalism. We will explore the reasons for this in a later section of this chapter when we discuss ideology.

DIALECTICAL MATERIALISM

In any event, in Marx's theory, history does not progress in a smooth, linear manner. Each historical-economic epoch (e.g., slave society, feudalism, capitalism) is characterized by tensions or contradictions, and change emerges only when these contradictions, and the social forces and relations which reproduce those contradictions, are exposed and ruptured through social revolution – "revolution is the driving force of history" (GI 29). Marx's view of history, then, is one which emphasizes that the human-created economic conditions in place at a given historical moment give rise to particular economic and social practices, out of which emerge challenges by particular groups or social classes to the conditions of their existence, thus opening the way for the emergence of new material conditions and social relations.

This historical process, for Marx, is dialectical materialism. The word "dialectic" derives from the Greek word *dialegein*, meaning "to argue," and was used by philosophers from Plato down to Hegel to draw out the contradictions in the logic used in intellectual arguments and the structure of ideas. This method typically follows not a linear but a pendulum-like, thesis–antithesis–synthesis form. Marx – given his focus on what he considered *real* history, i.e., the history not of ideas but of "the production of material life itself" (GI 16) – used the term to capture the human-social activity involved in the historical transformation of contradictory or antithetical economic forces and relations. In this dialectical framing, existing material conditions (e.g., capitalist class inequality – the thesis) produce opposition (class revolt – the antithesis) which in turn leads to a new economic system (communism – the synthesis). In a similar fashion, slave-based economies gave way to feudalism with indentured peasants only to be superseded by capitalism with its rising middle class of small shop owners.

Although the dialectic sounds complicated, we basically see a dialectical process in the regular cycle of democratic politics. In the US, for example, no one political party dominated the White House for more than 12 years or so over the course of the twentieth century. This is partly because when the Republicans are in power, their policies (thesis) eventually produce a backlash (antithesis) among the electorate that then sees the Democrats elected. Once in power, the Democrats have to deal with the new reality created by Republican policies and thus modify their own agenda, producing new policies (synthesis), which, after creating a temporary balance, in turn lead eventually to disaffection among the electorate, who then return the Republicans to power. Once in power, the Republicans must again adjust their policies to deal with the new social reality that emerged during the Democratic administration. This process of policy adjustment and change is evident, for example, in welfare reform. According to the dialectical view of development the successive stages of equilibrium (syntheses) are marked by higher levels of integration or progress (social improvement).

For Marx, dialectical materialism means that historical change (i.e., material/economic change) is the result of conscious human activity emerging from and acting on the socially experienced contradictions of historically conditioned (i.e., human-made) economic forces and relations in order to produce a new form of social existence:

> History is nothing but the succession of separate generations, each of which exploits the materials, the forms of capital, the productive forces handed down to it by all preceding ones, and thus on the one hand, continues the traditional activity in completely changed circumstances, and on the other, modifies the old circumstances with completely changed activity. ... It shows that circumstances make men just as much as men make circumstances. (GI 38, 29).

In Marx's evolutionary view, communism is the type of society that would emerge following the overthrow of capitalism. It would be a society characterized by the abolition of private property, profit, the division of labor, and social classes. The logic of material production in communist society would require each person to contribute their labor to the everyday material and social good of the community on the basis of their diverse and multifaceted abilities (to build cabins, grow tomatoes, cook, sew, sing). Communism would deprive

> no man of the power to appropriate the products of society: all that it does is to deprive him of the power to subjugate the labour of others by means of such appropriation ... In place of the old bourgeois society, with its classes and class antagonisms, we shall have an association [a community] in which the free development of each is the condition for the free development of all. (CM 99, 105)

In contrast, therefore, to the unequal relations of capitalist production between owners and wage-workers, there would be equality between people (no one would be particularly rich or poor), thus terminating the structural conflict that inheres in capitalism – the division between the social classes, between the property-owning bourgeoisie and the property-less proletariat. Marx outlined this vision in his most publicly well-known or infamous statement, *The Communist Manifesto*. Labor, he argued, would "no longer be converted into capital, money, or rent, into a social power capable of being monopolized" (CM 98). Rather, all individuals would be entitled to "appropriate the products of society" (CM 99); hence the division of labor, private property, profit, and class inequality would disappear (CM 104–105; GI 21–23).

Consequently, communism would represent the "end of history," so to speak; it would mark the end of the periodic historical ruptures from ancient times, through the slave-owning Roman and Classical epoch (from 500 BC to AD 999), the Feudal Age (1000 to 1490), and through the various stages of capitalism. In a communist society – i.e., a society in which private property, profit, and inequality would be eliminated and thus no one class (e.g., slave-owners, feudal lords, capitalists) would control the means of production (slaves, land, capital) – there would be no more tensions and contradictions to resolve. Hence the dialectic of history (dialectical materialism) would come to a close.

Marx's vision of communism, therefore, would entail the emancipation not only of the working class, but of all people; it would represent "universal human emancipation" (EPM 82). Thus: "All previous historical movements were movements of minorities, or in the interests of minorities. The proletarian movement is the self-conscious, independent movement of the immense majority, in the interests of the immense majority" (CM 92). It would produce a communal society wherein each person would have rights and responsibilities toward the maintenance of their shared material and social existence.

The communes that have sprung up occasionally in the US and which are prominent in other societies (e.g., Israeli kibbutzim) provide a glimpse of communally cooperative societies and how they work. These "utopian" experiments, however, tend to be short lived due to the challenges confronted in trying to build a truly egalitarian communal living situation and adapt it to a larger and more complex society. The Soviet Union was organized as a socialist society – a step away from the final communist stage envisaged by Marx, but it was characterized by stark inequality and oppression (as is also evident in North Korea).

THE MILLENNIUM'S GREATEST THINKER

Although capitalism has not collapsed and yielded to communism as Marx predicted (or has not *yet* collapsed, as contemporary Marxists who have not ruled out its possible downfall might aver; e.g., Wallerstein; see chapter 15), Marx's analysis provides a trenchant critique of capitalism's underlying structure and how it works. This analysis is all the more necessary today given that capitalism is such a pervasive force across the world. Capitalism has changed a lot over the past several decades, and especially since the late 1990s, propelled by the rise of internet technology. Today's capitalist structures are much more complex than they were in the mid-to-late nineteenth century when Marx was writing. And then too there was a lot more economic and social deprivation in people's lives and a lot more industrial strife than we see today in western societies. Just think of America or England in the 1890s when child labor was a normal part of everyday life, a theme vividly portrayed in Charles Dickens's novels.

WEB 1.1

Yet, despite the changes that have occurred over the last century, Marx's ideas still help us to make sense of the ways in which capitalism infuses everyday life. The breadth and continuing relevance of Marx's analysis help explain why, as documented by the (pro-capitalist) *Economist* magazine, British public opinion at the end of the millennium (10 years after the collapse of Soviet communism) resoundingly favored Marx as the "millennium's greatest thinker" (followed by Einstein, Newton, and Darwin).

NEWS 1.4

The logic of capitalism does not just apply to one slice of everyday life – such as the economy or paid work. It also pervades the world of sports, medicine, education, Hollywood, politics, and even romance and marriage. We can still enjoy living in a capitalist society and the freedoms associated with capitalism, most especially the freedom to shop and consume. But while reading Marx, we also have to step back from our complete immersion in capitalism and all that we take for granted about capitalist society. Instead, we begin to critique it, to cast what Elvis Presley calls a suspicious mind, one that makes us probe beneath surface appearances to discern the multiple ways in which the logic of capitalism works. It makes us probe, for example, why hotel housekeepers receive low wages for their hard labor (cf. Introduction), whereas multimillionaire salaried CEOs (even in times of recession) receive additional multimillion dollar bonuses even as their company's stock declines.

> ## Topic 1.1   Corporate executive pay: Some highlights
>
> - 2008: Wall Street companies paid out $18.4 billion in bonuses.
> - 2007: Wall Street companies paid out $32.9 in bonuses.
> - 2007: Kenneth Lewis, CEO of Bank of America, was paid $14.4 million.
> - 2007: Rick Wagoner, CEO of General Motors, was paid $11.7 million.
> - 2007: CEOs' average base pay was $11.2 million.
> - 2007: Kenneth Chenault, CEO of American Express, was paid $53.2 million.
> - 2007: Robert Nardelli, Home Depot's ousted chairman and CEO, received an exit package worth more than $210 million, on top of the $64 million he was paid during his six years at the company.
> - 2006: Pfizer's CEO, Hank McKinnell, received a pension worth $83 million (though under McKinnell, Pfizer's stock fell 50 percent; and in January 2007, Pfizer announced it would be closing several manufacturing plants and cutting 7,800 jobs).
> - 2005: James J. Kilts, chief executive of Gillette, received $175 million as a "change of control" payment after agreeing to sell Gillette to Procter & Gamble.

NEWS 1.5

HUMAN NATURE

Marx's view of human nature is frequently misunderstood. Because Marx is critical of the inequality structured into capitalist society, people who have not studied him tend to think of him as being opposed to work. This is far from true. Marx, in fact, has a very positive view of work, of labor, and he saw the individual's productive skills and capacities as integral to what it means to be human. Through work, the ability to work with and transform nature, individuals demonstrate the higher consciousness of the human species. In *The German Ideology*, Marx celebrates those traits that are distinctively human. He emphasizes:

> The first premise of all human history is, of course, the existence of living human individuals. Thus the first fact to be established is the physical organization of these individuals and their consequent relation to the rest of nature ... Man can be distinguished from animals by consciousness ... [Humans] begin to distinguish themselves from animals as soon as they begin to *produce* their means of **subsistence** [their livelihood]. (GI 7)

This is a process "which is conditioned by their physical organization" and through which (i.e., by producing their means of subsistence), "men are indirectly producing their actual material life" (ibid.). The creativity shown by individuals in producing material life – their actual physical existence – something that whole populations have necessarily done throughout history as they adapt to the physical and material conditions existing in any given geographical area, is exclusive to the human species. Engagement in this process of transforming nature is integral to what Marx calls our species being (humanity); we don't just simply perform basic bodily functions (e.g., eating, sleeping, procreating) but we also creatively work in and on our physical (and social) environment and adapt it to our needs. In sum, Marx emphasizes, our ability to produce an existence – e.g., food, tools, entertainment – is what distinguishes us as humans.

The activities that individuals do in order to live and in order to reproduce their mode of existence (way of life) are what set humans apart from other species. We live with nature and we embrace our natural surroundings but we also act on nature, and in acting on nature we produce and continually reproduce our means of life, of subsistence. We don't simply accommodate to nature, but we transform nature through what we make of it and out of it, i.e., what we produce; we are what we produce. Marx argues:

> The way in which men produce their means of subsistence depends first of all on the nature of the actual means of subsistence they find in existence and have to reproduce. This mode of production must not be considered simply as being the reproduction of the physical existence of the individuals. Rather it is a definite form of activity of these individuals, a definite form of expressing their life, a definite *mode of life* on their part. As individuals express their life, so they are. What they are, therefore, coincides with their production, both with *what* they produce and with *how* they produce ... This production ... presupposes the intercourse of individuals with one another. (GI 7–8)

MATERIAL AND SOCIAL EXISTENCE INTERTWINED

Through production, we create and recreate the material world for our subsistence – to subsist not simply as animals do, but to live out a mode of existence that is compatible with who we are as a species. As humans, we are physical beings, but not that alone. Rather, we have a consciousness which allows us to be aware that we exist in relation to other individuals, and we maintain that existence by producing and interacting with other individuals. Marx elaborates:

> In production men not only act on nature but also on one another. They produce only by co-operating in a certain way and mutually exchanging their activities. In order to produce, they enter into definite connections and relations with one another and only within the social connections and relations does their action on nature, does production, take place ... Thus the social relations within which individuals produce, the social relations of production, change, are transformed, with the change and development of the material means of production, the productive forces. The relations of production in their totality constitute what are called the social relations, society, and specifically, a society at a definite stage of historical development, a society with a peculiar, distinctive character [e.g., ancient, feudal, bourgeois society]. (WLC 29–30)

Throughout history, individuals have always existed in relation to other individuals, both physically and socially. As Marx notes, Robinson Crusoe, the epitome of the lone individual favored by economists in discussing the laws of capitalism, is a fictional character. In historical fact, there is no Robinson Crusoe. Explorers, settlers, immigrants have always adapted to their physical surroundings by working collectively to transform their surroundings and in the process to create society. Society is made up of

> real individuals, their [practical] activity and the material conditions under which they live, both those which they find already existing and those produced by their activity ... Life is not determined by consciousness, but consciousness by life ... the real living individuals themselves ... men, not in any fantastic isolation and rigidity, but in their actual, empirically perceptible process of development under definite conditions. (GI 7,15)

Individuals' material existence, therefore, *what* people do in everyday life and *how* they do it is what matters; it is this "practical activity" (GI 15) that we need to focus on, Marx says. Existence, for Marx, is not something abstract or philosophical. Questions about the meaning of existence have a place in human thinking – we may all have some existential doubts and this may be a good topic for late-night conversations propelled by reading existentialist writers (e.g., Jean-Paul Sartre, Albert Camus). But Marx is not interested in looking at existence this way. He wants us to focus on the actuality of our existence, the concrete things we do, the living conditions and practices that characterize everyday reality, because through practical activity "definite individuals who are productively active in a definite way enter into ... definite social and political relations" (GI 13). Hence if we want to apprehend what is going on in society, the nature of social structures and of social relations, we must study the "life-process of definite [real] individuals ... [who] produce materially, and are active under definite material limits" (GI 13). This is what sociologists do. We don't simply theorize about social life; we go out into society and investigate how real people live in definite social contexts.

CAPITALISM AS A DISTINCTIVE SOCIAL FORM

PRIVATE PROPERTY

Marx emphasizes that the notion of private property developed as the world became more populated and more complex in its social organization. Private ownership was the norm in ancient Rome (e.g., ownership of slaves) and in the feudal system of organization that characterized Europe during the Middle Ages, and it is a core characteristic of capitalism. In capitalist society, ownership of the means of production – of land, oil wells, factories, capital – differentiates the bourgeoisie from the proletariat, and on this unequal division rests the whole system of economic, i.e., class, and social relations (GI 8–13).

Society, therefore, has long been stratified (organized into unequal classes or strata). Inequality is not the result of the transition to capitalism or the result of industrialized, factory production; rather, from as early as the slave-owning Roman Empire, inequality has characterized social organization and social relationships.

THE PRODUCTION OF PROFIT

Marx singles out capitalism for specific critique, however, largely because in his assessment (and in accord with his progressive view of the march of history), capitalism had outlived its usefulness. Therefore while Marx appreciated the economic and technological advances achieved by capitalism, and recognized it as a progression over previous modes of production (e.g., feudalism), he also emphasized what he saw as its regressive aspects. In particular, Marx underscored the fact that capitalism is a system of commodity production – its fundamental objective is the production of commodities whose sale in the marketplace produces capital (money/economic resources) which accumulates as profit for the capitalist. With the production of capital/profit as the prime objective in a capitalist society, this means that the ties among individuals are purely determined by economic interests, their ties to capital. Capitalism requires a mass of individuals who must sell their labor power, and the only relevance wage-workers have for the capitalists is the extent to which they can be used (employed) to produce profit for the capitalist.

This, according to Marx, is what sets capitalist social relations apart from those in ancient Roman or in feudal social systems. In Roman society, slavery was the norm and inequality clearly existed between slaves and masters (and there was also inequality between free men and women). Notwithstanding this blatant inequality, however, slave-masters also had a certain commitment to the welfare of their slaves, as did feudal lords toward their serfs – even if these commitments were driven largely by self-interest. Feudal lords, for example, did not abandon the serfs in times of famine – they felt obliged to still feed the serfs even though the serfs were (temporarily) unable to produce food for the manor.

Conversely, under capitalism, when there is an economic downturn or when profits are sluggish for whatever reason, factory owners and corporations fire many of their workers; they downsize and retrench – thus Pfizer laid off over seven thousand workers in Brooklyn, New York, when its profits were hurt by other companies' sales of generic drugs. And notwithstanding any personal regrets that a given individual capitalist might have, he or she is obliged to terminate a worker's employment – this is what "the economy" (i.e., capitalism, "Wall Street") requires. Capitalism as a system of profit production requires the factory owner or corporation to maintain economic competitiveness vis-à-vis other companies, to cut production costs and maintain profitability, or else face the collapse of the company.

NEWS 1.6

In capitalist society, the capitalists, the owners of capital, the owners of the means of the production of capital – whether of land, factories, railroads, or technological systems – and additionally in today's economy, the owners/executives of television networks, oil companies, and of high-tech, financial and other corporations – what Marx would call the bourgeoisie – care about workers, the proletariat, only to the extent that they have use-value, i.e., the extent to which they can be put to use in producing something useful, something that results in producing capital and profit for the capitalists. Marx elaborates: "The capitalist buys labour-power in order to use it; … The purchaser of labour-power consumes it by setting the seller of it to work … on something useful" (Cap 197). Thus, the extent to which use-value converts into capital, into profit, becomes the criterion determining social relations in a capitalist society. The ties between individuals are based on "naked self-interest," and sentiment and honor are displaced by the only value that matters in a capitalist society, the "callous 'cash payment'" (CM 82); in short, "Show me the money" is the catch-cry informing social relations under capitalism.

What is especially distinctive about capitalism vis-à-vis other historical systems of inequality is that under capitalism, workers are free – this is a mark of progress; workers are not owned by masters, even though historically, slavery was integral to the expansion of capitalism (e.g., Patterson 1982; cf. chapter 12). In democratic capitalist societies, political and economic freedom tend to go together (though there are historical exceptions, such as South African apartheid). The entwining of economic and political freedom produces the historically unusual circumstance whereby in capitalist societies, free workers sell their labor or, more specifically, their labor power on the market. And in doing so, wage-workers themselves become commodities, to be bought and sold. Capitalism thus requires, and is defined by, the commodification of labor. Marx explains:

> what [workers] sell to the capitalist for money is their labor *power*. The capitalist buys this labor power for a day, a week, a month etc. And after he has bought it, he uses it by having the workers work for the stipulated time. For the same sum with which the capitalist has bought their labor power, for example, two marks [German currency], he could have bought two pounds of sugar or a definite amount of any other commodity. The two marks with which he bought two pounds of sugar, are the *price* of the two pounds of sugar. The two marks, with which he bought twelve hours' use of labor power, are the price of twelve hours' labor. Labor power, therefore, is a commodity neither more nor less than sugar. The former is measured by the clock, the latter by the scales. Labor power is, therefore, a commodity which its possessor, the wage worker, sells to capital … Labor power was not always a commodity. Labor was not always wage labor, that is, free labor. The slave did not sell his labor power to the slave owner anymore than the ox sells its services to the peasant. The slave [in ancient Rome], together with his labor power, is sold once and for all to his owner. He is a commodity which can pass from the hand of one owner to that of another. He is *himself* a commodity, but the labor power is not *his* commodity. The serf [in medieval/feudal times] sells only a part of his labor power. He does not

receive a wage from the owner of the land; rather, the owner of the land receives a tribute from him ... The free laborer, on the other hand, sells himself and indeed sells himself piecemeal ... The worker belongs neither to an owner nor to the land, but eight, ten, twelve, fifteen hours of his daily life belong to him who buys them. (WLC 17–21)

Thus the freedom under capitalism is really an illusion, Marx argues, because in reality capitalism is a coercive system of labor exploitation. In capitalist societies, the commodities produced are not solely the sorts of things we typically think of, such as manufactured goods, our clothes and food, or even information and service goods. Labor power itself is a commodity. Wage-workers are exchanged and traded on the market and their market value, as with other commodities, is given a price. And although wage-workers, unlike slaves and serfs, are free to leave a particular employer because they do not like the price they get for their labor or do not like their general working conditions, this freedom is always constrained. The movement of labor may appear on the surface to be done freely, but it is in fact required, demanded, and coerced by capitalism.

Marx explains:

The worker leaves the capitalist to whom he hires himself whenever he likes, and the capitalist discharges him whenever he thinks fit, as soon as he no longer gets any profit out of him, or not the anticipated profit. But the worker, whose sole source of livelihood is the sale of his labor power, cannot leave the *whole class of purchasers,* that is, the capitalist class, without renouncing his existence. He belongs not to this or that capitalist but to the *capitalist class,* and, moreover, it is his business to dispose of himself, that is, to find a purchaser within this capitalist class. (WLC 21)

Accordingly, for Marx, wage-labor is in essence "forced labour." (EPM 74) Whereas slavery is "*direct* forced labour," wage-labor is "*indirect* forced labour."

In a capitalist society, workers are obligated to present their labor power, their usefulness to a prospective employer, as a commodity for sale. In sum, laborers "live only so long as they find work, and ... find work only so long as their labour increases capital. These labourers, who must sell themselves piecemeal,

Wal-Mart's employee policies epitomize the low-wage, cost-reduction strategies required by contemporary capitalism.

45

are a commodity, like every other article of commerce, and are consequently exposed to all the vicissitudes of competition, to all the fluctuations of the market" (CM 87).

PROFESSIONAL SPORTS: THE COMMODIFICATION OF LABOR IN ACTION

The commodification of labor is well demonstrated in professional sports. We see this in several ways. The very language that professional sports organizations and teams use in talking about their hiring practices ensures that there is no ambiguity about the fact that football or basketball players are evaluated as commodities; as underscored in the US by the annual National Football League (NFL) draft day. We hear about the *trading* that occurs prior to draft day; one team exchanges their #5 pick in exchange for two lower-ranked choices from a different team; we hear how much a prospective player is willing to settle for, what price he will accept for his labor power; and we are left in no doubt that the quarter-back (QB) is being selected (and subsequently assessed) not for his all-around athletic ability or leadership qualities, but for his *piecemeal* value – his arm, his ability to throw the ball, his "passing efficiency." Despite the glamour (think of Tom Brady, the Patriots QB), the quarter-back more than any other player – and especially compared to defensive backs whose whole bodies are commodified – is reduced to the value of one body piece, the usefulness of his arm. And the efficiency of the arm is determined statistically: the number of completed passes and the ratio of touchdowns to interceptions thrown.

We see similar efficiency-evaluation scales used across all professional sports. Players' usefulness is determined by their productivity; their statistics (e.g., the velocity with which baseball pitchers hit the ball, the number of three-point shots in basketball, the number of goals scored, etc.) provide a shorthand metric determining their market value. And while some players are "free agents," not bound by their contract to a previous team-owner, they are nonetheless, as Marx reminds us, not really free; they must find another team-owner to whom to sell themselves;

Topic 1.2 Scouting new football recruits

The evaluation of football players as efficient physical objects – as future profit-generating commodities – is the primary purpose of the NFL's annual Scouting Combine. At this week-long event, college football players are evaluated by NFL coaches and scouts. Several tough physical tests assess the players' physical strength and especially their speed – because in the NFL "each second makes a difference" to the player's and the team's success. It is not all about speed, however. At the Combine, "the least exhaustive test ... often takes the longest to prepare for ... the look test ... During a medical exam, the prospects strip to their shorts to reveal whether they look the part of a football player." For some, this means bulking-up, for others, slimming down.

NEWS 1.7

---

they are not free to leave the capitalist class of team-owners. They can leave one but not all; otherwise they would not subsist. Wage-workers, whether professional sports players or waitresses, have to sell their labor power. Why do they sell it?

> In order to live. But the exercise of labor power, labor, is the worker's own life activity, the manifestation of his own life. And this life activity he sells to another person in order to secure the necessary *means of subsistence*. Thus his life activity is for him only a means to enable him to exist. He works in order to live. He does not even reckon labor as part of his life, it is rather a sacrifice of his life. It is a commodity which he has made over to another. (WLC 19)

Clearly, professional sports players earn huge sums of money; many garner multimillion dollar deals and these earnings allow them to meet their subsistence needs far more easily than is the case for waitresses, sales people, skilled workers, and most professional workers (e.g., lawyers, doctors). Nonetheless, despite their exceedingly high income, the truth remains that professional sports players are commodities, and perhaps more than many other workers, they literally sacrifice their lives in order to work. How many sports players retire with a lot of money, but severely disabled from a career marked by repeated concussions and other injuries which have a long-term debilitating impact on the player's physical and mental functioning? This is a topic garnering increased attention in football circles, despite the NFL's relative silence on the issue.

NEWS 1.8

Not only do professional athletes endure these injuries as simply an incidental part of their job, they willingly choose to actively harm their bodies over the long term by taking steroids to build up their short-term strength. As early as high school, young men are taking steroids – substances that over time build up cumulative negative effects on an individual's physical and mental health – in order to enhance the price they can get for themselves when (in actuality, *if*) they make it to draft day and a professional career.

NEWS 1.9

WORK: LIFE SACRIFICE

There is compelling evidence from professional sports of workers' willingness to sacrifice their health for someone else's profit. But many other wage-workers sacrifice their health by working in dangerous jobs in return for relatively low earnings. Meat-packers, miners, firefighters, police officers, soldiers, and construction workers confront the threat of injury and death on a regular basis. But even apart from these particularly life-threatening jobs, all wage-workers, Marx reminds us, sell their labor power "in order to live" (WLC 19), to exist. Work thus becomes a means to an end rather than an end in itself; it loses its potential to be a creative and cooperative activity reflective of humans' higher consciousness (as would occur in the communist society envisaged by Marx). Its value is instead determined by its usefulness in the production of capitalist profit.

Furthermore, even if steroid-using athletes were assured of success – of getting drafted (bought) or getting a contract extension – a Marxist-derived analysis

> **Topic 1.3**   Occupational injuries in the meat-packing industry
>
> A recent report by Human Rights Watch concluded that "Meatpacking work has extraordinarily and unnecessarily high rates of injury, musculoskeletal disorders (repetitive stress injuries), and even death. Whatever the inherent dangers of meatpacking work, they are aggravated by ever-increasing line speeds, inadequate training, close-quarters cutting, and long hours with few breaks … Almost every worker interviewed … for this report began with the story of a serious injury he or she suffered in a meat or poultry plant, injuries reflected in their scars, swellings, rashes, amputations, blindness or other afflictions." Among the meat-industry injuries recorded by the US federal Occupational Safety and Health Administration (OSHA) were the following:
>
> - "Worker killed when hog-splitting saw is activated."
> - "Worker dies when he is pulled into a conveyor and crushed."
> - "Worker loses legs when a worker activates the grinder in which he is standing."
> - "Worker loses hand when he reaches under a boning table to hose meat from chain."

NEWS 1.10

would argue that they are deluded by a false consciousness, a consciousness that is itself the historical product of capitalism. Because, as Marx tells us, we embrace the "illusion" of the capitalist epoch in which we live (GI 30) – its affirmation and celebration of freedom, equality, money, and consumption (GI 40) – we willingly and freely sell ourselves because we believe that we are profiting through our particular actions.[2] But this is false: the capitalist will always profit more than even the most highly paid professional athlete. And the capitalist's profit, by definition, comes at the expense of the wage-worker's life. Wage-workers, though consciously working to produce capital (and hence to reproduce capitalism as a system), work under the historically produced illusion that capitalism is a natural economic system rather than a historically specific and humanly produced economic system that favors some (the owners/capitalists) at the expense of others (wage-workers). Under capitalism, therefore, wage-workers are unable to develop a true consciousness of how their economic interests are in contradiction with those of capitalism; they cannot see that their objective class position and economic interests are in contradiction with the class position and economic interests of the capitalists (for whom belief in the naturalness of capitalism fits with their economic interests).[3]

WAGE-LABOR

Whereas slaves knew they were slaves, and serfs knew they were indentured to a lord, wage-workers think they are free; they may think of themselves as just trying to make a decent living, but in essence, as we recall, they are commodities bought and sold on the market for others' pleasure and profit accumulation.

> What [a wage laborer] produces for himself is not the silk that he weaves, not the gold that he draws from the mine, not the palace that he builds. What he produces for himself is wages, and silk, gold, and palace resolve themselves for him into a definite quantity of the means of subsistence, perhaps into a cotton jacket, some copper coins and a lodging in a cellar. And the worker who for twelve hours, weaves, spins, drills, turns, builds, shovels, break stones, carries loads etc., – does he consider this twelve hours' weeding, spinning, drilling, turning, building, shoveling, stone-breaking as a manifestation of his life, as life? On the contrary life begins for him when this activity ceases, at table, in the public house, in bed. The twelve hours labor, on the other hand, has no meaning for him as weaving, spinning, drilling etc., but as *earnings*, which bring them to the table, to the public house, into bed. (WLC 20)

WAGE-LABOR AND SURPLUS VALUE

What the high-income professional sports player and the low-income hotel housekeeper have in common is that surplus value is extracted from both by their respective employers. Since the logic of capitalism is the accumulation of profit, this profit has to come from somewhere. It comes from the extra value – the surplus value – and hence the extra capital that is created by wage-workers' labor. As you may know, the laws of supply and demand influence how much a given worker or a group or class of workers, electricians say, can earn in a given place at any given time. How well the economy is doing, and whether there is an under- or over-supply of qualified workers available in a particular locale to make or distribute a particular commodity for which there is a market demand (e.g., new housing, dentists, restaurant services at a seaside resort), impact how much money workers can command for their labor power.

Marx recognizes these factors in determining wages. But he also highlights an even more basic way in which wages are determined – the actual cost of production. Marx argues:

> the price of labor will be determined by the cost of production, by the labor time necessary to produce this commodity – labor power. *What then is the cost of production of labor power? It is the cost required for maintaining the worker as a worker and of developing him into a worker. ... The price of his labor* will, therefore, be determined by the *price of the necessary means of subsistence* ... Another consideration ... in calculating the cost of production of simple labor power, there must be included the cost of reproduction, whereby the race of workers is enabled to multiply and to replace worn-out workers by new ones. Thus the depreciation of the worker is taken into account in the same way as the depreciation of the machine. The cost of production of simple labor power, therefore, amounts to the *cost of existence and reproduction of the worker*. The price of this cost of existence and reproduction constitutes wages. Wages so determined are called the *wage minimum*. (WLC 27–28)

In other words, the capitalist pays the worker the minimum necessary to ensure the worker's physical subsistence as a worker, and his or her social existence so that it is conducive to the actual physical and social reproduction of a new generation of workers. These are necessary costs that the capitalist encounters in reproducing current and future workers who can be put to work creating capital and profit. In return for these wages, the capitalist receives "the productive activity of the worker, the creative power whereby the worker not only replaces what he consumes [as a worker] but gives to the accumulated labor a greater value than it previously possessed … he produces capital" (WLC 32). And, this capital has a surplus value for the capitalist above and beyond the worker's production cost (i.e., the cost to the capitalist of the worker's subsistence and reproduction as a worker).

Marx explains surplus value as the differential between a worker's exchange-value – simply another way to refer to a worker's wages; the market value of a worker's labor – and his use-value:

> The daily cost of maintaining [labor] and its daily expenditure in work, are two totally different things. The former [the cost of maintaining labor, i.e. the subsistence and reproduction of the worker] determines the exchange value of the labour-power, the latter [the living labor that it can call into action] is its use-value … Therefore, the value of labour power, and the value which that labour-power creates in the labour process are two entirely different magnitudes, and this difference of the two values was what the capitalist had in view, when he was purchasing the labour power … What really influenced him was the specific use-value which this commodity possesses of being a source not only of value, but of more value than it has itself. This is the special service that the capitalist expects from labour power, and in this transaction he acts in accordance with the 'eternal laws' of the exchange of commodities. The seller of labour-power, like the seller of any other commodity, realizes [acquires] its exchange value, and parts with its use-value. He cannot take the one without giving the other. The use value of labour-power (labor) … belongs just as little to its seller, as the use-value of oil after it has been sold belongs to the dealer who has sold it. (Cap 215–216)

THE GAP BETWEEN EXCHANGE-VALUE AND USE-VALUE

Consequently, what workers are paid – their earnings/market value or exchange-value – and what they are paid for – their labor power/use-value, their usefulness in creating capital/profit – are two very different things. The capitalist pays the exchange-value (wages) of 20 hours' labor power but gets the use-value of 40 hours' labor; the wage-workers' usefulness in creating capital extends beyond what they are paid for, and this difference between their exchange-value (wages) and their use-value to the capitalist is what constitutes surplus value, or profit (Cap 207–217). For workers to subsist and to physically maintain themselves as workers, they may need only to work for 4 hours a day, but they work for 8 hours a day. A worker may need to prepare and cook 12 cheese pizzas every day in exchange for the wages he is paid by the restaurant owner. But in fact, he prepares

48 pizzas every day; thus he creates surplus value for the owner through his labor in producing the 36 additional pizzas. The additional hours worked, or the additional pizzas prepared by the worker, over and above his production cost to the capitalist (including the costs of the ingredients, electricity, building maintenance, etc.), is the surplus value that is taken by the capitalist. And it is this surplus value, produced by the worker, that constitutes the capitalist's profit.

Accordingly, the capitalist's surplus value is the worker's surplus labor (Cap 207–217), and the production of this surplus value/surplus labor is what is necessary to capitalism, to the pursuit of profit, the engine that drives capitalism. The more productive workers are, the more surplus value they create for the capitalist, and therefore, the cheaper they are for the capitalist to buy. Just as we sometimes comment to a friend that something we bought was "good value," that we got, for instance, a long-desired pair of jeans on sale below their typical retail cost, so too "productive" workers, i.e., surplus value/profit-producing workers, are good value for the capitalist. Just consider why the US has so many undocumented workers that continue to find employment. It is because they are useful to the capitalists in creating profit, and as Marxist sociologists would also emphasize, they are easy to exploit. Moreover, their availability expands the pool of wage-labor from which capitalists can pick and thus adds to the competition between workers that capitalism fosters (and exploits). It is not accidental, therefore, that business organizations are among the most vocal supporters of immigration reform in the US. Illegal immigrants, as Senator John McCain, the 2009 Republican presidential candidate, stated, should be treated with dignity "because they are God's creatures." But they are also resources – commodities – to be exploited by the pro-business lobbies supporting and funding McCain.

📰 NEWS 1.11

Remember that workers are commodities; their proportional cost to the capitalist decreases the more surplus value or capital they produce for the capitalist. So the more they work – the more surplus labor they do (beyond the cost to the capitalist of their subsistence and reproduction as workers) and the more surplus capital they create for the capitalist – the further their cost to the capitalist decreases. Hence Marx's comment: "The worker becomes all the poorer the more wealth he produces ... The worker becomes an ever cheaper commodity the more commodities he creates" (EPM 71). The workers' use-value to the capitalist increases but their exchange-value, the cost of maintaining them as workers, decreases in inverse proportion to their use-value. The workers' use-value (to the capitalist) is greater than their exchange-value is to themselves, as indicated by the wages they earn in exchange for selling their labor power, their use value (Cap 215–216). In short, workers are more useful to the capitalist than they are to themselves.

In sum, Marx sensitizes us to the inequalities in capitalism, inequalities that are not simply a side effect or a result of capitalism, but which are built into the very structure and organization of capitalism as a mode of production. Capitalism requires inequality; it requires workers to produce commodities that are sold by the capitalist for profit. The wage-worker's surplus sweat in producing surplus value beyond the worker's cost to the employer allows the employer (the purchaser of that labor power) to cool off at his or her Caribbean beach house bought with the profit from the surplus value produced by surplus labor.

THE DIVISION OF LABOR AND ALIENATION

The division of labor, or economic and occupational specialization, is a dominant feature of modern capitalist society, and has progressively evolved over time (GI 8). Thus, agricultural production is separated from industrial and commercial production, and both, in turn, are separated from cultural and financial production. The division of labor thus separates sectors and workers into exclusive spheres of ever-more specialized activity. Adam Smith (1776/1925), the eighteenth-century Scottish philosopher and advocate of free market capitalism, emphasized the material advantages that derive from exchange based on occupational specialization and the division of labor. Marx, by contrast, underscores its negative, fragmentary effects. Marx argues that individuals have the human ability to do many things and to have many creative interests and hobbies. But the division of labor as a thing-like, objectified structure of capitalism reduces the individual to the performance of the specialized activity for which each has the most use-value in the production of capital (e.g., football quarterback Tom Brady's arm-throwing labor).[4] Thus, Marx states, "as soon as labor is distributed, each man has a particular exclusive sphere of activity, which is forced upon him and from which he cannot escape. He is a hunter, a fisherman, a shepherd, or a critical critic, and must remain so if he does not want to lose his means of livelihood; while in communist society where nobody has one exclusive sphere of activity, but each can become accomplished in any branch he wishes ... makes it possible for me to do one thing to-day and another to-morrow, to hunt in the morning, fish in the afternoon, rear cattle in the evening, criticize after dinner, just as I have a mind, without ever becoming hunter, fisherman, shepherd or critic" (GI 22).

THE PRODUCTION PROCESS

The organization of capitalist production – whether in factories, construction sites, or corporate offices – ensures the usefulness or efficiency of workers in the creation of surplus value, capitalist profit. Workers' tasks are divided into minute elements so that each individual is responsible for a very specific aspect of the production process. The diversity of occupations that exist in any industrialized country in the world today underscores the point that to make a living in today's economy, a worker must specialize in a highly defined labor activity. Just picking a random page in the US Census occupational code, we see the following specialized jobs: "aircraft cleaner, aircraft communicator, aircraft designer, aircraft electrician, aircraft engine specialist, aircraft instrument tester, aircraft lay out worker, aircraft log clerk, aircraft machinist, aircraft metalsmith, aircraft painter, aircraft riveter, aircraft stress analyst," and so on.

The fast-moving, assembly-line production we associate with the manufacture of goods (whether cars, pizzas, or candy) epitomizes the division of labor under capitalism (see Lucille Ball in the *I Love Lucy* Candy Factory comedy episode, available on YouTube). Assembly-line production assigns specific tasks to each worker (or worker team), whose speedy task accomplishment is essential to the smooth, uninterrupted operation of commodity production. A similar division of labor is evident in the production (construction) of houses: a primary contractor is hired to build the house and in turn hires a whole retinue of subcontractor specialists: laborers, plasterers, plumbers, carpenters, electricians, roofers, and landscapers.

ALIENATED LABOR

The division of labor may seem necessary to dividing responsibility and expertise for the many complex jobs that need to be done in society, and ensuring that labor is used efficiently to produce the vast amount of commodities that are needed to meet consumer demand. But Marx wants us to see it differently – to see it as dehumanizing of the individual and of society. Marx argues that the commodification of labor such that workers are reduced to commodities (with exchange- and use-value) produces alienation, or alienated labor. Alienated labor is the result of the economic and social organization of capitalism, and specifically of the division of labor. The alienation of labor manifests itself in four interrelated ways (see EPM 71–81).

(a) Alienation of workers from the products they produce

Workers are alienated or estranged from the products their labor produces; both their labor and the product of their labor is *external* to them both literally and in terms of ownership. A worker's labor is not his or her own, but is "forced labour" (EPM 74), it belongs to the employer. Similarly, the products of the worker's labor do not belong to the worker, but to someone else – the employer who sells the product/commodity and the consumer who buys it. The commodities that workers produce are not theirs to use despite their having made them; they are only theirs to buy. Thus the product of a worker's labor (like the labor itself) becomes a force that is external to the worker. Rather than being the objective reflection of the worker's transformation of raw materials into something new – an object available to the worker – the product of the worker's labor becomes an object, an object for someone else's disposal on the market; "it exists outside him, independently, as something alien to him; ... it becomes a power of its own confronting him: it means that the life which he has conferred on the object confronts him as something hostile and alien" (EPM 72). Marx refers to this process as the objectification of labor. The products produced by a worker's labor exert a power over the worker; the worker must keep producing more and more products (and service workers must serve more and more customers, or, like hotel housekeepers, clean

53

more rooms, change more beds, etc.) – but the value of this extra work returns to the capitalist and not to the worker.

This idea fits with Marx's thesis (see p. 51 above) that the more commodities the worker produces the relatively poorer the worker himself or herself becomes. Wages can increase, but the profit return to the capitalist from the wage-worker's labor will always be proportionally greater than the wages paid to (for) the worker. Wage-labor thus differs from the labor done, for example, under feudalism, where the farmer-serfs ploughed the land, planted the seeds, tilled and cultivated the furrows, and then harvested the crops and kept what was necessary for their and their family's subsistence. The farmers experienced the complete cycle of production and produced for their own needs while also producing for others; as did the blacksmith, the tanner, and all the other farmers and craft workers under the feudal lord's tutelage.

(b) Alienation of workers in the production process

The worker is also alienated through the **production process** itself. The process of production is "active alienation," whereby the "worker's own physical and mental energy" is turned against him (EPM: 74, 75). Labor is not for the worker an end in itself and freely chosen, but is coerced by and performed for someone else; most immediately, the capitalist employer. Wage-labor is "activity performed in the service, under the dominion, the coercion and the yoke of another" (EPM 80). In short, wage-workers do not determine what they produce or how they produce it; but are simply objects in the production process. As those of you who have worked in restaurants know, your daily schedule and the number of tables/customers you serve are not spontaneously determined by you but by your supervisor/employer. And the speed with which you serve the customers is also not yours to decide; each employer sets prior standards and rules that you have to abide by, irrespective of how you are feeling on a given day. (See Topic 1.4, p. 57.)

(c) Alienation of workers from their species being

The production process reduces workers to objects with use-value in commodity production, and thus alienates them from their species being, from the creativity and higher consciousness that distinguish humans from animals (EPM 76–77). Wage-labor coerces us to use work – our life activity – as a means to our physical existence rather than using our physical existence to realize our humanity and to engage in the freely chosen physical and mental activities of which our species is capable. Therefore, while in principle, work can be a creative extension of our selves – "the productive life is the life of the species. It is life-engendering life" – under capitalism, "life itself appears only as a means to life" (EPM 76) – i.e., we work to live (to subsist) rather than (creatively) working as part of a fully human-social life. Alienated labor strips work of its intrinsic human meaning and its potential to express human creativity, and in this process, humans are reduced essentially to an animal-like status; they are alienated from the very things that distinguish them as humans. Marx writes:

First, the fact that labor is external to the worker, i.e., it does not belong to his essential being; that in his work, therefore, he does not affirm himself but denies himself, does not feel content but unhappy, does not develop freely his physical and mental energy but mortifies his body and ruins his mind. The worker therefore only feels himself outside his work, and in his work feels outside himself. He is at home when he is not working, and when he is working he is not at home. His labor is therefore not voluntary, but coerced; it is *forced labor*. It is therefore not the satisfaction of a need; it is merely a *means* to satisfy needs external to it ... man (the worker) no longer feels himself to be freely active in any but his animal functions – eating, drinking, procreating, or at most in his dwelling and in dressing-up, etc.; and in his human functions he no longer feels himself to be anything but an animal. What is animal becomes human and what is human becomes animal. Certainly eating, drinking, procreating, etc., are also genuine human functions. But in the abstraction which separates them from the sphere of all other human activity and turns them into sole and ultimate ends, they are animal. (EPM 74)

(d) Alienation of individuals from one another

Although humans are a social species who relate to and cooperatively interact with others, capitalism produces "the *estrangement of man* from *man*" (EPM 78), of individuals from one another. Work becomes the individual's life, rather than the means by which individuals enjoy their life with others. The demands of work, whether for wage-laborers (e.g., hotel housekeepers) or for professionals in corporate suites (e.g., Epstein et al. 1999), are not conducive to workers' family life or to their participation in community activities; the demands of work require that work rather than non-work activities receive priority. At Wal-Mart, for example, new workplace policies "to create a cheaper, more flexible work force by capping wages, using more part-time workers and scheduling more workers on nights and weekends" mean that workers are pressured to be available 24/7. This strategy is seen as an attempt by Wal-Mart to have more part-time than full-time employees, thus reducing Wal-Mart's wage costs, expanding its profits, and enhancing its stock rating on Wall Street. Workers are worried, however, that awkward time scheduling and around-the-clock, shift-availability demands will negatively impact their family and other commitments – making it difficult for them to care for their children, to attend school functions, or to go to church. One worker said: "it makes it hard to establish routines like reading to your kids at night or having dinner together as a family."

NEWS 1.12

And at work, the alienation of workers from one another is accomplished through the production process: its demands of speed and efficiency – the number of beds made, of customers served, of hours billable to a client – require workers to work rather than to socialize. Another way in which workers are alienated from one another is through the competitive nature of the workplace. Who will be the employee of the month? Who will get a bonus? Who will get the most valuable player award? These are competitive awards of which there are winners and losers, thus pitting workers against one another, and they exist across all work sectors, from fast-food restaurants to Wall Street. The worker who receives an award will be the one who has been the most productive (i.e., created the most surplus value/profit) during a given time interval: who delivers more pizzas, sells more condominiums, logs more billable hours. So, even when it seems that companies (including universities) are being nice to workers by giving them bonuses and prizes, from a Marxist perspective, these incentives are nothing more than another capitalist strategy to ensure that more and more surplus value, more and more profit is being produced by workers for their respective employers and for the capitalist class as a whole.

Capitalist production, moreover, is structured so that the livelihoods of employed workers are in constant threat from those on the sidelines (e.g., due to seasonal work, unemployment, immigration flows). The capitalist always has access to the labor power of the unemployed; current employees can be fired and replaced by other workers who must necessarily find work in order to live, to make a living wage. This is yet another way in which labor is coerced and by which capitalism sets individuals against one another. Further, interworker competition is geographically globalized; hence workers in the US, for example, are stripped of sympathy for their fellow-workers in the sweat shops of China, whom they see largely as undermining their own continuing employment (thus further dampening the development of the class consciousness of the proletariat envisaged by Marx).

Box 1.1 Four types of alienation produced by capitalism

1. Alienation from the products produced
2. Alienation through the production process
3. Alienation of individuals from their species being (human essence)
4. Alienation of individuals from one another

THE OPPRESSION OF CAPITALISTS

In Marx's analysis, it is not just wage-workers who are alienated under capitalism – so are the capitalists. Thus factory owners and corporate executives are also in servitude to production demands, i.e., the production of capital. There are, for example, at least two competing firms in the poultry industry (Koch Foods and Sun Kist); and thus both must compete with one another to cut production costs and increase profits and market share.

NEWS 1.13

Although capitalists' relation to capital – as owners of land, factories, corporations – is quite different to that of workers, and although the production process is organized to maximize the capitalists' accumulation of capital, nevertheless the capitalists themselves are controlled by capital, though it may seem that they are its masters. In actuality, their life-activity is driven toward the accumulation of capital. To succeed as capitalists they must defer their non-economic interests and activities to the pursuit of profit; this activity takes on a life of its own and renders the capitalists "under the sway of [the] inhuman power" of capital" (EPM 125).

There is much evidence of this in the business world. For example, James Kilts, the retired, highly successful former chairman and chief executive of Gillette, accepted a post-retirement appointment managing a private investment firm. He

Topic 1.4   Laboring in the poultry factory

If we were to step inside the poultry plants in Tennessee and Alabama, we would see what is entailed in the alienation of labor that Marx discusses. At these plants, there is a highly specialized division of labor; the women who work in the plant's "deboning line" are not just *poultry* workers, but, more specifically, chicken deboners or "wing cutters." Their personal identity is reduced to this highly specific wing-cutting activity such that they are described as if they were machines, as objects rather than humans (i.e., alienated in the production process and from their human species being). The production process, i.e., the factory owner's production demands on these cutters, is very specific: to maintain a "42 chickens a minute line speed" – almost a chicken per second. One consequence of this production speed pressure is that workers are not allowed to have bathroom breaks and thus are unable to attend to their basic physical needs. Similarly, there is no time for chatting with other workers on the line. These demands thus produce alienated labor; the workers' physical and social needs are subjugated to the demands of profit production as the workers, who make approximately 18,000 deboning cuts during a typical shift (eight hours), prepare the chicken pieces for supermarket sales to consumers. The deboned chicken breasts and fillets etc. thus come to exist as objects that have an external, controlling power over the workers; they are not for the workers' consumption, for satisfaction of their physical hunger, but are tallies of the workers' speed and productivity (thus producing workers' alienation from the products of their labor). Most chicken deboners, even those with a lot of experience, earn less than $8 an hour. Given that a packet of chicken tenders sells in the supermarket for about $7, we can readily see that, even taking account of the expense incurred in raising a chicken, and the production costs and profit margins in the distribution chain from factory owners to shop owners, there is a substantial gap between the worker's exchange-value (approx. $8 per hour) and their use-value (deboning over 2,000 chickens per hour) – the surplus value or profit their labor produces for the factory owner. Chicken-cutters produce a lot of surplus value. Nevertheless, their profit usefulness is lessened if they take bathroom breaks – thus this activity is regulated. It is not the worker who freely decides when she needs to go to the bathroom; like the amount of wing-cuts required, this need is determined externally – by factory owners who are mindful only of profit production demands. And Wal-Mart has similar restrictions on rest breaks for its employees. Thus capitalism produces workers' alienation because workers' basic human-physical and social needs are suppressed in order to meet production demands that are set to ensure the highest possible surplus value/profit for the factory owner.

NEWS 1.13

NEWS 1.12

commented that, unlike some of his peers at other firms who work *part-time* (i.e., 5 days a week), his was a 24/7 commitment. The need for Mr Kilts to work seven days a week was not driven by his lack of personal wealth; when Gillette was sold to Procter & Gamble (P & G) in 2005, he received $175 million, and an additional $19.1 million subsequently as vice-chairman of P & G. Yet, despite his extensive economic assets, he is still enchanted by the prospect of making even more money; this is the lure of capitalism and capital accumulation.

NEWS 1.5

The pressure exerted by capital accumulation on the everyday, capital-accumulation habits of corporate executives gives flesh to Marx's argument that:

> The less you eat, drink and read books; the less you go to the theater, the dance hall, the public house; the less you think, love, theorize, sing, paint, fence etc., the more you save – the *greater* becomes your treasure which neither moths nor dust will devour – your *capital*. The less you *are*, the more you *have*; the less you express your own life, the greater is your *alienated* life – the greater is the store of your estranged being ... all passions and all activity must therefore be submerged in *avarice*. (EPM 118–119)

This avarice is not necessarily a personal trait of any individual capitalist but is demanded by capitalism: the accumulation of capital and of profit is a ceaseless task; it is a seven-days-a-week commitment.

And if the capitalist fails to serve capital by accumulating profit in an ever-greater amount, he or she will have to leave the capitalist class or, in today's more differentiated corporate structure, leave its higher echelons, at least for a while (like Robert Nardelli who was fired as CEO of Home Depot). As the business news attests, the firing and demotion of corporate executives is quite common. The everyday, profit-oriented activities of corporate executives are beholden to "Wall Street"– how economists and media commentators customarily refer to the US stock market and investment banking industry, as if they are things separate from and beyond the control of individuals, rather than a product of capitalist social relations (cf. Marx, CM 97; Cap 83). Corporate value and the productivity of companies and their executives are the objects of several economic indexes and ratings. Therefore, just as the productivity of factory workers and football players is easily assessed, we can also readily see the stock performance and capital rankings of corporations and their executives, whether companies and their executives are making enough profit to satisfy the corporate owners or the company's shareholders.

Corporate owners/executives are thus subservient to Wall Street's capital growth demands over a particular interval; each business quarter – 3 months: not such a long time, the same interval as a semester – brings the threat of failure, of having a profit sheet that shows less capital than anticipated by Wall Street. In sum, although capitalist owners/executives are much wealthier than workers, nonetheless, given Marx's explication of the creative potential endowed in humans, the capitalists too, because of the hold of capital accumulation on their lives, are self-alienated. The objective alienation that capitalism produces is all the more dehumanizing given, as Marx recognized, the vast resources that capitalism generates and which could be used to create a society in which individuals are free to pursue hobbies without being so tied to the unceasing obligation to produce more and more surplus value. In short, under capitalism, both the capitalists and the workers are servants of capital.

NEWS 1.5

Recognizing exploitation

It is more difficult, however, for the capitalists than it is for the proletariat to recognize the self-alienation and objectification that capitalism produces. After all, it is wage-workers – chicken deboners, Wal-Mart shelf-stockers, hotel house-keepers – who most immediately experience the dehumanization of the production process on a daily basis. By contrast, the bourgeoisie, "the possessing class" (e.g., corporate executives), experiences the profit production process and its results, i.e., private property, as affirming their own abilities and power. Consequently, they misrecognize the alienation that capitalism produces for capitalists and wage-workers alike, and unlike wage workers, they "experience alienation as a sign of their own [bourgeois] power" (ASC 133). Partly for this reason, according to Marx, the overthrow of capitalism will originate with the workers (see p. 36 above), or with what the Hungarian Marxist theorist Georg Lukacs (1968: 149) refers to as the standpoint of the proletariat; given the inequality between the bourgeoisie and the proletariat, Marx states, "the proletariat … is compelled to abolish itself and thereby its conditioning opposite – private property – which makes it a proletariat" (ASC, 133).

ECONOMIC INEQUALITY

The different positions that capitalists and workers objectively occupy in relation to capital – what is surplus value for the capitalist is the worker's surplus labor – produce the oppositional standpoints and polarized class structure that Marx emphasizes as inherent in capitalism. Therefore, while politicians celebrate worker productivity and job creation as signs of a strong economy, Marx offers a different view. He argues that the more industry prospers and the more the mass of workers grows, the more "the domination of capital extends over a greater number of individuals" (WLC 34). For Marx, increased employment and increased productivity – even if accompanied by an increase in wages – mean that more and more surplus labor is being extracted from more and more workers to provide more and more wealth for the bourgeoisie, with the effect that the economic and social gulf between capitalists and workers widens (WLC 34–35).

Marx argues that an increase in wages does nothing to change the structural inequality that is inherent in capitalism (between capitalists and workers), and nor does it diminish the capitalists' privileged access to capital, a privilege seen in corporate executive pay. This inequality derives from the fact that "the existence of a class which possesses nothing but its capacity to labor is a necessary prerequisite of capital" (WLC 31). Accordingly,

NEWS 1.1

> to say that the most favorable condition for wage labor is the most rapid possible growth of productive capital is only to say that the more rapidly the working-class increases and enlarges the power that is hostile to it, the wealth that does not belong to it and that rules over it, the more favorable will be the conditions under which it is allowed to labor anew at increasing bourgeois wealth, at enlarging the power of capital, content with forging for itself the golden chains by which the bourgeoisie drags it in its train. (WLC 41)

WEB 1.1

The chains in which workers are enmeshed were more vividly apparent during Marx's day. He was writing when factory conditions were appalling, child labor was the norm, and extreme poverty was visible on the streets and in the housing tenements of the increasingly populous cities. During the twentieth century, working conditions changed for the better in most sectors of the economy notwithstanding the dangerous conditions that still exist in many workplaces (e.g., meat factories, mines) and especially in the factories and construction sites of expanding capitalist countries (e.g., China). However, despite economic growth and a general improvement in working conditions, Marx's claim of persistent inequality between wage-workers and capitalists finds strong empirical support.

INCOME DISPARITIES

NEWS 1.14

The US Census reports that while men and women earned less in 2005 than 2004, median household income slightly increased because "more family members were taking jobs to make ends meet." Economic inequality has in fact grown since the late 1980s, as has the gap between the highest and lowest income groups (Glassmeier 2005: 2). Notwithstanding the many changes that have occurred since the 1970s – an increase in the number of college graduates, advances in computer technology, and the shift from private to publicly traded companies – the greatest increase in household income has occurred among those families who were already well-off, thus leading to an increased concentration of economic assets among fewer households – the top one-fifth of Americans own 84 percent of the nation's wealth (Glassmeier 2005: 2).

NEWS 1.15

The concentration of wealth among fewer Americans is giving rise to comparisons not, as in the past, between the rich and the middle-class, but between the rich and the "super-rich" – whose expanse of capital is creating a "yacht parking problem" for ocean resorts around the world; they need more space for more and for bigger, super-size yachts. At the same time, while the proportion of poor Americans has declined over the last four decades (from 23 percent in 1959 to 13 percent in 2003), "the absolute number of people in poverty has changed remarkably little" during this interval (Glassmeier 2005: 1–2), and there has been a significant increase in family income inequalities (e.g., Chevan and Stokes 2000). The starkness of economic inequality in America, one of the most affluent and economically advanced societies in the world, is that the life expectancy of poor Americans has actually *declined* since the late 1980s, decline that was further accelerated by the recession of 2008–2009.

NEWS 1.16

MAINTAINING THE STATUS QUO

Why, you may well ask, are wage-workers seemingly content to accept the status quo? Why do workers work as hard as they do (e.g., Burawoy 1979). And why do we not see much evidence today of the class antagonism that Marx regarded as integral to capitalism, and which was evident in the US in the 1920s and 1930s during the Great Depression? Many reasons are likely. For one, the huge post-World War II expansion in education, the expansion of service occupations, occupational mobility, and a growing middle class (largely comprised of professional, service, and sales workers) has made a relatively affluent consumer lifestyle available to a huge sector of the population in western societies and especially in the US (Fischer and Hout 2006). Second, even among the working class (comprised largely of skilled, semi-skilled, and unskilled workers), an increasing proportion of wage-worker households do not rely solely on wages for their livelihood. Almost a half of all American households and about a quarter of British households own investment stock (Halle and Weyher 2005: 209). The transformation in capitalism away from family or individual company ownership toward the shareholder society ushered in by the public flotation of company shares on the stock exchange means that many wage-workers have a specific economic interest in corporations, through either personal or work-related pension investments. And although workers own fewer shares than company executives, their shares can constitute a significant proportion of wage-workers' overall economic assets, thus making them highly protective of corporate interests and vested in the positive functioning of the economy as a whole.

In short, many wage-workers are owners of capital (though they own a much smaller proportionate share than the financial and corporate executives). Accordingly, the line between capitalists and wage-workers is not as clear cut as it was in Marx's time and for much of the twentieth century, when owners' and workers' relations to property and capital were simpler. The shift toward a stock-owning society means that workers, even though they may grumble about the extraordinarily high salaries and benefits that corporate executives receive, are also keenly aware that the fortunes of a particular company and economic growth in general directly affect their fortunes, the value of their stock/pension fund. Stock investment, then, gives workers a particular stake in the production of capital, notwithstanding the empirical truth in Marx's point that the expansion of the economy does not alter the inequality between the capitalists – the industrial and media tycoons and the corporate executive elite – and the proletariat – all those who rely primarily, if not solely, on wages for their livelihoods.

Third, the state intervenes not just to dampen some of the most severe effects of capitalist crises by propping up financial institutions and markets (e.g., following the collapse of the mortgage industry in 2007–2008), but also by buffering individuals against some of the excesses of the profit logic of capitalism; e.g., by giving unemployment benefits. The state, therefore, has a more active role in capitalist society than envisaged by Marx, and it is a role that allows the state to maintain the status quo (of economic inequality) while also appearing to be on the side of wage-workers (e.g., Block 1987; Przeworski 1985) – hence politicians frequently refer to their support for economic policies that help hard-working ordinary individuals.

Fourth, worker unionization and the legal right of unionized worker groups to strike also help to quell workers' concerns that they are being exploited by

WEB 1.3

NEWS 1.13

NEWS 1.17

employers. Although many employers resist unionization and in some cases prohibit workers from joining unions, many poultry workers, for example, believe that union membership is necessary if they are to be protected from employer mistreatment. Overall, however, this is a minority view. Today, the labor movement in the US is relatively moribund, as unions represent "ever-smaller proportions of the workforce" despite some evidence of local revitalization (Voss and Sherman 2000: 303). In the 1950s, 35 percent of employees in the US were union members; this proportion declined to 20 percent in 1983, and to 12 percent in 2007. In Europe, by contrast, which has a much stronger labor movement and social welfare tradition, trade unions are still relatively strong and in some countries (e.g., Ireland) are part of the institutionalized policy-making process; they are considered "social partners" along with the government and employers' organizations, who together cooperate in establishing pay scales, benefits, etc.

All of these adaptations of capitalism (e.g., expanding middle class, changes in capital ownership, an activist state, unionization) contribute to workers' acceptance of economic and social inequality. But perhaps the most significant reason workers are willing to accept the status quo is their immersion in an ideological system which makes inequality seem fair and justified, a topic to which we now turn.

IDEOLOGY AND POWER

To talk of ideology is basically to refer to the everyday ideas that circulate in society. Marx underscored the importance of everyday, lived, material-social existence in determining our ideas about what we consider normal:

> Consciousness can never be anything else than conscious existence, and the existence of men in their actual life-process ... [i.e.] developing their material production ... Life [social/economic existence] is not determined by consciousness, but consciousness by life [by material-social existence]. (GI 14, 15)

The everyday activities and experiences in capitalist societies make it seem normal that wage-workers and owners and executives should work as hard as they do. Although the financial rewards differ, most people consent to produce the surplus labor and surplus value that create the profit needed to sustain capitalism.

EVERYDAY EXISTENCE AND THE NORMALITY OF IDEAS

More generally, the ideas we have about what is normal, about what is inane and what is cool, whether we go to college and what to do afterwards, do not just pop into our heads out of nowhere; these ideas come from our everyday existence, from what we have already lived and experienced in our families and neighbor-hoods. Marx's insight that everyday material and social existence determines our consciousness is well recognized by many educators today (though they may be unaware of Marx's thesis). Many universities, concerned that there are too few students enrolled from low-income families, are making efforts to make college more affordable. These individuals don't apply to college, not because they are not interested in education but because their material existence essentially rules out the normalcy of this idea or option. Beyond financial considerations, some universities are trying to change the everyday consciousness of young people by going out into their communities to persuade them and their parents that college is a viable option. The University of Montana organizes whistle-stop train trips through rural communities where faculty and administrators meet local residents and through conversations and exhibits try to get teenagers thinking about col-lege. Having grown up in families and communities where mining and ranching were for generations the dominant occupations, and ones that did not require col-lege education, these young people now confront a changing economy where such jobs are in decline. This new economic reality requires a different consciousness – to see other possibilities as "normal." By going out into these communities, the university is itself impacting these residents' social existence – making a dent on their experiences, and one which may encourage rural families to consider college (and, of course, increased enrollments might, in turn, increase the amount of money the university accumulates from fees).

FREEDOM TO SHOP

Individuals' social experiences vary in all kinds of intersecting ways from place to place and by gender, race, socio-economic class, etc. But, across today's globalizing economy (see chapter 15), the one common cultural denominator is the primacy of consumption in everyday life (notwithstanding the persistence of poverty). A snapshot of any major city in the world will testify to the prominence of consumer culture, highlighted by the well-known brand names that dominate shop-fronts, billboards, and other public advertisements. We live, as we are frequently told, in a consumer society and many partake directly and vicariously of the great range of commodities available. Again, as Marx noted, "The bourgeoisie has through its exploitation of the world-market given a cosmopolitan character to produc-tion and consumption in every country ... In place of the old wants, satisfied by the productions of the country, we find new wants, requiring for their satisfaction the products of distant lands" (CM 83).

As I have noted, freedom and capitalism tend to go together – hence we talk about democratic capitalist societies such as the US (though for Marx "free" labor is coerced; see p. 45 above). The links between capitalism and freedom, however, are not all-encompassing. In countries such as China or Russia, for example, a growing capitalist economy coincides with and requires the freedom of consumer choice, but not the freedom of the press, the freedom to vote, to

NEWS I.3

criticize the government, or to publicly assemble, etc., the freedoms that are institutionalized in the everyday culture of the US and most other western societies. Each semester when I ask students to list what it means to be American, they invariably name all of these political freedoms without much prompting. These are the freedoms that democratic societies take for granted.

Additionally, in capitalist societies – societies in which the production of commodities is crucial to capital and profit accumulation – one of the most expansive and ingrained freedoms is the freedom of choice, and its twin, the freedom to shop. Yet it is rare for students to mention these freedoms in an initial listing of American values. Because the freedom to shop and to make choices everyday at the vending machine and in the supermarket and on the Abercrombie and Fitch and American Eagle websites is so much a part of our social existence, we don't think of it as something special; it is simply what we do. It is an everyday freedom as opposed to one we might avail ourselves of on more formal occasions by voting, worshiping, or attending a political rally.

IDEOLOGY OF CONSUMPTION

Consumption pervades our existence – that is why so many people work as hard as they do; they endure the burdens of work so that they can use their pay check to buy the things they covet. They work to live, Marx tells us (see p. 47 above), and they define their life by what it is they own. The power of money to buy all of the things we do not ourselves possess – including beauty, popularity, friends – Marx argues, lures us into reproducing capitalism through consumption. "All the things which you cannot do, your money can do. It can eat and drink, go to the dance hall and the theater; it can travel, it can appropriate art, learning, the treasures of the past, political power – all this it can appropriate for you – it can buy all this for you" (EPM 119). It is so "natural" for us to be consumers, to shop, to consume and to own things, that we don't consider it a special freedom or privilege. We consider it our existence. This is the power of ideology in everyday existence: consumption, and ideas about consumption, structure who we are and what we do.

Furthermore, we rarely wonder where the impulse to buy comes from, and nor do we wonder about how things get produced (e.g., the labor invested in making commodities) – nor the service production process either (e.g., how heavy it is for hotel housekeepers to lift the super-thick mattresses in the Westin hotel's "heavenly" beds). It is only when a favorite brand is missing from the shelf that we wonder what unnatural thing might have happened to account for its mysterious absence. It is the expected and coveted presence of commodities in our lives, in defining and anchoring our everyday social existence, that makes capitalism so alluring and which makes critique of capitalism so difficult, even at an intellectual level (i.e., while studying Marx). We are so fixated with consumption – that is what is real to us – we tend to ignore our other freedoms: we are more likely to shop than to worship, vote, or assemble for a political or civic event. Public

NEWS I.1

holidays – e.g., Labor Day, Thanksgiving, Veteran's Day – days on which we might well ponder the value of labor, are instead occasions for shopping, promoted by the allure of big "sales events."

THE MYSTICAL VALUE OF COMMODITIES

We relish being consumers and by extension living in a capitalist society, and because its freedom of choice is so routinized in daily life, we remain blissfully unaware of the social relations that underlie our freedom to shop, i.e., the social relations vis-à-vis commodity production and by extension the different, unequal relations of workers and capitalists to capital and profit. Marx calls this the fetishism of commodities. We are so fixated with the commodity as an object in itself, we don't recognize what it really is: raw materials transformed by human labor for someone else's profit. As with other aspects of capitalism, we reify commodities as if they are things that have a life of their own, as if they are mysteriously independent of the social organization of production (and consumption). But as Marx emphasizes, production is "always production ... by social individuals ... Production mediates consumption; it creates the latter's material; without it, consumption would lack an object" (Gru 85, 91). Marx elaborates:

> A commodity appears at first sight, a very trivial thing, and easily understood ... So far as it has a value in use, there is nothing mysterious about it, ... it is capable of satisfying human wants, ... [and is] the product of human labour. It is as clear as noon-day, that man, by his industry, changes the ... materials furnished by Nature, in such a way as to make them useful to him. The form of wood, for instance, is altered by making a table out of it. Yet, for all that, the table continues to be that common, every-day thing, wood. But, so soon as it steps forth as a commodity, it is changed into something transcendent ... The mystical character of commodities does not originate, therefore, in their use-value ... A commodity is ... a mysterious thing, simply because in it the social character of men's labour appears to them as an objective character stamped upon the product of that labour ... the products of labour become commodities, social things whose qualities are at the same time perceptible and imperceptible by the senses ... There is a physical relation between physical things. But it is different with commodities. There, the existence of the things qua commodities, and the value-relation between the products of labor which stamps them as commodities, have absolutely no connection with their physical properties and with the material relations arising therefrom ... the definite social relation between men [as producers of the products of labor] ... assumes ... the fantastic form of a relation between things. (Cap 81–83)

Marx is not opposed to consumption. His writings continually acknowledge that needs are not just physical but social, and that each mode of existence produces new needs. Thus, being a college student today may require you to have an iPod. But what Marx critiques is how we let our obsession with commodities obscure the social relations that underpin commodity production (and consumption), and how in this process we objectify the workers as well as ourselves. We see

Early morning customers on Fifth Avenue, Manhattan, await the freedom to shop.

NEWS 1.18

a clear example of our own objectification in the content of a recently created website, Zebo, which boasts "the world's largest repository of what people own." The site is owned by an internet and advertising technology company who presumably have an explicit interest in knowing who owns and who wants what kinds of things. Young people, mostly ages 13–25, post a profile of themselves in terms of what they own or what they aspire to own. It attracts people, or more accurately, *lists*, from all across the globe. There is nothing mysterious about this website: it's all about what you own. Once you log on, after an initial greeting, "Hi. What do you own?" you are commanded: "List what you own and then see who else owns that. You are known by what you own, so list your best stuff."

"You are known by what you own." This is not simply a cliché. It is, rather, one of the dominant ideas in society and a primary organizing principle of capitalist production – the class that owns the means of production (e.g., land, oil, etc.) also owns more things, has more wealth, than the working class. We are reduced to what we own; and whereas we own our labor power but must sell it (in order to live), we can consume the (other) commodities we possess. "We are what we own" is the ideology that circulates in capitalist societies. And although we ourselves are active promoters of this ideology in our everyday social relations, we are also heavily encouraged, even bombarded, by the advertising industry to do so. Advertising celebrates consumption and in doing so celebrates capitalism as a system of commodity production; it "glorifies the pleasures and freedoms of consumer choice" (Schudson 1984: 218). Every advertisement we see – on the highway, riding the subway, at the bus stop, in the football stadium, on television and the internet, in magazines and church bulletins – even if it is not showcasing a product that we ourselves want, is celebrating the everyday capitalist freedom to shop. We might not be persuaded to buy a given advertised item, but each advertisement reminds us of the American dream: affirming what we have and, importantly, reminding us of what we can own and what we should aspire to own (e.g., Marchand 1985).

Our ideas about shopping and consumption do not come from nowhere. And nor do those of the capitalists; their promotion of consumption has a clear economic logic: Consumption produces profit while simultaneously distracting consumers from the unequal social relations underlying the labor–capital process. Thus, social existence determines consciousness; our social existence is determined by capitalism. And though we make our own history, as Marx tells us, it is not under conditions of our own choosing: "Men make their own history, but they do not make it just as they please; they do not make it under circumstances chosen by themselves, but under circumstances directly found, given, and transmitted from the past" (Bru 595). We freely consume, but in ways and under conditions not chosen by us but by the capitalist class, and by the advertising industry which is one of its core channels of power.

The allure of consumption further dampens the development of class consciousness; if we can all go to the mall, and consume the commodities produced by capitalism (some more, some less), why should we fixate on the fact that some have more things to consume than others? We all partake of the freedom to shop; we all partake of the goods produced within our capitalist society. False consciousness, therefore, means not just that we freely consent to selling ourselves on the employment market such that we are cheaper than the commodities our labor produces and cheaper than the commodities we buy (see pp. 50–51 above). Additionally, we deceive ourselves that we will be worth more if we buy more. Marx presumed that in pushing through a revolution against capitalism, "The proletarians have nothing to lose but their chains" (CM 121). The failure of Marx's prophecy (so far), however, is itself a testament, in part, to the insight of his analysis of the power of money and of consumer ideology within capitalism. Commodity consumption is such an integral part of lived existence in economically developed societies that it makes a vision of society in which "we are *not* what we own" beyond the imagination of most of us. Consumption, and the ideology of consumption, binds us to capitalism; it is the mark of global civilization.

🔲 NEWS 1.19

THE CAPITALIST SUPERSTRUCTURE

The advertising industry is just one, albeit a powerful, element in the larger ideological system that governs our everyday existence. And while we might not be too surprised that advertising promotes consumption/capitalism, Marx highlights that other institutions in society, those not tied directly to economic markets, also, nonetheless, promote capitalist ideology. Marx argues that because the social institutions in a capitalist society evolved in ways that are compatible with capitalism, they serve the economic interests of the bourgeoisie. The ideology of "free competition [is] accompanied by a social and political constitution adapted to it, and by the economic and political sway of the bourgeois class" (CM 85). In this view, the political, legal, educational, family, religious, and cultural institutions – all those spheres of social existence whose (apparent) purpose is not economic/capital production – promote ideas and practices that support capitalist production and accumulation and suppress those that might in any way challenge the capitalist status quo (EPM 102–103; CM 100).

Marx refers to these institutions as the superstructure; their existence and activities bolster the foundational, economic base of capitalism, and the structural inequality of capitalists and wage-workers.

> In the social production of their life, men enter into definite relations that are indispensable and independent of their will, relations of production which correspond to a definite stage of development of their material productive forces. The sum total of these relations of production constitutes the economic structure of society, the real foundation, on which rises a legal and political superstructure and to which correspond definite forms of social consciousness. The mode of production of material life conditions the social, political and intellectual life process in general. It is not the consciousness of men that determines their being, but, on the contrary, their social being that determines their consciousness. (Preface 5)

Hence, the everyday practices that characterize the state, the media, education, the church, the family, the courts, and the parliament, in executing their specialized institutional routines and determining individuals' social experiences, are, at the same time, practices that support capital accumulation and the ideology of capitalism that underpins and justifies it. Thus Marx argues, the organization of the bourgeois family and the gender inequality and exploitation it institutionalizes is "based on capital, on private gain ... the bourgeois [man] sees in his wife a mere instrument of production" (CM 100–101; see also Engels 1844); she produces the next generation of wage-workers and capitalists and her everyday (unpaid) labor in the home (as well as her paid labor if she is employed) contributes to the surplus value required and appropriated by the capitalist class.[5]

When we look at education, we see that schools and colleges (and parents) emphasize daily practices affirming disciplined work habits, focus, and productivity; and you are required to major in a specialized field of study rather than develop several of your intellectual and creative interests. And although colleges verbalize the intellectual value of an allegedly wide-ranging "liberal arts" education, this must be balanced with training graduates who are able to meet the economy's demand for specialized workers. In the domain of law, for example, the courts protect individuals' property rights, and in politics, notwithstanding the hand-wringing that occurs on a frequent basis over the fact that big business and corporate donations have too much influence on the political process, the right of business leaders and political lobbyists to make large campaign donations is defended as part of their constitutional rights, i.e., their (political-economic) freedom of expression.

NEWS 1.11

In a capitalist society, the rights of capital are more strongly protected than the rights of workers and of the poor. As Marx emphasizes, you "cannot give to one class without taking from another" (Bru 616). Hence when Congress is passing legislation (e.g., freezing the minimum wage), or universities are revising the curriculum, or the Supreme Court is evaluating some particular law (e.g., workplace discrimination), we are prompted to ask: "Who benefits?" The answer in most instances will be the capitalist class. Moreover, even when economically struggling individuals, many of whom are wage-workers whose earnings are insufficient to maintain their basic needs, are given welfare benefits, this too is an effort by the state to prop up capitalism, to suppress its contradictions (e.g., unemployment, recession, etc.).

What the poor do have, Marx argued, is religion, yet another institution that upholds capitalist ideology and the status quo. For Marx, religion distracts workers from consciousness of their exploitation; just as wage-labor (coerced by capitalism) produces estrangement or alienation (see pp. 52–56 above), so too Marx argues, does religious faith; "The more man puts into God, the less he retains in himself" (EPM 72) – religion becomes an alien power over the individual. The core ideas in Christianity, for example, can be seen as an ideology that promotes the interests of the ruling class; it is meekness and non-material values that Christian scripture affirms – e.g., we are commanded to love one another and not to envy our neighbor's possessions: "Blessed are the meek, for they will inherit the land; blessed are the poor for theirs is the Kingdom of God." And although individuals and activists in poor inner-city neighborhoods frequently use religion to challenge the status quo of economic and social inequality (e.g., McRoberts 2003), for the most part, religion has a stabilizing rather than a revolutionary impact in society.

Across various social institutions, therefore, we see that the ideas articulated on a routine, everyday basis are ideas that serve the interests of the capitalist class – i.e., the ruling class – and of capitalism as a system (of inequality). Marx explains:

> The ideas of the ruling class are in every epoch the **ruling ideas**, i.e., the class which is the ruling material force of society, is at the same time its ruling intellectual force. The class which has the means of material production at its disposal, has control at the same time over the means of mental production, so that thereby, generally speaking, the ideas of those who lack the means of mental production are subject to it. (GI 39)

In addition, therefore, to the multiple ways in which the interests and ideas of the ruling class are affirmed and protected across non-economic social institutions (e.g., education, law, etc.), the ruling class also has the capital to directly purchase media and other opportunities to directly disseminate advertisements and political and economic messages that serve its interests. The class which owns or controls access to capital gets to define literally what we are reading or watching and, by extension, the sorts of things and issues we are prompted to think about and how to think about them (e.g., Gitlin 1980). Even with the opportunities provided by internet blogging, many of us do not have the time and resources that corporations have to publicize their ideas. It is hard for ordinary individuals to compete, for example, against the American beverage and restaurant industry, which places full-page advertisements in large circulation news media to oppose in-car breathalyzers (ignition interlocks), an initiative they oppose because it would mean not just fewer drunk drivers but the end of "moderate responsible drinking prior to driving" and thus "no more champagne toasts at weddings … no more beer at ballgames." Clearly, it is relatively easy for the capitalist class to disseminate ideas that protect their economic interests.

THE RULING POWER OF MONEY IN POLITICS

The ideas of the ruling class also get directly transmitted into the halls of political power as a result of the ruling class's political spending. Once again, we can refer to Marx's analysis of the power of money in a capitalist society. Just as the capitalist can buy bravery, culture, glamour, love (a trophy wife; e.g., Perelman's ex-wife; see p. 64 above), so too he can buy political power. Although in a democratic society it is commonly said that it is "the people and not the purse" that elects candidates – i.e., that money cannot buy votes – it is nonetheless evident that money is crucial in determining who runs for and gets elected to political office; the financial disclosure forms of several of the 2008 presidential candidates indicate their hefty multimillion dollar personal assets, and similarly, the US Senate is aptly referred to as a "millionaires' club."

And, if capitalists are not themselves running for office, they are able to buy access to those who have political power and who make the rules in society – the elected legislators, whose decisions affect the spending and distribution of billions of federal dollars (i.e., taxpayers' money) every year and who make and oversee the laws regulating society. Money can buy access to politicians in multiple ways. For example, company owners and corporate executives move in much the same social circles as politicians, making it easy for them to press their economic and policy concerns. But corporations do not have to wait for fundraisers, golf tournaments, and other social events to communicate with Congress; the extensive lobbying system in Washington, DC, provides a well-organized, routinized way for corporations and other groups to advance their legislative interests. And many paid lobbyists have themselves been political office-holders (or intimately related to legislators). The line, therefore, between money and politics is blurry at best, notwithstanding politicians' repeated claims of clamping down on the influence of money in politics. In short, networks matter (see chapter 7), and in a capitalist society money buys network connections. Corporate interests readily receive greater priority from politicians than the everyday issues that matter to ordinary wage-workers and their families, despite the opportunity all citizens have to visit their local representatives during public constituency meetings.

Further, as underscored by several political corruption scandals, some politicians sell their political (labor) power (as either legislators or lobbyists) in exchange for free dinners, golf trips, and cash. And, as is true of all wage-labor, the politician's

KARL MARX

📖 NEWS 1.20

📖 NEWS 1.3

📖 NEWS 1.21

📖 NEWS 1.22

use-value to the capitalist extends beyond his or her exchange value; the use-value continues long after the politician has consumed free dinners and vacations as a result of his or her ongoing policy interventions aiding capitalist profit accumulation.

In sum, the power of money in the political process and in determining the political agenda illustrates Marx's thesis that the ruling ideas in society (e.g., "free trade," the triumph of economic priorities over human rights or environmental considerations, as in US trade with China) will be those that accord with the interests of those who are the ruling material force in society. And these ideas serve not simply the individual interests of a given entrepreneur, but more importantly, the interests and ideology of capitalism as a whole – the ongoing expansion of capitalist markets and of profit.

SUMMARY

Marx's progressive view of history argued that each mode of production (e.g., imperial Rome, feudal Europe, capitalism) contains the seeds of its own destruction; the mode that was once an improvement over its predecessor will eventually suffer its own demise and be replaced with a system that improves on it, until history ends with the destruction of capitalism and its replacement by communism. This latter stage has (so far) not emerged. To the contrary, capitalism has shown itself to be remarkably adaptive to integrating the crises and contradictions that challenge its supremacy. Its underlying structure (e.g., division of labor, surplus value), moreover, has not changed and, indeed, with the global expansion of capitalism and consumer culture, Marx's analysis remains highly applicable to understanding contemporary society.

POINTS TO REMEMBER

- Marx's focus was on the structure of capitalist society
- Marx saw history as a progression in material forces and conditions:
  - Slave society
  - Feudal society
  - Capitalism
  - Communism
- Marx emphasized that capitalism and all existing societies are characterized by inequality

Characteristics of capitalism emphasized by Marx:
- The objective of capitalism is the production of capital/profit
- Capitalism is a system of structured class inequality based on differential relations to capital

- Two dichotomously opposed classes:
  - The bourgeoisie (capitalists/owners)
  - The proletariat (wage-workers who produce capital/profit)
- Capitalism is a system of commodity production
- Labor power is itself a commodity
- Wage-labor is exploited labor; labor power is used by the capitalist to produce profit for the capitalist
- Surplus value produced by wage-workers becomes the capitalist's profit
- Surplus value derives from the gap between a worker's exchange-value and his or her use-value to the capitalist
- The division of labor produces alienated labor
- Alienated labor takes four forms:
  - Alienation from the product produced
  - Alienation in the production process
  - Alienation from our own species being
  - Alienation from other workers
- Economic power determines political and social power
- Social/material being determines consciousness; how we live determines what we know and think
- Economic relations determine ideology
- Economic/profit logic (base) determines the logic/practices of all social institutions (superstructure)

GLOSSARY

alienated labor the objective result of the economic and social organization of capitalist production (e.g., division of labor); takes four forms:

(a) alienation from products produced: Wage-workers are alienated from the product of their labor; a worker's labor power is owned by the capitalist, and consequently the products of the worker's labor belong not to the worker but to the capitalist who profits from them.

(b) alienation within the production process: Wage-workers are actively alienated by the production process; labor is not for the worker an end in itself, freely chosen, but coerced by and performed for the capitalist; the worker is an object in the production process.

(c) alienation of workers from their species being: By being reduced to their use-value (capitalist profit), workers are estranged from the creativity and higher consciousness that distinguish humans from animals.

(d) alienation of individuals from one another: The competitive production process and workplace demands alienate individuals from others.

bourgeoisie the capitalist class; owners of the means of production, who stand in a position of domination over the proletariat (the wage-workers).

capital money and other resources invested in the production of commodities whose sale accumulates profit for the capitalist.

capitalism a historically specific way of organizing commodity production; produces profit for the owners of the means of production (e.g., factories, land, oil wells); based on structured inequality between capitalists and wage-laborers whose exploited labor power produces capitalist profit.

class consciousness the group consciousness necessary for wage-workers (the proletariat) to recognize that their individual exploitation is part and parcel of capitalism, which requires the exploitation of the labor power of all wage-workers (as a class) by the capitalist class in the production of profit.

class relations unequal relations of capitalists and wage-workers to capital. Capitalists (who own the means of production used to produce capital/profit) are in a position of domination over wage-workers, who, in order to live, must sell their labor power to the capitalists.

commodification of labor the process by which, like manufactured commodities, wage-workers' labor power is exchanged and traded on the market for a price (wages).

communism envisaged by Marx as the final phase in the evolution of history, whereby capitalism would be overthrown by proletarian class revolution, resulting in a society wherein the division of labor and private profit would not exist.

dialectical materialism the idea that historical change (i.e., material/economic change) is the result of conscious human activity emerging from and acting on the socially experienced inequalities (and contradictions) in historically conditioned (i.e., human-made) economic forces and relations.

division of labor the separation of occupational sectors and workers into specialized spheres of activity; produces for Marx, alienated labor.

economic base the economic structure or the mode of production of material life in capitalist society. Economic relations (relations of production) are determined by ownership of the means of production and rest on inequality between private-property-owning capitalists (bourgeoisie) and property-less wage-workers. Economic relations determine social relations, and social institutional practices (i.e., the superstructure).

exchange-value the price (wages) wage-workers get on the market for the (coerced) sale of their labor power to the capitalist; determined by how much the capitalist needs to pay the wage-workers in order to maintain their labor power, so that the workers can subsist and maintain their use-value in producing profit for the capitalist. The workers' exchange-value is of less value to the worker than their use-value is to the capitalist.

exploitation the capitalist class caring about wage-workers only to the extent that wage-workers have "use-value," i.e., can be used to produce surplus value/profit.

false consciousness the embrace of the illusionary promises of capitalism.

fetishism of commodities the mystification of commodities whereby we inject them with special properties beyond what they really are (e.g., elevating an Abercrombie and Fitch shirt to something other than what is really is, i.e., cotton converted into a commodity), while remaining ignorant of the exploited labor and unequal class relations that determine its production and consumption.

historical materialism history as the progressive expansion in the economic-material-productive forces in society.

ideology ideas in everyday circulation; determined by the ruling economic class such that they make our current social existence seem normal and desirable.

inequality structured into the profit objectives and organization of capitalism whereby the exploited labor power of wage-workers produces surplus value (profit) for the capitalist class.

means of production resources (e.g., land, oil wells, factories, corporations) owned by the bourgeoisie and used for the production of commodities/profit as a result of the labor power of wage-workers.

mode of production how a society organizes its material-social existence (e.g., capitalism).

objectification the dehumanization of wage-workers as machine-like objects, whose maintenance (with subsistence wages) is necessary to the production of commodities (objects) necessary to capital accumulation/profit. The term is interchangeable with "alienation."

private property accumulated by capitalists from profits produced by wage-workers' labor; both a source and consequence of the inequality between capitalists and workers.

profit accumulation of capital as a result of the gap between commodity production costs (e.g., raw materials, production facilities, wages) and their market price.

proletariat wage-workers who, in order to live, must sell their labor power to the capitalist class, which uses them to produce commodities creating capitalist surplus value/profit.

ruling class the class which is the ruling material force in society (capitalists/bourgeoisie) being also the ruling intellectual/ideological force, ensuring the protection and expansion of capitalist economic interests.

ruling ideas ideas disseminated by the ruling (capitalist) class, invariably bolstering capitalist economic interests.

species being what is distinctive of the human species (e.g., mindful creativity).

standpoint of the proletariat the positioning of the proletariat vis-à-vis the production process, from within which they perceive the dehumanization and self-alienation structured into capitalism, unlike the bourgeoisie, who experience capitalism (erroneously) as self-affirming.

subsistence wage minimum needed to sustain workers' existence (livelihood) so that their labor power is maintained and reproduced for the capitalist.

superstructure non-economic social institutions (legal, political, educational, cultural, religious, family) whose routine institutional practices and activities promote the beliefs, ideas, and practices that are necessary to maintaining and reproducing capitalism.

surplus value capitalist profit from the difference between a worker's exchange-value (wages) and use-value; the extra value over and above the costs of commodity production (i.e., raw materials, infrastructure, workers' wages) created by the labor of wage-workers.

use-value the usefulness of wage-workers' labor in the production of profit.

RELEVANT NEWSPAPER STORIES

All news stories are from the *New York Times* unless otherwise noted, and can be accessed via www.wiley.com/go/dillon. See NEWS icons in the margins above.

NEWS 1.1 "In Siberia, malls are sprouting all over," May 17, 2008.
NEWS 1.2 "Bouquet of roses may have note: 'Made in China'," September 25, 2006.
NEWS 1.3 "Ellen unloads: Dumped by the billionaire Ronald O. Perelman, Ellen Barkin dumps $15 million of his jewels," September 21, 2006.
NEWS 1.4 "Marx after communism," *The Economist*, December 21, 2002.
NEWS 1.5 Executive Pay, Special Report, April 6, 2008.
"What red ink? Wall Street paid hefty bonuses," January 29, 2009.
"Executive pay limits seek to alter corporate culture," February 5, 2009.
"Corporate America's pay pal," October 15, 2006.
"An ousted chief's going-away pay is seen by many as typically excessive," January 4, 2007.
NEWS 1.6 "Pfizer, hurt by generic drugs, will lay off 7,800," January 23, 2007.
NEWS 1.7 "A job interview where each second makes a difference," February 8, 2007.
NEWS 1.8 "High school players shrug off concussions, raising risks," September 15, 2007.
"Sixth N.F.L. player's brain is found to have damage," January 28, 2009.
"Ex-players dealing with not-so-glamorous health issues," February 1, 2007.

"Dark days follow hard-hitting career in NFL," February 2, 2007.

"NFL culture makes issue of head injuries even murkier," February 3, 2007.

"Study of ex-NFL players ties concussion to depression risk," May 31, 2007.

"Player silence may be hurdle for the NFL on concussions," June 20, 2007.

NEWS 1.9 "Baseball is challenged on rise in stimulant use," January 16, 2008.

"In baseball, fear bats at the top of the order," January 16, 2008.

"Issue may really be how far players will go to gain an advantage," January 7, 2008.

"With no answers on risks, steroid users still say 'yes'," December 2, 2002.

NEWS 1.10 "Blood, Sweat and Fear: Workers' Rights in the U.S. Meat and Poultry Plants." Human Rights Watch Report, 2005: http://hrw.org/reports/2005/usa0105/summary-eng.pdf. Retrieved October 11, 2006. See also "Rights group condemns meatpackers on job safety," January 26, 2005; "Child labor charges are sought against kosher meat plant in Iowa," August 6, 2008.

NEWS 1.11 "McCain's lobbyist-laden group," July 28, 2008.

NEWS 1.12 "Wal-Mart to add more part-timers and wage caps," October 2, 2006.

"Wal-Mart to settle suits over pay for $352 million," December 24, 2008.

"Wal-Mart loses a suit over work breaks," July 2, 2008.

NEWS 1.13 "Union organizers at poultry plants in South find newly sympathetic ears," September 6, 2005.

NEWS 1.14 "Census reports slight increase in '05 incomes," August 30, 2006.

NEWS 1.15 "Resorts respond to the yacht parking problem," September 5, 2007.

"The millionaires who don't feel rich: In Silicon Valley, a small fortune can seem meager," August 5, 2007.

NEWS 1.16 "The short end of the longer life," April 27, 2008.

NEWS 1.17 "Sharp decline in union membership in '06," January 26, 2007.

"Union membership up 310,000 in '07, biggest rise since '83," January 26, 2008.

NEWS 1.18 "Sense of belonging among belongings," September 17, 2006.

NEWS 1.19 "Chasing Utopia, family imagines no possessions," May 17, 2008.

NEWS 1.20 "Ignition interlocks." Advertisement by the American Beverage Industry, an Association of America's Restaurants, May 20, 2008.

NEWS 1.21 "Reports show wealth as a common factor among 2008 contenders," May 17, 2007.

"Big donors, too, have seats at Obama fund-raising table," August 6, 2008. See also News 1.11 above.

NEWS 1.22 "Senator charged in scheme to hide gifts of oil firm," July 30, 2008.

NEWS 1.23 "In economics departments, a growing will to debate fundamental assumptions," July 11, 2007.

"The free market: A false idol after all?" December 30, 2007.

All web supplements are available at www.wiley.com/go/dillon. See WEB icons in the margins above.

WEB SUPPLEMENTS

WEB 1.1   The Industrial Revolution
WEB 1.2   Census list of occupations; a selection
WEB 1.3   Labor strikes and the regulation of industrial conflict

NOTES

1   In citing Marx's writings (and subsequently Durkheim's, chapter 2, and Weber's, chapter 3), I reference the book initials rather than the date of publication. I do this to make it easier for students to keep in mind the classical theorists' main books, which comprise the core foundation of sociological theory. A list of these theorists' writings, their dates, and the book title initials for referencing them appears after the biographical notes in these three chapters.

2   Marx argues that we misunderstand history because we do not perceive the real conditions of everyday life, instead preferring to talk in general terms of some universal spirit or universal idea (e.g., freedom). Under capitalism and the division of labor to which we must consent, individuals' material activities become divorced from their real interests and hence their economic activities "become an alien power opposed" to them. (GI 22), a power that makes us desensitized to the real, unequal, material forces in society (GI 20–24). See earlier section in this chapter on historical materialism.

3   The influential Hungarian Marxist theorist Georg Lukacs (1885–1971) elaborates on Marx's theory of class consciousness. He emphasizes that Marx's collaborator Friedrich Engels pointed out that while humans make history and do so consciously, this consciousness is false insofar as it is part of "the historical totality" of class-conditioned social relations of inequality which exist under capitalism, and which can only be transcended by the class-conscious revolutionary political action of the proletariat (see Lukacs 1968: 48–55).

4   Lukacs (1968: 83–222), elaborates the centrality of the concept of reification in Marx's writing.

5   There are times when superstructural institutions critique capitalism – for example, the critique by the Catholic church of consumerism and of the extremes of economic inequality within the West and between the so-called first and third worlds; or the fledging discussion among university economists of the limits of free market ideology. These critiques, however, tend to be of specific capitalistic practices and ideas, rather than of the system of capitalism as a whole.

NEWS 1.2

CHAPTER TWO
EMILE DURKHEIM (1858–1917)

KEY CONCEPTS

functionalism

social facts

sui generis reality

morality

solidarity

interdependence

collective conscience

mechanical solidarity

division of labor

physical density

moral density

organic solidarity

contract

moral individualism

social integration

altruistic suicide

egoistic suicide

anomic suicide

sacred

profane

symbol

religion

collective representation

rituals

church

moral community

civil religion

sociology of knowledge

CHAPTER MENU

Timeline 2.1	Major events in Durkheim's lifetime (1858–1917)
1861	Telegraph line across the USA completed
1863	Football Association (soccer) established in Britain
1864	Red Cross established
1867	US purchases Alaska from Russia
1872	Friendly (charity) Societies in Britain report 4 million members
1873	Herbert Spencer, *The Study of Sociology*
1879	Church of Christ Scientist (Christian Science) established in Boston
1883	Statue of Liberty presented by France to the US
1889	Compulsory old-age and incapacity pensions introduced in Germany
1896	First modern Olympic games held in Athens
1900	10-hour working day mandated in France
1902	Public Health Act in France leads to better living conditions for the working class
1903	Formation of the Women's Social and Political Union in Britain by Emmeline Pankhurst, demanding votes for women
1906	Alfred Dreyfus, French Jewish army captain (and Durkheim's brother-in-law), cleared of treason, having been wrongly accused due to anti-Semitism
1908	Separate courts established for juveniles in Britain
1909	National Association for the Advancement of Colored People (NAACP) founded
1910	A ratio of one car to every 44 households in the US
1914	Outbreak of World War I; Germany declares war on Russia and France
1915	Einstein, *General Theory of Relativity*
1917	US declares war on Germany; Proletarian Revolution in Russia – abdication of the tsar, triumph of Lenin
1918	End of World War I

WEB 2.1

Emile Durkheim lived in Europe – in France – during much the same era as Karl Marx (1818–1883), though unlike Marx, his life extended into the twentieth century, to World War I (1914–1918), in which his only son, Andre, was killed. Living through a time of social, economic, and political upheaval, it is not surprising that, like Marx, Durkheim focused on social change and industrial society. But unlike Marx, who focused on the structural contradictions in capitalism (e.g., class inequality), Durkheim was preoccupied with the question of social and moral order.

Like Saint-Simon, Comte, and Rousseau (cf. Introduction), he was interested in probing how social order is achieved and maintained amidst social progress (Bellah 1973: xviii). He gave particular attention to how, in the progressive evolution from traditional to modern society, the forms of social organization and social relationships adapt so that society, social life, continues to maintain its effective functioning.

Durkheim conceptualized society as a complex system whose component parts or structures (e.g., economic activity, science, family structure, religion, etc.) are all interrelated but whose independent functioning is necessary to the functioning of the whole society. For this reason, his sociology is often referred to as functionalism or structural functionalism. Social structures, Durkheim argues, necessitate "a certain mode of acting" (DL 272–273), a particular way of being and of organizing social life whose consequences, in turn, function to maintain society, and which make other modes of being "almost impossible" (DL 273, 276).[1] Durkheim, therefore, offers a very different perspective on the organization of society and social relations than does Marx. In fact, among the theorists discussed in this book, the greatest theoretical divide is between Marx and Durkheim. Durkheim's contributions to sociology are both methodological and substantive, and although these intertwine in his writings, in this chapter I first discuss his methodology and then focus on his more substantively driven questions.

BIOGRAPHICAL NOTE

Emile Durkheim was born in April 1858 into a middle-class orthodox Jewish family in northeastern France. His father, grandfather, and great-grandfather were rabbis; and his mother ran a successful embroidery business. Emile was the youngest of four children; his family emphasized hard work, morality and duty – habits maintained by Durkheim throughout his life. He married Louise Dreyfus in 1887, and with their two children, Marie and Andre, enjoyed an idyllic family life despite his serious personality. Louise helped with Durkheim's writing: "she copied manuscripts, corrected proofs and shared in the administrative editorial work of the *Annee sociologique*" (Lukes 1973: 99), a prestigious multivolume journal that Durkheim founded, edited, and wrote for, using it to establish what he considered sociology's specialized content. Always concerned with the varying forces that undermine and produce social order, the end of Durkheim's life coincided with the ravages and disorder produced by World War I, and the death of his son in military action in 1915 was "a blow from which he would never recover" (Lukes 1973: 554). Durkheim continued to lecture and write, though with a marked social and emotional detachment, and he died two years later, in 1917, at age 59 (Lukes 1973: 39–40, 99–100, 554–559).

Durkheim's Writings
1893: *The Division of Labour in Society*, DL
1895: *The Rules of Sociological Method*, RSM
1897: *Suicide*, Su
1912: *The Elementary Forms of Religious Life*, EFRL
1914: "The Dualism of Human Nature and its Social Conditions," HN

DURKHEIM'S METHODOLOGICAL RULES

SCIENTIFIC SOCIOLOGY: THE STUDY OF SOCIAL FACTS

Although Durkheim is less popularly known than Marx, his enduring influence on the everyday practice of sociology is probably greater. This is particularly true of American sociology. Although many sociologists today might not acknowledge any debt to Durkheim, the dominant way sociologists go about studying the world owes much to his methodological approach. He outlined a scientific socio-logical methodology in *The Rules of Sociological Method*, first published in 1895, and in a pioneering study of suicide rates in nineteenth-century Europe (published in *Suicide*) demonstrated the scientific method that has influenced what sociolo-gists do when they conduct quantitative research. This includes, most notably, the definition and measurement of social variables and the statistical study of the relations between various independent and dependent variables.

Following the view of sociology as science elaborated by Saint-Simon, Comte, and Martineau (cf. Introduction), for Durkheim, sociology was the "science of civilization" (HN 149). He thus embarked on the analysis of what he called social facts, that is, all those *external* and *collective* ways in which society shapes, structures, and constrains our behavior. Durkheim states: "A social fact is any way of acting ... [that is] capable of exerting over the individual an external con-straint; or which is general over the whole of a given society, whilst having an existence of its own, independent of its individual manifestations" (RSM 59). Social facts – "the beliefs, tendencies, and practices of the group taken collec-tively" (RSM 54) – are, therefore, what sociologists study (and not individual psychological facts or physical or biological facts, though these may impinge on social facts).

For Durkheim, society is not simply a collection of individuals but is a collectiv-ity with features and characteristics of its own. Society is more than the sum of the individuals that comprise it; it is also comprised of social relationships (e.g., family, friends, community) and forms of social organization (e.g., occupational divisions, marriage, church, various groups), and these collective forces independ-ently regulate individual and collective behavior. Thus, Durkheim argues, society has its own reality, what he calls a *sui generis* reality, that is, a collective reality that exerts its own force *independent* of individuals (*genus* is the Latin for group; *sui generis* refers to "of the group in and of itself").

Society, therefore, through its various social structures and everyday customs and norms, constrains how we think, feel, and act. These external constraints exist outside of the self; they have an independent existence in society and cannot be willed out of existence by the individual. A 19-year-old man who doesn't go to college does not internalize society's expectations of how college students should act, and a college graduate may forget these expectations soon after she leaves college and has a full-time job – but these expectations still exist nonetheless in society. As social facts, they have an objective, external existence independent of any given individual; moreover, the *collective* existence of a social phenomenon can vary from its expression in any given individual's life.

The collective incidence of something in society – of divorce (or immigration, or economic inequality, etc.), for example – is separate from any one individual's experience of divorce, though at the same time, that individual's divorce contributes to the collective (social) phenomenon of divorce. By the same token, the incidence of divorce, how prevalent it is in a particular community, and public opinion about divorce are all social facts external to the individual. And as such, these social facts shape individual attitudes toward divorce in general and individuals' decisions about marriage and divorce (RSM 55).

Social facts, then, should not be equated with "statistical facts," such as the percentages of girls and boys who go to college, or the divorce or birth rates, though all of these facts too are social facts because they shape social behavior: they structure social policies, cultural expectations, and individuals' decisions about various things. But social facts encompass much more than statistical facts; they include all the ways in which social structures and social norms and collective expectations constrain social behavior.

STUDYING SOCIAL FACTS AS THINGS

How, as sociologists, should we scientifically study social facts? According to Durkheim, "the first and most basic rule is to consider social facts as things" (RSM 60) – as things that objectively exist in society and which can be studied

---

Topic 2.1 Born on the Bayou and barely feeling any urge to roam

The constraining power of society on individual (i.e., social) behavior is evident in Vacherie, Louisiana. Vacherie is one of the most settled places in the U.S. Almost all (98%) of Vacherie's residents were born in Louisiana, compared to an average of 60% for other American states. In this bayou town on the Mississippi River less than 30 miles west of New Orleans, families stay put over several generations and there are strong cultural and family expectations that they will do so. In the Reulet family, for example, whose descendants settled in Vacherie from France in the 1820s, all eight adult children live within a five mile radius of their parent's home; middle-age sons drop by for coffee and hot chocolate at the start of the work-day before heading to nearby manufacturing plants and oil refineries, while Sunday brings the obligatory extended-family dinner of Cajun pork and potatoes prepared every week by the Reulet adult daughters. Alongside Cajun food and culture, fishing and hunting are the main leisure activities in Vacherie, not surfing the internet.[2] [Among the social facts evident in Vacherie are population mobility patterns, immigration history, the occupational structure, family and gender structures, and collective expectations of everyday food, leisure, and gender behavior.]

NEWS 2.1

(as Comte too envisaged) with objectivity (see glossary at the end of the book). While the command to investigate "social facts as things" may sound straightforward, it is deceptively so. We cannot, for example, objectively see friendship or social ties – we cannot put them under a microscope in the same way that biologists study cells or microbes. And yet, social relationships are a core part of social life. Durkheim acknowledges the difficulty in measuring social phenomena – the fact that in and of themselves they are "not amenable to exact observation and especially not to measurement" (DL 24).

What then are we to do? How can we be scientists of social life if we cannot measure what constitutes social life? The answer, Durkheim states, is that while we cannot observe social processes directly we can study them scientifically by defining (or operationalizing) the things we study in terms of directly observable manifestations or indicators of the phenomenon in question: "We must ... substitute for [a particular social phenomenon] ... an external [measure] which symbolizes it, and then study the former through the latter" (DL 24). Definition is critical, because otherwise we don't know what we are looking for, or how to categorize and differentiate among things; "moreover, since this initial definition determines the subject matter itself ... that subject matter will either consist of a thing or not, according to how this definition is formulated" (RSM 75).

This is precisely what sociologists do. If you look in the "Methods" section of any quantitative research article you will see that sociologists discuss how they define and measure the particular variables of interest. Thus, for example, a recent article that studied older adults' social connectedness *defined* social connectedness as interpersonal ties and community participation. They *measured* the respondents' interpersonal social ties by the frequency of their interaction with, and subjective emotional closeness to, individuals in their circle (or network); and they measured the respondents' community participation (or integration) by the frequency of their neighborly socializing, religious participation, volunteering, and organized group involvement (Cornwell et al. 2008).

Sociological objectivity

Importantly, for Durkheim, by considering social facts as things that objectively exist outside of us and which can be objectively measured using various indicators, we can study social phenomena irrespective of our own views of, or feelings toward, the particular phenomenon. Consider religion. Religion is about a lot of unknowns. Does God exist? Does God answer prayers? Is there an after-life? These are questions that no researcher, and not even the most devout faith believer, can verify empirically. Nonetheless, many sociologists, following Durkheim, study religion as a social fact, as an objective thing in society – using indicators of its thing-ness, such as how often individuals attend church. These sociologists then investigate how frequency of church attendance constrains other forms of social behavior, such as volunteering in the community, alcohol consumption, voting.

Sociologists similarly study crime, homelessness, friendship, divorce, income inequality, etc. These are all social facts that have an external, independent existence in society. Moreover, all of these "social phenomena ... must be considered in themselves detached from the conscious beings who form their own mental representations of them" (RSM 70). Therefore, although "man cannot live among things without forming ideas about them according to which he regulates his behavior" (RSM 60), as social scientists, we must leave aside our preconceived ideas about society and how it works – ideas that necessarily derive from our own immersion in society – and instead focus on what comprises the (objective) social reality (social facts). As such, sociologists' empirical findings and conclusions about religion, crime, or any social fact are independent of their own personal beliefs about God, crime, etc. Further, since, as Durkheim argues, all social facts are produced by other social facts, we should see all social facts in terms of their social context – thus, for example, we should study the social conditions and circumstances that give rise to crime and to particular types of crime – rather than psychologically, in terms of a particular criminal's individual psyche (RSM 134).

Data-centered sociology

The relationship between the sociologist and the things we study is more complicated than Durkheim acknowledged; a point highlighted by Harriet Martineau (cf. Introduction), and developed by Max Weber (chapter 3) and elaborated especially by contemporary feminist theorists (chapter 10). Durkheim's scientific method, nonetheless, still informs much of what comprises empirical sociology. Research proceeds from things (data) to ideas and not the reverse (RSM 60); "to treat phenomena as things is to treat them as data and this constitutes the starting point for science" (RSM 69). In this scientific process, the whole of social reality is open to empirical investigation, wherein "the conventional character of a practice or an institution should never be assumed in advance" (RSM 70). Therefore, although we study things that may seem obvious or that we think we already know, such as friendship, crime, families, by studying these social phenomena scientifically – using data and making inferences based on data – we will likely discover or clarify characteristics about the phenomenon.[3]

SOCIAL FACTS AND SOCIAL PROBLEMS

An emphasis on social facts as objective things also means that crime, homelessness, and other things we might consider "social problems" are in fact sociologically "normal." They are things that exist in society, that are part of the collectivity. As such, we can measure and compare the occurrence and prevalence of these things (social facts), and their relation to other things (social facts) across different cities or countries that share a similar level of socio-economic development (RSM 92).

Durkheim argues, for example, that "crime [defined as any action that is punished] is normal because it is completely impossible for any society entirely free of it to exist" (RSM 99). Further, he notes that the criminal "plays a normal role in social life" (RSM 102), alongside judges, laws, prisons, etc. All "social problems" raise important political and policy-making questions. But for the Durkheimian-inspired sociologist, they are first and foremost social facts worthy of investigation, and social facts whose investigation will show how they vary in different social contexts, and variously relate to other social facts (e.g., unemployment). A normal social phenomenon (e.g., unemployment, drug addiction) becomes problematic – or for Durkheim, "pathological" – only when its incidence becomes abnormally high compared to its regular incidence in society or in other similarly developed countries. In the US, for example, a 4 percent unemployment rate is considered normal in times of economic prosperity, but a 6 percent unemployment rate is a sign of recession, i.e., of an abnormality in the economy/society. Politicians and policy-makers thus make great efforts to dampen the negative effects of recession (e.g., factory and bank closures, home foreclosures); they want to limit the disruptive impact on the normal functioning and cohesiveness of particular communities and of society as a whole. The maintenance of social cohesion was Durkheim's core preoccupation, and it is this substantive focus to which we now turn.

THE NATURE OF SOCIETY

Durkheim emphasized the uniquely specific and collective nature of social life – i.e., social facts have an external existence independent of any individual and constrain social behavior. Yet it is individuals who live in society. How then do individuals whose (individual) nature is different from the (collective) nature of society manage to live in society? This for Durkheim is the core task of sociology: analyzing social morality (Bellah 1973: xv). Essentially for Durkheim, morality comprises the social ties, the social solidarity, that binds individuals to other individuals and to the larger society; "morality consists in solidarity with the group, and varies according to that solidarity" (DL 331). Durkheim argues that society could not exist – it could not hold together in a relatively ordered and cohesive fashion – if each individual were to simply pursue his or her own individual, sensation-seeking ends, physical impulses and appetites to eat, drink, etc. We certainly act on those impulses, but we do so while simultaneously orienting ourselves to, and being regulated by, others, by society. Durkheim explains:

> Our sensory appetites are necessarily egoistic: they have our individuality and it alone as their object. When we satisfy our hunger, our thirst and so on, without bringing any other tendency into play, it is ourselves, and ourselves alone that we satisfy ... moral activity ... on the contrary, [is] distinguished by the fact the rules of conduct to which they conform can be universalized. Morality begins with disinterest, with attachment to something other than ourselves. (HN 151)

In other words, humans have certain basic biological drives that, according to Durkheim, are necessarily selfish. For example, we have a sexual drive and a need to procreate and pass on our genes. The view that these are selfish drives is most pronounced today among socio-biologists; they emphasize strategic mate-selection impulses whereby individuals ruthlessly vie for mates who will maximize their chance of having healthy and successful children who in turn will successfully procreate (e.g., Buss 2003). We see some evidence of this selfish impulse in advertisements seeking egg donors; as these advertisements state, "choosing an egg donor has lifelong implications," and, therefore, egg-donor agencies work to fulfill the "high expectations of sophisticated parents" and their precisely defined specifications in regard to intelligence, physical beauty, talents and accomplishments.

📰 NEWS 2.2

But as a social species who need others in order to live and reproduce, this also involves a learned capacity to transcend self-centered appetites so that, as Durkheim argues, we are able to cooperate with others and become attached to "something other than ourselves" (HN 151) – the external society of our family, neighborhood, school, our sports team, nation, etc. The functioning of all of these groups and of society as a whole is contingent on our learned ability to conform (more or less) to the respective norms and expectations within each of these multiple communities. This is why socialization is so important; from early infancy, we are taught how to interact and behave as social beings; to sacrifice a certain amount of self-interest to the interest of the collectivity – the community or society – that is external to us but of which we are a part. Socialization

> consists of a continual effort to impose upon the child ways of seeing, thinking and acting which he himself would not have arrived at spontaneously. From his earliest years we oblige him to eat, drink and sleep at regular hours, and to observe cleanliness, calm and obedience; later we force him to learn how to be mindful of others, to respect customs and conventions, and to work, etc. If this constraint in time ceases to be felt it is because it gradually gives rise to habits, to inner tendencies which render it superfluous; but they supplant the constraint only because they are derived from it. (RSM 53–54)

SELF-INTEREST VERSUS COLLECTIVE INTEREST

Through socialization, therefore, we learn to maintain society by cooperatively co-existing as friends, family members, work-mates, house-mates, team-mates, citizens – collectively tied by our shared interdependence. The relation of the individual to society is one which necessitates regulation and constraint precisely because of the collective (*sui generis*) nature of society. As Durkheim states, society has its own nature, and consequently, its requirements are quite different from those of our nature as individuals: the interests of the whole are not necessarily those of the part. Therefore, society cannot be formed or maintained without our being required to make perpetual and costly sacrifices. Because society surpasses us, it obliges us to surpass ourselves; and to surpass itself, a being must, to some degree, depart from its nature – a departure that does not take place without causing more or less painful tensions ... we must ... do violence to certain of our strongest inclinations. (HN 163)

You and your room-mates probably know well what Durkheim means about tension emanating from competing inclinations – when the nature of community/ society and the impulses of individuals are at odds. Your dorm-room (or apartment) mimics the tension that confronts society as a whole. This tension may be especially pronounced when you first come to college and share a dorm-room with someone you had not previously known. One likes to go to sleep early and another likes to socialize late in the evening with friends over to your room. The resolution of these conflicting impulses necessitates reciprocal compromising whereby both room-mates rein in their individual desires in order to preserve the effective functioning of college society, i.e., dorm cohabitation. And this scene wherein different individuals and groups must necessarily curb their selfish or self-oriented impulses occurs daily across diverse locales – in families, at church, in the workplace, and in the conduct of national and global politics. Reciprocity is central to social life and hence to all forms of social interaction; it is, as Durkheim's contemporary, the German social theorist Georg Simmel (1858–1918), would say, a "sociologically oriented ... feeling" (1908/1950: 384).[4]

THE CONSTRAINT OF SOCIETAL EXPECTATIONS

The multiple expectations associated with being a friend or daughter or student, and the rules of neighborhood and workplace culture, are institutionalized and exert an external constraint on our behavior. These are not our rules but society's rules, most of which were in place long before we were born and will still matter long after we have died. Moreover, even when we create what we think of as our very own individualized rules and norms for certain things, these too come from society. And even though we may not subjectively feel any social pressure to conform to being a certain kind of friend, daughter etc., and even when it seems natural for us to behave in certain ways toward others, that behavior is, nonetheless, socially inherited; it is externally given to us from society and it exists independent of us. Durkheim elaborates:

When I perform my duties as a brother, a husband or a citizen and carry out the commitments I have entered into, I fulfill obligations which are defined in law and custom and which are external to myself and my actions. Even when they conform to my own sentiments and when I feel their reality within me, that reality does not cease to be objective, for it is not I who have prescribed these duties; I have received them through education [socialization]. Moreover, how often does it happen that we are ignorant of the details of the obligations that we must assume, and that, to know them, we must consult the legal code and its authorized interpreters! Similarly, the [religious] believer has discovered from birth, ready fashioned, the beliefs and practices of his religious life; if they existed before he did, it follows that they exist outside them. The system of signs that I employ to express my thoughts, the monetary system I use to pay my debts, the credit instruments I utilise in my commercial relationships, the practices I follow in my profession, etc. all function independently of the use I make of them ... Thus there are ways of acting, thinking and feeling which possess the remarkable property of existing outside the consciousness of the individual. Not only are these types of behavior and thinking external to the individual, but they are endued with a compelling and coercive power by virtue of which, whether he wishes it or not, they impose themselves upon him. Undoubtedly, when I conform to them of my own free will, this coercion is not felt or felt hardly at all, since it is unnecessary. None the less, it is intrinsically a characteristic of these facts; the proof of this is that it asserts itself as soon as I try to resist. If I attempt to violate the rules of law they react against me so as to forestall my action, if there is still time ... If I do not conform to ordinary conventions, if in my mode of dress I pay no heed to what is customary in my country and in my social class, the laughter I provoke, the social distance at which I am kept, produce, although in a more mitigated form, the same results as any real [legal] penalty. In other cases, although it may be indirect, constraint is no less effective. I am not forced to speak French with my compatriots, nor to use the legal currency, but it is impossible for me to do otherwise. If I try to escape the necessity, my attempt would fail miserably. (RSM 50–51)

AN ARMY OF ONE

Some of you, understandably, may be surprised by Durkheim's emphasis on the necessarily constraining force of society. His view may seem especially jarring in America, which has an accentuated emphasis on individualism and individual rights, and where socialization emphasizes self-reliance and the uniqueness of individual habits and aspirations (e.g., Bellah et al. 1985). This ethos is so deeply present that even recruitment advertisements for the American army, an institution that necessarily demands cooperative teamwork and a strong sense of group bonding, nonetheless advertises itself as "An army of one," as if the lone individual soldier is equal to the entire army – as if the parts are greater than the whole, rather than the inverse.

It is important to keep in mind, however, that in emphasizing the external and constraining force that society exerts on the individual, Durkheim is not discounting the role of individual reason and free will in a person's actions, and nor is he dismissing the unique nuances of personality in how individuals may respond to social customs and conventions (RSM 52). He is simply highlighting that society exists independent of the individual, and that it necessarily constrains individual and group behavior. Durkheim argues that rather than being diminished by the awareness that we are not dependent on ourselves alone, we are in fact enriched by our social dependence; "it is indisputable today that most of our ideas and tendencies are not developed by ourselves, but come to us from outside, they can only penetrate us by imposing themselves upon us" (RSM 52). And they impose themselves through society, through socialization and social interaction. Durkheim's core thesis is that individuals are socially interdependent. Social cohesion comes from individuals' ties to others; our sense of social belonging comes from ties to other people, and not from our belongings, as the consumer product-owning website Zebo claims.

NEWS 1.18

CHANGE AND RESISTANCE

Although Durkheim's emphasis on society's existence prior to and beyond individual existence might seem to imply that social change never occurs, this, of course, is not the case. Social change happens, as Durkheim was well aware. Political and social upheaval was normal in France immediately prior to and during his early years: France had seen "three monarchies, two empires, and two republics in the period between 1789 and 1870" (Bellah 1973: xvi). But social change, whether large-scale or local (e.g., change in a bus or subway schedule), does not occur without a struggle; most change is initially resisted as a result of the collective force of existing social facts. The patterns and structures already in place cast a long shadow on people's expectations of what is normal, or of what functions effectively. As things external to us, social facts are "principally recognizable by virtue of not being capable of modification through a mere act of the will. This is not because it is intractable to all modification. But to effect change the will is not sufficient; it needs a degree of arduous effort because of the strength of the resistance it offers, which even then cannot always be overcome" (RSM 70).

Just think for a moment of marriage. It is a social fact that constrains collective expectations, as well as the actuality, of who can marry whom, and it dims our ability to recognize alternative possibilities. It was only in 1967, for example, that the US Supreme Court struck down state laws (e.g., Virginia) banning inter-racial marriage. And today, same-sex partners can marry in Vermont and

NEWS 2.3

Massachusetts but not in all American states. And as highlighted in the movie *Meet the Parents*, although it is not against the law, there is still a strong cultural expectation that women should marry men who have traditional male occupations (e.g., that women, not men, are nurses). It is hard to escape the constraining power of society. Although social change occurs, it is not simply willed by individuals. It has to be accomplished collectively and in tune with collective forces (e.g., public opinion at large, economic transformation). Durkheim comments: "As an industrialist, nothing prevents me from working with the processes and methods of the previous century, but if I do I will most certainly ruin myself. Even when in fact, I can struggle free from these rules or successfully break them, it is never without being forced to fight against them" (RSM 51). Similar challenges confront any individual or group who tries to defy any social convention.

Today, there is a lot of talk about the immensity of the social changes occurring due to economic and cultural globalization (see chapter 15). There was also, however, a lot of economic, social and technological change happening in the latter part of the nineteenth century when Durkheim and Marx (and Max Weber) were writing. Like Marx, Durkheim was preoccupied with the changes around him: industrialization, urbanization, immigration, and population growth – changes that sociologists typically see as differentiating modern from traditional societies. From the 1840s to the end of the nineteenth century, the US, for example, experienced a massive amount of immigration (e.g., Fischer and Hout 2006: 23–56). Thousands of Irish, Italians, Germans, Swedes, and Poles, among others, made their way to America and found jobs in its rapidly expanding manufacturing industries. The invention of the power loom moved textile production from a household-based craft to cloth-making by a highly specialized workforce producing standardized output in highly regulated factories (Smelser 1959; Williams 1990: 94–95). The convergence of these population and technological changes transformed society, speeding its transition from traditional to modern forms of social organization.

WEB 1.1

Durkheim was particularly interested in how such large-scale social change impacts social relations and the overall order and cohesion of society. In times of societal change and upheaval, what holds society together? Can we assume that society will more or less gel together regardless of the changes it undergoes? These are the very same questions percolating in public discussion in several countries today as people grapple with the globalizing impact of economic and population change – what, for example, is the impact of the current large-scale immigration of Polish and Brazilian and Kenyan workers and their families on the social structure and social relationships in Ireland, a small and homogeneous society?

contemp link.

NEWS 2.4

Following Ferdinand Tonnies (1855–1936), who distinguished between small-scale local community (*Gemeinschaft*) and large-scale, impersonal, urban society (*Gesellschaft*), Durkheim makes a clear analytical distinction between traditional and modern societies. He does so to elaborate how differences in social structure produce different mechanisms that function to create social cohesion or solidarity.

TRADITIONAL SOCIETY

Traditional (pre-industrial or agricultural) societies and communities tend to be characterized by *sameness*, by the similarities that exist among people. Anyone who has lived in a rural community knows this. In farming communities today, for example in rural Nebraska or Iowa, farmers do a similar kind of farming (e.g., wheat and cattle) using similar methods and tools (e.g., same-brand tractors, combine harvesters, pickup trucks, etc.), and each one is able to do the breadth of farm-related chores (e.g., harvesting, fixing tractors, butchering cattle for beef for the family freezer) required on any neighboring farm, as we see when farmers help one another in emergencies. Thus, rather than specializing in one very specific aspect of one very specific farm chore (the specialization seen in the division of labor in modern factory production; cf. chapter 1), these farmers have a breadth of competence, and one farmer's breadth of competence is similar to that of the next. Each farmer lives, moreover, in a relatively homogeneous community comprised of more or less similar-looking farms, farmers, and farm-families. This is the sort of sameness that captures the social organization seen in traditional societies and communities.

In traditional societies, social ties and relationships – bonds of social solidarity – are relatively easy to maintain because people share a lot in common. In the absence of the geographical and occupational mobility required by industrialization, the same individuals and families tend to live in the same place and engage in similar occupations over several generations. And similarly, there is a sameness of ethnicity, of religious and political beliefs, and of culture.

The organization and structure of everyday life in traditional communities are such that people meet each other in all kinds of overlapping contexts over the course of their daily or weekly routines; they meet at the same one or two churches, the same diner, the same post office, the same stores, and their children go to the same school, play on the same football team, etc. It's the type of society or community in which everyone basically knows everyone else; and even if they do not know them personally they know who they are, who their mother or brother is. Family, school, work, and leisure are all intersecting domains of activity and of social ties. In traditional communities characterized by overlapping ties, the maintenance of social solidarity does not require much effort, because as Durkheim states: "The more closely knit the members of a society, the more they maintain various relationships either with one another or with the group collectively. For if they met together rarely, they would not be mutually dependent, except sporadically and somewhat weakly" (DL 25).

Small towns and rural communities have different characteristics and different types of social relations than those found in urban centers.

There are many places in the US and in other modern societies where overlapping social ties are the norm. Grover's Corners on the Hudson, a town of 10,000 people in New York state, is one such place. Commenting on the community's intense grief following the death of one of its own, the third soldier from the town to be killed while serving in Iraq, one man who had been the dead soldier's high school teacher, soccer coach, and friend pointed out that in his town there are many layered relationships: "You know people, you know their brothers and their parents, you know them for generations ... You don't experience that most places in the world but you do here."

NEWS 2.5

THE SOCIETAL ABSORPTION OF THE INDIVIDUAL

We would expect Grover's Corners, and other traditional communities, to have a robust collective conscience. Durkheim uses this term (translated from the French *conscience collective*) to refer to a society's or community's collectively shared feelings, values (e.g., patriotism) and ideals (DL 43). He explains:

> The totality of beliefs and sentiments common to the average members of a society forms a determinate system with a life of its own. It can be termed the collective or common consciousness [conscience] ... By definition it is diffused over society as a whole ... it is independent of the particular conditions in which individuals find themselves. Individuals pass on, but it abides ... [and] links successive generations to one another. (DL 38–39)

Although Durkheim gives a lot of emphasis in his writings to the strong hold of the collective conscience and of society's "collective feelings" (RSM 99; DL 39) on a community's beliefs and practices, we should note, as feminist theorists like Dorothy Smith would point out, the allegedly objective "collective feeling" frequently excludes those who are not part of the dominant (white male) group in society (see chapter 10).

The collective conscience, nevertheless, exerts a strong authority over the whole community; maintaining social order and cohesiveness by tightly regulating the expectations and behavior of individuals. In Vacherie, for example, it would be hard for a woman to defy the expectation of helping to prepare the extended family's Sunday dinner (see Topic 2.1). In traditional communities there is little individualism, little personal freedom and anonymity – the individual, rather, "is absorbed into the collective" (DL 242). This brings a strong feeling of social belonging but it also means that the individual has little freedom to stray from the norms and authority of the community. Anyone who has grown up in places akin to Vacherie or Grover's Corners knows this feeling well; it's hard to escape your neighbor's watchful eyes, and particularly as you move through your teenage years looking for excitement, you might find the community's "social horizon" (DL 242) too limiting, too constraining and overpowering of your individual desires.

NEWS 2.1

Nonetheless, the authority of the collective conscience is keenly felt if you don't toe the line; and the repressive, punishing power of gossip, shame, and ostracism is felt not only by the individual deviant, but by his or her whole family and friends too in the loss of honor imposed on them (DL 47).[5] More generally, a community's informal sanctions and conventions function to affirm the collective conscience by elaborating particular expectations as well as variously punishing those who offend against strongly held collective feelings. "Punishment constitutes an emotional reaction" (DL 44) aimed at avenging and pouring scorn on the deviant act – the violation of the collective conscience – and defending the community against further challenges to the authority of its collective beliefs (DL 44). Through punishment, therefore, we "stir up [and reaffirm] the social sentiments that have been offended" (DL 47–48); punishment thus functions to repress the threat to societal cohesion that the deviance represents.

MECHANICAL SOLIDARITY

The sameness that characterizes the beliefs and social relationships in traditional societies produces what Durkheim calls mechanical solidarity; the creation and maintenance of social ties are fairly mechanical, i.e., they are built into the very structure of the community. When people in a community have relatively similar occupations, family histories, experiences, and beliefs, and overlapping social relationships, these similarities make it relatively easy to produce social cohesion. The similarity in what people do (e.g., farming, mill work, etc), and in who and what they know, means that no one individual or family is necessary to the functioning of the whole community; e.g., in Iowa farming communities, each individual/family basically replicates the next (like segments in an orange). Hence the absence of any one individual/family from the community (due to death or ostracism, for example) does not impact the overall functioning of the community. We see a parallel in the mechanical working of a car engine: only four cylinders are necessary for a car to work, to function; thus cars with six or eight cylinder engines basically have cylinders that replicate rather than add to the functioning of the other four (notwithstanding the fact that an eight-cylinder engine may function to enhance the car owner's social status).

📖 NEWS 2.1   Vacherie, Louisiana, the most rooted town in the most rooted state in America, is a good illustration of the mechanical solidarity that Durkheim attributes to traditional communities. Its tightly bounded and overlapping family and neighborhood relationships, the force of its collective expectations on everyday routines (e.g., Sunday dinner for the extended family), and long-established shared occupational histories and leisure routines ensure a fairly mechanical maintenance of the community's social ties, order, and cohesion.

MODERN SOCIETY

Even in Vacherie, however, there are some emerging threats to the maintenance of tight social solidarity. Well-paid blue-collar work is on the decline, thus pushing
📖 NEWS 2.1   Vacherie's young people to continue education beyond high school. Those who

leave Vacherie to go to college are less likely to return and settle there, and with more young people availing themselves of the college and post-college economic opportunities outside of Vacherie, this trend may weaken the strong family and community bonds that have characterized Vacherie for several generations. Such mobility (a social fact) is precisely one of the defining characteristics of modern society. Is it possible then for solidarity (social cohesion) to characterize modern societies that, by definition, do not have the overlapping social relationships seen in traditional societies?

Modern societies, after all, look almost exactly the opposite of traditional societies. They are characterized by population density, urbanization, geographical and social mobility, and a diversity of occupational, religious, political, ethnic, and cultural groups. Diversity brings a lot of personal freedom, anonymity, and impersonality; individual difference rather than sameness is the norm. If we think of densely populated cities like New York, Toronto, or Mumbai (Bombay), or even of smaller cities like Glasgow or Cleveland, we have a snapshot of a modern society. The urban metropolis, as Georg Simmel, elaborated, produces an "intensification of nervous stimulation ... With each crossing of the street, with the tempo and multiplicity of economic, occupational and social life, the city sets up a deep contrast with small town and rural life ... [where] the rhythm of life ... flows more slowly, more habitually, and more evenly" (1903/1950: 410).

In modern, urban societies, unlike in traditional societies, Durkheim argues, the collective conscience is less forceful and is less encompassing and less controlling of the individual:

> As society spreads out and becomes denser, it envelops the individual less tightly, and in consequence can restrain less efficiently the diverging tendencies that appear ... in large towns the individual is much more liberated from the yoke of the collectivity ... the pressure of opinion is felt with less force in large population centers. It is because the attention of each individual is distracted in too many different directions. Moreover we do not know one another so well. Even neighbors and members of the same family are in contact less often and less regularly, separated as they are at every moment by a host of matters and other people who come between them. (DL 238–239)

Thus the solidarity that derives from shared beliefs, experiences and sentiments is harder to find in modern societies, notwithstanding the existence of many enclaves of traditional community within the urban metropolis (e.g., Boston's North End) and within modern societies more generally (e.g., Grover's Corners; Vacherie).

SPECIALIZED DIVISION OF LABOR

Yet, despite the individual freedom and the mobility, diversity, and weaker collective feelings that characterize modern society, there is still social cohesion. How is this possible? The reason, Durkheim argues, lies in the highly specialized division of labor that characterizes America and other modern societies. The crucial variable differentiating modern from traditional societies is the extent to which there is specialization across and within various sectors of society. Durkheim wrote about these processes in a book of this very title, *The Division of Labor in Society* (DL). Sounding a lot like Karl Marx (see chapter 1, p. 52), Durkheim identified an increasingly specialized division of labor that coincides with the expansion of modern industrialization. It

> involves increasingly powerful mechanisms, large-scale groupings of power and capital, and consequently an extreme division of labor. Inside factories, not only are jobs demarcated, becoming extremely specialized, but each product is itself a specialty entailing the existence of others ... the division of labor is not peculiar to economic life. We can observe its increasing influence in the most diverse sectors of society. Functions, whether political, administrative, or judicial, are becoming more and more specialized. The same is true in the arts and sciences. (DL 1–2)

Thus, modern societies are characterized by specialization. There is a division of labor not only in the economy (e.g., factory production) and in the functions of government but also in the responsibility for child socialization, for example, whereby socialization functions are dispersed across institutions – with the family, the church, and the education system all having discrete and specific institutional roles. And within the university, for example, education is further divided across specialized colleges and schools (of business, law, liberal arts) and still further specialized departments and disciplines (sociology, economics, history, English, etc.). Similarly, the government has its specialized divisions and departments, as does the judicial system. Traditional societies, by contrast, or rural communities, have a limited division of labor (as we discussed; see pp. 90–91).

SOCIAL INTERDEPENDENCE

Population growth and concentration *necessitate* a division of labor. Durkheim states, "The division of labour varies in direct proportion to the volume and density of societies and if it progresses in a continuous manner over the course of social development it is because societies become regularly more dense and generally more voluminous" (DL 205). The increasingly specialized division of labor that thus characterizes modern society, Durkheim argues, affects "profoundly our moral constitution" (DL 3) – our social ties and relationships, social solidarity. But Durkheim, unlike Marx, did not see the division of labor as producing alienation (cf. chapter 1). Rather, Durkheim argued that the specialized division of labor creates social interdependence. This is because occupational specialization *requires* individual specialization, and each individual's specialty contributes to the functioning of the whole.

Thus the division of labor produces "a moral effect" (DL 17). "The division of labor can only occur within the framework of an already existing society. By this we do not just simply mean that individuals must cling materially to one another, but moral ties must also exist between them" (DL 218). Accordingly, for

Dukheim, individual interdependence creates and regulates social solidarity because of the social-moral ties that underlie interdependence, ties which exist outside of, but which are also encompassed in, the division of labor (DL 219); the division of labor "creates between men a whole system of rights and duties joining them in a lasting way to one another" (DL 337–338). Thus, contrary to Marx (cf. chapter 1), Durkheim argues that there is "nothing antisocial" or alienating about the division of labor. It is not antisocial "because it is a product of society" (DL 221), and it organically connects and integrates individuals. Moreover, the division of labor – contrary to the utilitarian view of unregulated individual self-interest advocated by Adam Smith and John Locke (cf. Introduction) – enables and requires cooperation among individuals in modern society; thus "moral life permeates all the relationships that go to make up co-operation" (DL 220–221).

For Durkheim, therefore, the division of labor produces interdependence and social cohesion; it is a functional accommodation to the increase in population growth and the concentrated population density (urbanization) associated with the development of modern societies. He explains: "the number of social relationships increases generally with the number of individuals … [who] must be in fairly intimate contact so as to act and react upon one another"; they cannot be separated by "mutually impenetrable" environments (DL 205). With more and more people moving within an increasingly concentrated or dense space, there is, by default, increased social interaction and dependence. The division of labor not only makes it possible for, but requires, increasing numbers of individuals to act and interact with one another – "for functions to specialize even more, there must be additional cooperating elements, which must be grouped close enough together to be able to co-operate" (DL 205).

THE DENSITY OF SOCIAL INTERACTION

We generally do not have the same regularity of contact with family and relatives as would occur in a traditional society, but we are in contact with the many others who literally cross our path every day. As we go about our daily business (getting coffee, at work or school, working out, attending a ball game), many of the people we meet are different from us in some way – a different family background, different ethnicity, different occupational aspirations, different political and religious beliefs, etc. These many individuals comprise and contribute to the physical density of our environment; literally, the number of people we encounter during the day. (Census reports use *population density*, i.e., the number of people per specified area, to differentiate among places; cities have high, and rural areas low, population density.) What is significant about physical density for Durkheim is the social or moral density that it gives rise to; the more people we meet, the more social interacting we have to do, however fleetingly.

The division of specialized labor brings us into contact with more and more people not like us (occupationally, economically, culturally, etc.) and makes us dependent on one another: "Each one of us depends more intimately upon society the more labour is divided up ... Society becomes more effective in moving in concert, at the same time as each of its elements has more movements that are peculiarly its own" (DL 85). Georg Simmel similarly observed that "specialization makes each man the more directly dependent upon the supplementary activities of all others" (Simmel 1903/1950: 409).

ORGANIC SOLIDARITY

The interdependence that results from the highly specialized division of labor produces what Durkheim calls organic solidarity. "This solidarity resembles that observed in the higher animals. In fact each organ has its own special characteristics and autonomy, yet the greater the unity of the organism, the more marked the individualization of the parts. Using this analogy, we propose to call 'organic' the solidarity that is due to the division of labor" (DL 85). Thus we recognize that while each organ in the body (e.g., lungs, kidneys, stomach) performs a very specialized function, a healthy body is dependent on the effective simultaneous functioning of each independent and interdependent organ. So too with modern society; social cohesion (social health) results from the interdependence of individuals, each with his or her own specialty. Modern society not only affirms but requires individualism; an individualism, however, that produces inter-individual dependence rather than individual isolation.

Roofers at work. The specialized division of labor makes individuals dependent on one another; interdependence creates solidarity.

Durkheim points out, moreover, that the interdependence in modern society is not determined solely by contractual exchange (even though laws proliferate in modern society). Contract certainly matters; it regulates social relationships and behavior in all sorts of ways (e.g., marriage; club membership; housing mortgages and leases; almost all financial transactions). And when contracts get broken, modern societies have laws in place that seek to restore the order that the laws were intended to protect (see note 3). But, as Durkheim argues, "if a contract has binding force, it is society which confers that force" (DL 71). Contracts have legitimacy only because they institutionalize (or legalize) the expectations and customs that we in society believe should be enforced regarding how we should treat one another, how relationships should be regulated.

Durkheim argues that contracts are an expression not of utilitarian exchange based on individual self-interests (as Adam Smith or John Locke would argue; cf. Introduction), but of social morality (DL 221). Like all social facts, contracts originate within society and it is society which gives them their obligatory (moral) force. They simply represent the inter-individual cooperativeness that society considers moral in the first place; they do not have an existence or a power independent of society. Hence "the contract is not sufficient by itself, but is only possible because of the regulation of contracts, which is of social origin" (DL 162).

All contractual relationships thus also have at the same time a pre-contractual, moral (social) element over and above the protection of the individual interests at stake. In this view, contracts are not simply formal legal rules established to restrain individuals' avaricious appetites (cf. Hobbes), or even a social mechanism to protect individual rights (as in Rousseau's *social contract*). Rather, for Durkheim, contracts are thoroughly social; they both originate in and function to protect *society*, i.e., the functioning of society and its various, interdependent social relationships as collective forces that impact the moral (constraining) ties among individuals (see pp. 80–81 above).

When we do things that go beyond the requirements stipulated by contract, this vividly demonstrates the moral-social basis of society that Durkheim emphasizes. Volunteering in the community, for example, and the generosity that is observed following natural disasters, when people travel miles to help others whose homes and livelihoods have been destroyed by hurricanes or earthquakes – these social facts crystallize the moral force exerted by society: the attachment of individuals to something other than themselves (i.e., to society; see pp. 84–85 above) – demonstrated by individuals' collective awareness of the social interdependence that underlies and builds society.

NEWS 2.6

Thus while we have self-interests (and appetites), it is not these interests alone that make us social and that enable us to build solidarity with one another and the collectivity:

> if mutual interest draws men closer, it is never more than for a few moments. It can only create between them an external bond. In the fact of exchange the various agents involved

remain apart from one another, and once the operation is over, each one finds himself again "reassuming his self" in its entirety. The different consciousnesses are only superficially in contact: they neither interpenetrate nor do they cleave closely to one another ... For where interests alone reign, as nothing arises to check the egoisms confronting one another, each self finds itself in relation to the other on a war footing ... Self-interest is, in fact, the least constant thing in the world. Today it is useful for me to unite with you; tomorrow the same reason will make me your enemy. (DL 152)

The individualism of modern society, therefore, does not preclude a felt responsibility toward others; it is, for Durkheim, a moral individualism that goes beyond our contractual obligations (while also shaping them). Society – moral life – is possible only because individuals are attached to something other than themselves; they recognize the necessity of cooperative interdependence with others, an interdependence demanded by the ever-increasing complexity in the organization of modern society. Consequently, while the solidarity in traditional societies derives from the sameness of the community, in modern societies the cooperation required by the specialized division of labor is moral too, producing social interdependence (organic solidarity). In sum, traditional and modern societies can both be described as moral societies but the source of their morality/solidarity derives from different social structures (different social facts).

Box 2.1 Contrasts between traditional and modern society

Traditional society	Modern society
Pre-industrial/rural society	Industrialized, urban society
Sameness	Diversity
Strong collective conscience	Weak collective conscience
Limited division of labor	Highly specialized division of labor
Repressive, punitive law	Contract-type law stipulating reciprocal rights
Mechanical solidarity	Organic solidarity

SOCIAL CONDITIONS OF SUICIDE

As part of his focus on the social mechanisms (e.g., the division of labor) that create social solidarity and integrate individuals into society, Durkheim wrote extensively about the social conditions that are conducive to, and weakening of, social integration. He did so primarily in *Suicide* (1897), a major empirical study of suicide rates in nineteenth-century Europe (and the first to demonstrate the methodology of scientific sociology that he advocated; see pp. 81–83 above). Using suicide as the dependent (outcome) variable, he examines how social integration or regulation varies by several independent (predictor) variables to increase the likelihood of suicide. In addition to its methodological importance, Durkheim's

Suicide is important theoretically because, first, it further elaborates his core theoretical emphasis on the significance of social interdependence and how social structures function to attach the individual to society. And second, his highlighting of particular categories or types of suicide allows him to show how different social conditions or circumstances can produce different social consequences.

SUICIDE: A SOCIAL FACT

Although suicide is an individual act, it is also a social phenomenon. And although we might think of suicide as a "social problem," it is "normal" in the Durkheimian sense (see pp. 83–84 above) because every society has a certain level of suicide. Already in the early nineteenth century, Harriet Martineau had defined suicide as "the voluntary surrender of life from any cause" (1838: 103), and as Durkheim would too, she recognized it as a normal social fact, and one indicative of varying levels of social regulation and integration. Martineau stated: "Every society has its suicides, and much may be learned from their character and number, both as to the notions on morals which prevail and the religious sentiment which ... controls the act" (1838: 105).

From a sociological perspective, therefore, notwithstanding the unique personal circumstances in which individuals commit suicide, suicide can – and should, according to Durkheim – be studied in terms of its antecedent social context, specifically, its relation to social integration. From his analysis of suicide rates in Western Europe, Durkheim concluded that "suicide varies inversely with the degree of integration of the social groups of which the individual forms a part" (Su 209). Social groups and the extent to which those groups are tightly integrated exert a constraining influence on the individual, because, Durkheim explains,

> a collective force is one of the obstacles best calculated to restrain suicide, its weakening involves a development of suicide. When society is strongly integrated, it holds individuals under its control, considers them at its service and thus forbids them to dispose willfully of themselves. Accordingly, it opposes their evading their duties to it through death ... they cling to life more resolutely when belonging to a group they love, so as not to betray interests they put before their own. The bond that unites them with the common cause attaches them to life. (Su 209–210)

So while many people think of suicide in psychological terms (e.g., related to depression), Durkheim sees it and studies it as a social fact, a social fact that sheds light on the social or group relationships that constrain individuals and thus regulate the social cohesion that is critical to the maintenance of society (DL xxxv).

In accord with differences in the social relationships that characterize traditional (mechanical solidarity) and modern society (organic solidarity), Durhkeim argues that different societal contexts produce different conditions leading to suicide. He identified *egoistic* and *anomic* suicide as more characteristic of modern

99

society, and *altruistic suicide* as more likely to be found in the pre-modern era or in specific, tightly bonded social circumstances in contemporary times.[6]

ALTRUISTIC SUICIDE

In traditional societies or communities, suicide can occur as result of individuals' excessively tight relation to, or absorption by, the community. In these circumstances of high social integration, individuals are so closely oriented to fulfilling the social expectations of the community or group that suicide becomes the obligatory or honorable option when they fail to meet those expectations (Su 221). Durkheim calls this altruistic suicide (altruism is the word used to describe selfless commitment to others). Japan, for example, has a long history of high rates of suicide attributed to individuals' loss of honor in the community whether due, historically, to defeat in military battles, or in current times, to economic failure. This type of obligatory suicide can emerge in any tightly bonded community where individuals acutely feel the moral sanction of the collective conscience. Two miners whose jobs included watching for safety hazards committed suicide shortly after twelve of their close "comrades" were killed in a blast at the Sago mine in West Virginia in the summer of 2005; their action might be seen as an instance of altruistic suicide. Although they were not blamed for the disaster – the blast was caused by lightning – the miners, nonetheless, may have felt responsible for their workmates' loss and an inability to imagine continuing to work and live in the tightly bonded community in their absence.

NEWS 2.7

EGOISTIC SUICIDE

Egoistic suicide, as the label suggests, refers to suicide under social conditions in which individuals are excessively self-oriented, and hence only very loosely bound to other individuals and social groups. In modern western society individualism is highly valued; the advanced division of labor associated with industrialization requires, as Durkheim emphasized, individual specialization. The collective conscience does not rein in the individual's egoistic appetites, and indeed celebrates individual freedom and ambition. It is not so surprising, then, that some individuals become so self-oriented they have fewer outlets and opportunities for social relations (family, friends, community).

Young graduates who aspire to successful corporate careers in law and finance work long hours, often spending weekends in the office rather than with friends and in social activities (e.g., Epstein et al. 1999). Although these people are well compensated financially, the demands of work do not end once they get a coveted promotion. The egoistic culture of the corporate world is not conducive to individuals developing supportive social ties. Thus, if confronted with some personal crisis, whether regarding work (e.g., sharp income decline due to a recession) or health or some other personal matter, they are not as cushioned as someone who has managed to maintain close family, friendship, and other bonds. The egoistic individual, in short, lacks the social constraints, the social attachments, that can protect against suicide.

Topic 2.2 Terrell Owens

Although Durkheim focused on suicide *rates*, not individual suicides, we can use the alleged suicide attempt of the US football player Terrell Owens to illustrate the type of social conditions that are conducive to egoistic suicide. When the media reported that Owens, the controversial wide-receiver for the Dallas Cowboys football team, allegedly tried to commit suicide in September 2006, his agent denied the suicide attempt, declaring that Owens had "25 million reasons why he should be alive." These reasons derived from the three-year, $25-million contract that Owens had signed with Dallas earlier that year. But from a Durkheimian perspective we should not be too surprised if Owens had, in fact, attempted suicide. His history of mobility from one football team to another over a relatively short span of time (San Francisco Forty-Niners, Philadelphia Eagles, Dallas Cowboys), and the ongoing disruptions created by his self-celebrating antics, suggest that Owens is a maverick, a lone rider, and not very attached to either his team-mates or a particular team or city. Independent of any psychological processes motivating Owens's alleged suicide attempt, the egoistic conditions in modern society and in professional sports, where team mobility (e.g., teams move to new cities if they get a better financial deal) and player mobility rather than social attachment are rewarded, make it difficult to restrain egoistic behavior (including attempted suicide) either on or off the field.

Social structures and social relationships

Social relationships are constraining forces, tying us into social commitments. Thus Durkheim found that single people were more likely to commit suicide than married people: marriage is a constraining condition; it literally binds you to someone else and thus has a regulatory and socially integrating force in the individual's life (Su 196–198). Similarly, Durkheim noted that suicide varied inversely with the number of children per marital household; marriage is a constraint but having children is even more constraining – the responsibility to and for others which it entails is especially pressing.

Accordingly, Durkheim emphasized that it is not just social relationships in general but differences in the structure of social relationships that also matter: some social structures (e.g., marriage, parenthood) are more likely than others to integrate individuals into society. This point is well exemplified for Durkheim (Su 152–154) by the lower incidence of suicide in predominantly Catholic (e.g., Spain, Portugal, Italy) than in predominantly Protestant countries (e.g., Germany, Denmark). This statistical difference seems initially puzzling: if participation in a social group is functional to social integration, and churches are social groups that have a regulatory force in individuals' lives (as Martineau too observed),[7] then why would Catholics and Protestants vary in the propensity to commit suicide? You might reasonably suggest that perhaps the doctrines of the two churches differ on suicide; if Catholicism were more opposed than Protestantism to suicide, we might expect fewer Catholic suicides. Both churches, however, are equally condemnatory of suicide. What, then, explains their different suicide rates? Durkheim argues that it is not doctrine, but variation in the structure or social organization of the churches that accounts for variation in religious adherents' suicide rates.

The Catholic church is much more socially constraining of the individual than is Protestantism. Protestants emphasize the individual's ability to interpret the Bible, whereas Catholics are obliged to defer to the interpretive authority of the church hierarchy (pope, bishops, etc.). Indeed, Protestantism is strongly associated with the individualism (the egoism) of modern capitalist society (cf. Weber; see chapter 3). Catholicism, by contrast, embeds the individual Catholic in layered church relationships and practices (e.g., weekly Mass) that require the individual's integration (communion) with the Catholic collectivity, and by extension, the social integration that more strongly buffers against suicide. Durkheim elaborates:

> All *variation* is abhorrent to Catholic thought. The Protestant is far more the author of his faith. The Bible is put in his hands and no interpretation is imposed upon him ... The proclivity of Protestantism for suicide must relate to the spirit of free inquiry that animates this religion ... Free inquiry itself is only the effect of another cause ... if Protestantism concedes a greater freedom to individual thought than Catholicism, it is because it has fewer common beliefs and practices. Now a religious society cannot exist without a collective credo, and the more extensive the credo the more unified and strong is the society ... It socializes men only by attaching them completely to an identical body of doctrine and socializes them in proportion as this body of doctrine is extensive and firm. The more numerous the manners of action and thought of a religious character are, which are accordingly removed from free inquiry, the more the idea of God presents itself in all details of existence, and makes individual wills converge to one identical goal. Inversely, the greater concessions a confessional group [a specific religious denomination/ church] makes to individual judgment the less it dominates lives, the less its cohesion and vitality. We thus reach the conclusion that the superiority [higher incidence] of Protestantism with respect to suicide results from its being a less strongly integrated church than the Catholic church. (Su 158–9)

In short, we learn here from Durkheim's discussion of suicide that different forms of social organization have different social effects, an insight that sociologists apply to the study of a whole range of social processes (e.g., gender equality in the workplace; Kanter 1977).

ANOMIC SUICIDE

Although the egoistic individualism of modern society can weaken our ties to others, societal upheaval produces anomic conditions that can also disrupt the individual's bond with society, producing what Durkheim calls anomic suicide. Anomie is a French word meaning the absence of norms or of established standards; it refers to circumstances when the normal patterns of social life are suddenly uprooted. In contemporary times, many people live in communities that are aptly characterized as "places without roots," places that attract transients, people on the move for various economic and personal reasons, and as such it is difficult for these communities to provide a socially integrating anchor for individuals and families. In these anomic places, we would expect suicide rates to be high. Nevada, home to Las Vegas, is the most rootless place in America, and it has the nation's highest suicide rates for teenagers, adults, and the elderly (it also has high rates of alcoholism, high school dropouts, child abuse deaths, teenage pregnancy, smoking and compulsive gambling).

🖹🖹 NEWS 2.10

But anomie can also strike communities and places that have deep roots. This happens during times of rapid social change or cultural turmoil and crisis – when the norms, those ways of acting, thinking, and feeling that we understand to be normal, get uprooted and overturned. Anomic suicide results from social conditions when

> the scale is upset; but a new scale cannot be immediately improvised. Time is required for the public conscience to reclassify men and things. So long as the social forces thus freed have not regained equilibrium, their respective values are unknown and so all regulation is lacking for a time. The limits are unknown between the possible and the impossible, what is just and unjust, legitimate claims and hopes and those which are immoderate. Consequently there is no restraint upon aspirations ... Appetites, not being controlled by a public opinion, become disoriented, no longer recognize the limits proper to them. (Su 253)

During times of social upheaval, the force of collective (public) opinion, of society, weakens precisely because what the collectivity thinks is itself in turmoil; it is unable to make sense of what it is experiencing. The terrorist events of September 11, 2001, in New York exemplify a crisis that caused anomic societal conditions. In addition to the severed ties it caused for the thousands of families and co-workers directly affected by the deaths on that day, 9/11 also upended Americans' expectations about all kinds of things: their everyday security, their trust in airlines and airports, their trust in technology, their belief in America as an open and welcoming immigrant society, and their trust in government and its various agencies. In short, 9/11 ruptured much of what had long rooted and anchored Americans.

Societal dislocation: Hurricane Katrina

Natural disasters also create anomic social conditions. Tsunamis, hurricanes, earthquakes, floods, and fires literally uproot whole communities to varying degrees and in the process uproot people from the structures and the many social groups and relationships (of family, school, work, church, friends, etc.) that regulate their daily lives and integrate them into society. In the United States, for example, Hurricane Katrina (which hit Louisiana and neighboring states in September 2005) "produced a diaspora of historic proportions" with thousands of families displaced from their homes, schools and neighborhoods, from all their familiar anchors. This is an uprooting that still continues for thousands of evacuated families who are shifted by the government from one temporary trailer park to another, thus impeding their ability to put down roots, however fragile, in new neighborhoods. The negative consequences of such displacement were exacerbated for many families by the fact that their government-issued trailers were subsequently found to have been contaminated with poisonous construction materials that cause serious respiratory and other illnesses.

In the aftermath of Hurricane Katrina, medical sociologists documented a two-fold increase in the incidence of serious mental illness (e.g., depression, anxiety, and post-traumatic stress) among individuals in the New Orleans area (a population that had also been studied prior to Katrina) – thus underscoring the negative social impact of disruptive events. But, despite the greater prevalence of mental illness, the prevalence of suicide and of suicide plans was lower among those diagnosed with mental illness after Katrina than it was in the mentally ill population in New Orleans prior to Katrina. While this finding might be seen to challenge Durkheim's specific claims about the positive relation between anomie and suicide, Durkheim's larger point that social relationships integrate individuals into society and buffer against suicide is also borne out by the data. The researchers attribute the lower incidence of suicide to, among other factors, the increased social support given to individuals in Katrina's aftermath (Kessler et al. 2006).

Clearly, different social conditions and circumstances, as Durkheim emphasizes throughout his writing, produce different social consequences, and the sociologist's task is to identify the specific social conditions that give rise to particular social patterns. We know, for example, that the disruptive and traumatizing effects of military combat on soldiers' lives and their families increases the incidence of

suicide and suicide-like symptoms in the military. Notably, the military is responding to this by, among other things, making efforts to increase the social support (e.g., marital counseling, family social activities) available to soldiers and their families and thus buffer them with a "chain of care" against the negative personal consequences of serving in Iraq and Afghanistan. (See also chapter 9.)

Economic transformation

Economic events too can cause anomie – whether due to a sharp downturn in financial markets, the crash of a staple food crop, or the closing of a large factory in a local community. Similarly, changes that bring a lot of new wealth to a community can weaken social cohesion; "boomtown blues" – whether in Wyoming cowboy country or high-tech Bangalore, India's suicide capital – can result from the transformative effect of new money on a community's (and individuals') previously existing ways of being. In sum, as Durkheim states, "when society is disturbed by some painful crisis or by beneficent but abrupt transitions, it is momentarily incapable of exercising [a restraining] influence; thence come the sudden rises in the curve of suicides" (Su 252).

Although societal anomie produces conditions that increase suicide – detachment from society – it is also the case, Durkheim argues, that societal crises can have a socially unifying effect too. He cites war as an example of a social disturbance that can strengthen rather than weaken social cohesion. Observing that the incidence of suicides decreased in urban but not in rural areas in France in 1870–1871 (during the Franco-Prussian War), Durkheim sought to identify the larger societal circumstances that accounted for this (having ruled out recording errors). He concluded:

> The war produced its full moral effect only on the urban population, more sensitive, impressionable and also better informed on current events than the rural population. These facts are therefore susceptible of only one interpretation; namely that great social disturbances and great popular wars rouse collective sentiments, stimulate partisan spirit and patriotism, political and national faith, alike, and concentrating activity toward a single end, at least temporarily cause a stronger integration of society. The salutary influence which we have just shown to exist is due not to the crisis but to the struggles it occasions. As they force men to close ranks and confront the common danger, the individual thinks less of himself and more of the common cause. (Su 208)

Thus, some disruptive events can have a socially binding effect, leading individuals to affirm their shared life in society – this is highlighted, for example, by the collective response of so many volunteers helping others rebuild their lives following Hurricane Katrina, the Indonesian tsunami, and the Sichuan earthquake. Indeed, while 9/11 certainly caused anomie, it also resulted in collective gatherings across the US, at memorial services and in informal public spaces, that produced and strengthened solidarity among those present.

NEWS 2.14

Topic 2.3   When tragedy brings strangers together

In the week after the 9/11 terrorist attacks, crowds of people spontaneously gathered in Union Square in Manhattan, to express grief, anger, and loss, or simply "just to be around other people," during that unsettling, tragic time. Thousands of people brought flowers, photographs, and candles to makeshift shrines near the square's equestrian statue of George Washington. What happened at Union Square was the coming together of strangers, causing a "sense of unity," as one person who had visited the park several nights in a row since 9/11 said. She further commented: "We all feel differently about what to do ... but everybody seems to agree that we've got to be together no matter what happens. So you get a little bit of hope in togetherness." A similar collective affirmation of strangers coming together occurred in the streets of London following Princess Diana's tragic death.

NEWS 2.14

Although suicide is a normal social fact, if suicide (or, e.g., crime) rates are abnormally high in a given historical or socio-cultural context, this can suggest a social pathology reflecting a rupture in social ties. Durkheim argued that this can occur in modern societies as a result of "abnormalities" in the division of labor, such as would happen if functional interdependence was displaced by a situation in which one social group "seeks to live at the expense" of another (DL 291). Sounding here like Marx, Durkheim suggests "the hostility between labour and capital" as an example, and elaborates how this relation has deteriorated over time:

> As industrial functions specialize more the struggle becomes more fierce, far from solidarity increasing. In the Middle Ages the workman everywhere lived side by side with his master, sharing in his work "in the same shop, on the same bench." ... Both were almost equal to one another ... conflicts were completely exceptional. From the fifteenth century onwards things began to change. (DL 292)

Unlike Marx, however, who argued that conflict between workers and their capitalist masters would lead to the overthrow of capitalism (chapter 1), Durkheim saw such conflict as simply an abnormality in the division of labor and in the functioning of society, but not one that threatens the demise of industrial society.

Another abnormality for Durkheim occurs if the individualism required by the division of labor becomes excessive, so that the individual isolates himself from others, believing that his specialized activity is superior to that of others (DL 294). In these circumstances, the moral (socially anchored) individualism that Durkheim saw as inherent in modern society gets displaced by what some sociologists today would call a narcissistic, self-seeking, and self-satisfied individualism (e.g., Bellah et al. 1985). In sum, abnormalities in the functioning of society (e.g., in the division of labor) that attenuate either inter-individual or inter-group ties threaten social interdependence and solidarity.

RELIGION AND THE SACRED

As part of his expansive theoretical interest in the societal circumstances that impact social cohesion, Durkheim also wrote extensively about the social nature and functions of religion. We already know from his *Suicide* that religion acts as a social integrating force. And this is still the case today, even though religion is frequently intertwined with divisive conflicts – in national and world politics, and even among church members challenging church teaching on various issues (e.g., women's ordination, same-sex marriage). Durkheim wrote extensively about religion, recognizing it, once again, as a social fact, and as such, something that can be studied objectively, and in relation to other social facts (see above, pp. 80–82).

Durkheim's definition of religion, or more precisely, the sacred, is remarkably broad. He argued that all societies, from the most "primitive" – such as Australian Aboriginal society, which he studied intensively (see EFRL) – to the most modern, invariably categorize all things in society into two mutually exclusive categories: the sacred and the profane. We might generally tend to think of religion as institutionalized churches and established religious traditions, and we might readily call to mind well-known sacred sites, religious prayers, and collectively recognized religious symbols such as the Cross (Christianity), the Star of David (Judaism), and the Crescent (Islam). Durkheim argues that the sacred includes all of these things. But, importantly, the sacred also includes many other things so defined as sacred by any given society.

SACRED THINGS

The sacred is all things "set apart" (sanctified), and whose devaluing is prohibited (EFRL 46). The collectivity, society, requires us to have a certain reverential attitude toward them, and if some individuals do not partake in worshipping the sacred things in a particular community, this detaches the individual from the community in which these sacred things are worshipped. The sacred thus refers to all those things that have a special symbolic significance in a given community; we isolate and protect sacred things from being violated or contaminated by the profane, the ordinary mundane things in which we have invested no special symbolic significance.

Every religion, and hence every community or society too, according to Durkheim, recognizes a "plurality of sacred things" (EFRL 40); "What makes a thing holy is … the collective feeling attached to it" (EFRL 308). And these sacred things are not divinely ordained or historically predetermined but are defined by the particular society. "Since neither man nor nature is inherently sacred, this quality of sacredness must come from another source" (EFRL 76); that source is society – the many different groups and communities to which we belong and which comprise the larger society. Hence, "it is the unity and the diversity of social life that creates both the unity and the diversity of sacred beings and things" (EFRL 309).

In the US, for example, the nation's flag is sacred – it is a symbolic, collective representation of Americans' shared national identity, a shared sacred history of freedom, democracy, patriotism. The flag's sacredness is visible in its prominent public presence in people's yards and especially in the nation's collective civic life – at official events and in official places (e.g., the White House).

SACRED BELIEFS AND RITUALS

We know what things and ideas a society or religion deems sacred by the beliefs and rituals (rites) that they classify as, and attach to, the sacred: "Religious phenomena fall quite naturally into two basic categories: beliefs and rites. The first are states of opinion and consist of representations [symbols]; the second are fixed modes of actions [specific practices]" (EFRL 36). Thus, what we believe or worship and how we worship comprise religion. And not surprisingly, given Durkheim's emphasis on the thoroughly *social* and *collective* nature of social facts, religious beliefs and rituals are not unique to the individual but are, and must necessarily be, shared collectively.

> Religious beliefs proper are always held by a defined collectivity that professes them and practices the rites that go with them. These beliefs are not only embraced by all the members of this collectivity as individuals, they belong to the group and unite it. The individuals who make up this group are bound to one another by their common beliefs. A society whose members are united because they share a common conception of the sacred world and its relation to the profane world, and who translate this common conception into identical practices, is what we call a **church**. (EFRL 42–43)

Church, then, is the collective coming together of people with similar beliefs and rituals, the practice of which further unites and solidifies the group and the solidarity of its members. It is in, and through, and around sacred things that individuals collectively unite as a **moral community** affirming a shared solidarity: "A religion is this unified system of beliefs and practices relative to sacred things, that is to say, things set apart and surrounded by prohibitions – beliefs and practices that unite its adherents in a single moral community called a church" (EFRL 46).

Importantly, since Durkheim's definition of the sacred includes all things that a community collectively holds sacred, religion/church (for Durkheim) can take many forms. In many societies, sports, for example, is sacred; e.g., soccer in England and Brazil, football and baseball in the US, or cricket in Australia, India, and Pakistan. The collective awe and reverence that collectivities (fans, local communities, nations) have toward particular sports teams, the sacred space in which the teams play and fans congregate (worship), and the various sacred symbols (logos, clothing), icons (stars, heroes), hymns (songs), and rituals (seventh inning stretch) that they have, mean – following Durkheim – that sport functions as a social equivalent of (institutionalized) religion. Thus, for Red Sox baseball fans, church is Fenway Park; for Manchester United soccer fans, it is Old Trafford; for cricket fans in Australia, it is the Melbourne Cricket Ground – these are the sacred sites at which people collectively worship and unify around all that is sacred in sport.

NEWS 2.15

THE ASSEMBLING OF COMMUNITY

As moral communities, we worship something other than ourselves; and what we worship is, in essence, our shared collective life. Coming together as one – whether in church, at a sports event, or at other public gatherings – affirms a shared solidarity – the fact that we belong to this particular community – and the process of shared interaction itself strengthens our shared bonds (see Topic 2.3). Robert Bellah (1967) uses the term civil religion to refer to the civic-political ceremonies and rituals (e.g., presidential inaugurations, State of the Union addresses) that characterize the public life of American society and which function to affirm and maintain the (political) unity of the nation (indivisible, under God), notwithstanding partisan political affiliations. Special ritualized events – whether with family and friends or within larger community or national gatherings – remind us of the interdependent communal bonds we have with one another and with society as a whole.

The regulatory significance of communal gatherings on social integration is particularly well illustrated by funeral rituals and memorials; they affirm the social bonds of the living to the deceased person(s), to one another, and to society (see Topic 2.3). Durkheim states:

> When an individual dies, the family group to which he belongs feels diminished, and in order to react against this diminishment, it assembles. A common misfortune has the same effects as the arrival of a happy event: it awakens collective feelings that impel individuals to seek each other out and come together. We have even seen this need affirmed with special energy – people kiss, embrace, and press against one another as much as possible. But the emotional state in which the group finds itself reflects the immediate circumstances. Not only do the relatives most directly affected bring their personal pain to the gathering, but society exerts a moral pressure on its members to put their feelings in harmony with the situation. To allow them to remain indifferent to the blow that strikes and diminishes them would be to proclaim that society does not hold its rightful place in their hearts, and this would be to deny itself. A family that tolerates a death among its members without weeping bears witness that it lacks moral unity and cohesion. It abdicates, it renounces its being. (EFRL 296–297)

The assembling family's response to the death of one of its members extends more generally to any community/society which suffers a loss. Thus the public response to 9/11, for example (see p. 105 above), is both the collective mourning of society's loss and, simultaneously, the collective affirmation of the bonds that unite those remaining and which regenerate society.

When we as individuals remain aloof from such rituals, and from joyous events (e.g., a family wedding, a celebration of a sports team's accomplishments, a local community festival), our indifference both reflects and further debilitates our weakened ties to the collectivity, and moreover, dampens the collective effervescence of those participating. Durkheim argues:

> For his part, when the individual is firmly attached to the society to which he belongs he feels morally compelled to share its joys and sorrows; to remain a disinterested observer would be to break the ties that bind him to the collectivity, to give up wanting the collectivity, and to contradict himself ... We know from other sources how human feelings

are intensified when they are affirmed collectively. Sadness, like joy, is exalted and amplified by its reverberation from [individual] consciousness to [individual] consciousness ... Each person is led along by all the others ... [individuals] weep together because they value one another and because the collectivity, despite this blow [e.g., death], is not damaged. Of course, in this instance they share only sad emotions; but to commune in sadness is still to commune, and every communion of consciousness, of whatever kind [sadness or joy], increases the social vitality ... [and makes] society even more vigorous and active than ever. (EFRL 297, 299)

Precisely because Durkheim saw religion – the sacred – as that which compels us to assemble, to act in unison together (thereby bending our individual impulses to the collective moral/social force), and as a consequence to be strengthened in our individual and collective ability to cope with life's joys and sorrows (EFRL 311, 313, 309), he regarded religion as eternally necessary.

There is something eternal in religion ... that is destined to survive all the particular symbols in which religious thought has successfully cloaked itself. No society can exist that does not feel the need at regular intervals to sustain and reaffirm the collective feelings and ideas that constitute its unity ... this moral remaking can be achieved only by means of meetings, assemblies, or congregations in which individuals, brought into close contact, reaffirm in common their common feelings: hence those ceremonies whose goals, results, and methods do not differ in kind from properly religious ceremonies. (EFRL 322)

In sum, the sacred is present in each and every collective assembly.

RELIGION AND SCIENCE

Durkheim recognized that with the rise of modern society – in particular, the increase in individualism (required by the specialized division of labor) and the expansion of science as the basis of knowledge – the dogmatic hold of traditional religious systems would wane (EFRL 325). Nonetheless, as the above quote underscores, Durkheim also recognized that scientific knowledge alone is not sufficient to tie people together. He did not see science and religion in conflict with one another, but as having interdependent functions. Science provides knowledge, but religion (and its functional equivalents such as baseball, etc.) provides action – the "moral remaking" that exists around its rituals. Hence, "science could not possibly take religion's place. For if science expresses life, it does not create it" (EFRL 325). It does not revitalize social ties. Thus, Durkheim argued, religion would maintain itself as an eternal social fact; it would adapt and transform rather than disappear (EFRL 324–326). As we see today, although traditional religion is a significant source of social integration in many societies (and especially in the US), there are also many other sacred things (e.g., sports events, knitting groups) that draw people together and invigorate social cohesion and solidarity.[8]

Durkheim's writings demonstrate the content and rules of a scientific sociology. In particular, his discussion of social facts; his differentiation between traditional and modern society and of the different forms of social organization that produce mechanical and organic solidarity; his analysis of suicide as a function of social integration; and his study of religion as the collective representation of the sacred in society all serve to show the breadth of Dukheim's sociological focus and the range of topics that sociologists study.

POINTS TO REMEMBER

For Durkheim

- Sociology: science of moral life
- Morality: social ties; bonds attaching individuals to something other than themselves, society
- Society is greater than the sum of its individuals; has its own social logic
- Society exists independently of the individuals who comprise it; exerts a collective force that is external to the individual
- Sociological method: "Treat social facts as things"
- Social facts: objective, collective forces that are external to and constrain the individual
- Mechanical solidarity; characteristic of traditional, homogeneous societies
- Organic solidarity; characteristic of modern, heterogeneous societies
- Modern society: division of specialized labor creates interdependence among individuals
- Collective conscience: beliefs and sentiments shared in common
- Social integration: a function of social ties
- Suicide: a social fact; a function of social integration
  - Altruistic suicide; a function of excessive communal orientation
  - Egoistic suicide; a function of excessive individualism, lack of social ties and constraints
  - Anomic suicide; a function of societal upheaval, normlessness, rootlessness
- Religion: a social fact or social phenomenon; concern with the sacred in society
- All societies classify things/ideas into two mutually exclusive categories
  - Sacred (holy) things/ideas
  - Profane (mundane, ordinary) things/ideas
- Symbols: collective representations; represent collective life, values
- Rituals: collective celebrations that reaffirm and strengthen social solidarity
- Religion: collectively shared beliefs and rituals in regard to the sacred
- Church: a single moral community united by shared beliefs and rituals pertaining to the sacred

GLOSSARY

altruistic suicide results from tightly regulated social conditions in which the loss of comrades, or an individual's loss of honor in the community, makes suicide obligatory.

anomic suicide results when society experiences a major disruption that uproots the established norms.

church any moral community unified by sacred beliefs and practices.

civil religion the civic-political symbols, ceremonies, and rituals (e.g., presidential inaugurations) that characterize society's public life and reaffirm its shared values.

collective conscience a society's collectively shared beliefs and sentiments; regulates social life.

collective representation the symbols and categories a society uses to denote its commonly shared, collective beliefs, values, interpretations, and meanings.

contract society's legal regulation of the obligations it expects of individuals in their relations with one another; its regulatory force comes from society.

division of labor the separation of occupational sectors and workers into specialized spheres of activity; produces, for Durkheim, social interdependence.

egoistic suicide results from modern societal conditions in which individuals are excessively self-oriented and insufficiently integrated into social groups/society.

functionalism term used (often interchangeably with "structural functionalism") to refer to the theorizing of Durkheim (and successor sociologists, e.g., Parsons) because of a focus on how social structures determine and are effective in, or functional to, maintaining social cohesion/ the social order.

interdependence ties among individuals; for Durkheim, the individualism required by the specialized division of labor creates functional and social interdependence.

mechanical solidarity social bonds and cohesion resulting from the overlapping social ties that characterize traditional societies/communities.

moral community any group or collectivity unified by awareness of their shared social interdependence.

moral density social ties created as a result of interaction with the multiplicity of diverse others encountered in modern society.

moral individualism individuals (as social beings) interacting with others for purposes other than simply serving their own selfish or material interests.

morality social life; the social ties that regulate individual appetites; sociology's subject matter; can be studied with scientific objectivity.

organic solidarity social ties and cohesion produced by the functional interdependence of individuals and groups in modern society.

physical density the number of people encountered in the conduct of everyday life.

profane ordinary, mundane, non-sacred things in society.

religion a social phenomenon, collectively defined by the things, ideas, beliefs, and practices a society or community holds sacred; socially integrating.

rituals collectively shared, sacred rites and practices that affirm and strengthen social ties, and maintain social order.

sacred all things a society collectively sets apart as special, requiring reverence.

social facts external and collective social things (structures, practices, norms) regulating and constraining individual and social behavior.

social integration degree to which individuals and groups are attached to society. Individuals are interlinked and constrained by their ties to others.

sociology of knowledge demonstrates how the organization and content of knowledge is a social activity contingent on the particular socio-historical circumstances in which it is produced.

solidarity social cohesion resulting from shared social ties/bonds.

sui generis reality the idea that society has its own nature or reality – its own collective characteristics or properties, which emerge and exist independent of the characteristics of the individuals in society.

symbol any sign whose interpretation and meaning are socially shared; collective representation of a society's collectively shared beliefs and values.

RELEVANT NEWSPAPER STORIES

All news stories are from the *New York Times* unless otherwise noted, and can be accessed via www.wiley.com/go/dillon. See NEWS icons in the margins above.

NEWS 2.1   "Born on the Bayou and barely feeling any urge to roam," September 30, 2002.

NEWS 2.2   "Donor egg: Immediate availability." Advertisement by the Genetics and IVF Institute, *New York Times Magazine*, December 17, 2006.

NEWS 2.3   "California court overturns a ban on gay marriage," May 16, 2008.
"A poll finds Californians still oppose gay marriage," May 24, 2008.

NEWS 2.4   "Does the real Ireland still exist?" May 18, 2008.
"Born Irish but with illegal parents," February 25, 2008.

NEWS 2.5   "3rd Iraq death has one town shaken to core," October 11, 2006.

NEWS 2.6   "Many hands, not held by China, aid in quake," May 20, 2008.

NEWS 2.7   "2 at Sago mine on day of blast commit suicide," September 28, 2006.

NEWS 2.8   "Who's cuddly now: Law firms," January 24, 2008.
"Wall Street exodus: Fear, panic and anger," May 25, 2008.

NEWS 2.9   "Owens denies he attempted to take own life with pills," *Boston Globe*, September 28, 2006.

NEWS 2.10   "A place without roots that some call home," September 30, 2002.

NEWS 2.11   "Uprooted and scattered far from the familiar," September 11, 2005.
"Many children lack stability long after storm," December 4, 2008.

NEWS 2.12   *Invisible wounds of war*. April 2008. www.rand.org
"Talking veterans down from despair," April 22, 2008.

NEWS 2.13   "Boomtown blues: How natural gas changed the way of life in Sublette County," *New Yorker*, February 5, 2007.
"Elusive, but not always stoppable," *The Economist*, June 23, 2007.

NEWS 2.14   "In a square, a sense of unity," September 19, 2001.

NEWS 2.15   "An elite pastime that became a passion of the masses," October 7, 2008.

WEB SUPPLEMENTS

All web supplements are available at www.wiley.com/go/dillon. See WEB icons in the margins above.

WEB 2.1   World War I

WEB 2.2   Suicide rates in the US and cross-nationally

NOTES

1 In citing Durkheim's writings, I reference the book's initials rather than the date of publication. A list of Durkheim's core writings, their date of publication, and the book title initials I use to reference them follows the biographical note above.

2 Vacherie is located in St James Parish in Louisiana, a parish/ Census unit that borders the New Orleans parishes that were hardest hit by Hurricane Katrina in September 2005. The Census has recorded a slight increase in the population of St James since 2005, suggesting perhaps that some of the people displaced by Katrina moved to St. James Parish.

3 Durkheim's emphasis on empirical data as the starting point for social science is referred to as *induction*; we induce or infer from data an explanation about how the social world works. This approach contrasts with *deduction*, which uses theoretical and non-empirical statements about a particular phenomenon as the starting point for making generalizable claims about the class of phenomena more broadly; deduction proceeds by logically deducing from one idea other similar or parallel processes in the logic of the social world. Most sociologists today tend to be inductive in their approach to describing and explaining society.

4 For a detailed introduction to Simmel, see Frisby (1994).

5 Durkheim differentiates between the *repressive* penal laws that characterize traditional societies – stripping individuals and groups of honor (and social rights) – and the *restitutive* laws that tend to characterize modern societies – laws that seek to restore the status quo to what it was before the deviant act; e.g., individuals pay damages to an injured or third party to offset their culpability (DL 68–70).

6 Durkheim (Su 276) also briefly noted a fourth category: "*fatalistic* suicide," typical of social circumstances which are characterized by "excessive regulation" wherein individuals (e.g., slaves) see no alternatives to their current situation. Martineau highlighted suicides due to duty or loss of honor in the community – e.g., "the defeated warrior," "the injured woman," and situations "when men and women destroyed themselves to avoid disgrace" (1838: 103), as well as the suicides of "those who have devoted themselves to others." According to Martineau's biographer (Hoecker-Drysdale 1992), Durkheim had read but did not acknowledge Martineau.

7 Martineau noted the regulatory impact of religion on suicide, which she inferred from the higher rates of suicide in non-religious French society than in religiously devout Ireland (1838: 106–107).

8 Durkheim's emphasis on the social origins of the sacred is an important contribution to the **sociology of knowledge**. Durkheim argued that all categories, and hence all ideas or concepts, are collective representations; they provide members of a society with a common, shared system of communication and interpretation. Just as members of a given nation recognize the national flag, so too the members of a given society use a language that derives from and can be used to describe and categorize their particular societal characteristics and experiences. In other words, there is no conceptual logic – no language or concepts – independent of, or prior to, society. Rather, concepts and language are "eminently social" (EFRL 11); they "express collective realities" (ibid.). Durkheim's emphasis on the social origins and functions of concepts (as collective representations) is regarded as a "crucial first step" in the sociology of knowledge (Lukes 1973: 448); it helps us see that concepts and knowledge emerge out of particular socio-historical and generational contexts (cf. Mannheim 1936/1968).

CHAPTER THREE

MAX WEBER (1864–1920)

KEY CONCEPTS

subjectively meaningful
   action
interpretive understanding
Verstehen
this-worldly
other-worldly
asceticism
calling
rationality
Calvinism
predestination
Puritan ethic
individualism
ideal type
value-rational action
instrumental rational
   action
non-rational action
emotional action
traditional action
power
domination
legal authority
traditional authority
nation-state
bureaucracy
charisma
charismatic community
routinization of charisma
stratification
class
status
parties
values
value neutrality
objectivity

CHAPTER MENU

Timeline 3.1   Major events in Weber's lifetime (1864–1920)

1864	Pope Pius IX criticizes liberalism, socialism, and rationalism in the *Syllabus of Errors*
1865	US President Lincoln assassinated
1865	John D. Rockefeller, Sr, establishes Standard Oil
1866	Mary Baker Eddy introduces Christian Science
1867	Karl Marx, *Capital* (*Das Kapital*)
1870	Vatican One: Declaration of Papal Infallibility
1870	Diamonds discovered in South Africa
1873	Design of the first commercially successful typewriter
1876	Alexander Graham Bell invents the telephone
1877	Thomas Edison patents his phonograph
1883	Standardization of Greenwich Mean Time
1883	Completion of the Brooklyn Bridge linking Manhattan and Brooklyn
1887	German domination of the chemical industry
1889	T. H. Huxley, *Agnosticism*
1890	Fall of Bismarck in Germany
1892	Gold discovered in Western Australia
1895	Gillette invents the safety razor
1900	Expansion of the German navy
1903	Henry Ford sets up the Motor Company
1904	Separation of church and state accomplished in France
1907	Pope Pius IX denounces Modernism
1909	Women admitted to German universities
1911	Standard Oil Trust split up into 33 companies; Rockefellers retain a major interest in Exxon, Mobil, Amoco, and Standard Oil of California
1914	Outbreak of World War I; Germany declares war on Russia and France and invades Belgium
1918	Republic declared in Germany; Germany agrees to Armistice; end of World War I
1920	Prohibition in effect throughout the US

Like his fellow-German Karl Marx, **Max Weber** had much to say about the structure of capitalism and inequality, but unlike Marx, Weber also paid a lot of attention to the cultural and non-economic motivations underlying social action. Like Durkheim, Weber wrote extensively about religion, but in contrast to Durkheim, Weber was more concerned with the substantive content of religion – the subjective meanings and worldviews that particular religions give rise to at a given point in history – and how they get translated into institutional practices, than with the

BIOGRAPHICAL NOTE

Max Weber was born in Germany in 1864. His father came from a business family and was active in industry and politics; his mother was a devout and well-educated Protestant. Weber grew up in a suburb of Berlin and his neighborhood included several important intellectual and political figures who socialized with his parents. Even as a child, Weber had expansive intellectual interests. Subsequently, he studied law, economics, history, and philosophy at Heidelberg University and, though studious, he also actively participated in the university's robust social life; he joined a dueling fraternity (that his father had also belonged to) and was also a regular afternoon card-player. At age 19, while enrolled at Heidelberg, Weber moved to Strasbourg to complete a mandatory year of army training; he had a hard time adjusting to military discipline and mechanical drills but became a commissioned officer, highly respected by his peers and superiors.

After Heidelberg, Weber returned to Berlin, where he practiced law and completed his PhD on the history of trading companies during the Middle Ages. In 1893, he married Marianne Schnitger, following a remorseful break-up with another woman with whom he had been in love for six years, and he assumed the career of a hard-working and successful academic with positions at prestigious German universities. As time went on, Weber suffered recurring episodes of severe depression and fatigue but he nonetheless managed to lecture and write prodigiously. He and Marianne had no children, and they traveled extensively in Europe for rest and respite (including to Ireland, Scotland, Spain, and Italy). In 1904, Weber visited the United States. He presented a paper at a congress in St Louis organized as part of the Universal Exposition that year, and he also visited New York, other east coast cities (Boston, Baltimore, Washington, DC, Philadelphia), Chicago, and several southern states. Weber was mesmerized by what he saw of life in America – by both the good and the bad of capitalism – and was enthralled by the tenor of American life. He was, for example, "fascinated by the rush hour in lower Manhattan, which he liked to view from the middle of the Brooklyn Bridge as a panorama of mass transportation and noisy motion" (Gerth and Mills 1946: 15). Following his return to Germany, Weber finished writing *The Protestant Ethic and the Spirit of Capitalism*. At the beginning of World War I (1914), Weber was a captain in the reserve corps and for a year had responsibility for running nine hospitals in the Heidelberg area, an experience that gave him first-hand knowledge of the workings of bureaucracy. Although energized by the politics surrounding the war, Weber did not live long enough to see the aftermath of its resolution. He died in 1920, at age 56, from pneumonia (Gerth and Mills 1946: 3–31).

Weber's Writings

1904–1905: *The Protestant Ethic and the Spirit of Capitalism*, PE
1909–1920: *Economy and Society*, ES*
1915: "The Social Psychology of the World Religions," in *From Max Weber: Essays in Sociology*, FMW
1919: "Politics as a Vocation," in *From Max Weber: Essays in Sociology*, FMW
"Science as a Vocation," in *From Max Weber: Essays in Sociology*, FMW
1903–1917 The Methodology of the Social Sciences, MSS

* Several of the sections in ES are reprinted in condensed form in FMW

social function of religion in general. In the process, moreover, Weber discussed and compared the major world religions (Christianity, ancient Judaism, and Islam, which are all God-centered religions; and Confucianism, Hinduism, and Buddhism, which affirm an impersonal, cosmocentric force).

SOCIOLOGY: UNDERSTANDING SOCIAL ACTION

For Weber, the domain of sociology is subjectively meaningful action:

> Sociology ... is a science concerning itself with the **interpretive understanding** of social action and thereby with a causal explanation of its course and consequence. We shall speak of "action" insofar as the acting individual attaches a subjective meaning to his behavior ... Action is "social" insofar as its subjective meaning takes account of the behavior of others and is thereby oriented in its course. (ES 4)[1]

It is the sociologist's task to make sense of all the varying motivations that propel social action, and to do so by reaching an understanding – *Verstehen* (see Introduction) – of why individuals and institutions and whole societies behave in certain ways: why they attach meaning to some goals and not others, and why certain behavioral patterns and consequences emerge in a given socio-historical context. Unlike Durkheim, therefore, who focused on the external manifestations of social phenomena (social facts as things) and how they constrain social behavior (e.g., integration; see chapter 2), Weber probed the historical and cultural origins of social phenomena (e.g., capitalism) and the particular institutional practices they produced (e.g., bureaucracy).

Following Weber, sociologists aim to achieve either an emotional-empathic or a rational-logical understanding of motivation "by placing the observed act in an intelligible and more inclusive context of meaning" (ES 8). In order to get a strong interpretive grasp or a deep understanding of social action, therefore, we have to immerse ourselves in the world and the worldviews of those we are studying. As Harriet Martineau (1838: 25, 52) advised, we have to adopt a non-judgmental attitude, and sympathetically "find our way to the hearts and minds" of those whom we are studying (see Introduction).[2]

We do not have to be Caesar to understand Caesar (ES 5), Weber tells us, but we do have to commit to research aimed at understanding the meaning of social action. Thus sociologists seek to explain the context in which particular social patterns and meanings emerge. This is why they conduct qualitative, in-depth interviews with individuals to understand the meanings that they, and their peers who are involved in a particular activity, inject into that activity. Similarly, we conduct historical and comparative research to understand why some communities, organizations, and societies do things in one particular way whereas others do things differently. This rich research legacy comes from Weber; an interpretive-hermeneutic, qualitative methodology that complements sociology's quantitative survey methods (see Introduction).

CULTURE AND ECONOMIC ACTIVITY

Weber's best-known book, and one which demonstrates what is entailed in the task of interpretive understanding, is *The Protestant Ethic and the Spirit of Capitalism*, published in 1904–1905. As is evident from the title, Weber illuminates the links between two domains of activity, *religion* and *economics*, that are generally thought of as separate, or, as in Marx's analysis of base–superstructure, reducible to one another (cf. chapter 1). Weber probes the relation between the this-worldly concerns that orient economic activity, material acquisition, and wealth; and the other-worldly concerns (e.g., after-life, salvation) of religious belief. The impetus for Weber's study came from his empirical observation that Protestants rather than Catholics predominated in business occupations: "A glance at the occupational statistics of any country of mixed religious composition brings to light with remarkable frequency … the fact that business leaders and owners of capital, as well as the higher grades of skilled labour, and even more the higher technically and commercially trained personnel of modern enterprises, are overwhelmingly Protestant" (PE 35). Weber acknowledged that the over-representation of Protestants in industry and business may have been due to historical circumstances favoring them (e.g., English penal laws in Ireland from the seventeenth to the early nineteenth century prohibited Catholics from owning property and going to college). Nevertheless, Weber observed that even in those countries where Catholics were unrestricted, they, unlike Protestants, tended to opt for non-business occupations, and among skilled workers, tended to remain in crafts rather than pursue clerical or skilled employment in the newly established factories (PE 38).[3]

THE PROTESTANT-CAPITALIST PUZZLE

Weber, therefore, starts with what for Durkheim would be an objective social fact (i.e., denominational differences in occupational specialization), explainable by other social facts, namely, the different social integrating structures of Catholicism and Protestantism, and their varying constraints on individual ambition (cf. *Suicide*; see chapter 2). For Weber, however, these social phenomena in and of themselves beg for further understanding. Thus, in accord with his own definition of sociology, he proceeded to investigate what underlying religious-doctrinal or cultural beliefs gave rise to different religious and social structures (institutions) in the first place, and specifically, what was culturally peculiar to Protestantism that would account for the discrepancy between Catholics and Protestants in their affinity for business and industry.

A second puzzle noted by Weber was the extent to which the character or spirit of modern capitalism (approximately from the seventeenth through the mid-nineteenth century) was marked by asceticism – the disciplined imposition of a frugality and sobriety regarding the wealth accumulated through hard work. This contrasted with material acquisition in pre-industrial eras, which was driven by individuals' basic survival needs, and also differed from the greed of adventurers and pirates.

THE PROTESTANT ETHIC

Probing this ascetic attitude, Weber was intrigued that it was cogently summarized in the infamous maxim of one of America's founding fathers, the prolific writer and inventor Benjamin Franklin (1706–1790): "*Time* is money" (PE 48–50). This saying clearly has a utilitarian thrust – the more time you spend doing useful things, the more productive you are and the more money you make. But, Weber argues, "Time is money" also has a larger meaning, one grounded in a religious ethic. Weber states that although Franklin was not religiously devout, he was nonetheless heavily influenced by his strict Protestant upbringing and his father's endless sermonizing about the virtues of work. Franklin knew these virtues well, and as Weber notes, he readily quoted from the Bible's Book of Proverbs, "Seest thou a man diligent in his business? He shall stand before kings" (PE 53). Wasting time, therefore, not being diligent, takes on a religious meaning – it offends against God.

Accordingly, Weber argues, "the earning of money within the modern economic order is, so long as it is done legally, the result and the expression of virtue and proficiency in a calling [selfless, diligent commitment to a vocation/work] ... [the idea of] duty in a calling, is what is most characteristic of the social ethic of capitalistic culture. It is an obligation which the individual is supposed to feel and does feel towards the content of his professional activity" (PE 53–54). This ethic – embracing work as a duty with its own intrinsic reward of giving glory to God, and thus working hard irrespective of the job, or its fit with one's talents, or its material reward – preceded the expansion of capitalism. Medieval monks, for example, lived a life of simplicity and asceticism (disciplined frugality), laboring in the monastery fields cultivating crops to meet their own needs and those of the local beggars.

But, Weber notes, under capitalism this work ethic got harnessed to a disciplined, methodical, and rational pursuit of profit. Economic success, not mere survival, became the objective. The accumulation of money/profit resulting from diligent work and a frugal lifestyle led to the investment and re-investment of the capital necessary to building the factories and plants and general infrastructure (e.g., railroads) essential to the expansion of capitalism (PE 17).

THE REFORMATION

In the *Protestant Ethic*, Weber thus traces how the idea of work as a duty or calling got entwined with profit-oriented, everyday, economic activity. To understand its evolution, we first need to review the Protestant Reformation, a critical event

WEB 3.1

Timeline 3.2	The emergence of Protestantism and the expansion of capitalism
1495–1498	Leonardo da Vinci paints *The Last Supper*
1504	Michelangelo's statue of *David* installed in Florence
1517	Martin Luther nails his theses denouncing the Catholic church to the doors of Wittenberg cathedral
1527	Sweden becomes Lutheran
1531	In England, Henry VIII forces the (Catholic) clergy to recognize him as head of the (Protestant) Church of England
1539	First printing of the English (Protestant) Bible
1545	The Council of Trent: the beginning of the Catholic Counter-Reformation
1546	Martin Luther dies
1553	Queen Mary returns England to the Catholic fold
1558	Queen Elizabeth I re-establishes Protestantism in England
1564	John Calvin dies
1583	Jesuit missionaries settle in China
1584	Potato introduced to Europe
1607	Tea introduced to Europe
1607	English found Jamestown, Virginia
1611	Publication of the authorized King James (Protestant) Bible
1620	English pilgrims land at Plymouth, Massachusetts
1626	Dutch found New Amsterdam on Manhattan Island (New York)
1630	John Winthrop founds Boston, Massachusetts
1683	First German immigrants arrive in North America
1701	Founding of Yale College, New Haven, Connecticut, as a Protestant Congregational seminary
1706	Benjamin Franklin born
1730	John and Charles Wesley found the Methodist Society at Oxford University, England
1746	Princeton University (College of New Jersey) founded as a Presbyterian seminary
1760	Expansion of British cotton production
1776	Declaration of Independence by American colonies
1790	Beginnings of multistory factory blocks bigger than mills

shaping western modernity, and especially American culture and society. In 1517, when Martin Luther (1483–1546), a German monk and theology professor, nailed 95 theses to the doors of Wittenberg cathedral, protesting the abuses and excesses in the Catholic church, his break with the church established Protestantism (derived from the word *protest*).

Luther disagreed with many aspects of Catholicism. Foremost was his rejection of the church's emphasis that the individual believer needed the intervention of the church hierarchy (the sacred authority of the pope, bishops, and priests) to interpret scripture and God's intentions, and that of the sacraments to confer the divine grace necessary for salvation. And even more objectionable to Luther was the church's use of special indulgences (e.g., forgiveness of sins) given in exchange for good works, pilgrimages, or financial donations to the church. Instead, Luther maintained, the individual believer was directly given grace and salvation by God, and hence did not need the church's indulgences and sacraments, and nor, by extension, its intermediaries (pope, etc.).

Luther is important because he did the groundwork for the emergence of Protestantism (and specifically Lutheranism). Protestantism quickly evolved into a variety of separate traditions or denominations (e.g., Presbyterians, Congregationalists, Methodists, Quakers, Baptists). The history of Protestantism, especially in the sixteenth and seventeenth centuries in England and Northern Europe, and subsequently in the seventeenth and eighteenth centuries in North America –

following the arrival of the first Puritans in Massachusetts Bay in 1620 – was characterized by several theological disputes as different groups argued over what constituted core doctrines and beliefs, and established new denominations that affirmed the purity of their particular beliefs.

SALVATION AND PREDESTINATION

Among the early Protestant strands, Calvinism, so called because it derives from John Calvin (1509–1564), a French-Swiss reformer, has particular significance for Weber's thesis. Although Calvin was one of Luther's successors and disciples, his beliefs departed in important ways from Luther's. Most notably, Calvin disagreed with Luther about God directly giving grace to the lowly individual. Calvin instead postulated the doctrine of predestination – the belief that the individual's salvation was already predetermined, predestined, by God. In other words, at birth, your salvation – whether you are going to heaven or hell – is already known to God and no matter how you live your life, no matter how many good works you do or how much you seek God's grace, you can do nothing to affect your after-life destiny. This dogma was expressed in the "authoritative Westminster Confession," which Weber quotes: "By the decree of God, for the manifestation of His glory, some men and angels are predestined unto everlasting life, and others foreordained to everlasting death" (PE 99–100).

While busy with your college life, you may not give much thought to the after-life. But the question of eternal salvation was very important to many people in the sixteenth and seventeenth centuries, and is still important for many people today – in the US, for example, approximately 80 percent believe in life after death (Pew Forum 2008). For Calvin and his followers who believed in predestination, the dilemma of what to do about salvation became an enormous psychological challenge. If you believe in an all-powerful and glorious God, and you believe that God has already sealed your fate, and you know that you cannot know God's plans, what are you to do? Unlike the Lutherans, who could believe in God reaching down to give them grace and, ultimately, salvation, and unlike the Catholics, who could earn grace and salvation through the church (e.g., confession), the Calvinist could turn to no one for hints or assurance about salvation.

Weber writes:

> In its extreme inhumanity this doctrine [predestination] must above all had one consequence for the life of a generation which surrendered to its magnificent consistency. That was a feeling of unprecedented inner loneliness of the single individual. In what was for the man of the age of the Reformation the most important thing in life, his eternal salvation, he was forced to follow his path alone to meet a destiny which had been decreed for him from eternity. No one could help him. No priest, for the chosen one can understand the word of God only in his own heart. No sacraments, for though the sacraments had been ordained by God for the increase of His glory, and hence must be scrupulously observed, they are not a means to the attainment of grace ... No church ... Finally, even no God. For even Christ had died only for the elect, for whose benefit God had decreed His martyrdom for eternity. (PE 104)

The Calvinist's inner loneliness, his "deep spiritual isolation" (PE 107), did not lead, however, to either self-indulgence or fatalism. It did not make the Calvinist feel that one should live life as one pleases and throw caution to the wind seeing that in any event there was nothing one could do to change one's predestined fate. This attitude would have contravened the Calvinist and general Puritan belief in asceticism, and the related view that self-indulgence, emotional spontaneity, and sociability were to be avoided. These were all seen as unholy distractions, tempting the individual from the purpose of diligently glorifying God (PE 105–106). For Calvinists, Weber argues,

> The world exists to serve the glorification of God and for that purpose alone. The elected [saved] Christian is in the world only to increase this glory of God by fulfilling His commandments to the best of his ability ... The social activity of the Christian in the world is solely activity [for the glory of God]. This character is hence shared by labour in a calling which serves the mundane [ordinary] life of the community. (PE 108)

PROVING ONE'S SALVATION

Weber argued that the rationalization of the Calvinist, as a God-fearing believer faced with the nagging question "Am I one of the elect?" was to convince himself or herself of his or her salvation and to justify that conviction through intense activity in the world – glorifying God in everyday activity, specifically, as the Biblical proverb instructs (see p. 120), through diligence in business. Hence success, resulting from hard work in this world, would be a *sign* of one's salvation – but not a *means* to salvation; it would signify one's membership among the elect, the saved. Taking the pragmatic view that "God helps those who help themselves" (PE 115), the Calvinists took it as their duty to demonstrate (prove) their salvation to themselves and to others through evidence of material success. Weber states that the Calvinist "creates his own salvation, or, as would be more correct, the conviction of it" (PE 115). And the Calvinist did it not like Catholics through the gradual accumulation of credit (from indulgences, the sacraments, etc.), but through "systematic self-control which at every moment stands before the inexorable alternative, chosen or damned" (PE 115). Faith in the conviction that you were one of the chosen was demonstrated not by emotional feelings of closeness to God (e.g., mysticism), but by the objective *proof* provided by the visible results of your morally disciplined and methodical worldly activity, the fruits of your labor. "The God of Calvinism demanded of his believers not single good works, but a life of good works" (PE 117), a life that allowed for no temporal failures or lapses in glorifying God through disciplined, everyday activity.

RATIONAL SELF-REGULATION AND SELF-CONTROL

Thus as Weber notes, the sermons of Richard Baxter (1615–1691), one of the leading English Puritans, repeatedly emphasized the ethical importance of "hard, continuous bodily or mental labour" (PE 158), because "every hour lost is lost to labour for the glory of God" (PE 158). Moreover, the impulse not to work, regardless of one's wealth, is itself "symptomatic of the lack of grace" (PE 159). Therefore, the Puritan ethic not only affirmed the idea of work as a calling; it also denounced time spent not in work but in leisure as sinful, departing as it does from the command to glorify God through work. Weber's interpretive analysis of the sermons and writings of several of the leading Puritans showed that the asceticism of the Calvinist ethic "turned with all its force against one thing: the spontaneous enjoyment of life and all it had to offer" (PE 166). The Puritans had an aversion to sport, for example, accepting it only if it

> served a rational purpose, that of recreation necessary for physical efficiency [in work]. But as a means for the spontaneous expression of undisciplined impulses, it was under suspicion; and in so far as it became purely a means of enjoyment, or awakened pride, raw instincts or the irrational gambling instinct, it was of course strictly condemned. Impulsive enjoyment of life, which leads away both from work in a calling and from religion, was as such the enemy of rational asceticism. (PE 167)

What the Calvinists accomplished, therefore, was to infuse rationality, a deliberate, planful, methodical focus, into everyday life; their cultural legacy was "the rationalization of conduct within this world ... [penetrating] the daily routine of life with methodicalness" (PE 154). Hence we see that the regulation and control of the Catholic church that Martin Luther protested was replaced with the *self-regulation* of the individual over all aspects of daily life; it required the individual "to bring his actions under constant self-control with a careful consideration of their ethical considerations [to serve God]" (PE 119). In turn, this self-regulation and self-discipline animated the expansion of capitalism.

Thus, an *unintended* consequence of Calvinism was the expansion of capitalism. Calvinist religious beliefs – in particular, predestination and attendant concerns about salvation in the next world – and the rationalization of those beliefs through activity in *this* world, led to the harnessing of a disciplined work ethic to the accumulation of capital. It is not that Protestantism created capitalism; but as evidenced from history, it accelerated its development – notably, capitalist industrialization expanded in the eighteenth and nineteenth centuries in countries where rational, ascetic Protestantism predominated (e.g., England, Germany, America).

PROTESTANT-WESTERN INDIVIDUALISM

More generally, Calvinism sowed the seeds of individualism. If the individual stands alone before God in a state of inner loneliness, and is alone responsible for establishing proof of his or her salvation, this requires the cultivation of individual independence, self-reliance, self-regulation, and personal responsibility (PE 105–106). These are habits and values that many parents and teachers today seek to instill in children, especially in American society, and the cultural affirmation of these values is further underscored by the extent to which they underlie public policy debates in the US on government versus individual responsibility regarding poverty, health, and welfare. Thus, Weber, argued there is a fit, an "elective affinity," between a particular culture or a particular religious belief-system, and the particular personality type that it fosters and which gets translated into a country's national character and its social institutions (PE 105–106). Protestantism produces individualism, "respect for quiet self-control ... [, and] the destruction of spontaneous, impulsive enjoyment" (PE 119), values that are conducive to achievement and economic productivity. By contrast, world-rejecting Buddhism, for example, fosters a personality type of "concentrated contemplation ... regarding the solidarity of all living, and hence transitory, beings" (ES 627–628), an ethic which may help account, in part, for the "slower" economic development of Vietnam, for example, a country with a strong Buddhist history and culture.

NEWS 3.1

Weber's discussion of the links between culture (e.g., religious beliefs) and the expansion of capitalism is important for social theory because it opens up the analysis of capitalist society beyond an economic framing. Unlike Karl Marx, who, accentuating the economic logic of capitalism (property relations, profit), saw culture and beliefs as not independent of, but serving, capitalist ideology/practices (see chapter 1), Weber emphasizes that cultural beliefs and values matter in and of themselves. Moreover, they shape social institutions (including the economy). Calvinists did not set out to influence the development of capitalism. But, as a result of their particular religious beliefs and their this-worldly rationalization, they chose a course of action – rational methodical asceticism in work and in all aspects of everyday activity – whose consequences produced profit and capitalist investment, and importantly, too, institutionalized the cultural values of hard work and individualism.

IDEAL TYPES

Weber's discussion of the planful, methodical individualism associated with Protestantism (and its contrast with the Buddhist mystical contemplative) is illustrative of a crucial aspect of his methodology, namely, his use of ideal types. For Weber, ideal types are basically yardsticks – just as we use yardsticks to measure and compare the length of different physical objects, we can use ideal types to describe and compare different social phenomena by accentuating the differences between them. Ideal types are a useful way of orienting sociological research as we seek to explain the array of social action and the diverse social relationships that comprise society (ES 26). Thus Protestantism, in its ideal typical form, has characteristics that are different to Buddhism or Islam, and each of these religions has different social origins and different consequences for everyday social action (FMW 323–359; ES 576–634).

> The ideal typical concept will help to develop our skill in imputation in *research*: it *is* no "hypothesis" but it offers guidance to the construction of hypotheses. It is not a *description* of reality but it aims to give unambiguous means of expression to such a description … An ideal type is formed by the one sided *accentuation* of one or more points of view and by the synthesis of a great many diffuse, discrete, more or less present and occasionally absent *concrete individual* phenomena, which are arranged according to those one-sidedly emphasized viewpoints into a unified *analytical* construct. In its conceptual purity, this mental construct cannot be found empirically anywhere in reality … Historical research faces the task of determining in each individual case, the extent to which this ideal-construct approximates to or diverges from reality … When carefully applied, those concepts are particularly useful in research and exposition. (MSS 90)

Thus Weber regarded the characteristics he outlined as distinctive of a certain type of religion (and of different types of social action, authority, etc.; see below) as the set of characteristics that we should expect to see if the construct being studied empirically were to approximate the "pure" or "ideal" type of the construct so theorized (or defined). For him, the usefulness of any ideal-type categorization was to be judged in terms of the empirical results it yielded in a particular socio-historical context (ES 26). He emphasized that precisely because his ideal types are (theoretically) pure, "it would be very unusual to find concrete cases of social action which were oriented *only* in one or another of these ways" (ES 26).

This becomes especially clear when we study the different types of social action that Weber identified, the subject to which we now turn.

SOCIAL ACTION

VALUE-RATIONAL ACTION

Weber's *Protestant Ethic* demonstrated that values are a well-spring or motivator of social action. And while we might be inclined to think of values as being non-rational – it is, after all, hard to rationally defend the superiority of one belief or value to that of another – the important point for Weber is that values, irrespective of their content or substance (e.g., equality, multicultural diversity, beauty), not only motivate action but can motivate rational action, i.e., motivate individuals and groups to act in a highly planful, rational, methodical way in the pursuit of those values. For him, this is one (ideal) type of social action, what he calls value-rational action. Value-rational action occurs when an individual or a group or organization or whole society values some ideal or belief such that they decide to rationally act on that value, to demonstrate their commitment to that value, regardless of the (expected or unexpected) costs of that action to them. "For my country, right or wrong!" is the cry of the soldier heading to war. "Here I stand, I can do no other" (FMW 127) is the voice of a principled person explaining his or her decision about a particular course of action – whether demonstrating commitment to country, family, friendship, religious faith, the poor, education, the environment. Value-rational action is "determined by a conscious belief in the value for its own sake of some ethical, aesthetic, religious, or other form of behavior, independently of its prospects for success" (ES 24–25).

When our siblings or friends choose to enlist in the military and, by extension, choose to put themselves in the face of great personal danger, many do so because of their commitment to the value of patriotism (and independent of the social and economic benefits and costs of enlistment). Once committed to that value, they then methodically proceed to act on that value; i.e., their military training and participation are rational actions in the service of their values. Similarly, many childless couples go to great lengths to have a child; they invest a lot of time and money and endure a lot of heartache (expectation and disappointment) as they experiment with various fertility programs or go through the arduous process of trying to successfully adopt a child from a foreign country. These are all rational, well-thought-out options they deliberately pursue because of their commitment to the value of children.

When you help out a friend or neighbor even though doing so involves a great personal cost to you in terms of time, energy, money, or other opportunities lost, your conduct is rational vis-à-vis your values – your valuing of friendship, loyalty, etc. By the same token, a university's commitment to the value of multicultural diversity can lead it to rationally implement recruitment and admission policies and changes in curriculum offerings and faculty hiring plans that, though economically costly to the university, produce a more diverse student body and a more diverse learning environment for all its students. The rationally deliberate, planful steps the university makes toward accomplishing its goal (despite its costs) make sense given its valuing of diversity.

In sum, many different values – duty, loyalty, an aesthetic of beauty – can motivate rational action; "value-rational action always involves 'commands' or 'demands' which, in the actor's opinion, are binding on him" (ES 25). Anytime, therefore, that we express puzzlement at why some individuals, or some religious or political activist groups, or whole countries act as they do – what may seem like "irrational" behavior to us (like the Calvinists working so hard but not enjoying their money) – we should probe whether their behavior is being driven by commitment to some particular value. We might not personally approve of the particular value, but from Weber we learn to recognize that values can motivate highly rational, deliberative action.

INSTRUMENTAL RATIONAL ACTION

Another type of rational behavior and one Weber sees as dominating modern capitalist society is what he calls instrumental rational action. In contrast to value-rational action, which is driven by our commitment to a particular value (irrespective of the costs imposed on us), instrumental rational action is strategic, cost–benefit action; we are interested in achieving a particular, rationally calculated goal or end (e.g., economic wealth) and we assess the most effective means to achieve that end among the options available. "Action is instrumentally rational when the end [goal], the means, and the secondary results are all rationally taken into account and weighed" (ES 26).

Instrumental rational action thus captures the calculating means–end behavior that individuals, organizations, and societies engage in when they make cost–benefit decisions about a course of action (e.g., college education) whose planned outcome (high post-college income) is intended to benefit the actor making the decision. We make instrumentally rational decisions about all sorts of things on the basis of their perceived costs to us – what college to attend, which highway route to take when going to visit a friend who has moved to a different city, how much time to spend studying for a particular class, etc. Instrumental rational action is, according to Weber, "determined by expectations as to the behavior of objects in the environment [e.g., the housing market] and of other human beings; these expectations are used as 'conditions' or 'means' for the attainment of the actor's own rationally pursued and calculated end" (ES 24). In capitalist society, cost–benefit rationality predominates; profit-and-loss is the ledger used, with net profit or net gain being the decisive criterion in determining behavior.

The world of work and economic relations provides much evidence illustrating the pervasiveness of instrumental rational action in contemporary society. The article on poultry workers we discussed in highlighting Karl Marx's ideas about surplus value, exploitation, and alienated labor (chapter 1, Topic 1.4), can also be used to illustrate Weber's concept of instrumental rational action. Notably, Weber's construct applies equally to the factory owners and to the workers seeking unionization. Both groups are trying to maximize their benefits: for the owners, profit resulting, for example, from the speed of the line-production process; and for the workers, the economic and health and safety benefits that would result from better working conditions. Similarly, when General Motors (GM) made sweeping cost cuts to bolster its tenuous economic status in mid-2008, these cuts included eliminating the health benefits of its older white-collar retirees. Although GM is renowned for its value commitment to workers' health, it acted in an instrumental rather than in a value-rational way: maintaining its cash reserves has greater strategic value for GM than does preserving its retirees' health benefits.

▤▤ NEWS 3.2

The iron cage of contemporary capitalism

When Weber writes about the pervasiveness of instrumental rationality in modern society he sounds a lot like Marx (chapter 1). Although Weber highlighted the historical role of religious values in capitalist expansion (cf. *Protestant Ethic*), his conclusion about modern-day capitalism (at the beginning of the twentieth century) was that it had *lost* its religious, ethical foundations. He believed it was no longer driven by non-material (e.g., religious) values but, as Marx argued, by economic interests. Rather than making work our calling, our vocation, the demands of capitalist society have become so all-pervasive and controlling that we are coerced into fulfilling the rational cost–benefit expectations of the capitalist marketplace. Thus:

> The Puritan wanted to work in a calling; we are forced to do so. For when asceticism was carried out of monastic cells into everyday life, and began to dominate worldly morality, it did its part in building the tremendous cosmos of the modern economic order. This order is now bound to the technical and economic conditions of machine production which to-day determine the lives of all individuals who are born into this mechanism, not only those directly concerned with economic acquisition, with irresistible force. Perhaps it will so determine them until the last ton of fossilized coal is burnt. In Baxter's view the care for external goods should only lie on the shoulders of the "saint like a light cloak, which can be thrown aside at any moment." But fate decreed that the cloak should become an iron cage ... material goods have gained an increasing and finally an inexorable power over the lives of men as at no previous period in history. (PE 181)

Today, given the ethos of instrumental rationality which pervades so many aspects of our lives and of the culture as a whole – constituting an "iron cage" of economic and technological determinism – we make decisions based on a calculating, methodical assessment of the opportunities and alternatives available in terms of their "marginal utility." We opt (and are expected to opt) for the course of action whose immediate and secondary consequences are most likely to best serve our strategic interests.

Box 3.1 Types of meaningful social action	
Rational or purposive action	**Non-rational action**
1 Instrumental rational action	3 Emotion
2 Value-rational action	4 Tradition

Value-rational and instrumental-rational action are examples of the meaningful social action that, for Weber, is the focus of sociology. Not all meaningful action, however, is rational action. We know from our own everyday lives that emotion, for example, underlies many of the things we do. Emotion is at the root of much social interaction, and this is true even in places where we might think that emotion and non-rational action in general don't belong – in the halls of Congress and parliament, for example, where, following the Enlightenment conception, we would expect to find only well-argued rational debate (cf. Introduction), not angry outbursts; or on Wall Street, where we might expect that money trading decisions would not be driven by fear and panic but by calculated plans designed to ensure long-term financial gains. Yet just a cursory eye on the day's news reminds us of the extent to which emotion pervades the public world of politics and economics.

Weber recognized the socially meaningful significance of emotion – categorizing affectual or emotional action as a third type of social action, that which is determined by the actor's specific feeling states: "Action is affectual [emotional] if it satisfies a need for revenge, sensual gratification, devotion, contemplative bliss, or for working off emotional tensions" (ES 25). A second type of non-rational action (and Weber's fourth type of social action) is that determined by tradition. Many American families have particular Thanksgiving and other traditions, habits, and customs they follow simply because they have always done things that way. Tradition matters. (See Topic 3.1.)

Topic 3.1   Muslim women and virginity: Two worlds collide

In private clinics in fashionable neighborhoods in Paris, hymen-restoration surgery is increasingly sought by young Muslim women who, despite the modern freedoms they enjoy, are under intense pressure to provide certificates of virginity prior to their wedding night. These certificates are demanded by their own fathers and brothers as well as by their future in-laws. Thus hymenoplasties are on the rise: short cosmetic surgical procedures "involving one semicircular cut, 10 dissolving stitches and a discounted fee of $2,900" allow Muslim women to avoid becoming targets of the anger and degradation that is invariably directed toward them once it is publicly announced that they had lost their virginity prior to marriage. One young Muslim female student explained: "In my culture, not to be a virgin is to be dirt." The hymen-replacement surgery is non-detectable and provides the necessary proof of vaginal bleeding on the wedding night.

NEWS 3.3

THE INTERPLAY OF RATIONAL AND NON-RATIONAL ACTION

We see that tradition is a powerful motivator of social action, and it frequently collides with modern lifestyles (as young Muslim women know well). But

Muslim women also demonstrate that the force of tradition can in turn spur rational strategic decisions (e.g., hymen-restoration surgery). As Weber fully recognized, social action does not necessarily correspond to any one type alone; rather, various types of action can co-exist in any given context, something that will become even more apparent in the next section as we consider additional examples of social action and assess them in terms of Weber's four types of social action.

VALUES AND EMOTIONS IN THE CORPORATE WORLD

Although we can predict that almost any story about corporate hiring and investment practices will testify to the pervasiveness of instrumental rationality, being aware of Weber's four-fold classification of social action helps us notice how, in any given context, different types of action co-exist. Value-rational and emotional action can occur even in corporate boardrooms typically dominated by instrumentally rational action. This mix of motivating forces is seen in the response of Sandler O'Neill, a small investment-banking firm that lost many employees in the 9/11 terrorist attacks in Manhattan. In the immediate aftermath of the attacks, the firm not only set up a foundation to pay for the education of the 71 children of its deceased employees, it also made an 8-year commitment to pay the bereaved families the full health benefits that its employees receive. Moreover, it paid out bonus and stock money to the deceased employees' families. One senior partner explained that the firm had so many close-knit, family-like ties with the (deceased) employees and their families that it could not imagine not making a systematic effort to care for them in tangible ways. We thus see that on Wall Street, despite the constant pressure of a profit-oriented strategic rationality, firms occasionally reject instrumental criteria (e.g., self-profit and company profit) in favor of non-economic considerations. Similarly when Pfizer, the pharmaceutical company, acting in an instrumental rational way, let go thousands of workers in Brooklyn, New York, it nonetheless continued to subsidize housing and schools in the community, thus acting on its values, i.e. its commitment to neighborhood well-being. It was also motivated by tradition – Brooklyn is Pfizer's birthplace; and by emotion – its sentimental attachment to the place.

NEWS 3.4

NEWS 3.5

WANTING A CHILD: EMOTION, VALUES, AND INSTRUMENTAL RATIONALITY

Clearly, value-rational and non-rational (emotional and traditional) action can penetrate corporate behavior, notwithstanding the larger instrumental, strategic context in which businesses operate. By the same token, instrumental rationality can penetrate areas of life that we generally regard as motivated primarily by emotion or values. Take, for example, the decision to have a child. When a person or couple decide they want a child, we generally assume that this is driven by emotional fulfillment, as well as by commitment to the value of family. But we

NEWS 3.6

> **Topic 3.2** Egg donors wanted
>
> Help loving couples who want to have a baby. 20–29 years of age, physically/emotionally healthy, college-educated, no anti-depressant use or history of mental illness, non-smoking or smoke-free for at least one year, height/weight proportionate, no drug use or alcohol abuse ... $5–10 K compensation.

also see evidence that couples' decisions to have children are not entirely lacking instrumental motivation. The classified personal advertisements for egg donors that we typically see in college newspapers indicate that some couples have very specific requirements about the kinds of children they want.

The highly specific requirements in Topic 3.2 suggest the calculated presumption that egg donors who can meet the requirements will most likely produce emotionally, cognitively, and physically high-functioning children. These donor-seeking couples, therefore, do not seem to want children solely because they value children; rather, while they value children, they seem to value a particular type of child – one who starts out with a higher than average probability of being strategically poised to have a successful life.

NEWS 3.7

It is more surprising, perhaps, that there are also couples who seek to have children with specific disabilities. Some prospective parents intentionally choose to undergo invasive genetic diagnoses and related fertility implants by which they choose "malfunctioning genes that produce disabilities like deafness or dwarfness ... [a] painful and expensive fertility procedure for the express purpose of having children with a defective gene." From a Weberian perspective, these parents are acting in a highly rational, methodical, and calculating manner, choosing defective genes in order to realize their commitment to the value of deafness. These parents have a concern that in contemporary society, where we glorify perfection and expect people to screen out for disability, those with a disability will become increasingly marginalized. In this context, intentionally choosing to have embryonic implants that will ensure deafness can be seen as a value-rational act. There is also an element of tradition; maintaining the culture and traditions of deaf

NEWS 3.8

people and their particular communities. Similarly, too, there is an emotional component; like non-deaf parents, deaf people love their children and, as deaf people themselves, may feel especially close emotionally to a deaf child.

In sum, as Weber's analysis of social action demonstrates, social behavior is complex. While it can frequently be characterized as illustrating one type of social action rather than another, in many instances, the social action we observe variously combines instrumental rational and value-rational motivations as well as elements of emotion and tradition. More generally, Weber's analysis of social action demonstrates his commitment to understanding the broad gamut of social behavior. Thus, unlike Marx, he does not see social behavior as reducible to economic or property relations, and unlike Durkheim, is not concerned primarily with explaining social solidarity.

Social action and social relationships do not occur in a vacuum, but in societal and institutional contexts characterized by different forms of power and authority, different sources of legitimation. This is a subject extensively addressed by Weber, who tended to interchangeably use the terms power, authority, domination, and legitimation. For Weber, power is "the probability that one actor within a social relationship will be in a position to carry out his own will despite resistance" (ES 53). More precisely, domination or authority is:

> the probability that certain specific commands (or all commands) will be obeyed by a given group of persons … Domination may be based on the most diverse motives of compliance: all the way from simple habituation to the most purely rational calculation of advantage. Hence every genuine form of domination implies a minimum of voluntary compliance, that is, an interest (based on ulterior motives or genuine acceptance) in obedience. (ES 212)

Weber gave particular attention to distinguishing between the (ideal) types of domination in modern society compared to earlier times. Thus he noted that authority in modern society is typically legal authority, i.e., based on norms (or rational rules) grounded in a society's collective and intentionally established, impersonal force of law (ES 954), and imposed by "ruling organizations" (ES 53) such as the state and other bureaucracies (ES 217–220). By contrast, feudal society and other traditional societies and communities are characterized by traditional authority. In these contexts, it is personal loyalty to an estate lord or master – or to a community elder or religious leader – and loyalty to the estate's or community's traditions, which secure individual obedience and compliance (ES 226–241). Thus, "Authority will be called traditional if legitimacy is claimed for it and believed in by virtue of the sanctity of age-old rules and powers. The masters are designated according to traditional rules and are obeyed because of their traditional status" (ES 226).[4]

We see evidence of the legitimacy of traditional authority today in countries that still have a monarchy (e.g., the UK), and even more visibly in the global presence of the Catholic church. As Weber emphasizes regarding all ideal typical classifications, "The forms of domination occurring in historical reality constitute combinations, mixtures, adaptations, or modification of these 'pure' [or ideal] types" (ES 954). Highlighting the blurred lines that exist between traditional and rational-legal authority, the church, for example, establishes legitimacy through its many age-old traditions, symbols, and rules, but it also relies on a highly rational (and periodically updated) set of modern laws – canon law – outlining the property and other rights of the church as an institution vis-à-vis its own members and vis-à-vis other institutions (e.g., the state). Notably, the church in the US relied more heavily on its legal than its traditional authority in dealing with the fall-out from the sex abuse crisis that came to the fore in 2002, though it was traditional authority (e.g., the special, sacred authority of priests and bishops as perceived by its members as well as by the government) that largely enabled priests to engage in the sexual abuse of children, and of bishops to suppress it (e.g., Bartunek et al. 2006).

THE LEGAL AUTHORITY OF THE STATE

In general, however, the state has much greater power and authority than the church in modern society. The state's ability to impose its will despite resistance comes from its unique power: The nation-state is legally entitled to engage in violence against other states and against individuals and groups within its borders.

> A state is a human community that (successfully) claims the monopoly of the legitimate use of physical force within a given territory. Note that "territory" is one of the characteristics of the state ... the right to use physical force is ascribed to other institutions or to individuals only to the extent to which the state permits it. The state is considered the sole source of the "right" to use violence. (FMW 78)

There are two important points to emphasize regarding Weber's definition of the state. First, he defines the nation-state primarily in terms of its legal-political territory and structure; thus, shared ethnic roots, language, or cultural sentiments are not sufficient to constitute a nation (FMW 172–173). Second, he underscores the specific means or instruments which are peculiar to the state, namely legal violence. The state uses physical violence to defend itself (and society) against threats to its security that come both from within the state and from other states and other entities. "The state is valued as the agency that guarantees security, and this is above all the case in times of external danger, when sentiments of national solidarity flare up, at least intermittently" (FMW 177). The terrorist events of 9/11 dramatically violated the physical and cultural security of the US, and the government's response demonstrates the power of the state to strike with physical-military force against the ongoing security threat posed by terrorism. Post-9/11 world events underscore that the state (acting alone or jointly with other nation-states) engages in physical violence – warfare – against other nation-states (e.g., Afghanistan, Iraq) and against terrorist individuals and groups (e.g., Al-Qaeda, Hezbollah) who may or may not be supported financially or logistically by a given state (e.g., Iran) or by a formal or informal alliance among a few states.

Again, highlighting the blurred lines between legal and traditional authority, we see, for example, that when the US president – who has extensive legal authority – makes important speeches announcing military action, or outlining a new domestic policy program, he does so amidst some of the nation's most powerful symbols of tradition: he customarily speaks from the Oval Office in the White House, a space embodying the historical authority which inheres in the tradition of American democracy. Further underscoring the power of tradition which surrounds presidential authority, whenever the president makes a speech there is, typically, an American flag draped in the background.

Unlike Marx, who would emphasize the economic motivation underlying state violence against other states – the claim, for example, that US military action is "all about oil" (Harvey 2003: 25) – Weber notes that political expansion is not always motivated by economic objectives (FMW 164). The glory of power and national prestige for its own sake drives competition between nation-states. Similarly, a nation's interest either in maintaining a historical tradition of geo-political dominance, or in asserting a newly found national pride, can also motivate state action vis-à-vis other states. Political expansion, moreover, does not always involve the use of coercion and violence. States seek to dominate other states and to ensure their own prestige and their military, economic, and cultural security through diplomatic initiatives and alliances. Weber argues: "The prestige of power, as such, means in practice the glory of power over other communities; it means the expansion of power, though not always by way of incorporation or subjection. The big political communities are the natural exponents of such pretensions to prestige. Every political structure naturally prefers to have weak rather than strong neighbors" (FMW 160). And, as witnessed since the collapse of the Soviet Union in 1989, when weak states (e.g., Georgia, Poland) have strong neighbors (e.g., Russia), they build economic, defensive, and cultural bridges with other strong states (e.g., the US, the European Union) that can, in principle, buffer them against their strong neighbor. Given the complexity of geo-political networks (see chapter 7), however, this does not always happen; thus, the US did little to intervene when Russia invaded Georgia in August 2008.

NEWS 3.10

The state's response to internal threats

The modern state also uses coercion and violence in policing behavior as it responds to criminal activity and other perceived threats to social order within its borders, including that posed by public mass protests. Specifically, the police force is the institutionalized, legal-rational, bureaucratic structure that monitors behavior within the state. The police are sanctioned and obliged by the state to use physical force in order to restrain individuals and groups. Most people in society accept the police's use of physical violence as a routinized form of social control; generally, it is only when the police act with what is perceived as *excessive* physical force that individuals are collectively mobilized to comment on what are, essentially, state-enforced, rational-legal procedures. And even then, notwithstanding the public controversies occasioned by "police brutality" (e.g., Blauner 2001: 193–196), these instances tend to seen as aberrations rather than a likely consequence of institutionalized police procedures for enacting their state-affirmed legal right to use violence.

In sum, the state has a monopoly on the use of violence. Violence alone, however, is not necessarily the first, and typically not the only, action engaged in by the state in protecting security. The state's use of violence and the degree to which it uses it are themselves determined by a given nation's regard for human rights and political values (e.g., the right to a fair trial; eschewal of torture). Weighing competing values is a challenging task, and state policies that favor one (e.g., security) over another (e.g., individual freedom) ignite heated public debate. Weber argued: "All political structures use force, but they differ in the manner in which and the extent to which they use or threaten to use it against other political organizations. These differences play a specific role in determining the form and destiny of political communities" (FMW 159).

This point applies well to ongoing debates in the US about the use of torture in interrogating terrorists. The arguments back and forth are complex, but a dominant theme is that the US, because of its constitutional and political history affirming democracy, freedom, and the dignity and rights of the individual, should not engage in the kinds of physical force that are most usually associated with non-democratic, authoritarian regimes, such as Iraq under Saddam Hussein. Thus the state's use of physical force, though guaranteed by state law, is constrained by value-rational, cultural norms. Indeed, admission to the club of high-status (economically, socially, and politically) modern nations is contingent on members' demonstrated commitment to human rights; e.g., this is an obstacle blocking (democratic) Turkey's admission to the European Union. In short, as Weber would affirm, the political destiny of countries rests on the degree to which their respective states use physical violence and to what ends they use it.

📰 NEWS 3.11

BUREAUCRACY

The state's legal authority is typically institutionalized and exercised through bureaucracy (e.g., the Pentagon, the Department of Justice, federal regulatory agencies, the military, etc.). But in contemporary society, bureaucratic organization is also evident across all domains of daily life – in economic corporations; churches, universities, and non-profit organizations; dentists', doctors', and lawyers' offices; and professional sports teams. The bureaucracies that many of us might encounter on a given day include, most immediately, the university, as well as the federal government (when you apply for financial aid), your local bank (when you apply for a supplementary student loan), the Registry of Motor Vehicles (when you renew your driver's license), your car insurance company, your health clinic. The list is long. What all of these organizations have in common is that they have a legally recognized set of technical or procedural rules, and official policies and regulations that guide their specific activities and the social relationships in which they are engaged, whether these relationships are with individuals, government departments, corporations, or other bureaucratic organizations.

Bureaucratic authority

Bureaucracies, Weber states, are legitimate structures of domination in modern society. They are formal organizations exerting legal authority over us, making us behave in specific, required ways. Most of the time, we may have little awareness of the multiple ways in which bureaucratic authority pervades daily life. Yet we are readily reminded of bureaucratic authority any time we try to bypass official rules; any student who has "petitioned" the dean's office for a waiver on some rule is well aware of what bureaucratic authority can entail: if the right form is not completed, if we get in the "wrong" line to speak to the official in charge of these (and not other) specific petitions, if we fail to meet the specified deadline, if we fail to submit all of the required supporting documents, if we forget to secure all the required signatures from other various officials, etc. We are often frustrated by what we see as the inefficiency of bureaucracy, especially when dialing a 1–800 number to inquire about a credit card charge. Weber recognized that bureaucracy can produce inefficiencies. But he also saw it as the most rational, i.e., the most efficient way of accomplishing tasks and values (e.g., fairness, equal treatment) in modern society.

Impersonal criteria

Bureaucratic rationality is institutionalized through the application of specific practices and procedures designed to ensure that impersonal (rational) criteria rather than personal or other considerations (of values, emotion, or tradition) determine the outcome of the exchange. For example, when you request a waiver from the dean's office on some college graduation requirement, the person you talk to does not determine your fate on the basis of whether she or he likes or dislikes your mother, or whether you are or are not related to a prominent person in the community. If the college administrator were to be swayed by such considerations, she or he would not be acting in accord with the (legally enforced) rules of bureaucratic rationality. In traditional (patrimonial) societies, personal criteria (e.g., knowing you or your family) might well play a large part in determining the outcome of your interaction with officials (e.g., college administrators, police officers, school principals), officials who, in turn, likely owe their position to family connections. In modern society, by contrast, impersonal technical rationality informs the behavior of, and within, social organizations. And this rationality is institutionalized and routinized through the hierarchical division of labor and the corresponding rules and authority structure that characterize bureaucracies; for example, under the triage system in medical offices you are first screened by a receptionist, then by the nursing assistant, then by the nurse practitioner, then (if you are *really* sick) by the doctor, and then perhaps subsequently by an even more specialized doctor.

Thus, Weber states:

> The purest type of exercise of legal authority is that which employs a bureaucratic administrative staff. Only the supreme chief of the organization occupies his position of dominance by virtue of appropriation, of election, or of having been designated for the succession. But even *his* authority consists in a separate sphere of legal "competence." The whole administrative staff under the supreme authority then consists, in the purest type, of individual officials ... who are appointed and function according to the following criteria: (i) They are personally free and subject to authority only with respect to their

impersonal official obligations. (ii) They are organized in a clearly defined hierarchy of offices. (iii) Each office has a clearly defined sphere of competence in the legal sense. (iv) The office is filled by a free contractual relationship. Thus, in principle, there is free selection. (v) Candidates are selected on the basis of technical qualifications. In the most rational case, this is tested by examination or guaranteed by diplomas certifying technical training, or both. They are *appointed* not elected. (vi) They are remunerated by fixed salaries in money, for the most part with a right to pensions. Only under certain circumstances does the employing authority, especially in private organizations, have a right to terminate the appointment, but the official is always free to resign. The salary scale is graded according to rank in the hierarchy; but in addition to this criterion, the responsibility of the position and the requirements of the incumbent's social status may be taken into account. (vii) The office is treated as the sole, or at least the primary, occupation of the incumbent. (viii) It constitutes a career. There is a system of "promotion" according to seniority or to achievement or both. Promotion is dependent on the judgment of superiors. (ix) The official works entirely separated from ownership of the means of administration and without appropriation of his position. (x) He is subject to strict and systematic discipline and control in the conduct of the office. (ES 220–221)

Bureaucratic rules and procedures thus minimize the interference of non-rational forces (e.g., emotional likes and dislikes) in social organizational relationships. Similarly, with a premium on efficiency and competence, the hierarchical organization of expertise and responsibilities ensures that you seek assistance from those most qualified, an expertise that is certified or credentialed by an external, objective authority based on rational evaluative criteria of competence.

Certified expertise

We see much public evidence of certification (itself a rational process to help us avoid wasting time seeking unqualified help or faulty services/products). Certificates on the walls of various establishments attest to individuals' qualifications: doctors, dentists, beauticians, garage mechanics. And on construction vans, we see that plumbers, carpenters, and electricians are licensed to do the work they advertise. Certification shadows our everyday movements: when we ride the elevator, we see a certificate testifying to its safety; in restaurants, we see certificates of the restaurant's hygiene standards, in car sales showrooms, we see certificates clarifying the technical and sales information about the car, and, as we noted earlier, some Muslim women need certificates of virginity (see Topic 3.1).

NEWS 3.3

CHARISMATIC AUTHORITY

Alongside legal and traditional authority, Weber discusses the significance of a third (ideal) type of legitimation or domination in society: the non-rational authority that derives from charisma, that special charm that gives an individual power over others. When charismatic authority is present, it always and only resides in a particular *individual*. Groups and organizations do not have charisma (although their leaders may, and hence may be able to expand or consolidate the organization's

In modern society, even those not working in a bureaucratic organization are subject to rational bureaucratic authority; a mobile food vendor prominently displays his license.

The state protects its citizens from internal (and external) threats; government agencies warn people against using unlicensed business providers and contractors.

power as a result). Charismatic authority is an attribute of an individual's personality; we acknowledge this anytime we comment that someone is a "natural" or "born" leader. Weber tells us:

> The term charisma will be applied to a certain quality of an individual personality by virtue of which he is considered extraordinary and treated as endowed with supernatural, superhuman, or at least exceptional powers or qualities. These are such as are not accessible to the ordinary person, but are regarded as of divine origin or as exemplary, and on the basis of them the individual concerned is treated as a "leader." (ES 241)

We all probably have a friend whom we would describe as charismatic, that person who has the extra spark and energy, the one who always seems to manage to authoritatively persuade us to do something or other. And in the public world we can think of individuals who many people would likely describe as charismatic – who have shown remarkable ability in persuading people to act in particular positive or negative ways. Across history, those who have had charismatic authority include Jesus Christ, John F. Kennedy, Charles Manson, Nelson Mandela, the Dalai Lama, Pope John Paul II, Princess Diana, and Oprah Winfrey, among others.

Anticipating Weber's construal of charisma, Harriet Martineau observed that

> Man-worship is as universal a practice as that of the higher sort of religion ... Every community has its saints, its heroes, its sages, – whose tombs are visited, whose deeds are celebrated, whose words have become the rules by which men live ... Now the moral taste of a people is nowhere more clearly shown than in its choice of idols. (1838: 126)

Today, pop cultural idols Bono, Bob Geldof, and Willie Nelson use their celebrity status and charismatic power to persuade world political leaders and ordinary people to work to redress poverty and hunger. In corporate America, Lee Iacocca and Jack Welch have a charisma that gives an extra edge to their business reputation, allowing them (even in retirement) to command financial rewards and acclaim even when their actual track record may not fully support their gilded reputation.

NEWS 3.12

The perception of charisma

Individuals who follow and defer to a charismatic leader comprise a charismatic community; they accept the leader's authority not because this is required by the leader's official authority or credentials, or because of his or her traditional status in the community. They do so rather as "disciples" involved in "an emotional form of communal relationship" (ES 243), and because they *perceive* the charismatic figure as "qualified" to lead them (ES 242). Charismatic leaders are perceived, essentially, as "prophets" or "messiahs," or at least as approximating someone with messianic promise. Charismatic figures, in turn, comport themselves in ways that befit a messiah, projecting the self-confident conviction that they truly are uniquely able to lead their followers to achieve whatever the designated goal may be (ES 631).

Charismatic leaders preserve charismatic authority by showing indifference to the material cares and concerns of the everyday world (e.g., like Jesus; ES 633);

they cannot be perceived as personally benefiting from their charisma. This can be a challenge, especially for corporate and celebrity charismatic leaders; Jack Welch received negative publicity when it was revealed that he billed General Electric for flowers and groceries for his Manhattan home despite his extensive pension and accumulated economic fortune. By contrast, although the Dalai Lama writes best-selling books that earn a lot of money, his public demeanor is always one of simplicity; he is dressed in plain, unadorned robes; his eschewal of consumer ostentation strengthens his followers' convictions about his lofty mission.

The temporality and routinization of charisma

Because charisma inheres in a person (and not in bureaucratic office), when the person dies (or loses credibility), the charisma dies too. This poses a problem: how can the mission or agenda of the charismatic leader continue after his or her death? If the mission is to continue, the only way it can, Weber argues, is by being rationalized, i.e., converted into an organizational goal. In other words, the charismatic leader's (non-rational) personal (emotional) power must be converted into the rational, impersonal, administrative power of official authority (ES 246–251). This can happen if the goals of the charismatic leader are taken over and routinized through the establishment of a bureaucratic organization rationally equipped to execute those goals; thus, for example, Oprah Winfrey does not rely solely on her own personal charisma but has also established a business corporation (Harpo Productions Inc.) to ensure the (long-term) success of her goals.

The Catholic church exemplifies the successful routinization of charisma (ES 246–249) – the translation of Jesus's personal charismatic authority into enduring symbolic traditions and into bureaucratic organizational hierarchies, rules, and procedures. Weber states:

> In its pure form charismatic authority has a character specifically foreign to everyday routine structures. The social relationships directly involved are strictly personal, based on the validity and practice of charismatic personal qualities. If this is not to remain a purely transitory phenomenon, but to take on the character of a permanent relationship, a community of disciples or followers or a party organization or any sort of [formal] organization, it is necessary for the character of charismatic authority to become radically changed … It cannot remain stable but becomes either traditionalized or rationalized, or a combination of both. (ES 246)

In sum, charismatic authority, though highly effective, is always temporary; it inheres in an individual and ceases with the death (or disgrace, or lack of mission-success) of that individual. Charismatic power, therefore, is unstable – very different to the institutionalized permanence of bureaucratic and traditional forms of authority. Organizational goals and routines precede and outlive the individual incumbents of office, including organizational leaders; and do not need to rely on the creative energy of any one particular individual in ensuring organizational success. Witness the speed with which the charismatic leader of a Colorado evangelical mega-church, and incoming president of the National Association of

Evangelicals, was fired (in November 2006) by the board of overseers when it recognized that the fortunes of the mega-church congregation would be damaged by the pastor's personal transgressions. Despite the creative energy charismatic leaders contribute to an organization's success, the organization's structures are highly rationalized (bureaucratized) so that any fall from grace of the leaders will be smoothly accommodated by the organizational procedures and routines already methodically in place.

SOCIAL STRATIFICATION

Like Marx, Weber wrote about inequality or stratification, i.e., the processes in society which determine individuals' objective location in a hierarchical system of social classes or strata based on their differential access to resources. Unlike Marx, however, Weber focused not just on economic resources, but also on how non-economic resources, namely social status and political power, create and maintain class inequality. "Man does not strive for power only in order to enrich himself economically. Power, including economic power, may be valued for its own sake. Very frequently the striving for power is also conditioned by the social honor it entails ... 'classes,' 'status groups,' and 'parties' are phenomena of the distribution of power within a community" (ES 926–927).

GRADIENTS OF ECONOMIC INEQUALITY

Weber uses the word class to denote individuals' shared economic situation: individuals who have similar economic interests and assets and who have similar life-chances as a result of property, income, and labor market opportunity (ES 927). In particular, he distinguishes between property and the lack of property as a major factor differentiating classes, and further, among property owners, its scale and purpose (e.g., entrepreneurial or commercial) (ES 302–304).

Whereas Marx posited two dichotomously opposed classes – capital owners (bourgeoisie) and wage-workers (proletariat) – Weber outlined a more differentiated class structure. He argued that between the "positively privileged property classes," typically including "rentiers" receiving income from land, mines, factories, ships, creditors, and securities; and the "negatively privileged property classes" of debtors and paupers are the "middle classes." The middle classes broadly encompass individuals variously dependent on income earned from property or acquired skills. They include the "positively privileged" commercial classes – including entrepreneurs, bankers, and professionals with sought-after expertise or training (e.g., lawyers, doctors, artists) and the "negatively privileged" commercial classes comprised of "laborers with varying qualifications; skilled, semi-skilled, and unskilled." Weber summarized four different classes: (a) the working class as a whole (laborers); (b) the petty bourgeoisie (self-employed farmers, grocers, and craftsmen); (c) the property-less intelligentsia and specialists (e.g., white-collar employees, civil servants); and (d) the classes privileged through property and education (ES 303).

Given the complexities in today's economy – the extent to which many people work in corporate finance and in upper-managerial and professional strata within corporations – Weber's differentiated class model is more applicable than Marx's to analyzing the specific characteristics of the occupational and class structure. As Weber recognized, investment managers and professional and expert employees occupy a "positively privileged" location vis-à-vis corporate capitalism (without necessarily owning the corporation); they have access to highly rewarding economic opportunities, and ones typically less accessible to clerical, skilled, and unskilled workers. At the same time, however, Marx's emphasis on the profit logic and economic inequality structured into capitalist society (chapter 1) continues to make analytical sense in assessing the organization of work and other social phenomena (e.g., sports), and highlighting the economic interests that underpin social relations.

SOCIAL STATUS

Independent of people sharing a common economic class, they can share a similar social status. Status is "an effective claim to social esteem in terms of positive or negative privileges," which typically, according to Weber, are founded on style of life, education, and hereditary or occupational prestige (ES 305–306). In American society, for example, the highest status group historically was comprised of white Protestant males, from the upper socio-economic echelons, and educated at elite private schools and universities (e.g., Harvard, Yale, and Princeton) whose admissions policies excluded those whose profile did not match the chosen criteria of privilege (Karabel 2005: 22–23). This relatively closed system of privilege and inequality began to crack somewhat in the late 1960s when elite universities expanded the admission of women, blacks, Jews, and Catholics (Karabel 2005). Nonetheless, race and gender continue to be major sources of status (and economic) inequality, as underscored by the exclusion of women and blacks from full membership in some elite golf and country clubs, or in the race self-segregation apparent among the upper-middle class in their summer residence habits; on prestigious Martha's Vineyard (an island off the coast of Massachusetts), upper-class blacks tend to "summer" in certain towns and upper-class whites in others.

Status and class

Weber emphasizes that status and prestige are not solely determined by economic class, even though the costly fees entailed in admission to exclusive housing developments and prestigious colleges and country clubs points to the close relation between economic class and social status. Nevertheless, a person might have a lot of wealth but little prestige or honor in the community, perhaps because the individual's family "pedigree" is less "pure" than that of others – his or her wealth might be "new" rather than accumulated over many family generations.

As Weber notes: "Mere economic power, and especially 'naked' money power, is by no means a recognized basis of social honor" (ES 926). Money, nonetheless, makes it easier for families to send their children to elite private colleges, which, in turn, confer prestige of their own as well as enhancing the occupational, lifestyle, and related status (and economic market) opportunities available to those graduates. Similarly, some country clubs are more elitist (and more costly) than others. Gaining access to the more prestigious club readily confers status on a given individual, and establishes additional opportunities for consolidating one's status in the community, through sponsorship of charity or philanthropic causes, hosting political events, etc.

Membership of a particular status group confers prestige, but it also obliges one to have a certain "style of life" (ES 932–933): the maintenance of a particular lifestyle visibly shared with others of similar status – e.g., what neighborhoods or towns to live in; who to marry; what restaurants to dine at; what kind of architect-designed kitchen to choose; where to summer. Thus, "a specific style of life is expected from all those who wish to belong to the [status] circle" (ES 932). Weber presciently recognized the consumption-driven status lifestyles prevalent today, stating: "Every status society lives by conventions, which regulate the style of life, and hence creates economically irrational consumption patterns" (ES 307). "Keeping up with the Joneses" in order to signal social status (or status aspirations) can be economically costly, leading to the (non-rational) embrace of particular consumption fads. At the same time, of course, such behavior has a rational dimension insofar as purchases are instrumentally used to achieve a rationally calculated social end (status). Importantly, too, independent of consumption, laws determine status behavior; all formally organized clubs and associations are bound by legally enforced rules regulating members' behavior (a point highlighted on HBO's television show *Curb Your Enthusiasm*, when the show's main protagonist, Larry David, is expelled from his golf club for rude behavior).

One final point on the class–status relation: Weber notes that in times of economic and technological transformation, it is typically class situation (economic power) that comes to the fore as the primary source of social stratification, whereas in economically settled or stable contexts, it is status that tends to have primacy (ES 938). This insight helps to illuminate the apparent primacy of "naked money power" (ES 926) in stratifying individuals today, whether in the US or in China and India, where historically, status-honor (e.g., related to family caste) was somewhat independent of economic assets, but where currently the transformative impact of economic globalization makes economic capital (rather than honor) and what it can buy the most salient status marker. We will return to the impact of economic globalization in chapter 15.

NEWS 3.14

POLITICAL POWER

Economic classes and social statuses can influence and overlap one another. An additional source of stratification is differential access to social power. Political groups and associations, or parties, therefore, engage in action "oriented toward the acquisition of social power, that is to say, toward influencing social action no matter what its content may be. In principle, parties may exist in a social club as well as in a state" (ES 938). Thus, politics is "the striving to influence the distribution of power, either among states or among groups within a state" (FMW 78). Within any given club, community, or society, we all engage to varying degrees in political behavior, seeking to influence the distribution of power.

The goals toward which parties plan their actions may be issue-oriented or ideological (e.g., workers' safety, gender and racial equality in golf clubs, environmental protection). Or the goals may be personal – seeking prestige and honor for a party leader and/or for specific party members (ES 938). Typically, political power aims toward the achievement of both ideological/issue and personal goals; Weber notes, "*all* party struggles are struggles for the patronage of office, as well as struggles for objective goals" (FMW 87). Indeed, at times, it is hard to differentiate between these goals insofar as an individual's reputation and the ideological issues he or she fights for get entwined.

Parties gain power by several avenues. Voting and campaign behavior certainly matter but so too do other means (ES 938). Weber points out that political power can be achieved through the influence of money (as also emphasized by Marx; see chapter 1), but also by social status, and through coercive, illegal, and sometimes even violent means. Although democracies emphasize the procedural and substantive value that inheres in the legally rational, democratic electoral process, there is evidence from almost all western democracies that parties use illicit means toward achieving political objectives. And in fledgling democratic societies (e.g., Kenya, Iraq, Lebanon), violence by one party against another is a frequent occurrence, though violence between political parties NEWS 3.15 within the same democratic state tends to be rare and illegal; as discussed above, violence is the legal right of the state, and can only be legitimately approved by the state.

MODERNITY AND COMPETING VALUES

Another subject which Weber addressed and which has much salience today is the tension among conflicting values and their negotiation; this is a core dilemma of modern society. The unfettered march of progress, propelled by advances in science and technology, means that modern societies have the capability to accomplish many goals. The triumph of reason and science over mythical and magical thinking, first celebrated by Enlightenment thinkers (cf. Introduction), has not freed us, however, from confronting the question: "What is the value of science?" (FMW 140). What values, what ends, should science serve? The great discoveries of science – regarding brain cancer, stem cells, genetic engineering, life on Mars – do not give any hint as to what we should do with them.

SCIENCE AND VALUES

Science does not, and cannot, tell us how to use science. This is a point strongly emphasized by Weber. Scientific tools and data do not help us rank priorities regarding what topics merit scientific investigation, which projects should be funded with federal money, and who should benefit from scientific discovery. These are all questions about values. And the tension that invariably emerges between competing values and value-stances is glaringly obvious in public debates about evolution, abortion, end of life care, DNA testing, space exploration, etc. Weber quotes the great Russian novelist Leo Tolstoy to underscore the enormous challenge that modern societies encounter in deciding among diverse values: "Science is meaningless because it gives no answer to our question, the only question important for us: 'What shall we do and how shall we live?'" (FMW 143).

Many in our society fully embrace the intrinsic and practical value of scientific knowledge and its relevance to advancing economic and social progress. But as Weber reminds us, it cannot "be proved that the existence of the world which these sciences describe is worth while, that it has any 'meaning,' or that it makes sense to live in such a world. Science does not ask for the answers to such questions" (FMW 144). And we should not expect it to. Scientists, no matter how well qualified and distinguished they are as scientists, cannot use their scientific expertise to answer society's questions about what is meaningful, worthwhile, or morally right. And neither can sociologists, nor experts in any field of study (FMW 145). What shall we do? And how shall we arrange our lives (FMW 152–153)? These are questions that transcend science. Scientific data certainly inform our debates about values, as we see on abortion and stem-cell research, for example. But scientific data alone can never determine how we use scientific data, nor how we decide among competing values.

THE VALUE NEUTRALITY OF SCIENCE

It is our duty as scientists and sociologists, Weber argues, to present all the data pertaining to a given topic, and not simply to document that which agrees with our personal opinions. We are not politicians or demagogues, who, at political meetings, are obliged to take a political stand; who are legitimately expected to be partisan, and to strongly canvass and defend that stance against opposing views. Conversely, politics, Weber emphasizes, does not "belong in the lecture room." And equally important, the "prophet and the demagogue do not belong on the academic platform" (FMW 145–146); to each his or her own distinct sphere. Moreover, "'scientific' pleading is meaningless in principle because the various value spheres of the world stand in irreconcilable conflict with each other … different gods struggle with one another, now and for all times to come" (FMW 147–148). Our fate is to decide which of the warring gods to serve, and, Weber argues, only prophets or saviors can help us with this, not bureaucrats, nor scientists, whose credentialed, professional expertise requires them to maintain value neutrality.

The principle of value neutrality or objectivity is the professional ethic of the scientist. Thus, while we as individuals have our own values and passions, we do not, and should not, Weber argues, let them impose on the conduct of our research or on our sociological interpretations. We should be passionate about our work – as Weber states, "nothing is worthy of man as man unless he can pursue it with passionate devotion" (FMW 135). But regardless of our own opinions and values we must be open to the findings we uncover in our data gathering and analyses. And in particular, sociologists (and all scientists) must be open, and teach students to be open, to recognizing "inconvenient facts" (FMW 147). In other words, we need to be open to any and all ideas and data and occurrences which contravene our personal beliefs and opinions about how the world works.

Objectivity in cultural context

Durkheim also emphasized sociological objectivity, but Weber's understanding is much more contextual. Recall that Weber defined sociology as a science concerning itself with the interpretive understanding of subjectively meaningful social action (ES 4; p. 118 above). The objectivity he proposes, therefore, requires the sociologist to investigate and understand (i.e., interpret) the subjective meanings that social actors inject into behavior. Such understanding is impossible without appreciation of the cultural and historical context in which meaningful behavior occurs (as Weber himself showed in the *Protestant Ethic*). Therefore, whereas Durkheim's command to "treat social facts as things" (chapter 2) suggests that social facts objectively present themselves regardless of the societal context of the facts and of the sociologist, for Weber, the objective analysis of social phenomena (e.g., religion, capitalism, bureaucracy) is always historically and culturally grounded. Thus Weber emphasized that knowledge, including what we study and how, is shaped by cultural context:

> All knowledge of cultural reality … is always knowledge from *particular points of view*. When we require [researchers to] … distinguish the important from the trivial … we mean that they must understand how to relate the events of the real world … to universal "cultural values" and to select out those relationships which are significant for us. If the notion that those standpoints can be derived from the "facts themselves" continually recurs, it is due to the naïve self-deception of the specialist who is unaware that it is due to the evaluative ideas with which he unconsciously approaches his subject matter … cultural science … involves subjective presuppositions insofar as it concerns itself only with those components of reality which have some relationships, however indirect, to events to which we attach cultural significance. Nonetheless, it is entirely causal knowledge exactly in the same sense as the knowledge of significant concrete natural events which have a qualitative character. (MSS 82–83)

For Weber, then, the attainment of objectivity is not at the expense of either scientific rigor or the historical and cultural context in which science, and social life as a whole, occur. Recognition of how different contextual standpoints inform everyday experiences and social relations, and disrupt notions of an allegedly pure objectivity, is a critical theme elaborated by contemporary feminist theorists (as we discuss in chapter 10).

SUMMARY

Weber's theorizing engages with a remarkable breadth of topics – how culture and ideas, and not just material interests, matter in shaping social and institutional behavior; the myriad ways in which rational and non-rational motivations permeate everyday individual and institutional practices; the various sources of authority and legitimation in society; the multiple sources of social stratification; value dilemmas; and contextual objectivity in science.

POINTS TO REMEMBER

- Weber defined sociology as the interpretive understanding of subjectively meaningful social action in its historical and cultural context
- Weber uses ideal types – accentuated descriptions of the characteristics of a particular social phenomenon – to assist in comparative analysis of social structures/social action

Weber analyzed the relation between ideas and economic structures and modern capitalist culture in his study of the Protestant/Calvinist ethic

- This entails historical understanding of the Reformation, its core leader, Martin Luther, and Luther's disciple, John Calvin
- Calvinist tenets:
  - Purpose of this-worldly activities to serve God
  - Individual stands alone before God
  - God's will cannot be known
  - Predestination: one's fate (heaven/hell) already decided by God
    - Deal with uncertainty about salvation through this-worldly rationalization
      - Work as a calling; hard work for the glorification of God
      - Time not spent in work is sinful, i.e., not glorifying God
      - Ascetic conduct in this world, frugality
      - Doctrine of proof; this-worldly success (based on methodical hard work) a *sign* of other-worldly salvation
- Calvinist ethic expands capitalism: economic profits from work invested (not spent on non-work activities)
- Protestant ethic contributed to advancing an ethos of individualism

Weber identified four (ideal) types of social action:

- Instrumentally rational action: strategic means–end, cost–benefit analysis
- Value-rational action: values (e.g., patriotism, loyalty) set the ends/goals pursued irrespective of costs
- Emotional action
- Traditional action; habit, custom

Weber identified three (ideal) types of authority/domination:

- Traditional authority

- Rational legal authority:
  - The state
  - Bureaucratic organizations
- Charismatic authority; individual; unstable, needs to be routinized to ensure the continuation of goals

Stratification

- Class; economic
- Status; prestige, lifestyle
- Party; political power

Science and values

- Science cannot tell us what goals to pursue
- Value neutrality or objectivity; personal and political values have no place in the conduct of research and academic analysis
- Objectivity does not preclude attentiveness to historical and cultural context

GLOSSARY

asceticism avoidance of emotion and spontaneous enjoyment as demonstrated by the disciplined, methodical frugality and sobriety of the early Calvinists.

bureaucracy formal organizational structure characterized by rational, legal authority, hierarchy, expertise, and impersonal rules and procedures.

calling intrinsically felt obligation toward work; work valued as its own reward, an opportunity to glorify God.

Calvinism theology derived from John Calvin; emphasis on the lone individual whose after-life is predestined by God.

charisma non-rational authority held by an individual who is perceived by others to have a special personal gift for leadership.

charismatic community group of individuals (disciples) who follow and defer to a charismatic individual's authority.

class individuals who share an objectively similar economic situation determined by property, income, and occupational resources.

domination authority/legitimacy; the probability that individuals will be persuaded/obliged to comply with a given command.

emotional action subjectively meaningful, non-rational social action motivated by feelings.

ideal type an exhaustive description of the characteristics expected of a given phenomenon.

individualism cultural ethos of individual independence, responsibility, and self-reliance.

instrumental rational action behavioral decisions or action based on calculating, strategic, cost–benefit analysis of goals and means.

interpretive understanding *Verstehen*; task of the sociologist in making sense of the varied motivations that underlie meaningful action; because sociology studies human lived experience (as opposed to physical phenomena), sociologists need a methodology enabling them to empathically understand human-social behavior.

legal authority based on rational, impersonal norms and rules; imposed by the state and other bureaucracies; dominant in modern societies.

nation-state rational, legal, bureaucratic actor; has specific territorial interests; entitled to use physical force to protect and defend its internal and external security.

non-rational action behavior motivated by emotion and/or tradition rather than by reasoned judgment.

objectivity the professional obligation of scientists, researchers, and teachers to report and discuss "inconvenient facts," i.e., facts that disagree with or contradict their personal feelings and opinions.

other-worldly non-material motivations; e.g., after-death salvation; the opposite of this-worldly.

parties political groups or associations which seek to influence the distribution of power in society.

power the probability that a social actor (e.g., the state, an individual) can impose its will despite resistance.

predestination Calvinist doctrine that an individual's salvation is already determined at birth by God.

Puritan ethic emphasis on methodical work, sober frugality, and the avoidance of spontaneous emotion.

rationality emphasis on the authority of reason in deliberating about, and evaluating explanations of, the nature of reality/social phenomena.

routinization of charisma the rational translation of individual charisma into organizational goals and procedures.

status social esteem or prestige associated with style of life, education, and hereditary or occupational prestige.

stratification inequality between groups (strata) in society based on differences in economic resources, social status and prestige, and political power.

subjectively meaningful action wherein the individual attaches subjective meaning to his or her behavior and takes account of, and is oriented to, the behavior of others.

this-worldly the material reality of the everyday world in which we live and work.

traditional action non-rational, subjectively meaningful social action motivated by custom and habit.

traditional authority derived from long-established traditions or customs; dominant in traditional societies but co-exists in modern society with legal-bureaucratic and charismatic authority.

value neutrality the idea that scientists and researchers do not inject their personal beliefs and values into the conduct, evaluation, and presentation of their research.

value-rational action rational, purposeful behavior motivated by commitment to a particular value (e.g., loyalty) and independent of its outcome or success probability.

values questions concerning the goals or ends that individuals, organizations, institutions, and societies should purposefully embrace or pursue.

Verstehen German for "understanding"; refers to the process by which sociologists seek interpretive understanding of the subjective meanings that individuals and collectivities give to their behavior/social action.

RELEVANT NEWSPAPER STORIES

All news stories are from the *New York Times* unless otherwise noted, and can be accessed via www.wiley.com/go/dillon. See NEWS icons in the margins above.

NEWS 3.1   "Vietnam's remarkable recovery," *The Economist*, April 24, 2008.
NEWS 3.2   "With warning, G.M. takes wide cost cuts," July 16, 2008.
NEWS 3.3   "In Europe, debate over Islam and virginity," June 11, 2008.

NEWS 3.4   "After 5 years, his voice can still crack," September 9, 2006.

NEWS 3.5   "Pfizer's birthplace, soon without Pfizer," January 28, 2007.

NEWS 3.6   *Wellesley News* (Wellesley College Newspaper), September 20, 2006.

NEWS 3.7   "Wanting babies like themselves, some parents choose genetic defects," December 5, 2006.

NEWS 3.8   "Where sign language is far from foreign: Community embraces the deaf, and vice versa," December 25, 2006.

NEWS 3.9   US flag in government or official political settings: President Obama, February 25, 2009; President Bush, March 20, 2007; Attorney General Gonzales, March 14, 2007.

NEWS 3.10   "Taunting the bear: Russia and Georgia were going to erupt. It was really just a question of time," August 10, 2008.

NEWS 3.11   "EU warns Turkey on human rights," *The Times*, September 5, 2006.

NEWS 3.12   "Good charisma, bad business," September 13, 2002.

NEWS 3.13   "Layoffs follow scandal at Colorado megachurch," March 6, 2007.

NEWS 3.14   "Inside gate, India's good life; outside, the servants' slums," June 9, 2008.

NEWS 3.15   "Signs in Kenya that killings were orchestrated," January 21, 2008.

WEB SUPPLEMENTS

All web supplements are available at www.wiley.com/go/dillon. See WEB icons in the margins above.

WEB 3.1   The Reformation and Martin Luther

WEB 3.2   Luther's space

WEB 3.3   John Winthrop and the Puritans

NOTES

1   In citing Weber's writings, I reference the book's initials rather than the date of publication. A list of Weber's core writings, their date of publication, and the book title initials I use to reference them follows the biographical note above.

   Some everyday personal routines, e.g., brushing teeth, can be considered *social* action insofar as we are keenly aware that not brushing our teeth would diminish our status among friends; action is social action if it is meaningfully oriented to and takes account of the reactions of others (cf. ES 23–24).

2   There is no apparent evidence that Weber was familiar with Martineau's ideas (see Hoecker-Drysdale 1992).

3   Weber is criticized for exaggerating the occupational and economic differences between Catholics and Protestants (e.g., Giddens 1976: 12). Nonetheless, whatever the historical-empirical accuracy of Weber's claims, the thesis he outlines in *The Protestant Ethic* is still highly relevant in helping us understand the cultural origins of western (and indeed today's globalizing capitalist) economy and society.

4   Weber tends to refer to feudal relationships and to other similarly traditional social arrangements as representing a *patrimonial* system of authority; this refers essentially to a system of personal loyalty to, and dependence on, a lord or master (e.g., ES 231–236; 1070–1073). In contemporary society, we might think of the relationships depicted in *The Godfather* and *The Sopranos* as approximating patrimonial relationships – the pre-eminent criterion determining the behavior of the Godfather's associates, subordinates, and bodyguards (and the privileges they receive) is loyalty or fidelity to the Godfather.

KEY CONCEPTS

grand theory
social system
functions
structural-functionalist
subsystems
adaptation
goal attainment
integration
pattern maintenance
unit act
voluntaristic action
cultural system
value system
personality system
secularization
Christianizing of secular
   society
pattern variables
universalistic versus
   particularistic
specificity versus diffuseness
achievement versus ascription
neutrality versus affectivity
self- versus collectivity
   orientation
modernization theory
status differentials
uneven modernization
cultural lag
middle-range theory
functional analysis
manifest functions
latent functions
deviance
institutionalized means
cultural goals
conformist
innovator
ritualist
retreatist
rebel
neofunctionalism

CHAPTER MENU

TALCOTT PARSONS (1902–1979)

Talcott Parsons is a towering figure in American sociology. Although his name is not explicitly invoked in as many sociology classrooms today as a few decades ago (the 1940s–1970s), his impact on the development of American sociology is immense. His theorizing provides both a bridge to the classical tradition and the stimulus that led many of his peers and successors to enrich contemporary theory as a result, in part, of their critique of what they saw as Parsons's highly generalizing grand theory. And, though criticized for his tendency toward abstraction and social conservatism, recent years have seen a revival of interest in Parsons's ideas (see, e.g., Alexander 1985; Moss and Savchenko 2006).

BIOGRAPHICAL NOTE

Talcott Parsons was born in Colorado in 1902. His father was a (Protestant) Congregational minister who served on the faculty and as dean at Colorado College; the family emphasized a modest and disciplined lifestyle. Parsons completed his undergraduate education at Amherst College (in Massachusetts), and subsequently studied at the London School of Economics (LSE), and the University of Heidelberg (Germany), where he received his PhD, based on his analysis of capitalism in German thought (including Weber's). In 1927, Parsons became an instructor in the Department of Economics at Harvard University; he transferred in 1930 to the newly created Sociology Department, where he eventually received tenure, and subsequently was a founding member of Harvard's interdisciplinary Department of Social Relations, which combined sociology, cultural anthropology and social psychology. Parsons married Helen Walker, whom he had met while at the LSE, and they had three children. He remained at Harvard until his death in 1979. During his lifetime, Parsons received many national and international awards and honors, and served as president of the American Sociological Association (1949–1950) (Lidz 2000: 389–398).

In the 1930s, when Parsons returned to the US having completed his PhD at the University of Heidelberg (where Max Weber had been professor until his death in 1920), American sociology was still finding its feet. Its main focus was empirical studies of urban communities, a rich ethnographic tradition pioneered by W. E. B. Du Bois's study of *The Philadelphia Negro* (1899) (Anderson and Massey 2001: 3–4), and consolidated in the 1920s by sociologists such as William Thomas (1864–1947) at the University of Chicago (the location of the first academic department of sociology in the US). The highly respected Chicago School of Sociology (1915–1935) focused on the spatial and social organization of particular urban communities. Though still sociologically interesting, these micro studies both reflected and fed into a reluctance among sociologists to discuss American society as a whole (as a macro unit), and to generalize from local studies to the larger society. Additionally, there was little attention given to sociology's historical and intellectual roots (e.g., Rocher 1974).

Into this context Parsons marched, determined to provide a systematic, abstract, and generalizable theory of social action. He wanted sociology to be a theoretically informed science whose analytical laws would be applicable to any society, and he saw the development of such a theory as essential to the growth and maturation of sociology. Parsons explained:

> It is scarcely too much to say that the most important single index of the state of maturity of a science is the state of its systematic theory. This includes the character of the generalized conceptual scheme in use in the field, the kinds and degrees of logical integration of the different elements which make it up, and the ways in which it is actually being used in empirical research. On this basis, the thesis may be advanced that sociology is just in the process of emerging into the status of a mature science ... Theory is a term which covers a wide variety of different things which have in common only the element of generalized conceptualization. The theory of concern to the present paper [essay] in the first place constitutes a "system" and thereby differs from discrete "theories," that is, particular generalizations about particular phenomena or classes of them. A theoretical system in the present sense is a body of logically interdependent generalized concepts of empirical reference ... The two most general functions of theory are the facilitation of description and analysis. The two are most intimately connected since it is only when the essential facts about a phenomenon have been described in a carefully systematic and orderly manner that accurate analysis becomes possible at all. (1949/1954: 212–213)

BLENDING THEORY AND DATA

Despite Parsons's strong commitment to developing a broad, general, and integrated theory about how society, the social system, works, he was not interested in theory for the sake of theory. He was committed to developing a generalizable theory of society that other sociologists would apply in specific societal contexts and use to make sense of the empirical data they gathered. In turn, he believed that the empirical puzzles sociologists encountered on the ground would propel him and others to rework and modify their theories to take account of such realities. Therefore, while Parsons repudiated an empiricism which "blindly rejects the help of theoretical tools" (1949/1954: 220), he strongly argued for a synthesis between theory and data, stating:

> we cannot achieve a high level of dynamic generalization for processes and interdependencies even *within* the same society, unless our ranges of structural variability are really systematized so that when we get a shift from one to another we know *what* has changed, *to what* and *in what degree*. This order of systematization can, like all theoretical work, be verified only by empirical research. But experience shows that it cannot be worked out by sheer *ad hoc* empirical induction, letting the facts reveal their own pattern. It must be worked out by rigorous theoretical analysis, continually stimulating

and being checked by empirical research. In sum I think this is one of the very few most vital areas for the development of sociological theory, and ... the prospects are good ... [I have been] careful to note ... that however important an ingredient of the scientific brew theory may be, it is only one of the ingredients. If it is to be *scientific* theory it must be tied in, in the closest possible manner, with the techniques of empirical research by which alone we can come to know whether our theoretical ideas are "really so" or just speculations of peculiar, if not disordered minds ... If I correctly assess the recipe for a really good brew of social science it is *absolutely imperative* that these two basic ingredients [theory and data] should get together and blend with each other. (1949/1954: 364, 366)

PARSONS'S INTELLECTUAL DEBT TO WEBER AND DURKHEIM

The Structure of Social Action (1937), one of Parsons's most renowned (and hard to read) books, provides a densely argued analysis of the writings of Weber and Durkheim (and of the Italian economist Alfred Pareto), and became the gateway to sociological theory for American and other English-speaking students. Additionally, Parsons played a critical role in making Weber's work accessible, having translated *The Protestant Ethic* (in 1930), for example. Parsons's theorizing is clearly influenced by Weber, but it also integrates distinct elements from Durkheim. For Parsons, as for Weber and Durkheim, individual behavior cannot be understood in terms of individuals' internal processes (what psychologists study), but in the context of the social structures and the cultural values that invariably constrain the individual and determine all social action.

THE SOCIAL SYSTEM

Parsons regarded all social units, whether groups, institutions or whole societies as self-contained social systems (1949/1954: 13) or social action systems; each could be studied and analyzed in its own right. Like Durkheim, who underscored the functions of specific social structures (e.g., division of labor, crime, religion), Parsons is regarded as a structural-functionalist, because his core focus was the analysis of the structure of the social system (society) and its subsystems (social institutions and structures), and their functional relevance in maintaining society, social order, or system equilibrium (1951: 21–22).

Society, for Parsons, is an action system "analytically divisible into four primary subsystems" of action (1971: 10). These four subsystems comprise the core institutional structure of modern societies, established to accomplish the economic, political, societal integration, and cultural socialization functions necessary for societies to maintain themselves and adapt to change. These core functions are: (1) adaptation to the environment (e.g., economic production); (2) goal attainment (the political system with its goals of equality and universal rights);

(3) integration, by articulating and enforcing society's collective norms (e.g., the legal system); and (4) latency or pattern maintenance, i.e., transmitting society's generally shared values through socialization (e.g., the family; education) so that the value-orientations of society effectively regulate individual behavior and social action (1971: 10–15).

A functionalist analysis of the education system, for example, would show that in the mid-nineteenth century, high school education was not necessary (or adaptive) to the basic functioning of the economy: industrial and factory production did not need young men and women to have skills beyond basic math and literacy (e.g., Smelser 1959). Moreover, it was working side by side with parents, not high school courses, which socialized children into the work ethic and other norms necessary to being a productive worker. Today, by contrast, college education in science and math is required for the effective functioning of the hi-tech economy, and internships function to socialize students into corporate work habits.

SOCIAL ACTION

Core to Parsons's theory of action was the construct of the unit act. A unit act is comprised, at a minimum, of (a) a social actor (e.g., a person, a family, an occupational group); (b) an end (a goal or objective), a concrete future state of affairs toward which the action is directed; (c) a concrete situation in which the act must be initiated and in which certain social and physical conditions will apply; and (d) a normative (value-)orientation which regulates the relationship between these elements (1937: 43–45). In other words, in a given situation or context, social actors choose (among culturally bounded) goals and the (culturally and structurally available) means toward achieving those goals.

The conditions of the situation (e.g., social class) determine some of the social actor's options. But, Parsons emphasized, the social actor has freedom to choose among various goals and means. Hence, Parsons called his a theory of voluntaristic action (1937: 11); choices are voluntary rather than coerced. This freedom, nonetheless, is always culturally bounded; social action is, and must necessarily be, restrained by the societal norms and values that predominate in a given socio-historical context (1937: 75). For example, while Americans have a lot of freedom regarding occupational choices, their choices are ultimately constrained by the strong cultural expectation that individuals will be self-reliant in adulthood, and not dependent on parents or on the state for economic support. Similarly, some Muslim women in France who have sex before marriage make choices that are influenced by French cultural norms (i.e., that sex before marriage is acceptable). And, by the same token, when some of these women subsequently choose to have restorative surgery to demonstrate that they are virgins to their future Muslim husbands (and their families), this action is also culturally constrained – by the social and gender expectations in Muslim communities (see chapter 3, Topic 3.1).

Having read Weber (chapter 3), you may find the thesis that values matter in shaping social action is not surprising. What is noteworthy in Parsons's argument, however, is his emphasis on the essential systemic and structural importance of a normative orientation to action. Parsons insists that all social action is contingent on a normative or values orientation. Weber concluded *The Protestant Ethic* (1904–1905) with the assertion that in modern society values were becoming less salient in motivating social action, being displaced by the increasing domination of instrumental rational action. Yet, writing in 1937, Parsons was very clear that by contrast with the social disorder that would likely result if social actors were to follow utilitarian or instrumental ends, all social action is produced by, and needs to be regulated by, a normative orientation. When utilitarianism (or instrumental rationality) dominates social action, he argues, there is a "precariousness of order" (1937: 95), an argument that clearly echoes Durkheim's emphasis on the instability of purely contractual social ties (chapter 2). Parsons states: "A purely utilitarian society is chaotic and unstable, because in the absence of limitations on the use of means, particularly force and fraud, it must ... resolve itself into an unlimited struggle for power; and in the struggle for the immediate end, power, all prospect of attainment of the ultimate [end, social order,] is irreparably lost" (1937: 93–94).

For Parsons, a consensual value-orientation necessarily imposes a discipline on conduct; it restrains people's immediate "satisfaction of the appetites, the pursuit of wealth and power" (1937: 284–285). The cultural system, specifically, "a common value system, manifested in the legitimacy of institutional norms" (1937: 768), is seen by him as being so central to societal order that he defines the study of this domain of social action as the core of sociology: sociology is the "science which attempts to develop an analytical theory of social action in so far as these systems can be understood in terms of the property of common-value integration" (1937: 768). Thus, for Parsons, culture has a causal role (along with social structures) in social action. Today, the sociology of culture is a vibrant area of inquiry, and although it has moved beyond Parsons's emphasis on consensual values to instead focus on the varied cultural scripts and cultural repertoires that produce social action (e.g., Swidler 2001), its development, nonetheless, owes much to the earlier theorizing of Parsons (and Weber).[1]

SOCIALIZATION AND SOCIETAL INTEGRATION

For Parsons (1951), social action emerges from the interdependence of social, cultural, and personality systems. It is the outcome of the interaction of a plurality of social actors whose expectations and behavior are oriented to a situation and for which there is "a commonly understood system of cultural symbols" (1951: 5).

As Parsons emphasized, "even the most elementary communication is not possible without some degree of conformity to the 'conventions' of the symbolic system" (1951: 11). It is through the socialization of the individual personality that culture – symbols, meanings, norms, and expectations held in common – is transmitted, learned and shared (1951: 13). Socialization into the norms and behavior required across the varied social roles and relationships in which the individual participates is thus a core functional requirement of society:

> Since a social system is a system of processes of interaction between actors, it is the structure of the relations between the actors ... involved in the interactive process which is essentially the structure of the social system. The system is a network of such relationships ... Without the requisite cultural resources to be assimilated through internalization it is not possible for a human level of personality to emerge and hence for a human type of social system to develop. (1951: 25, 34)

Socialization is necessary because individuals have to be adequately motivated to fulfill the functional requirements of the social system; individual needs must be more or less in synchrony with the functional needs of the social system. Using Parsons's language, we can say that in America, for example, the smooth functioning of the economy (economic subsystem) requires and rewards (through the stratification sub-system) well-trained (educated) and "goal-directed" individuals with the analytical skills to be productive in today's economy, and hence requires that children be socialized into developing both the good work habits necessary (for educational and economic success) and the desire or motivation for achievement (e.g., Parsons 1949/1954: 72). If there is too much slippage between the social system's requirements and individual desires, this produces strain and tension in the social system which can result in dysfunctional consequences (e.g., high school drop-out rates which in turn impact the economy, the socialization of the next generation, etc.). The social system relies on mechanisms of social control (e.g., laws mandating school attendance and levels of performance) as a way to ensure that tendencies toward deviant behavior can be regulated to the extent that deviance does not result in producing dysfunctional consequences (1951: 35). The objective, in short, is to integrate the social, personality-motivational, and cultural elements so that "they are brought together in an ordered system" (1951: 36).

VALUES CONSENSUS

The idea that a common value system is necessary to society may strike many of us today as archaic and even insulting. This criticism, indeed, was leveled at Parsons back in the 1960s and 1970s, a time when American and western society was becoming aware of the multiculturalism and values diversity in its midst. Grassroots protesters, many of them college students, rallied against "The Establishment" and its presumption of a unitary values consensus. The social protest movements of that era – advocating women's rights, civil rights, and gay rights – directly challenged the values and institutional practices of the (white male) Establishment in everyday life, and especially targeted the government, the military, the churches, and universities for their inattentiveness to social inequality.

Understandably, Parsons's theorizing was seen as socially conservative. If institutions must necessarily maintain the particular norms already in place, how is social change possible? How can change occur when the newly proposed norms – e.g., greater equality for women and minority racial groups – are at odds with the norms already institutionalized? Of course, as Parsons repeatedly emphasized, he was concerned with providing a generalized theory of society, not an analysis of any one particular societal context. This abstract intellectual preoccupation, however, reinforced the perception that Parsons simply favored the status quo, a perception further fueled by his thesis that religion provides an integrating value system.

SOCIAL DIFFERENTIATION, CULTURE, AND THE SECULARIZATION OF PROTESTANTISM

Following Weber (cf. chapter 3), Parsons argued that religion is a significant cultural determinant of social action. He also argued that just as modern society evolves, and becomes more complex in its structure and institutions (and has a more differentiated division of labor, as elaborated by Durkheim; cf. chapter 2), so too does religion. With industrialization, social institutions – e.g., the economy, the family, religion, the legal system – become more differentiated both internally and with respect to one another; they become more specialized in the societal functions they perform. This thesis was empirically demonstrated by Parsons's student and collaborator Neil Smelser (1959), who studied the impact of the industrial revolution on family and social change.

Smelser shows, for example, that the shift from the domestic hand-loom to cotton factories, and the subsequent reduction (in the 1830s) in the number of hours that children worked compared to their parents, changed the structure both of the economy and of family functions and relationships, among other things. As children's labor became separated (or differentiated) from that of their parents, new forms of social organization emerged in order to perform the functions previously carried out by the family in its fusion of economic and other functions. Structural differentiation emerged in part as a result of the need to "redefine the [non-economic] family functions (education, recreation, moral training, etc.) ... which had been performed hitherto *on the factory premises* [and] were now moved outside the factory" (Smelser 1959: 307). Hence the establishment of schools to perform the education and training functions previously performed by the family, and further, the differentiation of education from religion, which assumed its own specialized domain of religious/moral training (Smelser 1959: 402–408).

Religion, therefore, is differentiated from other social institutions and has its own (relatively narrow) functional specialization (e.g., worship, religious practices). This general process of functional differentiation and specialization is, for Parsons and Smelser, critical to the evolution and modernization of society; illustrated, for example, in the separation of church and state in the US, each with its own autonomous functions. Secularization, understood in terms of the increased institutional differentiation of society, does not, however, mean the disappearance of religion as a normative or cultural system. It means, rather, that while the church has (allegedly) a narrower and more specific function in individual lives, Christianity as a value system (in the US) exerts leverage on the society as whole: it provides the value system underlying social action across all institutional spheres. Parsons argues: "A true differentiation always involves at the same time an allegiance to common values and norms. In terms of the ultimate trusteeship of these values, the church is the higher authority" (1967: 396). And in the American and western context, largely as a result of the links between Protestantism and capitalism (discussed by Weber; see chapter 3), it is specifically Protestantism that provides the common cultural reference point. Parsons called this the Christianizing of secular society – the extension of the idea of the calling and of individual responsibility beyond religious salvation (cf. Weber; see chapter 3) and into every aspect of secular society.

Institutional differentiation and specialization characterize modern society. The tasks of economic productivity and values transmission have their own particular spaces; corporate offices and churches amicably co-exist side by side.

RELIGION AS SOURCE OF CULTURAL INTEGRATION

In the modern world, Parsons argues, there are two layers of religious commitment. One is the individual's denominational membership. In the context of Christianity, this refers to the post-Reformation differentiation between Protestantism and Catholicism, and within Protestantism between denominations (e.g., Presbyterians, Southern Baptists, etc.). In line with secularization processes, Parsons saw denominational attachment per se becoming less significant as societies progressively modernize (see below, pp. 168–169).

The second layer, for Parsons, is more crucial for social integration. This refers to the way in which religion provides

a common matrix of value-commitment [values] ... broadly shared between denominations, and which forms the basis of the sense in which the society as a whole forms a religiously based moral community. This has, in the American case, been extended to cover a very wide range. Its core certainly lies in the institutionalized Protestant denominations, but with certain strains and only partial institutionalizations, it extends to ... the Catholic Church, the various branches of Judaism, and not least important, those who prefer to remain aloof from any formal denominational affiliation. To deny that this underlying consensus exists would be to claim that American society stood in a state of latent religious war. Of the fact that there are considerable tensions every responsible student of the situation is aware. Institutionalization is incomplete, but the consensus is very much of a reality. (1967: 414)

Religion, therefore, notwithstanding its institutional differentiation from other spheres (e.g., political, economic, legal), its narrower role in individuals' lives – and we should add, its frequent role in driving social conflict rather than consensus – can nonetheless be described as being functionally necessary "to the maintenance of the main patterns of the society" (1967: 418). In other words, it provides the core underlying values that orient action across all spheres of society. These values include individualism, achievement, and pluralism or respect for difference (derived from denominationalism, i.e., religious group differentiation), a functional pluralism or differentiation evident in the differentiation across social institutions.

VALUE-ORIENTATIONS IN A TIME OF GLOBAL SOCIAL CHANGE

Parsons argues that precisely because of the complex technical and moral problems that confront modern society, there is all the more need of values, of "moral orientations toward the problems of life in this world" (1967: 420). He was careful to note, however, that Christianity as a religion per se was not necessarily the answer to contemporary problems. Moreover, he presciently commented on the emergence of what we would today call globalization (a topic I discuss in chapter 15), and notably too, its cultural divisions: "For the first time in history something approaching a world society is in process of emerging. For the first time in its history Christianity is now involved in a deep confrontation with the major religious traditions of the Orient" (1967: 420–421).

Parsons did not greet this new historical situation with dismay but as an opportunity for the further adaptation of religion and of other societal structures. He argued:

any relative success in the institutionalization of Christian values cannot be taken as final, but rather as a point of departure for new religious stock-taking ... We are deeply committed to our own great traditions. These have tended to emphasize the exclusive possession of the truth. Yet we have also institutionalized the values of tolerance and equality of rights for all. (1967: 421)

Thus, Parsons concluded that just as Christianity had adapted historically to changes in the evolving structure of society, it could also adapt to new societal challenges and draw on its values of tolerance to embrace the increasing religious and cultural pluralism of society. In this, we see a hint that Parsons is both less parochial and more open to the adaptive requirements of societal change than some of his critics acknowledge.

PATTERN VARIABLES

In emphasizing the centrality of institutionalized norms and values in social action, Parsons argued that there are many different kinds of value-orientation patterns and systems of patterns and "many different ways in which role-expectations may be structured relative to them" (1951: 43). He proposed a set of five dichotomous value-orientations which shape social behavior and in terms of which it can be analyzed. What is helpful about this schema is that we can apply it anywhere social action occurs – to characterize whole societies or the structures within a given society (or across several societies). Parsons called his schema of contrasting value-orientations or normative orientations pattern variables. Unlike earlier models of society (e.g., Durkheim's distinction between mechanical and organic solidarity; see chapter 2), Parsons's schema, by using five categories rather than just one, offers a more precise and detailed, multi-dimensional way of analyzing, and comparing across, societies and social structures. This means that as Parsons emphasized, we can be attentive to the ways in which different combinations of elements or normative orientations charac-terize social processes.

THE DOCTOR–PATIENT RELATIONSHIP

We can see the application of Parsons's patterns variables (and their possible multiple combinations) in how, for example, a society's occupational system is structured (1949/1954: 34–37). Parsons himself, in fact, focused on the medical system and the doctor–patient relationship to illustrate "the major structural outlines of the social system" (1951: 428). And, in support of his insistence that both theory and data are necessary to the development of sociology, his theoretical analysis of the medical system derived in part from time he had spent earlier in his career doing fieldwork in Boston area hospitals (1951: 428, n2).

Accordingly, his analysis of the medical system, though still fairly abstract, is empirically informed.

Parsons defines illness as a "state of disturbance in the 'normal' functioning of the total human individual," and medical practice as a "mechanism in the social system for coping with the illnesses of its members" (1951: 431–432). When people get sick, their functional contribution to the family, at work, and to society as a whole is diminished; i.e., they are not fully functioning. Society, therefore, needs to ensure that illness does not threaten the functioning of society and its subsystems. Straightaway, therefore, Parsons makes us think of health, illness, and medicine as systemic phenomena. In other words, health and medicine are social phenomena, and how we deal with them is not based on an individual's ad hoc, idiosyncratic ideas but is institutionalized as a system of social action. There are patterned or institutionalized ways in which the medical system works, in how sick people behave, and in how doctors and patients behave toward one another. And there are similarly institutionalized, patterned ways characterizing how society and all of its subsystems (the economy, the family, the university, etc.) function.

The doctor–patient relationship (and any professional relationship, including the professor–student one), in contrast, for example, to the parent–child relationship, is based on universalistic criteria. This means what whereas a mother responds to her child based on a very particularistic and personal sense of who the child is (my very special son or daughter), the doctor treats her patient in ways that are guided by objective, impersonal criteria applicable to all the patients she sees (1951: 438). The doctor uses a process of technical (medical) judgment and classification about sickness and treatment that extends beyond the symptoms of any particular individual to encompass ailments and patients in general. The code of ethics of the American Medical Association (or of any professional association) institutionalizes these universal criteria, i.e., the judgment and classificatory criteria that all doctors should use in treating all patients.

> **Box 4.1** Parsons's five sets of patterned value-orientations (pattern variables)
>
> - Universalistic versus Particularistic
> - Specificity versus Diffuseness
> - Achievement versus Ascription
> - Neutrality versus Affectivity
> - Self versus Collectivity

Doctors and patients have very specific functions vis-à-vis one another; their role expectations and domains of interaction are well defined and they relate to one another in very specific ways. We go to the doctor because we have a specific ailment. We do not go to the doctor to seek financial or gardening advice, or to get advice about whether we should split up with a boyfriend. By the same token, the doctor is not expected to ask the patient about these aspects of the patient's life, and can ethically do so only insofar as this information might cast some light on the patient's health (e.g., stress, allergies, partner violence). In contrast, our family and friend relationships generally have a diffuse orientation. We talk about all sorts of things and the expectations of reciprocity are much broader and more encompassing than in a professional or business setting;

when you borrow money from your mother, there may be a lot of vagueness about when she expects you to pay her back or whether in fact she even expects repayment; she may expect other things (visits home over spring break, or a promise to do something – get good grades in school?). The boundaries defining expectations and behavior are much more narrowly and clearly drawn in the public world of occupational relationships than in the private sphere of family and friendship.

Similarly, related to the doctor's specific expertise is the very specific training that she or he has received to ensure proficiency in treating patients. The doctor's professional status is achieved rather than ascribed (or inherited); doctors have to pass several examinations and demonstrate competence to perform the role of doctor. The professional role of doctor cannot simply be claimed as a person's birthright regardless of his or her medical training and expertise. On the other hand, family social roles are ascribed. We inherit particular (socially institutionalized) sex (and racial) statuses upon birth: a social inheritance that largely circumscribes the individual's status – the "institutionally defined position of an individual in the social structure" (Parsons 1949/1954: 76) – and hence his or her social experiences, life-chances, and outcomes. Thus regardless of achieved competence, women and men are expected in many quarters still today, by virtue of their ascribed sex, to do (and only do) certain things, a point underscored by the male heckler who commanded Hillary Clinton in the 2008 presidential campaign to "Iron my shirt."

NEWS 4.1

Additionally, the smooth functioning of professional roles and relationships requires emotional neutrality rather than affectivity or emotional engagement. The doctor is expected to behave as "an applied scientist," to "treat an objective problem in objective, scientifically justifiable terms," irrespective of whether or not she or he likes the patient (1951: 435). By contrast, the parent–child relationship is built on and maintained by affective or emotional ties. Thus, medical doctors typically avoid performing the role of doctor in their own family; close emotional ties would likely impair the doctor's medical judgment, and the consequences of misdiagnosis would not only be detrimental to the patient but dysfunctional for society's subsystems (e.g., his or her role functioning in the family, at work, etc.).

Finally, Parsons argues that professional roles are structured such that the doctor, for example, is expected to put the welfare of the patient before his or her own welfare. This altruistic prioritization of others – a collectivity orientation – contrasts with the self-orientation of the business person, who is expected to advance personal interests over other considerations. In short, the institutional and cultural (normative) expectation is for business executives to be motivated by profit motives, but not so the physician (1951: 435), or for that matter, family members.

CHANGE IN THE MEDICAL SYSTEM

Following Parsons's emphasis that pattern variables are useful in assessing social change, let us consider the extent to which the present-day doctor–patient relationship demonstrates the norms Parsons outlined. Medicine has certainly changed since the 1950s (e.g., Starr 1982). Indeed, Parsons recognized its emerging transformation already in the late 1940s, noting that "an increasing proportion of medical practice is now taking place in the context of organization" (1951: 436). He argued that this was primarily "necessitated by the technological development of medicine itself" (ibid.), making it difficult for doctors to practice without access to a medical-technological complex.

Hence, today, the traditional practice of the local family doctor making home visits to patients (whom he or she personally knows) is no longer adaptive to the changes that have occurred in society. The increased technological sophistication of medicine in the diagnosis, treatment and tracking of patients has contributed to the development of HMOs, health maintenance organizations. HMOs are bureaucratic organizations characterized by impersonality, a hierarchical division of specialized expertise, efficiency (including economic efficiency as determined by the HMO's medical insurance professionals rather than its doctors), and routines and other features common to bureaucracies (as outlined by Weber; cf. chapter 3). This organizational shift fundamentally alters the structure of the doctor–patient relationship, i.e., the value-orientations determining the behavior of both patients and doctors. Despite the "sacred bond" many of us may have with our doctor, the doctor–patient relationship is shifting more toward self-interested (business-like) considerations – as we see with dermatologists who have separate waiting rooms and shorter appointment delays for their (higher-paying) cosmetic patients than for their skin-cancer patients.

NEWS 4.2

NEWS 4.3

The economic corporatization of medicine

This is a much changed social reality. Although Parsons, a non-Marxist, noted that many Marxist-oriented critics focused on the economic exploitation and other "evils of our capitalistic society," he argued that, indicatively of the professional esteem enjoyed by physicians, such criticism "tends to spare the physician. The American Medical Association tends to be attacked, but in general not the ideal-typical physician. This is significant of the general public reputation for collectivity-orientation of the medical profession" (1951: 445, n7).

Parsons would find evidence in contemporary American society that might lead him to revise his conceptualization of the altruism of the medical profession. Today, medicine, and the medical profession, are increasingly intertwined with economic corporate interests (see Topic 4.1). From a functionalist perspective, this might be explained as a necessary adaptation by medical doctors and hospitals to the high financial costs imposed on the practice of medicine as a result of technological-organizational change and the general increase in the competitive character of the health-care sector. The intermixing of medicine and corporate finance, whatever adaptive functions it may serve, also threatens the professional status of the medicine being delivered. It raises questions as to whether the medical diagnosis and treatment are influenced by the doctor's or hospital's economic ties, rather than by the altruism and impartiality necessary to ensure effectively functioning doctor–patient relationships (and by extension, a smoothly functioning society).

Topic 4.1 Blurring the lines between medical diagnoses and economic profit

One indicator of the increasing commercialization of medicine is the trend whereby hospitals pay professional sports teams for the status of being designated as the team's doctors or hospital. Seeking to capitalize on the promotional advantage of being affiliated with a sports franchise, some hospitals pay teams as much as $1.5 million annually for the right to treat their high-salaried players. In addition to the revenue, sports franchises get the services of the provider's physicians either without charge or at severely discounted rates. In return, the medical groups and the hospital are granted the exclusive right to market themselves as the team's official hospital, HMO, or orthopedic group. Among those who have million-dollar team–hospital contracts are the New York Mets – New York University Hospital for Joint Diseases; the Boston Celtics – New England Baptist Hospital; and the Houston Astros – Texas Methodist Hospital. Hospitals and medical groups are not just teaming up with professional sports franchises. Manufacturing companies are sponsoring medical services. For example, Clinique, the global cosmetics company, made a $4.75-million donation to the Weil Medical College of Cornell University (Manhattan, New York) to finance a new "Clinique Skin Wellness Center," which includes examination rooms where doctors conduct skin examinations, focused on educating patients in how to prevent skin cancer and maintain skin health. Not coincidentally, patients at the Center may also make "on-site appointments with Clinique representatives to learn about makeup that can cover skin redness or facial scars." Further evidence of the blurring of the lines between medicine and industry is the increasing trend of doctors investing in medical companies, highlighted in particular by the close ties between doctors and the rapidly expanding spinal implants sector. Coinciding with an increase in spinal fusion surgery (a highly lucrative area in medicine), there is a growing trend of doctors investing in the stock of companies that produce the highly profitable screws and other hardware that are part of the spinal fusion surgery that many doctors recommend as a remedy for patients' back pain (despite evidence that spinal surgery may not be effective).

NEWS 4.4

NEWS 4.5

NEWS 4.6

MODERNIZATION THEORY

These examples pointing to the shift in the commercialization of the doctor–patient relationship illustrate the analytical usefulness of Parsons's pattern variables in describing, and identifying changes in, institutions and social processes. Parsons also used his pattern variables to conceptualize the analytical characteristics of modern society, outlining what sociologists refer to as modernization theory.

Taking the US as the "lead society" in the latest phase of modernization (1971: 114), Parsons argued that the system of modern societies is characterized by its positioning along each of the five pattern variables. In Parsons's analysis, the US and other societies with a high degree of modernization, i.e., societies that have undergone democratization, industrialization, and the expansion of education and literacy (see also Smelser 1959, and Smelser 1968: 125–146), can be described as favoring or institutionalizing in their societal structures the following norms:

1 Criteria of achievement over ascription. Modern societies are democratic rather than aristocratic or monarchic, and hence political, occupational, and social status is achieved rather than inherited or ascribed at birth. Modern societies are stratified societies, but the system of stratification is based on differential rankings based on achieved competence and merit rather than characteristics and outcomes ascribed on the basis of family or ethnicity.

2 Universalistic over particularistic criteria. Modern societies are pluralistic and diverse and no one group in society is favored. Instead, individuals are socialized into being citizens of the nation rather than primarily associating with a particularistic ethnic, tribal, social class, or religious community. Societal structures and values affirm generalized rather than particularistic values; e.g., laws and public policies respect religion in general rather than a particularistic, denominational affiliation.

3 Specific over diffuse criteria. Modern societies require individuals to master certain bodies of basic knowledge and the ability to specialize in specific competencies. The occupational structure requires specific qualifications; in modern politics, there is a tendency toward role specialization rather than the diffuse obligations associated with traditional patronage. Additionally, the system of stratification in modern society is, in principle, according to Parsons, based on the acquisition of specific competencies; e.g., because of the specific "competence gap" between doctors and patients, for example, there is a social status differential between them. By the same token, inequality based on membership of a diffuse group (e.g., a racial, ethnic, gender, or religious group) would be a vestige of a less modernized or more traditional society (1971: 110).

4 Emotional neutrality over affectivity. In modern societies, there is a differentiation between public (e.g., work occupations) and private (e.g., family) spheres and their respective normative orientations to emotion. Unlike in traditional societies, where family and work tasks commingle (e.g., "the family farm"), modern societies maintain a clear functional separation between work (the factory, the office) and family (the home). The public sphere is based on an emotionally neutral instrumentality (expressed in the execution of specific functions) whereas the private sphere is oriented by expressivity and emotion (in dealing with family relational diffuseness).

5 Modern societies are characterized by self-orientation rather than collective or other-orientation. Individuals are expected to follow their desires in choosing an occupation, a marriage partner, etc., unlike in more traditional societies, where family, ethnicity, and religious affiliation would constrain certain

choices. "Following in father's footsteps" is the hallmark of occupational histories in traditional societies (e.g., Hout 1989), whereas in modern societies, the individual is free to be an entrepreneurial trail-blazer. Individual self-determination is reflected in the stratification system. With status achieved as a result of individual choices rather than family ascription, some individuals experience upward mobility, and others downward mobility, relative to the socio-economic status of their family of origin.

AMERICAN SOCIETY AS THE PROTOTYPE OF MODERNIZATION

Parsons maintained that American society, as the most developed and advanced modern society, is characterized by the orientations listed above; i.e., its generalized value-orientations are achievement, universalism, specificity, emotional neutrality, and self-orientation. In particular, it has ensured its economic and social progress by embracing generalized values of achievement; "American society has gone farther than any comparable large-scale society in its dissociation from the older ascriptive inequalities and the institutionalization of a basically egalitarian pattern" (1971: 114). This imperative, according to Parsons, must permeate the whole modern and modernizing system (not just the US).

Parsons's modernization theory stimulated a large body of macro-societal empirical research, as sociologists including his student Neil Smelser (1968) and other scholars (e.g., Black 1966; Gerschenkron 1962; Inkeles and Smith 1974) investigated the extent to which various societies could be described as modernized, modernizing, or economically and culturally "backward." Many neo-Marxist critics (e.g., Gunder Frank 1967; Cardoso and Faletto 1979) contended that modernization theory was essentially ethnocentric because of its presumption of American society as the prototype and any societal deviations from it as inferior. Parsons's conceptualization, these scholars pointed out, ignored the different histories (e.g., of colonialism) and political cultures of different countries, and the impact of these differences on how different societies modernize or evolve over time (see chapter 6). Notwithstanding the validity of these criticisms, modernization research provided a richly informative series of country case studies that illuminated the diverse social processes within, and differences among, countries. These studies (inadvertently) highlighted the process of uneven modernization, i.e., variation in a country's simultaneous embrace of economic, social, and cultural change, and the societal conditions in which they overcome cultural lag, i.e., the gap between their achieved economic modernization and the persistent vestiges of cultural traditionalism (e.g., Ireland in the 1970s and 1980s; Dillon 1993).

STRATIFICATION AND INEQUALITY

Parsons's modernization theory was also criticized for its inattentiveness to the unevenness of modernization *within* American society. In particular, the ongoing

169

gender and racial inequality in America challenged his argument that individual achievement, rather than the status inherited (or ascribed) at birth on the basis of sex and race, characterizes modern society. Parsons acknowledged these sources of societal strain, but nonetheless argued that "equality of opportunity" and the ethos of "accountability" (performance) institutionalized in American society meant that social status "cannot be determined primarily by birth or membership in kinship units" (1971: 118; 1949/1954: 79). Parsons regarded status differentials – individual differences in income and occupational prestige – as functionally necessary to reward individuals for their comparatively greater technical/professional achievement and competence in contributing to the specialized functioning of society (1949/1954: 83–84) (a thesis further explicated by Davis and Moore (1945), who elaborate a functionalist explanation of social inequality). But, Parsons contended, these status differentials derived largely from individual achievement within the occupational system rather than from any ascribed privilege (notwithstanding inherited wealth): "We determine status very largely on the basis of achievement within an occupational system which is in turn organized primarily in terms of criteria of performance and status within functionally specialized fields" (1949/1954: 78–79).

In line with his systems perspective on society, Parsons maintained that the occupational system, which is crucial to the functional imperatives of the economy (adaptation), necessarily "coexists in our society with a strong institutional emphasis on membership in kinship [family] units" (1949/1954: 79), one befitting the family's socialization function (pattern maintenance). The functioning of, and the maintenance of solidarity within, the family system is based on emotion, relationship quality, particularism, diffuseness, and collective orientation. These orientations are, however, incompatible with the achievement and other normative orientations of the occupational system. The societal strain that could emerge from this incompatibility is partially resolved by the institutionalization of children's role in society: "Dependent children are not involved in competition for status in the occupational system, and hence their achievements or lack of them are not likely to be of primary importance to the status of the family group as a whole" (1949/1954: 79).

FUNCTIONALISM OF SEX ROLES

But what about the strain on society that would come from status competition between parents? Parsons argued that strain is avoided by having a clear sex-role separation, whereby men compete in the occupational structure and women occupy the home-based roles of wife and mother. He explained:

> If both [parents] were equally in competition for occupational status, there might indeed be a very serious strain on the solidarity of the family unit, for there is no general reason why they would be likely to come out very nearly equally, while, in their capacity of husband and wife, it is very important that they should be treated as equals. One mechanism

which can serve to prevent the kind of "invidious comparison" between husband and wife which might be disruptive of family solidarity is a clear separation of the sex roles such as to insure that they do not come into competition with each other. (1949/1954: 79–80)

Aware that even in the 1940s (when he first published this essay), many married women were working outside the home, Parsons observed nonetheless that it is "for the great majority, in occupations which are not in direct competition for status with men of their own class" (ibid.: 80).

Moreover, Parsons claimed:

Women's interests and the standards of judgment applied to them, run in our society, far more in the direction of personal adornment and the related qualities of personal charm than is the case with men. Men's dress is practically a uniform ... This serves to concentrate the judgment and valuation of men on their occupational achievements, while the valuation of women is diverted into realms outside the occupationally relevant sphere. (1949/1954: 80)

In short, for Parsons, sex-role segregation is functionally necessary to maintaining societal equilibrium; clearly defined sex-role boundaries, norms, and expectations maintain social order and avoid the dysfunctional consequences that would arise from status competition between women and men.

Not surprisingly, Parsons's sex-role thesis came to be viewed with skepticism by the emerging women's movement – Betty Friedan's best-selling book *The Feminine Mystique*, published in 1963, ignited public debate about the alleged emptiness of the lives of stay-at-home wives and mothers. Although Parsons's theoretical interest was in explaining how various social structures (e.g., gender roles, occupations) function to maintain a particular social order, his sex-role theory was seen as undermining women's equality and stalling the fledgling efforts to grant women greater equality in the public sphere (of work, mass media, and politics) as well as in the home. Parsons further annoyed advocates of women's equality with his claim that because sex role segregation is structurally crucial to the effective functioning of society, "the feminist movement has had such difficulty in breaking it down" (1949/1954: 80).

Time, of course, would prove Parsons partially wrong. Sex-role segregation is, at least officially and legally, largely a thing of the past in the US and in other western societies. Nevertheless, in line with his theoretical emphasis on the relative resistance of social systems and institutionalized patterns notwithstanding the efforts to change them (e.g., the women's movement), there are still many structural and cultural obstacles impeding women's full equality with men. Moreover, as Parsons anticipated, the blurring of sex-role boundaries has given rise to certain "disequilibrating" effects: a cultural backlash against working mothers (Jacobs and Gerson 2004) and against women who seek to enter previously male-dominated arenas (e.g., Faludi 1991); and the over-burdening of women more than men with the logistical (e.g., time-management) and emotional challenges associated with maintaining both career and parenting/family aspirations

171

(e.g., Bianchi et al. 2006; Jacobs and Gerson 2004). We will explore sociological theorizing on gender equality in chapter 10.

ROBERT MERTON'S MIDDLE-RANGE THEORY

Among a core group of influential sociologists who studied and worked closely with Parsons, **Robert Merton** (1910–2003) most forcefully argued against the generalized theorizing Parsons favored. Merton instead emphasized the value of what he called middle-range theory. He carefully explained:

> sociological theory refers to logically interconnected conceptions which are limited and modest in scope, rather than all embracing and grandiose [or "grand"] ... I focus attention on what might be called theories of the middle range: theories intermediate to the minor working hypotheses evolved in abundance during the day-to-day routines of research, and the all-inclusive speculations comprising a master conceptual scheme from which it is hoped to derive a very large number of empirically observed uniformities of social behavior. (1949: 5)

Middle-range theories are those that are closely tied in to the empirical realities in societies, articulating the relationships that exist among particular variables, as exemplified by Weber's *Protestant Ethic* and Durkheim's *Suicide* (Merton 1968: 63).

BIOGRAPHICAL NOTE

Robert Merton was born in 1910, in Philadelphia, to a working-class Jewish immigrant family. From childhood he was a voracious reader; after graduating from Temple University he won a scholarship to Harvard, where he studied under Parsons. Merton spent most of his career at Columbia University (New York), where he collaborated with Paul Lazarsfeld in pioneering studies of mass media and public opinion. Merton is most renowned for middle-range theory and extensive contributions to the sociology of deviance and the sociology of science. He was active in national and international professional associations, and, like Parsons, served as president of the American Sociological Association (1956–1957). He died in 2003 at age 92.

Like Parsons, Merton emphasized the interrelation between theory and data, but he rejected Parsons's presumption that data had to be fitted into a general theoretical system applicable to all societies and which would explain all inter-societal structures and subsystems. Instead, Merton emphasized that the main task should be the development of "social theories applicable to limited ranges of data – theories for example, of class dynamics, of conflicting group pressures, of the flow of power and the exercise of interpersonal influence – rather than to seek at once the 'integrated' conceptual structure adequate to derive all these and other theories" (1949: 9). In this endeavor, moreover, Merton emphasized that empirical research does not simply test pre-established hypotheses – it "also initiates, reformulates, re-focuses (or deflects), and clarifies the theories and conceptions of sociology" (1949: 12, 98). For Merton, therefore, theory and data impact each other in a reciprocal way rather than theory requiring, but ultimately having primacy over, data, as Parsons envisaged.

MANIFEST AND LATENT FUNCTIONS

Showing his intellectual debt to Parsons, nonetheless, Merton too emphasized a functional analysis of society, one that depended on the interplay of theory, method, and research data (1949: 21). He maintained, moreover, that "the clues to the imputed functions [of a given societal pattern – conspicuous consumption, for example,] are provided almost wholly by the description of the pattern itself" (1949: 56–58). He distinguished between two types of functions: manifest functions, "those objective consequences contributing to the adjustment or adaptation of the system which are intended and recognized by participants in the system," and latent functions, those objective consequences which "are neither intended nor recognized" (1949: 51).

In Merton's framing (and following Durkheim; cf. chapter 2), the punishment of crime, for example, has both manifest and latent functions; the manifest function of sending a criminal to prison is to punish the criminal for his wrong-doing, and its latent function is the affirmation of the behavioral norms institutionalized for the community as a whole (Merton 1949: 62). Similarly, knowledge of Latin as a requirement for admission to Yale until the 1930s can be seen as having the manifest function of demonstrating the university's aspiration to emulate the classical model of education valued historically in Britain (and seen as essential to the intellectual and character building of leaders who would maintain the imperial power of the British Empire). However, given the fact that Latin was not taught in most public schools but was taught in elite private (preparatory) schools populated by children (boys) from the upper class (see Karabel 2005: 22–23, 47, 52), the latent function of this policy was to maintain the exclusive, elite character of Yale.

In short, structures and functions mutually impact one another. And the discovery of latent functions, Merton argued, represents important advances in sociological knowledge (1949: 68), in part because such discoveries typically highlight the interdependence of the various elements of a given social structure (1949: 53), and the interdependence of various structures in society (e.g., family, education, and the stratification system).

SOCIAL CONSEQUENCES

All social actions can have multiple consequences, either for the whole society or for just some individuals and sub-groups. Some of these consequences may be unanticipated insofar as they were not intended to occur, and though unintended, can be (a) functional, (b) dysfunctional, or (c) irrelevant in a given societal context (1949: 51).

Topic 4.2 Unintended consequences

Riverside, a run-down factory town in New Jersey, enacted legislation that penalized employers who hired illegal immigrants and the home-owners who rented to them. Within a short interval of time, many of the town's illegal immigrants – mostly from South American countries – had left the area; "The noise, crowding and traffic that had accompanied their arrival over the past decade abated." The law was obviously having its intended effect. However, with the immigrants gone, so too was their business; hairdressers, restaurants, and convenience stores were among the businesses that were quick to experience a notable decline in earnings. Consequently the town rescinded the anti-immigration ordinance; similar laws are being re-evaluated in other towns in the US too as a result of their unintended economic consequences. In New York State, farmers are cutting down acres of decades-old cherry and peach trees because of the shrinking availability of immigrant fruit pickers – one unintended consequence of the farmers' actions is a dampening of the region's agricultural economy; another is a dent in the quality of life of affluent urban consumers who seek fresh, hand-picked produce.

Similarly, if health-insurance reform is introduced in the US to make health insurance more affordable to lower-income Americans, one unintended and dysfunctional consequence of this action will likely be a reduction in the number of military recruits, many of whom are attracted by the army's health insurance benefits.

📰 NEWS 4.7

📰 NEWS 4.8

📰 NEWS 4.9

Dysfunctional consequences, or social strains and tensions in the social system in its existing form (e.g., regarding immigration or health insurance), can, however, have a positive function. As Merton notes, they can be instrumental in leading to changes in that system (1949: 116). Whether and how this occurs are questions for empirical investigation.

STRAIN BETWEEN CULTURE AND SOCIAL STRUCTURE

One of Merton's most significant contributions is his analytical framework explaining the links between social structural and cultural determinants of deviance. Merton showed that deviance is not simply due to an individual's faulty socialization (as a Parsonian analysis would suggest). Rather, Merton argued:

some social structures exert a definite pressure upon certain persons in the society to engage in nonconformist rather than conformist conduct. If we can locate groups primarily subject to such pressures, we should expect to find fairly high rates of deviant behavior in these groups, not because the human beings comprising them are compounded of distinctive biological tendencies but because they are responding normally to the social situations in which they find themselves. (1949: 125–126)

Thus Merton argued, socially deviant behavior, just like conformist behavior, is a product of a given social structure (1949: 115).

Merton distinguished between the goals, purposes, and interests that a given society defines as culturally acceptable, and the acceptable norms and institutionalized means for attaining those goals. Individuals have freedom in choosing the means used to attain desired cultural goals – for example, the money to support the culturally valued goal of a consumer lifestyle can be attained through a variety of means: family inheritance, winning the lottery, working in a financially rewarding occupation, stock market investment, theft, or embezzlement.

Merton's framework highlights the outcomes that are likely when individuals' social structural location prevents them from being able to attain desired cultural goals (e.g., prestige, success). He argues that when a gap or discrepancy exists between the goals affirmed in society and access to the institutional means to attain them – or, we should note, when institutional access is blocked as a result of poverty, racism, sexism, etc. – individuals adapt their behavior, either rejecting the culturally acceptable goals, or rejecting the institutional means for their attainment. These options lead to various socially patterned ways by which individuals respond to the goals – means dilemmas encountered, adaptations which Merton (1949: 140) sketched; see Box 4.2.

Merton's typology thus introduces the conformist, who accepts cultural goals and society's approved means for their attainment; the innovator, who accepts the goals but finds new ways to achieve them; the ritualist, who, though rejecting the culturally sanctioned goals, nonetheless passively goes along with the behavior necessary to achieve those goals; the retreatist, who opts out of both the goals and the goal-behavior; and finally, the rebel, who rejects the cultural goals and the institutionalized means but who substitutes new goals and means of his or her own. The conformist accepts the cultural goal of academic success and conforms to professors' expectations of course-work requirements toward excellence; the innovator accepts the goal of academic success but finds ways to circumvent the professor's assignments by stealing ideas and papers posted on the internet and passing them off as his or her own work; the ritualist rejects academic ambition but dutifully goes along with all of the required course work; the retreatist disavows any interest in

---

Box 4.2 Modes of individual adaptation to societal conditions

Modes of adaptation	Cultural goals	Institutionalized means
I Conformity	+	+
II Innovation	+	–
III Ritualism	–	+
IV Retreatism	–	–
V Rebellion	+/–	+/–

Note: + = acceptance; – = rejection; +/– = rejection of prevailing goals and means and substitution by new goals and means.

academic work and makes no effort to do well in class; the rebel rejects offers of admission from elite colleges and instead goes off to the mountains, spending time perfecting his skiing technique but with no interest in enhancing his status or prestige (culturally acceptable goals) by participating in ski competitions.

Because Merton's typology highlights "individual" adaptation, this may obscure how the access of whole groups in society to the institutional means toward the achievement of cultural goals gets blocked by the larger social structure. For example, inner-city adolescents in the US, like those in the suburbs, accept the cultural goals of economic success and consumption – something highlighted by the popularity of rap songs celebrating consumption (e.g., Kanye West's "Flashing Lights" or Blood Raw/Young Jeezy's "Louie"). But the interrelated effects of poverty and racism on the education provided in some inner-city neighborhoods mean that the relevance of school fades as the appropriate institutional means toward economic success. In such contexts, some inner-city residents (whether innovators or rebels) might turn to (illegal) means (e.g., selling drugs, crime) as a way of acquiring the culturally affirmed consumer lifestyle (e.g., MacLeod 1995: 231). Similarly, the high incidence of drug use among adolescents in isolated, poor rural communities in the US that have limited economic opportunities (VanGundy 2006) might be seen as indicating retreatist behavior; namely, the teenagers' rejection of both the unattainable goals of, and the unattainable means toward, economic success.

Merton's typology is useful, therefore, because it highlights how a functional analysis can be helpful in explaining "social problems," and more generally, in highlighting the conjoint institutional and cultural conditions that can variously produce and predict social deviance. It also illuminates the several possible sources of strain toward deviance (or anomie) that can exist in society, given that so many diverse goals can characterize any individual's social context. Different forms of success – economic, academic, athletic, artistic, military – are given greater affirmation by some families, groups, or communities than by others; and, in addition to success and prestige, society also emphasizes the values of civic duty, loyalty, neighborhood spirit, etc. There are, therefore, many opportunities for discrepancies to arise between cultural goals and the institutionalized means toward achieving them, depending on the individual's social situation.

SUMMARY

The recent revival of interest in Parsons's theory, referred to as neofunctionalism (e.g., Alexander 1985; Moss and Savchenko 2006), stresses the value of the multidimensionality found in Parsons. (*Neo* is Greek for "new," and thus when contemporary theorists revise elements of classical or established theories such as Parsons's functionalism, the revised formulation is referred to with the prefix *neo*). Some neofunctionalists tend to probe the implications of the interaction between different societal spheres (economic, political, cultural), and the micro–macro implications of Parsons's attention to the significance of both personality and culture in producing social action. Other neofunctionalists (e.g., Luhmann 2002) stress the relevance of an abstract, self-contained systems approach to understanding modern society; the idea, for example, that contemporary communication relies on and requires universal as opposed to specific linguistic or symbolic codes across multiple societal subsystems.[2]

We do not have to get too embroiled in the systems analysis Parsons favored in order to appreciate, nonetheless, the theoretical schemas he articulated. In particular, his pattern variables offer an important set of conceptual dimensions that can be used for extensive descriptive and comparative analysis of social processes. The legacy of Parsons's focus on the functioning of the social system (e.g., status rewards, role structures), and of Merton's functionalist analysis, is indirectly apparent, moreover, in the search by contemporary researchers to identify the social mechanisms that help explain differential outcomes in inequality, health, crime, and many other domains. And, of course, both Parsons's and Merton's insistence on the necessary blending of theory and data is the dictum that anchors the practice of sociology today.

POINTS TO REMEMBER

Talcott Parsons:
- Sought to develop a highly abstract, generalizable sociological theory that would be universally applicable
- Adopted a systems approach to society
- Each societal system has four primary subsystems of action
  - Adaptation; e.g., the economy
  - Goal attainment; e.g., politics
  - Integration; e.g., legal/regulatory functions
  - Pattern maintenance or latency; cultural socialization, transmission of values and norms
- Social action voluntaristic; actors choose among various, culturally bounded, goals and means
- Structural functionalism: focus on the functional relevance of societal structures (e.g., occupational structure; stratification) in maintaining system equilibrium or social order
- Pattern variables: patterned value-orientations determining how society and its subsystems function
  - Universalistic – Particularistic
  - Specificity – Diffuseness
  - Achievement – Ascription
  - Neutrality – Affectivity
  - Self – Collective (other) orientation

STRUCTURAL-
FUNCTIONALISM

Robert Merton:

- Middle-range theory: close ties between conceptual hypotheses and empirical realities
- Manifest functions: intended and recognized consequences of a given social phenomenon
- Latent functions: unintended and unrecognized consequences of a given social phenomenon
- Deviance a function of strain between cultural goals and institutionalized means toward their attainment
- Different types of individual adaptation to cultural/institutional strain

GLOSSARY: PARSONS

achievement versus ascription one of Parsons's five patterned value-orientations whereby modern society emphasizes achievement rather than ascriptive (e.g. inherited status) criteria.

adaptation economic function (or institutional subsystem) necessary in all societies and societal sub-units.

Christianizing of secular society the thesis that Christian-derived values (e.g., Protestant individualism, the Golden Rule) would penetrate the everyday culture and non-religious institutional spheres of modern secular society.

cultural lag when societies that experience economic and social modernization experience a delay in adjusting their (traditional) values to accommodate change.

cultural system institutionalized norms, values, motivations, symbols, and beliefs (cultural resources).

functions necessary tasks accomplished by specific social institutions (e.g., family, economy, occupational structure) ensuring the smooth functioning of society.

goal attainment – political function (or institutional subsystem) necessary in all societies and societal sub-units.

grand theory elaborate, highly abstract theory which seeks to have universal application.

integration regulatory function (or institutional subsystem) necessary in all societies (and societal sub-units).

modernization theory the thesis that all societies will inevitably and invariably follow the same linear path of economic (e.g., industrialization), social (e.g., urbanization, education), and cultural (e.g., democracy; self-orientation) progress achieved by American society.

neofunctionalism refers to the approach of contemporary sociologists who embrace Parsons's theoretical perspective but who amend some of its claims.

neutrality versus affectivity one of Parsons's five patterned value-orientations whereby modern societies differentiate between institutional spheres and relationships based on impersonality (e.g., work) rather than emotion (e.g., family).

pattern maintenance (latency); socialization function (or institutional subsystem) necessary in all societies and societal sub-units.

pattern variables Parsons's schema of five separate, dichotomously opposed value-orientations determining social action.

personality system the individual's inculcation of the values and habits necessary to effective functioning in a given society (e.g., ambitious, hardworking, and conscientious personality types favored in the US).

secularization the thesis that religious institutions and religious authority decline with the increased modernization of, and institutional differentiation in, society.

self- versus collectivity orientation one of Parsons's five patterned value-orientations whereby modern society emphasizes individual over communal interests.

social system(s) interconnected networks of institutional subsystems and relationships that comprise society and all of its sub-units.

specificity versus diffuseness one of Parsons's five patterned value-orientations whereby modern society emphasizes role specialization rather than general competence.

status differentials comprise social inequality (stratification); gap in achievement and rewards based on differences in individuals' achieved competence (doctor/patient) and ascribed social roles (male/female).

structural-functionalism term used to refer to the theorizing of Durkheim and Parsons because of their focus on how social structures determine, and are effective in (functional to) maintaining, the social order, society (social equilibrium).

subsystems spheres of social (or institutional) action required for the functioning and maintenance of the social system (society) and its sub-units (institutions, small groups, etc.).

uneven modernization when societies experience modernization more quickly in one sphere of society (e.g., the economy) than in another (e.g., education; developing the educated workforce necessary to the changed economy).

unit act analytically, the core of social action; comprised of a social actor, a goal, specific circumstances, and a normative or value orientation.

universalistic versus particularistic one of Parsons's five patterned value-orientations whereby modern society emphasizes impersonal rules and general principles rather than personal relationships.

value system shared value-orientation (culture) that functions to maintain societal cohesion/integration.

voluntaristic action the thesis that social actors are free to choose among culturally constrained goals and the means to accomplish those goals.

GLOSSARY: MERTON

conformist individual who accepts cultural goals and institutionalized means toward their achievement.

cultural goals objectives and values affirmed in a given society; e.g., economic success.

deviance the result of discrepancies between society's culturally approved goals and the institutional means toward their realization.

functional analysis the combination of theory, method, and data to provide a detailed account of a given social phenomenon such that the description illuminates the phenomenon's particular social functions.

innovator individual who accepts cultural goals but substitutes new means toward their attainment.

institutionalized means approved practices in society toward the achievement of specific goals (e.g., a college education as the means toward achieving a good career or economic success).

latent functions unanticipated and unrecognized (functional or dysfunctional) consequences of an intended course of action.

manifest functions intended and recognized consequences of a particular course of action.

middle-range theory generates theoretical explanations grounded in and extending beyond specific empirical realities.

rebel individual who rejects cultural goals and institutionalized means, and who substitutes alternative goals and alternative means toward attaining those goals.

retreatist individual who rejects cultural goals and institutionalized means, and who, by and large, withdraws from active participation in society.

ritualist individual who rejects cultural goals but who accepts and goes along with the institutional means toward their achievement.

RELEVANT NEWSPAPER STORIES

All news stories are from the *New York Times* unless otherwise noted, and can be accessed via www.wiley.com/go/dillon. See NEWS icons in the margins above.

NEWS 4.1   "Should Hillary pretend to be a flight attendant?" November 14, 2007.
"What Hillary won," June 7, 2008.
"Pantsuits and the presidency," June 22, 2008.

NEWS 4.2   "Recognizing a sacred bond sometimes obscured," January 23, 2007.

NEWS 4.3   "As doctors cater to looks, skin patients take a seat and wait," July 28, 2008.
See also: "Doctors and drug makers: A move to end cozy ties," February 12, 2007.
"Survey of medical schools is critical of perks," June 3, 2008.

NEWS 4.4   "Sports turnaround: The team doctors now pay the team," May 18, 2004.

NEWS 4.5   "A word from our sponsor," January 25, 2007.

NEWS 4.6   "The spine as profit center," December 30, 2006.

NEWS 4.7   "Towns rethink laws against illegal immigrants," September 26, 2007.

NEWS 4.8   "Farm machines replacing shrinking migrant work force," May 27, 2008.

NEWS 4.9   "Health gains may be army's loss," May 30, 2008.

NOTES

1   Contrary to Parsons's view of the endurance of particular values in shaping individual and social action, Ann Swidler (2001: 80), a leading sociologist of culture, argues that people change their goals (and values) depending on changed circumstances; thus an immigrant in the US is motivated to pursue wealth whereas in his or her home country he or she might have sought the preservation of family ties.

2   Luhmann (2002: 125) states, for example, that "society is an operationally closed, autonomous system of communication. Consequently everything it observes and describes (everything that is communicated about) is self-referentially observed and described. That holds for the description of the societal system itself, and it also holds with the same necessity for the description of the environment of the societal system ... It is as though the distinction between a map and a territory – a territory in which the map has to be made – itself has to be inscribed on the map."

CHAPTER FIVE

THE FRANKFURT SCHOOL

TECHNOLOGY, CULTURE, AND POLITICS

KEY CONCEPTS

critical theory
controlled rationality
emancipated society
Enlightenment
technical rationality
technological rationality
instrumental domination
normative rationality
scientific rationality
dialectic of Enlightenment
social control
scientific management
mass culture
culture industry
homogenization
standardization
technological determinism
reification
hegemony
promotional culture
one-dimensionality
false needs
celebrity
cultural totalitarianism
administered world
steering problems
crisis
political dependency
lifeworld
legitimation crisis
public sphere
civil society
communicative action
colonization of the
    lifeworld
systems of domination
ideal speech situation
communicative rationality
distorted communication

CHAPTER MENU

Timeline 5.1	Major events in the decades of the Frankfurt School (1918–present)		
1918	End of World War I
1919	Jazz arrives in Europe
1920	First radio broadcasting station opens in Pittsburgh (US)
1922	BBC (British Broadcasting Company) established as state broadcaster in Great Britain
1923	Hitler attempts to overthrow Bavarian government in Munich
1923	Mussolini begins to turn Italy into Fascist state
1923	Collapse of German currency due to inflation
1924	Italian elections: Fascist majority win
1924	Establishment of Chrysler (car) Corporation
1926	Kodak produces first 16 mm movie film
1927	Introduction of sound into movies
1928	Discovery of penicillin
1929	Wall Street Crash: economic Depression
1929	Pope recognizes Mussolini's Fascist government in exchange for establishment of Catholicism as Italian state religion
1929	Museum of Modern Art, New York, founded
1931	Empire State Building in New York completed
1932	Aldous Huxley, *Brave New World*
1933	Hitler appointed chancellor of Germany with dictatorial powers
1933	President Roosevelt launches New Deal in US
1936	Hitler and Mussolini establish Rome–Berlin Axis
1936	BBC announces a television service
1936	Charlie Chaplin stars in *Modern Times*
1937	Movies become fourteenth largest business in US
1938	Germany invades and annexes Austria
1938	Munich Pact made, with Britain agreeing to Hitler's take-over of German-speaking region of Czechoslovakia
1938	Anti-Semitic legislation passed in Italy
1938	Disney, *Snow White and the Seven Dwarfs*

1938	Principle of paid vacations established in Britain
1939	Germany invades Poland; start of World War II
1940	30 million homes in US have radios
1941	Japan attacks US fleet at Pearl Harbor, Hawaii; US declares war on Japan
1941	First Jewish extermination camps set up in Poland and Russia
1941	Manhattan Project of intense nuclear research gets underway to develop atomic bomb
1941	Orson Welles, *Citizen Kane*
1942	First nuclear reactor established at University of Chicago
1942	First automatic computer developed in US
1942	Magnetic recording tape invented
1943	Allied forces begin round-the-clock bombing of Germany; Allies invade Italy
1944	Allied forces land at Normandy beaches (France); liberate Paris and Belgium
1945	Hitler kills himself (April 30)
1945	US drops atomic bombs on Hiroshima and Nagasaki
1947	Christian Dior opens fashion salon in Paris
1948	United Nations Declaration of Human Rights
1948	Long-playing record invented
1948	USSR withdraws from coalition with war allies
1949	USSR explodes its first atomic bomb; escalation of arms race with US
1951	First peaceful use of atomic energy in producing electric power in US
1952	Britain explodes its first atomic bomb
1952	First commercial jet airline service launched
1953	Discovery of DNA structure
1954	29 million homes in US have television
1955	Bill Haley, "Rock Around the Clock"
1958	Stereophonic records come into use
1962	First American (John Glenn) to orbit space
1966	Wide adoption of color television in US
1967	Marshall McLuhan, *The Medium Is the Message*

cont'd

1967	100 million telephones in use in US
1968	Student protests in US and Europe
1969	American astronauts land on moon
1973	World Trade Center Twin Towers, New York, completed; 411.5 meters high
1977	Research indicates smoking unhealthy
1978	World's first test-tube baby born
1988	US B-2 "Stealth Bomber" unveiled
1993	World's first human embryo cloned
2008	135 million internet users watch videos on YouTube and other websites

The core theorists associated with the Frankfurt School (*FS*) include **Theodor Adorno, Max Horkheimer,** and **Herbert Marcuse,** whose lives spanned much of the twentieth century, and whose societal critique is maintained today, but also pushed in new directions, by Jurgen Habermas, currently a retired sociology professor at the University of Frankfurt. The Frankfurt School is so named because of its founding as an independent Institute for Social Research (ISR) in Frankfurt, Germany, in 1923. Marxism was the Institute's "ruling principle" (Jay 1973: 8–9), and in 1930, Horkheimer (at age 35) became its director. The Nazis came to power in 1933, however, and Adolf Hitler soon shut down the Institute for "tendencies hostile to the state" (Jay 1973: 29); its vast library was seized by the government but not its financial endowment, which Horkheimer had earlier transferred to Holland (Jay 1973: 26). Exiled from Germany, Horkheimer and his colleagues settled in the US (initially at Columbia University, New York City) and after the war traveled back and forth to Europe (see biographical notes). They continued to write in German – partly to demonstrate that not all things German were tainted with Nazism (Jay 1973: 40) – though this restricted their accessibility to English-speaking audiences; their important book *Dialectic of Enlightenment* (DE), for example, was not translated into English until 1972 (though its first German edition was published in 1944).

🖥 WEB 5.1

CRITICAL THEORY

The body of writing produced by the *FS* is typically referred to as critical theory. It is so called because its central objective is to highlight how critical, reflective thought – the democratically empowering use of reason and rationality (see glossary at the end of the book) institutionalized as a result of the Enlightenment (see Introduction) – is suppressed in society by the mass media and other institutions (e.g., corporations, education, politics), which instead extend an instrumental, strategic, or controlled rationality into all domains of society. *FS* theorists argue that the elimination of critical thought and the suppression of meaningful dissent, whether in political opinions, social values, or fashion choices, strips individuals and society (whether Soviet socialism or western capitalism) of

BIOGRAPHICAL NOTE

Max Horkheimer was born in 1895 in Stuttgart, Germany; his father was a prominent Jewish manufacturer who encouraged Max to travel throughout Europe. Horkheimer worked for a few years in his father's business but then pursued academic studies. After completing his military service, he wrote his doctoral thesis on Immanuel Kant and subsequently became director (in 1930) of the Institute of Social Research. In the US, in exile as a result of the rise of German Nazism, Horkheimer suffered from heart disease and at his doctor's urging moved to Pacific Palisades, where he and Adorno wrote *Dialectic of Enlightenment*. Horkheimer traveled back and forth between Frankfurt and the US in the years after the war, and he died, an American citizen, in Germany in 1973 (Jay 1973: 6–7, 234, 254).

BIOGRAPHICAL NOTE

Herbert Marcuse was born in 1898 in Berlin, Germany; he too had prosperous Jewish parents, and also completed military service. Subsequently, he studied philosophy and received his doctorate from the University of Freiburg. While in the US, he worked with the State Department (until 1950), then returned to Columbia University, and subsequently went to Brandeis University and the University of California, San Diego. Marcuse become highly identified with the New Left and the student and anti-war protest movements of the 1960s and 1970s. He died in 1979 (Jay 1973: 28, 71, 80, 284).

BIOGRAPHICAL NOTE

Theodor Adorno was born in 1903 in Frankfurt, Germany, to prosperous Jewish-Catholic parents. He studied music composition in Vienna, Austria, and also pursued philosophy, writing his doctorate on Edmund Husserl. Adorno joined the Institute for Social Research in Frankfurt in 1938. He subsequently spent four years at Oxford University in England before moving to America to join his exiled colleagues until the re-opening of the Institute in Frankfurt after the war. With a strong personal and intellectual interest in classical and contemporary music, he worked at the renowned Columbia University Institute of Radio Research (which pioneered survey research of radio audiences) before moving to Pacific Palisades, near Los Angeles. He continued to write prolifically on wide-ranging topics, including a cultural analysis of jazz and its liberating (though ultimately repressed) potential to break the individual free of the constraints of the status quo. He also conducted content analyses of television shows and of newspaper astrology columns, and contributed to pioneering survey research on authoritarianism and prejudice (Adorno et al. 1950). Adorno, who became an American citizen, died in 1969 (Jay 1973: 22, 172, 188, 196–197).

the ability to form an egalitarian and fully democratic society. It is only through a critical theory of society – by using reason to critique how society works – the *FS* argued, that we can collectively create an emancipated society in which we are not beholden to, but are autonomous from, the controlling demands of competitive capitalism that penetrate every aspect of everyday life, including our inner desires: "Critical thought strives to define the irrational character of the established rationality" (Marcuse 1964: 227). Accordingly, *FS* theorists advocate that individuals should engage in a systematic critique of the ways in which society is organized and of the goals served.

TECHNOLOGY AND SOCIAL PROGRESS

Notwithstanding the very different – pre-internet – society in which *FS* theorists wrote, their analysis of technology and culture is highly applicable today given the pervasiveness of technology in our lives. Horkheimer and Adorno (H & A) recognize that technology is crucial to ensuring efficiency in goal accomplishment – clearly, most of the technological devices we use every day make our lives more smoothly efficient and give us more control over our activities. Just think about how much time and trouble we save by using email, cell-phones, and texting, or how internet access gives us so much information about so many things (books, politics, restaurants), and how we, in turn, actively use technology to personally add to the flow of images, information, and opinion (through blogs, YouTube, etc.).

    FS theorists are fully cognizant of the many positive ways that technological advances can enhance social institutions and everyday life. In fact, they remind us of the great promise of social progress that was instilled by the Enlightenment affirmation of scientific reasoning as the way forward from the non-rational myths and traditions that legitimated social inequality (e.g., the unquestioned divine rights of monarchies; see Introduction). H & A state, "Enlightenment, understood in the widest sense as the advance of thought, has always aimed at liberating human beings from fear and installing them as masters … Enlightenment's program was the disenchantment of the world. It wanted to dispel myths, to overthrow fantasy with knowledge" (DE 1).

Normative evaluation of technological and social progress

The emancipatory progress promised by advances in knowledge has not, however, H & A argue, come to fruition. Instead they argue, following Weber (cf. chapter 3), that it is stalled by an instrumental or technical rationality detached from the reasoned commitment to norms of social equality. Thus, it is not that H & A are opposed to rationality, but that they want us to evaluate the goals to which science and technology, these "gifts of fortune" (DE xviii), are applied. H & A contend that scientific and technological progress, removed from commitment to broader societal values (e.g., social equality), is driven by a technological rationality – the use of technology to expand the instrumental domination of individuals and groups across all spheres of society, as well as of the natural environment. This is a very broad theoretical and values-based or normative claim; its core thesis, however, can be empirically evaluated across various societal domains by systematically identifying specific contexts which support or, importantly, challenge *FS* assumptions.

Not coincidentally, H & A made this claim in the wake of World War II – a war precipitated by the instrumentally planned and rationally executed destruction of human life crystallized by the Holocaust. World War II, an event of our Enlightened modern epoch, demonstrates "one of the most vexing aspects of advanced industrial civilization: the rational character of its irrationality" (Marcuse 1964: 9); rational humans' rational pursuit of humans' irrational destruction. Similarly, advances in scientific and technological knowledge have made nuclear energy possible; a knowledge that is used in a highly rational way not only for energy-efficiency purposes, but also for militaristic purposes (e.g., atomic bombs) that fuel the ongoing global nuclear arms race and the threat of nuclear destruction.

Whereas Weber argued that science cannot provide answers to ethical questions regarding how society should use scientific knowledge – it cannot tell us how we should live or what values should guide us (cf. chapter 3) – H & A argue that we need to inject an ethical or normative dimension into our evaluation of how societies use scientific and technological knowledge. And those norms, H & A argue, should come from the Enlightenment's understanding of reason and progress as an emancipatory force; we should thus employ a normative rationality (as opposed to only instrumental or strategic rationality) and assess the extent to which we use reason for destructive and controlling purposes rather than to advance the norms of social equality and human flourishing.

In other words, we should not be deceived by the mystique of scientific rationality: the presumption that the application of science and technology is invariably good and that the proliferation of technology across all domains of everyday life demonstrates the uncontestable fact that we live in a time of social progress. We believe we are in control – of our lives, of our government, of nature – but in actual fact, H & A argue, we are the ones being dominated and controlled, and we stand powerless in the face of the corporate and political bureaucratic actors that control and administer our lives. Thus while the great advances in scientific and technological knowledge give us the means available to eliminate many societal ills (e.g., poverty) and to create a society in which all members can fully participate and realize their humanity, instead, H & A argue, we collectively use technological knowledge for strategic purposes, to serve the interests of those individuals, groups, and corporations who are already economically and politically powerful (DE 30–31, xvii).

WEB 5.1

DIALECTIC OF ENLIGHTENMENT

This general state of affairs – the strategic harnessing of technological and economic rationality for domination rather than emancipation – H & A (1972) call the dialectic of Enlightenment. Don't be intimidated by this phrase. In essence, it simply means that the Enlightenment has given us the contradictory opposite or antithesis of what it promised, and this has resulted in our being less free, less autonomous, and less enlightened than we believe ourselves to be. Instead of progress, our technologically advanced society is characterized by regression; instead of freedom, by domination.

The social, political, and economic use of technology today is more complicated than *FS* theorists envisaged. Cell-phones and the internet, especially text-messaging, MySpace, and YouTube, clearly increase the everyday autonomy of individuals and groups, and in many instances, allow them to bypass the gate-keeping power of political, mass media, and other authorities (e.g., parents and teachers). Public protests in fall 2007 against the ruling military junta in Myanmar/Burma provided a good example of the grassroots, democratic ends to which internet technology can be used. Instant messaging and cell-phone photographs taken by protesters and onlookers were critical to gaining western support for the protests and against their military crushing. However, soon after these images appeared on the internet and on western television and newspapers, the military

NEWS 5.1

government cut off internet access in Myanmar, an action that reminds us that the internet is not as free as it seems, but is controlled, rather, by states and corporations. Thus while we find many advantages in using MySpace and Facebook, their corporate owners have technologically sophisticated ways to mine the information on users' personal pages for personally targeted advertising that translates

NEWS 5.2

into increased corporate profits.

H & A emphasize that technological rationality has a clear economic logic; following Marx, they contend that technology is used to extend the economic interests of capitalism and of capitalist institutions (e.g., the state, the university, the media). Thus, *FS* theorists meld Weber's focus on instrumental rationality with Marx's emphasis on the profit logic of capitalism. Analytically, then, the dialectic of Enlightenment is driven by capitalist forces, whose ethically unrestrained, strategic economic use of technology directly penetrates all spheres of society. Technological knowledge

> serves all the purposes of the bourgeois economy both in factories and on the battlefield, it is at the disposal of entrepreneurs regardless of their origins ... [Technology] is as democratic as the economic system with which it evolved. Technology is the essence of this knowledge. It aims to produce neither concepts nor images, nor the joy of understanding, but method, exploitation of the labor of others, capital ... What human beings seek to learn from nature is how to use it to dominate wholly both it and human beings. Nothing else counts. (DE 2)

TECHNOLOGY AS SOCIAL CONTROL

A couple of examples help illustrate *FS* ideas about technology as an instrument of domination or social control. We can begin right on campus. Most colleges today use electronic swipe-card systems to provide students with access to various

> **Topic 5.1**   UNH swipe cards linked to Social Security numbers
>
> "In case you forgot what time you arrived home last night, UNH knows. The identification card used to gain access to UNH facilities such as dining halls, computer clusters, and residences around campus are doing more than opening doors. Logged in a confidential database is the place, the date, and the time of each individual swipe, allowing the university to know where you are and when. Because each card is embedded with a Social Security number or student identification number, the cards that many of us swipe multiple times each day are unique. Each SSN is followed by a two-digit issue code, indicating the number of times the ID card has been reissued. The inconspicuous card-readers are hardwired into a subnet, which is fed large amounts of numerical information each day … [According to UNH officials] the subnet that collects all of this information is entirely separate from that which is accessible by UNH students ensuring the sensitive data's security. The card readers are efficient, specific and secure, all at a cost of up to $1000 per reader … the system allows for a new keycard to be issued to the student without the added expense of changing the locks. The keycard system enables the university to grant or deny access to any person at any door on campus. The card readers can detect which doors are open and where, notifying the university of potential breaches in security. UNH can use this data in a variety of ways according to [officials]. For instance, the records that they collect are accessible to many UNH employees including the UNH police. If a crime were committed within one of the residence halls or off-campus apartments, the university could provide law enforcement with records of who had recently entered the building."
>
> 🗏🗏 NEWS 5.3

campus facilities. These systems are generally seen as efficient and secure, and they are also effective tracking devices, as seen at the University of New Hampshire (UNH); see Topic 5.1.

And similarly, E-ZPass and other GPS devices can be used to track our movements. These systems are so effective that parents are using such devices to control their teenagers' movements, so that they always know whether they are where they are supposed to be. Other devices (e.g., car ignition locks, electronic bands) are pre-programmed by parents and others (e.g., police) to prohibit certain activities (e.g., driving after drinking alcohol, going over the speed limit, or roaming beyond a specified location), and by adult children who monitor their ailing parents' daily habits from afar. Electronic forensic evidence (e.g., of emails from computer hard drives, etc.) is becoming a staple of divorce cases, and at work and in public places, the "camera's eye" is pervasive, monitoring activities and communication.

🗏🗏 NEWS 5.4

Clearly, while some of these devices can have beneficial effects (e.g., reducing drunk-driving injuries and deaths; ensuring older people take their medicine), this list underscores the penetration of technology as a means of control into domains of life that in the past were unburdened by constant surveillance. Thus, they

From the ATM to
E-ZPass, new
technological devices
enhance efficiency
while also tracking
our movements.

illuminate the core *FS* thesis that: "Technology serves to institute new, more effective, and more pleasant forms of social control and social cohesion … the traditional notion of the 'neutrality' of technology can no longer be maintained. Technology as such cannot be isolated from the use to which it is put; the technological society is a system of domination" (Marcuse 1964: 158, xv–xvi).

Rational, scientific management

Long before GPS technology, **scientific management** became the catch-phrase in the world of business. Inspired by the early twentieth-century experiments and ideas of Frederick Taylor (1911) on managerial control of work processes and workers' tasks, this method focused on making workers' physical movements as automated as the machines they were working on. Hence, "time and motion" studies emerged as a popular way of finding the most efficient use of workers' hand and body movements while executing the production tasks assigned; the method was exemplified by workers on the automated assembly lines of Henry Ford's then-fledgling car industry plant in Michigan (and thus is often called Fordism). Today, Wal-Mart uses standardized, automated temperature controls set at headquarters (in Bentonville, Arkansas) and imposed throughout all of the company's approximately 3,500 worldwide stores, irrespective of the physical climate of the place where the Wal-Mart store is located; the controlling reach of scientific-technological management is thus extensive.

📖 NEWS 5.5

SOCIETY'S RATIONAL CONTROL OF NATURE

As *FS* theorists would underscore, society has long used technology to advance economic interests and in particular to control the physical environment, nature. Today the pervasive extent of our manipulation and control of nature is such that Dubai, for example, a city in the middle of the desert, boasts the world's third largest indoor ski slope. Our control of nature, however, while increasing our freedoms in some ways (e.g., where and when we ski), also exacts a high economic and environmental cost. The expense of buying and maintaining snow-making machines has driven many small ski-resort operators out of business in favor of large resorts confined to a few select locations. And, as a result of the global warming that snow-making and other machines have contributed to, there is less natural snow due to the buildup of greenhouse gases that are warming the climate.

📖 NEWS 5.6

📖 NEWS 5.7

It is not just snow that we try to control. When houses are decimated as a result of earthquakes, wildfires, and floods, we are reminded that we rational humans choose time and again to build against the irrational force of nature even though we are well aware at the time that nature has its own logic, a logic that we irrationally believe we can control. The devastating impact of Hurricane Katrina underscored the non-rationality of the historically long, economically driven desire to rationally control nature: New Orleans is a city built below sea level, which means that quite apart from hurricanes, it "must run pumps simply to keep from being flooded in an ordinary rainstorm."

📖 NEWS 5.8

📖 NEWS 5.9

In sum, H & A would emphasize that the domination of nature, rationally executed in the pursuit of economic profit, fails to control nature and (frequently too) to be rationally cost-effective. "In the mastery of nature ... enslavement to nature persists" (DE 31). Such is the dialectic of Enlightenment; the mastery of nature (thesis) becomes its antithesis (domination by or enslavement to nature). We literally sink money into building projects that are destined to collapse (from floods, fires, earthquakes, etc.) and to destroy lives as well as local economies (thus further alienating us from cooperative existence with nature).

Caring for nature and society

Notwithstanding *FS* insights about the rational exploitation of nature, there is some evidence today that amidst a growing environmental awareness in society,

191

corporations are exploring ways to use technological knowledge to arrest the negative effects of global warming and other societal problems (e.g., poverty, disease). Dell's plant-a-tree program, Google's generosity toward the development of a commercial plug-in car, Wal-Mart's selling of environmentally friendly light bulbs, and the Gates Foundation's efforts in fighting poverty, among other initiatives, are glimmers that technology is being used toward "the fulfillment of past [Enlightenment] hopes" but in ways that move us beyond the past (unenlightened practices) (DE xvii).

NEWS 5.10

These initiatives suggest that, as the *FS* would maintain, *normative* rational action, i.e., action that recognizes our ethical obligations to one another and to our larger physical and social environment, may ensure that "the gifts of fortune themselves [will not] become elements of misfortune" (DE xviii). Rather, we can use the gifts of nature – human potential, reasoned insight, environmental beauty – for constructive rather than destructive ends.

MASS CULTURE AND CONSUMPTION

FS theorists also focused on mass culture, the media content produced by the technologically sophisticated, profit-driven culture industry, and gave it a searing, though perhaps overly pessimistic, critique. Although the early decades of television saw a corporate commitment (e.g., by NBC, CBS, and ABC in the US, and the BBC in the UK) to edifying the public – keeping viewers well informed about politics and world events and providing them with entertainment that would elevate rather than dumb down their intellectual and cultural interests and their psychological understanding of the human condition – this aim has been increasingly displaced by a concern with corporate profit margins. Thus, for example, today, the US television networks are *entertainment* businesses (cf. DE 108–109; e.g., news shows are entertainment), businesses that are part of much bigger global economic conglomerates (e.g., GE owns NBC).

WEB 5.2

The mass media, therefore, are an industry, and as such the production, packaging, marketing, and distribution of media products (entertainment) are driven by the same profit criteria as in any other industry. Long before the media industry became as profit-oriented as it is today, H & A emphasized both the capitalist economic structure of the culture industry and the mass production and mass homogenization (sameness) and standardization of the (cultural) goods produced.

Culture today is infecting everything with sameness. Film, radio, and magazines ... no longer need to present themselves as art. The truth that they are nothing but business is used as an ideology to legitimize the trash they intentionally produce. They call themselves industries, and the published figures for their directors' incomes quell any doubts about the social necessity of their finished products. (DE 94–95)

Some might argue that television and film, for example, because they are visual media must necessarily use content that strikes our visual senses – and hence the tendency for action images and adventure stunts to be given much greater emphasis than the narrative plot itself; as if with special effects, we don't need much plot (DE 132). This argument is referred to as technological determinism, and it can be applied to any instance in society where technology is used as the logic (or excuse) for why something occurs (e.g., "the computer is down and so I can't access your reservation/account," etc.). In this view, "technology has become the great vehicle of reification – reification in its most mature and effective form. The social position of the individual and his relation to others appear … as calculable manifestations of (scientific) rationality. The world tends to become the stuff of total administration, which absorbs even the administrators" (Marcuse 1964: 168–169). Reification means that technology is seen as having a life of its own; technological tools are treated as if they themselves have an inherent rationality (and a political neutrality) such that decisions about their use in society are beyond human control.

FS theorists, however, reject technological determinism. They emphasize instead that economic interests determine how technology is used, and in the case of mass media, determine the content used to make profit and, by extension, to control audiences (for profit):

> Interested parties like to explain the culture industry in technological terms. Its millions of participants, they argue, demand reproduction processes which inevitably lead to the use of standard products to meet the same needs at countless locations … What is not mentioned is that the basis on which technology is gaining power over society is the power of those whose economic position in society is strongest. (DE 95)

Because the culture industry is so tied into economic profit, it produces entertainment standardized to have mass appeal to audiences who will watch (buy) that content and, importantly, buy the products advertised around, and as part of, that entertainment. And the most efficient way for television and other media businesses to make money is through selling their own products (shows), and the products that other businesses produce, to the people who are most likely to buy those products. In a word, advertising is the real business of the culture industry. The best way to ensure that the largest possible audience of consumers gets to see the paid advertising and product placement on television (and in/at the movies) is to produce content standardized to fit targeted consumer demographic segments. According to H & A, the media industry manipulates us into watching only that which they predict will sell – a manipulative logic similarly used by politicians: messages are tailored to themes that controlled focus-group research indicates will sell (convert into money or votes). Moreover, even with this targeted slicing or squeezing of the audience into different groups, the content produced remains standardized; the differences are not of substance but of packaging. A culture of sameness – whether in media entertainment or in politics – is what is being sold. H & A elaborate:

The dependence of the most powerful broadcasting company on the electrical industry [i.e., General Electric owns NBC], or of film on the banks, characterizes the whole sphere [the whole culture industry], the individual sectors of which [film, television, music production, etc.] are themselves economically intertwined. Everything is so tightly clustered that the concentration of intellect reaches a level where it overflows the demarcations between company names and technical sectors. The relentless unity of the culture industry bears witness to the emergent unity of politics. Sharp distinctions like those between [allegedly different] films ... do not so much reflect real differences as assist in the classification, organization, and identification of consumers. Something is provided for everyone so that no one can escape; ... Everyone is supposed to behave spontaneously according to a "level" determined by indices and to select the category of mass product manufactured for their type. On the charts of research organizations, indistinguishable from those of political propaganda, consumers are divided up as statistical material into red, green, and blue areas according to income group ...

That the difference between the models of Chrysler and General Motors is fundamentally illusory is known by any child who is fascinated by that very difference. The advantages and disadvantages debated by enthusiasts serve only to perpetuate the appearance of competition and choice. It is no different with the offerings of Warner Brothers and Metro-Goldwyn-Mayer. But the differences, even between the more expensive and cheaper products from the same firm, are shrinking – in cars to the different number of cylinders, engine capacity, and details of the gadgets, and in films to the different number of stars, the expense lavished on technology, labor and costumes, or the use of the latest psychological formulae ... The budgeted differences of value in the culture industry have nothing to do with actual differences, with the meaning of the product itself. (DE 96–97)

CULTURE OF ADVERTISING

The culture industry advertises (sells) consumption and keeps our attention focused on consumption, thus underscoring what the Italian Marxist and political activist Antonio Gramsci (1891–1937) would call the hegemony of consumption. This refers to the many intersecting and overlapping ways by which, in a capitalist society, consumption (and the ideology of consumption) is organized and promoted such that consumption appears as the most attractive and natural thing to do. No matter where we go, whether we stay at home and watch television or take a ride on the subway, we are flooded with information. And this is a very particular kind of information – it is promotional information about products to buy; we are thus encircled and surrounded by a promotional culture – notice how the judges on *American Idol* sip from Coca-Cola cups. And it is a never-ending stream. If we try to escape by going out to lunch – to the popular Cheesecake Factory, for example – even as we flip through the menu we encounter large ads for several luxury products (diamond jewelry, cruise vacations, leather bags). Our promotional culture smoothly reproduces the capitalist status quo.

With further advances in technology – and its harnessing to economic profit – internet and consumer brand companies continuously seek and develop new ways to target us: as noted at the outset of this chapter, MySpace uses new

> ## Topic 5.2   Advertising, advertising everywhere
>
> So pervasive is advertising in contemporary society that "Anywhere the eye can see, it's now likely to see an ad." Supermarket eggs advertise television shows, subway turnstiles promote Geico insurance, Continental Airlines is promoted on Chinese take-out cartons, while US airways sells its air-sickness bags as advertising space. Digitalized advertising screens dominate not only in Times Square but also along the highway, on the sides of buildings and at bus stops, and in elevators in department stores, hotels, and dental offices. In short, "in blank spaces in public places, advertisers see branding opportunities."

NEWS 5.11

technology programmed to scan the information on users' personal pages and summon targeted ads; Google scans email users' in-boxes to deliver ads related to those messages; and other companies listen in on internet phone users' conversations so that they can deliver same-time ads related to the phone message content. And most of us don't even give this constant scanning of our lives a second thought; that's the way it is. While lying on the beach we are accustomed to seeing messages in the air; and now while in the air we can expect to see some ads. A company called "Ad-Air" has created what it calls the "first global aerial advertising network" – giant, billboard-like ads that will be visible from the air as planes approach runways. "What an incredible advertising opportunity – all these passengers with nothing else to do, staring down at the ground below."

NEWS 5.2

NEWS 5.12

CONTROLLED CONSUMPTION

Although the advertising industry appeals to our individual vanity, it essentially promotes a culture of sameness – a one-dimensionality which suppresses individuality (Marcuse 1964: 1) in favor of sameness in how we look, feel, and think. Thus, *FS* theorists argue, the culture industry does not respond to our real needs, but to fabricated or false needs which it controls; fabricated, because rather than trying to establish what our real needs might be, the media industry determines our needs as evidenced by what we buy from what it makes available to us:

> False needs are those which are superimposed upon the individual by particular social interests in his repression: the needs which perpetuate toil, aggressiveness, misery and injustice. Their satisfaction might be most gratifying to the individual but this happiness is not a condition which has to be maintained and protected if it serves to arrest the development of this ability (his own and others) to recognize the disease of the whole and grasp the chances of curing that disease ... Most of the prevailing needs to relax, to have fun, to behave and consume in accordance with the advertisements, to love and hate what others love and hate, belong to this category of false needs. (Marcuse 1964: 4–5)

What we "need" or "buy" – at the mall or on television – is controlled by the culture industry, which, *FS* theorists argue, manipulates us into buying from among the artificial choices it makes available to us; we cannot buy what is not offered. It is also apparent, however, that contrary to the *FS* theorists' exaggeration of the controlling power of the culture industry, individuals find ways to make their needs known to manufacturers, and companies respond accordingly; this is seen, for example, in the decreased popularity of soda drinks and the expanded range of more health-conscious (manufactured) water and energy drinks available in their stead. Similarly, when television audiences indicate their pleasure with a particular show, the media industry responds to audience interests (needs) with a slew of similar-themed shows (e.g., the popularity of *American Idol*-like contests, and reality shows).

In any event, the media and other consumer conglomerates use technology to track both what we buy and, by extension, what we are likely to buy. Thus Wal-Mart, for example, is able to closely track its customers' preferences from purchases made, and is able to use that detailed information to confidently predict the kind of things its customers will likely want in the future. And, largely reflecting the "insatiable uniformity" (DE 97) that characterizes choice in a capitalist society, Wal-Mart is able to strategically divide its millions of customers into just three types of shoppers; see Box 5.1.

⊞ NEWS 5.13

The sociological power of fashion imitation, as first noted by Georg Simmel – with whom Adorno studied – "gives to the individual the satisfaction of not standing alone in his actions. Whenever we imitate, we transfer not only the demand for creative activity, but also the responsibility for the action from ourselves to others. Thus the individual is freed from the worry of choosing and appears simply as a creature of the group" (Simmel 1904/1971: 295). We are content with similarity and uniformity (ibid.). In this framing, there seems to be only one way to be a 20-something today; you must look like you stepped out of an advertisement for Abercrombie and Fitch.

Box 5.1   Wal-Mart shoppers

1 *Brand aspirationals*, people with low incomes who are obsessed with names like Kitchen-Aid.
2 *Price-sensitive affluents*, wealthier shoppers who love deals.
3 *Value-price shoppers*, who like low prices and cannot afford much more.
⊞ NEWS 5.13

Through the language they speak, the customers make their own contribution to culture as advertising … the language and gestures of listeners and spectators are more deeply permeated by the patterns of the culture industry than ever before … all are free to dance and amuse themselves … But freedom to choose an ideology, which always reflects economic coercion, everywhere proves to be freedom to be the same. The way in which the young girl accepts and performs the obligatory date, the tone of voice used on the telephone and in the most intimate situations, the choice of words in conversation, indeed the whole inner life compartmentalized according to the categories of vulgarized depth psychology, bears witness to the attempt to turn oneself into an apparatus meeting the requirements of success, an apparatus which, even in its unconscious impulses, conforms to the model presented by the culture industry. The most intimate reactions of human beings have become so entirely reified, even to themselves, that the idea of anything peculiar to them survives only in extreme abstraction: personality means hardly more than dazzling white teeth and freedom from body odor and emotions. That is the triumph of advertising in the culture industry: the compulsive imitation by consumers of cultural commodities which, at the same time, they recognize as false. (DE 133, 135–136)

MEDIA REALITY

Whatever the content, all media content – whether billed as fact (e.g., news, interviews) or fiction (drama) – is advertising, according to H & A, aimed at making us buy more media and other products. Thus, "Every film is a preview of the next, which promises yet again to unite the same heroic couple under the same exotic sun. Anyone arriving late cannot tell whether he is watching the trailer or the real thing" (DE 132). And we see promotional advertising not just in the movie theater, but across all media sectors. *ABC World News Tonight* will have a segment on an issue that is also being featured on one of ABC's sitcoms or dramas; the commentators on *Monday Night Football* will interrupt their play-

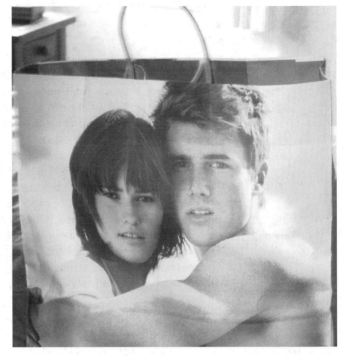

According to Frankfurt School theorists, the sameness that characterizes mass media content also extends to a sameness in individual appearance and personality.

by-play analysis of the live action on the field while they take a few minutes to chat with the celebrity star of a soon-to-be-released movie owned by their parent company (Disney) or of a new show starting on its network; and so on.

The mass mediated reality and the real reality frequently blur. This is especially evident in the so-called "reality" shows – which we eventually learn are not really reality shows but fictionalized and stylized enactments of a reality scripted by the TV producers. And celebrities further blur TV reality and real reality. Thus Richard Gere, who played a man who fell in love with a high-end prostitute (played by Julia Roberts) in the 1990 movie *Pretty Woman*, can urge a gathering of "some 10,000 Indian prostitutes" to refuse sex without condoms to prevent the spread of HIV/AIDS. And Harrison Ford is inducted into the Archaeology Hall of Fame, not because he is an archaeologist but because he is Indiana Jones (a popular movie character). The legitimacy of celebrities persuading us to behave in particular ways might be explained from a Weberian perspective as being due to charismatic authority (see chapter 3). Nonetheless, most of us don't think it unusual to see celebrities engaging in public health or environmental etc. advocacy. It seems natural to us that media reality is the reality. We (more or less) accept its definitions of the world as if they are, and should be, the only ones that count.

NEWS 5.14

NEWS 5.15

197

CULTURAL TOTALITARIANISM

FS theorists thus conclude that mass consumer society produces a new form of totalitarianism, a cultural totalitarianism crystallized by the creation of false needs and the attendant suppression of ideas and needs that are at odds with those mass marketed and promoted as being necessary to the perpetuation of capitalism. Marcuse argues:

> By virtue of the way it has organized its technological base, contemporary industrial society tends to be totalitarian. For "totalitarian" is not only a terroristic political coordination of society, but also a non-terroristic economic-technical coordination which operates through the manipulation of needs by vested interests ... All liberation depends on the consciousness of servitude, and the emergence of this consciousness is always hampered by the predominance of needs and satisfactions which, to a great extent, have become the individual's own ... the optimal goal is the replacement of false needs by true ones ... The range of choice open to the individual is not the decisive factor in determining the degree of human freedom but *what* can be chosen and what *is* chosen by the individual. The criterion for free choice can never be an absolute one, but neither is it entirely relative. Free election of masters does not abolish the masters or the slaves. Free choice among a wide variety of goods and services does not signify freedom if these goods and services sustain social controls over a life of toil and fear, that is, if they sustain alienation. And the spontaneous reproduction of superimposed needs by the individual does not establish autonomy; it only testifies to the efficacy of the controls. (1964: 3, 7–8)

ACTIVE CONSUMERS AND AUDIENCES

Although the *FS* arguments about consumer culture accurately capture much of what surrounds us today, they exaggerate the extent to which individuals passively embrace mass media and consumer culture. Sociological research indicates that consumers and audiences are not as passive or as disengaged as the *FS* theorists suggest. Several wide-ranging studies from as early as the mid-1970s (e.g., Hall and Jefferson 1976; Ang 1985; McRobbie 1991; Fiske and Hartley 1978) document that while many of us might be avid consumers of television dramas, soap-operas, and romance and fashion magazines, we nonetheless bring our own interpretations to bear on some of that content. At times, we even subvert the show's dominant message in favor of interpretations that fit better with our own experiences of reality, experiences that are invariably shaped by our own particular socio-biographical and socio-economic situation. Thus, for example, while many people enjoy seeing the glamorous and lavish lifestyles celebrated in the content of several television shows, this does not prevent them from actively comparing the television reality with the more burdensome and economically strained circumstances in their own lives, and from criticizing the economic structures that produce stark inequalities (e.g., Ang 1985).

The current popularity of interactive-audience shows (such as *American Idol* with its phone/text audience votes), and the participatory culture required by internet blogging and YouTube (e.g., Burgess and Green 2009), further challenge the *FS* presumption of passive audiences. Additionally, many internet users actively protest against the tracking devices and advertising that clutter their favorite websites, as underscored by controversies in response to Facebook's policies regarding its ownership of users' personal information and other internet advertising initiatives. And the political success of users in getting these technology and media companies to change their policies suggests a slightly greater democracy in technology-media control than intimated by the *FS* assessment.

📖 NEWS 5.16

POLITICS: ONE-DIMENSIONAL RATIONALITY

As already noted, *FS* theorists argue that the sameness characterizing consumer culture also extends to politics. Politicians are packaged and advised by a bevy of well-paid media handlers, and their "off-message" spontaneity is further curbed by their entangled ties to lobbyists and the media industry, which suppress any ideologically challenging views that politicians might be tempted to occasionally voice. In branding and frequently re-branding their candidate-clients, the handlers also brand (and seek to control) the electorate, comprised of (controllable) homogenized groups: soccer moms, NASCAR (competitive car-racing) dads, angry white men, and Wal-Mart women (voters with lower incomes and lower education, who tend to be conservative and to have been impacted by economic difficulties). These homogenized groups are assumed to think alike, thus making it easier for political candidates and their media consultants to target them with clichéd policy messages that will feed into their perceived (short-term) needs, rather than opening up a sustained discussion of the many pressing issues that voters, irrespective of demographics, are concerned about (e.g., health care). Thus, "One dimensional thought is systematically promoted by the makers of politics and their purveyors of mass information. Their universe of discourse is populated by self-validating hypotheses which, incessantly and monopolistically repeated, become hypnotic definitions or dictations" (Marcuse 1964: 14).

📖 NEWS 5.17

TECHNOLOGY AS POLITICAL CONTROL

And like the media industry (and universities, stores, governments, parents), political consultants too use new technologies to control people. Brain-scanning, MRI technology (like other new technologies) has many benefits; it can be used to help people as a result of the early detection and treatment of brain tumors. But MRI technology can also apparently detect political partisanship. We are accustomed to researchers conducting focus groups and surveys to find out what issues motivate voters' choices and what kinds of campaign advertising strategies they are likely to favor or frown upon. Now, technology can circumvent this kind of research by allowing researchers to conduct experimental MRI assessments of voters' brains. As one of its sponsors (a former campaign strategist and aide to President Clinton) stated: "These new tools could help us someday ... put a bit more science in political science." Science, as *FS* theorists emphasize, offers the promise of social and political progress. But what will this extra political science accomplish? It will likely be used, as the *FS* would predict, to further assist political campaign strategists and the advertising and media industry in their ceaseless efforts to gain strategic advantage over the competition, whether they are trying to sell a political candidate, a movie, or any other product.

It is unlikely that MRI or any other new technologies will be used to implement more egalitarian public policies (on health, education, etc.), but as Marcuse predicted, to further sustain the status quo:

Today political power asserts itself through its power over the machine process and over the technical organization of the apparatus. The government of advanced and advancing industrial societies can secure and maintain itself only when it succeeds in mobilizing, organizing, and exploiting the technical, scientific, and mechanical productivity available to industrial civilization ... the machine [is] the most effective political instrument in any society whose basic organization is that of the machine process. (1964: 3)

It is also important to note, however, that although politicians and their handlers resort to manipulative techniques to win votes, voters are not as stupefied by politicians (and by advertising) as the *FS* theorists maintain. Many voters query the motivations and arguments put forward by political candidates, a deliberative process most easily observed in America during the presidential primary process. Moreover, as opinion polls indicate, voters do not like "mud-slinging" or negative campaigning and want greater attentiveness to policy issues (e.g., Pew Research Center 2004).

As Jews who had to flee Nazi Germany, *FS* theorists saw first-hand the prejudice and horror (e.g., the Holocaust) that are unleashed when passivity is the response to totalitarian control (e.g., Hitler). For this reason, the *FS* theorists urge us to reject the relative homogenization (sameness) that pervades contemporary culture, whether in political debate, media content, or consumer lifestyles. They instead advocate our engagement in a rational critique of the economic, political, and cultural forces that seek to control us – though it is of course hard to do this – immersed as we are in this everyday reality. Nevertheless, the many explosive, geo-political conflicts in the world today, and the accelerating expansion of global consumerism, make the remarks of H & A, written in the aftermath of World War II, a useful reminder that the thoughtful use of reason may be ever-more necessary to stem the destruction that results from the systematic recourse to instrumental domination:

In a period of political division into immense blocs driven by an objective tendency to collide, horror has been prolonged. The conflicts in the third world and the renewed growth of [political, economic, and cultural] totalitarianism are not mere historical interludes any more than ... fascism was ... [in the 1930s and 1940s]. Critical thought ... requires us to take up the cause of the remnants of freedom, of tendencies toward real humanity, even though they seem powerless in face of the great historical trend ... What matters today is to preserve and disseminate freedom, rather than to accelerate, however indirectly, the advance toward the **administered world** [of government/state- and corporate-bureaucratic manipulation and control]. (DE xi–xii)

JURGEN HABERMAS: THE STATE AND SOCIETY

The curtailment of individual and group freedom as a result of an increase in government/state and economic-corporate intervention in everyday life in democratic societies is a major concern of **Jurgen Habermas**. He highlights how the government intervenes more and more in trying to administer or control various crises in society (e.g., the collapse of the mortgage industry in the US in 2007–2008), crises that frequently result from a narrowly conceived, strategic rationality in the first place. Writing in the 1970s, Habermas argued that "in liberal capitalist societies ... crises become endemic because temporarily unresolved steering problems which the processes of economic growth produces at more or less regular intervals, *as such* endanger social integration" (1975: 25). Habermas does not use the term crisis lightly. To the contrary, he states: "only when members of a society experience structural [institutional] alterations as critical for continued existence and feel their social identity threatened can we speak of crises" (1975: 3). Thus, for example, Americans' social identity and their pursuit of home ownership as part of the American Dream are threatened currently (2009) by the failure of the mortgage industry and the high incidence of home foreclosures, a crisis that forced the US government to take several historically unprecedented measures starting in the spring of 2008 to begin radically altering the institutional organization of the banking industry.

BIOGRAPHICAL NOTE

Jurgen Habermas was born near Cologne, Germany, in 1929. He studied philosophy, history, psychology, and German literature, and received his doctorate from Bonn University in 1954. Soon thereafter, he became Adorno's research assistant at the Institute, then re-established back in Frankfurt. Currently retired, Habermas has held important sociology professorships at a number of German universities as well as delivering public lectures in the US. In addition to writing his many scholarly works, he is a frequent commentator on German and western politics (Outhwaite 2000: 659–661).

The perception of crisis is not driven, as Marx envisaged, by economic inequality (cf. chapter 1). The likelihood of class consciousness developing has long been obliterated, *FS* theorists argue, by the media industry and its promotion of consumption-driven lifestyles – and we should add, by the vast improvements in the standard of living of most people across the globe, notwithstanding persistent inequality (cf. Giddens 2003). Habermas argues that in western capitalist societies, where citizens (more or less) have access to the same consumer goods, social class becomes "depoliticized" (1975: 25). Why should we make a political issue of economic inequality when we can all (more or less) go to the mall, and when we can all (allegedly) achieve the American Dream (of home ownership, consumer lifestyle)?

ECONOMIC AND POLITICAL STEERING PROBLEMS

Yet, despite class depoliticization and the general public acceptance of the idea that the market's invisible hand works to produce both economic growth and social integration, ongoing crises within capitalist society (e.g., recession) indicate otherwise. The economic system is not as free from tension as we might presuppose. It has, rather, as Habermas states, steering problems in the circulation of money that make it periodically veer off track. Stock markets experience sudden declines, banks and corporations go bankrupt as a result of market forces (loss of profit) and/or financial corruption (e.g., embezzlement; manipulation of trading markets), and other corporations encounter severe financial shortfalls (e.g., General Motors, Chrysler) due, in large part, to cost and product mismanagement and the lack of prudent planning such that they request (and receive) multibillion dollar loan guarantees (bailouts) from the government, as occurred in the US during the

📖 NEWS 5.19   2008–2009 recession.

These problems might appear to you as narrow economic problems whose discussion should be confined to business executives and bankers. But, in fact, these problems are not just economic but social and political. As Habermas notes, "In liberal capitalism, crises appear *in the form* of unresolved economic steering problems" (1975: 24). Because the economic system is not just responsible for economic productivity but plays a major role in the task of societal integration, i.e., through the ideology of consumption, equality, and the depoliticized notion that "we are all middle-class," economic problems threaten the whole structure of society. This is a direct result of the system interdependency within modern capitalist society. Although there is institutional specialization, all institutions and spheres of activity are interdependent; thus, for example, the financial losses of Citibank, JP Morgan and other banks in the US in 2007 led, among other things, to these banks' severe curtailment of loans to community college students – they simply cut several 2-year colleges from even the possibility of their students apply-

📖 NEWS 5.20   ing for loans. Thus, precisely because the economic system has its own economically unresolvable steering problems, and because these problems can cause problems in society as a whole, the state (i.e., the government) needs to step in to prop up the economy, to steer it on a different course. This is why the US Federal Reserve Bank assisted the financial company JP Morgan Chase when it came to the rescue of the privately owned Bear Stearns bank in March 2008, and a couple of months later (in October 2008), the government launched its historically unprecedented rescue of several other financial companies and of the Wall Street

📖 NEWS 5.21   financial markets.

Similarly, when we read stories, regularly recurring since the late 1990s, that GM is threatened with bankruptcy we realize there is a potential crisis that needs to be offset. GM is not only a major employer whose collapse would seriously disrupt the lives of its employees, their families, and their communities. Additionally, if GM were to go bankrupt, it would be unable to pay the health insurance costs of its (ex-)workers and of its retired employees (as is already happening). Hence, the masses of newly uninsured Americans would impose such vast economic demands on the already stressed American health-care system that it would be likely to literally collapse. This would affect not only GM's ex-employees and families, but the provision and distribution of health care across the country as a whole. Clearly, then to avert such a crisis, or to manage and control the emerging crisis, the state (the government) needs to do something. It could, among policy alternatives, prop up GM with short-term loans and fiscal write-offs, or it could re-examine and re-imagine the financing of the whole health and health-insurance industries in the US. Independent of GM's problems, the ongoing reports of systemic failures and high costs in American medicine – many patients are in severe debt due to medical costs – suggest that this is a society-wide systems crisis.

📰 NEWS 3.2

📰 NEWS 5.22

LEGITIMATION CRISES

The home-mortgage crisis, with its deep effects on economically struggling families as well as in spurring the collapse in 2008–2009 of large banking and financial corporations (e.g., Countrywide, Bear Stearns, Lehman Brothers), uncovered systemic cracks not only in investment and lending practices but in individual and corporate financial decision-making more generally. Among other consequences, the government bailout of Wall Street during the 2008–2009 recession underscored the political dependency of economic and financial markets; the economic steering mechanism is neither invisible – as some economists would argue – nor a self-contained system.

Political dependency becomes apparent when ongoing, systemic problems in the economy and in interrelated systems (housing mortgages, health care, welfare, education, etc.) come to the fore. In such circumstances, we as citizens – no longer thinking of ourselves in terms of Marx's categories of wage-workers and capitalists – look to the state to manage or administer the crises and problems in society. Specifically, these problems pertain to what Habermas calls the lifeworld (following Alfred Schutz's conceptualization; cf. chapter 9) – our everyday world, the normative (values) and institutional (workplace, school, family, etc.) context in which we organize and live our lives (Habermas 1984: 70). We look to the state to fix the systems that break down or threaten to break down, and to compensate for the dysfunctional consequences of capitalism (1975: 54).

The state frequently fails to respond adequately to systemic problems. It is not clear as yet (May 2009) whether the government's Wall Street and other corporate

🗐 NEWS 5.23

🗐 NEWS 5.24

🗐 NEWS 5.25

bailouts will be effective. In recent times, failure was apparent in the government's handling of the immediate and long-term aftermath of Hurricane Katrina, and regarding problems in the economic and civic reconstruction in Iraq – some of the construction work of US companies with million-dollar building projects was so shoddy that, for example, the internal sewage system in the newly constructed police headquarters collapsed, and US soldiers were electrocuted while showering in their barracks as a result of faulty wiring that the US government ignored. In other instances, the state may over-reach into individuals' lives, trying to regulate individuals' highly complex personal decisions (e.g., abortion, end-of-life decisions) and to wire-tap and listen in on private email and text-messaging conversations.

When individuals perceive the state as either having failed to intervene sufficiently or having over-reached into the lifeworld, then we have what Habermas calls a legitimation crisis. This occurs when "the legitimizing system does not succeed in maintaining the requisite level of mass loyalty while the steering imperatives taken over from the economic system are carried through" (1975: 46). In other words, it constitutes a sort of "identity crisis" (ibid.) among the citizenry, because "the people," the governed, feel they can no longer consent to the tasks the government sets for itself (and the nation), nor to the methods the state uses in attempting to manage those tasks. Such crises typically mobilize individuals and groups to engage in political action - such as mass protest (e.g., in response to the Vietnam War or the Iraq War, or with regard to immigration), participation in social movements advocating specific reforms (e.g., the women's movement, the civil rights movement, the green movement), or simply voting.

COMMUNICATION AND THE PUBLIC SPHERE

Political protest, and political discussion in general, are a core characteristic of democratic society, and can also be a significant engine of change in non-democratic societies; e.g., Poland before the collapse of the Soviet Union, or currently in China. Habermas has long emphasized the centrality of communication and of communicative freedom as among the requisite norms of democratic society. In particular he has focused on the historical significance of the emergence of a vibrant public sphere or civil society, comprised of private individuals coming together in, and as, a public (Habermas 1989: 27). Initially (e.g., in late seventeenth/eighteenth-century Europe), this sphere of informal public debate was relatively autonomous of government, church, and mass media. Today, however, a democratic public sphere wherein individuals come together in small groups and informal public settings (e.g., the coffee shops, the hairdresser or barber shop) to talk with one another and argue over political and economic issues is increasingly colonized, taken over, by corporate economic and cultural influences; e.g., Starbucks makes its pre-selected background music available to customers for instant iPod downloading. (Moreover, the constant piped music that serves as background in many coffee shops can make conversation difficult.) Habermas argues that this colonization needs to be resisted and supplanted by the re-activation of engaged, reasoned conversation.

According to Habermas, communication with partners with whom we disagree (whether individuals, groups, organizations, or governments) is the only way forward toward the retrieval of a rational democratic society. This is the core idea of Habermas's (1984; 1987) theory of communicative action (TCA), which he elaborates in a dense and lengthy two-volume treatise of the same title. Habermas's intent in TCA is to retrieve reason from its distorted, one-sided association with instrumental rationality – the over-reach of technical rationality criticized by his predecessor *FS* colleagues (Horkheimer, Adorno, Marcuse; see McCarthy 1984). Instead, Habermas focuses on how reason can be used to resist and move beyond the colonization of the lifeworld (the domination of everyday life) by systems of domination (the state, media, corporations). He argues that reason can be used not just to dominate and control but to emancipate (as Enlightenment thinkers envisaged), to secure our freedom from the iron cage imposed by instrumental technical rationality. We can use language, he argues, rational, reasoned arguments, to critique domination and find ways out of it.

Habermas introduces the construct of an ideal speech situation – a theoretically imagined context in which participants use reason not to dominate or bully one another but to seek to reach a common understanding of the question at issue and of plans for mutually agreed, future action. The ideal speech situation, therefore, would be characterized by communicative rationality: participants would use reasoned arguments to query or raise validity claims about (a) the propositional (objective) truth, (b) the normative or values rightness, and (c) the sincerity of statements made by one another (1984: 86, 75). The purpose of reciprocal, reasoned deliberation is to find a reasoned consensus that, in turn, becomes the basis for action. Communicative action is thus a cooperative process of reasoned interpretive negotiation "in which no participant has a monopoly on correct interpretation" (1984: 100).

We can see, therefore, that the creation of an ideal speech situation for communicative exchange might begin to move us beyond the stalemates that characterize everyday culture and politics. Whatever the issue (e.g., Iraq/Middle East; abortion, immigration reform, health insurance) and whether it is local or global in scope,

> Communicatively achieved agreement must be based in the end on reasons. And the rationality of those who participate in this communicative practice is determined by whether, if necessary, they could under suitable circumstances provide reasons for their expressions … The "strength" of an argument is measured in a given context by the soundness of the reasons; that can be seen in, among other things, whether or not an argument is able to convince the participants in a discourse, that is, to motivate them to accept the validity claim in question. (1984: 17–18)

REASONED ARGUMENTS

In other words, individuals (or political parties or nation-states) cannot enter communication situations with a preset, stubborn notion of the only outcome that is acceptable to them. Instead, there has to be openness to the reasoned arguments of others, and we must be able to reason against the arguments others put forward and respond with new counter-arguments. And, by the same token, our communication partners must be open to our arguments and prepared to counter-argue. Such reasoned, discursive exchange pushes us toward reaching a decision on which there is a consensus, an outcome decision that the communicative parties may not even have thought of before entering the speech situation.

The stakes are certainly high when it comes to finding an action consensus among competing groups in the US abortion debate, for example, or among nation-states competing for economic and political influence. Habermas's TCA suggests, however, that reasoned communication rather than competitive law suits (between pro-life and pro-choice groups using strategic arguments) or political strategies of non-communication offers the possibility of reasonable rather than destructive outcomes. Notably, the Baker-Hamilton Report (published December 2006), commissioned by the US Congress to evaluate the ongoing and increasingly destructive conflicts in the Middle East, recommended that the US engage in dialogue with Iran and Syria (countries with whose representatives the US had adamantly declined to talk). In the absence of communication, hostility festers and the non-rational force of intimidation (and terror) can take over. In any context, the alternative to communicative rationality is domination, as we bully others into agreeing to go along with our preferences. At a macro level, domination is achieved by whichever state (or state alliance), political group, or industry has the greatest access to technological and economic resources, and systematically uses those resources to achieve strategic ends. Technical-instrumental rationality will most likely lead to coerced rather than (communicatively rational) consensual action.

NEWS 5.26

DISTORTED COMMUNICATION

Although Habermas's ideal speech situation offers a hopeful way of thinking about the resolution of conflict, it is difficult to realize in practice. Even negotiating a restaurant choice with our friends, it is difficult to transcend our own individual assumptions and preferences and to not act in a calculating and strategic fashion, no matter what surface appearance we may present. We are so accustomed to exchange in social life (see chapter 7), we tend to think of compromise as something we do today with the expectation that someone will do something for us later. Compromise, however, is not the same as reaching consensus. A rationally achieved consensus requires the crafting of what may be a totally new strategy of action, one not initially intended by any of the participants. Compromise, by contrast, tends to be a solution that honors, however partially, the initial agendas of the participants, and it typically does not require the participants to re-examine the very assumptions informing what they consider to be their preferences, interests, or values. Compromise often works well, whether politically or among friends, but it may not do much to alter deeply ingrained inequalities.

At a societal level, our various forms of social organization mean that there are many institutional blocks to communicative rationality. Habermas highlights how the steering mechanisms within capitalist society, i.e., money and power, and the range of economic, social, and ecological problems they have exacerbated (1996: xlii), produce distorted communication; they distort the possibilities for communicative rationality. Thus, for example, the resolution of the health-care crisis would necessarily require an examination of the fundamental ways in which health-care distribution is managed and organized. This would inevitably raise basic questions about the economics of health care, and by extension, spotlight the fundamental assumptions built into capitalism, not least of which is its structurally inherent economic and social inequality. No matter how well intentioned any player in the health sector may be, the many and varied vested economic and political interests at stake among the participants – hospitals, insurance companies, pharmaceutical drug companies, doctors' and nurses' professional organizations, corporate and small business employers, federal and state government, medical malpractice lawyers – distort the possibility that all of the players would be willing to reflexively examine how their particular strategic interests may be getting in the way of creating a more equitable and more efficient health-care system. This distortion – deeply grounded in the very structure of our capitalist society and its forms of institutional and social organization – thus impedes the likelihood of communicative rational action in regard to health care.

REASON IN THE CONTEXT OF EVERYDAY LIFE

In general, given everyday lived realities, the application of Habermas's concept of an ideal speech situation ruled by communicative reason seems somewhat unrealistic, notwithstanding the hope it stimulates for realizing a more rationally engaged and participative democracy. Indeed, Habermas has been criticized by feminist scholars and political theorists on several points. In particular, he marginalizes the impact of the power inequalities in social interaction and the different interests, experiences, traditions, language capabilities, and informal narrative storytelling styles that participants variously bring to a particular communicative context (e.g., Calhoun 1995; Collins 1990: 212; Frazer and Lacey 1993: 19–21, 144–147). Further, Habermas's embrace of what Iris Young (1990: 125) calls "the disembodied coldness of modern reason" excludes the play of emotions despite their obvious centrality to communication and social interaction; an exclusion in sociology more generally that is redressed by feminist theorists (see chapter 10).

Moreover, notwithstanding the institutionalized and informal ways in which religious involvement, for example, can at times facilitate reasoned communication and social critique (e.g., Dillon 1999), Habermas has expressed a skeptical view toward religion in the public sphere, seeing it as distorting institutional critique. His TCA, for example, requires the (evolutionary) attainment of societal conditions such that "the authority of the holy is gradually replaced by the authority of an achieved consensus. This means a freeing of communicative action from sacrally protected normative contexts ... [and] the spellbinding power of the holy" (Habermas 1987: 77).

Habermas recently appeared to modify his understanding of religion and rationality. He now argues that much of the affluent western world can be characterized as a *post-secular* society. Unlike a secular society, in which religion (allegedly) loses its public authority, a post-secular society sees religion maintaining "a public influence and relevance" (Habermas 2008: 4), and is one which presumes that religious believers and secularists "can live together in a self-reflective manner" (Habermas 2008: 12). The post-secular society is thus for Habermas still secular in that it is rationality that orients the public sphere. A primary difference between secular and post-secular society is that the persistence of religious individuals and communities "robs the secular understanding of the world of any triumphal zest" (Habermas 2008: 4). The post-secular political culture requires inclusion of religious perspectives, but importantly, it is not religious faith per se but the translation of religious beliefs into a rational-secular discourse that is required. This, Habermas argues, can help society deal with "a miscarried life, social pathologies, the failures of individual life projects, and the deformation of misarranged existential relationships" (Habermas, quoted in Nemoianu 2006: 26). Thus Habermas states: "It is in the best interest of the constitutional state to act considerately toward all those cultural sources [including religion] out of which civil solidarity and norm consciousness are nourished" (ibid.: 27).

What Habermas means by the state "acting considerately" is vague. As the sociologist Robert Bellah (2005) argues, because of historical religious influences on the formation of the state, the state is not a neutral actor. Think, for example, of the influence of Protestant individualism in the US (cf. Weber, chapter 3; and Parsons, chapter 4) and how its derived discourse of individual rights influences American law, social policy (e.g., Glendon 1987), and economic inequality (fueled by the cultural emphasis on self-reliance). The state itself needs to be resisted, as indeed Habermas emphasizes, and this resistance requires a robust normative or values framework, whether these values come from within a religious framework as Bellah (2005) would recommend – or from a secular ethic of equality and communal responsibility. In sum, Bellah and Habermas agree that communicative rationality is necessary against the totalitarian forces that threaten democratic society (e.g., state coercion, consumerism, and extremes of wealth and poverty). But Bellah sees a more explicit and vigorous role than Habermas does for the place of religion-derived norms in informing the rational critique necessary to advancing social and political equality.

SUMMARY

FS theorists offer a searing critique of contemporary culture, society, and politics. They argue that while we use reason to produce new scientific knowledge and sophisticated technologies that enhance our lives, at the same time we use much of this knowledge for social control, and to advance capitalist economic, political, and cultural domination. This is the "dialectic of Enlightenment" – seen, for example, in the one-dimensional content (the sameness) that characterizes the (false) choices celebrated in the consumer marketplace and in political discourse. Jurgen Habermas glimpses a (somewhat utopian) way out of this domination. He argues that we need to retrieve an emancipatory, communicative rationality such that through un-coerced communication with others in the public sphere, we can commit to consensual actions undistorted by economic, political, and other self-serving interests. There is much evidence to support the pessimistic view of mass culture, politics, and technological colonization articulated by the *FS*. But, importantly, too there are many instances that challenge their theoretical claims.

POINTS TO REMEMBER

Enlightenment: the valuing of:
- Reason
- Equality
- Emancipation

Dialectic of Enlightenment (Horkheimer and Adorno):
- Critique of the selective implementation of Enlightenment ideals
- Reason becomes equated with instrumental reason
- Domination and subjugation, not emancipation
- Not illumination, but repression
- Not progress, but regression
- Not evaluative-normative reason, but a strategic, technical rationality
- One-dimensional thought and behavior
- Homogenization and standardization
- Sameness evident in mass culture and politics; controlled choices

Theory of communicative action (Habermas):
- Rational domination
  - Money
  - Power
    - The colonization of the lifeworld
    - An administered, controlled society
- Habermas's goal: rescue reason from its one-sided association with instrumental rationality/domination
- Retrieve reasoned communication; communicative rationality
- Ideal speech situation; validity claims concerning assumptions and goals
- Communicative action: build a reasoned consensus, avoid domination
- Impeded by structures within capitalism: produce distorted communication

GLOSSARY

administered world bureaucratic-state regulation and control diminishing the political autonomy of individuals and the public sphere.

celebrity mass media celebration of the public legitimacy and influence of actors and other media personalities irrespective of their credentials.

civil society sphere of society mediating between individuals and the state; e.g., informal groups, social movements, mass media.

colonization of the lifeworld the idea that the state and economic corporations (including mass media) increasingly penetrate and dominate all aspects of everyday life.

communicative action the idea that social action should be determined by a rationally argued consensus driven by rationally argued ethical norms rather than strategic partisan interests.

communicative rationality back-and-forth reasoning and reflexive examination of various claims made in a given communicative exchange. The reasonableness of the arguments articulated rather than the power or status of the communication partners determines the communicative outcome.

controlled rationality strategic use of instrumental reason to attain a particular (controlled) end.

critical theory Frankfurt School critique of the one-sided, strategic use of reason in democratic capitalist societies to advance economic, political, and cultural power, and suppress critique of social institutions and social processes, rather than to increase freedom, social equality, and democratic participation.

cultural totalitarianism the repression of diversity in the expression of individual needs and opinions; accomplished by the restricted sameness of content and choices available in the economic, political, and cultural marketplace.

culture industry corporate economic control of the mass media and its emphasis on advertising and business rather than providing cultural content (e.g., ideas,

story plots) that would challenge rather than bolster the status quo.

dialectic of Enlightenment the thesis that the ideas affirmed by the Enlightenment (e.g., the use of reason in the advancement of freedom, knowledge, and democracy) have been turned into their opposite (reason in the service of control, inequality, political passivity) by the instrumentally rational domination exerted by capitalist institutions (e.g., the state, economic and media corporations).

distorted communication ways in which current economic and political arrangements and cultural assumptions (e.g., free markets; individual self–reliance) impede communicative rationality.

emancipated society when previously marginalized individuals and groups are free to fully participate across all spheres of society; one in which freedom rather than domination is evident in institutional practices.

Enlightenment eighteenth-century philosophical movement emphasizing the centrality of individual reason and scientific rationality over against non-rational beliefs and forms of social organization (e.g., monarchy).

false needs the fabrication or imposition of consumer wants (needs) as determined by mass media, advertising, and economic corporations in the promotion of particular consumer lifestyles; and which consumers (falsely) feel as authentically theirs.

hegemony process by which the institutions (e.g., mass media) and culture in capitalist society are orchestrated to produce consent by the masses to the status quo.

homogenization standardization of products and choices in consumption and politics driven by the mass orientation (sameness) most profitable to the culture industry.

ideal speech situation when communication partners use reason (communicative rationality) to seek a common understanding of a question at issue, and to embark on rationally justified, mutually agreed, future action.

instrumental domination strategic use of reason (knowledge, science, technology) to control others.

legitimation crisis when national or other collectivities lose trust in the ability of the state (or other institutions) to adequately respond to major systemic disruptions in the execution of institutional tasks (e.g., the effective functioning of the banking system).

lifeworld from the German word *Lebenswelt*; the world of everyday life and its taken-for-granted routines, customs, habits, and knowledge.

mass culture advertising and other mass mediated content delivered by a technologically sophisticated, profit driven, corporate culture industry.

normative rationality evaluative use of reason to advance values (or prescriptive norms) of equality and freedom.

one-dimensionality sameness; lack of meaningful alternatives in mass culture and politics.

political dependency dependence of citizens on the state to resolve problems and crises created, by and large, by the state and economic institutions.

promotional culture constant stream of consumer advertising dominating mass media content and public space (e.g., highways).

public sphere public, relatively informal spaces (e.g., coffee shops, public squares) and non-state-controlled institutional settings (e.g., mass media, voluntary and non-profit organizations) where individuals and groups freely assemble and discuss political and social issues; produces "public opinion." *See also* civil society.

reification from the Latin word *res*, "thing"; process whereby we think of social structures (e.g., capitalism), social institutions and other socially created things (e.g., language, technology, "Wall Street") as things independent of human construction rather than as social creations that can be modified and changed to meet a society's changing needs and interests and to accomplish particular normative or strategic goals.

scientific management industrial method introduced in the early twentieth century by Frederick Taylor to increase worker efficiency and productivity by controlling workers' physical movements.

scientific rationality use of scientific information to advance planful precision in task execution.

social control methodical regulation curtailing the freedom of individuals, groups, and society as a whole.

standardization imposition of sameness or homogenization in culture and politics.

steering problems emerge when economic and political institutions do not work as functionally intended and as ideologically assumed (e.g., the market's "invisible hand" working to produce economic growth and social integration), thus causing problems (e.g., recession) whose resolution demands state intervention in the system (e.g., shift in federal monetary policy).

systems of domination penetration of the regulatory control of the state and other bureaucratic and corporate entities into everyday life.

technical rationality calculated procedures and techniques used in the strategic implementation of instrumental goals.

technological determinism the assumption that the use of a particular technology is determined by features of the technology itself rather than by the dominant economic, political, and cultural interests in society.

technological rationality proliferation of technological devices and procedures in strategically managing and controlling everyday corporate and individual activities.

All news stories are from the *New York Times* unless otherwise noted, and can be accessed via www.wiley.com/go/dillon. See NEWS icons in the margins above.

NEWS 5.1   "Monks are silenced, and for now, internet is, too," October 4, 2007.

NEWS 5.2   "Jockeying for a stake raises value of Facebook," September 25, 2007.

"An oracle part man, part machine," September 23, 2007.

"A company will monitor phone calls and devise ads to suit," September 24, 2007.

"Intimate shopping. Should everyone know what you bought today?" December 3, 2007.

"Facebook is marketing your brand preferences," November 7, 2007.

NEWS 5.3   "UNH swipe cards linked to Social Security numbers," *The New Hampshire*, December 8, 2006.

NEWS 5.4   "A new strategy to discourage drunk-driving," November 20, 2006.

"Tell-all PCs and phones transforming divorce," September 15, 2007.

"New York plans surveillance veil for downtown," July 9, 2007.

"Where little is left outside the camera's eye," July 8, 2007.

"AT&T to sell equipment to monitor workplaces," November 14, 2007.

"Peace of mind when they ask to borrow the car," November 3, 2007.

NEWS 5.5   "Wal-Mart, a nation unto itself," April 17, 2004.

NEWS 5.6   www.skidubai.com

NEWS 5.7   "Forgotten trails and frozen lifts of winters past," January 25, 2008.

NEWS 5.8   "Experts warned of quake risk in China," June 5, 2008.

NEWS 5.9   "After centuries of 'controlling' land, Gulf residents learn who's really the boss," August 30, 2005.

NEWS 5.10   "Buy a laptop for a [third world] child, get another laptop free," September 24, 2007.

"Dell says plant a tree, help the environment," January 10, 2007.

"Google offers a map for its philanthropy," January 18, 2008.

NEWS 5.11   "Anywhere the eye can see, it's now likely to see an ad," January 15, 2007.

"This air sickness bag is brought to you by ...," March 6, 2007.

"As the fall season arrives, TV screens get more cluttered," September 24, 2007.

"When traffic piles up, drivers sit and publishers see new opportunity," October 8, 2007.

NEWS 5.12   "The view from your airplane window was brought to you by ...," September 25, 2007.

NEWS 5.13   "It's not only about price at Wal-Mart," March 2, 2007.

NEWS 5.14   Video available on YouTube.

NEWS 5.15   "World Briefing,"May 16, 2008.

NEWS 5.16   "Apologetic Facebook changes ad program," December 6, 2007.

"Facebook's users ask who own information," February 16, 2009.

"Billboards that look back," May 31, 2008.

NEWS 5.17   "Soccer moms are so 1996. Try Wal-Mart women," September 23, 2007.

NEWS 5.18   "Politics on the brain? Resorting to MRIs for partisan signals," April 20, 2004.

NEWS 5.19   "GM lays its future on Washington's doorstep," February 26, 2009.

"In aid filing, GM reduces fuel economy estimate," February 26, 2008.

"GM speeds hat in hand to treasury," October 27, 2008.

NEWS 5.20   "Student loans start to bypass 2-year colleges," June 2, 2008.

NEWS 5.21   "Seeking fast deal, JPMorgan quintuples Bear Stearns bid," March 25, 2008.

"Paulson's deal making revives Treasury's relevance," January 28, 2008.

"Democrats see a need for further economic stimulus," July 16, 2008.

"Bailout plan wins approval; Democrats want tighter rules," October 4, 2008.

"Latest Citigroup rescue may not be its last," February 27, 2009.

NEWS 5.22   "Your Mastercard or your life," January 22, 2007.

NEWS 5.23   "Report issued on FEMA trailers," March 4, 2008.

"Holdouts test aid's limitations as FEMA shuts a trailer park," June 7, 2008.

NEWS 5.24   "An American builder's failures in Iraq are found to have been more widespread," January 29, 2008.

"U.S. Agency finds new waste and fraud in Iraqi rebuilding projects," February 1, 2007.

"GI's death prompts 2 inquiries of Iraq electrocutions," March 20, 2008.

"Electrical risks worse than said at bases in Iraq," July 8, 2008.

"Failure to fix base hazards worried Pentagon official," July 19, 2008.

"Occupation plan for Iraq faulted in Army history," June 29, 2008.

NEWS 5.25   "Democracy is about the government listening. Not listening in," American Civil Liberties Union (ACLU) one-page advertisement, July 17, 2008.

NEWS 5.26   "A blueprint for a different course," December 7, 2006.

"A new openness to talks with that 'axis of evil'," July 22, 2008.

The Baker-Hamilton Report can be downloaded from the website of the United States Institute of Peace, www.usip.org

WEB SUPPLEMENTS

All web supplements are available at www.wiley.com/go/dillon. See WEB icons in the margins above.

WEB 5.1   World War II
WEB 5.2   Media ownership concentration

CHAPTER SIX
CONFLICT, POWER, AND DEPENDENCY IN MACRO-SOCIETAL PROCESSES

KEY CONCEPTS

group conflict

power

dialectic of power and
   resistance

interest group

manifest interests

latent interests

democratization of conflict

functions of social conflict

post-capitalist society

conflict groups

authority structures

new middle class

power elite

triangle of power

mass society thesis

development

underdevelopment

world system

neo-Marxist

center–satellite

dependence

situations of dependency

CHAPTER MENU

Talcott Parsons's influence on American and much of European sociology from the 1940s to the 1970s (see chapter 4) was such that students might have had little familiarity with the ideas of other theorists writing at that time. Frankfurt School writings had a narrow circulation in the English-speaking world until the 1970s (see chapter 5), and other European theorists of that generation, most notably Louis Althusser (1969), Georg Lukacs (1968), and Antonio Gramsci (1929/1971) – all intellectually indebted to Karl Marx – remained similarly inaccessible to English-speaking audiences. Nevertheless, these same decades saw important challenges to Parsons's core ideas. While Parsons was emphasizing the importance of shared values in society, Ralf Dahrendorf was emphasizing the centrality of conflict; while Parsons was emphasizing the smooth functioning of institutional structures, C. Wright Mills was highlighting the matrix of power within the institutional system; and while Parsons was elaborating an allegedly universal, American-centered modernization theory, Latin American-based scholars (e.g., Andre Gunder Frank, Fernando Cardoso) were emphasizing the structurally dependent economic relations between countries and geographical regions. This chapter briefly traces these diverse perspectives to highlight how they conceptualize macro-societal processes in ways that build on and move beyond classical theory (especially that of Marx and Weber; see chapters 1 and 3), as well as challenging Parsons's framework.

RALF DAHRENDORF'S THEORY OF GROUP CONFLICT

Ralf Dahrendorf is a German-born sociologist who spent most of his career in England. He is most associated with underscoring the normalcy of group conflict in society, a thesis he counterposed against Parsons's emphasis on values consensus. For Dahrendorf, society is comprised of unequal power and competing group interests, and should be understood in terms of coercion and constraint rather than voluntary obedience or consensus. Power, he argues, "is unequally divided, and therefore a lasting source of friction" (1968: 138), a point we see underscored time and again with the various ethnic and other group conflicts that characterize society (e.g., Sunni versus Shia in Iraq; Luos versus Kikuyus in Kenya; Bloods versus Crips in Los Angeles). Thus, Dahrendorf claims, any given political situation can be described in terms of the antagonism between power and resistance (1968: 145). He explains:

🖽 NEWS 6.1

> Power always implies non-power and therefore resistance. The **dialectic of power and resistance** is the motive force of history. From the interests of those in power at a given time we can infer the interests of the powerless, and with them the direction of change ... Power produces conflict, and conflict between antagonistic interests gives lasting expression to the fundamental uncertainty of human existence, by ever giving rise to new solutions and ever casting doubt on them as soon as they take form. (1968: 227)

In this view, then, justice is "the permanently changing outcome of the dialectic of power and resistance" (ibid.: 150).

BIOGRAPHICAL NOTE

Ralf Dahrendorf was born in Hamburg, Germany, in 1929. He received his PhD from the London School of Economics (LSE), and subsequently had a distinguished academic and political career, holding professorships of sociology at several German universities and serving as director of the LSE. He retired as warden of St Anthony's College in Oxford in 1997. In the early 1970s, he served in the German parliament and was Germany's European Commissioner in Brussels (the location of one of the EU headquarters). Dahrendorf became a British citizen in 1988. Among many honors, he was granted a peerage by the queen in 1993, thus privileging him with a seat in the British Parliament's upper House of Lords. Dahrendorf continues to engage in scholarly and political debates as a frequent contributor to many newspapers.

Dahrendorf does not see conflict as a threat to society – even though some conflicts produce violence that severely undermine a given society's social order (e.g., Kenya). For the most part, however, non-violent conflict characterizes democratic industrial societies; conflict inheres in social life, a result of the unequal distribution of power and authority, and does not necessarily produce disorder or chaos. Dahrendorf explains:

NEWS 6.1

> Institutions have to be set up in such a way as to accommodate change, conflict, and the interplay of power and resistance. There is no foolproof recipe for creating such institutions, and someday we may well conclude that parliaments, elections, and the other traditional democratic political machinery are only one of many arrangements of roughly equal effectiveness. In any case, such institutions should allow for conflict; they should be designed to control power rather than to camouflage it behind an ideology of consensus, and they should permit change even in the unwieldy structure of a complex modern society. (1968: 149)

The establishment of such institutions, however, is difficult – as highlighted by the ongoing obstacles encountered in efforts to establish civic structures in Iraq, for example, that would be fair to all competing groups (and perceived as such). We see similar hurdles in the various community-policing initiatives toward building trust among competing gangs in inner-city neighborhoods. Nonetheless, Dahrendorf emphasizes that conflict is part and parcel of social life and that society, rather than ignoring conflict, deals with its normalcy by institutionally regulating it. Bureaucratic division within organizations is one relatively effective way to regulate different groups' differential access to power and authority (e.g., between engineers and accountants in a construction firm).

CONFLICT GROUPS

Formally organized interest groups such as labor unions, other employee and professional groups, and owner/management associations are all part of the institutionalization of conflicting interest groups and of class conflict in democratic industrial societies (1959: 257). An interest group is any "organized collectivity of individuals sharing manifest interests," i.e., interests which the collectivity is consciously aware of and articulates as being their interests. Groups, by virtue of their organizational position vis-á-vis other groups, also have interests of which they may be unaware; they are unspoken and hence referred to as latent interests. The establishment of diverse interest groups and organizations, and of conflict-mediating/negotiating bodies (e.g., labor courts for the mediation of employee – management disputes, especially apparent in Western Europe) – what Dahrendorf calls the democratization of conflict – is itself a structural change "which is due to no small extent to the effects of industrial conflict" (1959: 257).

Class antagonisms between factory workers and owners, vividly apparent as a result of unsafe working conditions in late nineteenth-century factories and mills, gave rise to political solutions establishing new norms (e.g., legislation regulating work-hours) and new structures and opportunities (e.g., legalization of unions) for the airing and negotiation of grievances. Dahrendorf argues that the establishment of trade unions reduces the intensity of conflict between workers and owners. With the democratization of conflict, "Organized groups stand in open, and therefore in controllable, conflict" (1959: 259). This process is well exemplified in the US in the relations between the car manufacturing companies (e.g., GM, Ford, Chrysler) and the car workers' union, the United Auto Workers (UAW); though they frequently have tense relations, both sides ultimately resolve their disputed issues (at least temporarily). Perhaps for this same reason, Wal-Mart appears to be rethinking its overtly hostile attitude toward unionization, recognizing that conflict is more easily controlled when it is institutionalized rather than suppressed.

▤▤ NEWS 6.2

Therefore, although Dahrendorf positions himself as a critic of functionalism, it is more accurate to say that he is a critic not of functionalism but of Parsons's emphasis on shared social values i.e., the generalized value system in society. We see, in fact, that Dahrendorf emphasizes the functions of social conflict. Social conflict has an integrative function insofar as it is an essential feature built into the structures of social life, allowing for the co-existence and interdependence of numerous groups with diverse, overlapping, and conflicting interests (Dahrendorf 1959: 206–207). At the same time, social conflict also functions as a mechanism of social change (1959: 206–207), to the extent that conflicts can result in structural changes instituted to resolve given conflicts, and which, in turn, most likely give rise to new conflicts (see Coser 1956).

CLASS CONFLICT IN INDUSTRIAL SOCIETY

Dahrendorf's emphasis on the normalcy of interest-group conflict, his language discussing the "dialectic of power and resistance as the motive force of history"

(1968: 227), and his denunciation of equilibrium models in favor of what he contends is the superior, more plausible and informative, coercion theory of society (1968: 150) might suggest that he is a theorist in the tradition of Marx. But, although Dahrendorf is intellectually engaged with Marx's theory, he is very critical of its core assumptions and their applicability to contemporary society.

In his influential book *Class and Class Conflict in Industrial Society* (1959), Dahrendorf subjects Marx's theory of capitalism to a detailed critical reassessment in light of the changes in capitalism in the first half of the twentieth century. Dahrendorf argues that the dichotomized property and class relations assumed by Marx no longer characterize capitalism (1959: 244–245), and hence it is more appropriate to refer to contemporary capitalist economies as advanced or post-capitalist society (as Dahrendorf does).

THE CHANGING CHARACTER OF CLASS CONFLICT

Dahrendorf highlights several structural changes in capitalism. Among these is the decomposition of the capitalist class, i.e., the fact that the capitalist class is no longer simply the owners of capital, factories, etc., but is differentiated between ownership and management (1959: 44–45). There is thus, as Weber recognized (chapter 3), a stratum of business executives and professionals who manage, but don't own, capital; and the ownership of capital itself has become more differentiated with the emergence of public shareholder companies. Similarly, there is the decomposition of the working class: "the working class of today, far from being a homogeneous group of equally unskilled and impoverished people, is in fact a stratum differentiated by numerous subtle and not-so-subtle distinctions" (1959: 48). As Weber also recognized, there are numerous categories of semi-skilled and highly skilled workers whose skills require hefty economic compensation in the market. Dahrendorf argues, therefore, that while the "increasing uniformity of the working class was an indispensable condition" for the intensification of class conflict and the anticipated proletarian revolution (for Marx), the changing conditions of capitalism make that presumption implausible (1959: 51). Additionally, Dahrendorf argues, the structural opportunities provided by occupational and social mobility and the rise of the salaried middle class (ibid.: 51–61) further complicate any discussion of the working class and class conflict.

In post-capitalist society there is, similarly, no one ruling class, because the decomposition of the capitalist class means that no one class controls the means of production (capital ownership). Instead, Dahrendorf argues, there is a plurality of ruling groups or ruling elites.

> Ruling groups are ... no more than ruling groups within defined associations. In theory, there can be as many competing, conflicting, or coexisting dominating **conflict groups** in a society as there are [industrial, social, political] associations ... it is analytically necessary

and empirically fruitful to retain the possibility of a competition or even conflict between the ruling groups of different associations. In this sense, the expression "ruling class" is, in the singular, quite misleading. (1959: 197–198)

In short, contemporary capitalism has a plurality of classes and of non-economic interest groups, thus diffusing class relations and the conflicting interests between various class and non-economic interest groups. Thus Dahrendorf maintains that while there is inequality between classes, "to conclude merely that we are still living in a class society is as insufficient as it is unsatisfactory" (1959: 247). Instead, echoing Weber's elaboration of the multiple sources of stratification, and of authority in society (chapter 3), he argues that there are different authority structures, variously based on diverse economic, political, social status, and bureaucratic resources and interests (1959: 248, 256–257).

THE MULTIPLICITY OF CONFLICT GROUPS

Given these multiple authority structures, therefore, Dahrendorf argues that we should think of economic classes as conflict groups. And as conflict groups, classes co-exist and compete with other (conflict) groups and quasi-groups in society – all those organized and semi-formal groups and associations that have social, political, cultural, religious, etc. interests. A core proposition in Dahrendorf's theory is that "Any antagonistic relationship between organized collectivities of individuals that can be explained in terms of patterns of social structure (and is not, therefore, sociologically random) shall be called *group conflict*" (1959: 238). In sum, Dahrendorf sees society as comprised of diverse interest groups that operate in an open but regulated social and political environment in which they variously compete for available resources. Inter-group conflict emerges when one group becomes aware of the threat posed to its interests by the legitimate existence and behavior of some other group.

C. WRIGHT MILLS

While Dahrendorf was challenging Parsons's emphasis on societal consensus, the influential American sociologist C. **Wright Mills** was critiquing the conceptual abstraction in Parsons's writing, which he referred to sarcastically as "grand theory" (Mills 1959: 33–59). Mills, by contrast, argued that because sociology is (or should be) concerned with "all the social worlds in which men have lived, are living, and might live" (1959: 147), it must necessarily be attentive to the empirical realities in individual lives, and their intersection with history and social structures: "Biography, history, society … are the coordinate points of the proper study of man" (1959: 159), a theme Mills elaborated in his widely read book *The Sociological Imagination* (1959).

BIOGRAPHICAL NOTE

C. Wright Mills was born in Waco, Texas, in 1916. He completed his undergraduate education at the University of Texas, Austin, and received his PhD from the University of Wisconsin. He was subsequently professor of sociology at Columbia University. As well as writing many influential books and articles, Mills also edited and translated several of Weber's essays in *From Max Weber* (with H. H. Gerth). An avid motorcyclist, Mills was killed in a motorcycle accident in 1962, at age 46.

THE NEW MIDDLE CLASS

Mills himself wrote about many social issues, but most especially, he was at the forefront of documenting the changing composition of the class structure that began to emerge in the US in the 1940s. Mills (1951) documented, for example, the transition from the "old middle class" comprised of farmers, business, and independent professionals (e.g., family doctors) to the "new middle class," comprised of managers, salaried professionals, sales people, and office workers, a shift driven by the changing post-World War II American consumer economy and the expansion of government, corporate, professional, and service-sales bureaucracies, including the expansion of media, advertising, and public relations companies. Critical of the penetrating control exerted by bureaucratic organization (and its emphasis on rationality, impersonality, hierarchy, etc.; cf. Weber; see chapter 3), Mills argues (1951: 182) that the bureaucratization of work has produced a "personality market," requiring employees to have standardized, self-alienated personalities molded by "the market mentality" that dominates the bureaucratic society. Thus Mills identified the emergence of the "managerial type of man" (1951: 77) – the standardized, managerial-entrepreneurial personality who, essentially, bends and blends his own personality and interests to fit with the strategic interests of the organization he serves (1951: 77–111). The control institutionalized in bureaucratic organization extends to self-control; self-control over the employee's own feelings and desires, as exemplified by "the salesgirl," who must maintain a "friendly" personality – "a commercial mask" – to impress customers, remembering that she represents the organization, not herself (1951: 182–184). (We will return to the theme of personality control and self-alienation at, and as, paid work when we discuss Arlie Hochschild's contributions to the sociology of emotions; see chapter 10.) Succumbing to the demands of the bureaucratic and consumer society, it is status and prestige (e.g., 1951: 240–241), rather than political or civic commitment, Mills argues, that characterizes the character of the "politically indifferent" (1951: 327) new middle class.

Most notably, Mills underscored the impotence of the salaried middle class and of blue-collar workers (the working class) against what he called the power elite – the decision-makers in the upper echelons of the political, economic, and military institutions. Of Mills's several books, *The Power Elite* (1956) is still especially relevant to highlighting the overlapping composition of the institutional power structure in contemporary American society. Contrary to Dahrendorf's group-conflict theory of society, Mills emphasized the unilateral and far-reaching, consolidated power of the ruling institutional elite. Elaborating on the expansion of the bureaucratic, administrative authority of the state and the extending reach of economic and technological rationality first highlighted by Weber (chapter 3), Mills argued that "there is an ever-increasing interlocking of economic, military, and political structures" constituting a "triangle of power ... In each of these institutional areas, the means of power at the disposal of decision makers have increased enormously; their central executive powers have been enhanced ... As each of these domains become enlarged and centralized, the consequences of its activities become greater, and its traffic with the other increases" (1956: 8, 7).

Mills argued the power elite possess power, wealth, and celebrity, and by definition, present themselves, and are perceived, as being of superior moral and psychological character to those beneath them (1956: 13). Arguing against the view that it is Fate or Chance or some Unseen Hand that determines history, Mills instead emphasized that: "The course of events in our time depends more on a series of human decisions than on any inevitable fate ... in our time the pivotal moment does arise, and at that moment, small circles do decide or fail to decide. In either case, they are an elite of power" (1956: 21, 22). And he argued that the power elite have at their disposal the ever-expanding and concentrated power of the latest technology and the most efficient tools for logistics planning and other organizational effectiveness (1956: 23). (See also Frankfurt School, chapter 5.)

SHIFTS IN THE COMPOSITION OF THE POWER ELITE

Mills noted that the institutional composition of the power elite was not set once and for all time; "No matter how we might define the elite, the extent of its members' power is subject to historical variation" (1956: 20). He thus recognized that the institutional domains comprising the power structure can vary over time, though he also argued that such changes were usually a matter of relative degree rather than challenging the power elite's basic authority (ibid.: 269). The continuing interlocking power of corporate economic and political decision-makers is readily apparent today, as documented by Domhoff (2006a). What is new today is the ascendancy (since the 1970s) of a media elite to prominence and power far

WEB 5.2   beyond Hollywood and media circles. This is underscored by the narrow concen-
NEWS 6.3   tration of media owners (e.g., Rupert Murdoch) and executives who control a

greatly expanded world media industry, and whose power commands the attention of political and economic elites.

The defense industry continues to be a major corporate-political force (e.g., General Electric, Haliburton, Lockheed Martin, Boeing), and one much in the news as a result of controversies over US rebuilding contracts in Iraq (cf. chapter 5). And military-defense industry executives, as is true of all corporate executives, have a network of cross-cutting ties with several diverse corporations (banks, food manufacturers, etc; Domhoff 2006a: 27–28, 35). Unlike defense industry executives, however, military commanders have limited political influence. As underscored in military and other accounts of the Iraqi war, the assessments and judgments of senior military commanders are frequently ignored if they do not fit the agenda established by political elites (e.g., decision-makers in the White House, non-military Pentagon officials, etc.). Major General Taguba, a distinguished two-star army general who was assigned by the Army to investigate the Abu Ghraib prisoner abuse scandal in Iraq in late 2003, reported to his superiors that "Numerous incidents of sadistic, blatant, and wanton criminal abuses were inflicted on several detainees ... [indicating] systemic and illegal abuse." Subsequently told to retire earlier than he had planned, Taguba commented: "They always shoot the messenger ... I was being ostracized for doing what I was asked to do." Military decision-makers today thus seem to have less autonomy than argued by Mills, and it is likely that back in the 1950s too, they had less power than their economic and political counterparts (Domhoff 2006b).

📖 NEWS 6.4

WOMEN IN THE POWER ELITE

One aspect of the power elite that has not changed very much since the 1950s is its gendered character. In the 1950s the exclusion of women from the halls of power was so taken for granted that Mills, "an outspoken radical but a product of his times on matters of gender ... did not even mention [women's] absence among corporate and military leaders" (Karabel 2005: 410). Today, although there are more women in the upper echelons of government (e.g., Senators, cabinet secretaries), and more women corporate executives, judges, and military generals (one – appointed in 2008), they nonetheless comprise a small minority; for example, less than 2 percent of CEOs at Fortune 500 companies today are women. We will elaborate on the institutional and cultural barriers to women's equality and power in chapter 10.

📖 NEWS 6.5

THE PASSIVE, MASS SOCIETY

Unlike Dahrendorf, who noted the differentiation within the upper class between owners and executives, and thus the possibility for inter-group conflict within that stratum, Mills highlighted what he saw as the overall unity of the ruling elite, notwithstanding differences among them based on family wealth (Mills 1956: 62–65).

Topic 6.1   The gender power gap

A recent study commissioned by the World Economic Forum documents a persistent gender gap in access to resources and opportunities in countries across the globe. The Global Gender Gap Index uses United Nations' databases to measure labor-force participation, wages, and economic opportunity; literacy and access to education; participation in high-level political decision-making; and health, nutrition, and life expectancy. The study found that while women have almost closed the gap with men on access to education and health, they lag far behind when it comes to economic and political empowerment. The United States ranked 27th, placing above Canada (31st), Russia (42nd), Israel (56th), China (57th), Chile (65th), Brazil (73rd), Japan (98th), and India (113th). Those countries that scored higher than the US include Ireland (8th), Germany (11th), the UK (13th), France (15th), Trinidad and Tobago (19th), Australia (21st), South Africa (22nd), Argentina (24th), and Cuba (25th). Iran, Turkey, Egypt, Saudi Arabia, and other Middle Eastern and North African countries received the lowest rankings.

Further, he contrasted elite unity with what he saw as the powerlessness and fragmentation of other classes and groups. Thus, contrary to Marx's view that revolutionary social change would inevitably emerge from class antagonism between capitalists and workers, and contrary to Dahrendorf's construal of inter-group conflict and social change, Mills regarded those outside of the power elite, including the new middle class, as incapable of effecting social change – they stand powerless in the face of the ruling elite's decisive and consequential power.

Essentially, Mills (1956: 302–303) articulated a mass society thesis, namely, the idea that the vast majority of people, who are outside the corporate power structure, are both helpless and uninterested in influencing the ruling decisions determining their fate; as the early Frankfurt School theorists argued, they are manipulated and controlled by the mass media into passivity (cf. chapter 5). Mills argues that "mass education" fulfills a similar function. Education is not a prerequisite for "political alertness," a point highlighted by the active political interest and involvement of earlier uneducated generations (1951: 338). Nonetheless, "mass education" today – criticized by Mills for its narrow, unimaginative and boring content – trivializes politics and, Mills maintains, contributes to the masses' greater fascination with media entertainment than with politics (1951: 338–339).

This political indifference and passivity stand in sharp contrast to the democratic ethos and its affirmation of citizen participation and voluntary groups and associations in shaping society (1956: 28–29). In this context, social change, for Mills, is contingent not on political activism but on changes in the institutional landscape (ibid.: 280) – shifts in the mix of whichever institutional sectors become more prominent than others (e.g., resulting from how changes produced by internet technology get adapted by existing institutions). Thus Mills did not recognize the protest-mobilizing impact of Martin Luther King, Jr, in the mid-1950s (e.g., Halberstam 1993: 423–424), and nor did he anticipate the subsequent expansion in grassroots civil rights activism that was robust in the 1960s and 1970s, and which succeeded in achieving gains in equality for blacks, women, gays and lesbians, and physically disabled individuals (Domhoff 2006b). Despite these omissions, Mills's (1951) attentiveness to "managerial culture," and to the consequential significance of an interlocked network of powerful political, military, and economic figures in shaping the history of the present, finds considerable support in the several "insider" accounts of the planning and aftermath of the US invasion of Iraq in March 2003 (e.g., McClellan 2008).

DEPENDENCY THEORY: NEO-MARXIST CRITIQUES OF ECONOMIC DEVELOPMENT

Despite the different orientations of Dahrendorf (interest-group conflict) and Parsons (values consensus); and of Mills (power elite) and both Dahrendorf (multiple power groups) and Parsons (power equilibrium); the societal context informing their respective analyses was the US, and additionally for Dahrendorf, European industrialized countries. This US/western focus is in part due to the fact that in the post-World War II period, with the triumph of democracy over Nazism and Fascism, the US was seen as the prototypical modern society, and as crystallized in Parsons, the presumption was that all countries would eventually take on the same dimensions of modernization as the US (cf. chapter 4).

Although women and members of racial minorities are slowly penetrating the ranks of the power elite, they continue to be under-represented in the US Congress (seen here) and in other decision-making institutions.

There were challenges from within America and western Europe to the unevenness of modernization – the fact that in the US, for example, despite an expanding middle class, there was still large numbers living in poverty. It was also becoming apparent that modernization had its costs – the fledgling environmental movement in the 1970s highlighted the impact of unregulated economic growth on local communities and on the natural environment. The more visible social movements of the 1960s and 1970s highlighted the unevenness for blacks, women, and gays and lesbians in the realization of social equality, while the student anti-war movement protested what it regarded as American/western imperialism, an imperialism primarily located in America's protracted military presence in Vietnam, and one that loomed large over protesters' own immediate future as a result of the US military draft (e.g., Gitlin 1980). In short, in the US, the modernization narrative of a progressive expansion in economic and social prosperity had its many vocal detractors, among both the elite and those on the margins.

CAPITALIST DEVELOPMENT OF UNDERDEVELOPMENT

Although American sociologists were among those critiquing American domestic and foreign policy in the 1970s, the theoretical challenges to the modernization paradigm came from those scholars who, extending the lens beyond the US and Europe, took a more global perspective on economic development and social change. In particular, scholars in Latin America associated with the Economic Commission for Latin America (ECLA), an organization sponsored by the United Nations, directly challenged the assumptions of modernization theory. Notable among these, **Andre Gunder Frank**, a European-born, American/European academic, established an explicitly Marxist-derived framework for thinking about development. Against the backdrop of heated political debate in the US and Europe (the so-called "first world," which also includes Canada, Japan, Australia, and New Zealand) about how to deal with economic underdevelopment in the so-called "third world" (South and Central America, Africa, and much of Asia), the self-avowedly "political" Gunder Frank (1967: xiv) argued that the historical analysis of underdevelopment in Chile and Brazil provided clear evidence of the *capitalist* development of underdevelopment. He stated: "I believe with Paul Baran [neo-Marxist economist] that it is capitalism, both world and national, which produced underdevelopment in the past and which still generates underdevelopment in the present" (1967: vii).

BIOGRAPHICAL NOTE

Andre Gunder Frank was born in Germany in 1929, but his family fled the country with the rise of Hitler and eventually settled in the US. He received his PhD in economics from the University of Chicago (in 1957) and soon thereafter moved to Latin America, where he completed several country case studies of development. As professor of sociology and economics at the University of Chile in Santiago, Gunder Frank was involved in implementing the democratic reforms of the Allende government, but after its military overthrow in 1973, he moved back to Europe. He retired from the University of Amsterdam in 1994, and died in 2005.

By highlighting the significance of capitalism in producing and deepening underdevelopment in poor countries, Gunder Frank thus argued against the common view of modernization and development, and one that he states was his too until he went to live and do research in Latin America. The assumed view was that underdevelopment was due to the "backward" country's own internal problems, to: "largely domestic problems of capital scarcity, feudal and traditional institutions which impede saving and investment, concentration of political power in the hands of rural oligarchies" (1967: vii), and many other domestic obstacles to economic development. Instead, Gunder Frank argued that underdevelopment was generated and persisted in Latin America because of the innate contradictions in the capitalist production of capital/profit – the inherent structure of capitalism such that profit must always, and can only, be generated at the expense of workers' labor and the surplus value (profit) it produces for the factory owners and landowners (and corporations, etc.). This is the core Marxist point about the inequality and exploitation structured into capitalist relations of production (chapter 1). Gunder Frank insightfully extended this analysis to the unequal relations of production within not just one country but the world system, between developed and underdeveloped economies, a structural inequality that, he argued, is required by capitalism in the pursuit of its core goal: profit accumulation. (**Neo-Marxist** is the term sociologists apply to any theorist who, like Gunder Frank, employs Marx's core framework but then extends it in a new (*neo* in Greek) way or to a different unit of analysis.)

Center–satellite relations in global capitalism

Specifically, Gunder Frank argued that to understand underdevelopment in Chile or Brazil or any other Latin American country, we "must locate it in the economic structure of the world system as a whole," and in particular, in the concentrated monopolization of capital accumulation in the metropolitan center, profit accumulated from the expropriation of value and wealth produced in peripheral satellite locations (1967: 8). This analysis of center–satellite polarization in access to surplus capital (money) was applicable, Gunder Frank argued, not only externally, i.e., in Chile's relations to foreign capital, but also to economic relations within the country. Within Chile, the center appropriates the economic surplus (profit) produced in its satellite regions and localities; but in turn, the (internal) center is converted into a satellite country in the world system, "its surplus being appropriated by others before [Chile] can firmly launch its own development" (ibid.: 10).

It is this center–satellite (or core–periphery) dynamic, according to Gunder Frank, that explains the ongoing generation and appropriation of capital such that capitalism produces *underdevelopment* rather than development at the periphery. In short, the periphery lacks access to its own surplus capital, to its own wealth, which becomes profit for the core (1967: 9) – just as for Marx, the wage-laborer does not have access to the surplus value (profit) produced by his or her work; rather, the surplus value is profit for the capitalist. Similarly, core economies profit as a result of their exploitation of peripheral economies. Thus Gunder Frank argued:

> Economic development and underdevelopment are the opposite faces of the same coin.
> Both are the necessary result and contemporary manifestation of internal contradictions

in the world capitalist system. Economic development and underdevelopment are not just relative and quantitative, in that one represents more economic development than the other; economic development and underdevelopment are relational and qualitative, in that each is structurally different from, yet caused by its relation with, the other. Yet development and underdevelopment are the same in that they are the product of a single but dialectically contradictory, economic structure and process of capitalism. (1967: 9)

Consequently, Gunder Frank maintained, underdeveloped countries are condemned to underdevelopment, unless capitalism dissolves or they abandon the capitalist world system and opt for a "rapid passage to socialism" (1967: 9, 277).

Clearly, the emergence of what economists and sociologists call newly industrializing countries (NICs) challenges the empirical validity of Gunder Frank's prediction. And while some neo-Marxists concede that enclaves of economic prosperity and social development are possible in the underdeveloped or third world even if such enclaves ultimately reproduce "First World–Third World exploitation within Third World cities and rural areas" (Sklair 2002: 32–33), Gunder Frank unequivocally rejects the idea that "that capitalism could ever develop the Third World" (Sklair 2002: 32). Gunder Frank's view, therefore, is at odds with what has happened since the early 1990s in some third world countries, e.g., Vietnam, and also goes against the traditional Marxist idea that countries go through various evolutionary stages of economic development (cf. chapter 1).

NEWS 6.7

In sum, Gunder Frank's thesis of the capitalist development of underdevelopment is theoretically interesting, especially his insight pointing to the determining relevance of a country's colonial-economic history. However, although it may have empirical application in some socio-historical contexts, it is insufficiently nuanced to explain the economic and social development that is occurring as a result of the impact of economic globalization on societies heretofore deemed underdeveloped (see chapter 15). Other neo-Marxist scholars who have focused on the historical world context in which economic development occurs, such as the American sociologist Immanuel Wallerstein, also take a skeptical view of economic globalization; we will discuss Wallerstein's perspective in chapter 15.

DEPENDENCY RELATIONS IN ECONOMIC UNDERDEVELOPMENT

Other Latin American scholars associated with ECLA also elaborated strands in the neo-Marxist sociology of development. Among these, **Fernando Cardoso** is the best-known, having been president of Brazil (1995–2002), though notably in that role, his economic policies were more aligned with the "Washington consensus" (e.g., World Bank policies, etc.) promulgating global capitalist development (cf. Held 2004). In *Dependency and Development in Latin America* (Cardoso and Faletto 1979), Cardoso clearly stated the theoretical goal:

We seek a global and dynamic understanding of social structures instead of looking only at specific dimensions of the social process ... we stress the socio-politico nature of the economic relations of production ... This methodological approach, which found its highest expression in Marx, assumes that the hierarchy that exists in society is the result of established ways of organizing the production of material ... life. This hierarchy also serves to assure the unequal appropriation of nature and of the results of human work by social classes and groups. So we attempt to analyze domination in its connection with economic expansion. (1979: ix)

BIOGRAPHICAL NOTE

Fernando Cardoso was born in Rio de Janeiro, Brazil, in 1931. Trained as a sociologist, for many years he was professor of political science and sociology at the University of Sao Paulo, prior to becoming president of Brazil (1995–2002). Over the years, Cardoso has lectured at many American and European universities, and received numerous academic and international public policy awards. He continues to write about economic development and globalization and is currently a professor-at-large at Brown University in Providence, Rhode Island.

Societal context and economic development

Thus, like Gunder Frank, Cardoso was interested in the inequalities that inhere in societal development, but he was also committed to outlining how economic development is interdependent with non-economic, social and political processes; how a given country's specific patterns of social change or continuity are related to the specific socio-historical and structural contexts in which they emerge. Cardoso noted that any given developing country's historical and structural context is impacted by *external* forces – e.g., western empires or superpowers, multinational corporations, foreign technology, international financial systems and policies (e.g., World Bank), and foreign embassies and armies (Cardoso and Faletto 1979: xvi). Additionally, he highlighted the *internal* societal forces that matter; the cultural (e.g., religious ties, political ideologies) and structural (e.g., class structure; church–state links) factors that impact political mobilization, specific ideologies, and patterns of class inequality within the society at any given historical moment.

For Cardoso, the interplay of internal and external forces means that any analysis of political and economic domination necessarily involves the analysis of class inequality and class conflict (manifest or latent) within the developing country (e.g., Chile, Bolivia, etc.), and of the structural inequality of that country as a geo-political-economic unit vis-á-vis other developing and developed countries. He thus recognized that some underdeveloped countries undergo economic development, but that their development is contingent on dependency relations. He places his analysis squarely in terms of the unequal (economic and political) dependence of peripheral economies on those at the center. And, in contrast to what structural functionalists and others might more benignly call functional "inter-dependence" (Cardoso and Faletto 1979: xxi), he underscores the exploitative nature of dependence – as highlighted, for example, by the US intervention against neo-Marxist socialist governments in South and Central America (e.g., Guatemala, 1954; Chile, 1973; Panama, 1989) and the close ties maintained by the US government with military dictatorships in the 1980s (e.g., Brazil, Argentina).

For Cardoso, the dynamic interplay between external and internal forces produces complicated relations and situations of dependency that invalidate the assumption "that *all* forms of dependency had common features" (Cardoso and Faletto 1979: xxiii, xiii). Rather, dependence produces (or at least can produce) multiple sets of dependency relations. This construal deviates from the colonial model whereby the developing country is dependent solely on the capital, technology, and expertise of the richer and more powerful country. It also deviates from the neocolonial model whereby the newly decolonized country remains unilaterally dependent for resources on the colonizer, and thus (in the modernization paradigm) remains backward because, by itself, it is unable to modernize its own country's economic, social, and cultural processes.

One of the key points Cardoso emphasizes is that there are "coincidences of interests between local dominant classes and international ones," and these interests "are challenged by local dominated groups and classes" (Cardoso and Faletto 1979: xvi). Thus there are not simply "external forms of exploitation and coercion," but more complex "networks of coincident or reconciled interests" between and among specific groups or classes within the developing country, and between these and dominant interests in the external country (1979: xvi). And these varying interests get advanced and/or contested by the active mobilization of groups pursuing their particular goals; thus political mobilization and social movements matter in shaping the structural contours of developing (and developed) societies. Cardoso states:

> Social structures impose limits on social processes and reiterate established forms of behavior. However, they also generate contradictions and social tensions, opening the possibilities for social movements and ideologies of change ... In this process, subordinated social groups and classes, as well as dominated countries, try to counterattack dominant interests that sustain structures of domination. ... social structures are the product of man's collective behavior. Therefore, although enduring, social structures can be and in fact are continuously transformed by social movements. (1979: xi, x)

While Cardoso affirms the significance of social movements in bringing about change, he is also realistic about the extent to which they can resist structures of domination. Although the interests of (select) local groups can coincide with foreign interests, he notes that, ultimately, the system of domination represented by external domination (imperialism) can mean that external foreign interests co-opt local interests in the pursuit of their own (foreign) interests (ibid.).

In any event, how various local and international interests intersect within the specific political and economic context in a given developing country is what determines the particular ways in which capitalism evolves in that country. Moreover, as Cardoso underscores, not all developing economies are in a similar situation of dependency. For example, social and economic inequality in Latin America varies from country to country as a result of internal industrialization and the local structures in place to expand capital. But in all situations of dependency (and in all capitalist countries), Cardoso emphasizes (Cardoso and Faletto 1979: xvii), it is not the logic of capital accumulation alone, but its interpenetration with a number of other historical and societal factors, including the political implications of particular alliances of local and foreign interests, that matters. It is important that Cardoso sensitizes us to the varied ways in which countries develop and their varied situations of dependency. However, because he does not specify how particular internal and external factors would likely interact, it is difficult to generate empirically testable hypotheses from his dependency thesis, though it can be drawn on for post hoc interpretations of a given set of case study findings.

CHALLENGES TO MODERNIZATION THEORY

Despite the theoretical shortcomings in both Gunder Frank's and Cardoso's elaboration of underdevelopment/dependency, we can appreciate how their arguments would have prompted sociologists to rethink the applicability of Parsons's modernization thesis that all societies would follow a uniform, linear path toward economic and social development (cf. chapter 4). Cardoso's move slightly away from Gunder Frank's sweepingly general accent on economic exploitation, to spotlight the internal social and political forces (e.g., social movements) that contribute to the evolution of change in developing societies, provided sociologists with a more thoroughly sociological view of development, and one that simultaneously challenged modernization theory.

In sum, dependency theory underscored three major, interrelated points challenging modernization. One, development is not an automatic process driven by industrialization or economic modernization alone but by an intermix of interrelated economic, social, historical, and cultural factors, including the developing country's unequal relations with already-developed countries. Two, development is not a universal process with each developing country progressing in the same unilinear and inevitable fashion; rather, different societies have different patterns of development (due to factors cited in the first point), notwithstanding commonalities of history, culture, etc. Three, by highlighting the political significance of class alliances and the mobilization of elite and/or grassroots efforts to implement particular ideologies, dependency theory redressed Parsons's emphasis that values, though central to the consensus legitimating social structure, are relatively static and in the background. Dependency theory recognized a more dynamic relation between culture and structure, whereby ideologies and values are actively articulated and contested by social movements and political alliances and used to prod and reshape existing economic and political structures.

SUMMARY

This chapter traversed wide-ranging ground highlighting theoretical contributions that add nuance to classical theory as well as challenging Parsons's post-war dominance. We discussed Dahrendorf's delineation of the normalcy of societal/group conflict, and his critique of the applicability of Marx's analysis of capitalism and class polarization to contemporary, post-industrial society. We then highlighted Mills's challenge to the consensus/power-equilibrium view of society (and to the group-conflict model), explicated in his construal of the relatively unchecked and unified power wielded by decision-makers in the core intersecting economic, political, and military institutions. Shifting focus from western society, we then discussed the challenge posed to modernization theory by the Latin American-based dependency relation theory of economic development, elaborated by Gunder Frank and Cardoso. Although the theorists in this mix do not share a coherent intellectual perspective, their joint relevance lies in their respective contributions to articulating alternative ideas to Talcott Parsons's about how macro-societal processes work. And each in his own right also advanced sociological thinking about specific phenomena, i.e., conflict, power, and economic change and development.

POINTS TO REMEMBER

Ralf Dahrendorf
- Normalcy of inter-group conflict in society in response to unequal distribution of power and authority
- Group conflict arises when the manifest interests of one group are at odds with those of another
- Group conflict can function to produce social change resulting from its institutional resolution
- Inter-group conflict is institutionally regulated in democratic, industrial societies and hence typically does not lead to violence
- In post-capitalist society, occupational mobility and the existence of many occupational groups and economic classes undermine the applicability of Marx's understanding of polarized class conflict
- Economic classes should be considered as conflict groups similar to other interest groups

C. Wright Mills
- Post-World War II, US society: expansion of the new middle class, bureaucratization, and consumerism
- Interlocking, elite concentration of power among decision-makers in political-economic-military institutions
- Disregarded the role of social movements in challenging the institutional power structure

Dependency development theory
- Analyses of economic development in Latin American countries
- Explicitly Marxist/neo-Marxist framework
- Structural existence of center–satellite inequality between capitalist and developing economies (Gunder Frank)
- Coinciding economic and political interests between select local and foreign interests in developing countries (Cardoso)

- Significance of social movements and alternative ideologies in resisting capitalism (Cardoso)
- Emphasized that situations of dependency vary between and within Latin American countries

GLOSSARY

authority structures varied sources of legitimation, authority, or power in modern society; possible sources of ongoing normal conflict.

center–satellite the idea that some states/regions are dominant in (core to) world economic production whereas others are marginal or peripheral (e.g., the North–South divide).

conflict groups competing interest groups in society.

democratization of conflict establishment of formally organized interest groups and of institutional mechanisms (e.g., labor courts, mediation panels) to regulate group conflicts.

dependence an underdeveloped or peripheral country's relation to a developed country due to the historical economic and structural inequalities between them.

development economic growth and related societal changes in previously undeveloped countries.

dialectic of power and resistance ongoing conflicts (and changes) in society produced by group power inequalities and group resistance to those inequalities.

functions of social conflict social integration due to the interdependent coexistence of conflict groups, and social change resulting from institutional resolution of group conflict.

group conflict emerges when the manifest interests of one group conflict with those of another.

interest group any group whose members consciously share and express similar interests.

latent interests unspoken, tacit interests of one group vis-à-vis another.

manifest interests explicitly stated objectives.

mass society thesis idea that individuals in society are passive, unaware of and uninvolved in politics.

neo-Marxist ideas derived from Marx's theory of capitalism but reworked in new ways and/or with new applications to take account of the transformations in capitalism.

new middle class the expanding sector of educated (but politically indifferent) salaried managers, professionals, and sales and office workers that resulted from the post-World War II expansion of bureaucracy and the consumer economy.

post-capitalist society the result of transformations in the economy and in the occupational and class structures since the mid-twentieth century that make capitalist society structurally different from its late nineteenth-century incarnation.

power an unequally divided, perpetual source of conflict and resistance.

power elite upper echelon in the interlocking network of economic, political, and military decision-makers; holders of power and wealth in society.

situations of dependency term used to highlight the social, historical, and economic variation that exists among developing economies.

triangle of power the intersection of economic, political, and military institutions.

underdevelopment economies in the third world whose development is hindered by their relational dependence on, and exploitation by, the economically developed first world.

world system the world as a relational system comprised of structurally unequal, developed and underdeveloped economies.

RELEVANT NEWSPAPER STORIES

All news stories are from the *New York Times* unless otherwise noted, and can be accessed via www.wiley.com/go/dillon. See NEWS icons in the margins above.

NEWS 6.1 "Kenya: Ethnic cleansing amid political talking," *The Economist*, February 7, 2008.
"Signs in Kenya of a land redrawn by ethnicity," February 15, 2008.
"As Kenya bleeds, tourism also suffers in land of safaris," March 1, 2008.

NEWS 6.2 "Wal-Mart's detractors come in from the cold," June 5, 2008.

NEWS 6.3 "Murdoch moving to buy Newsday for $580 million," April 23, 2008.
"Murdoch, ruler of a vast empire, reaches out for even more," June 25, 2007.

NEWS 6.4 "The general's report," *New Yorker*, June 25, 2007.

NEWS 6.5 Catalyst (a non-profit, business member organization focused on expanding opportunities for women and business), Pyramid of Women CEOs: www.catalyst.org

NEWS 6.6 *The Global Gender Gap Report*: www.weforum.org/en

NEWS 6.7 "Vietnam's remarkable recovery," *The Economist*, April 24, 2008.

CHAPTER SEVEN

EXCHANGE, EXCHANGE NETWORK, AND RATIONAL CHOICE THEORIES

KEY CONCEPTS

social exchange
behavior conditioning
action-reward/punishment
   orientation
power imbalances
scarcity value
trust
diffuseness of expectations
exchange network
power dependence
encapsulated interest
social capital
strong ties
weak ties
micro-economic model
economic efficiency
maximization of utility
marginal utility
systems of trust
human capital
net gain
analytical Marxism
game theory
organization assets
contradictory class
   locations

Although exchange, exchange network, and rational choice theories comprise discrete perspectives on social life, I group them together in this chapter because they variously focus on the processes whereby individual or collective actors (e.g., couples, teams, etc.) seek and exchange resources (money, status, power, influence, information). To think of social relations in terms of exchange is not new. Enlightenment philosophers conceptualized the social contract as a form of political exchange (cf. Introduction); classical anthropology highlighted the centrality of gift-exchange in everyday life (e.g., Mauss 1967); classical economics underscored the productive efficiency and utility of exchange in human relations (e.g., John Stuart Mill, Adam Smith; cf. Introduction); and of course, among classical sociologists, Karl Marx stressed the unequal exchange that is structured into capitalist relations (cf. chapter 1).

EXCHANGE THEORY

Whereas Marx focused on economic exchange relations at a macro level, subsequent theorists shifted attention to also encompass the many non-economic forms of social exchange characterizing interpersonal and group relations. Georg Simmel observed: "Most relationships among men can be considered under the category of exchange. Exchange is the purest and most concentrated form of all human interactions in which serious interests are at stake ... every conversation, every love (even when requited unfavorably), every game, every act of looking one another over" (1907/1971: 43, 33). In this view, whether in the marketplace, politics, the classroom, or at home, social exchange is the core social process underlying relations between individuals, and within and between groups (cf. Blau 1964: 4); "Two conditions must be met for behavior to lead to social exchange. It must be oriented toward ends that can only be achieved through interaction with other persons, and it must seek to adapt means to further the achievement of these ends" (Blau 1964: 5).

GEORGE HOMANS: INDIVIDUAL ACTORS IN SOCIAL EXCHANGE

One of the leading theorists associated with social exchange was the Boston-born Harvard sociologist **George Homans**. In the post-World War II era dominated by a focus on impersonal social systems (following Parsons; cf. chapter 4), Homans sought to return attention to individual and small-group behavior and away from the macro structures, organizations, and processes that sociologists tended to emphasize. He argued that all elementary forms of social behavior could be explained in terms of the psychological motives of the individual (1961/1974: 12). For him, individual motives explain why institutions exist; they exist only because they enlist and coordinate the motives of individuals in support (or in spite) of the institution's aims (1961/1974: 372–373).

Thus, while Durkheim insisted that the behavior of individuals in society (manifest in social facts) could (and must) only be explained sociologically, i.e., by other social facts (cf. chapter 2), Homans took the opposite view. For him, in effect, sociology was a corollary of psychology – of individuals in interaction with other psychologically motivated individuals, whether in small groups or in organizations. Weber affirmed the significance of individual actors engaged in subjectively meaningful rational action (cf. chapter 3), but he also highlighted the specific sociological characteristics of groups and organizations (e.g., bureaucracy). By contrast, Homans argued that organizations do not have a sociological character of their own; organizations are simply "shorthand for the persistent, concerted activities of a number of persons" (1961/1974: 357). For him, all social behavior is a manifestation of *individually* motivated behavior and, further contrary to Weber, is independent of the historical, cultural, and organizational context in which individuals act.

BIOGRAPHICAL NOTE

George Homans was born into a well-established upper-class Boston family in 1910. He spent most of his life at Harvard University, first as a student – concentrating on English and American literature as an undergraduate, and sociology and economics for his PhD – and subsequently as a professor. He married Nancy Parshall, whom he credits (1950: xxvi) for drawing the various charts he used to illustrate relations among individuals in dyads and groups. Homans was president of the American Sociological Association in 1964; he died in Cambridge, Massachusetts, in 1989.

Exchange behavior

The elementary basis of all individual/social behavior, Homans argued, has to do with the fact that the individual's behavior "is a function of its payoffs, of its outcomes, whether rewarding or punishing, and they hold good whether or not the payoffs are provided by the non-human environment or by other human beings" (1961/1974: 12). In other words, we can only begin to understand human behavior, human interaction, if we consider it exchange behavior (ibid.: 56). The exchange that occurs in interpersonal face-to-face interaction covers a wide gamut: we exchange opinions about all kinds of topics, we exchange advice, CDs, friendship, clothes, favors, etc. In any exchange, "There are two kinds of dimensions along which a person and others who observe him assess his status. He is ranked on what he does himself – that is, on what he gives in social exchange – and on what he gets from others" (Homans 1961/1974: 225).

Following the behavior conditioning thesis popularized in psychology by B. F. Skinner (1938), Homans outlined a set of deductive propositions that emphasized a basic action-reward/punishment orientation to social behavior. Among other propositions, he argued that

For all actions taken by persons, the more often a particular action of a person is rewarded, the more likely the person is to perform that action … If in the past the occurrence of a particular stimulus, or set of stimuli, has been the occasion on which a person's action has been rewarded, then the more similar the present stimuli are to the past ones, the more likely the person is to perform the action, or some similar action, now … the more valuable to a person is the result of his action, the more likely he is to perform the action. (1961/1974: 16, 22–23, 25)

Power in social exchange

Social action and interaction, therefore, are driven by the individual's experience and learned anticipation of rewards and punishment. This is not, however a simple calculus. Because social exchange is characterized by power imbalances such that one person within the interaction gets more out of the exchange than the other person (1961/1974: 70–71), the value of the exchange has to be weighed in relatively subtle ways. Further, the power dynamics shift once a third person is involved in the interaction – a situation typifying small-group interaction. "A difference between men in their capacity to change the behavior of others and to change it in their favor is what we mean by a difference in power" (ibid.: 73); "what a person … gives in social exchange … determines his power" (ibid.: 223). Because of imbalances in power, in what people give and are able to give, individuals make choices among alternative courses of possible action on the basis of their projected assumptions as to which course of action will yield greater rewards.

For example, three of four roommates sharing a campus apartment may do all of the cleaning chores because they want their apartment to look well when other friends visit (the reward of both a tidy apartment and their friends' approval); they thus invest in this activity even though the fourth roommate gets to similarly enjoy the rewards of the others' efforts. There is a clear exchange imbalance in the group's relationship. But this chore imbalance might be offset by other resources the fourth roommate contributes; she may be a good cook or have an extensive CD collection, and generously share these resources with her roommates.

In all one-to-one or group relationships, Homans argues, "Power … depends on an ability to provide rewards that are valuable because they are scarce … What determines the scarcity value of a reward is the relation between the supply of it and the demand for it" (1967: 55). Thus, the fourth roommate will only retain the power not to be kicked out of the apartment by the others if she cooks things they really like and cannot get or afford elsewhere. If, by contrast, a roommate or friend continues to disappoint, to violate your expectations of how she or he should behave, and to give "nothing" in exchange – not even affirmation of your chore efforts – you will likely engage in deprivation or punishment behavior by withholding your approval or other symbolic rewards (e.g., your company, by declining to attend a party with her). But you will only engage in such behavior to the extent that it does not simultaneously deprive you of rewards. Therefore, while you might in frustration refuse to tidy the apartment, you too, and not just your roommate, will be deprived of the rewards of your (time and effort) investment in chores.

Taking an example from the higher stakes of presidential election politics, the end of the Democratic presidential nomination contest between Barack Obama and Hillary Clinton in June 2008 clearly underlined the centrality of exchange in social life: that "One never gets [or gives] something for nothing" (Homans 1967: 73). Despite the power imbalance – the fact that Clinton did not win sufficient primary delegates and, therefore, really had no other option but to concede her support to Obama – the conditions for her doing so were nonetheless framed unambiguously in terms of the reward expected in exchange for her support. The question asked by political commentators and by Hillary herself and her aides, namely, "What does Hillary want?" crystallizes Homans's core assumption: all behavior, whatever its appearance and outcome, is exchange behavior, motivated by the individual's anticipated rewards (and punishment avoided) as a result of their action. (As it turned out, Hillary Clinton became President Obama's secretary of state, a highly prestigious and powerful cabinet post – though there is no evidence that this coveted position was promised to her in advance of the election outcome.)

NEWS 7.1

But why some rewards are prioritized and others dismissed, and in what circumstances – key questions of sociological interest – remain unaddressed by Homans. He does not acknowledge the larger societal context and how, for example, it shapes relationships (e.g., marriage) and individuals' expectations of and within relationships. Individuals have different expectations of friends than of work colleagues, and of teammates than of roommates. These varied expectations are also contingent on and mediated by intersecting differences in gender, class, racial, and other social locations. Therefore, while an exchange–rewards logic characterizes social relations, how it unfolds and plays out in interpersonal and group relationships is more complicated than the individual-motives logic outlined by Homans.

PETER BLAU: SOCIAL EXCHANGE IN ORGANIZATIONS

Homans's perspective is also of limited use in explaining the behavior of organizations, a challenge taken up by **Peter Blau**. In his influential book *Exchange and Power in Social Life* (1964), Blau stated:

> The core of a theory of society has to explain the complex interdependence between substructures of numerous kinds ... The foundation required for a systematic theory of social structure is a thorough knowledge of the processes of social association, from the simplest that characterize the interpersonal relations between individuals to the most complex that pertain to the relations in and among large collectivities. (1964: 2)

Blau studied how social exchange (defined above, p. 236) operates in organizations by investigating workers' behavior in several different bureaucratic settings. His research findings showed how the characteristics of organizations, such as occupational rank and status among workers, lead to social exchanges that (contrary to Homans) are not reducible to workers' individual psychological characteristics. Blau noted that employees in a government agency are required to defer to a hierarchical order of authority (e.g., to consult about a work-task problem with their supervisor rather than with co-workers) and to follow highly specified impersonal rules and procedures for accomplishing tasks (cf. Weber on bureaucracy; see chapter 3). But Blau also discovered that employees' work is dependent too on social exchange and the trust it implies. For example, when work colleagues informally seek advice from one another about a task, this builds esteem among colleagues (flattered that their colleagues recognize their competence) and contributes to the effective completion of the work-task at hand (1974: 6–8, 157–169).

BIOGRAPHICAL NOTE

Peter Blau was born in Vienna, Austria, in 1918; his parents were secular Jews who were imprisoned with the rise of Nazism and subsequently executed in Auschwitz (in 1942). Blau managed to escape from Europe and settled in New York, where he completed his PhD in sociology under the guidance of Robert Merton. Blau held distinguished faculty appointments at the University of Chicago, Columbia University, and after his retirement (in 1988), at the University of North Carolina, Chapel Hill. He was president of the American Sociological Association. He married Judith Blau, also a sociologist (at the University of North Carolina), and they had two daughters. He died in 2002, at age 84.

Trust relationships

Blau's insights into social exchange and trust relationships in organizations are supported in today's corporate workplace. There is much recognition that the effectiveness of teamwork in task accomplishment is dependent not just on everyone following the correct technical procedures, but on worker-team cohesiveness, a point underscored in many corporate advertisements, and in the prevalence of company-financed, team-building fun activities (e.g., Outward Bound weekend camps, treasure hunts etc.) and in-house employee clubs.

📰 NEWS 7.2

📰 NEWS 7.3

Beyond the workplace, politicians have long known the value of developing personal relations of reciprocity and trust that encompass but extend beyond strategic interests. Especially in the international political arena, the development of personal trust between potential allies and adversaries is seen as core to building and maintaining inter-country ties. This accounts for the frequency with which political leaders visit each other not just at their official residences and offices but also at their personal or family vacation homes; such social exchange creates both the structure and the expectation for future interpersonal and strategic exchanges.

However, unlike economic exchange relationships, wherein we typically pay a specified amount of money in return for a specified product or service, the sociological significance (and intrigue) of social exchange lies largely in its diffuseness of expectations:

> Social exchange ... entails supplying benefits that create diffuse future obligations. The nature of the return is invariably not stipulated in advance, cannot be bargained about,

In giving we expect to receive something in return, sometime in the future.

and must be left to the discretion of the one who makes it ... Generally, a [person] expects some expressions of gratitude and appreciation for favors he/she has done for others, but he/she can neither bargain with them over how to reciprocate nor force them to reciprocate at all ... The distinctive significance of social obligations requires that they remain unspecific and the fact that social, as distinguished from economic, commodities have no exact price facilitates meeting this requirement. Since the recipient is the one who decides when and how to reciprocate for a favor, or whether to reciprocate at all, social exchange requires trusting others, whereas the immediate transfer of goods or the formal contract that can be enforced obviates such trust in economic exchange. Typically, however, social exchange relations evolve in a slow process, starting with minor transactions in which little trust is required because little risk is involved and in which both partners can prove their trustworthiness, enabling them to expand the relation and engage in major transactions. (Blau 1974: 209)

Balancing the imbalances in social exchange

Moreover, Blau notes: "A paradox of social exchange is that it serves not only to establish bonds of friendship between peers but also to create status differences between persons" (Blau 1974: 210; see also 1964: 88–114), differences that invariably revolve around differences in power and rank. Thus "there is a strain toward imbalance as well as toward reciprocity in social associations," including friendship and marriage (Blau 1964: 26–27). We give birthday presents to our friends with the (unspoken) expectation (or trust) that they will reciprocate and not only give us a present on our birthday but give us one of comparable value to the gift we gave them. This seems like a fairly balanced social exchange. A "strain toward imbalance" emerges, however, when Friend A has more friends than Friend B. This gives Friend A more power in the A–B relationship because she has

241

more alternative friends to hang out with (and more birthday presents to buy), and hence may not feel constrained to give B a gift of comparable value to the one received from B. Giving a less expensive (or no) gift may have negative consequences (e.g., losing a friend), but these consequences will be greater for B than for A. Unlike B, A does not have a scarcity of friends. The (less expensive) gift A gives B, therefore, affirms the friendship, but it simultaneously affirms the power imbalance in the friendship. In short, friendship (and marriage) are exchange relationships, and they tend toward imbalance, given the variation in the resources (of money, skills, popularity, beauty, etc.) that individuals bring to the relationship.

The differentiation of power, however, does not necessarily lead to change in the structure of social relationships. Change only occurs in circumstances where those involved in the (imbalanced power) exchange perceive that change might enhance their net access to greater rewards (e.g., nicer friends, a promotion, votes). In many relationships – between spouses and friends, in bureaucratic work settings, or in politics – the perceived negatives are neutralized by the perceived advantages. This occurs because of a general overall reciprocity (rather than a unilateral dependence) in the exchange relationship such that the exchange more or less balances power (Blau 1964: 29) (as we discussed in the roommate example earlier).

EXCHANGE NETWORK THEORY

How power imbalances impact the development of trust is one of the questions explored by contemporary sociologists who elaborate a social psychological approach to the study of social exchange networks. The study of exchange networks is heavily indebted to the social exchange theory of **Richard Emerson**, who is widely recognized for developing Homans's individual exchange model to make it applicable not just to dyads (two-person units) and small groups but to larger social units. The now-common idea that organizations, corporations, and states are actors involved in networks of unequal exchange relationships owes much to Emerson's theorizing (see Cook and Whitmeyer 2000).

BIOGRAPHICAL NOTE

Richard Emerson was born in Utah; he majored in sociology at the University of Utah and received his PhD in sociology and psychology from the University of Minnesota. He spent most of his career at the University of Washington. During World War II, he served in an elite mountaineering army division, and subsequently participated in the first successful US mountaineering expedition to climb Mount Everest (in 1963), during which he also conducted prize-winning sociological fieldwork on communication networks; he was also an accomplished mountain photographer. He and his wife, Pat, had two children. Emerson, who suffered from cancer, died unexpectedly in 1982 (Cook and Whitmeyer 2000: 486–488).

For Emerson, an exchange network "is a set of actors linked together directly or indirectly through exchange relations. An actor is then conceived as a point where many exchange relations connect" (Emerson 1972: 57; also quoted in Cook and Whitmeyer 2000: 495). Importantly then, as Cook and Whitmeyer elaborate, "a connection exists not between actors but between exchange relations. A connection between two exchange relations is either *positive* or *negative* ... use of power in an exchange relation entails obtaining terms of exchange more favorable to oneself. Therefore, the more powerful actor in an exchange relation should obtain more favorable terms of exchange" (2000: 495–496, 497–498).

Emerson's focus on exchange relations has been useful in studying organizations, marriage and family dynamics, marketing, and geo-politics (Cook and Whitmeyer 2000: 501), and as world politics and economics lead to more intricately intertwined global networks (cf. chapter 15), we can assume that its usefulness will expand. Network alignments help to explain why the US took a relatively low-key approach toward Russia when it invaded Georgia in August 2008. Although the US is an ally of Georgia (and needs it as part of its western political-economic-military network bloc), the US also needs to maintain cordial relations with Russia. Russia has greatly expanded its own global economic power; it is a major supplier of oil, which if disrupted in any way by US actions would increase the price of gas in the US (and elsewhere); and further, Russia is also a key player in a network of allies that includes China, Iran, and North Korea – all countries that the US needs to contain to protect its political/economic/military interests.

NEWS 7.4

POWER AND MISTRUST IN SOCIAL EXCHANGE NETWORKS

Karen Cook and her collaborators (e.g., Cook et al. 2005) use Emerson's (1962) conceptualization of power dependence to assess how power differences militate against the development of trust across different types of relationships. Cook et al. explain:

> The main power-dependence proposition is that *dependence is the basis of power in an exchange relation* ... That is, the power of actor A over actor B in the A–B relation is a function of B's dependence on A. This general proposition relating power and dependence has been demonstrated to apply in many types of relations, including employer–employee relationships, marital relationships, friendship and dating relationships, and other social exchange relations involving mutual dependence that can be defined as relations of **encapsulated interest** [the idea that we trust someone because we believe that they take our interests to heart and encapsulate or merge our interests in/with their interests] ... In addition, the power-dependence proposition applies to other types of social units, including relations between groups, organizations and even nation-states. (2005: 42–43)

They note that while trust may emerge in unequal power relationships, it tends to be fragile, because individuals' (and groups' or nations') relative power impacts how they perceive the relationship (Cook et al. 2005: 43).

THE INSTITUTIONAL REGULATION OF TRUST

Because power inequalities weaken trust, and because trust is seen as an important element in smooth interpersonal and societal functioning, there are institutional mechanisms designed to supervise and enforce trust (a development that has parallels with Dahrendorf's democratization of conflict; cf. chapter 6). For example, the expectation of trust in professional relationships (e.g., doctor–patient, banker–client) is strengthened by external agencies and associations that impose detailed codes of ethics, and the mistrust that may characterize bankers and their clients is

---

BIOGRAPHICAL NOTE

Karen Cook received her undergraduate and graduate education at Stanford University, and after many years on the faculty at the University of Washington, where she collaborated with Richard Emerson, returned to Stanford, where she is currently a distinguished profes-sor of sociology. She has published widely and has received many awards, including election to the National Academy of Sciences, and to the American Academy of Arts and Sciences. Cook served as vice-president of the American Sociological Association in 1994–1995.

---

dampened to some extent by the guarantees of financial security (e.g., Federal Deposit Insurance Corporation; FDIC) and oversight (e.g., the Securities and Exchange Commission; SEC) provided by federal agencies. Notably, investor and public trust in these institutionalized trust mechanisms is weakened considerably when financial crises occur that are due, in part, to regulators' failures to exercise the supervision of banking and investment practices that they are entrusted with by the government. During the Wall Street financial crisis of fall 2008, the head of the SEC acknowledged lapses in the agency's regulatory practices.

NEWS 7.5

Belief in the social value of trust as a remedy against crime is so strong in law enforcement that many police departments invest great resources in developing personal relationships among police and residents in crime-prone neighborhoods. Similarly, independent mediating agents are frequently appointed to help cultivate feelings of trust between marriage partners, or among the parties to trade and other economic disputes within countries (e.g., between employer and employee groups) and between countries (e.g., tensions over free trade policies), and impartial monitors are dispatched to oversee the fairness of elections in fledgling democracies, in the belief that their presence on the ground will increase the trust of minimally empowered individuals in the country's voting procedures and election outcomes.

Clearly, trust-nurturing bodies are not always successful in maintaining trust in the relationships in question. And indeed, as Cook et al. note, in circumstances of declining trust, "reliance on interpersonal mechanisms for maintaining trust gives way to organizational mechanisms that ensure trustworthiness through increased monitoring and sanctioning, ironically reducing the possibility for ongoing trust relations" (2005: 47).

Cook and other exchange network scholars argue that one reason why networks are sociologically important is because they function effectively even in the absence of trust relations (Cook et al. 2005: 103). Trust can play a role in initiating your social contacts and acquaintances, but it does not have to; people can do things for you for reasons other than trusting you – out of professional duty, or for money (ibid.: 86–87), or for altruistic reasons (e.g., Dillon and Wink 2007: 158–179). The important thing is to have (direct or indirect) connections to people who are willing and able to commit to do things on your behalf. This is social capital. For network scholars, "Social capital enables us to get things done by people with whom we do not have a substantial trust relationship – indeed, people whom we need not even know" (Cook et al. 2005: 87). This is what we see, for example, in addiction-companion networks: paid "sober companions," whom alcohol and drug addicts may or may not trust, nonetheless help the addicts-in-recovery maintain an alcohol- and drug-free daily routine.

NEWS 7.6

THE STRENGTH OF WEAK TIES

Thus, sociologists who study social networks are interested not so much in whom we trust or like as whom we spend time with (irrespective of whether we trust or like them).[1] As underscored by Mark Granovetter (1973; 1974), overlapping interpersonal ties among individuals even, or *especially*, when the ties are weak rather than tightly knit are effective in enhancing individuals' life-chances (e.g., economic success) as well as community well-being. Granovetter shows that strong ties among a small group of individuals may reduce their ties to others outside the group, and hence close off their access to information and opportunities that might be effective for them either as individuals or collectively (e.g., in achieving community goals). When individuals have weak ties to several different people (e.g., an old high school friend, a former workmate) who themselves have weak ties to many others, this invariably opens up the individual's access to new information and opportunities (which may include jobs on Wall Street).

NEWS 7.7

Although, as Granovetter (1973: 1371) notes, it might intuitively seem that "those with whom one has strong ties are more motivated to help with job information … those to whom we are weakly tied are more likely to move in circles different from our own and will thus have access to information different from that which we receive [from our close friends]." In short, word-of mouth information or recommendations shared across several weakly connected people can create a large domino effect. This, in fact, is how the use of steroids in baseball seems to have expanded, as documented by the Mitchell Report (see Topic 7.1).

Trust certainly matters in social relationships, and closed sanctuaries such as locker rooms are certainly conducive to the development of social solidarity (cf. Durkheim; see chapter 2) and of trusting relationships. From a social network

NEWS 7.8

Topic 7.1 Steroid report depicts a two-player domino effect

The Mitchell Report on steroid abuse in professional baseball identified a former club-house attendant for the New York Mets, Kirk Radomski, as a major supplier of steroids. Among those whom he supplied, David Segui, a Mets player, subsequently went on to play for seven other teams, and he introduced Radomski to players on each of these teams. One of his contacts, in turn, was a trainer on one of those teams, and that trainer became a supplier to Roger Clemens and two other players. As the *New York Times* reported, "The use of steroids and human growth hormone seemed to multiply and stretch after the most ordinary interactions. Introductions were made over lunch or advice was doled out in the locker room, one place that players congregated every day."

perspective, however, what is more crucial is the existence of multiple connections across several different contexts – in the case of steroids, across several different teams.

Beyond the relatively confined network of steroid users, weak ties also impact macro-level processes – in the steroids case, leading to congressional investigations, public debate, and likely changes in drug policy for both professional and amateur baseball (and for other sports too). Weak ties can also facilitate the development of bridges to several other individuals when there is a need for community activism; bridging ties between loosely connected individuals and groups in the larger society, therefore, can thus breed social cohesion rather than alienation or fragmentation (Granovetter 1973: 1378).

In short, the maintenance of weak ties facilitates more connections among loosely tied individuals and groups. Tightly bonded, closed cliques, by contrast, are strongly tied to one another but with few ties to individuals outside the group, and thus a likely source of community fragmentation – a society of similarly minded cliques that do not communicate with others. Accordingly, the analysis of networks and of micro-level interpersonal ties illuminates how "The personal experience of individuals is closely bound up with larger-scale aspects of social structure, well beyond the purview of particular individuals" (Granovetter 1973: 1377). In sum, interpersonal ties – whom you talk to – are important; they are a core component of the social or network capital you (and your community) can use to accumulate additional resources.

RATIONAL CHOICE THEORY

All theories that focus on exchange project a certain utilitarian or self-interested understanding of the individual and of social relationships. It is rational choice theory (*RCT*), however, that makes utilitarianism (see glossary at the end of the book) – the utility of a course of action to the self – a core axis of explanation. **James Coleman**, influenced by Homans's exchange theory (Marsden 2005: 12), and impressed by how economists link micro – and macro-economic behavior (e.g., the translation of micro, individual demands onto macro supply processes), became a leading proponent of *RCT* for sociology. Coleman embraced the micro-economic model of the self-interested individual in his efforts to understand the mechanisms that link individual behavior to larger, macro processes.

BIOGRAPHICAL NOTE

James Coleman was born in Bedford, Indiana, in 1926. He received his BA in chemical engineering from Purdue University and later studied for his PhD in sociology at Columbia University, where he was deeply influenced by Robert Merton, to whom he dedicated his American Sociological Association (ASA) award-winning book *Foundations of Social Theory*. Coleman spent much of his early academic career as a sociology professor at Johns Hopkins University and then moved to the University of Chicago. His research on race, inequality, and education (Coleman et al. 1966) was highly influential in public policy debates. Coleman was elected president of the ASA in 1991 and was also an elected member of the National Academy of Sciences. He married Zdzislawa Walaszek, and they had four sons. He died in 1995, at age 68 (Marsden 2005).

Although you might be inclined to equate self-interest with selfishness, this is not entirely accurate. Acting on self-interest, as John Stuart Mill (1806–1873) noted long ago, does not necessarily prevent one from serving the interests of others. For example, although we might think of altruism – selfless concern for others – as the opposite of selfishness, many would argue that altruism is driven by many different motives, including self-interest (cf. Dillon and Wink 2007). In any case, the behavior of the self-interested individual reverberates well beyond the individual alone, and impacts macro processes across multiple domains (e.g., the economy, family relations, politics, religion).

Coleman (1961) first highlighted micro–macro connections when he studied how American adolescents' choices or values – whether they emphasize peer popularity over scholastic achievement – feed into aggregate, nation-wide patterns of educational and occupational success/failure. It was in his later theoretical work, however, that Coleman developed his ideas about the economic efficiency or rationality of human behavior and its implications for social processes that would seem to have little to do with economics. Coleman offers a social theory based on the "purposive action of individuals" (1990: 17). We know from Weber (cf. chapter 3), that purposive action can have several different motivational sources, but Coleman narrowly defines it as the maximization of utility – the usefulness of action to advancing the actor's own interests. Coleman frames it this way, in part, he states, because he wants to trade off as much psychological complexity as possible so as not to complicate his theory of the linkages between individual actions and their manifestation in social organizational processes (1990: 19).

MAXIMIZATION OF INDIVIDUAL INTEREST

For Coleman, an individual's rational cost–benefit evaluations in deciding whom to trust (1990: 177–196), whom to marry, whether and when to have children and how many, whether to pursue a college education, what church to attend, etc., can predict aggregate societal processes and trends (e.g., Coleman 1990: 21–22). Given the individual's (economic and non-economic) resources, the marginal utility of one course of action as opposed to another is what determines human behavior. Thus:

> The types of action available to the actor are severely limited. All are carried out with a single purpose – to increase the actor's realization of interests ... Actors are connected to resources (and thus indirectly to one another) through only two relations: their control over resources and their interest in resources. Actors have a single principle of action, that of acting so as to maximize their realization of interests. (1990: 32, 37)

The purposive maximization of interests is bolstered in modern societies, Coleman argues, by the development of systems of trust (or institutionalized trust mechanisms; see above, p. 244) that contribute to modifying "the decisions of individual actors to place trust and to be trustworthy" (1990: 175). According to *RCT*, trust in individual and collective others, including those "intermediaries in trust" (e.g., brokers, lobbyists) who act on behalf of "interested parties" (1990: 180–183), is a function of the likely future benefits to the (trusting) actor as a result of the negotiated deal. "The expansion of trust leads to increased potential for social action [motivated by its anticipated benefits] on the part of those who are trusted ... and the contraction [diminishment] of trust has the opposite effect" (1990: 196).

HUMAN CAPITAL AND SOCIAL CAPITAL

Coleman's colleague Gary Becker, a Nobel award-winning economist who elaborated "the economic approach to human behavior" (1976), argues that the rate of return on investments in human capital (by the individual and others) determines not only individual behavior but how couples, organizations, institutions, and societies behave. Human capital refers to the "resources in people," such as education, health, job training, and other non-monetary assets, that "influence future monetary and psychic income" (Becker 1964: 1). Just as we create physical capital by transforming raw materials (e.g., wood) "so as to form tools that facilitate production, human capital is created by changing persons so as to give them skills and capabilities that make them able to act in new ways" (Coleman 1990: 304).

Hence today when we hear business and university executives and politicians talking about investing in human capital, this is what they mean – retraining and retooling and re-educating workers so that they can be productive in a changing hi-tech economy.

NEGOTIATING SCARCE RESOURCES

Individuals need to maximize human capital, the economists argue, because there is a scarcity of resources in society: there is a market squeeze in, and hence increased competition for, job opportunities, houses, classroom seats, specialty restaurants, ski slopes, eligible marriage partners. Those who get to maximize utility in these markets will be those who are best able to use their human capital, and their social capital. Human capital can complement social capital if we use it (i.e., our abilities, health, skills, beauty, friendliness, etc.) to develop connections with others (social capital) (Coleman 1990: 304–305). As Coleman emphasizes – following Pierre Bourdieu (whom he cites, 1990: 300; cf. chapter 13) – social capital, unlike human capital, is not lodged in individuals but "inheres in the structure of relations between and among persons ... it is embodied in the relations among persons" (Coleman 1990: 302, 304). And, like other forms of capital, "social capital is productive, making possible the achievement of certain ends that would be unattainable in its absence" (1990: 302). By the same token, "a given form of social capital that is valuable in facilitating certain actions may be useless or even harmful for others" (ibid.).

Whom we hang out with, therefore, may facilitate or be functional to our access to certain opportunities that enhance the realization of our academic and occupational goals; and by the same token, some of our friends may hinder the realization of our interests by distracting us with less productive activities or getting us into trouble with the police, etc. This line of argument is reminiscent of the significance sociologists, including Coleman (1961), attach to the role of peers and peer *culture* in influencing adolescents' study and leisure habits. Hence for Coleman, "effective *norms* can constitute a powerful form of social capital ... This social capital not only facilitates certain actions but also constrains others" (1990: 311; emphasis mine). Coleman, then (unlike Bourdieu; cf. chapter 13), subsumes culture within social capital. He sees culture (like Parsons; cf. chapter 4; and Becker 1996: 16) in terms of the individual's internalization of the culturally affirmed norms and values that are conducive to achievement, for example, rather than a separate capital resource that can be actively drawn on to pursue various objectives (Bourdieu 1984; cf. chapter 13; see also Swidler 2001).

Economic theory, according to its proponents, provides a "unified framework for all behavior involving scarce resources, nonmarket as well as market, monetary as well as non-monetary, small group as well as competitive" (Becker 1976: 205). Thinking of marriage, for example, as a "productive" household unit, the prediction would be that "marriage occurs if, and only if, both [Person A and Person B] ... are made better off – that is, increase their utility [or expect to increase their utility]" (Becker 1976: 207). Marriage makes sense, has utility, if by pooling their resources, marriage partners are more productive and efficient as a household unit than either would be acting alone (as consumers and producers of goods and services – e.g., meals, leisure, etc.). In Becker's view, the division of labor between spouses, for example, would be based on evaluating the net gain in efficiency and resources for the family unit as a whole that would result from considering various alternative arrangements; whether one spouse should work for pay and one stay at home minding the children and doing housework; or if efficient for both to work, who should work more and/or do more household chores (so that the family will have more money, more leisure time, etc.).

MARRIAGE: STRUCTURAL AND CULTURAL CONSTRAINTS ON SELF-INTEREST

Paula England is a feminist sociologist who has written extensively on gender inequality, work and family (e.g., England 2005a; 2006; England and Farkas 1986), and specifically on exchange relations in marriage. While England accepts that optimizing individuals are self-interested actors (as *RCT* assumes), she argues, along with exchange theorists (cf. Homans, Blau), that self-interest is not confined to economic rewards, and she points out that Becker and others in the *RCT* tradition do not consider power imbalances or power dependence relations in their calculations. Going beyond both *RCT* and exchange theory, England offers a more nuanced understanding of individual and household behavior. In particular, she underscores the structural (e.g., wage and occupational structures) and cultural constraints (e.g., gender-role expectations in marriage and at work) that actively impinge on optimizing individuals pursuing their self-interests (England and Farkas 1986: 20–21).

England's research with colleagues, using time-management data from the US and Australia (Bittman et al. 2003), partially supports the claims made by exchange theorists (e.g., Homans, Blau; see above, pp. 237–242), namely, that "power flows from bringing resources to a relationship and that a spouse can use economically based bargaining power to get the other partner to do housework" (Bittman et al. 2003: 187).

Exchange-bargaining works such that women decrease their housework when they increase their earnings; in short, "money talks in marriage" (2003: 209). But that is not the whole story. Wives' increased income does not seem to push husbands to do more housework; rather, they pay for outside help and services (ibid.). Further underscoring the larger significance of gender in determining social patterns and processes, England and her collaborators also find that exchange-bargaining and the marital division of household labor are not simply a function of financial resources. For example, not only do women do a larger baseline amount of housework than men, but the research also shows that in the minority of households where women earn 51 percent or more of the household's total income, "gender trumps money" – meaning that women do more, not less, housework. They do so, England and colleagues argue, to compensate for the "gender deviance" of husbands earning less than wives in a society that still expects men not to be economically dependent on women (Bittman et al. 2003: 192, 210; England and Farkas 1986: 96). This is a cultural expectation internalized by the high-earning women in Manhattan, whose impression management strategies include keeping their lower-earning boyfriends from seeing their affluent apartments.

England and other sociologists thus challenge the narrow, micro-economic, efficiency-maximization approach used in *RCT* and its eschewal of the interpersonal, institutional, and cultural contexts in which actors make decisions. More generally, *RCT* fails to account for the many instances in which individuals and collectivities apparently act against their own utilitarian self-interests. Research (e.g., Bittman et al. 2003) suggests that the press of cultural expectations (e.g. of gender roles), institutional arrangements (e.g., the split between work and family domains; e.g., Jacobs and Gerson 2004), political ideology, and/or love, loyalty, and other emotions also need to be fully acknowledged as factors determining social behavior.

ANALYTICAL MARXISM

Although *RCT* seems far removed from Marxist theory (cf. chapter 1), some of its micro-economic principles are used by some contemporary scholars working within the Marxist tradition. Known as analytical Marxism, this empirically oriented school of thought emerged in the late 1970s as various neo-Marxist sociologists and economists sought to re-conceptualize some of Marx's core assumptions (e.g., historical materialism) in the context of late twentieth-century capitalist society (Roemer 1994: ix). Analytical Marxists seek to explain how, for example, occupational mobility and the emergence of an economically strong middle class – characteristics of contemporary capitalism that undermine Marx's stress on class polarization (between the proletariat and the bourgeoisie) – can be nonetheless understood in Marxist terms (e.g., Wright 1997).

Scholars associated with analytical Marxism vary in the specifics of the arguments they elaborate; their chosen unit of analysis – individuals (e.g., Roemer 1982), social classes (e.g., Wright 1984), or the state (e.g., Block 1987; Przeworski 1985); and their research methods. John Roemer, one its founding theorists, probes whether workers in modern capitalist societies should be considered economically "exploited" (as Marx would aver). Roemer (1982), an economist, draws on game theory models of inter-individual cooperation and competition to hypothesize a general theory of exploitation. Roemer conceptualizes the actors in an economy as "a set of agents, each of whom is characterized as having preferences over goods and leisure, and … an initial endowment of goods which can be used as inputs in the production process" (1994: xi). From experiments that impose varying degrees of difference in individuals' assets and preferences (on "labor market island"), Roemer argues, for example, that individuals basically select their own class position as a result of the asset-allocation decisions they make. In this view, therefore, it is individuals and not the capitalist class structure per se (as it is for Marx) that locks individuals into unequal relations. Roemer states: "People are not born into classes, so to speak, but choose their own class positions as a rational (i.e., preference maximizing) response to their wealth constraints. Thus capitalism induces [produces] a class structure in which those who are poor systematically work for those who are rich and are exploited by them in the classical Marxian sense" (1994: xi; see also 1982: 259–263).

CLASS LOCATIONS

Taking a different tack, the prolific American sociologist **Erik Olin Wright** focuses on the changing composition and dynamics of the class structure in contemporary capitalist societies. Using aggregate data from a large-scale, cross-national survey of class structure and class consciousness, Wright argues that "There are class locations that are neither exploiters nor exploited" (1984: 399). This is evidenced by the large sector of self-employed owners/workers, and by professionals and managers who occupy the senior ranks of corporate and non-economic bureaucratic organizations. These employees have access to organization assets – i.e., technical knowledge and expertise which they effectively control (as opposed to privately owning the means of production – property, capital), and which may be used by them to exploit others (Wright 1984: 399). Wright refers to these workers as occupying contradictory class locations, i.e., they are simultaneously in more than one class. Thus, "Managers, for example, should be viewed as simultaneously in the working class (in so far as they are wage laborers dominated by capitalists) and in the capitalist class (in so far as they control the operation of production and the labor of workers)" (Wright 1984: 384).

The interests, therefore, of those who occupy contradictory class locations do not correspond *a priori* to any one class. This, Wrights notes, is especially characteristic of state and non-economic managerial bureaucrats; "state managers ... unlike corporate managers, are less likely to have their careers tightly integrated with the interests of the capitalist class" (1984: 402). But as Block (1987) would emphasize, the capitalist context in which the state operates means that it will most likely bolster rather than undermine business interests over the long term,

BIOGRAPHICAL NOTE

Erik Olin Wright was born in Berkeley, California, in 1947. He received his BA from Harvard College and his PhD from the University of California, Berkeley. He has spent his career at the University of Wisconsin, Madison, where he is currently professor of sociology.

Wright is the sociologist most intimately associated with analytical Marxism; he has written several books and research articles documenting and elaborating his innovative analysis of the class structure of contemporary capitalist societies.

even if it at times it acts against specific interests of the capitalist class (e.g., taxation policy that redistributes wealth from the rich to the less well off).

In any event, Wright's identification of a contradictory class location upends the traditional Marxist conceptualization of a "one-to-one correspondence between structural locations filled by individuals and classes" (1984: 384). This re-conceptualization of class illuminates the complex nature of class exploitation and of the interrelation between class location and individual interests, a complexity that highlights the open-endedness of class conflict and class alliances. Wright argues that

> Individuals in contradictory locations within class relations face three broad strategies in their relationship to class struggle: they can try to use their position as an exploiter to gain entry as individuals into the dominant exploiting class; they can attempt to forge an alliance with the dominant exploiting class; or they can form some kind of alliance with the principal exploited class. (1984: 405)

In sum, class alliances are somewhat open-ended, contingent as they are on the interests and interest-maximization strategies of those occupying a contradictory location in the system of class relationships.

SUMMARY

Exchange, exchange network, and rational choice-influenced theorists variously underscore that social life can only be understood by recognizing that the exchange of resources underlies and characterizes the range of interpersonal, group, and organizational relationships that constitute society. Although there are different emphases among the approaches we have discussed, taken as a whole, this body of theory alerts us to the relevance of utilitarian motivational principles in shaping cooperative behavior; the relevance of power imbalances in exchange relationships; the centrality of trust in social life and of institutional mechanisms that build and regulate trust; the productive significance of social ties even in the absence of trust; the application of a cost–benefit, economic efficiency assessment to areas of social life that may seem at odds with economic maximization criteria (e.g., marriage); and how asset-maximization strategies produce exploitation, and shape and alter the composition of the class structure.

POINTS TO REMEMBER

Exchange theory
- George Homans: interpersonal exchange based on reward/punishment is the basis of all sociological action
  - Social exchange refers to what we give to, and get from, others
  - Social exchange is characterized by power imbalances

- Peter Blau: extended the analysis of social exchange to organizational behavior
  - Power imbalances get neutralized in social exchange relations of interdependence
  - Social exchange generates trust and diffuse expectations of reciprocity

Exchange network theory

- Exchange networks (Emerson, Cook):
  - Exchange networks are comprised of sets of exchange relations
  - Dependence is the basis of power in exchange relations
  - Trust may emerge in unequal power relationships, but tends to be fragile
  - Trust relations are institutionally regulated
  - Networks are effective independent of relations of trust
- Social networks (e.g., Granovetter):
  - Significance of overlapping weak ties in developing social connections between diverse individuals and groups

Rational choice theory (e.g., Coleman)

- An emphasis on the self-interested, utility-maximizing individual
- Focus on the economic efficiency of human capital/behavior in non-economic markets (marriage, etc.)
- Systems of trust facilitate self-interested decision-making and gain-maximization behavior
- Emphasizes complementary links between human capital and social capital
- Criticized for its inattentiveness to power dependence and the interpersonal, institutional, and cultural contexts shaping social behavior

Analytical Marxism (e.g., Roemer, Wright)

- Uses an empirically grounded, economistic, rational actor perspective to re-conceptualize the class structure of contemporary capitalist societies
- Exploitation remains a central construct, though its dynamic in class formation and class relations is more complex than originally theorized by Marx

GLOSSARY: EXCHANGE THEORY

action-reward/punishment orientation behavior as motivated by the individual's perception of its likely rewards and punishments.

behavior conditioning human behavior as determined (conditioned) as a function of previous experience of, and/or perceived future, rewards and punishments.

diffuseness of expectations unspecified expectations characterize non-economic and non-contractual social relationships (e.g., friendships).

power imbalances in any social exchange relation, interaction is contingent on differentiation between and

among the actors in terms of who gets more out of the relationship.

scarcity value determines power imbalances in any exchange relationship; a function of the relation between the supply of, and demand for, rewards.

social exchange all forms of social behavior wherein individuals exchange resources with others in order to attain desired ends.

trust confidence in the reciprocity and sincerity of economic, professional, and other social relationships.

GLOSSARY: EXCHANGE NETWORK THEORY

encapsulated interest in exchange relations of mutual dependence, we trust individual and other social actors, believing that they sincerely appreciate our interests and merge (encapsulate) our interests with theirs.

exchange network sets of actors linked together directly or indirectly through exchange relations.

power dependence basis of power in an exchange relation; the power of actor A over actor B in the A–B relation is a function of B's dependence on A.

social capital individuals' ties or connections to others; can be converted into economic capital.

strong ties exist when people are closely bonded to others (e.g., cliques); close off interaction or sharing of information with individuals or groups outside the group; source of community fragmentation.

weak ties when people have loose ties to acquaintances across several different social contexts. Weak ties expand individuals' access to information and opportunities, and can facilitate community cohesion.

GLOSSARY: RATIONAL CHOICE THEORY

economic efficiency purposive utility and resource rationality of a given course of action.

human capital skills, education, health, and other competences/resources that individuals possess; influences their future economic and social-psychological functioning.

marginal utility extent to which one course of action rather than another proportionally increases an individual's resources or advances their interests.

maximization of utility behavior motivated by principles advancing self-interest.

micro-economic model presumes that individuals act to maximize their own self-interests and self-satisfaction.

net gain when the benefits of a course of action outweigh its costs.

systems of trust establishment of organizations and groups to mediate transactions between social actors. These systems influence the decisions of self-interested actors to place trust and to be trustworthy in order to maximize gains.

GLOSSARY: ANALYTICAL MARXISM

analytical Marxism use of social scientific methods to highlight how the interest maximization strategies of individual and collective rational actors impact class formation, exploitation, and class alliances.

contradictory class locations employees, such as professionals, managers, and bureaucrats, whose objective location in the class-occupational structure as members neither of the capitalist nor of the proletarian class means

that their economic interests are not *a priori* allied with any one particular class.

game theory a scientific experimental method used mostly by economists to predict interest maximization decisions.

organization assets specific skills and resources controlled by the class of professionals/bureaucrats/managers who have technical knowledge and expertise.

RELEVANT NEWSPAPER STORIES

All news stories are from the *New York Times* unless otherwise noted, and can be accessed via www.wiley.com/go/dillon. See NEWS icons in the margins above.

NEWS 7.1   "Roles of Clintons at convention start to clear," August 8, 2008.

NEWS 7.2   "Pulling for each other works in the office, too," February 18, 2008.

NEWS 7.3   "The workplace as clubhouse," February 16, 2008.

NEWS 7.4   "Russia steps up its push; West faces tough choices," August 12, 2008.

NEWS 7.5   "Fed sets rules meant to stop deceptive lending practices," July 15, 2008.

"Lessons from a credit crisis: When trust vanishes, worry," October 1, 2008.

NEWS 7.6   "A companion to protect addicts from themselves," April 15, 2007.

NEWS 7.7   "The Facebook of Wall Street's future," October 3, 2007.

NEWS 7.8   "Steroid report depicts a 2-player domino effect," December 16, 2007.

The Mitchell Report can be downloaded from the MLB website: www.mlb.com

NOTE

1   Early studies of networks, such as the sociometry used by Parsons and Bales (1955) in analyzing friendship patterns in small groups, focused on personal likes and dislikes rather than ties or connections per se. Granovetter (1973: 1376) points out that his network "model differs from sociometric models in that most sociometric tests ask people whom they *like* best or would *prefer* to do something with, rather than with whom they actually spend time."

CHAPTER EIGHT
SYMBOLIC INTERACTIONISM

KEY CONCEPTS

self
pragmatism
I
Me
looking-glass self
socialization
primary group
generalized other
definition of the situation
behaviorism
meaning
symbols
conversation of gestures
language
symbolic interactionism
interpretive processes
cues
social roles
presentation of self
performance
actors
parts
routines
stage
setting
props
audience
dramaturgical
front
appearance
manner
interaction rituals
ritual
encounters
rituals of subordination
body idiom
impression management
team
back-stage
front-stage
region
total institutions
segregated audiences
stigma
passing
frame
on-the-ground observation

CHAPTER MENU

There is a lot of emphasis these days on the self – especially on television talk-shows like *Oprah!* and *Dr. Phil*, and in interviews with celebrities. Whether talking about self-esteem, self-aspirations, self-identity, self-fragmentation, or self-discovery, these stories remind us, as we tend to know from our own lives, that the self is precious. And if there is something gone awry with the self, it affects our relationships and our general everyday functioning in society. Although studying the self is generally seen as the domain of psychologists and psychotherapists, there is a strand in sociological theory that focuses on the self, and, in particular, on the interpretive work of the self in social interaction. This theoretical perspective is called symbolic interactionism (*SI*).

SI is indebted to the insights of **George Herbert Mead,** who was associated with a school of American philosophy called pragmatism, an approach emphasizing the practical conditions under which action occurs, and its practical consequences.[1] Mead's core thesis was that we are not born with an already-made self. Rather, the self emerges out of, and in turn influences, the practical conduct of social interaction.

DEVELOPMENT OF THE SELF THROUGH SOCIAL INTERACTION

Mead (1934: 137) argued that the self is active; it is always reflexively processing what's going on – we are engaged, if you will, in an ongoing internal conversation with ourselves, using the self to monitor and evaluate the self. Even when we are alone we are thinking back on some experience – how we looked, how we came across to others at last night's social gathering – or thinking about something that

BIOGRAPHICAL NOTE

George Herbert Mead was born in South Hadley, Massachusetts, in 1863 into a strongly Protestant family. Mead, who was "shy, studious, and deferential to his parents" (Shalin 2000: 303), attended Oberlin College, a Congregationalist institution, where he studied classics and moral philosophy. Although he pondered becoming a pastor, he eventually opted to pursue academic study at Harvard, where his professors included the philosopher Josiah Royce and the psychologist William James. Mead secured an academic position at the University of Michigan, where he became a close friend of his colleague, the philosopher John Dewey; both subsequently moved to the University of Chicago. Before heading to Ann Arbor, Mead married Helen Castle, an heiress to the Dole Pineapple fortune. Mead had a strong sense of social justice and took a keen interest in politics; he suffered, however, from "writer's block," a condition exaggerated by his personal meekness about the originality and importance of his highly original approach to social interaction. Fortunately, his students (including Herbert Blumer) transcribed his lectures, thus making Mead's thinking publicly accessible. Mead died in 1931. (Shalin 2000).

someone said to us, or anticipating what we might say to someone when we next meet them. We simultaneously process what others are saying or communicating to us, what we should think about the said thing or what it means, and how we should respond to and act on what they have communicated. This, in essence, is what it means to have a self.

We are simultaneously both subjects, and objects to, ourselves. Mead's insight becomes clear if we consider what happens when we look in the mirror. When I look in the mirror I am a subject (Michele) looking in the mirror, and the object I see in the mirror is Me (Michele). When I (subject) see Me (object), I ask: "How do I look?" I might give different answers (depending on the day), but Mead argues that all of these responses originate with my cognitive interpretation of the responses of others to me; e.g., how my mother, sister, or friend would say that I look. This is how we develop a sense of Me (my self as an object) – it is socially created as part of ongoing interpersonal contact or interaction. The Me that I see is a Me that I have learned to see and evaluate from what others have told me about looking good in general, and about how I in particular look.

This for Mead is the dynamic interaction of the I and the Me, an ongoing interaction that, he argues, is critical to the emergence and development of the self. "the essence of the self is ... cognitive," that is, the individual takes on or internalizes the attitudes of others toward him or her, and responds or reacts to those attitudes (Mead 1934: 173, 174–175). The self can only exist because you as an "I" have internalized the "Me," i.e., the attitude/response toward you expressed by others. The "I," the (subjective) acting self, is only able to act because the "I" internalizes the attitudes toward him or her – toward "Me" (as an object) – received from others' behavior toward him or her. I know who I am and I know how to respond and behave in a given situation because I have learned from others' attitudes toward me (the self that I am aware of) and from how they behave (as selves) in a similarly given situation or in a common social activity or undertaking (ibid. 155). Thus Mead states: "The 'I' reacts to the self which arises through the taking of the attitudes of others. Through taking those attitudes we have introduced the 'Me' and we react to it as an 'I'" (1934: 174); I see the "Me" (as an object) through how others see me as indicated by their attitudes toward me. The "I "is the response of the organism to the attitudes of others" (ibid.: 175).

The individual, therefore, develops, and can only develop, a self (and a sense of self) out of social interaction and social experience. It is social interaction that enables the self to become an object to itself (Mead 1934: 138, 142). Accordingly, "Selves can only exist in definite relationships to other selves" (1934: 164), interacting selves whose behavior is shaped by the family, community, and society in which the individual lives (1934:155).

THE LOOKING-GLASS SELF

The ongoing subject–object (I–Me), self–other conversation in which the individual is engaged is illuminated by Charles Horton Cooley. It is he who uses the metaphor of the looking-glass self to vividly illustrate the self's dynamic interpretive processes. When we look at ourselves in the mirror, Cooley reminds us:

> As we see our face, figure, and dress in the glass, and are interested in them because they are ours, and pleased or otherwise with them according as they do or do not answer to what we should like them to be; so in imagination we perceive in another's mind some thought of our appearance, manners, aims, deeds, character, friends, and so on, and are variously affected by it. A self-idea [self-image] of this sort seems to have three principal elements: the imagination of our appearance to the other person; the imagination of his judgment of that appearance; and some sort of self-feeling, such as pride or mortification ... The thing that moves us to pride or shame is not the mere mechanical reflection of ourselves, *but an imputed sentiment, the imagined effect of this reflection upon another's mind*. This is evident from the fact that the character and weight of that other, in whose mind we see ourselves, makes all the difference with our [self]-feeling. We are ashamed to seem evasive in the presence of a straightforward man, cowardly in the presence of a brave one, gross in the eyes of a refined one, and so on. We always imagine, and in imagining share, the judgment of the other mind. (1902/1998: 164–165; emphasis mine)

Thus the self is formed and maintained through ongoing interaction with others.

SOCIALIZATION

Because the self can only emerge out of social interaction, this means that we are not born with an already-made self. This is what socialization accomplishes: it teaches us how to be social, how to use and interpret symbols and language, and how to interact with others. The importance of the social is clearly seen in autism,

---

Topic 8.1   The talking mirror

Cooley emphasizes that your distinct self, your self-feelings of pride, joy, embarrassment, shame, etc., are always felt and interpreted in relation to others. This is an insight long understood by the fashion industry and finds a new reality in today's internet-wired age. At Bloomingdale's department store in Manhattan, New York, there is a digitalized interactive mirror positioned amidst the many high-end Nanette Lepore dresses and suits that customers try on. The full-length mirror, wired to the internet, allows customers to send live video images of how they look in a particular dress or when they mix and match various items of clothing to online viewers – off-site friends and family members – who can instant-message their immediate feedback to the mirror's screen, telling the customer how she looks and whether the clothes suit her. Online viewers can also import from the store various clothing items and accessories that might work well with what the customer is trying on; these suggestions get translated into video holograms that appear on the customer alongside or over whatever else she is (actually) wearing.

NEWS 8.1

a disorder which prevents children from learning to take the perspective of the other, and hence giving rise to a range of other developmental and behavioral problems. Socialization is both the means of teaching us to internalize and adopt the perspective of others, and at the same time the means of our individualization, our development of particular individual selves (Schubert 1998: 22). Mead tells us: "The self is something which has a development; it is not initially there, at birth, but arises in the process of social experience and activity, that is, develops in the given individual as a result of his relations to that process as a whole and to other individuals in that process" (1934: 135).

The family is the primary, most important agent of socialization. And sociologists think of the family as a primary group – primary in the sense that it is typically the first source of children's socialization, and because its influence tends to endure over a long period (Cooley 1909: 23–31; Thomas 1923: 43). Socialization teaches us how we should perceive and interpret all of the things in our social environment. It orients us to the expected behavior in our particular families, as well as to that expected by the generalized other – the community and society in which we live (Cooley 1902/1998: 157, 163; Mead 1934: 154).

As William I. Thomas explained, socialization teaches us the generalized definitions of social conduct that society imposes on the individual:

> Preliminary to any self-determined act of behavior there is always a stage of examination and deliberation which we may call *the definition of the situation* ... the child is always born into a group of people among whom all the general types of situation which may arise have already been defined and corresponding rules of conduct developed, and where he has not the slightest chance of making his definitions and following his wishes without interference. (1923: 42)

Thus, echoing Durkheim's emphasis on the social regulation of individual appetites (cf. chapter 2), "There is therefore always a rivalry between the spontaneous definitions of the situation made by the member of an organized society and the definitions which his society has provided for him" (Thomas 1923: 42).

Mead, Cooley, and Thomas took it for granted (like Parsons; see chapter 4), that the generalized other represented the collectively shared consensual meanings in society; e.g., the valuing in the US of individual achievement and economic success. Today, however, we are much more aware that the generalized other, especially in culturally diverse and economically unequal societies such as the US or the UK, for example, comprises a lot of variation in terms of individuals' and groups' everyday experiences. These differences, in turn, shape the attitudes and expectations of these individuals and groups (and their children), making it difficult for poor inner-city children, for example, to internalize the view that they can do well in school (e.g., MacLeod 1995). We should also keep in mind that the generalized other encountered by many individuals, especially if they are outside of the dominant gender, class, racial, and sexual-orientation categories in society, will be comprised of several, often conflicting, socialization influences (e.g., Collins 2004). In general, different family structures and differences in the individual's social environment relating to gender, race, social class, etc., provide different influences on, and contexts for, the development of the self.

SHARED SYMBOLS: THE CONVERSATION OF GESTURES

In the early decades of the twentieth century, when Mead was writing, behaviorism was prominent in intellectual thought, associated with psychologists such as the American John Watson (1930) and the Russian Ivan Pavlov (1927). Behaviorism presumed that, like animals, humans can be conditioned to respond in predictable ways to external stimuli in their environment, and that this conditioned behavior can be explained without presuming that individuals have selves. Just as the infamous dogs in Pavlov's experiments predictably salivated when stimulated by the sound of a bell (the cue for dinner), so the presumption was that human behavior is also governed or conditioned by external forces in the environment. Contrary to the behaviorists, Mead argued that because humans have a cognitively reflexive self, i.e., they are able to see and think about themselves as objects (as discussed above), human interaction is qualitatively different to animal behavior.

Today, our view of animal (and human) behavior is more complex. Biologists and primatologists document the intelligence and sociability of animals and show that some (e.g., monkeys, elephants, whales), like humans, have sophisticated social structures (hierarchical or more communal) and networks, and engage in social and strategic behavior (finding a mate, avoiding predators). Scientists are uncertain, however, whether animals are self-consciously aware of why they behave in particular ways. Therefore, while there are fascinating similarities between animal and human behavior, there are nonetheless degrees of difference between animals and humans. One of these differences pertains to the relevance of meaning.

NEWS 8.2

Mead argued that humans give significance, give meaning, to what they are communicating or intending to communicate, and these meanings derive from our consciousness of and ability to manipulate, interpret, and use shared symbols, language, gestures, etc. Mead explains:

> Self-consciousness ... lies in the internalized **conversation of gestures** which constitutes thinking ... the origin and foundations of the self, like those of thinking, are social ... In the conversation of gestures what we say [or signal] calls out a certain response in another and that in turn changes our own action, so that we shift from what we started to do because of the reply [or signal] the other makes. The conversation of gestures is the beginning of communication. The individual comes to carry on a conversation of gestures with himself. He says something, and that calls out a certain reply in himself which makes him change what he was going to say. (1934: 173, 140–141)

In other words, we learn to think about and anticipate the consequences of our everyday interactions, of our words and gestures, on creating a response in the other. When I am in a restaurant with a friend, as soon as I pick up the menu to start examining it, my friend interprets this gesture as a signal to stop talking and to give her attention too to the menu; this is the generally accepted "definition of the situation" into which we have both been socialized – we know how to interpret the communication of the other (though we may at times try to impose an alternative definition, and ignore our friend's gesture). Gestures become "significant symbols" when their meaning is shared by the interacting individuals; this is what language is:

> a significant symbol [that] signifies a certain meaning ... Gestures become significant symbols when they implicitly arouse in an individual making them the same responses which they explicitly arouse, or are supposed to arouse, in other individuals, the individuals to whom they are addressed; and in all conversations of gestures ... the individual's consciousness of the content and flow of meaning involved depends on his thus taking the attitude of the other toward his own gestures. (Mead 1934: 46, 47)

Communication can only occur because "through gestures responses are called out on our own attitudes, and as soon as they are called out, they evoke, in turn, other attitudes" (1934: 181).

In short, communication is impossible without symbols and language whose meanings are shared among those in a given social setting. The universality of symbols means that they produce shared responses and understandings; "A symbol is nothing but the stimulus whose [interpreted] response is given in advance" (Mead 1934: 181). Symbols require and produce shared meanings; symbols have "the same meanings for all individual members of the given society or social group" (1934: 47), whether among roommates greeting each other (e.g., US, "What's up?"; UK "How are you?"), at a baseball game (seventh inning stretch), for a whole country (national flag), or globally (McDonald's golden arches). We should also recognize, however, that as feminist (e.g., Collins 1990; Smith 1987; cf. chapter 10) and race and cultural theorists (e.g., Gilroy 1987; Hall 1990; cf. chapter 12) would emphasize, symbols and meanings are often contested, especially by minority racial and cultural groups and others in society whose everyday experiences make them feel excluded rather than included by the established meaning-system.

THE PREMISES OF SYMBOLIC INTERACTIONISM

Symbolic interactionists build on Mead's and Cooley's insights on the centrality of symbolic exchange to human social life and the development of the self. The focus of symbolic interactionism is the exchange of symbols that inheres in the ongoing, self–other interpretive processes that characterize social interaction. "Symbolic interactionism" is thus an apt description for this perspective; it was **Herbert Blumer** who coined the term – initially using it "in an offhand way" (in 1937), but it caught on and quickly came into general use in sociology to describe "a relatively distinctive approach to the study of human group life and human conduct" (Blumer 1969: 1).

BIOGRAPHICAL NOTE

Herbert Blumer, born in 1900, was a member of the sociology faculty at the University of Chicago during the heyday of the Chicago school of sociology, when Robert Park and other colleagues produced many distinguished community studies of urban life. Blumer studied under and was heavily influenced by Mead, whose ideas he elaborated. Blumer left Chicago in 1952 to help found the sociology department at the University of California, Berkeley, where he maintained a large presence as a much-loved and sought-after figure until his death in 1987. Among many honors, Blumer served as president of the American Sociological Association in 1956.

SI emphasizes that society is human group life – human beings engaging in social (symbolic) interaction (Blumer 1969: 7); as such, for symbolic interactionists, society is an ongoing process of symbolic interaction wherein we continuously interpret and respond to the cues, i.e., signals or messages, in our social environment. Thus, *SI* sees institutions not in terms of organizational structure (of hierarchically organized, impersonal offices and duties) and norms of bureaucratic rationality, but, according to Blumer, as "arrangements of people who are interlinked in their respective actions," and who act and interact as they handle "situations at their respective positions in the organization" (1969: 58). Therefore, unlike Marx, Durkheim, Weber, and other theorists we have discussed, whose writings are concerned with large-scale social structures and processes (capitalism, division of labor, the state, bureaucracy, inequality, the occupational structure, the culture industry), *SI* focuses primarily on the **micro-level** processes and outcomes of everyday, face-to-face interaction. Micro-level interactions occur, nonetheless, in socially structured interaction contexts (Goffman 1959, 1971), and moreover, have broad, **macro-level** consequences (e.g., maintaining social inequality).

According to Blumer, *SI* rests on three basic premises:

[a] Human beings act toward things on the basis of the meanings that the things have for them [including other human beings and physical things in the person's environment, social institutions] ... [b] The meaning of such things is derived from, or arises out of, the social interaction that one has with one's fellows ... [c] These meanings are handled in, and modified through, an interpretive process used by the person in dealing with the things he encounters. (1969: 2)

Because meaning arises out of (interpretive) social interaction, it is not something that is pre-given independent of language; it does not inhere in things per se but in the linguistic and social meanings in a given societal context (meanings that, though social in origin, are nonetheless well established and highly constraining).

By the same token, we cannot take the meaning of things (of other individuals, social institutions, physical things) for granted; meaning is neither marginal to social interaction nor set in stone, inscribed once and for all time (Blumer 1969: 3). Rather, because meaning derives from social interaction, from social actors' ongoing definition and redefinition of situations, the meanings that we give to symbols and other things can vary across time and from one social context to another (e.g., the meaning of hard work; cf. Weber, chapter 3).

THE SOCIAL CONTEXT OF HUMAN INTERACTION

Precisely because people act on the basis of the meanings that objects (cars, clothes, wrinkles, other things, people, social institutions) have in their social environment (world of objects), "the life and action of people necessarily change in line with the changes taking place in their world of objects" (Blumer 1969: 12). We interact with ourselves and others differently in different social environments because of the different meanings and expectations characterizing those contexts. After you graduate from college and secure a job at an insurance company where you receive a commission for every new customer you enroll, you will interpret your world of objects differently. At college, when you look in the mirror (Cooley's looking-glass), you are imagining how your friends would respond to how you look and what you are wearing; "Am I cool?" you wonder, and evaluate your appearance accordingly. But in your new job, you will look in the mirror and respond to what you imagine will sway your potential customer; "Do I look like I have a solid grasp of actuarial projections?" and judge yourself accordingly and make adjustments. Further, these evaluations (of you and by you) will also be influenced by your gender, race, and age, among other things. Particular others – e.g., airline passengers (Hochschild 1983), corporate male professionals (Pierce 1995) – and the generalized other (society) impose different expectations on women than men (cf. chapter 10), on blacks than whites (cf. chapter 12).

ERVING GOFFMAN: SOCIAL EXCHANGE AS RITUALIZED SOCIAL INTERACTION

Although many social theorists discuss social roles (e.g., Parsons; see chapter 4), it is the elements of symbolic exchange in the face-to-face performance of social roles that is of most interest to *SI*. **Erving Goffman** uses the metaphor of a theatrical performance to elaborate the many elements that go into face-to-face interaction in everyday life. For Goffman (1959), social life, the presentation of self in everyday life, is the performance by social actors of different roles, parts, and routines on various stages with different settings and props. And, as in the theater, the success of any role performance is contingent, in part, on the particular audience that is present and that responds to the cues and miscues (mistaken signals) actors convey. Goffman's perspective, therefore, offers a dramaturgical approach to social life.

BIOGRAPHICAL NOTE

Erving Goffman was born in Alberta, Canada, in 1922, to immigrant Ukrainian Jewish parents. After receiving his undergraduate sociology degree at the University of Toronto, he pursued graduate studies at the University of Chicago. His dissertation research, based on observing everyday life on one of the small Shetland Islands (Scotland), formed the basis of his theory of face-to-face interaction. He spent many years at the University of California, Berkeley, invited there by Hebert Blumer, and later moved to the University of Pennsylvania.

Goffman was not only a prolific and accessible writer (writing 11 major books), but an enthusiastic gambler and a successful stock-market strategist. On a darker note, his wife, Angelica Choate, experienced severe mental health problems and committed suicide in 1964, leaving Goffman alone with their young son. Almost twenty years later, Goffman remarried but within a few months of having a daughter, he died of stomach cancer, in 1982, the same year he was president of the American Sociological Association (Fine and Manning 2000).

Goffman's concepts provide a rich vocabulary for describing face-to-face interaction across the broad range of everyday social settings. He highlights the socially structured expectations imposed on the performance of social roles, and as such provides a "social anthropology" (Collins 1986: 109) of the rituals of everyday social interaction (ordering coffee at Starbucks; waiting for and riding the elevator, the bus, etc.). Not surprisingly, many researchers draw on Goffman's concepts in making sense of social life and its many complex social processes (e.g., Snow and Anderson's 1993 study of homeless adults).

SOCIAL ROLES

We all perform many social roles in life as we enact the expected behavior associated with "the rights and duties attached to a given status" (Goffman 1959: 16) – the roles of student, daughter or son, friend, roommate, girlfriend or boyfriend, sister or brother, waitress, teammate, church member, etc. The content of all these and myriad other social roles is pre-established for us by society. Social roles are socially scripted and we learn how to perform the scripts through socialization; as daughters we play the part (or enact the routine) of the dutiful daughter, and sometimes the part of the ungrateful daughter; in performing the role of customer, we sometimes play the part of the disgruntled customer, and sometimes that of the impatient customer, etc.

But although social roles and their various parts or routines are scripted, this does not mean that our role-playing is fake or artificial. While we certainly might enjoy or more readily identify with some roles than others, all social behavior is necessarily role-playing behavior. For *SI*, social life, society, would be impossible without social roles; pre-defined social roles provide the structure for the social interaction required in everyday life (in classrooms, dorms, offices, stores, courts, subways, Congress, etc.): the "pattern of appropriate conduct ... that must be enacted, portrayed ... and realized" (Goffman 1959: 75).

Here, Goffman, like Mead discussing the generalized other (see p. 261 above), does not problematize what might be entailed in "appropriate conduct." He takes it for granted that what is appropriate is the role patterns and expectations already in place and established toward "maintaining the normative social order" (Collins 1986: 107). Thus, "When an individual presents himself before others, his performance will tend to incorporate and exemplify the officially accredited values of the society ..." (1959: 35). Goffman (1959: 188–189) acknowledges that performers can disrupt social roles by not playing the part their audience expects, or indeed exaggerating it (as if in parody). However, he does not probe how, or the settings in which, "accredited values," role scripts, and traditional role boundaries get contested, as occurs when individuals cross over traditional gender-occupational role boundaries – e.g., male nurses (e.g., Williams 1993a) or women coal miners (Tallichet 2006).

In any case, if you were to list all of your social roles, three things would be apparent. One, it would be hard to imagine having a self, an identity, that is independent of the several roles you play. Two, you are always acting in reciprocal relation to someone else (who is playing his or her role); e.g., you are a daughter to your mother and father. And, even when we are not in others' company, our self-interaction means that we rehearse or imagine our performance of a particular role for some imaginary other (remember the looking-glass self). Social roles thus capture the Mead–Cooley–Blumer emphasis that the self is always a relational self; we cannot have a self without other selves. Three, while we tend to be aware of playing certain roles – e.g., the good student – Goffman would remind us that we are always playing some role; we are never not performing a role. In addition to the roles we have listed, we play many other roles: customer sales attendant, cafeteria diner, house guest, airline passenger, dental patient, marathon runner, etc. Moreover, we are always an audience responding to someone else's role performance. In sum, social life is the ongoing and continuous enactment of role performances, performances that give rise to and structure our social relationships. Thus, "when an individual or performer plays the same part to the same audience on different occasions, a social relationship is likely to arise" (Goffman 1959: 16).

PERFORMANCE PRESSURE

Goffman primarily emphasizes that the presentation of self in everyday life – the individual's execution of multiple social roles – is an ongoing task of symbolic exchange, inference, and interaction; we control (or try to control) the cues we emit to others so that we can manage our audiences' impressions of us. Just as an actor in a play does not want to be booed off the stage for a lousy performance, we too want to convey a good impression and hence put on a successful perform- ance. We don't want our supervisors to think we are lazy; our parents to think we are ungrateful; our friends to think we are disloyal. And by the same token, we want the waitress to know we are annoyed by the slow service, and the judge that we are ashamed of speeding.

As Goffman argues (1959: 3–4), in face-to-face interaction it is in everyone's interest to control the conduct of others through their own performance and the response it elicits:

> When an individual plays a part he implicitly requests his observers to take seriously the impression that is fostered before them. They are asked to believe that the character they see actually possesses the attributes he appears to possess, that the task he performs will have the consequences that are implicitly claimed for it, and that in general, matters are what they appear to be. (1959: 17).

Goffman's emphasis on social life as role performance has been criticized for its relative lack of attention to the relevance of individuals' feelings and emotions. Arlie Hochschild, a sociologist whose research and theorizing draw on Goffman, argues, "Goffman gave us actors without psyches ... the characters in Goffman's books actively manage outer impressions but they do not actively manage inner feelings, a habit itself distributed variously across time, age, class, and locale" (2003: 7, 91). The marginalization of emotion by Goffman and in sociological theory in general is redressed by Hochschild, and we will discuss her sociology of emotions in chapter 10.

ESTABLISHING THE DEFINITION OF THE SITUATION

Goffman (1959) argues that the most effective way to ensure a convincing role performance is to influence the definition of the situation that others come to have of a given interaction. How things (a setting or a situation) get defined matters enormously to what can subsequently occur in the situation and what is subse- quently evaluated as appropriate or convincing behavior. How we initially define the situation will determine how we behave (perform) in that situation – does it require formal dress? joviality? deference toward others? – and if we misidentify the situation, however slightly, we will suffer at least embarrassment, and perhaps ostracism. The initial defining information we convey to our audience therefore is crucial because, as many advertisements warn, first impressions last. And the con- sequences of our failure to define the situation in ways that foster a good impres- sion of the performance we want to pull off can seriously impact our life-chances; if we fail to convince the judge of our remorse, we may have to spend a few months in jail; if we fail to make a good impression at a coveted job interview, our long-term chances of carving out a particular career may be jeopardized.

According to Goffman, we create a particular definition of a situation by the front we maintain: "that part of the individual's performance which regularly functions in a general and fixed fashion to define the situation for those who observe the performance" (1959: 22). Thus, the Wal-Mart sales associate helping a customer has a different front than that same individual when she is at home with her children, or at church, or at the doctor's office.

The "fronts" actors present and maintain in interacting with others are made possible because all social interaction occurs in particular settings supported by an array of props, elements that signal the kind of role performance expected. A particular setting and its customary props implicitly authenticate the validity of our face-to-face interactions and define the expectations of the performances that are to be enacted. And when the setting has somehow been tampered with or when the customary props are not present, we are thrown as to how we should interpret the situation and define what's really going on. It is easy to perform in a deferential manner toward the airport security screener because we are alerted to do so by the message communicated by the security agent's federal badge, the presence of beeping screens being reviewed by other security agents in our presence, and the visible holding-area for those passengers who are deemed worthy of further personal screening.

Similarly, the doctor's office or clinic provides a setting that readily establishes that he or she has the expertise to assist us – its furniture and sterile decor, the range of medical equipment and paraphernalia, and the certificates of qualification and specialization hanging on the wall. In all settings and among all social actors, appearance and manner are critical to the symbolic work of imposing and sustaining the definition of the situation (Goffman 1959: 24–26). Goffman refers to an individual's appearance as those signals that indicate his or her social statuses and their "temporary ritual state," as indicated by whether they are dressed for work, formal social activity, or informal recreation (ibid.: 24). Thus when the doctor makes an appearance you know it is the doctor because of the white coat, the stethoscope around the neck, and the name or status badge on the coat lapel (cf. 1959: 22–24) – all of these things (props) convey the message that this really is a medical doctor you can trust. As research confirms, patients in the US overwhelmingly prefer and are more likely to confide in doctors who are dressed in white coats than in surgical scrubs, or business or casual attire.

NEWS 8.3

In some social settings, the presence of certain props can hinder social interaction. High-earning women in New York fear that if they invite their dates – who usually earn less – back to their apartments, the dates will be put off by the evidence of the high-class apartment and lifestyle the woman can afford. Because more women than men are currently graduating from college, women may be increasingly likely, on average, to earn more money than men. Yet cultural expectations of behavior are such that men (and many women too) still expect that male dates and potential future husbands should be the higher-earning partners.

NEWS 8.4

Topic 8.2   Body appearance and cosmetic dermatology

The soaring increase in dieting programs and in elective plastic surgery and cosmetic dermatology attests to Goffman's insight that appearance and body display are crucial elements in the presentation of self and in creating and maintaining a good impression among one's role-performance audiences. Non-invasive medical cosmetic procedures increased by more than 700 percent between 1997 and 2006, and elective plastic surgery is one of the fastest-growing surgical procedures in the US. Body makeovers are no longer the province of the rich and famous; a recent survey by the American Society of Plastic Surgeons found that a third of people considering plastic surgery reported average household incomes below $30,000. Older women who want to re-enter the workforce or change jobs increasingly contemplate the possibility of Botox and cosmetic surgery because a strong resume alone may not be sufficient for them to secure a job. Similarly, politicians, both male and female, are increasingly availing themselves of the services of cosmetologists to remove spots, broken capillaries, wrinkles and other blemishes. Appearance matters.

NEWS 8.5

NEWS 8.6

INTERACTION RITUALS

For Goffman, everyday life is comprised of interaction rituals, and the ritual is "accomplished through doings – through making appearances ... performing gestures" (1979: 10). Goffman does not use the term ritual in quite the same way as Durkheim does (e.g., to mean collective events that affirm social ties and, by extension, social order). What interests Goffman is ritualized self-presentation behavior, and how such everyday interaction behavior maintains social order. For Goffman, ritual refers to all those simplified, exaggerated, stereotyped behaviors that signal or display particular emotions or social statuses in various interaction situations. Such ritualized display behavior signals to those present something about the individual's "social identity, ... mood, intent, and expectations, and about the state of his relation to them" (1979: 1). Goffman's interest in ritual is largely in its micro-level expression: the signaling role of ritualized expression in face-to-face interaction and its function in establishing the definition of the situation, but these micro-situational definitions, in turn, maintain the larger social order.

Interaction rituals are the institutionalized, though frequently unspoken, ways of behaving in society – whether with friends or with strangers in the elevator. They are "found in all peopled places, whether public, semi-public or private, and whether under the auspices of an organized social occasion or the flatter constraints of merely a routinized setting" (Goffman 1967: 2). For example, we have many ritualized ways of greeting and bidding farewell in social interaction, and depending on the nature of the relationship, we perform interaction rituals – handshakes, hugs, kisses – that signal varying degrees of friendship or intimacy. When we mistake the greeting rules governing a given relationship, this causes much fumbling and embarrassment (1971: 74–77).

The interaction rituals of public behavior range from fleeting gestures and facial movements that may initiate a social encounter with a stranger to the enactment of formalized ceremonial rules for terminating a social gathering. Symbolic exchange is so central to everyday behavior that, though we may not always be consciously aware of its demands, it necessarily impinges on the most apparently trivial and minor of encounters. As Goffman elaborates, everyday "encounters are organized by means of a special set of acts and gestures comprising communication about communicating" (1963b: 99). Thus:

> An encounter is initiated by someone making an opening move, typically by means of a special expression of the eyes but sometimes by a statement or a special tone of voice at the beginning of a statement. The engagement proper begins when this overture is acknowledged by the other, who signals back with his eyes, voice, or stance that he has placed himself at the disposal of the other for purposes of mutual eye-to-eye activity – even if only to ask the initiator to postpone his request for an audience. (1963b: 91–92)

All of us have initiated such overtures and have tactfully (or non-tactfully) disengaged from similar overtures made by others toward us.

Rituals of subordination

Although interaction rituals occur or are observed in face-to-face interaction, they reflect the norms of the larger social order and, in turn, function to impose that order on and across micro-level interactions. Thus, among various interaction rituals, Goffman wrote extensively about rituals of subordination: all those behavioral displays by which we indicate and recognize the difference in rank or hierarchy between individuals of different social statuses – most especially in the objective stratification system, the differential status attendant on gender, race, and socioeconomic location. Goffman observes: "A classic stereotype of deference is that of lowering oneself physically in some form or other of prostration. Correspondingly, holding the body erect and the head high is stereotypically a mark of unashamedness, superiority, and disdain" (1979: 40). In analyzing advertisements, Goffman noted, for example, that the interaction rituals between women and men typically signal women's socially subordinate status relative to men, as indicated by their deferential physical posture toward the man (ibid.: 42–45) and/or by their emotional display – "in cross-sexed encounters in American society, women smile more, and more expansively, than men" (ibid.: 48). (See also chapter 10.)

NON-VERBAL RITUALIZED INTERACTION

Whether in the classroom, in the cafeteria, or on the street, and regardless of whether we want to communicate or not, we cannot stop communicating. We may cease talking but our body idiom (body language and display) continues to communicate with those around us. It cannot say nothing (Goffman 1963b: 35). Indeed, so long as there is even one person co-present, there is an obligation to convey certain information and not to convey other impressions, just as others present must too ... when individuals come into one another's immediate presence in circumstances where no spoken communication is called for, they none the less inevitably engage one another in communication of a sort [through] ... bodily appearance ... dress, bearing, movement and position, sound level, physical gestures such as waving or saluting, facial decorations, and broad emotional expression. In every society, these communication possibilities are institutionalized ... Half aware that a certain aspect of his activity is available for all present to perceive, the individual tends to modify this activity, employing it with its public character in mind ... a body symbolism, an idiom of individual appearance and gestures that tends to call forth in the actor what it calls forth in the others ... immediately present. (1963b: 35, 33–34)

We can stare at someone (because we are appalled that they are speaking so loudly on their cell-phone) or we can look away (because we are embarrassed to overhear the details of their relationship), but in either case we are communicating a message, and it will always be a message that requires them to respond to our response, to our performance in presenting our selves (as they too must present their selves). The meanings of "the stare" are institutionalized such that it is a major mechanism of social control; we stare in disapproval, and when someone stares at us we tend to alter or cover up our behavior, and even literally cover our selves. "Given the pain of being stared at, it is understandable that staring itself is widely used as a means of negative sanction, socially controlling all kinds of improper public conduct. Indeed it often constitutes the first warning an individual receives that he is 'out of line' and the last warning that it is necessary to give him" (Goffman 1963b: 88).

IMPRESSION MANAGEMENT

Across all social encounters, we engage in impression management, symbolic work that we strategically do to orchestrate a good performance in our various roles.[2] Performance strategies and situational definitions are better institutionalized in some settings than others (e.g., occupational roles). And in some settings, it is a team performance that needs to be managed. For Goffman, a performance team

refers to any set of individuals who co-operate in staging a single routine ... while a team-performance is in progress, any member of the team has the power to give the show away or to disrupt it by inappropriate conduct. Each teammate is forced to rely on the good conduct and behavior of his fellows, and they, in turn, are forced to rely on him. There is then ... a bond of reciprocal dependence linking teammates to one another. (1959: 79, 82)

A team can be a couple – e.g., a husband and wife putting on a front of amicability in front of their guests (or for the media if they are a political couple); the dentist and receptionist putting on a front of office efficiency and professionalism for the waiting patient. Or a team can be a group of three or more, as, for example, in a restaurant with the waitresses colluding to convey the impression that it's the friendliest restaurant in town; such teamwork, though easily disrupted, is generally effective, notwithstanding the fact that, as Marx (chapter 1) and other theorists would underscore, the waitresses' labor, including their friendliness (e.g., Hochschild; see chapter 10), is being exploited by the restaurant owner for profit.

Self-presentation of the politician

Any individual or team performance can falter, especially if there is inconsistency between the performer's appearance and manner. We see much evidence of this in politics. When the 2004 Democratic presidential candidate John Kerry, a man of high-status bearing and elitist reputation, tried to project an everyday, casual, and outdoorsy manner by going hunting in a brand new, well-tailored hunter's outfit, the impression he wished to convey backfired. Similarly, discrepancies can arise between the expressions a social actor gives, i.e., what we say, and the expressions given off – the many contextual and non-verbal cues we unintentionally emit and which are interpreted as being symptomatic of the actor – thus derailing a good impression. George Bush Sr learned this first-hand: when running for re-election in 1992, he was dogged by claims that he was out of touch with and uninterested in ordinary Americans. He argued against this, but his non-verbal behavior (cues and signals emitted) spoke louder than words when, during one town-hall meeting with voters, the cameras focused on him checking his watch – "Will I ever get out of here?" was the expression given off – while candidate Bill Clinton engagingly answered a question. (Clinton won the election.) Similarly during the 2008 presidential election, when news leaked that Sarah Palin's designer wardrobe had cost $150,000 (paid for by the Republican National Committee), commentators argued that it contradicted the Republican vice-presidential nominee's carefully honed image of being an ordinary soccer mom with frugal tastes.

Politicians, more than other role-performing professionals in society, have almost incessantly to maintain a front, especially given our 24/7 television-mediated reality. This is partly why so much attention is given even to their physical appearance, especially when they are women or black – it is treated as a reflection of their competence and electability; not surprisingly, politicians are among the increasingly growing numbers seeking cosmetic surgery. Politicians, moreover, must maintain their front across many different audiences in many varied settings; they have to look good and put on a deft performance with talk-show hosts, and whether meeting skilled workers at the factory gates, attending a celebrity-studded Hollywood fundraiser dinner, presenting a policy address to New York financial and media moguls, or simply ordering breakfast before they head out on the campaign trail. Even when male politicians are allegedly backstage, relaxing and engaged in leisure activities, then too, typically, they are actually engaged in front-stage behavior; in the presence of press photographers,

NEWS 8.6

273

projecting the impression of how cool or relaxed or masculine they are – sailing, hunting, golfing, biking, clearing brush, playing basketball, etc.

Goffman distinguished between front- and back-region (or front- and back-stage) to underscore that role performance is contingent on the presence of an actor's primary audience. A region is "any place that is bounded to some degree by barriers to perception" (1959: 106). Such barriers are most visibly marked by the walls dividing a restaurant's kitchen from its dining area, a family's living rooms from its bedrooms, the company executive's office from the pool of administrative assistants, the football team's dressing rooms from the pitch area, and so on. The "front-region" refers to the place where the performance is given (e.g., waitresses perform for guests in the restaurant's dining area), and the "back-region" is literally the staging area for the front-region behavior; it is where actors do the preparatory work to ensure a successful performance.

As in the theater, actors can be more relaxed back-stage; there is less performance pressure. Goffman notes, "One of the most interesting times to observe impression management is the moment when a performer leaves the back region and enters the place where the audience is to be found, or when he returns therefrom, for at these moments one can detect a wonderful putting on and taking off of character" (1959: 121). However, as Goffman elaborates, the back-stage has its own audience and performance expectations. Thus when waiters return to the kitchen they are still performing – but for a different audience: for the chefs and other kitchen workers and for the other waiters and waitresses as they come and go. As anyone of you who has ever worked in a restaurant will appreciate, waiters and waitresses behave very differently in the restaurant dining area than in the kitchen; front-stage and back-stage, they are performing different roles to different audiences. And similarly too doctors, teachers, sales assistants, etc.

Day spas in the mall and on Main Street make it easy for individuals to do some of the back-stage body work necessary to make a good impression. There are cosmetic dermatological treatments for unwanted hair, sunspots, age spots, acne, uneven skin tone, thin lips, folds, wrinkles, crows' feet, scowl lines, laugh lines, fat accumulation, leg veins, and spider veins. And among the surgical procedures offered are: facelift, eyelid surgery, chin implants, browlift, nose reshaping, breast augmentation, breast lift, breast reduction, liposuction, arm lift, tummy tuck, and thigh lift.

TOTAL INSTITUTIONS

Although politicians choose their role and in so doing voluntarily accept (and reinforce) the blurring between back- and front-stage behavior that society imposes on politicians, not all individuals have such freedom. Inmates in mental health hospitals, prisons, and other institutions to which individuals are confined either because of their inability to function in, or because of the threat they pose to, society do not have this option. These types of settings, what Goffman calls total institutions, remove the barriers that customarily separate individuals' basic everyday functions (e.g., sleeping, playing, working); instead all activities are performed in the presence of similarly regulated co-participants (e.g., inmates) and their supervisors (Goffman 1961: 5–6). And the same principle applies in institutional settings in which particular work-like tasks are assumed to be best accomplished, e.g., army barracks, boarding schools, monasteries (1961: 5).

All of these highly structured, highly regulated settings require highly specified role performances of inmates and of supervisory staff (e.g., wardens, headmasters, etc.), that, although they may seem punishing, serve, Goffman argues, "good functional reasons" (1961: 124). Total institutions use various strategies (e.g., mortification, denial of privileges) to produce a stripped-down self, rid of any autonomous signs of individuality (hence the required wearing of uniforms, short hair, etc.) (1961: 12–29, 71). This self is defined primarily (if not solely) in terms of a role performance that conforms to the institution's regimented authority structure (1961: 41–42) and for which there is no – even temporary or transitional – back-stage respite.

Recent decades have seen a trend toward the de-institutionalization of mental health services and a shift away from asylums toward community-based care. Nevertheless, many of the same self-stripping strategies identified by Goffman can be observed today in settings that care for the elderly and other special populations (e.g., those with a mental and/or physical disability). However unintentionally, when doctors, nurses, and care assistants talk to the elderly person in the third person – "How is Joan today?" rather than "Hi Joan. How are you doing?" – as if in fact Joan is an object rather than someone with a subjective, intact self, this strips the person of their individuality, and has been shown by researchers to have negative consequences for the long-term image and health of the elderly.   NEWS 8.7

MANAGING OUR AUDIENCES

Outside of total institutions, everyday life is structured such that individuals' various social roles are typically witnessed by segregated audiences; i.e., those who are audience to one of our roles will not see us perform in other roles (Goffman 1959: 137). Typically, your parents are not present when you are socializing with friends or in class, and your college friends are not present when you are socializing with old high school friends. The advantage of playing to segregated or compartmentalized audiences is that it decreases the likelihood that inconsistent or contradictory role information will enter and confuse the definition of the situation. Playing one role to one audience at a time generally means that we have less "covering up" to do (e.g., managing information flow to our parents).

Politicians, by contrast, encounter diverse overlapping audiences, a performance dilemma crystallized during election campaigns. Observers of the presidential election campaign in 2008 wondered whether John McCain's self-presentation, for example, could maintain role credibility simultaneously across diverse audiences: religious conservatives, fiscal independents, and social moderates (and thus get him elected). Because of the challenges associated with role performance to overlapping audiences, and given the gaps that may exist between politicians' front- and back-region behavior, it is not surprising that political candidates pay a lot of money to public relations consultants in order to influence (or manipulate) voters' knowledge and impression of them (cf. chapter 5). Indeed, the public relations industry is indebted to Goffman's insights on impression management.

NEWS 8.8

WEB 8.1

MISREPRESENTATION

A certain amount of misrepresentation is structured, however, into all face-to-face interaction. Tact, when we mask honesty with politeness or obfuscation, is critical, according to Georg Simmel (1917/1950: 45), to regulating and maintaining the sociability of human relations. This is as true of friendship as of politics, corporate relations, and international diplomacy. The management of politeness – an art accentuated at Disneyworld – is especially required across all service industries, from restaurants and airlines to banks and customer sales departments.

Politeness and good manners, social etiquette, are expected in civilized society, and thus society has institutionalized several ways of orchestrating good impression management in everyday behavior. Notwithstanding the capitalist logic underlying these practices (cf. Marx; see chapter 1), brides-to-be spend large sums of money on specialized bridal magazines that will help them to put on a successful wedding performance, and corporations send new recruits to table-manners workshops – for these corporations, the self-presentation of employees conveys the impression of the company as a whole; if the investment associate eats in a slothful manner, perhaps then too, the company has slothful accounting practices?

STIGMA

Impression management is all the more challenging for those individuals in society who are stigmatized because they carry some "undesired differentness" from what we consider "normal" (Goffman 1963a: 5). One of Goffman's most famous books, *Stigma: Notes on the Management of Spoiled Identity*, analyzes the sociological bases of stigma. Goffman differentiates among three sources of stigma:

> [a] abominations of the body – the various physical deformities ... [b] blemishes of character perceived as weak will, domineering or unnatural passions, treacherous and rigid beliefs, and dishonesty, these being inferred from a known record of, for example, mental disorder, imprisonment, addiction, alcoholism, homosexuality, unemployment, suicidal attempts, and radical political behavior ... [c] the tribal stigma of race, nation, and religion, these being stigma that can be transmitted through lineages and equally contaminate all members of a family. (1963a: 4)

Although Goffman compiled his list in the early 1960s, the kinds of people and attributes that society stigmatizes do not seem to have changed much since that era. Nonetheless, stigma – who or what is labeled "abnormal" – is socially defined and hence can vary as societal expectations and understandings change. Thus, for example, in 1980, partly as result of pressure from gay rights organizations and due to a more complex understanding of gay sexuality, the American Psychiatric Association's influential *Diagnostic and Statistical Manual of Mental Disorders* removed homosexuality from its list of mental illnesses.

Goffman observes that in everyday discourse, body language, and behavior "we exercise varieties of discrimination, through which we effectively, if often unthinkingly, reduce [the stigmatized person's] life chances" (1963a: 5). In essence, "we believe the person with a stigma is not quite human," and treat them accordingly (ibid.). Moreover, the stigmatized or discredited know that they fall short of "normal." Given that selves, as Mead (1934) argued, can only develop from interaction with other selves, the stigmatized individual comes to internalize the negative attitude that others have toward him. Stigma, therefore, is socially defined; deriving from and reinforced through social interaction.

PASSING

The stigmatized necessarily engage in impression-management behavior toward gaining acceptance and respect among "the normals," and hence work at presenting an uncontaminated or "unspoiled" identity when in the co-presence of others from whom they must hide their stigma. Goffman (1963a: 73) notes, for example, that while prostitutes have to present as prostitutes when dealing with their clients, they must hide this role-identity in the presence of others (e.g. the police, family members, etc.). Taking their cues from socially accepted identities and performances, stigmatized individuals learn to develop ways to correct for their stigma – the cancer survivor works at continuing to excel at sports (e.g., Lance Armstrong), the disabled veteran learns to perform a new athletic activity. And if the stigmatized condition cannot be physically or otherwise corrected, the stigmatized individual can learn to cover up the stigma and to pass as normal. Passing is always learned behavior; like all social interaction, it is about controlling the information, the "definition of the situation," and the impression that others come to have in interacting with you; thus in campaigning among white working-class men, Hillary Clinton drank whisky, and Barack Obama, beer.

Passing strategies, however, can only accomplish so much. The persistence of racism, for example, means that some individuals have a far higher bar to cross than others in making – and getting rewarded for making – a good impression. As documented by a recent study, skin tone matters: "light-skinned immigrants in the United States make more money on average than those with darker complexions," even after controlling for English-language proficiency, education, occupation or country of origin. Similarly, despite the success of the disability rights movement in increasing the access of physically disabled individuals to public places (e.g., restaurants, playgrounds, government offices), it is still difficult, nonetheless, for a blind person, for example, to pass as "normal" to a store cashier given that a \$5 bill and a \$10 bill are printed on paper of equal size and shape. Goffman's perceptive analysis of the various role-performance strategies required in the presentation of self allow us to look for and see the many "fronts" individuals put on as they interact with someone of a different race (or some other stigmatized status). These insights, however, then need to be harnessed to a broader level of analysis, one that seeks to also incorporate recognition of the underlying systemic ways in which social inequality – racism (cf. chapter 12) and sexism (cf. chapter 10), for example – are structured into everyday life irrespective of the interacting individuals in any given face-to-face setting.

INSTITUTIONAL FRAME ANALYSIS

SI's focus on face-to-face interaction clearly has implications for macro societal structures and processes; as we have noted, the smooth functioning of families, universities, service industries, corporations, and politics depends in part on the role performances of individuals. Moreover, it is not just individuals who have to impose definitions of the situation on everyday activities; so too do organizations, institutions, and social movements. Goffman argues that individuals make sense of the ongoing plethora of simultaneous activities surrounding them by selecting from the reality and imposing some kind of frame, a "unitary exposition and simplicity" on the situation (1974: 8–9). Building on Goffman's frame analysis, sociologists have examined how large-scale social actors such as mass media organizations frame or package (socially and organizationally defined) newsworthy events for readers/audiences. Just as individuals frame or characterize select happenings in their reality in order to manage and respond to that reality, the organizational news-gathering routines and divisions (e.g., crime, lifestyle, business) developed by media organizations allow them to manage, select, and pre-define "the news." All of the many happenings in the world on a given day are thus reduced to fit with the media frames that then serve as our (mass mediated) "definition of the situation."

The sociologist Todd Gitlin, following Goffman, argues that

> Media frames, largely unspoken and unacknowledged, organize the world both for journalists who report it and, in some important degree, for us who rely on their reports. Media frames are persistent patterns of cognition, interpretation, and presentation, of selection, emphasis, and exclusion by which symbol-handlers routinely organize discourse, whether verbal or visual. Frames enable journalists to process large amounts of information quickly and routinely: to recognize it as information, to assign it to cognitive categories, and to package it for efficient relay to their audiences. Thus, for organizational reasons alone, frames are unavoidable, and journalism is organized to regulate their production. (1980: 7)

How, of course, the media frames a given event, an anti-war protest march in Washington, DC, for example, or ongoing processes such as income inequality, can have important consequences for how readers/audiences come to interpret and act on that event or issue (e.g., Gitlin 1980; Gamson 1992).

SYMBOLIC INTERACTIONISM AND ETHNOGRAPHIC RESEARCH

SI's focus on face-to-face interaction and the practical implications of role performances in localized settings has been very influential in advancing qualitative, observation research. As Blumer argued (1969: 38), when we are interested in everyday interaction, we need to study through first-hand observation what is actually happening in a given area of social life. In this view, the dynamics of social interaction can be apprehended not by relying on survey responses or census data, but by looking carefully and closely and seeing how humans engage with and respond to one another. It is only through such first-hand, on-the-ground observation that we can "expand and deepen our perception of group life" (ibid.: 39), and get a more accurate awareness of what is taking place as individuals interact with one another in a given setting. Thus Blumer states:

> The metaphor that I like is that of lifting the veils that obscure or hide what is going on. The task of scientific study is to lift the veils that cover the area of group life that one proposes to study ... The veils are lifted by getting close to the area and by digging deep into it through careful study ... SI is a down-to-earth approach to the scientific study of group life and human conduct. Its empirical world is the natural world of such group life and conduct. (ibid.: 39, 47)

Many sociologists use on-the-ground methodology to systematically observe social behavior, conducting ethnographies of social interaction in varied work and organizational settings (e.g., Pierce 1995), on the streets (Snow and Anderson 1993), in the boxing gym (Wacquant 2004), and in inner-city neighborhoods (e.g., Anderson 1999a). These researchers invariably draw on insights from Goffman in making sense of some of the observation data they gather.

SUMMARY

Mead, Blumer, and Goffman vary in the specifics of their analytical focus. Common to all, however, is an emphasis on the interpretive, symbolic inferential work that is essential to and structured into human, i.e., social, interaction.

POINTS TO REMEMBER

George H. Mead (1863–1931) emphasized that:
- The self is a reflective, thinking self
- The self is an object to itself (I can see myself)
- The self is comprised of the interaction of the "I" and the "Me"
- The "I" is the response of the self to the attitudes of others
- The "Me" is the self taking on of the attitudes of others
- The self develops out of social interaction
- Individuals communicate through symbols, language, and gestures
- Symbols are universally shared (though contested)

Charles H. Cooley (1864–1929)
- Looking-glass self; we see ourselves through how (imagined) others see us

Herbert Blumer (1900–1987)
- Social interaction is the interpretation of symbols, gestures, and language
- Society: an ongoing process of symbolic interaction
- We respond to the meanings that things (cues, people, structures, processes) have in our social environment
- We deepen our understanding of group life through on-the-ground, systematic observation

Erving Goffman (1922–1982)
- Dramaturgical perspective
- Face-to-face interaction – reciprocal influence of individuals upon one another's actions when in one another's immediate physical presence
- Role: enactment of rights and duties attached to a given status (student, daughter) and performed on a series of occasions to the same kinds of audience
- Performance: activity of a given individual on a given occasion which serves to influence in any way any of the other participants
- Audience: performance observers and co-participants
- Front: that part of the individual's performance which regularly functions in a general and fixed fashion to define the situation for those who observe the performance
- Setting: stage, scenery, props, and audience informing role-performance execution
- Props: contribute to defining the situation; (e.g., office insignia, personal effects, clothing)
- Definition of the situation: how we convey and infer the type of socially expected behavior required in a given situation; process by which we control the conduct of others

- Impression management: fosters successful role performance; establishes definition of the situation

- Front-stage behavior: role behavior in the setting where the performance is given (e.g., waitresses perform for guests in restaurant dining area)
- Back-stage behavior: preparatory behavior in the staging area for front-region behavior
- Individuals and organizations impose particular frames on everyday life to selectively negotiate among simultaneously occurring activities

GLOSSARY

actors dramaturgical – individuals performing roles.

appearance signals indicating the individual's social statuses and "temporary ritual state" (e.g., a nurse dressed for work).

audience individuals who witness our role performance and for whom we perform.

back-stage staging area for front-region behavior, where actors do the preparatory work to ensure a successful performance.

behaviorism strand in psychology emphasizing that humans behave in predictable ways in particular situations.

body idiom information conveyed through body language/display.

conversation of gestures process by which our signals bring forth a meaningful response in another.

cues verbal and non-verbal signs, signals, messages.

definition of the situation socialization of individuals into a society's generalized expectations of behavior across an array of social settings (Thomas); crucial to how actors interpret and perform in a particular role-performance setting (Goffman).

dramaturgical perspective using the metaphor of drama to describe social life.

encounter acts and gestures comprising communication about communicating (e.g., how we initially respond when someone steps into an elevator we are riding; or when we encounter an acquaintance on the street).

frame simplifying reality by selectively interpreting, categorizing (and prioritizing) simultaneously occurring activities.

front the self-presentation maintained by the individual to project an intended definition of the situation in executing a particular role performance.

front-stage area where role performances are given.

generalized other community or society as a whole.

"I" part of the self; the "I" is the (subjective) acting self, and is only able to act because it internalizes the attitudes toward the "Me" (as an object) received from others' behavior/responses toward the acting "I."

impression management symbolic and strategic communicative work toward orchestrating a particular definition of the situation and a successful role performance.

interaction rituals routinized ways of self-presenting/behaving in the co-presence of others (e.g., greeting rituals).

interpretive process interpretation of the meaning of individuals' verbal and non-verbal communication and of the meanings of other things in our environment is an ongoing activity.

language a socially shared meaning system.

looking-glass self self-perception and behavior contingent on our knowing (or imagining) how others (would) respond toward us.

manner signals which function to indicate the tone in the interaction role a performer expects to play in an oncoming situation (e.g., the sympathetic grief counselor).

"Me" part of the self; the self as object ("Me"); the internalization of the expectations and attitudes of others toward "Me" and to which "I" (as the acting subject) respond.

meaning significance given to particular symbols and things in our environment.

on-the-ground observation data gathering in the everyday social context or setting in which individuals interact; ethnography.

part aspect of a social role.

passing the impression management and self-presentation symbolic work an individual must do in order to cover up or secretly maintain a stigmatized identity.

performance the idea that social life, society, is based on the socially structured, acting out (performance) of particular social roles.

pragmatism strand in American philosophy emphasizing the practicalities that characterize, and the practical consequences of, social action and interaction.

presentation of self ongoing symbolic work the role-performing actor does to project an intended definition of a situation.

primary group has a critically formative and enduring significance in child socialization (e.g., family).

props things in a setting that bolster (prop up) the actor's intended definition of the situation.

region any role-performance setting bounded to some extent by barriers to perception (e.g., walls divide a restaurant's kitchen from its dining area).

rituals routinized ways of acting and interacting that reflect status differences and maintain social order (Goffman).

rituals of subordination symbolic signals in self-presentation (e.g., body posture of one actor vis-à-vis another) indicating status differences or social inequality.

routines socially prescribed, ordered ways of accomplishing particular things or establishing particular

situational definitions and meanings in executing a role performance.

segregated audiences when role-performing actors are able to keep the audiences to their different roles separate from one another; facilitates the impression management required in a particular setting.

self reflexively active interpreter of symbols and meanings in the individual's environment; comprised of the "I" and the "Me."

setting the bounded social context in which a social role is performed.

socialization process by which individuals learn how to be social – how to participate in society – and thus how to use and interpret symbols and language, and interact with others.

social roles socially scripted role-performance behavior required of a person occupying a particular status and/or in a particular setting.

stage specific setting or place where the role-performing actor performs a particular social role.

stigma society's categorization or differentiation of its members as inferior based on the social evaluation and labeling of various criteria of undesired difference.

symbol any sign whose interpretation and meaning are socially shared.

symbolic interactionism sociological perspective emphasizing society/social life as an ongoing process wherein individuals continuously exchange and interpret symbols.

team when role-performers co-operate to stage a single routine or performance and project a shared definition of the situation.

total institutions highly regimented establishments (e.g., prisons) in which the barriers that customarily divide individuals' everyday functions (sleeping, eating, and working) are removed.

All news stories are from the *New York Times* unless otherwise noted, and can be accessed via www.wiley.com/go/dillon. See NEWS icons in the margins above.

NEWS 8.1   "If the mirror could talk (it can)," March 18, 2007.

NEWS 8.2   "Political animals (yes, animals)," January 22, 2008.

NEWS 8.3   "When young doctors strut too much of their stuff," November 21, 2006.

NEWS 8.4   "Putting money on the table: With rising incomes, young women discover the pitfalls of 'dating down,'" September 23, 2007.

NEWS 8.5   "Nice resume: Have you considered Botox?" January 24, 2008.
            "Who is the real face of plastic surgery?" August 16, 2007.
            "Feeling pudgy? There's a shot for that," September 20, 2007.
            "As doctors cater to looks, skin patients take a seat and wait," July 28, 2008.
            "Having a little work done (at the mall)," January 13, 2008.
            "For top medical students, an attractive field," March 19, 2008.
            "Penny-wise, not pound-foolish; city cashes in as mecca for the hefty (with wallets to match)," May 19, 2006.

NEWS 8.6   "The new political fixer: The skin doctor," March 22, 2007.

NEWS 8.7   "In 'sweetie' and 'dear,' a hurt beyond insult for the elderly," October 6, 2008.

NEWS 8.8   "McCain extends his outreach, but evangelicals are still wary," June 9, 2008.

NEWS 8.9   "With right props and rights stops, a transformation into working-class hero," May 6, 2008.

NEWS 8.10   "Study of immigrants links lighter skin and higher income," January 28, 2007.

NEWS 8.11   "Clearly, frankly, unabashedly disabled," May 13, 2007.
            "The blind welcome a court ruling that may help them count their paper money," May 22, 2008.

WEB SUPPLEMENTS

All web supplements are available at www.uriley.com/go/dilon. See WEB icons in the Margins above.

WEB 8.1   The emergence of the public relations industry

WEB 8.2   The disability rights movement

NOTES

1 The founder of pragmatism was Charles Peirce (1839–1914), and among sociologists, in addition to Mead, Alfred Schutz is highly influential (cf. chapter 9). Other pragmatists include the psychologist William James and the philosopher John Dewey, probably best known among the public for inventing the Dewey decimal system used in libraries as an effective and efficient way to categorize books by subject and author.

2 Instead of *SI*, Goffman (1969) occasionally called his approach "strategic interaction." He elaborated: "Strategic interaction is, of course, close to Meadian social psychology and to what has come to be called 'symbolic interaction' – since nowhere more than in game analysis does one see the actor as putting himself in the place of the other and seeing things, temporarily at least, from his point of view ... Strategic interaction appears to advance the symbolic interactionist approach in two ways. [i] the strategic approach, by insisting on full interdependence of outcomes, on mutual awareness of this fact, and on the capacity to make use of this knowledge, provides a natural means for excluding from consideration merely any kind of interdependence ... [ii] strategic interaction addresses itself directly to the dynamics of interdependence involving mutual awareness; it seeks out basic moves and inquires into natural stopping points in the potentially infinite cycle of two players taking into consideration their consideration of each other's consideration, and so forth" (1969: 136–137). Goffman frequently used the example of a poker game to illustrate the interdependent awareness of individuals engaged in strategic interaction. This point is underscored by James Bond in the movie *Casino Royale*. About to embark on a critical game of poker, Bond states: "You never play your hand. You play the man across from you." And presumably (in support of strategic interdependence) that is what the man across from him would say too.

CHAPTER NINE

PHENOMENOLOGY AND ETHNOMETHODOLOGY

KEY CONCEPTS

phenomenology
natural attitude
wide-awake attention
here and now
practical knowledge
scheme of reference
lifeworld
stock of preconstituted
    knowledge
typifications
common-sense knowledge
recipe knowledge
social construction of
    reality
objective reality
externalization
internalization
subjective reality
in-group
out-group
symbolic universe
subuniverse of meaning
plausibility structures
ethnomethodology
accomplishment of social
    reality
members
accounts
background knowledge
breaching experiments
conversation analysis
glossing practices

CHAPTER MENU

There has been a lot of talk over the last few years about the adjustment problems faced by soldiers returning home from the wars in Iraq and Afghanistan. You might think that after a long deployment in a war zone, where you must constantly be alert to the threat of insurgent sniper attacks and roadside bombs, not to mention witnessing the death and paralyzing injuries of fellow-combatants, and so constantly and anxiously alert that when you "sleep," you sleep in combat gear with your rifle to the ready, coming home could only be a relief. Yet the new, everyday reality of home presents soldiers and their families with difficult readjustment challenges. This is because, quite apart from the added trauma of a war zone, the practical, everyday realities of life in any one particular social context and what is "natural" and relevant in that context are very different from those in another – something you become acutely aware of the first time you return home from college for a break.

NEWS 9.1

PHENOMENOLOGY

The significance of the everyday reality and everyday experiences in how individuals construct knowledge of their social world, and the practical implications of that knowledge in informing the sense of order we impose on how the world works, is the focus of a strand in sociological theory called phenomenology. In contrast to the focus on societal structures and institutions that is the primary interest of many sociological theorists (e.g., Marx, Durkheim, Weber, Frankfurt School, Parsons), for phenomenologists, the core focus is the "analysis of the world of everyday life" (Schutz 1970: 72). Phenomenology is attentive to how individuals recognize and make sense of the experiences that characterize their everyday reality. This approach is called "phenomenology" because it probes how particular experiences or *phenomena* (things as perceived by us) are selected and given attention from the ongoing, flowing stream of experiences that exist.

EXPERIENCE, MEANING, AND SOCIAL ACTION

Phenomenological sociology has its roots in twentieth-century philosophy, in the ideas elaborated by the German philosopher Edmund Husserl (1859–1938). Husserl argued that the consciousness of human beings is *intentional* – it is intentionally directed toward objects in individuals' socio-cultural environment; it is thus a consciousness of certain particular experiences rather than of a general or some outer reality beyond individual experience. Husserl's student **Alfred Schutz**, an Austrian who emigrated to New York in the 1930s, applied this idea to underscore the significance of everyday life, everyday experiences, in how individuals construe and act in and on a particular social reality. Schutz explained:

The world of everyday life is the scene and also the object of our actions and interactions. We have to dominate it and we have to change it in order to realize the purposes which we pursue within it among our fellow-men. Thus we operate not only within but upon the world ... a pragmatic motive governs our **natural attitude** toward the world of daily life. (Schutz 1970: 72–73)

BIOGRAPHICAL NOTE

Alfred Schutz was born in Vienna, Austria, in 1899; he served in the Austrian-Hungarian army during World War I, and studied law and social sciences in Vienna. In 1938, with the rise of Hitler and Nazism in Germany, he, with his wife, Ilse, and their two children, emigrated to Paris and then to New York, where (along with many other war-exile intellectuals) he was affiliated with the New School for Social Research. Schutz founded the International Phenomenological Society in 1941; he died in New York in 1959.

In other words, individuals live in the everyday world as subjectively engaged social actors. This was something emphasized, of course, by Max Weber, who defined sociology as the study of "subjectively meaningful action" (cf. chapter 3). Weber's thinking influenced Schutz (Luckmann 1978: 10). But Weber was more interested in how different historical and cultural-interpretive contexts (e.g., Calvinism) and different social structures (e.g., bureaucracy) shape social action than in individuals' experience of everyday reality and their interpretation of that reality – the focus of phenomenology. Similarly, although symbolic interactionists (*SI*) underscore the processes of meaning exchange and interpretation that occur in the face-to-face interactions comprising society (cf. chapter 8), their interest is in the socially structured nature of interaction, meaning (symbols, language), and role performance, and not, for example, the individual's experiences of his or her role behavior. It is precisely the individual's experience of everyday reality that preoccupies phenomenologists.

HERE-AND-NOW, EVERYDAY REALITY

Phenomenology emphasizes that we don't simply see the social world as detached observers (though many sociologists adopt this detached approach as social scientists conducting research on social life). The practical tasks of getting on with everyday life demand our wide-awake attention to the here and now of everyday reality. For Schutz, wide-awakeness is a critical notion, central to understanding what consciousness entails, i.e., "full attention to life and its requirements" (1970: 69; see also ibid.: 129).

The reality to which individuals are most wide awake is their here-and-now, everyday reality, a reality that is highly pragmatic. Amidst all the big and small things going on in society, on campus, in the classroom, it is your particular "here and now" that is of most relevance to you. Irrespective of any big existential questions we might ask about life and irrespective of the political debates at the United Nations or the academic discussions in the university provost's office, we are most alert to the practical tasks, the "natural" routines, in our particular here and now. Making breakfast, starting the car, finding a seat on the train, taking notes in class, planning dinner with a friend – these are just a few of the many ordinary things we do routinely. We don't give much attention to these daily tasks because they are so familiar, so apparently natural. We know how to do these things because we inherit a way of doing them, doing what is considered normal or natural by those around us, from those with whom we live. It is only when the car doesn't start that we begin to wonder, and to do so rather urgently, "How does this car work?" "What do I need to do to get it moving?" This is an everyday knowledge I really don't need to know, because most of the time my car works fine and because it works, I don't need to know how and why it works; I can trust in, or suspend disbelief about, the mechanics of car engines. But I do need to know how to use the ignition key and how to drive, and how to use my computer and send email. This is my social world and I have a great deal of the practical knowledge necessary to smoothly negotiate its everyday tasks. By contrast, the social world of the car mechanic down the road, the everyday knowledge he or she has, is very different.

The here-and-now reality of everyday life requires individuals to master many practical tasks.

What is deemed relevant knowledge – engine mechanics, or what to eat for dinner and when and how to eat it – is variously shaped by the family, community, and society in which we live. It is from the everyday practical context in which we live our lives that we learn to identify and compartmentalize relevant experiences (e.g., whether we need to know the differences between types of car engines). Our interpretation of everyday reality "is based upon a stock of previous experiences of it, our own experiences and those handed down to us by our parents and teachers, which in the form of 'knowledge at hand' function as a scheme of reference" (Schutz 1970: 72) that anchors and orients us.

The paramount nature of any particular individual's here-and-now reality – the fact that you have to file a study-abroad petition with the dean's office while your roommate has to rush to her medical appointment or to her job – means that although you both share a common reality as college students, the specific pragmatic tasks that inhere in your respective here-and-now realities vary tremendously. Each individual necessarily inhabits a unique "biographically determined situation" (Schutz 1970: 163) – your sister and you, although close in age and interests, will invariably have different apperceptions and experiences of growing up in your shared family world. Similarly, no two students in a particular theory class on a particular day will have the same subjective experience of that shared classroom reality. Each person's consciousness of, attentiveness to, and feelings about their particular, subjective here-and-now reality will vary (Schutz 1970: 165).

INTERSUBJECTIVE, OBJECTIVE REALITY

Nevertheless, although any individual's specific here-and-now reality differs from a sibling's or a classmate's, this does not mean that individuals create their own reality and that reality can be whatever we deem it to be. Quite the contrary. Despite the uniqueness of subjective experiences, it is the intersubjectivity of human life that demarcates human consciousness and human society;

> the world of my daily life is by no means my private world but is from the outset an intersubjective one, shared with, ... experienced and interpreted by others ... The unique biographical situation in which I find myself within the world at any moment of my existence is only to a very small extent of my own making. I find myself always within an historically given world which, as a world of nature as well as a sociocultural world, had existed before my birth and which will continue to exist after my death. This means that the world is not only mine but also my fellow men's environment; moreover, these fellow men are elements of my own situation, as I am of theirs. (Schutz 1970: 163–164)

In other words, our reality is always social, always shared with others. As Mead emphasized (chapter 8), the self can only emerge out of social interaction. Similarly, the world of everyday life, what Schutz calls the lifeworld (1970: 72), is a world shared with other selves; it is a thoroughly social world and we come to know that world through its everyday ways of organizing reality. As individuals we bring into each concrete situation a **stock of preconstituted knowledge** [experience] which includes a network of **typifications** of human individuals in general, of typical human motivations, goals, and action patterns. It also includes knowledge of expressive and interpretive schemes, of objective sign-systems and in particular, of the vernacular [local] language. In addition to such general knowledge I have more specific information about particular kinds and groups of men, of their motivations and actions. (1962: 29–30)

Everyday reality is experienced by us through its many typifications – the typical ways we expect individuals of varying statuses, roles (e.g., police officers, celebrities, Americans, Europeans), and institutions (e.g., the state, the economy, the church) in our social world to act. Typifications provide the individual with "appropriate tools for coming to terms with things and men, accepted as such by the group into which he was born" (Schutz 1970: 119).

EVERYDAY REALITY AS *THE* SOCIAL REALITY

Phenomenologists thus emphasize that we experience and know everyday social reality as a natural reality whose common-sense knowledge we take for granted. Schutz emphasizes that the everyday ways of doing things in a particular community (or among members of a particular group) are accepted as the right way to do things; they work and make sense and have stood the test of time. Hence this recipe knowledge is taken for granted; it provides ready-made ways of doing things and these tried-and-true ways don't need to be explained or justified (Schutz 1970: 80–81).

ORDERED REALITY

Consequently, as emphasized by **Peter Berger** and **Thomas Luckmann** – sociologists who popularized Schutz's ideas in their well-known book *The Social Construction of Reality* (1966) – social reality, human-made and human-experienced, is a highly ordered reality. Berger and Luckmann explain: "Social order is a human product, or more precisely, an ongoing human production" (1966: 52). Reality production is thus a social process. The social construction of reality means that individuals collectively create an objective social reality whose objects (e.g., things, tools, institutions) they designate and arrange or order in ways that make sense to them as they subjectively experience that reality. Social reality is produced as a result of individuals' ongoing negotiation and experience of the external, objective reality – of the socially institutionalized processes and practices in a given society. Thus the "institutional world" is "experienced as an objective reality" (ibid.: 60), i.e., it is an objectification of the product of human-social activity and given externalization in the institutions and order created by humans in society. This objective, externalized reality is, through a process of internalization, appropriated by individuals on the basis of, and out of, the particular (objective) social reality which they experience and make sense of from within their own particular family-community-social environment (1966: 130–132). The objective social reality (e.g., economic inequality) is thus internalized and interpreted, in part, on the basis of idiosyncrasies that characterize the individual's family reality (e.g., whether the family mood is one of contentment with, or resentment of, the status quo).

BIOGRAPHICAL NOTES

Peter Berger was born in Vienna in 1929; he and his wife, Brigitte Berger, also a sociologist, moved to the US after World War II. After many years on the faculty at Rutgers University, New Jersey, the Bergers moved to Boston University, where Peter is currently an emer-itus professor and director of the Institute for the Study of Economic Culture.

Thomas Luckmann was born in Germany in 1927 and is currently an emeritus professor of sociology at the University of Konstantz.

The individual's subjective internalization and experience of (the externalized) reality is the reality in and from which he or she participates in the ongoing creation and maintenance of an external social reality. The individual internalizes an objectified reality, makes it his or her own subjective reality, and in turn acts backs on that reality – the objectified reality can be readily translated into subjective reality, and vice versa (1966: 22, 35, 37, 129–130). In short, there is an ongoing creative, back-and-forth relationship or translation between the individual and society (1966: 61), through the processes of internalization and externalization. Language is the principal vehicle of this ongoing translation (1966: 133). Language names all of the things in our everyday environment – our country, our town, our family, the occupations in our society, the cars people drive, the kitchen utensils we use, the food we eat, etc., and thus gives them an objective existence; they constitute the external reality – one that has existed before we were born – an objective reality that we encounter and which we must negotiate. Thus:

> The reality of everyday life appears already objectified, that is, constituted by an order of objects that have been designated as objects before my appearance on the scene. The language used in everyday life continuously provides me with the necessary objectifications and posits the order within which these make sense and within which everyday life has meaning for me ... The reality of everyday life is not only filled with objectifications; it is only possible because of them. (Berger and Luckmann 1966: 22, 35; see also Schutz 1970: 80–81)

We use language to construct and to label and to maintain our reality. And when the language we have no longer works to label our experiences, we devise new words, new ways of labeling those experiences, thus objectifying and legitimating the validity of these experiences as part of everyday reality. Hence, today, we have new words and new experiences – googling, friending, remix – and these words, in turn, shape our everyday reality. Language, and all social institutions (e.g., marriage, divorce), are human-created realities – they are social constructions, and hence their definition evolves and changes in tandem with other changes in society, including individuals' experiences of and responses to their changing, lived reality. This does not mean that social institutions are not "real." Clearly, they have an objectified reality. But as human products, they do not have a reified existence. Reification, as Berger and Luckmann explain, is:

> the apprehension of human phenomena as if they were things ... *as if* they were something else than human products – such as facts of nature, results of cosmic laws, or manifestations of divine will. Reification implies that man is capable of forgetting his own authorship of the human world ... The reified world is, by definition, a dehumanized world. It is experienced by man as a strange facticity ... over which he has no control rather than as ... his own productive activity ... As soon as an objective social world is established, the possibility of reification is never far away. The objectivity of the social world means that it confronts man as something outside of himself. The decisive question is whether he still retains the awareness that, however objectified, the social world was made by men – and therefore can be remade by them. (1966: 89).

PHENOMENOLOGICAL DIVERSITY

Because we take the naturalness of our everyday reality for granted, it is easy to think of that reality as a reified rather than a socially constructed reality. The taken-for-grantedness of our everyday world becomes apparent to us generally only after we step out of that reality. This happens when we move from the everyday reality of our (phenomenological) in-group – the reality of our family, our neighborhood, our college campus, etc. – to that of someone else's everyday reality, the social world of an out-group (those whose everyday typifications and experiences are different to ours). It seems trivial, but how we set the dinner table and do several other basic everyday things is core to how we experience and make sense of everyday life; it comprises our natural common-sense knowledge. But this common sense may not work as smoothly when in the company of a particular "out-group" (e.g., visiting your boyfriend's family, who have different ways of organizing dinner and other routine tasks), because you and they have different schemes of reference.

Once we recognize that something as ordinary as having dinner at a friend's home can challenge what we consider to be the common-sense way to do things, we can, by extension, begin to appreciate the enormous diversity in everyday lived experience of individuals and groups who live in social environments very different from ours. Intersecting differences across race, income, gender, ethnicity, occupation, sexuality, region, country, etc., produce diverse lived experiences that make it problematic to make knowledge claims that are presumed to be universal, i.e., applicable to everyone's experiences.

Because of the wide-ranging everyday experiences that differently situated individuals have, there are different ways of knowing and different ways of evaluating the knowledge that is handed down as the objective, one, true knowledge. This phenomenological insight informs the work of feminist theorists such as Dorothy Smith (1987) and Patricia Hill Collins (1990), whose ideas we discuss in chapter 10; they argue against the presumption that there is one (objective) reality and one knowledge. The divergent phenomenological realities to which individuals are sensitized or "wide awake" are underscored by the contrasting views of motherhood and abortion among (mostly) white middle-class mothers in Kristin Luker's (1984) study of pro-choice and pro-life activists.

THE STRANGER

Schutz elaborates on the typifications of the *stranger* and the *homecomer* to highlight the contrasting realities, perceptions, and experiences of everyday life. A *stranger*, by definition, is one for whom the everyday habits in a given community are strange, and whose own habits appear strange to those settled there. Following Georg Simmel, who construed the stranger "not as the wanderer who comes today and goes tomorrow, but rather as the person who comes today and stays tomorrow" (1908/1950: 402), similarly, for Schutz, a stranger is not simply a tourist. He or she is, rather, someone who wants to be a member of, or permanently accepted or tolerated by, a specific group (Schutz 1962: 91).

The immigrant clearly is a stranger but so too is anyone who wants to be a member in a "closed club" – whether this is a family into which you marry, a person from a working-class background who graduates from college and moves into the middle class, an urban cosmopolitan who moves to a rural area, etc. (Schutz 1962: 91). Indeed, we tend to see as strange all those who are in any way culturally different to us, and this is especially true of those who are racially different, as underscored by the phenomenological experience of "the fact of blackness," recounted by Frantz Fanon (1967) (cf. chapter 12).

The stranger, then, is someone who has a history and a set of habits different to those of the host or dominant cultural group. As such, strangers invariably challenge the typifications and ways of being they necessarily encounter in their new social environment. Thus, as Simmel first wrote, the stranger "is not radically committed to the unique ingredients and peculiar tendencies of the group, and therefore, approaches them with the specific attitude of 'objectivity.' But objectivity does not simply involve passivity and detachment; it is a particular structure composed of distance and nearness, indifference and involvement" (Simmel 1908/1950: 405). Strangers find as strange the everyday, recipe knowledge that those at home in the environment take for granted as they go about everyday tasks. The stranger, therefore, Schutz argues, basically questions all of the things, all of the everyday ways of doing things, that are taken for granted by the in-group (the community in which he or she seeks acceptance); their ways are not his or her (taken-for-granted) ways (Schutz 1962: 96–97). The stranger will continue to maintain the natural attitude that worked in his home group because that is his history, his way of interpreting reality: "the stranger starts to interpret his new social environment in terms of his thinking as usual," but this scheme of reference will not work in the new situation (1962: 97). Accordingly, the stranger has to learn new ways of orienting him/herself and of doing things; acquiring the in-group's recipe knowledge for interpreting and understanding this new social environment so that the "strange" ways in this newly entered social world can acquire sufficient coherence and make sense to him/her (1962: 95).

THE HOMECOMER

We expect the stranger to undergo a process of social adjustment – an insight reflected in the first-year orientation programs universities provide. But Schutz alerts us that the *homecomer* too needs to adjust to "home." The homecomer's experience, perhaps even more than the stranger's, highlights how the experience of everyday life is so thoroughly a subjectively experienced reality. The homecomer is someone who is returning home after an absence and who is returning not simply for a temporary stay, like you for an end-of-semester vacation, but permanently – "who comes for good to his home" (Schutz 1962: 107). The idea of "home" connotes many varied things; "Home means different things to different people ... home means one thing to the man who has never left it, another thing to the man who dwells far from it, and still another to him who returns" (1962: 108).

Whatever particular connotation home has for you, one thing is fairly certain:

> Life at home follows an organized pattern of routine; it has its well-determined goals and well-proved means to bring them about, consisting of a set of traditions, habits, institutions, timetables for activities of all kinds, etc. Most of the problems of daily life can be mastered by following this pattern ... The way of life at home governs as a scheme of expression and interpretation not only my own acts but also those of the other members of the in-group. I may trust that, using this scheme, I shall understand what the Other means and make myself understandable to him. (1962: 108)

But precisely because the homecomer is someone who has left home, she has become familiar with a different set of typifications, a different "system of coordinates" than that used as the scheme of reference for life at home (1962: 111).

The homecomer, then, unlike the stranger, returns to a social environment which she has committed to memory and which she thinks she already knows. But while away from home, she has changed – she has had different everyday experiences – and in her absence, the family members left at home have also had different everyday experiences, from which the homecomer is excluded. The homecomer's stock of knowledge, of (remembered) home typifications, has not changed, but the remaining family members have devised some new typifications as they go about the everyday reality experienced in her absence and, consequently, the old typifications or schemes of reference held by the homecomer may no longer work in her (old) home environment.

The phenomenology of the homecoming veteran

The phenomenological dilemma faced by the homecomer is well captured by the returning veteran, an example used by Schutz, and one that continues to be remarkably salient. Clearly, as we noted at the outset, anyone who spends time in a war zone experiences an everyday reality that is radically different from even the most tumultuous (and violent) home environment in their home-place. Although soldiers in Iraq, for example, face a highly threatening enemy, sociologically – or phenomenologically – they are armed to deal with this turbulent and anomic context (cf. Durkheim; see chapter 2) by the clearly defined norms of authority and the tight network of social relationships that typify their military in-group. The soldier's in-group knows (more or less) who the out-group is (the enemy) and what (more or less) is required in in-group/out-group encounters; the horrors of war, however, can distort these categorizations and responses, as highlighted by the Abu Ghraib prison abuse.

NEWS 6.4

When the soldier returns home, he or she encounters a reality that is also characterized by anomie – a shift in norms created largely by his or her absence; a home-anomie that is different to the anomie of war. Absence matters. The fact that the soldier had to leave home means that he or she thinks of and remembers "home" differently than if he or she had never left, and differently than if he or she had stayed away (cf. Schutz 1962: 108). The absence has also created a new reality for the family left at home. Families organize and experience things differently when one of their members is absent, producing a shift in the family's scheme of reference. And the soldier's war experiences and war typifications do nothing to prepare the veteran for making sense of his or her home-anomie experiences. At home, unlike in Iraq, the soldier is no longer battling an enemy to which he or she knows how to respond, but is now battling against his or her in-group, the very family of which the soldier was an integral part prior to going to war.

The gulf in the different experiential realities of the soldier and those of his or her family is exacerbated by the fact that those remaining at home have an image of the soldier's war-time experience that tends to be distorted by idealized television and movie images of war (Schutz 1962: 118–119). These distortions continue today, notwithstanding the coverage given to the "actual" reality of war by movies, newspapers, and internet blogs. But even in-depth accounts can never fully convey what it really means to be a soldier in Iraq (or elsewhere). Moreover, as the comparatively low box-office returns of war movies such as *In the Valley of Elah* indicate, we prefer not to know the experienced realities of war, something reinforced by the government's prohibition on news video documenting the return of dead soldiers' coffins to the US.

NEWS 9.2

NEWS 9.3

The severe social and psychological consequences of being a homecoming-veteran-stranger are underscored by the fact that an estimated 31 percent of troops returning from Iraq or Afghanistan have either major depression, post-traumatic stress disorder, or traumatic brain injury. Compounding the home-anomie, many

NEWS 9.4

📖 NEWS 9.5

homecomer-soldiers have to deal with problems stemming from the military's rejection of their medical insurance claims, acute economic pressures, and few educational opportunities (e.g., many veterans are ineligible for GI education benefits). The different worlds of everyday experience that the soldier *and* his or her family experience while the soldier is at war means that both the returning veteran and his or her family are, phenomenologically, strangers to one another, at least for a while, and in many instances, for a long time. War experiences and homecoming experiences converge to produce new everyday realities for both the homecomer and the home-family, conflicted and confusing realities that translate into high rates of marital strain, separation, divorce, and domestic violence,

📖 NEWS 9.6

including murder, among soldiers/veterans and their families.

Topic 9.1   After war, love can be a battlefield

At special weekend retreats organized by the Army for small groups of officers and their spouses, returning veterans squirm uncomfortably as they acknowledge to their own spouse and to the other couples present the emotional difficulties they are encountering in settling back to life at home. Officers talk about their feelings of detachment from their young children, of a general emotional numbness, and of anger and resentment toward their spouse. This emotional sharing, and the opportunity to spend a weekend at a relaxing resort reconnecting with their spouse and hanging out with other couples experiencing similar strains, is seen by the Army as one way to help stem the tide of marital dissolution that appears to be on the increase among its highly-valued, highly-experienced officer corps. Like the military's foot-soldiers, they too find it difficult to settle back into life at home after harrowing tours of duty in Iraq and

📖 NEWS 9.7

Afghanistan.

The gulf that necessarily separates the everyday realities of veterans and of their families prompted Schutz to argue that just as the military prepares its veterans for their return to their (strange) homeland, it should also prepare veterans' families for the return of their (strange) homecomer. "In the beginning it is not only the homeland that shows to the homecomer an unaccustomed face. The homecomer appears equally strange to those who expect him, and the thick air about him will keep him unknown. Both the homecomer and the welcomer will need the help of a Mentor to 'make them wise to things'" (1962: 119).

Thus, despite the political pressures on the military to make soldiers seem like heroes, as highlighted by the controversy over the US military's account of the murder of Corporal Tillman, a professional football star who enlisted in the army after 9/11 and who was subsequently killed in Afghanistan in 2004 by a fellow-

📖 NEWS 9.8

soldier, the military also recognizes the need to organize programs aimed at making the veterans and their families wise to one another's realities. Suicide hotlines provide a "chain of care" linking veterans to local care and emergency

📖 NEWS 9.9

response workers, and as we see from Topic 9.1, marital counseling retreats and other family programs are intended to help the adjustment experience of military families, notwithstanding the enormous gap that exists between the soldier's and the family's divergent schemes of reference.

SYMBOLIC UNIVERSES

Although individuals live in very specific, here-and-now realities, people also seek to integrate their myriad everyday realities into a larger system of meaning, a "meaningful totality" or a symbolic universe of meaning that helps to explain and even justify the nature of their experiences (Berger and Luckmann 1966: 96). "The symbolic universe provides order for the subjective apprehension of biographical experience. Experiences belonging to different spheres of reality are integrated by incorporation in the same, overarching universe of meaning" (1966: 97). For Berger and Luckmann, religion is one such symbolic universe; science is another. These are overarching meaning systems that help the individual make sense of experiences in their reality – of war, of tragic accidents or earthquakes, for instance – and that impose some interpretive order on the everyday disorder that can accompany life-course transitions (e.g., marriage) and ruptures (e.g., divorce), including the expected reality of death (1966: 97–102).

We typically come together with others with whom we share a subuniverse of meaning when we go to church or participate in various social support (e.g., Alcoholics Anonymous) and other particular groups. These groups objectively legitimate our subjective experiences and the meanings with which we interpret reality – as happens when veterans' wives have an opportunity to share their marital experiences. Similarly, when Native American gay men get together to talk about their lives, they learn that their subjective experiences of a doubly stigmatized racial and sexual identity are not the personal aberration they had individually assumed, but instead comprise an objective and collective reality indicated by the existence of several gay Native Americans with similar experiences. Participation in groups with others who have similar experiences and similar interpretive frameworks makes our particular feelings, experiences, and identities plausible (Berger 1967: 50). "Like all social edifices of meaning, the subuniverses must be 'carried' by a particular collectivity, that is, by the group that ongoingly produces the meanings in question and within which these meanings have objective reality" (Berger and Luckmann 1966: 85). Such collectivities thus form part of the plausibility structure that affirms and legitimates the facticity, the realness, of individuals' everyday reality, their everyday experiences.

In particular, groups whose members experience social marginality (e.g., gays), or a conflict between a subjectively experienced and objective reality, help to facilitate participants' questioning of the objective or institutionally defined reality. This process, in turn, can mobilize activism toward social and institutional change (e.g., the gay rights movement's advocacy of same-sex marriage). And when laws change, both reflecting and ushering in a new reality – e.g., gay marriage – this new objective reality further affirms both the subjective and the objective plausibility of

📖 NEWS 9.7

📖 NEWS 9.10

collectively shared meanings, typifications, and institutional practices. Thus, for example, one lesbian woman who married her partner (in California, during the interval when same-sex marriage was legal before being overturned by a state referendum in November 2008) commented on how astonished she was at the support she received from her straight friends. She learned, she said, the importance of marriage as a rite of passage: "With a real wedding – not a commitment ceremony, not a domestic partnership registry – we were initiated into a crowded circle of people who automatically affirmed our very beings. It was a club we never even knew existed until we joined."

▦▦ NEWS 9.11

ETHNOMETHODOLOGY

Schutz's focus on everyday reality influenced the development of ethnomethodology, a field of study founded by the American sociologist **Harold Garfinkel**. (The term "ethnomethodology" simply refers to the methods people use to make sense of their experiences; *ethnos* is the Greek word for people.) Garfinkel (1967), concerned with what he regarded as sociological theory's general tendency to take social order and social processes for granted, argued instead that these are things that need to be accomplished on an ongoing basis. Specifically targeting Durkheim's assumption of the given-ness (or thing-ness) of "social facts," Garfinkel's stated intention was to focus on the processes by which social facts get made, and thus on the accomplishment of social reality. He explained:

> in contrast to certain versions of Durkheim that teach that the objective reality of social facts is sociology's fundamental principle, the lesson is taken instead ... that the objective reality of social facts *as* an ongoing accomplishment of the concerted activities of daily life, with the ordinary, artful ways of that accomplishment being by members known, used, and taken for granted, is for members [of society] a fundamental phenomenon. (1967: vii)

BIOGRAPHICAL NOTE

Harold Garfinkel was born in Newark, New Jersey, in 1917. While taking business courses at the University of Newark, he learned the "theory of accounts," a method that would later impact his sociological thinking. He received his Master's degree at the University of North Carolina, and after serving time in the air force during World War II, he completed his PhD at Harvard, studying with Talcott Parsons. Garfinkel subsequently established a long and distinguished career at the University of California at Los Angeles (UCLA), making UCLA the center for ethnomethodological studies. He and his wife, Arlene, whom he married during the war, had two sons (Rawls 2000).

Ethnomethodologists thus concern themselves with documenting in detail how it is that individuals in society (what Garfinkel calls members) work at creating an ordered or organized social reality. As such, ethnomethodology is not a theory with an explicit set of concepts that can be used to explain social life. It is more accurately viewed as a way of looking at and describing how people process everyday experiences so that they can recognize and produce or accomplish a highly ordered everyday social reality.

THE ACCOMPLISHMENT OF SOCIAL REALITY

Ethnomethodologists emphasize that individuals (members of society) accomplish order as they go about their everyday business, recognizing and making sense of their experiences in ways that fit with the socially shared norms of order and reasonableness in society. "Ethnomethodological studies analyze everyday activities as members' methods for making those same activities visibly-rational-and-reportable-for-all-practical-purposes, i.e., 'accountable,' as organizations of commonplace everyday activities" (Garfinkel 1967: vii). In other words, the focus is on how individuals use society's expectations of how and why things happen (or are expected to happen) to explain "what really happened" (1967: 15) in a particular setting regarding a particular event or activity.

Garfinkel argues that we can discern how members accomplish social reality by looking at the usual organized practices (what he calls "artful practices") that underlie and shape how individuals go about everyday tasks (1967: 11). These routine tasks invariably demand the organization and categorization of things and experiences on the basis of past experiences and their categorization in everyday family, work, and other settings. In various institutional settings (classrooms, hospitals, courtrooms, science laboratories), the routines individuals follow as they go about various tasks are organized in an orderly and sequential manner. This ensures that the sequence adhered to will enable them to produce retrospective accounts (of procedures etc.) that will hold up under scrutiny were they to be asked to provide a defensible account of some event or decision (e.g., a final grade assigned).

All decisions have consequences; reality is consequential. Hence, societal members have to be able to establish a reasonable account of what really happened (e.g., for a student to deserve a C or an A, etc.) and of how we know what really happened, when so many reasonable category choices or decisions may be available to us. Notably, many corporate and public controversies – e.g., the US military's revised accounts of football star Corporal Tillman's death in Afghanistan from friendly fire, or US Attorney General Gonzales's firing of state district attorneys – stem from accounts by participants whose evasiveness and contradictions make it hard for others to believe what the accounts claim about what *really* happened with regard to a particular decision or event.

NEWS 9.8
NEWS 9.12

THE CORONER'S OFFICE: ESTABLISHING HOW INDIVIDUALS
DIED AND LIVED

How, for example, can workers in a coroner's office "formulate accounts of how a death really-for-all-practical-purposes happened," when they themselves have not witnessed the death first-hand? How do they decide, and account for, whether a particular death is the result of natural causes, a suicide, a homicide, or an accident (Garfinkel 1967: 13–14)? Garfinkel argues that in arriving at a decision, the coroner uses all the "remains" available to make a determination. There are the "physical remains" – how the body appeared upon death: was the throat slashed? And if so, did it show the "hesitation cuts" of a suicidal death or the less hesitant ones that might accompany a homicide? And of course "cuts that look like hesitation cuts can be produced by other mechanisms [not just a suicidal person's hesitation]" (1967: 17). Because

> other courses of action are imaginable ... one needs to start with the actual display and imagine how different courses of actions could have been organized such that *that* picture would be compatible with it. One might think of the photographed display [of the dead body] as a phase-of-the-action. In any actual display is there a course of action with which that phase is uniquely compatible? *That's* the coroner's question. (1967: 17–18)

The coroner also has access to what might be called the social "remains":

> rumors, passing remarks, and stories – materials in the "repertoires" of whosoever might be consulted via the common work of conversations. These *whatsoever* bits and pieces that a story or a rule or proverb might make intelligible are used to formulate a recognizably coherent, standard, typical, cogent, uniform, planful, i.e., a professionally [and culturally] defensible, and thereby for members, a recognizably rational account of how the society worked to produce those remains. (1967: 17)

"*Whatsoever* bits" are the rumors about a person – e.g., "He was having financial trouble" – and the extent to which proverbs are applicable to the dead person's life (and the circumstances of his or her death), common sayings such as "He who lives by the sword dies by the sword." The physical and social remains have to be woven into accounts that are seen as credible and defensible; they have to add up, they have to fit with what it is we believe or know to be in keeping with the person's everyday routines, the member's social repertoire. As such the coroner's report does not just tell us how someone died but also how he or she *lived* (e.g., death from occupational injuries or from a drug overdose).

Gendering of accounts

And, I should add, the coherence of the social remains, of the bits believed about a person, and what is imputed too to the physical remains are socially differentiated. If the dead person is black, a woman, or an immigrant, for example this information makes some presumptions and interpretations more culturally defensible than others. Indeed, some commentators have noted that female celebrities "behaving badly" receive much more negative media coverage than their male peers who also have a reputation for partying. As feminist sociologists have long emphasized, in a patriarchal society wherein women are unequal to men, women, and especially mothers, are expected to behave differently than men (cf. chapter 10). And, by the same token, racial Others (e.g., Said 1978), i.e., those outside the dominant racial group, are expected to behave in certain culturally stereotyped ways – to commit more crime, for example (Gilroy 1987; cf. chapter 12).

This gender difference played out in the aftermath of the actor Heath Ledger's death from an apparent (accidental) drug overdose in 2008. Although Ledger was separated from his wife and had a party-going reputation, media commentators nonetheless expressed surprise at the circumstances of his death. Yet, one year earlier (spring 2007), celebrity model Anna Nicole Smith's death from a mix of prescription medicines did not seem to generate the same element of surprise. Similarly, media commentators interpreted model and singer Lindsay Lohan's Marilyn-Monroe-like *New York* magazine photo spread (February 25, 2008) as anticipating the star's (predicted) imminent demise from drugs given the "bits and pieces" known about Lohan's drug/partying habits. The categorization of reality, therefore, by the accounts of coroners, and more generally, by lawyers, publicists, police officers, medical personnel, and all those ordinary individuals who just so happened to have gone to school, etc., with the person of note (whether dead or alive), imposes an order on reality that is informed by – and reaffirms – dominant societal expectations regarding what kinds of people should be doing what kinds of things.

NEWS 9.13

JURORS ACCOMPLISHING REALITY

Similarly of interest to how an ordered social reality gets accomplished is the work of jurors. Removed from their own everyday settings, jurors enter a courtroom trial setting and deliberate among many possible alternative accounts and alternative outcomes so as to render a verdict as to what *really* happened, as opposed to what *allegedly* happened, in a given criminal case (Garfinkel 1967: 104–115). And the ambiguity in finding out what really happened (the real sequence and circumstances of the alleged wrong-doing) is exacerbated because what seems credible is, as with coroners' accounts, socially differentiated. The gender, race, social class, and other social locations of the individual(s) being charged with a crime, of the person(s) bringing the charge, and of the jurors all matter in determining the accounts and the outcome of the case, patterns that are well documented by sociologists of law (e.g., Black 1976).

PRODUCING AN ORDERED REALITY

What jurors do in arriving at a credible account of an event is what we as individuals do in deciding among possible alternative scenarios and accounts of our reality (and this includes sociologists doing research about the social world). We make inferential judgments about the sorts of experiences we have day to day. We actively categorize, and know how to categorize, what we are doing or experiencing in the present from our already experienced, culturally learned everyday knowledge of social reality.

Garfinkel elaborates:

> jurors decide between what is fact and what is fancy; between what actually happened and what "merely appeared" to happen; between what is put on and what is truth, regardless of detracting appearances; between what is credible and ... what is calculated and said by design; between what is an issue and what is decided; between what is *still* an issue compared with what is irrelevant and will not be brought up again except by a person who has an axe to grind; between what is mere personal opinion and with what any right-thinking person would have to agree to ... Jurors come to an agreement amongst themselves as to what actually happened. They decide "the facts," i.e., among alternative claims about speed of travel or extent of injury ... They do this by consulting the consistency of alternative claims with common sense models. Those common sense models are models jurors use to depict, for example, what culturally known types of persons drive in what culturally known types of ways at what typical speeds at what types of intersections for what typical motives. The test runs that the matter that is meaningfully consistent may be correctly treated as the thing that actually occurred. If the interpretation makes good sense, then that's what happened. (1967: 105–106)

Social reality is thus accomplished by members' referencing the societal rules and norms regarding what will pass as being credible to all those who make it their business to know what *really* happened (1967: 15). Whatever reality we are accomplishing, our accounts of what really happened (at the party, missing a class assignment deadline, being late for work, etc.) have to demonstrate that a given outcome or course of action was justified by the actions and events preceding it; our accounts have to be "adequately told, sufficiently detailed, clear, etc., for all practical purposes" (1967: 15). Accounts, moreover, can be revised to create an ordered reality in light of the anticipated consequences of the decision (ibid.). Revising an account, however – calling a death a homicide after first categorizing it as a suicide – does not remove accountability – e.g., the coroner must now account for the revised decision and the changed account also needs to be credible; the re-ordering of reality must make the (revised) inferences and actions look sensible.

In sum, Garfinkel emphasizes, any account of reality has to make practical sense; it has to be believable and recognizably rational by the standards of the society in which the accounts are produced (cf. Garfinkel 1967: 12–13, 16–17). Again, however, what makes practical sense in one particular social context may not necessarily translate to another. This is why, for example, feminist (e.g., Smith 1987; see chapter 10), queer (e.g., Seidman 1997; see chapter 11) and race (see chapter 12) theorists highlight how particular categorizations, as the ruling or hegemonic norms in society, impose particular definitions of what is credible that exclude the practical, lived experiences and everyday knowledge of outsider individuals and groups (e.g., women, gays, blacks, disabled individuals).

GENDER AS AN ACCOMPLISHED REALITY

The accounts individuals provide of reality are not simply verbal or written but include actions too; how people behave (e.g., students, politicians, Lindsay Lohan) – how they *live*, what they *do* – is core to establishing the credibility and believability of accounts. Although Garfinkel did not acknowledge the gender and other power inequalities that comprise any social reality, nor indeed how social realities might be contested, he did recognize that gender – like everything else in society – is something that has to be accomplished. It is common for sociologists today to talk about "doing gender" – largely due to the highly influential essay by Candace West and Don Zimmerman (1987), whose ethnomethodological approach to disentangling sex and gender underscored that gender is something that emerges and gets accomplished in and through everyday social life. Their analysis builds on and considerably extends an insight first elaborated by Garfinkel (1967).

Garfinkel wrote about "Agnes," a person he interviewed and whom he said "was born a boy with normal-appearing male genitals" but who developed "secondary feminine sex characteristics" at puberty, and subsequently had a transsexual surgical operation that made her physically a woman (Garfinkel 1967: 120–121), which Agnes felt was her "natural, normal" self (ibid.: 119). Garfinkel's account of Agnes, her medical history, and his interpretations of that history is controversial among sociologists (e.g., Denzin 1990, 1991; Hilbert 1991), in part, because after completing his study, Garfinkel learned that Agnes had lied in her interviews and that in fact, "she was not a biologically defective male" (Garfinkel 1967: 285). Notwithstanding this critical revision to Garfinkel's account (ironic, given his concern with account credibility), from the point of view of pushing theoretical understanding of the relation between (biological) sex and (social) gender, his discussion of Agnes is still theoretically useful. Garfinkel's elaboration of Agnes's "abiding practical preoccupation with competent female sexuality" (1967: 121) and efforts to accomplish that reality, to "act in accordance with expected attitudes, appearances, affiliations, dress, style of life, etc." (ibid: 119), highlighted that what is considered appropriate sex/gender behavior is not natural but socially learned (notwithstanding biological influences).

Agnes knew what was expected of women though she also knew that her (biologically male) biographical history and experiences were at odds with what "normally" accompanies being a woman, despite her "convincingly female" appearance (Garfinkel 1967: 119). Therefore, she had to pass as a woman; she had, in Goffman's terms (cf. chapter 8), to perform the expected female role. And she had to accomplish this knowing that she had access to vitally relevant information about her own experiences that others with whom she was interacting did not have. Moreover, had they had such information, Agnes was aware that it would have led them to seriously question her ("natural") competence as a woman.

From Goffman's *SI* perspective, Agnes would need to ensure the presentation of an effective gender-role performance that would not be disrupted by an impression-management lapse revealing her (secret) stigma. For Garfinkel, however, an ethnomethodologist, background knowledge is not something to be managed or suppressed (in order for the individual to pass as normal); it inheres, rather, in the experiences individuals draw on as they anticipate and demonstrate the credibility of their gendered (and other accomplished) realities. Thus, Garfinkel argues, showing competence as a "natural" female against any anticipated claims that interested parties might make about one's gender competence is not a strategic game (or drama) that one engages in episodically (in performing the role of woman to particular audiences), but an ongoing accomplishment that has to be continuously accomplished.

The "ongoing-ness" of action with which ethnomethodologists are concerned leads Garfinkel to note: "it would be incorrect to say of Agnes that she has passed. The active mode is needed: she is passing" (1967: 167). She is, in short, actively engaged in accomplishing the ongoing social reality of being a "natural" woman. McCloskey's (1999) narrative of her own transgendered journey from being Donald (a 52-year-old man) to being Deirdre (a 55-year-old woman) discusses the routines and role expectations she follows in accomplishing a credible female identity.

In sum, for ethnomethodologists, social life, society, is not comprised of scripted roles (*SI*), nor of pre-given social facts. It is, rather, an ongoing social accomplishment, accomplished by accountable individuals actively producing behavioral claims and outcomes that are recognizable, credible, and rationally defensible in terms of established cultural and societal expectations.

RESEARCHING THE DOING OF REALITY-MAKING

Ethnomethodologists' attention to the order-creation processes in social reality means that they draw on a variety of research methods to show the experience categorization methods individuals use in order-making and (like jurors and coroners) accomplishing particular accounts of reality. The research methods include in-depth interviews, participant and non-participant observation (including videotaped observation), and especially "the documentary method of interpretation" (Garfinkel 1967: 78), first outlined by Karl Mannheim. Mannheim (1936/1968: 78–81, 184–191, 198–202) stressed that knowledge of, and from, a particular reality is always determined by the concrete socio-historical context in which that reality is known or experienced. Sociologists who use documentary or historical research methods thus identify the particular patterns of social structure and social order that emerge in their analysis of official reports, institutional records, newspapers, personal letters and diaries, etc.

Garfinkel (1967: 40) argues that this is the same method that all individuals basically use "in the conduct of everyday affairs."

BREACHING EXPERIMENTS

Ethnomethodologists' particular interest in "the routine grounds of everyday activities" (Garfinkel 1967: 35–75) leads them to conduct breaching experiments designed to disrupt the routines that comprise particular social realities so as to demonstrate the fragility that underlies everyday social order. They "modify the *objective* structure of the familiar, known-in-common environment by rendering the background expectancies inoperative. Specifically, this modification would consist of subjecting a person to a breach of the background expectancies of everyday life" (1967: 54).

For example, students are asked to act as strangers or as polite visitors in their own homes (1967: 44–49), or to have conversations with friends that keep questioning or asking for clarification of mundane and (apparently) self-evident statements – e.g. "What do you mean you had a flat tire?" "What do you mean your boyfriend is feeling fine?" (1967: 42–44). These experiments, the nature and purpose of which are not disclosed to family members or friends, are designed to make familiar details, objects, and scenes unfamiliar and strange. Typically, the consequences of these inversions of role behavior (e.g., daughter to visitor) and of conversational pickiness are far greater than one might expect. They generally cause much bewilderment (1967: 47, 53–65), a point used by Garfinkel to underscore how much work goes into the creation and maintenance of everyday reality, and to highlight "the role that a background of common understandings plays in the production, control and recognition" of reality (1967: 49).

Although effective in accomplishing their goal, breaching experiments raise ethical complications. They violate the requirement of university committees on research on human subjects (institutional review boards) that individuals be made aware of and freely consent to the research in which they are participating. Further, it is uncertain whether the benefits of the research outweigh the possible harm that the experiments can cause (e.g., bewilderment to unsuspecting family members or friends).

CONVERSATION ANALYSIS

Less controversially, ethnomethodologists also engage in conversation analysis aimed at detailing the specific, pragmatic steps that establish meaning, i.e., order, in everyday interaction, and this method has become popular in fields beyond sociology including linguistics, anthropology, and cognitive science (see Heritage 2009). The classical conversation analysis approach as outlined by Garfinkel and Sacks (1986) is to document how speaking individuals are able to master the natural language and understand one another in conversation so that they appear

305

to one another as "talking reasonably," as "speaking English (or French, or whatever)" and using "clear, consistent, cogent speech, i.e. rational speech" (Garfinkel and Sacks 1986: 165). This research shows that individuals are able to have efficient conversations because of glossing practices. "Glossing practices exist in empirical multitude. In endless, but particular, analyzable ways, glossing practices are methods for producing observable and reportable understanding, with, in, and of natural language" (ibid.: 164–165).

When we are interacting with our friends we generally use fewer words than would be grammatically required to say what we need to say in order to be understood. Typically, because there is an already established context for our relationship, we talk in shorthand – we gloss over a lot of specifics – and yet we expect the other person to know what we mean, and indeed, the person with whom we are communicating usually does know what we mean. Thus, "*Whatever* [a person] says provides the very materials to be used in *making out* what [he or she] says" (ibid.: 165). The way we gloss over many of the necessary-to-be-known background contextual assumptions and details allows us to order our reality claims to the other in ways that enhance their quick comprehension of how, for all practical purposes, things really happened.

The comprehension of claims is, however, more complicated than is fully acknowledged by Garfinkel. Because social interaction is, precisely, social, conversational practices, including interruptions, turn-taking, hesitations, pauses, and silences, as well as how language is used, are not independent of social class, gender, racial, and other everyday cultural differences. These differences matter in translating words and glossing practices from one family-societal context to the many other contexts in which individuals must necessarily interact with others (e.g., schools, playgrounds, doctors' offices, corporate offices, parliament). Thus, for example, as feminist sociologists (e.g., Thorne et al. 1983; West and Zimmerman 1983) highlight, women and men use different conversation tactics and strategies, and this in turn leads to and exacerbates female–male miscommunication.

Micro–macro linkages

These differences are not simply conversation differences, but differences that reproduce macro-societal inequalities in the gender order; inequalities in the intersectionality of gender, race, and class (e.g., de Vault 1991; Fenstermaker and West 2002); and power inequalities more generally – in doctor–patient encounters, for example (West 1984); see Box 9.1. These differences, moreover, tend to get glossed

---

Box 9.1 Conversation differences between women and men in the US

- Women use more indirect and euphemistic forms of speech than men
- Men are more likely than women to interrupt
- Male physicians are more likely than female physicians to interrupt their patients
- Patients in conversation with female doctors interrupt as much as, or more than, their physicians
- White male physicians are more likely to interrupt white female than male patients
- White male physicians are even more likely to interrupt black male and female patients

(*Sources*: Lakoff 1990; West 1984: 56–58)

over in ordinary, everyday conversation as well as in the (male-dominated) halls of power (cf. chapter 10). Therefore, although ethnomethodology maintains a core micro-focus, its insights can be applied beyond the specific micro-contexts in which accounts and conversations are accomplished (e.g., Hilbert 1990).

SUMMARY

Phenomenology focuses on everyday reality and how individuals recognize and organize their everyday experiences. It is a tradition indebted to the writings of Alfred Schutz, and elaborated by Berger and Luckmann (1966), who emphasize the social construction of reality. A second strand focusing on everyday reality is ethnomethodology, elaborated by Harold Garfinkel; it is concerned with the culturally determined categorizing methods societal members use to recognize, account for, and accomplish the everyday institutional and social routines that accomplish social order.

POINTS TO REMEMBER

Phenomenology
- A focus on the world of everyday life
- The world of everyday life is an intersubjectively shared social world
- The pragmatics of the "here and now" demand our full, wide-awake attention
- Though we live in a shared social environment, individuals' unique socio-biographical situations shape what is relevant for them in the here and now
- Common-sense knowledge derived from individuals' shared stock of social experience is the knowledge that anchors and orients everyday social reality
- Social reality is the product of human design
- Because humans have created society and social institutions, culture, etc., humans can change what they have created; i.e., social and institutional change is always a possibility
- Symbolic universes link individuals into a meaningful, collectively shared, integrated social reality

Ethnomethodology
- A strand of sociological thinking and inquiry influenced by Schutz's ideas and elaborated by Harold Garfinkel
- Individuals accomplish social reality in everyday life by categorizing experiences and producing accounts of those experiences so as to make an ordered social reality that fits with cultural assumptions of how things really happen in a given social and institutional setting
- The accounts produced must be culturally credible such that they provide a defensible account of how society works to produce certain outcomes

- For ethnomethodologists, gender is not a societal process or a social role performance but an ongoing, active, practical accomplishment
- The practical accomplishment of any ordered reality is contingent on the background of common understandings that determines the production, control, and recognition of reality
- The content and structure of everyday conversation play a key role in making accounts and their outcomes and consequences intelligible and credible

GLOSSARY: PHENOMENOLOGY

common-sense knowledge knowledge derived from individuals' everyday practices; what seems "natural" or obvious in their social environment.

externalization an aspect of the dynamic process by which individuals maintain social reality, whereby they act on and in regard to the already existing (human-created and externalized) objective reality (e.g., institutions, everyday practices in society).

here-and-now reality immediate pragmatic salience of individuals' everyday reality.

in-group particular community (or group/society) in which we are immersed, whose habits we have inherited, and with which we are "at home."

internalization an aspect of the dynamic process by which individuals create social reality such that, in experiencing an external, objective reality (e.g., institutional practices, social inequality), they translate (internalize) it into their own particular, subjectively experienced reality.

lifeworld from the German word *Lebenswelt*; the world of everyday life and its taken-for-granted routines, customs, habits, and knowledge.

natural attitude the individual's orientation toward his or her social environment, a reality which seems natural because it is the everyday reality which he or she knows.

objective reality the social reality, including objectively existing social institutions (economic, legal, etc.), language, and social processes (e.g., gender/race inequalities), into which individuals are socialized.

out-group everyday reality of those who have different everyday habits to us, and which to us seem "strange."

phenomenology focuses on the reality of everyday life and how individuals make sense of their everyday experiences.

plausibility structure group and institutional settings (e.g., churches) and laws that affirm (make plausible) the objective reality of individuals' subjectively experienced realities.

practical knowledge knowledge needed to accomplish routine everyday tasks in the individual's environment.

recipe knowledge particular ways of doing things in a particular social environment.

scheme of reference stock of accumulated knowledge and experiences we use to interpret and make sense of new experiences.

social construction of reality social reality as the product of humans acting intersubjectively and collectively. Social reality exists as an objective (human-social) reality to which individuals respond and which can be changed by individuals acting collectively.

stock of preconstituted knowledge cumulative body of everyday knowledge and experiences that individuals have from living in a particular social environment.

subjective reality the individual's subjective experience and interpretation of the external, objective reality.

subuniverses of meaning collectivities that share and objectify individuals' similarly meaningful interpretations of reality.

symbolic universes overarching meaning systems (e.g., religion, science) that integrate and order individuals' everyday realities.

typifications customary (typical) ways in which an individual's intersubjective social environment is organized; how things and individuals (as role/status types) are presumed to work/behave.

wide-awakeness the practical consciousness and attentiveness required in attending to the "here and now" tasks and realities of everyday life.

GLOSSARY: ETHNOMETHODOLOGY

accomplishment of social reality the idea that social reality does not have a pre-given objective order, but needs to be achieved on an ongoing basis by societal members.

accounts how individuals categorize events, experiences, and everyday reality such that their accounts produce an ordered reality that makes sense and is credible in a given societal context.

background knowledge an individual's stock of previous experiences and knowledge of reality; impacts how they categorize and evaluate current experiences.

breaching experiments designed to disrupt a particular micro-social reality in order to illustrate the fragility that underlies the order and routines of everyday reality.

conversation analysis detailed analysis of the specific, pragmatic steps in how language and speech are used in everyday conversation to create order.

ethnomethodology shared methods ordinary people (societal members) use to make sense of everyday experiences across different settings.

glossing practices shorthand ways in which language and speech utterances are used to communicate in particular social contexts.

members individuals who comprise society and accomplish social reality.

RELEVANT NEWSPAPER STORIES

All news stories are from the *New York Times* unless otherwise noted, and can be accessed via www.wiley.com/go/dillon. See NEWS icons in the margins above.

NEWS 9.1 "Weary soldiers, ready for rest, but not at ease," September 30, 2007.
NEWS 9.2 "While real bullets fly, movies bring war home," July 26, 2007.
          "A film year full of escapism, flat in attendance," January 2, 2008.
NEWS 9.3 "Not to see the fallen is no favor," May 28, 2007.
NEWS 9.4 RAND Corporation. 2008. *Invisible Wounds of War.* www.rand.org
          "Pentagon totals rise for stress disorder," May 28, 2008.
NEWS 9.5 "V.A. disavows combat stress memo," May 16, 2008.
          "Congress weigh veterans' adjustment aid," May 7, 2008.
          "Contenders spar on Veterans' Bill," May 23, 2008.
NEWS 9.6 "For soldiers' families, battles are not far off," November 3, 2007.
          "When strains on military families turn deadly," February 15, 2008.
NEWS 9.7 "After war, love can be a battlefield," April 6, 2008.
NEWS 9.8 "Panel hears about falsehoods in 2 wartime incidents," April 25, 2007.
          "Corporal Tillman haunts the Pentagon," editorial, April 27, 2007.
          "Politics during wartime," opinion editorial, April 27, 2007.
NEWS 9.9 "Talking veterans down from despair," April 22, 2008.
NEWS 9.10 "Moving far from home, finally able to feel at home, July 17, 2007.

NEWS 9.11 "The joy of marriage was ours, for a while," April 20, 2008.

NEWS 9.12 "Gonzales endures harsh session with senate panel: Doubt is raised about honesty and judgment," April 20, 2007.

NEWS 9.13 "Autopsy on actor is inconclusive as calls for help are revealed," January 24, 2008.

"Medical examiner rules Ledger's death accidental," February 8, 2008.

CHAPTER TEN
FEMINIST THEORIES

Timeline 10.1 Major events in the achievement of women's equality (1865–present)

1865	Women admitted to Cornell University at its inception; the only Ivy League University open to women
1869	National Women's Suffrage Association founded by Susan B. Anthony and Elizabeth Cady Stanton
1893	New Zealand first currently existing country to grant women voting rights
1903	Formation of Women's Social and Political Union in Britain by Emmeline Pankhurst, demanding votes for women
1903	Marie Curie awarded Nobel Prize in Physics for the discovery of radioactivity
1910	Increased public use of "feminism" as a term to summarize women's demands for equality
1918	Women over age 30 allowed to vote in Ireland, Britain; and over 18 in Canada
1920	American women receive right to vote
1944	Women receive right to vote in France (one of last western countries to grant this right)
1949	Women receive right to vote in China
1950	Women admitted to Harvard Law School
1952	Dorothy Swaine Thomas elected first woman president of the American Sociological Association
1963	Valentina Tereshkova, cosmonaut from the Soviet Union, first woman in space
1966	Bobbe Gibb first woman to complete the Boston marathon (but without an official number)
1969	Yale and Princeton universities admit women students
1972	Title IX US federal regulations prohibiting sex discrimination in education and sports programs
1978	Six women chosen by NASA (US space agency) as astronaut candidates
1979	Margaret Thatcher first woman prime minister of UK
1981	Sandra Day O'Connor first woman confirmed to US Supreme Court
1983	Columbia University admits women students
1983	Sally Ride first American woman astronaut in space
1986	*Oprah Winfrey Show*, produced and presented by Oprah Winfrey, goes into national syndication; currently broadcast in 134 countries

1990	Mary Robinson first woman president of Ireland
1993	Ruth Bader Ginsburg second woman confirmed to US Supreme Court
1993	Judith Rodin first woman president of an Ivy League university, University of Pennsylvania
1994	Women of all races in South Africa granted voting rights
1997–2001	Madeleine Albright first woman US secretary of state
2000	Vashti McKenzie first woman bishop of African Methodist Episcopal Church
2003	Eileen Collins first woman shuttle commander
2005	US Census data; majority of women (51 percent) living without a spouse
2005	16 percent of corporate officers at Fortune 500 companies are women; less than 2 percent are CEOs
2006	Katie Couric first woman to anchor US television evening newscast (CBS)
2006	Katharine Jefferts Schori first woman presiding bishop of Episcopal Church in US
April 2008	Danica Patrick first woman to win Indy 500 race (in Mootegi, Japan)
June 2008	Hillary Clinton comes close to becoming first woman nominee for president of US
June 2008	Lt. Gen. Ann Dunwoody first woman in US military chosen for promotion to four-star general

CONSCIOUSNESS OF WOMEN'S INEQUALITY

In 1985, two prominent feminist sociologists, Judith Stacey and Barrie Thorne, diagnosed the "missing feminist revolution in sociology." They argued that sociology was resistant to the theoretical challenges presented by feminism and the need to rethink sociological understanding of the permeation of gender inequality through all societal processes. Over twenty years later, many feminist sociologists voice frustration that gender is still marginalized within the discipline. Despite the noteworthy increase in empirical studies of gender, there is a lingering sense that, in particular, feminist theory is not really considered a core part of sociological theory (e.g., Ray 2006), but an add-on, something mentioned among other miscellaneous ideas. At the same time, however, women have achieved significant visibility in society and in sociology. Of particular note, one of sociology's leading feminist theorists, Patricia Hill Collins, was elected president of the American Sociological Association for 2009, joining Parsons, Merton, Goffman, and other distinguished theorists in sociology's "hall of fame." Nonetheless, within sociology

313

women confront many obstacles, as in society as a whole, in fields as varied as corporate finance, science, architecture, and music.

Feminist theory comprises several different strands and feminist sociologists research a great variety of topics. At the core of feminist theory, however, is a focus on women's inequality, and how that inequality is structured and experienced at macro and micro levels. As early as the 1830s, feminist sociologists such as Harriet Martineau (cf. Introduction) were highlighting the contradictions between societal ideals of equality, on the one hand, and on the other, social structures and practices which denied women's equality and curbed women's freedom to participate in the political, educational, occupational, and economic opportunities available to men. The women's movement in the US came to prominence in the late nineteenth century around an agenda that sought to establish voting rights (suffrage) and equal economic opportunities for women. The "most influential mentor" in this effort, according to historian Nancy Cott (1987: 40–41), was another feminist sociologist, **Charlotte Perkins Gilman** (1860–1935).

BIOGRAPHICAL NOTE

Charlotte Perkins Gilman was born in 1860 into a well-established Boston family, but her childhood was economically strained as a result of her father deserting the family. She studied at the Rhode Island School of Design and married Charles Stetson, a painter, at age 24. Soon thereafter, she suffered a nervous breakdown, and the couple divorced in 1890. Charlotte subsequently lived and raised her daughter in California, getting married in 1900 to George Houghton Gilman, with whom she seemed happy. By then, despite her nervous mental condition and the challenges of being a single mother, she was already a well-renowned and prolific book-writer and lecturer on women's issues in both the US and Europe. Diagnosed with breast cancer in 1932, she took her own life three years later, commenting in a suicide note, "I have preferred chloroform to cancer" (O'Neill 1972: vii–xi).

Gilman (1911) underscored that women and men live in a "man-made world," an "androcentric culture" in which one sex – man – is "accepted as the race type," as human, and women are considered a "sub-species"; thus men have "monopolized all human activities, called them man's work, and managed them as such" (1911: 18, 25). In our man-made world, women are restricted to a separate sex-specific sphere, the home:

> To the man, the whole world was his world; his because he was male; and the whole world of women was the home; because she was female. She had her prescribed sphere, strictly limited to her feminine occupations and interests; he had all the rest of life; and not only so, but, having it, insisted on calling it male. (1911: 23)

Gilman argued that the exclusion of women from the world of work, the industrial economy, was an "abnormal restriction" (1911: 38); it contravened the human desire to work and essentially reduced women to the inferior status of "domestic servant" (ibid.: 39). It is men who have defined the world, who have made its history and social organization, who have built an androcentric culture, none of which has a place for women. For Gilman, the right to work is core to *human* existence; it is neither male nor female: "Labor is not merely a means of supporting human life – it is human life" (1911: 231), life denied in man-made society in which "Economic Woman" does not exist.

True progress could only be achieved, Gilman argued, when society transcended its abnormal androcentric divisions and allowed women to be both workers and mothers. Gilman believed, somewhat ironically – and at odds with the feminist tendency today to reject natural biological reasons as explanations for the social differences between women and men – that both motherhood and economic labor were *natural* feminine-maternal instincts (ibid.: 233). She stated: "As a matter of fact industry is in its origin feminine; that is maternal. It is the overflowing foun-tain of mother-love and mother-power which first prompts the human race to labor" (1911: 233). And, Gilman maintained, when women are free to work, and thus able to realize their humanity, they will also become more, not less, efficient as mothers – not mothers androcentrically defined as personal servants in the home, but mothers of the next generation of the human race, "motherhood [being] the highest process" in the evolution of humanity (ibid.: 245), "the noblest and most valuable profession" (1903/1972: 122). Bolstering her view that women could/should mother *and* work for pay, Gilman envisaged the occupational pro-fessionalization of home cooking and home cleaning through the employment of those who are scientifically trained and best able to do such work (ibid.: 138).

Hence, for Gilman, women's equality rests on the socially institutionalized free-dom to act on what she alleged to be women's natural feminine instincts – to mother and work; a state of affairs that is only attainable once society ruptures the interwoven "concepts of maleness and humanness," i.e., the idea that while "men are people," women are "only females" and hence not deserving of human equality (1911: 237). For Gilman, it is only "When we learn to differentiate between humanity and masculinity [that] we shall give honor where honor is due" (1911: 6).

The validation of men's ideas and experiences as *the objective* and *legitimate* human experience continues to permeate gender structures and social relations, and as such is a prominent theme among contemporary feminist sociological theorists. Feminist theory resurged as part of the transformation in the public consciousness of social inequality that came to the fore in many western countries in the 1960s and 1970s as a result of that era's social and political protest move-ments. In particular, the women's movement challenged the status quo that saw biological differences between men and women as naturally legitimating social role and status inequality. Spurred by the increased political attentiveness to gender inequality, women sociologists turned their gaze to the discipline of sociol-ogy itself. The patterns they saw reflected trends in the larger society. Most notably, the canon was all-male, with an exclusive emphasis on the "founding fathers" – Marx, Durkheim, and Weber – and they and their successors (e.g., Parsons, Dahrendorf, Berger, Goffman) comprised a male-centered curriculum bolstered by the dominance of male sociology professors and graduate students (cf. Wallace 1989: 7–8). Thus feminist sociologists were prompted to ask, "Where are the women?" And they focused their efforts, as Jessie Bernard (1998: 6) phrased it, on "what women (and sympathetic men) can do for sociology" – and for society at large – to redress the androcentric biases (see also Laslett and Thorne 1997; Myers et al. 1998). These questions remain at the fore of feminist theorizing and research in sociology.

STANDPOINT THEORIES 1: DOROTHY SMITH AND THE RELATIONS OF RULING

RULING TEXTS IN A PATRIARCHAL SOCIETY

Dorothy Smith elaborates how the practices of sociology crystallize the larger structural and everyday dilemmas of gender in a patriarchal society. Smith argues that what counts for authoritative knowledge in sociology and in society is determined by standards that privilege men and exclude women. It is not that men are intent on sabotaging women, but that the structures and expectations institutionalized in society down through history are the creation of men. Men, not women, wrote the texts – they literally wrote the rules – that have come to define society and how we think about things.

BIOGRAPHICAL NOTE

Dorothy Smith was born into a middle-class family in Yorkshire, England, in 1926. Thinking that a college degree might land her a good job as a secretary, she applied and was admitted to the prestigious London School of Economics (LSE), where she majored in sociology and social anthropology. She met her husband, William Smith, while at the LSE and together they left England for graduate study at the University of California, Berkeley. Her two children were born while she was completing her doctoral dissertation in sociology, and soon thereafter, she and Bill divorced, leaving her to deal with the challenges of single motherhood and earning a living. After Berkeley, Smith and her sons returned to England for a few years; she then accepted a faculty position at the University of British Columbia, Vancouver, Canada, where she was influential in establishing the legitimacy of women's studies. In 1997, she accepted a faculty position at the Ontario Institute for Studies in Education. Currently retired, Smith has received several awards in recognition of her trail-blazing impact on feminist sociology, including the American Sociological Association's award for a Career of Distinguished Scholarship, and its Jessie Bernard Award for feminist scholarship.

We can readily list some of the ruling texts in western society. The Bible is one. It is a text written by men – the gospels of Matthew, Mark, Luke, and John; the epistles of Paul. And it is men who through history have been the Bible's primary interpreters – in the Catholic church, only men can be popes, cardinals, bishops, and priests; the Protestant Reformers were all men (e.g., Martin Luther, John Calvin), and still today in American society the leaders of the various religious denominations are men – with a couple of notable exceptions (see Timeline 10.1). In the US, another core text is the Declaration of Independence, written by a group of men; so too the US Constitution – written and signed by George Washington and 38 state representatives, all men. And the many significant Supreme Court cases that have so crucially defined the character of our legal rights have also been written by men: the justices on the Supreme Court – all men, until Sandra Day O'Connor became its first woman member in 1981 (see Timeline 10.1).

Texts are critical to organizing a society's ruling practices – they define who can do what, how it should be done, and how it should be evaluated. And these practices, in turn, determine the kinds of texts and ideas that are produced and validated. Texts are thus the centerpiece of what Smith calls the relations of ruling. She explains:

> When I speak here of governing or ruling I mean something more general than the notion of government as political organization. I refer rather to that total complex of activities, differentiated into many spheres, by which our kind of society is ruled, managed, and administered. It includes what the business world calls *management*, it includes the professions, it includes government and the activities of those who are selecting, training, and indoctrinating those who will be its governors. The last includes those who provide and elaborate the procedures by which it is governed and develop methods for how it is to be done – namely, the business schools, the sociologists, the economists. These are the institutions through which we are ruled and through which we, and I emphasize this *we*, participate in ruling. (1990a: 14)

The ruling texts are not confined to specific printed texts (e.g., the Bible, laws), but are far more encompassing. They include the many images in society – in stores, magazines, and advertising, for example, and the various discourses that circulate and which organize, reflect, and remind us of the practices and social relations that govern our everyday/everynight worlds (Smith 1990b: 164). As Smith would underscore, the texts that govern being a woman do not end – as they do for many men – at 5 p.m. (when the regular work-day ends), and nor do they end when the kids are settled in bed; the texts operate 24/7.

ADVERTISING FEMININITY

Among these ideologically powerful texts are all of those (often contradictory) texts that comprise a distinctive discourse of femininity. The ruling texts of femininity structure and are situated in the gender relations in society – relations organized around women as objects.

> Texts enter into and order courses of action and relations among individuals ... Texts ... must not be isolated from the practices in which they are embedded and which they organize ... In our time to address femininity is to address, directly or indirectly, a textual

discourse vested in women's magazines and television, advertisements, the appearance of cosmetics counters, fashion displays and to a lesser extent books ... Discourse also involves the talk women do in relation to such texts, the work of producing oneself to realize the textual images, the skills involved in going shopping, in making and choosing clothes, in making decisions about colors, styles, makeup, and the ways in which these become a matter of interest among men ... Ideologies and doctrines of femininity are explicit, publicly spoken and written ... [they] generate and interpret the visual images of femininity and interpret its embodied correlate in women's appearances. The doctrines ... are reproduced, revised, updated in popular philosophy, theology, and psychology, in magazines, in books, and as schemata governing the morality of soap operas, sit-coms, TV games shows, and so forth. Their interpretive paradigms are commercially produced on television, in movies, in advertising in multiple settings, including packaging, and shop-window and counter displays. (Smith 1990b: 162, 163, 170–171, 174)

And while Smith focuses on femininity, we should note that society also has clearly defined standards of masculinity – expectations that in turn differently impact gender relations. As Michael Kimmel (2005: 25–42) notes, the culture of masculinity in the US affirms a macho, though disguised, homophobia and the suppression in men of any signs of femininity in the self, a "fierceness" promoted in popular culture (see photo, p. 357).

THE RULES OF SOCIOLOGY AND THE EXCLUSION OF WOMEN'S STANDPOINT

Sociologists participate in the relations of ruling as teachers, researchers, writers, media commentators, etc. And Smith argues that the ruling text of sociology – the discipline's conceptual and methodological rules and procedures, the text that

---

Box 10.1   Objectification of women

Humanity is male and man defines woman not in herself but as relative to him; she is not regarded as an autonomous being ... Man can think of himself without woman. She cannot think of herself without man. And she is simply what man decrees ... she appears essentially to the male as a sexual being. For him, she is sex – absolute sex, no less. She is defined and differentiated with reference to man and not he with reference to her; she is the incidental, the inessential as opposed to the essential. He is the subject, he is the Absolute – she is the Other ... In men's eyes – and for the legions of women who see through men's eyes – it is not enough to have a woman's body nor to assume the female function as mistress or mother in order to be a "true woman." In sexuality and maternity woman as subject can claim autonomy; but to be a true woman she must accept herself as the Other. The men of today show a certain duplicity which is painfully lacerating to women; they are willing on the while to accept woman as a fellow being, an equal; but they still require her to remain the inessential. For her these two destinies are incompatible; she hesitates between one and the other without being exactly adapted to either ... With man there is no break between public and private life: the more he confirms his grasp on the world in action and in work, the more virile he seems to be; human and vital values are combined in him. Whereas woman's independent successes are in contradiction with her femininity, since the true woman is required to make herself object, to be the Other. (De Beauvoir 1949/1953: 16, 291)

organizes sociological practice – marginalizes women. The ethos of impersonal, scientific objectivity (see glossary at the end of the book) institutionalized in sociology (cf. Introduction) – the set of scientific procedures that "serve to separate the discipline's body of knowledge from its practitioners" (Smith 1990a: 16) – excludes women's everyday/everynight experiences as women and their first-hand knowledge of these experiences (1990b: 164). This ethos, Smith notes, is itself determined by a conceptual order that demands the exclusion of subjectively embodied, localized, particularized experiences. The pre-ordered concepts, categories, and definitions we use to study society – e.g., bureaucracy, race, family, crime, etc. – and the research methods we use to find evidence of these concepts are themselves ordered by the relations of ruling – by the (scientific) discipline of sociology itself. Thus as sociologists,

> we learn to think sociology as it is thought and to practice it as it is practiced. We learn that some topics are relevant and others are not. We learn to discard our personal experience as a source of reliable information about the character of the world and to confine our focus and insights within the conceptual frameworks and relevances of the discipline. (Smith 1990a: 15)

RULING TEXTS AND THE EXCLUSION OF EVERYDAY EXPERIENCES

Moreover, our learned, sociological way of thinking, of knowing what is relevant and what isn't, intertwines with other ruling institutions in society. In particular, what we research is contingent on the expectations of the government, industry, and other funding organizations that predetermine what topics and issues are worthy of research. And while much of this information has relevance for our lives, Smith underscores that it excludes the direct experiences of women and other subordinated (e.g., racial) groups in society

Despite advances in women's equality with men, women and men are reminded to see women as objects for men. This process starts early; young girls (and boys) making their way to toy stores at the mall are likely to see advertisements such as this for Victoria's Secret.

(1990a: 27). Nevertheless, the claim to scientific knowledge in which sociology shrouds itself presents this knowledge as a universally true, objective account of the world. We do not think of it as being partial, as privileging a particular set of (male) experiences; we think of it as neutral and not as a "sociology written from the standpoint of men located in the relations of ruling our societies" (Smith 1987: 1).

Missing from the sociological and the other texts that comprise our society's body of objectified knowledge, Smith argues, are the everyday experiences of particular people in particular situated contexts. Sociologists impose the discipline's generalized concepts of objective experience on people's subjective experiences. And typically we do not even pause to wonder whether in fact there is correspondence between our categories and the categories used by the people, the human subjects, we study; subjects, i.e., people, who are in every sense subject to – governed by – our scientific canon, our privileged knowledge, and who ironically, are stripped of their subjectivity by our privileging of objectivity. Consequently, Smith argues, "Sociological procedures legislate a reality rather than discover one" (1990a: 53).

We make the reality fit into the (objectified) conceptual order we impose rather than setting out to discover and understand how particularly situated people experience everyday reality. We suppress individuals' experiences under the objectified concepts we have been trained to use, as if concepts are sufficient to know and understand the gamut of people's everyday experiences. "Living individuals in their actual contexts of action have already been obliterated before their representation reaches the sociologist ... Who acts and how disappears" (1990a: 55). Thus Smith (1990a: 24–25) reminds us that although we talk in abstract conceptual terms about various social processes (e.g., stratification, domestic violence, etc.), these processes are not abstracted from but determine and are shaped by the embodied realities of real people in particular social locations (e.g., immigrant women deboning chickens in a poultry factory; see Topic 1.4).

📖 NEWS 1.13

Smith illustrates the divide between the presumed objectivity and objectified knowledge of the sociologist and our exclusion of the subjective relational context of those studied:

Riding a train not long ago in Ontario I saw a family of Indians [Native Americans] – woman, man, and three children – standing together on a spur above a river, watching the train go by. I realized that I could tell this incident – the train, those five people seen on the other side of the glass – as it was, but that my description was built on my position and my interpretations. I have called them "Indians" and a family; I have said they were watching the train. My understanding has already subsumed theirs. Everything may have been quite different for them. My description is privileged to stand as what actually happened because theirs is not heard in the contexts in which I may speak. If we begin from the world as we actually experience it, it is at least possible to see that we are indeed located and that what we know of the other is conditional upon that location. There are and must be different experiences of the world and different bases of experience. We must not do away with them by taking advantage of our privileged speaking to construct a sociological version that we then impose upon them as their reality. We may not rewrite the other's world or impose upon it a conceptual framework that extracts from it what fits with ours. Their reality, their varieties of experience, must be an unconditional datum. It is the place from which inquiry begins. (1990a: 24–25)

KNOWING FROM WITHIN LOCAL EXPERIENCES

The exclusion of the varieties of social experience produces distorted knowledge, and hence knowledge that, despite its promise, veils rather than illuminates social processes. There is, for example, a disjuncture between women's *experiences* and the objectified knowledge produced by sociology notwithstanding its claim to produce knowledge about the world women (and men) live in (Smith 1990a: 27). Smith argues that "The only way of knowing a socially constructed world is knowing it from within. We can never stand outside it" (1990a: 22). Knowing from within means that "sociological inquiry is necessarily a social relation" (1990a: 23).

Thus, contrary to the positivist tradition of objectivity, sociologists inhabit particular social worlds and the people we study also inhabit particular social worlds; we cannot take for granted that (as sociologists) we know and understand what is going on in those social worlds. We can only begin to understand social life when we begin to see how our social location affects how we see and interpret the experiences of those whose experiences are separate from ours, and when we see those people's experiences from within their subjectively embodied location. In short, the standpoint of the researcher and the standpoint of the individuals and groups we seek to know exist in relation to one another. Knowledge emerges from within this relation and cannot be independent of it. Awareness of this relation necessarily tempers the (positivist) view that sociology objectively studies an objectively observable, objective social reality.

Second, because social worlds must be understood from within a particular standpoint – from within the particular, localized contexts in which differently situated people experience everyday life (e.g., men's structural location and their experiences within that location are different to women's structural location and their experiences) – this means, Smith argues, that we cannot be content to talk about social reality as if there is just one common reality similarly experienced by all. The existence of different standpoints means we cannot accept as universally true the objectified (male-centered) reality given authority by ruling texts (e.g., sociological studies, newspaper reports, census classifications, medical records, etc.).

WOMEN'S REALITIES

Smith argues that women's phenomenological reality (cf. chapter 9), their everyday "here-and-now" relevances, also matter. These are legitimate and discoverable realities. She states: "The opening up of women's experience gives sociologists access to social realities previously unavailable, indeed repressed" (1990a: 12).

Women's reality is the domestic world – the worlds of household, children, and neighborhood. This domestic world is not just different from men's reality, the public world, but, as Smith argues, it must defer to men's reality; the male world stands in authority over the domestic world.

> The worlds of men have had, and still have, an authority over the worlds that are traditionally women's and still are predominantly women's – the worlds of household, children, and neighborhood. And though women do not inhabit only these worlds, for the vast majority of women they are the primary ground of our lives, shaping the course of our lives and our participation in other relations. Furthermore, objectified knowledges are part of the world from which our kind of society is governed. The domestic world stands in a dependent relation to that other, and its whole character is subordinate to it. (1990a: 13)

Women experience a reality that is not only different to men's but which they necessarily experience (and have interpreted) through the prism of the images, language, expectations, and laws determined by men, and by the overarching (male-constructed) ruling discourse of femininity that structures women's everyday subordination and objectification by men (see pp. 317–319).

Men know that paid work is valued, and women too learn to know that men's work/reality is more valuable than their home-based experiences. When women say "I'm just a housewife," they are not simply being humble about how they spend their time; they are speaking for society – they are speaking the father-tongue that tells men and women that housework and mothering are inferior realities – underscored, for example, by the absence of paid maternity leave in the

🗎 NEWS 10.2   US. And yet, at the same time, women know from their embodied experiences in the domestic world that it is different from that which men define it to be. Hence the disjuncture between what women know and what men tell them they should (objectively) know to be the objectified reality. Following a Marxist theoretical strand (cf. chapter 1), Smith argues that women are objectively alienated from their own everyday experiences by the systematic way in which the subordinated domestic world and their experiences within that world, are written off as irrelevant by the male ruling structure (in politics, industry, academia, medicine, mass media, etc.) (cf. Smith 1990a: 19). In our (patriarchal) society, the "real" world, the dominant and dominating reality, is the public world; that is where the action is, and women's standpoint is excluded.

And even when, as is increasingly the case, women participate in the public world of academia, law, medicine, corporate management, and politics (see Timeline 10.1), their experiences of that world are necessarily different from men's. The gender divide initially structured into the separation of the public and the domestic worlds continues to matter such that women's participation in the public world is not structured on their terms but by the terms and conditions laid down by men. We should not be surprised, then, that although women show higher levels of college achievement than men, once employed, they are paid

🗎 NEWS 10.3   less than male graduates. Women must play by the rules and the ruling texts, including pay scales and promotion criteria, created by men. And to be successful within this public world, women must suspend their knowledge of their experiences in the domestic world (Smith 1990a: 21). Even though the attitudes of women and men toward family life are increasingly converging, the pressures on women who move within and between family and work spheres remain unabated: At work, women have to behave as if they have no children, i.e., they have to be flexibly available for whatever Wal-Mart shift they are assigned on a given day, or show the extensive time commitment required on Wall Street; and at home they have to suppress the body aches and injuries that accompany them from work, e.g., as hotel maids, poultry deboners, etc.

FEMINIST THEORIES

📖 NEWS 10.4

📖 NEWS 1.12

📖 NEWS I.1

📖 NEWS 1.13

NEGOTIATING TWO WORLDS SIMULTANEOUSLY

Women who move between these two worlds, the public and the domestic, come to know from direct experience what Smith calls a bifurcation of consciousness (1990a: 17). The notion of bifurcation captures the conflicted realities that all women experience because of the split between objectified knowledge and women's everyday, localized experiences. But consciousness of this bifurcation becomes especially accessible to women who move between the domestic and the public worlds; their everyday experiences as workers (e.g., waitresses, professors, politicians, etc.) and as mothers, for example, expose them directly to the contradictions within and between the two worlds. Traditional gender roles – with men in the public world of work and politics, and women in the domestic world of home and family – Smith (1990a: 19) notes, "deny the existence of the contradiction; suppression makes it invisible."

Smith's view of gender, and the feminist view as a whole, contrasts sharply with Talcott Parsons's emphasis on the functional complementarity of male and female roles (cf. chapter 4). Parsons did not see role differentiation in terms of the invisibility or exclusion of women's experiences, or in terms of women's lack of power vis-à-vis men and the "real" world, but as a structural arrangement whereby different male and female roles were necessary to maintain order (avoid status competition) within and across the various institutional spheres in society.

The structure of work (and the public world in general) is such that it depends on the smooth functioning of the domestic world, the world wherein women do the work to maintain men's participation in the public world; it's hard to envision the president/governor without also thinking of the first lady who sits/stands by his side, who props him up, especially in times of scandal. But when women enter the public world, they still maintain a large responsibility for the domestic world (their "second shift"; e.g., Hochschild with Machung 1990), and hence must negotiate the contradictory demands of the two worlds simultaneously. Moreover, whether in the domestic world, or in the public world, or as they move in and between both worlds, women's relations to men are structured by the ruling discourse of femininity (see pp. 317–319), a discourse which exacerbates women's disempowerment rather than helping them deal with questions emerging from the everyday/everynight contradictions they necessarily experience. Smith emphasizes that these are not abstract but highly practical "here-and-now" questions that women confront in their everyday world. Smith, a woman, a mother, and a sociologist, outlines these conflicting practical demands and their implications:

> How are we to manage career and children (including of course negotiating sharing that work with a man)? How is domestic work to get done? How is career time to be coordinated with family caring time? How is the remorseless structure of the children's school schedule to be coordinated with the equally exigent scheduling of professional and managerial work? Rarely are these problems solved by the full sharing of responsibilities between women and men. But for the most part these claims, these calls, these somehow unavoidable demands, are still ongoingly present and pressing for women, particularly, of course, for those with children. Thus the relation between ourselves as practicing sociologists and ourselves as working women is always there for us as a practical matter, an ordinary, unremarked, yet pervasive aspect of our experience of the world. The bifurcation of consciousness becomes for us a daily chasm to be crossed, on the one side of which is this special conceptual activity of thought, research, teaching, and administration, and on the other the world of localized activities oriented toward particular others, keeping things clean, managing somehow the house and household and the children – a world in which the particularities of persons in their full organic immediacy (feeding, cleaning up the vomit, changing the diapers) are inescapable ... We have learned, as women in sociology, that the discipline has not been one that we could enter and occupy on the same terms as men. We do not fully appropriate its authority, that is, the right to author and to authorize the acts of knowing and thinking that are the knowing and thinking of the discipline. Feminist theory in sociology is still *feminist* theory and not just plain sociological theory ... The frames of reference that ordered the terms upon which inquiry and discussion are conducted have originated with men. (1990a: 20–21)

A FEMINIST SOCIOLOGY: THE STANDPOINT OF WOMEN

Smith wants validation given to the everyday/everynight realities of women's experiences. She thus proposes an alternative way of doing sociology and of governing society, that would take seriously women's particularized location(s). Smith advocates a sociology that would *begin* from women's standpoint and which would attempt to deal seriously with that standpoint (1990a: 12). She explains:

> Women's standpoint ... discredits sociology's claim to constitute an objective knowledge independent of the sociologist's situation ... I am not proposing an immediate and radical transformation of the subject matter and methods of the discipline nor the junking of everything that has gone before. What I am suggesting is more in the nature of a reorganization of the relationship of sociologists to the object of our knowledge and of our problematic. This reorganization involves first placing sociologists where we are actually situated, namely, at the beginning of those acts by which we know or will come to know, and second, making our direct embodied experience of the everyday world the primary ground of our knowledge. (1990a: 21–22)

In sum, "an alternative sociology, from the standpoint of women, makes the
everyday world [the real, actual world outside the text] its problematic [domain of
inquiry]" (ibid.: 27). Smith thus challenges sociology to address Marxist-inspired
questions about the relations of domination, questions whose answers will emancipate both women and men (Smith 2005: 1). These questions would necessarily
focus on women and their subordinate relation to the ruling male world, and inquire
into women's direct experience of the everyday/everynight world, and how those
experiences are organized and determined by forces beyond women's direct experience (ibid.: 27; see also Smith 1987: 47). We recall Marx's presumption (chapter 1)
that the standpoint of the proletariat, i.e., wage-workers' everyday experiences of
their objectification and dehumanization within the capitalist structure, their use-
value as producers of profit for the capitalists, gave them a clearer perception of and
ability to recognize the alienation that inheres in capitalism (as opposed to the bourgeoisie, who, despite their objectification, tend to equate their interests – accumulating money/profit – with capitalism). Following a similar line of argument, Smith
sees women's standpoint, women's experience, as the one from within which the
gender contradictions in society can be apprehended and transformed.[1]

She elaborates:

> the standpoint of women situates the inquirer in the site of her bodily existence and in the
> local actualities of her working world. It is a standpoint that positions inquiry but has no
> specific content [no predefined concepts]. Those who undertake inquiry from this stand-
> point begin always from women's experience as it is for women [and not as it is predefined
> by men]. We [women] are the authoritative speakers of our experience ... From this stand-
> point, we know the everyday world through the particularities of our local practices and
> activities, in the actual places of our work and the actual time it takes. In making the
> everyday world problematic we also problematize the everyday localized practices of the
> objectified forms of knowledge organizing our everyday worlds. (Smith 1990a: 28)

DOING ALTERNATIVE SOCIOLOGY

Doing sociology (and politics, business, etc.) from the standpoint of women would
entail taking seriously women's experiences and using the knowledge that comes
directly from those experiences to re-order social life and social institutions. The
knowledge produced from an alternative sociology that makes the everyday world
its domain of inquiry would produce knowledge that would be empowering for
all individuals – women and men; it would be political knowledge, i.e., knowledge that would stimulate "consciousness raising" about inequality (2005: 1).

Smith elaborates:

> an alternative sociology cannot be confined to a particular category of people. If it is a
> sociology that explores the social from women's standpoint and aims to be able to spell out
> for women just how the everyday world of our experience is put together by [institutional]
> relations that extend vastly beyond the everyday, then it has to work for both women and
> men. It has to be a sociology for people, as contrasted with the sociology in which I was

so properly educated, the sociology in which people were the objects, they whose behavior was to be explained ... Though it starts from where we are in our everyday lives, it explores social relations and organization in which our everyday doings participate but which are not fully visible to us ... [thus] expanding people's own knowledge. (2005: 1)

Such knowledge, in short, would not be androcentric (Gilman 1911: 6), but human-centered, producing a transformation which would rupture the unequal gender structures and relations on which a sociology and a society that privileges the male standpoint rely.

Many ethnographic studies in sociology reveal aspects of the mosaic of social inequality and illuminate the many ways in which inequality impacts individuals' everyday lived experiences (e.g., MacLeod 1995). This research, however, does not fully approximate the kind of alternative sociology envisaged by Smith (2005: 35–38). She argues that an alternative sociology "has no prior interpretive commitment" (2005: 36) – its process of discovery is not driven by theoretical concepts or by political agendas; and nor does it focus on places (research sites) or on people. Its sole focus, rather, is the standpoint that emerges from talking to one or more individuals, and using the experiences of those people as the starting point for investigating how their experiences (positively or negatively) intermesh with the institutional processes that determine their lives (2005: 36). Smith (2005) calls this approach institutional ethnography. She does not mean us to conduct ethnographies of specific institutional sites or settings, but to discover women's experiences and from those experiences explore and discover how institutions work (and might work better).

For example, Smith (2005: 205–222) approvingly cites the research of Pence (cf. Pence and Paymar 1993), who used battered women's experiences of abuse, and of the judicial system's prosecution of their abusive husbands, as a way to explore how the safety of women, from women's standpoint, may be very different to that institutionalized in the judicial system. Pence's research data follow from the abused women's first moment of contact with the 911 operator, to subsequent contact with the police and court officers, and include the various texts this process creates (police officers' reports of their original visits to the abused victim). Using these data, Pence subsequently helped to change police procedures in Minnesota and elsewhere; e.g., the adoption of a protocol indicating the degree of violence experienced by the victim, thus producing greater institutional alertness to the range and types of violence that impede women's safety (see Smith 2005: 205–222). This, for Smith, is a sociology *for* people.

DOROTHY SMITH'S INTEGRATED VISION OF SOCIETAL EQUALITY

In summary, Smith outlines the mechanisms that produce women's subjugation and the varied consequences of that subjugation not just for women, but for society as a whole. Drawing on phenomenology, Smith argues that we need to be attentive to the particular everyday/everynight experiences of women (and of other excluded groups) and to recognize how those localized voices and experiences are different from what sociologists and other ruling groups in society take to be the objective, relevant reality. At the same time, building on Marx's analysis of structural inequality, Smith underscores how the power structure in society – the institutional arrangements that determine the organization of work, politics, family life, education, mass media, etc. – relies on institutional texts (e.g., discourses of femininity) and practices (family/work divide) that are structured so as to maintain women's inequality vis-à-vis men. For Smith, a feminist standpoint is emancipatory; beginning with women's experiences, it would produce transformative knowledge and social equality.

STANDPOINT THEORIES 2: PATRICIA HILL COLLINS – BLACK WOMEN'S STANDPOINT

Dorothy Smith recognized that the eclipsing of women's voices from the ruling institutional texts was even more marginalizing of the experiences of non-white women (Smith 1987: 43, n. 45). **Patricia Hill Collins**, another major feminist and standpoint theorist, dissects how the absence of black women's voices from the structures of power has both defined black women and exacerbated their oppression.[2] Collins outlines the core themes constitutive of a black women's standpoint. She argues that:

All African-American women share the common experience of being Black women in a society that denigrates women of African descent. This commonality of experience suggests that certain characteristic themes will be prominent in a Black women's standpoint ... one core theme is a legacy of struggle. Katie Cannon observes, "throughout the history of the United States, the interrelationship of white supremacy and male superiority has characterized the Black woman's reality as a situation of struggle – struggle to survive in two contradictory worlds simultaneously, one white, privileged, and oppressive, the other black, exploited, and oppressed" (1985, 30). Black women's vulnerability to assaults in

BIOGRAPHICAL NOTE

Patricia Hill Collins was born to working-class parents in Philadelphia in 1948. After receiving her undergraduate education at Brandeis University and an MA in teaching from Harvard University, she worked in Boston community schools for many years. She was director of the Tufts University African-American Center before returning to Brandeis for her PhD in sociology. Collins subsequently received a faculty appointment at the University of Cincinnati, and upon her retirement held its distinguished Taft professorship of sociology and was director of African-American Studies. In 2006, she became a distinguished university professor of sociology at the University of Maryland. A prolific author, Collins has received numerous career awards, including the Jessie Bernard Award from the American Sociological Association and the C. Wright Mills Award from the Society for the Study of Social Problems. In 2009, Collins served as president of the American Sociological Association. She is married to Roger Collins, a professor of education at the University of Cincinnati.

the workplace, on the street, and at home has stimulated Black women's independence and self-reliance. In spite of differences created by historical era, age, social class, sexual orientation or ethnicity, the legacy of struggle against racism and sexism is a common thread binding African-American women. (Collins 1990: 22)

Because Collins recognizes that different black women have different localized experiences (depending on age, social class, sexual orientation, etc.) and thus respond to the black legacy of struggle in varying ways, she argues that this diversity makes it "more accurate to discuss a Black women's standpoint than a Black woman's standpoint" (1990: 24). She thus avoids making the essentializing claim that all black women think and act alike, whilst simultaneously recognizing the commonality of black women's shared history.

BLACK WOMEN'S HISTORY: SLAVERY AND COMMUNITY

☐ WEB 10.1

Black women's shared history of struggle includes the formative experience of slavery. Enslavement, Collins argues, was critical to the development of a different understanding among black women of the relation between family and work. Unlike the split between the domestic and public worlds that defined (middle-class) white women's experiences, slavery prompted a different way of organizing everyday life for black women. During the early nineteenth-century expansion of capitalism, white middle-class urban families adopted nuclear households units, whereas the majority of African-American families, the enslaved property of white owners, "had great difficulty maintaining private households in public spheres controlled by white slave owners." They thus recreated

> African notions of family as extended kin units. ... The entire slave community/family stood in opposition to the public sphere of a capitalist political economy controlled by elite white men. For Black women the domestic sphere encompassed a broad range of kin and community relations beyond the nuclear family household. The line separating the Black community from whites served as a more accurate boundary delineating public and private spheres for African-Americans than that separating Black households from the surrounding Black community. (1990: 48–49)

Hence, the gender divide institutionalized in the split between the (white) domestic and public sphere did not become a defining part of the black experience. Instead, enslavement pitted blacks (property), regardless of gender, against whites (property owners). Black women combined mothering and work (as slaves for their owners rather than for their own families); as workers, they were powerless, but as mothers and as enslaved workers they had the support of an extended black family-community.

The end of slavery expanded the opportunities for black women and men in the workplace. Nevertheless, because of the limited educational, work, and political opportunities available to African-American men in particular, and the resulting negative effects on black men's earning power, black women, Collins argues, continued to combine work and family to help ensure a sufficient family household income (1990: 52–55). And, despite the many changes entailed in late nineteenth-century migration from the rural South to northern cities, black families continued to live in largely black (neighborhood-segregated) communities, thus making it possible for black women to continue to draw on extended community support in combining work and family commitments (1990: 58). It is important to note, however, that "At all moments in time between 1880 and 1925 – that is, from an adult generation born in slavery to an adult generation about to be devastated by the Great Depression of the 1930s ... the typical African-American family was lower class ... and headed by two parents" (Gutman 1976: 455–456).

Although the recent expansion of the black middle class (e.g., Wilson 1978: 144–152) has highlighted the increasing salience of class divisions among blacks, Collins argues that diversity of experience has always been part of black women's experience (1990: 23–24, 66). The challenge today, as Collins sees it, is for black feminist scholars "to rearticulate these new and emerging patterns of institutional oppression that differentially affect middle-class and working-class Black women." And she warns that "If this does not occur, each group may in fact become instrumental in fostering the other's oppression" (1990: 66).

CONTROLLING IMAGES OF BLACK WOMEN

Collins (1990: 67) underscores that "Race, class, and gender oppression could not continue without powerful ideological justifications for their existence." In parallel fashion to Dorothy Smith's (1990b: 171) emphasis on how the discourse of femininity (through advertising, sitcoms, cosmetics displays, etc.) maintains women's presentation of self as an object for (and inferior to) men, Collins draws attention to the controlling images of black women that are used by the white male status quo in an attempt to suppress black women's vocal resistance to their subjugation and inequality. She argues:

> Portraying African-American women as stereotypical mammies, matriarchs, welfare recipients, and hot mommas has been essential to the political economy of domination fostering Black women's oppression. As part of a generalized ideology of domination, these controlling images of Black womanhood take on special meaning because the authority to define these symbols is a major instrument of power. In order to exercise power, elite white men and their representatives must be in a position to manipulate appropriate symbols concerning Black women. (Collins 1990: 67–68)

Rather than being allowed to define themselves, a definition that would likely draw on the diversity of black women's experiences and their active struggles against domination, black women are stripped of these experiences and portrayed in ways that distort the rich complexity of their diversity. They become defined as "Other" (cf. Said 1978), a threatening strangeness that needs to be controlled, suppressed, excluded. This depiction of Otherness, in its various guises, provides ideological justification for black women's gender, racial, and class oppression (Collins 1990: 68).

CULTURAL OPPRESSION

How do these controlling images maintain black women's oppression? The black *mammy* is the faithful, obedient servant, who loves her white family more than her own and thus, according to Collins, "symbolizes the dominant group's perceptions of the ideal Black female relationship [of subordination] to elite white male power" (1990: 71). One consequence of this enduring stereotype is that today black women professionals and executives are also expected to be nurturant and subservient, even though the corporate workplace financially rewards the opposite traits, i.e., instrumental and autonomous behavior (ibid.: 71). The *matriarch* symbolizes the "bad" black mother; "as overly aggressive, unfeminine women, Black matriarchs allegedly emasculate their lovers and husbands" (ibid.: 74), causing them to desert the family and thus exacerbating the social problems associated with single-parent families/households. As women who work outside the home, matriarchs are seen as failing to "fulfill the traditional 'womanly' duties" (ibid); thus matriarchs – rather than structural inequality – are blamed for black children's poor school performance and their continuing economic impoverishment (ibid.: 73–75). But if black women did not work outside the home, their children would have access to even fewer economic resources (given the continued economic disadvantage experienced by black men) and this in turn would contribute to the spiral of black poverty and inequality.

The *mammy* and the *matriarch* are powerful images, but perhaps not as ideologically controlling of the tripartite, race-class-gender matrix as that of the *welfare mother*. The welfare mother captures the deeply embedded racial stereotypes of blacks both as lazy and as the source of their own poverty, relying on government handouts rather than their own work ethic to compensate for their uncontrolled fertility. The ideological intertwining of poverty and fertility directs attention away from the structural sources of poverty, while simultaneously reaffirming the traditional white view that black fertility should be controlled because it produces too many economically unproductive and costly children. Additionally, the welfare mother, typically portrayed as a single mother, "violates one cardinal tenet of Eurocentric masculinist thought: she is a woman alone. As a result, her treatment reinforces the dominant gender ideology positing that a woman's true worth and financial security should occur through heterosexual marriage" (Collins 1990: 77).

And the fourth image, the *hot momma*, the whore, the sexually aggressive Jezebel, Collins argues (1990: 77), provides "a powerful rationale for the widespread sexual assaults by white men" on black women. In short, Collins argues, white men can only tolerate the de-sexed black woman, the *mammy* (who can nanny their children), and must control the sexuality of the matriarch, the teenage mother, and the Jezebel (1990: 78).

Black women have a long history of actively resisting these controlling images and articulating alternative definitions of their reality. Because, however, black women's experiences have historically been excluded from the traditional sites of knowledge – government agencies, academia, mass media, etc. – black women have voiced their knowledge of their reality in different sites: in everyday conversations with family, friends, and neighbors; through literature, poetry, art, music, and independent documentary films; and in the call-and-response discourse of church meetings (cf. Collins 1990: 91–114). Black feminist thought is thus produced by black feminist sociologists such as Collins and, importantly, by all black women who vocalize their experiences of and responses to the cultural contradictions they encounter as black women, caught between two histories of oppression (Collins 1990: 14–15). And, as the popularity of Toni Morrison's novels and Maya Angelou's poetry attests, when black women have the opportunity to speak and to act, many blacks and whites, women and men, want to hear and are moved by what they say and do.

Black feminist thought, somewhat akin to white women's knowledge, is outside the paradigm of objective knowledge, i.e., that which Smith (1987: 1) and Collins (1991: 201–206) debunk as the allegedly universal knowledge created from the standpoint of (Eurocentric white) men. Collins further underscores, however, that "Black feminist thought, like all specialized thought, reflects the interests and standpoint of its creators" (1990: 201). Therefore, while all women share a standpoint by virtue of their historical oppression as women, black feminist thought comes from a different standpoint than that of white feminist thought. It is knowledge that has a distinct African historical consciousness; "Black societies reflect elements of a core African value system that existed prior to and independently of racial oppression ... Moreover, as a result of colonialism, imperialism, slavery, apartheid, and other systems of racial domination, Black people [whether living in North America, South America, the Caribbean, or Africa] share a common experience of oppression," though their specific histories differ (1990: 206). Therefore, "Because Black women have access to both the Afrocentric and the feminist standpoints, an alternative epistemology used to rearticulate a Black feminist standpoint should reflect elements of both traditions," and by highlighting the points of contact between the two, enrich understanding of how the experiences of subordinate groups "create knowledge that fosters resistance" (1990: 207).

SOCIAL INTERSECTIONALITY

While emphasizing the specific standpoints from which knowledge is created, Collins calls for appreciation of the concrete intersectionality of all experiences – how experiences are shaped, interpreted, and talked about on the basis of the interlocking and interacting gender, race, social class, and other factors situating individuals. Different intersectional contexts give rise to different experiences and to different contradictions, and moreover, to how these contradictions are and can be negotiated. In Appalachia, West Virginia, a region with a long history of poverty, women miners in the male-dominated coal mines experience harassment. But black women miners experience different forms of harassment than white women miners, a racial-and-gender harassment of which white women are unaware – they literally don't see skin color as a source of discrimination (Tallichet 2006).

As theorists of race relations have long argued, who is Other and what it means to be Other is always relational (Fanon 1967; Said 1978; cf. chapter 12), as indeed Goffman elaborates in his discussion of stigma; who is "normal" and who is stigmatized depends on the social relational context of the groups who do the defining. Similarly, Collins observes:

> Privilege becomes defined in relation to its other ... Race, class and gender represent the three systems of oppression that most heavily affect African-American women. But these systems and the economic, political and ideological conditions that support them may not be the most fundamental oppressions, and they certainly affect many more groups than Black women. Other people of color, Jews, the poor, white women, and gays and lesbians have all had similar ideological justifications offered for their subordination. (1990: 225)

Whatever the sources of oppression, Collins argues, it is their intersectionality that matters. In everyday life, one is not just a woman, or black or Latina, or working-class, or poor or an immigrant, but typically, some combination of these subordinated statuses, as McDermott (2006) highlights in her study of racially mixed poor neighborhoods. The determining impact of such intersectionality on everyday experiences and life outcomes is institutionalized in the US stratification system: white men and black men, respectively, have higher median incomes than white women; and Latina women are at the bottom of the income ladder (Andersen and Collins 1995: 66). Different structural locations, therefore, interact and crisscross to produce different lived experiences and different conditions for the transformation of inequality and oppression. Collins thus pushes us to move beyond dichotomous either/or analyses of Otherness (e.g., women *or* men, black *or* white, gay *or* straight). This approach also opens up our awareness of the conflicting ways in which identities and the social relations that they produce are structured and experienced. As Collins notes, while "white women are penalized by their gender, they are privileged by their race; thus depending on the context, an individual may be an oppressor, a member of an oppressed group, or simultaneously oppressor and oppressed" (1990: 225).

ACTIVIST KNOWLEDGE

The activist knowledge generated from within intersecting matrixes of resistance is emancipatory – empowering individuals to take action against their oppression. Thus, Collins argues, although African-American women are victims of oppression, they are also active resistors of oppression: giving voice to oppression is an act of resistance, and resistance matters even if its voices are ignored by those in power. The interplay between oppression and activism is core to black feminist thought, Collins argues, and as such it advances the politics of empowerment:

> [Black feminist] thought views the world as a dynamic place where the goal is not merely to survive or to fit in or to cope; rather it becomes a place where we feel ownership and accountability ... there is always choice, and the power to act, no matter how bleak the situation may appear to be. Viewing the world as one in the making raises the issue of individual responsibility for bringing about change. It also shows that while individual empowerment is key, only collective action can effectively generate lasting social transformation of political and economic institutions. (1990: 237)

As Collins would affirm, speaking out with others of similar experience is a crucial step not only of resistance but of forcing accountability. Black feminist thought, therefore – knowledge derived from the daily experiences and activism of oppressed black women – is a knowledge that can be used by other oppressed people, whatever the source(s) of their marginality, to collectively transform the conditions of their daily existence. (See Topic 10.1.)

BLACK BODIES AND SEXUALITY

In her recent writing, Collins moves beyond her earlier emphasis on the oppressive intersectionality of gender, race, and class to address the intersectionality of gender, race, and *sexuality* in shaping black oppression and the possibilities for its

---

Topic 10.1 Domestic workers organize to end an "atmosphere of violence on the job"

We get a glimpse of what Collins means by activist knowledge in the collective organizing efforts of domestic housekeepers in the US. The housekeepers, most of whom are immigrants from Mexico, Central and South America, the Caribbean, the Philippines, and India, came to New York in June 2008 for a weekend of story-sharing and strategizing at the first National Domestic Workers Congress. At the Congress, they told of their own experiences and, as representatives of domestic workers' groups in about ten US cities, also recounted the experiences of others like them. The workers in attendance recounted various stories of physical abuse by their employers – one was slammed into a wall, another was struck as she hand-polished the floor. They also talked of the long days they worked, of being paid far less than the minimum wage, about their lack of health benefits, and their generally poor working conditions. Using their experiences of exploitation, they came together to build alliances with other domestic workers with a view toward achieving better rights and working conditions for all domestic workers. The political importance of giving visibility to domestic workers' everyday/everynight experiences was captured by the remarks of one worker present, who commented: "Many women feel they are alone ... and don't dare to come out in the light and speak."

📰 NEWS 10.5

transformation. In *Black Sexual Politics*, published in 2004, Collins argues that "moving from an exclusive focus on Black women to a broader one that encompasses how the politics of gender and sexuality frame the experience of women and men alike creates new questions for investigation and, perhaps, a new antiracist politics that might follow" (2004: 8). She asks: "What good is the empowerment of African American women if it comes at the expense of Black men?" (ibid.: 9), as indicated, for example, by the disproportionately high rates of black men who are in prison, who lack a college education, who have AIDS, or who are embroiled in black-on-black violence as perpetrators and victims (ibid.: 7) (see also chapter 12, box 12.1).

NEWS 10.6

In Collins's view, the pursuit of anti-racist policies cannot be successful unless black women and men confront intertwined questions of gender and sexuality, and in particular the oppressive ideology depicting them as the "embodiment of deviant sexuality" (2004: 35). Collins elaborates:

> Black gender ideology … draws upon widespread cultural beliefs concerning the sexual practices of people of African descent. Sexuality is not simply a biological function; rather, it is a system of ideas and social practices that is deeply implicated in shaping American social inequalities. Because ideas about sexuality are so integral to understandings of Black gender ideology [of femininity and masculinity] as well as broader gender ideology in the United States, neither Black masculinity nor Black femininity can be adequately understood let alone transformed without attending to the **politics of sexuality**. (ibid.: 6)

Thus while Collins (1990) previously elaborated on the politics of black women's sexuality apparent in the controlling images used by white male elite culture to maintain black women's inequality, she here extends her attention to the need for blacks themselves to rethink and reclaim their sexuality. This involves what she calls "the sexual autonomy of honest bodies," in contrast to the "Black gender ideology that encourages Black people to view themselves and others as bitches, hoes, thugs, pimps, sidekicks, sissies, and modern mammies" (2004: 282). This ideology is promulgated in the song lyrics and videos of top-selling black (and white) rappers. Many male rappers, like Tupac and Dr Dre, for example, articulate a politics of resistance to the police and the government, and insightfully name the institutionalized urban ills that so seriously undermine the life-chances of blacks in the ghetto. Yet these same rappers tend to reproduce rather than debunk the denigrating, stereotypical images of black women as sexual objects, bitches, and whores, and of black men whose virtue is defined by a hypermasculine virility focused on incessant sexual conquest (e.g., Dr Dre's song "Ed-Ucation").

SEXUAL INTEGRITY

Reclaiming "honest bodies," i.e., a sexual identity and sexual feelings and experiences that are real for the people involved rather than a distortion of sexuality by those who oppress black women (and black gays), presents a number of challenges. One of the challenges identified by Collins is that of integrating or rejoining "mind, soul, and body" (2004: 286), i.e., recognizing that bodies are not simply objects but embody the feelings, desires, and expressivity of individuals. In this view, sex is not a commodity to be distorted, packaged, and sold in songs, videos, movies, and advertising, but a desire and practice at the heart of relationships that are (or ought to be) based on mutual intimacy and love. A related "honest bodies" challenge is the "ability to select one's own sexual orientation" (Collins 2004: 286). This challenge is compounded by the heterosexism in society and its accentuation in black communities, a homophobia which in turn produces a silence about risky heterosexual and gay sexual behavior and the denial, for example, that HIV/AIDS affects African-Americans (2004: 288–295). (I further discuss heterosexism and gay sexuality in chapter 11.)

The reclaiming of sexual autonomy/honest bodies also challenges the association of the erotic with sexual violence and the extent to which intimate and family relationships involve violence (Collins 2004: 288). Approximately 29 percent of African-American women experience intimate-partner violence – rape, physical assault, or stalking – in their lifetime, and intimate-partner homicide is the leading cause of death among African-American women ages 15 to 45. Collins suggests that the entwining of sex and violence may also be used, in part, to think about forms of violence beyond intimate relationships, namely black male-on-male street violence; she wonders whether some of this violence may mask the repression of homoerotic feelings in the homophobic black community (ibid.), as indeed Kimmel would suspect (2005: 25–42).

Overall, Collins concludes, "African Americans certainly need to 'ready up for some honesty' in intimate love relationships" (2004: 292). The perpetuation of sexual oppression does violence not only to racial equality but also to the gender and sexual differences among blacks, undermining the building of solidarity within the black community between men and women, gay and straight. Collins warns: "As systems of oppression, racism, sexism, class exploitation, and heterosexism all gain power by denying sexual autonomy and annexing the power of the erotic for their own ends. In this context, reclaiming love and sexuality constitutes a necessary first step" (2004: 292–293). She also emphasizes, however, that "at the same time, love and sexuality are insufficient for confronting the economic exploitation, political powerlessness, and sexual violence of the new racism" (ibid.: 293), i.e., the persistence, but changing contours, of racial inequality in our globalizing world dominated by media conglomerates that propound ideologies that seek to deny racism and undercut mass awareness of its ongoing insidiousness (ibid.: 54; see also Gilroy 2000: 32). (I discuss racism in chapter 12, and globalization in chapter 15.)

SOCIOLOGY OF EMOTION

Through much of its history, sociological theory was relatively inattentive to emotion, though theorists did not completely ignore it. Georg Simmel (1921/1971) wrote about love, and more generally, highlighted the centrality of emotion in social-collective behavior (e.g., mass feelings and mass appeal; 1917/1950: 34–36).

NEWS 10.6

NEWS 10.7

Max Weber too recognized emotion as a significant motivator of social action, and saw Calvinists' fears about the after-life, for example, as a crucial component in the rationalization process accelerating modern capitalism. Overall, however, Weber emphasized emotion's secondary status vis-à-vis rational action; after all, the cultural contribution of the Protestant ethic is its suppression and methodical control of emotion (cf. chapter 3). Emile Durkheim gave more detailed attention to emotion, seeing the collective effervescence that emerges during ritual celebrations as a potent social force (cf. chapter 2). Nevertheless, in his analysis of the modern division of labor, Durkheim's focus was not the emotional bonds but the moral and functional interdependence that builds (organic) solidarity among individuals. More surprisingly, perhaps, Mead's focus on the practical consequences of face-to-face interaction essentially ignored the significance of emotion, instead emphasizing the cognitive aspects of interpretive action (cf. chapter 8).

At mid-twentieth century, Parsons's pattern variables confined emotion to the family sphere (cf. chapter 4; see also Smelser 1968: 132–134), and if emotion presented itself in the public realm, it was largely a non-rational strain on social action (e.g., the mob contagion effect of "hostile outbursts" in collective behavior; Smelser 1962: 222–269). In sum, emotion was just not something that many mainstream sociologists prioritized in their theory and research even as sociology of the family, of crime, and of health and illness, for example, all flourished – domains in which emotion surely matters. One exception was Goffman, but he emphasized the ritualization, rather than the *feeling*, of emotion in the signaling and performance of gender and other subordinated social statuses (cf. chapter 8). And emotion continues to be marginalized by influential contemporary theorists such as Habermas (cf. chapter 5).

ARLIE HOCHSCHILD: EMOTIONAL LABOR

It was **Arlie Hochschild** who turned the sociological spotlight on emotion. Her landmark book *The Managed Heart* (1983) succeeded in making sociologists recognize that feelings and emotions are of core relevance to societal processes. Today, the sociology of emotions is a well-established sub-field within the discipline (see, e.g., Stets and Turner 2006), and emotions are increasingly incorporated

BIOGRAPHICAL NOTE

Arlie Hochschild was born in 1940. She received her PhD in sociology from the University of California, Berkeley, and spent her entire faculty career there until her retirement in 2006. A prolific writer, Hochschild has focused much of her attention on themes of intimacy and the binds of home and work. Her major impact on the field, especially on feminist scholarship and qualitative research, has been widely recognized with several awards including, in 2000, the American Sociological Association's Award for furthering the public understanding of sociology. She is married to Adam Hochschild, a writer; they have two children.

within several other fields of sociological inquiry too (e.g., social movements; Polletta 2006). This transformation is largely due to the pioneering efforts of Hochschild and other feminist sociologists.[3]

While most of us tend to think of emotion as a natural reflection of how we are feeling at a given moment, Hochschild makes us think about emotions as work; she highlights the feeling rules that determine emotion. She emphasizes that emotion is not simply natural but is a socially structured, patterned way of feeling and of acting on feeling. We are socialized into learning how to recognize, and how and when to feel, certain emotions. We recognize a feeling rule, Hochschild explains,

> by inspecting how we assess our feelings, how other people assess our **emotional display**, and by sanctions issuing from ourselves and from them ... Sanctions common to the social scene – cajoling, chiding, teasing, scolding, shunning – often come into play as forms of ridicule or encouragement that lightly correct feeling and adjust it to convention ... What is taken for granted ... is that there are rules or norms according to which feelings may be judged appropriate [or inappropriate] to accompanying events. (1983: 57)

GENDERED DIVISION OF EMOTIONAL LABOR

Hochschild argues that while "both men and women do emotion work, in private life and at work" (1983: 162), "Our culture invites women, more than men, to focus on feeling rather than action" (1983: 57). There is a socially and culturally structured gendered specialization – a division of labor – in emotion work. Women are responsible more for smiling, being nice, celebrating others, empathizing with others, whereas men are expected to do the aggressive emotional tasks (1983: 163–165). And, by extension, when women engage in emotion work that is culturally unexpected of their gender – being angry – they are denigrated, and their credibility and femininity are called into question, even in professional-corporate contexts where one might think femininity would not impose on job-evaluation assessments. Further underscoring the gender contradictions in society, if women display stereotypically female emotions – e.g., crying – their professional credibility is questioned. Further, as Hochschild observes, women, because of their subordination to men in a patriarchal society, tend to have a "weaker 'status shield' against the displaced feelings of others" (1983: 163). Hence, they are more likely than men to be the object of emotional ridicule and attack.

NEWS 10.8

This gendering of emotion and its varied contradictory consequences was evident in the US, 2008 presidential election campaign process: It was apparently fine for John McCain to be an angry man, but not for Hillary Clinton to be either tearful (a sign of weakness in a leader unless at a funeral or memorial service) or angry (a weakness in a woman). The public's response to the emotion displays of these two candidates, the controversies surrounding any and all of Clinton's emotions, and the consensus among political pundits that Clinton is liked best when she smiles underscore the heavier emotion-work burden that women carry.

NEWS 10.9

Emotion work is, in a sense, easier for men: they simply have less emotion management to do; they can smile or be angry, and occasionally even cry; and they are more protected from the (negative) emotions of others.

Some feminist scholars, such as the psychologist Carol Gilligan (1982), argue that women *are* more emotional than men. In this (popular) view, women are seen as having a natural, gender-specific way of accessing emotions and hence are more emotional-relational than men. Men, by contrast, are seen as being more readily suited to tasks that are abstract, strategic, and rule-centered and to operating in contexts that marginalize emotion and relationships, an idea captured in the best-selling, light-hearted book *Women are from Venus, Men are from Mars*.

Hochschild and other sociologists fully acknowledge that emotion involves physiological and biological processes – emotions get displayed in physiological actions (crying, grimacing, shaking hands etc.); "thus when we manage an emotion, we are partly managing a bodily preparation for a consciously or unconsciously anticipated deed" (Hochschild 1983: 220). But sociologists also stress that the organization of emotion work is socially and culturally, not biologically, determined. Thus the gendering of emotion and of emotional tasks is not based on biology, but on society's evaluation of biological sex differences and their translation into social structures and cultural processes. It is not biology per se but socially structured gender differences in emotion specialization and social status that frame women as being less rational, over-emotional, and, therefore, difficult to vote for or promote, or simply hard to deal with, whether in romantic relationships or in the executive suite. As Hochschild observes: "Women's feelings are seen not as a response to real events but as reflections of themselves as 'emotional' women" (1983: 173).

Gendered feeling rules and habits also vary by, and interact with, social class. Hochschild elaborates:

> Especially in the American middle class, women tend to manage feeling more because in general they depend on men for money, and one of the various ways of repaying their debt is to do extra emotion work – especially emotion work that affirms, enhances, and celebrates the well-being and status of others ... The emotion work of enhancing the status and well-being of others is ... an unseen effort, which like housework, does not quite count as labor but is nevertheless crucial to getting other things done. As with doing housework well, the trick is to erase any evidence of effort, to offer only the clean house and the welcoming smile. (1983: 165, 167)

PAID EMOTIONAL LABOR

As wives and mothers, women do an inordinate amount of emotion work. And, they are also more likely than men to do emotion work for pay, to engage in emotional labor. "As traditionally more accomplished managers of feeling in private life," Hochschild notes, "women more than men have put emotional labor on the market, and they know more about its personal costs" (1983: 11). This is a core concern for Hochschild. She gives particular attention to the production and control of human emotion not just *as* work, but *at* work, and to what she refers to as the commercialization of feeling (her book's subtitle). Thus emotion work is not just the emotion management done in the home, typically for people with whom one has deep and continuous reciprocal relationships (children, spouse, parents, etc.), and where it is useful for maintaining relationships and gaining affirmation, respect, or gifts (i.e., has use-value). Emotion work also includes the work done by those whose labor-force participation – paid employment – is contingent on their continuous production of specific emotions as required by the marketplace. Hochschild explains:

> I use the term *emotional labor* to mean the **management of feeling** to create a publicly observable facial and bodily display; emotional labor is sold for a wage and therefore has *exchange value*. ›I use the synonymous terms *emotion work* or *emotion management* to refer to these same acts done in a private context where they have *use value*. (1983: 7)

THE MANAGEMENT OF FEELINGS

Hochschild's definition of emotional labor is influenced by Marx, C. Wright Mills, and Goffman. From Marx's discussion of the commodification of labor (cf. chapter 1), Hochschild construes emotions as commodities; they can (and must) be exchanged for money, i.e., bought and sold on the market. Like the manual and physical labor power that wage-workers in a factory sell to their employer, many professional and service workers sell their emotional labor power to the capitalist. And, once bought for a wage – its commercial or exchange-value in the occupational marketplace – the worker's emotional labor is used by the capitalist to produce profit for the capitalist (as a result of the difference between the worker's exchange-value and the surplus value it creates for the capitalist, i.e., the difference between the value of the emotion to the worker and its value to the capitalist; cf. chapter 1).

Once we sell our smile we no longer own it, and hence we must produce useful (i.e., profit-oriented) smiles on cue as deemed fit by our employer; this is what flight attendants typically do. Jobs that call for emotional labor "require face-to-face or voice-to-voice contact with the public; … require the worker to produce an emotional state in another person – gratitude or fear for example; [and] they allow the employer, through training and supervision, to exercise a degree of control over the emotional activities of employees" (Hochschild 1983: 147).

In today's post-industrial, information economy (where we are as likely to buy and sell information and personal services as factory-manufactured material goods), a broad array of professional, clerical, and service workers engage in emotional labor; a core component of their everyday job is the controlled presentation of feelings. This is especially true of the many service workers whose primary duties revolve around the greeting and personal care of (paying) customers – a point observed by C. Wright Mills (1951) in his discussion of the "personality market" and the commercial masking of feelings (cf. chapter 6). Receptionists,

WEB 10.2

339

retail workers, waitresses, air stewards, and child-care workers are among the emotional laborers who readily come to mind. Their labor power resides primarily in their smile and their repertoire of "niceness." They sell the ability to manage their emotions, irrespective of the feelings they are personally feeling at any given moment.

GOING BEYOND SYMBOLIC INTERACTIONISM

Hochschild's emphasis on emotion management is also very close to Goffman's theorizing (cf. chapter 8). Indeed, some textbooks include Hochschild's work as part of symbolic interactionism (*SI*). This categorization makes sense on one level – the fact that everyone who engages in face-to-face interaction must maintain a front in order to project a particular definition of the situation. But Hochschild's contribution, though influenced by Goffman, extends beyond *SI* in two major ways. First, as Hochschild points out, Goffman's analysis of social actors does not pay any attention to the actor's inner feelings and to how social actors actively name and manage inner feelings. She argues: "In Goffman's theory, the capacity to act on feeling derives only from the occasions [settings/situations], not from the individual. The self may actively choose to display feelings in order to give outward impressions to others. But it is passive to the point of invisibility when it comes to the private act of managing emotion" (1983: 218). In other words, Goffman takes it for granted that social actors manage the display of emotion in their self-presentation; he is not interested in the feelings beneath or behind the role performance, but in role performance irrespective of the actors' feelings.

Second, Goffman's analysis does not probe why emotion work is required in a capitalist (or socialist) society, nor how it is produced and regulated. Instead, Goffman is primarily interested in the social rules and implications (e.g., embarrassment) of face-to-face interaction, and not in how self-presentation rituals may vary depending on their structural context or their commercial value. By contrast, Hochschild argues that the habits individuals have or acquire in managing emotion vary by gender, social class, age, religion, and other socio-cultural locations (1983: 214–218; see also Hochschild 2003: 7, 91). Further, Hochschild probes beneath the inner feelings of the social actor and beyond the actor to the cultural and organizational rules determining emotion management and emotional labor.

Emotion work as self-alienation

In line with Marx's analysis of the alienation of labor (cf. chapter 1), and C. Wright Mills's (1951: 182–184) discussion of the standardized "personality market" that characterizes the service economy (cf. chapter 6), Hochschild argues that emotional labor constitutes self-estrangement or self-alienation. Drawing on observation research she conducted at Delta Airlines' training sessions, and interviews she conducted with Delta flight attendants, training supervisors, and company executives, Hochschild uses the flight attendant as the quintessential exemplar of emotional labor. She explains: the labor done in a factory calls for

a coordination of mind and arm, mind and finger, and mind and shoulder. We refer to it simply as physical labor. The flight attendant does physical labor when she pushes heavy metal carts through the aisles, and she does mental work when she prepares for and actually organizes emergency landings and evacuations. But in the course of doing this physical and mental labor, she is also doing something more ... emotional labor. This labor requires one to induce or suppress feeling in order to sustain the outward countenance that produces the proper state of mind in others – in this case, the sense of being cared for in a convivial and safe place. This kind of labor calls for a coordination of mind and feeling, and it sometimes draws on a source of self that we honor as deep and integral to our individuality. Beneath the difference between physical and emotional labor there lies a similarity in the possible cost of doing the work: the worker can become estranged or alienated from an aspect of self – either the body or the margins of the soul – that is *used* to do the work ... The company lays claim not simply to her physical motions – how she handles food trays – but to her emotional actions and the way they show in the ease of a smile. The workers I talked to often spoke of their smiles as being *on* them but not *of* them. They were seen as an extension of the make-up, the uniform, the recorded music, the soothing pastel colors of the airplane décor ... The final commodity is not a certain number of smiles to be counted ... For the flight attendant, the smiles are a *part of her work*, a part that requires her to coordinate self and feeling so that the work seems effortless. To show that the enjoyment takes effort is to do the job poorly. Similarly, part of the job is to disguise fatigue and irritation, for otherwise the labor would show in an unseemly way, and the product – passenger contentment – would be damaged. (1983: 6–8)

Emotional labor: External control of inner states

Manual workers engaged in physical labor can feel whatever (socially learned) emotions they feel like feeling and they can act on those feelings by smiling or frowning. From a capitalist viewpoint, it doesn't matter whether the chicken deboner is smiling or grimacing; she is not paid to feel, but to debone 42 chickens a minute (see Topic 1.4). Emotional labor is different, Hochschild argues, in that the emotional laborer's feelings must be given over to the work; they no longer belong to the person but to the employer who has purchased them for use in the creation of profit. Specific emotions must be produced by the worker as part of his or her labor, and they must be produced authentically and seem genuine so that they induce the correct emotional state in the customer. As Hochschild notes, "The airline passenger may choose not to smile, but the flight attendant is obliged not only to smile but to try to work up some warmth behind it" (1983: 19).

NEWS 1.13

Not all emotional labor is about smiling. The air hostess's smiling empathy must produce a sense of emotional security and feelings of welcome in the airline passenger, but the bill collector's gruffness and hostility must produce feelings of fear and shame in the bill defaulter. Irrespective, however, of the specific emotion that the emotional laborer must produce, emotional laborers no longer "own" their own emotions; they are owned by others (the employer) and regulated by others (the customers; e.g., the airline passenger who despite being obnoxious for the duration of a five-hour flight still expects the hostess to smile warmly at him as she reminds him for the third time to buckle his seat belt in preparation for landing).

Emotional laborers are thus trained to produce required emotions whose production is perceived as being sincere, not put on. Organizations and corporations train their workers to take an instrumental stance toward feeling, to see their feelings as a resource and thus to suppress the wrong feelings or induce the correct feelings, irrespective of how the worker is actually feeling. Hochschild explains:

> [Acting] in a commercial setting, unlike acting in a dramatic, private or therapeutic context, makes one's face and one's feelings take on the properties of a resource. But it is not a resource to be used for the purposes of art, as in drama, or for the purposes of self-discovery, as in therapy, or for the pursuit of fulfillment, as in everyday life. It is a resource to be used to make money. (1983: 55)

Unlike an actor in the theater, who knows, and whose audience knows, that she or he is acting, and temporarily feeling whatever emotions the acting part requires, the emotional laborer is supposed to *feel* the required emotions and make sure her customers feel that these emotions are real and sincere. The line between "surface acting" (in the theater) and the "deep acting" (inducing a specific felt emotion) required by the commercialization of feeling becomes blurred. Consequently, Hochschild argues, it is very difficult for the emotional laborer to know what is authentic to her own inner feeling state and what is phony. This splitting between felt and produced emotion, Hochschild argues, weakens the worker's ability to relate on a deep emotional level to others and can thus adversely affect her intimate relationships. A social theory of emotion, Hochschild contends, "must take into account that these emotional dues can be costly to the self. Institutional rules run deep but so does the self that struggles with and against them. To manage feeling is to actively try to change a preexisting emotional state" (1983: 219).

Most of us engage in deep acting occasionally as we try to really enter into feeling a particular emotion (of pride, sadness, gratitude, disappointment). But it is still we who are controlling the emotion and its expression. With the commercialization of feeling, however, Hochschild argues, it is corporate organizations that dictate to us how to feel; "some institutions have become very sophisticated in the techniques of deep acting; they suggest how to imagine and thus how to feel" (1983: 49).

Emotion training

As Hochschild saw at Delta Airlines, trainees undergo an arduous training program. Delta (and other airlines) screen trainees for a "certain type of outgoing middle-class sociability" – for those who are able "to project a warm personality" (1983: 97). The particular type of sociability required varies from company to company, with some airlines screening for more graciously reserved hostesses and others wanting them to be more sexy and brassy – depending on the corporate image of the airline itself (ibid.). Once screened, recruits are then systematically trained in how to "act as if the airline cabin (where she works) were her home (where she doesn't work)," and thus to act with the deep, inner-felt desire to treat passengers as family or friends (Hochschild 1983: 105). "Recruiters understood that they were looking for a 'certain Delta personality' ... The general prerequisites were a capacity to work with a team ... interest in people, sensitivity, and emotional stamina," though the trainees believed that they were chosen "because they were adventurous and ambitious" (1983: 98). And Hochschild saw more:

> The trainees, it seemed to me, were also chosen for their ability to take stage directions about how to "project" an image. They were selected for being able to act well – that is, without showing the effort involved. They had to be able to appear at home on stage ... they were constantly reminded that their own job security and the company's profit rode on a smiling face ... There were many direct appeals to smile: "Really work on your smiles." "Your smile is your biggest asset – use it."

And "Relax and smile," the trainees were instructed, in responding to troublesome passengers (ibid.: 105).

In short, stewardesses are trained to manage and modify their felt feelings. And like others in the service sector (e.g., waitresses, retail sales assistants), they must do this emotional labor while being relatively unshielded from customers who angrily abuse them (1983: 163) for failings over which typically they have no control (e.g., canceled flights, over-cooked steak, a store's returns policy). In one recent study, for example, almost three-quarters of retail workers reported that they have experienced verbal abuse from customers, mainly rudeness, curtness, and being the target of shoppers' anger.

NEWS 10.10

HOCHSCHILD'S CONTRIBUTIONS TO FEMINIST AND LABOR THEORIES

By focusing on emotional labor, Hochschild makes a two-fold feminist contribution. First, she redresses the male bias in sociology that downplays the social significance of emotion. Hochschild demonstrates that emotions matter, and they matter not only in the domestic sphere but in the workplace – they are an essential, and rationally instrumental, part of the commodities produced and sold in our (ever-expanding) service economy.[4] Second, as Hochschild (1983: 11) notes, women comprise a disproportionate number of workers employed in service occupations requiring a substantial amount of emotional labor. Currently, two-thirds of all occupational positions require a substantial amount of emotional labor; and while 44 percent of male workers are employed in such occupations, this is true of 89 percent of women workers. Focusing on emotional labor, therefore, directly accesses the everyday experiences of women, whether at home or in the workplace.

WEB 10.3

Further, Hochschild's attentiveness to the personal and social costs of emotional labor makes a substantial contribution not only to sociologists' understanding of the social and gendered contexts of emotion, but to broadening our understanding of occupations and labor-market processes. Hochschild makes a strong case that emotional labor is more costly to the self and social relationships than is manual-physical labor (because of the deep acting required). It is also important to keep in mind, however, that many manual laborers, especially the low-wage migrant and immigrant women workers (e.g., hotel maids and house-keepers) who comprise a larger part of the global service economy (e.g., Sassen 2007), also pay a steep emotional price. Many of them, for example, leave their children behind in their home countries and renounce the everyday routines of family life in order for their families to subsist (e.g., England 2005b: 392). Thus, in addition to their objective alienation by the production process (cf. Marx; see chapter 1), their self-alienation may be intensified by the emotion work they must necessarily manage, which is not only unpaid but frequently unacknowledged.

SUMMARY

Like society as a whole, sociology has been transformed by the changes in the status of women. Feminist sociological theorists have challenged the discipline's marginalization of women's realities so that sociology can in fact be what it claims to be: a theory about society, one which recognizes that social processes and insti-tutions shape, and are shaped by, the different gendered, racial, and other inter-secting locations of individuals. Early feminist scholars such as Harriet Martineau and Charlotte Perkins Gilman observed the contradictions between women's lives and the male world which defined and curtailed women's lives. Among contem-porary theorists, Dorothy Smith and Patricia Hill Collins underscore how every-day gendered experiences intersect with other historically marginalized standpoints, such as race, while Arlie Hochschild demonstrates how emotion work varies by social context and by the gendered and other socially differentiated statuses embedded in and determining institutional relations.

POINTS TO REMEMBER

Feminist standpoint theory:
- Challenges the male bias in allegedly objective knowledge
- Focuses attention on women's everyday/everynight knowledge and experiences
- Argues that sociological knowledge must begin from *within* the context of the people studied
- Women who move between the domestic and the public worlds develop a bifurcated consciousness of the split between objectified knowledge and women's everyday, local-ized experiences

Black women's standpoint:
- Underscores the specific racial history of oppression black women collectively share
- Ideologically controlling images –mammy, matriarch, welfare mother, whore – continue to define and oppress black women
- Black feminist thought produces activist knowledge from black women articulating their experiences of, and responses to, the everyday contradictions they encounter as black women oppressed by race, gender, and other intersecting marginalized statuses
- Sexual politics
  - Attentiveness to sexual politics highlights how ideologies of femininity and masculinity are variously used to disempower all subjugated groups in society, including black gay and straight men
  - An "honest bodies" project rejects the black gender ideology and commodification processes that subjugate black women
  - "Honest bodies" require the reclaiming of sexual identities and sexual feelings, especially by black women and gays

Emotional labor (Hochschild):
- The expression/display of feelings and emotion is socially regulated
- Women do more emotion management than men both in the home and at/as work
- Emotional labor is commodified; has exchange- and profit value
  - Involves face-to-face or voice-to-voice contact with the public
  - Requires the worker's production of an emotional state in another person
  - Is specified, supervised, and managed by employers

GLOSSARY

activist knowledge knowledge generated from within oppressed groups' lived experiences; empowers individuals to resist and take action against their oppression.

alternative sociology starts from the lived experiences and the standpoint of women and other minority groups rather than claiming an objectivity that largely cloaks male-centered knowledge; leads to the empowerment of women and men.

androcentric culture institutional practices and ideology whereby maleness defines humanity and the social reality of men and women.

bifurcation of consciousness knowledge that emerges from the contradictory realities women experience due to the split between objectified knowledge and women's everyday, localized experiences.

black feminist thought knowledge voiced by black women from within their lived experiences and across the different sites of their everyday reality.

black women's standpoint the common experiences that all African-American women share as a result of being black women in a society that denigrates women of African descent.

commercialization of feeling the training, production, and control of human emotions for economic profit.

controlling images demeaning images and representations of, for example, black women circulated by the largely white-controlled mass media and other social institutions.

discourse of femininity images, ideas, and talk in society informing how women should present themselves and behave vis-à-vis men and society as a whole.

domestic world home–neighborhood sphere of women's activity in a man-made world; deemed inferior to the public world in which men work, rule, and play.

emotional display socially learned and regulated presentation of emotional expression.

emotional labor emotion work individuals do at and as work, for pay; has exchange-value.

emotion work control or management of feelings in accordance with socially and culturally defined feeling rules.

everyday/everynight world continuous reality of women's lives as they negotiate the gendered responsibilities of motherhood, marriage, work, etc.

feeling rules socially defined, patterned ways of what to feel and how to express emotion in social interaction and in responding to and anticipating social events.

femininity (man-made) societal ideals and expectations informing how women should think and act in a society which rewards masculinity and male control of women.

feminist revolution transformation of knowledge and of social and institutional practices such that women are considered fully equal to men.

feminist theory focuses on women's inequality in society, and how that inequality is structured and experienced at macro and micro levels.

gender ideology a society's dominant beliefs elaborating different conceptualizations of women and men and of their self-presentation, behavior, and place in society.

honest bodies rejection of sexual exploitation and degradation (e.g., of women and gays), and the affirmation of sexual images, desires, and practices that recognize the emotional-relational context of sexual expression.

information economy dominance of information or service commodities, produced and exchanged for profit.

institutional ethnography an investigation that starts with individual experiences as a way to discover how institutions work, and how they might work better for people.

intersectionality multiple crisscrossing ways in which different histories and diverse structural locations (based on race, gender, class, etc.) situate individuals' experiences and life-chances.

knowing from within the idea that sociological knowledge must start from within the lived realities of the individuals and groups studied.

management of feeling control of emotion via the creation of a publicly observable and convincing bodily display.

masculinity societal expectations governing the self-presentation and behavior of men; accentuates characteristics and traits that are the opposite of femininity.

new racism symbols and ideas used (in politics and the mass media) to argue that race-based (biological) differences no longer matter even as such arguments reinforce racial-cultural differences and stereotypes.

patriarchal society one in which white men have a privileged position by virtue of the historically grounded, man-made construction of social institutions, texts, and practices.

politics of sexuality focus on the various ways in which ideas about sex and sexuality are used to create and contest divisions between and within particular social groups based on gender and sexual orientation differences.

public world the non-domestic arena; domains of work, politics, sports, etc., the sphere given greater legitimacy in society.

relations of ruling institutional and cultural routines which govern and maintain the unequal position of women in relation to men within and across all societal domains.

ruling practices array of institutional and cultural practices which maintain unequal gender relations in and across society.

ruling texts core man-made texts (e.g., Bible, Constitution, laws, advertising) which define gender and other power relations in society.

self-alienation produced as a result of emotional laborers' splitting of internal feelings and external emotion management.

standpoint a group's positioning within the unequal power structure and the everyday lived knowledge that emerges from that position.

RELEVANT NEWSPAPER STORIES

All news stories are from the *New York Times* unless otherwise noted, and can be accessed via www.wiley.com/go/dillon. See NEWS icons in the margins above.

NEWS 10.1   "How suite it isn't: A dearth of female bosses," December 17, 2006.
"Women in science: The battle moves to the trenches," December 19, 2006.
"Numbers are male, said Pythagoras, and the idea persists," October 3, 2006.
"Keeping houses, not building them," October 31, 2007.
"Career women in Japan find a blocked path," August 6, 2007.
"A rising [female conductor] star to shine briefly in New York," November 15, 2006.

NEWS 10.2   "Paid leave for maternity is the norm except in …," October 6, 2007.

NEWS 10.3   "At college, women are leaving men in the dust," July 9, 2006.
"Scant progress on closing gap in women's pay," December 24, 2006.

NEWS 10.4   "Signs of détente in the battle between Venus and Mars," May 31, 2007.

NEWS 10.5   "Domestic workers organize to end an 'atmosphere of violence on the job,'" June 9, 2008.

NEWS 10.6   "U.S. Blacks, if a nation, would rank high on AIDS," July 30, 2008.

NEWS 10.7   University of Minnesota School of Social Work – Institute on Domestic Violence in the African American Community, http://www.dvinstitute.org

NEWS 10.8   "A fragile foothold: The ranks of top-tier women on Wall St. are shrinking," December 1, 2007.

NEWS 10.9   "The world according to John McCain," *Newsweek*, April 7, 2008.
Clinton view expressed by David Gergen, a long-time White House insider and political commentator, on CNN's *360*, April 2, 2008.

NEWS 10.10   "Flying the unfriendly skies," September 14, 2008.
"Rise in verbal abuse of retail workers," *Irish Times*, December 9, 2008.

WEB SUPPLEMENTS

All web supplements are available at www.wiley.com/go/dillon. See WEB icons in the margins above.

WEB 10.1   Slavery
WEB 10.2   Census detailed table listing emotion workers
WEB 10.3   Interactive exercise using Census data on emotion workers classified by gender
WEB 10.4   Nancy Chodorow

NOTES

1 Outside of sociology, other influential and Marx-inspired feminist standpoint theorists include political theorist Nancy Hartsock (1998) and philosopher of science Sandra Harding (e.g., 1987; 1991).

2 Although Collins capitalizes "Black," the convention in sociology today is not to capitalize color words for race (black, white); I follow this convention in my discussion of race.

WEB 10.4

3 Nancy Chodorow (1978), using a psychoanalytical framework, has also made very important contributions to the understanding of emotion in gender-role reproduction.

4 Hochschild notes that service work is a requirement in capitalist and socialist economies. "Any functioning society makes effective use of its members' emotional labor. We do not think twice about the use of feeling in the theater, or in psychotherapy, or in forms of group life that we admire. It is when we come to speak of the exploitation of the bottom by the top in any society that we become morally concerned" (1983: 12).

CHAPTER ELEVEN
THEORIZING SEXUALITY AND THE BODY

KEY CONCEPTS

disciplinary practices

surveillance

docile bodies

Panopticon

bio-power

discourse

techniques of bio-power

genealogy

confession

regime of truth

ritual of discourse

power

heterosexist

essentialist view of
sexuality

constructionist view of
sexuality

semiotic code

queer theory

CHAPTER MENU

Sexuality and the body are intimately intertwined with emotions and with cultural definitions of femininity and masculinity (see chapter 10), as well as with a broad range of other social processes. Nevertheless, although the body has long been a focus for anthropologists, largely in relation to their interest in cultural rites of passage involving the body (Turner 1996: 4), sociological attention to it is a relatively recent development (see Turner 2009). Erving Goffman alerted sociologists to the social significance of body display and self-presentation (cf. chapter 8), while contemporary feminist sociologists (e.g., Conboy et al. 1997; Lorber and Moore 2006; Malacrida and Low 2008; Weitz 1998) unveil the many ways in which gender inequality is reflected, represented, and reproduced through cultural representations and talk of the body.

MICHEL FOUCAULT

The principal figure who transformed the body from a biological or physiological subject to an object of social inquiry was the late French philosopher **Michel Foucault**. Foucault wrote extensively on philosophical questions probing the nature of knowledge, truth, and power. And at the time of his death in 1984, he was regarded by some as "the most famous intellectual figure in the world" (Ryan 1993: 12). Foucault's fame derived in part from the wide range of topics he covered and his interest in challenging what we might generally tend to think of as the "natural" order of things; how, for example, societal definitions of sexuality are not natural or preordained categories but human-social creations, and thus *social* constructions (cf. Berger and Luckmann, chapter 9).

BIOGRAPHICAL NOTE

Michel Foucault was born in Paris, France, in 1926. He studied at the highly prestigious Ecole Normale in Paris and wrote his dissertation on the history of psychiatry, later published as *Madness and Civilization* (1965). During the course of his lifetime, Foucault held many distinguished posts including a faculty appointment at France's most prestigious university, the College de France. For many years he was also a visiting professor at the University of California, Berkeley, and was famously involved in the gay culture of San Francisco from the mid-1970s until his death in 1984, allegedly from AIDS, then a disease emerging into public notice (Eribon 1991). Many of Foucault's books were best-sellers in Europe and North America, and he wrote extensively about politics and culture for French newspapers and magazines.

DISCIPLINING THE BODY

Foucault would not be considered a feminist and, in fact, is heavily criticized by feminist scholars for his intellectual abstraction and disregard for the subjectively lived experiences of individuals (e.g., Hartsock 1998: 215–221; Hekman 1996;

Taylor and Vintges 2004). His work, nevertheless, is of particular relevance to sociologists interested in the body – and in institutional processes – because much of his writing was devoted to uncovering how the body came to have several disciplinary practices imposed upon it. Foucault investigated how institutional practices evolved so as to make control and regulation of the body, and hence the subjugation of individuals and society, a core preoccupation. The "birth" of the prison, of madness, the clinic, the asylum, and sexuality – all these topics converge in underscoring Foucault's interest, namely, how society develops ways of regulating and controlling, i.e., disciplining, the body/bodies. Therefore, despite Foucault's lack of attention to how disciplining practices are gendered and impact women and men differently (e.g., Bartky 1998), he stimulates us to think about the body and about social processes in new ways.

When we see the words "discipline" and "body" in the same sentence, we may well think of Max Weber, who drew attention to how the Protestant ethic's requirement of personal discipline and self-control over body and emotion provided the cultural-motivational energy for the expansion of capitalism (cf. chapter 3). Weber was interested in discipline insofar as it reflected and contributed to the increased rationality of modern society, but, unlike Foucault, he did not discuss the body as an object of rationality in and of itself.

For Foucault, the history of civilization can be told as an ever-expanding increase in rational surveillance of and over the body (bodies); modern, civilized society monitors, reins in, and disciplines the body. And while, historically, slavery regulated the body as a whole, Foucault argues that modern disciplinary practices target body details; "Discipline is a political anatomy of detail" (1979: 139), wherein body movements, gestures, attitudes, and behavior are subject to "a policy of coercions that act upon the body" with calculated manipulation (1979: 137–138). Through the physical-spatial layout, time scheduling, and supervisory and other organizational practices employed in prisons, hospitals, asylums, military academies, and schools, modern society, Foucault argues, produces docile bodies; "A body is docile that may be subjected, used, transformed and improved" (1979: 136). Thus, from our earliest days in pre-school, we learn (or are coerced) to sit attentively in a disciplined manner in class, and this body self-regulation continues right through college. "No slouching!" "Keep your hands to yourself!" "No looking around!" are the commands of parents, teachers, coaches, etc. Indeed it is so normal for us to expect children "to sit and be still" that it becomes front-page national news when an elementary school in Minnesota experiments with a new policy allowing pupils to sit or stand as they please while doing class-work and to fidget as much as they want. NEWS 11.1

Foucault used the Panopticon, a model of a prison proposed by Jeremy Bentham in the eighteenth century, to illustrate how disciplinary power works – how its continuous penetrating surveillance gives the individual no respite. The Panopticon is a large spatial area with a tower in the center, and surrounded by rows of buildings divided into multilevel cells with windows; the cells act as "small theatres in which each actor is alone, perfectly individualized and constantly visible" (Foucault 1979: 200). The inmate is an object, constantly observed, and constantly an object of information (derived from his or her constantly monitored actions), and visible only and at all times to the supervisor; the inmate cannot be seen by or have contact with the inmates in the other cells (1979: 200). The power of the Panopticon also lies in the fact that the inmate cannot see whether the supervisor is present or not, and hence must act as if he or she is being observed at all times. The supervisors, too, moreover, are enmeshed in the localization of power – "they observe, but in the process of so doing, they are also fixed, regulated, and subject to administrative control" (Dreyfus and Rabinow 1983: 189). In today's world, the reach of technological and electronic surveillance – the various uses of video and GPS tracking technology and the electronic monitoring of blogs, email, and Facebook (as we discussed in chapter 5) – might be seen as the new Panopticon. Technology is perhaps even more controlling, however, not just because of its unprecedented local and global reach but also because of its structural invisibility.

BIO-POWER

Foucault (1978: 140–141) argues that bio-power, i.e., the linking of biological processes (or body practices) to economic and political power, coincided with industrialization and capitalist growth in the eighteenth and nineteenth centuries, and in the related expansion of the nation-state and other social institutions. Foucault argues that although we associate the Victorian era (the nineteenth century) with sexual repression and silence (1978: 1–5, 17), that era, in fact, was one in which sex was a major preoccupation. It saw the transformation of sex into discourse, into something to be talked about, interrogated, and categorized. This transformation of sex, however, is not a liberation from repression as we might be inclined to think, but produces a discourse, Foucault argues, that regulates and controls sex and the body.

Foucault elaborates how, for example, the Census of Population – the great demographic data resource that many sociologists use, and that government officials and policy-makers also rely on – became one of a number of techniques of bio-power. It became an instrument for monitoring and controlling the practices of the body/bodies:

> One of the great innovations in the techniques of power in the eighteenth century was the emergence of "population" as an economic and political problem: population as wealth, population as manpower or labor capacity, population balanced between its own growth and the resources it commanded. Governments perceived that they were not dealing simply with subjects, or even with a "people," but with a population, with its specific phenomena and its peculiar variables: birth and death rates, life expectancy, fertility, state of health, frequency of illnesses, patterns of diet and habitation ... At the heart of this economic and political problem of population was sex: it was necessary to analyze the birth rate, the age of marriage, the legitimate and illegitimate births, the precocity [e.g., age of sexual initiation] and frequency of sexual relations, the ways of making them fertile or sterile, the effects of unmarried life ... the impact of contraceptive practices. (1978: 25–26)

In other words, demographers had to categorize, document, analyze, and publicize all those acts that people did with their bodies (as do medical doctors, medical insurance companies, etc.) – their various sexual habits and arrangements, and those "secrets" of sex that were already familiar to the people engaged in varied sexual practices/relationships. Foucault adds that while it was long accepted that countries needed to be populated if they wished to be prosperous,

> this was the first time that a society had affirmed, in a constant way, that its future and its fortune were tied not only to the number and the uprightness of its citizens, to their marriage rules and family organization, but to the manner in which each individual made use of his sex ... It was essential that the state know what was happening with its citizens' sex, and the use they made of it, but also that each individual be capable of controlling the use he made of it. Between the state and the individual, sex became an issue, and a public issue no less; a whole web of discourses, special knowledges, analyses, and injunctions settled upon it. (1978: 26)

THE INVENTION OF SEXUALITY

Accordingly Foucault argues, bio-politics, through its various technologies (its methods and procedures), *invented* sexuality. Through the Census, for example, we have invented the categories by which we come to label and enumerate different sexual circumstances and behaviors. There is nothing natural about these definitions or categories; they are administrative-bureaucratic constructs and, as such, are relatively arbitrary ways by which we carve up the use of sex, and also too, how society controls sex. If you look at the Census of Population today (see Box 11.1) you will readily see that the government makes several distinctions inferred from individuals' sexual habits and arrangements; who does what with whom and under what particular circumstances.

The government uses this information in making and administering policy decisions about the allocation of economic, health, social welfare, and other resources. But these categories, once they exist, also make available to us ways of thinking about sex and what we can do or should do with sex. We categorize ourselves – where we fit in terms of these categories; and, if our sexual habits and arrangements are not included in these lists, we wonder about the normalcy and social appropriateness of our practices. In short, sex is not only categorized but defined and regulated by society.

Box 11.1   Keeping a tab on bodies: Census categories

Marital status
- Currently married
  - *Spouse present*
  - *Spouse absent*
- Widowed
- Divorced
- Separated
- Never married

Households
- Married couple households
- Unmarried partner households
- Opposite-sex partners
  - With own children
  - With own and/or unrelated children
- Same-sex partners
  - With own children
  - With own and/or unrelated children

Births
- To teenage mothers
- To unmarried mothers

Notably, one way today that the US government is using the Census to regulate what comprises a "normal" household and hence what it (society) considers "normal" sexual behavior is that the Census Bureau – despite all the questions it asks – will *not* document the *marital status* of same-sex couples. Although same-sex marriage is legal in Massachusetts, for example, and although the Census counts same-sex couple households, it will not record whether these same sex-couples are married. The Census is prevented from doing so by the federal Defense of Marriage Act (passed in 1996), which defines marriage as between a man and a woman. And by officially not recording same-sex marriages, in this state document it is as if same-sex marriage does not exist.

NEWS 11.2

THE PRODUCTION OF BODY DISCOURSE

Historically, the bio-political production of discourse on sex (e.g., Census data and the absence of particular categories of data) meant that, like sex, the body too became something to be regulated and controlled. It produced a "constant alertness" among institutional authorities as to what was "normal" and "pathological" in regard to both sex and the body (Foucault 1978: 28). Teachers, doctors, psychiatrists, psychologists, and workers in the criminal justice system, among others, became experts in investigating, discovering, categorizing, and (allegedly) remedying sexual peculiarities and perversions (1978: 30–31). These experts produced discourses on sex "undertaking to protect, separate, and forewarn, signaling

---

Topic 11.1 The birth of obesity

Amidst today's bio-politics (seen in public debates over abortion, stem-cell research, sex education, physician-assisted suicide, etc.), we are witnessing "the birth of obesity," as the government, working in tandem with the medical profession and the health insurance industry, is imposing a new body category, obesity, one that must be institutionally monitored and controlled. In 1998, the US government-funded National Institutes of Health (NIH) created guidelines with a view toward defining and regulating obesity. Individuals whose Body Mass Index (BMI) rating is between 18.5 and 24.9 are categorized as "normal," a rating between 25 and 29.9 makes you "overweight," and you are considered "obese" if your BMI is 30 or higher. By these standards, two-thirds (66 percent) of American adults are either overweight or obese. The vocabulary of obesity has penetrated everyday life such that many schools monitor students' weight and send obesity reports to parents documenting their children's BMI score as well as an outline of recommended corrective dieting and exercise actions they should take to remedy their obesity. This in turn has led to an increase in specialized summer camps catering to obesity reduction.

NEWS 11.3

peril everywhere, awakening people's attention, calling for diagnoses, piling up reports, organizing therapies. These [institutional] sites radiated discourse aimed at sex, intensifying people's awareness of it as a constant danger, and this in turn created a further incentive to talk about it" (1978: 30–31).

CONFESSION

The incitement to talk about the body and about sex, Foucault argues, has a socio-historical genealogy originating in the sixteenth century. This was when the Catholic church (as part of the Counter-Reformation reforms accentuating its theological differences from the emerging Protestant church) gave increased emphasis to the obligatory ritual of confession. Because of the Catholic prohibition on sex outside of marriage, sex became a prime topic of confessional interrogation; the church made "sex into that which above all else, had to be confessed" (1978: 35). Thus the Catholic confession became one of the core techniques of bio-power; its procedures sought to extract truth about something that was omnipresent – sexual desire – yet repressed because of its sinful aura. The church targeted not only sexual acts but sexual *desires*.

> The scope of the confession – the confession of the flesh – continually increased ... [It] impose[d] meticulous rules of self-examination ... attributing more and more importance in penance ... to all the insinuations of the flesh: thoughts, desires, voluptuous imaginings, delectations, combined movements of the body and the soul; henceforth all this had to enter, in detail, into the process of confession and guidance. According to the new pastoral [the Catholic church's instructions in regard to confession], sex must not be named imprudently, but its aspects, its correlations, and its effects must be pursued down to their slenderest ramifications: a shadow in a daydream, an image too slowly dispelled, a badly exorcised complicity between the body's mechanics and the mind's complacency: everything had to be told. (Foucault 1978: 19)

As such, by interrogating and requiring the self-examination of every intricate and fleeting sexual desire, the confession shifted

> the most important moment of transgression from the act itself to the stirrings – so difficult to perceive and formulate – of desire ... Discourse, therefore, had to trace the meeting line of the body and the soul, following all its meanderings ... Under the authority of a language that had been carefully expurgated so that it was no longer directly named, sex was taken charge of, tracked down as it were, by a discourse that aimed to allow it no obscurity, no respite. (1978: 20)

In short, the penitent (the confessing person) was obliged through self-examination of conscience, and further interrogated by the priest – and the priest's language – during confession, to "transform desire, every desire into discourse" (1978: 21).

Discourse, therefore, according to Foucault, the ways in which we talk (and remain silent) about what we do and what we desire, produces truth. This "truth," however, is not some lofty philosophical or religious truth, but a truth produced by the institutional apparatuses, the system operating in a given society. Foucault argues that every society has its regime of truth. Just as political scientists in the West tend to refer to non-democratic, authoritarian governments as *regimes*, so too we can think of Foucault's use of *regime of truth* as indicating what he sees as the systemic, authoritarian, and controlling ways in which modern society produces particular truths. For Foucault, the confessional discourses extracted by the church, and the various discourses produced by the state, by the military, by the medical and the criminal justice systems, and by schools too are used not to establish some pure, disembodied truth but to categorize, govern, and regulate bodies. These are the institutional regimes that produce truth. Hence truth is not something that is independent of society, of the political and institutional contexts in which it is produced. In Foucault's (1984: 72–73) view, rather, the truths produced are coerced and power-ridden (a point that feeds into postmodern theory; see chapter 14).

SEX AND THE CONFESSING SOCIETY

Foucault argues that confession as a technique of truth/power subsequently expanded beyond the religious sphere (1978: 63), and alongside the development of scientific techniques and institutional discourses (of demography, medicine, psychiatry etc.).

> The confession became one of the West's most highly valued techniques for producing truth. We have since become a singularly confessing society. The confession has spread its effects far and wide. It plays a part in justice, medicine, education, family relationships, and love relations, in the most ordinary affairs of everyday life, and in the most solemn rites; one confesses one's crimes, one's sins, one's thoughts and desires, one's illnesses and troubles; one goes about telling with the greatest precision, whatever is most difficult to tell. One confesses in public and in private, to one's parents, one's educators, one's doctor, to those one loves; one admits to oneself, in pleasure and in pain, things it would be impossible to tell to anyone else, the things people write books about. One confesses – or is forced to confess. When it is not spontaneous or dictated by some internal imperative, the confession is wrung from a person by violence or threat; it is driven from its hiding place in the soul or extracted from the body. Since the Middle Ages torture has accompanied it like a shadow, and supported it when it could go no further: the dark twins. The most defenseless tenderness and the bloodiest of powers have a similar need of confession. Western man has become a confessing animal. (1978: 59)

It is body practices, moreover, that still comprise confessional discourse. Presidents, governors, Senators, Hollywood celebrities, sports stars, and even national governments (e.g., Australia, Canada, South Africa for their treatment of

The disciplined body. Church, state, and mass media regulate bodies and body desire.

minority populations) engage in ritualistic confessions. These confessions invariably revolve around the body – what individuals do with and to their bodies, and with and to other bodies. And these confessions are typically not spontaneous but coerced, coerced by the looming threat that particular sexual and body secrets will be exposed by media surveillance.

📖 NEWS 11.4

THE PRODUCTION AND CIRCULATION OF POWER

Confession, however, though it may unburden the confessing individual or organization, is, essentially, a power-ridden discourse:

> The confession is a **ritual of discourse** in which the speaking subject is also the subject of the statement; it is also a ritual that unfolds within a power relationship; for one does not confess without the presence (or virtual presence) of a partner who is not simply the interlocutor [the person(s) with whom we are speaking] but the authority who requires the confession, prescribes, and appreciates it, and intervenes in order to judge, punish, forgive, console, and reconcile; ... a ritual in which the expression alone, independently of its external consequences, produces intrinsic modifications in the person who articulates it: it exonerates, redeems, and purifies him; it unburdens him of his wrongs, liberates him, and promises him salvation. (1978: 61–62)

More generally for Foucault, power is relational rather than consolidated in specific institutional locations – in the state and bureaucracy, as Weber (cf. chapter 3), for example, would underscore. For Foucault, power does not flow in a top-down, hierarchical fashion, but has many sources and points of shifting impact and resistance. He states:

> Power is everywhere; not because it embraces everything, but because it comes from everywhere ... power is not an institution, and not a structure ... Power is not something that is acquired, seized, or shared, something that one holds on to or allows to slip away; power is exercised from innumerable points, in the interplay of nonegalitarian and mobile relations ... Power comes from below; that is, there is no binary and all-encompassing opposition between rulers and ruled at the root of power relations ... We must not look for who has the power in the order of sexuality (men, adults, parents, doctors) and who is deprived of it (women, adolescents, children, patients); nor for who has the right to know and who is forced to remain ignorant. (1978: 93, 94, 99)

In other words, for Foucault, power is not contained in any specific location, person, or social status; it is omnipresent and has no one anchor but continuously flows in all directions. And its pervasiveness is further underlined by the fact that all discourses are constituted and permeated by power. Remember that for Foucault, the transformation of sex into discourse was a bio-political strategy: a population's body practices (including desires) are documented, interrogated, and categorized (e.g., births outside of marriage, homosexuality), and in the process problematized into something to be administered and controlled. Power thus works through discourse; the very discourse produced on sex – even though it may seem liberating to us that we can talk about sex – is a strategy to demarcate what is sinful, normal, peculiar, etc.

Thus with confession, while the interrogator (especially when using physical torture) may seem to have more power than the interrogated individual, the discursive process of confession is not a zero-sum game. The questions asked by the interrogator (whether a priest, Oprah Winfrey, or a political reporter) are not spontaneously chosen by the interrogator but are determined externally by the discourse itself, by a given society's ways of naming and inquiring into what it is that is being interrogated. Power permeates all that is said, and not said. And similarly, the redemption and purification that derive from confessing further control the individual to think, desire, and behave within particular categories of normalcy. Both the interrogator and the interrogated are docile bodies, used and/or improved, i.e., controlled, by the confessional discourse (cf. Foucault 1978: 136).

MASKING POWER

The circulation of power as discourse is all the more controlling because it is essentially masked in and through discourse. When we are stopped by a police officer for speeding, we know we are looking at power, and that we are in an unequal power relationship with an authority figure. But when we are talking with our friends about the sex lives of celebrities we are not aware that the very discourse we use is itself subjecting *us* to a particular, regulated way of thinking/ talking about, categorizing, and practicing sex. We think we are just talking about sex, but we are really engaged in reproducing bio-power. Thus it is in discourse that power and knowledge are joined together ... we must not imagine a world of discourse divided between accepted discourse and excluded discourse, or between the dominant discourse and the dominated one ... Discourse transmits and produces power; it reinforces it, but also undermines and exposes it, renders it fragile and makes it possible to thwart it. In like manner, silence and secrecy are a shelter for power, anchoring its prohibitions; but they also loosen its holds and provide for relatively obscure areas of tolerance. (Foucault 1978: 100, 101)

Therefore, although we use a more explicit sexual vocabulary today, our sexual discourse also contains many silences about sex and the body. We silently collude in various forms of sexual exploitation including prostitution, which only gets discussed when it involves political scandal. Hence Patricia Hill Collins (2004) challenges us to create "honest bodies" (cf. chapter 10). All our silences about sex are an inherent part of discourse and how it works. Foucault argues that silence is not the opposite of discourse; rather, silence "functions alongside the things said, with them and in relation to them within over-all strategies ... silences permeate discourses" (1978: 27).

NEWS 11.5

For example, silence is required by the US military's gay policy: "Don't ask, don't tell" – a policy that the military sociologist Charles Moskos helped craft, and which allows gays to serve in the military as long as they keep their sexuality secret. This policy may expand career opportunities for gay soldiers and increase tolerance of gays in the military. At the same time, however, the necessary silence requires the closeted invisibility of gays and reproduces the social stigma attendant on being gay. It reinforces the idea that gays are different – they have a special secret that must be repressed – and that somehow, despite a long history of gays in the military (e.g., Berube 1990), their sexuality detracts from their ability to be good soldiers.

NEWS 11.6

NEWS 11.7

RESISTING/REPRODUCING POWER

The military, the state, and other institutions (the church, school, medicine, the criminal justice system) certainly use bio-power; their everyday practices – as Foucault documents – revolve around disciplining the body and regulating populations. But, for Foucault, these are not the only agents and locales of power. According to him, we are all engaged in the ongoing production of power, whether we want to be or not. Discourse *is* power and we cannot escape from producing it even as we try to thwart it. Individuals and groups are always in relational power struggles, struggles that are fluid but also never-ending – "there is no point where you are free from all power relations" (Foucault 1984/1994: 167). Resistance is itself critical to the ongoing circulation of power, but not to its elimination or transformation into something else; resistance is critical, not because it produces political opportunities for change, but simply because it maintains the circulation of power (ibid.).

This is where Foucault's understanding of discourse/power may make us feel entrapped and frustrated – though he argues that it is more correct to think of power as a (never-ending) struggle than as entrapment (1984/1994: 167). Nevertheless, we cannot use silence or language to reject power – even though it might seem to us that we can, and indeed we must if, for example, we wish to mobilize against social inequality and create a just society (e.g., Hartsock 1998: 221). This is because, for Foucault – unlike for Habermas, who affirmed the emancipatory power of reasoned argumentation (cf. chapter 5) – language is itself compromised by power. Because language comes out of and is conditioned in socio-historical contexts characterized by unequal power relations, it is impossible to change power structures and relations, since the only discourse which we can use against power is itself riddled with power. Therefore, although some arguments and silences (e.g., pleading the Fifth Amendment) may seem like resistance, ultimately they simply reproduce power, because, as Foucault emphasizes, all arguments, the language in which they are framed, and silence too, because silence is itself part of discourse/power, are impotent against power; it continues to circulate and flow. Thus while for him, discourse (including silence) is power, from a traditional sociological perspective it is ultimately impotent power because we cannot use it to get out of, or transform, the relations of economic, gender, racial, etc., domination that Marx-inspired and feminist theorists, among others, underscore as structured into society.

SEXUALITY AND QUEER THEORY

Not surprisingly, given Foucault's emphasis on the historical-institutional *invention* of sexuality, he was highly influential among scholars attentive to sexual politics. Feminist theorists, as we discussed (chapter 10), challenge the alleged objectivity and neutrality of (white male) sociological and other ruling knowledges in society. In similar fashion, **Steven Seidman** and other sociologists interested in sexual politics (e.g., Connell 1987, 1995; Kimmel 2005) seek to redress the long-time silence in social theory regarding sexuality. Seidman notes that despite the many sexual issues (e.g., divorce, homosexuality, prostitution, pornography, etc.) dominating public debate in the US and Europe at the beginning of the twentieth century, and the simultaneous rise of psychoanalysis, psychiatry, and Freudian theory – all of which gave prominence to sexuality – classical social theory maintained an oblivious silence on sexuality.

BIOGRAPHICAL NOTE

Steven Seidman is professor of sociology at the State University of New York (SUNY) at Albany. He received his undergraduate education at SUNY-Brockport, his MA from the New School for Social Research, New York, and his PhD in sociology from the University of Virginia (in 1980). Seidman has written several important books on sexuality and on social theory, and has been a highly influential scholar in elaborating a sociological interpretation and application of queer studies.

Seidman states: "Despite their aim to view the human condition as socially constructed, and to sketch a social history of the contours of modernity, the classical sociologists [Marx, Durkheim, Weber] offered no accounts of the social making of modern bodies and sexualities" (1996: 3). This silence fed into what Seidman sees as sociology's heterosexist bias, a bias stemming from the presumed naturalness of the founding fathers' "privileged gender and sexual social position" as heterosexual men. He elaborates:

> They took for granted the naturalness and validity of their own gender and sexual status the way, as we sociologists believe, any individual unconsciously assumes as natural those aspects of one's life that confer privilege and power. Thus, just as the bourgeoisie asserts the naturalness of class inequality and their rule, individuals whose social identity is that of male and heterosexual do not question the naturalness of a male-dominated, normatively heterosexual social order. It is then hardly surprising that the classics never examined the social formation of modern regimes of bodies and sexualities. Moreover, their own science of society contributed to the making of this regime whose center is the hetero/homo binary and the heterosexualization of society. (1996: 4; see also Seidman 1997: 81–96)

In other words, when we read social theory we take it for granted that when theorists write about "man in society" – whether the capitalist or the wage-worker, the bureaucrat or the Calvinist, the socially unmoored suicidal individual or the emotionally neutral doctor – they are assuming a heterosexual man whose sexuality is a given and about which there is nothing problematic.[1] It is telling that the one theorist who wrote about "the homosexual" – Erving Goffman (1963a) – did so to illuminate the self-presentation strategies that "abnormal" stigmatized individuals must use to pass as normal.

NORMALIZING HOMOSEXUALITY

The social movements of the 1960s and 1970s that transformed consciousness about gender and racial inequality also chipped away at the privileging of heterosexuality as the only normal sexuality. This political activism coincided with the emergence of scholarly histories of sexuality, pioneered by Foucault, and with the influence of Berger and Luckmann's analysis of the social construction of reality (cf. chapter 9). The public advocacy of the gay and lesbian movement for acceptance of gay sexuality and for equal civil rights for gays and lesbians helped shift attention to the idea that gays were more "normal" than many people, including homosexuals themselves, had assumed (i.e., had learned from society). Gays and lesbians argued that their everyday reality as gays and lesbians was indeed real, a paramount reality as relevant to them as the different realities experienced as real by heterosexual members of society. Rather than closeting this reality, the gay and lesbian movement argued for legal and institutional changes that would recognize homosexual realities.

📖 NEWS 11.8

📖 NEWS 11.9

📖 NEWS 11.10

📖 NEWS 11.11
📖 NEWS 11.12

The gay and lesbian movement, just like the feminist and the black civil rights movements, has had mixed success. On the one hand, as Collins (2004) reminds us, homosexuality is still heavily stigmatized in the black community (cf. chapter 10). Indeed, regardless of race and socio-economic class, gays continue to encounter discrimination and exclusion in the workplace and at school – as illustrated by the gay high school boy whose picture with his boyfriend was blacked out in the high school yearbook. On the other hand, a majority (57 percent) of Americans approve of gay relationships, and almost half (46 percent) support same-sex marriage, a substantial increase over the 27 percent who expressed approval for legalizing gay marriage back in the late 1990s. The increased recognition of the "normalcy" of gay relationships is reflected in the increased visibility of gay families, and in the fact that gays and lesbians can legally marry in the US in Massachusetts and Connecticut (and could for a while in California), as well as in Canada, Belgium, the Netherlands, Norway, Spain, Colombia, and South Africa.

Seidman, in fact, offers a generally positive assessment of the current status of gays' struggle for equality. He comments:

> Heterosexuality remains very definitely normative and homosexuality is still freighted with connotations of moral pollution ... concealment and disclosure decisions, and sexual identity management are still part of the lives of lesbians and gay men in America. Homosexuals still suffer and, for many, the closet and coming out remains not merely a phase of their lives but its center. Yet, [in individual lives, politics, and popular culture] ... a trend toward normalization and social routinization seems to be one prominent current in contemporary America. (2004: 259)

📖 NEWS 11.13
📖 NEWS 11.14

This normalization trend is apparent not only in large metropolitan centers but also in America's rural heartland, and among evangelicals and other religious groups who have traditionally opposed homosexuality.

PROBLEMATIZING SEXUALITY

In the 1980s and 1990s, sociologists, gay activists, and others spent much time debating the nature of homosexuality, a debate driven largely by the attempt to legitimate and normalize gay and lesbian sexuality. Theoretically innovative, it illuminated the social origins of sexuality and how socio-historical context shapes the definition and institutionalization of sexuality (e.g., Foucault 1978). This "sexual turn" in social theory thus ended sociological silence on sexuality and challenged the conventional sociological view of sex as an ascribed, i.e., biologically inherited, role status (cf. Parsons; see chapter 4).

Essentialist view of homosexuality

The debate on homosexuality has many strands but it has revolved around two contrasting perspectives (e.g., Epstein 1987). On the one hand are those who argue that homosexuality is a biological given. In this view, frequently reported in research interviews with gays and lesbians, gay people are born gay, something they long sense in their desires and experience as an essential part of their nature. This essentialist view of sexuality posits a core, natural difference between homosexuals and heterosexuals, a difference used by some activists to advocate a separatist identity politics that reinforces differences between homosexuals and heterosexuals. The essentialist view is also used to support the political claim that since gay people are born gay, it is not their "fault"; it is a natural orientation, they cannot do anything about it, and, therefore, they should not be discriminated against by social rules that exclude gays (e.g., from marriage to another gay person, church membership, certain occupations, sports, etc.).

Constructionist view of homosexuality

By contrast, the social constructionist view of sexuality emphasizes that all labels and categories in society and the meanings attached to them are socially defined (cf. Foucault above; and, more broadly, Berger and Luckmann's emphasis on the social construction of language and social institutions; see chapter 9). As homosexuality and heterosexuality (or any other categorical term) are human-created labels, what we mean by them varies by culture and time period; there is no one type of sexuality that is "natural." Rather, the meanings we assign to any and all sexuality are a human construction, and what sexuality is privileged in society (e.g., heterosexuality) is also a human construction.

Social constructionism sees homosexuality more as an identity choice than a biologically predetermined natural state. In this view, people learn how to present themselves as gay by internalizing what society labels as gay behavior; they seek out social ties with others whom they perceive to be gay, and form various gay subcultures. This perspective on sexual identity has parallels with how we commonly understand ethnic identity. Although ethnic identity can have a biological, genetic basis, in societal terms ethnicity is understood by individuals' patterns of association with others of similar ethnicity, and by the group's shared practices and meanings. Thus ethnic groups form subcultures affirming a particularized identity that accentuates its distinct heritage, and its difference from the mainstream culture (e.g., Italian-Americans, Brazilian-Americans). Homosexual constructionists argue that gay and lesbian identity can be similarly thought of as another ethno-social, subcultural identity; thus, like ethnic groups, gays and lesbians should be regarded as behaving in particular, meaningful ways that reflect and nurture their particular social identity. The social constructionist view of sexuality, though popular among sociologists, is increasingly challenged today, however, by cognitive psychologists and socio-evolutionary biologists who, in searching to demonstrate the genetic basis for many social characteristics and personality traits (e.g., shyness), talk about "the homosexual gene."

Irrespective of whether homosexuality is seen in essentialist (biological) or social constructionist terms, the gay and lesbian movement – and feminist and sexuality scholars – argue that it is a legitimate sexuality/identity and should not be grounds for discrimination. It is simply another source among the multiple, intersecting identities that variously shape people's everyday existence. In some contexts, moreover, an individual's sexuality can be paramount, whereas in another context their economic, racial, and/or regional and religious identities may be of greater salience.

THE QUEERING OF SOCIAL THEORY

Moving beyond the essentialist/social constructionist debate about the nature of homosexuality and who fits into the category of "the homosexual," Steven Seidman proposes the queering of social theory. This turn is influenced by academics outside of sociology and social science and whose theoretical background and methodology are very different from sociology. Most queer theorists are in the humanities, and they approach social categories and social identities just as they would the language used in literary texts. They regard the language used to categorize social behavior as a semiotic code – language used not simply to denote a particular reality but as a signifier, an indicator, of a more deeply structured and culturally understood context of meaning.

Through socialization we learn language, the words and symbols used to name and give meaning to all those things in our environment. We learn what goes with what, how things go together (salt and pepper) in a socially meaningful way (in setting the table; seasoning our food). Words have the property of turning the external reality into binary categories (salt, not-salt). But queer theorists argue that reality is not binary; it is more complicated (there are multiple shades of color

---

Topic 11.2   The fluidity of sexual and gender identity

Many individuals experience their sexual and/or gender realities in more fluid ways than typically acknowledged in the binary male/female and homosexuality/heterosexuality categories used in official and everyday discourse. The prevalence of gender-crossing highlights this fluidity (e.g., McCloskey 1999). Whether motivated by biological or/and by social reasons, individuals can remove themselves from the Census sex classification (male/female) assigned at birth on the basis of body-physiological characteristics, and cross over into a different category; an estimated 1,600 to 2,000 people a year undergo sex-change surgery in the US. One place in which there is strong cultural acceptance of the elasticity and fluidity of gender and sexual identities is among indigenous communities in Oaxaca, a state in Southern Mexico. There, the native Zapotec people recognize a third gender category, the muxes (derived from the Spanish word *mujer*, "woman"), which is used to refer to males who from boyhood have felt themselves female. Muxes are able to occupy social roles in the community that are traditionally associated with women (as garment workers or home-helpers). Acceptance of mixed gender identities has a long history among the Zapotec, as indicated by ancient Mayan gods who were simultaneously male and female.

NEWS 11.15

and flavor between (white) salt and (black) pepper). And we lose recognition of this complicated reality when we insist on its "either/or" binary classification.

For queer theorists, the key binary of interest is that of heterosexuality/homosexuality. Queer theorists argue that political and scholarly debates about the biological or social nature of homosexuality simply reproduce the pervasiveness of the binary, either/or categories we use to think about sexuality. They maintain that sexuality is far more *fluid* than allowed by the heterosexual/homosexual binary; it is more akin to a flowing continuum of variation. All binary categories contain an implicit hierarchy of difference or of Otherness. Dichotomized categories of opposites (e.g., heterosexual/homosexual; male/female) overstate differences as well as projecting the presumption that one side of the binary couplet has greater significance and value than the other; these binary categories are not simply descriptive of differences between and among individuals but are, in fact, political and prescriptive. Thus, in our society, heterosexuality is more valued (and connotes more symbolic and material power) than homosexuality; male is more valued (and has more power) than female. And these categorical differences get translated and embedded into institutional practices (in schools, churches, movies, music videos, laws, social policies, etc.).

The homosexual/heterosexual binary, queer theorists argue, reinforces the idea of sexuality as involving basic foundational differences (e.g., of sexual desire, attraction). Yet Arlene Stein (1997: 56) observes that being lesbian is not simply about sexual desire but about woman-identification and the development of a lesbian consciousness. Binary thinking also ignores the many social differences in lived experience that invariably characterize those singularly defined as gay or lesbian; this obscures recognition that among gays, just as among non-gays, there are differences of social class, race, generation, etc. – diverse intersecting differences that make talk of and knowledge about "the homosexual" rather superficial, as if gays are simply gay, with no other socially grounded identities.

THE RADICAL CHARACTER OF QUEER THEORY

Queer theory thus pushes for a move away from and beyond the homosexual/heterosexual categorization, whether on campus, at nightclubs, or in academic and policy debates. Therefore, while sociologists provide compelling research studies about the coming-out experiences of gays and lesbians, or how gays and lesbians negotiate the hurdles at work or in the legal system, or how they deal with illness and bereavement and other life transitions, these studies, according to queer theorists – whether their findings indicate gay emancipation or/and continuing discrimination - ultimately reproduce and reinforce how we conceptualize sexuality, and thus how we conceptualize and reaffirm the differences we impute to the categories of homosexual and heterosexual.

Seidman explains that queer theory seeks to "shift the debate somewhat away from explaining the modern homosexual to questions of the operation of the hetero/homosexual binary" (1996: 9) Accordingly, as Seidman elaborates:

Queer theorists have criticized the view of homosexuality as a property of an individual or group, whether that identity is explained as natural or social in origin. They argue that this perspective leaves in place the heterosexual/homosexual binary as a master framework for constructing the self, sexual knowledge, and social institutions. A theoretical and political project which aims exclusively to normalize homosexuality and to legitimate homosexuality as a social minority does not challenge a social regime which perpetuates the production of subjects and social worlds organized and regulated by the heterosexual/homosexual binary ... Moreover, in such a regime homosexual politics is pressured to move between two limited options: the liberal struggle to legitimate homosexuality in order to maximize the politics of inclusion and the separatist struggle to assert difference on behalf of a politics of ethnic [or homosexual] nationalism. (1997: 148–149)

The queering of social theory, then, aims to be disruptive. It is rebellious; "a theoretical sensibility that pivots on transgression or permanent rebellion" (Seidman 1996: 11). It challenges the very use of such words as "the closet" and "coming out" because these terms, whether used by gays and lesbians or by social researchers, yield power to the ascribed differences between homosexuals and heterosexuals that our society institutionalizes in its norms, laws, and everyday practices (Seidman 2004: 263). Queer theory contests this foundation – this culturally embedded definition of sexuality that permeates our society and which informs our knowledge of society (Seidman 1996: 22).[2]

Queer theory thus aims to decenter the normalcy of our categories – whether "the homosexual" is a category used to discriminate against gays, or as a social identity by gays to celebrate their difference and/or to claim equal rights with heterosexuals. Queer theory rejects all such packaged categorizations. Though sympathetic, Seidman (1996: 22) also is critical, however, of queer theorists for failing to recognize the institutional reality in which categorizations are anchored and which structure individuals' life experiences and life-chances. As sociologists emphasize, social reality is not solely about categories and language, but includes robust social structures and cultures that cannot simply be deconstructed by changing linguistic-semiotic codes.

Though queer theory's arguments can be dense, in practical terms its decentering challenge to sociology has very specific implications. Stein and Plummer elaborate, for example, on its implications for stratification and occupational mobility:

How can sociology seriously purport to understand the social stratification system ... while ignoring quite profound social processes connected to heterosexism, homophobia, erotic hierarchies, and so forth ... What happens to stratification theory as gay and lesbian concerns are recognized? What are the mobility patterns of lesbians? How do these patterns intersect with race, age, region, and other factors? What happens to market structure analysis if gays are placed into it? ... We need to reconsider whole fields of inquiry with differences of sexuality in mind. (1996: 137–138)

Clearly disruptive, queer theory requires sociologists to alter how we think not only about sexuality but about all social dynamics – how we study stratification, crime, family, religion, etc. The very use of the word "queer" in queer theory captures this disruptive strategy. This is a word that was traditionally used to refer to homosexuals in a pejorative way (homosexuals as queers), and subsequently re-appropriated by gay activists in the 1980s and 1990s as part of an energetic, in-your-face call to action at the height of the AIDS epidemic to redress the discrimination experienced by gays – summarized by their slogan, "We're here and we're queer." Queer theorists then inject this "disrespectable" word into respectable social theory. Queer theory thus seeks to destabilize the homosexual/heterosexual distinction and how it is used to reproduce power and inequality based on sexual orientation, and in sociology, to destabilize the discipline's core heterosexist assumptions and knowledge.

How effective queer theory can be in disrupting the heterosexist bias in sociology is uncertain. It seems to be of interest to a relatively small number of sociologists, and the writings of the queer theorists cited by Seidman and other sociologists are dense, opaque, and at times verging on incoherence; see, for example, Judith Butler's *Gender Trouble*. Nevertheless, the very radicalness of the idea of *queering* social theory is itself a contribution. Queer theory "aspires to transform homo-sexual theory into a general social theory or one standpoint from which to analyze social dynamics" (Seidman 1996: 13). It is another strand that makes us stop, if only momentarily, to reassess the language and categories we use to apprehend social reality. This can stimulate a broader reflection on how the master narratives we know and rely on to ground us – narratives about the foundation of sociology, of the US, of the Catholic church, the National Football League, etc. – may obfus-cate particular biases while simultaneously reproducing the language and rules that underlie the multiple forms of domination in our society. Queering (and querying) these narratives can disrupt our scholarly and everyday understandings of differ-ence, such that we might eventually move beyond the differences that divide us.

SUMMARY

Michel Foucault attuned sociologists to the many ways in which the body is institu-tionally controlled in modern society. As part of his broad analysis, he elaborated on the historical invention of sexuality, a theme that has been highly influential in advanc-ing scholarly and public understanding of homosexuality. Among sociologists inter-ested in sexual politics, Steven Seidman has played a lead role in bringing queer theory to the attention of sociologists, and at the same time, has tried to alert queer theorists, most of whom are not social scientists, to the importance of recognizing the structural significance of social institutions in shaping knowledge and individual experience.

POINTS TO REMEMBER

The body and sexuality:
- The body has been a targeted object of institutional surveillance and regulation especially since the sixteenth century

- The transformation of sexual desire and behavior into discourse was first accomplished by the Catholic confession and subsequently extended by the state (e.g., the Census) for political and economic purposes
- Discourses of sex/the body are imbued with, and add to the circulation of, power
- Debates about homosexuality contrast essentialist biological and social constructionist perspectives

Queer theory:

- Another standpoint from which to analyze social relations
- Rejects the binary, homosexual/heterosexual categories we use to think about and organize sexuality, instead emphasizing the fluidity of sexuality
- Focuses attention beyond sexual categories onto how sexuality and assumptions about sexuality are embedded in and constituted by institutional and everyday practices

GLOSSARY

bio-power the institutional use of bodies and body practices for purposes of political, administrative, and economic control.

confession production of discourse as a result of the interrogation of the self (by the self or others, real and imagined), typically with regard to body practices.

constructionist view of sexuality the idea that homosexuality and what it means to be gay has varied across history and social context; contrasts with an essentialist view.

disciplinary practices institutional practices (through schools, churches, clinics, prisons, etc.) used to control, regulate, and subjugate individuals, groups, and society as a whole.

discourse categorizations, talk, and silences pertaining to social practices.

docile bodies produced as a result of the various institutional techniques and procedures used to discipline, subjugate, use, and improve individual (and population) bodies.

essentialist view of sexuality the idea that being gay, and the social characteristics associated with being gay, are a natural and essential part of the gay individual's biology.

genealogy (of knowledge/power) interconnected social, political, and historical antecedents to, and context for, the emergence of particular ideas/social categories.

heterosexist presumption that heterosexuality is normative (and normal) and that other sexual feelings and practices are socially deviant.

Panopticon model (invoked by Foucault) to highlight how disciplinary power works by keeping the individual a constant object of unceasing surveillance/control.

power an ongoing circulatory process with no fixed location or fixed points of origin and resistance.

queer theory rejects the heterosexual/homosexual binary in intellectual thought, culture, and institutional practices; shifts attention from the unequal status of gays and lesbians in (heterosexist) society to instead focus intellectual and political agendas on the fluidity of all sexuality.

regime of truth institutional system whereby the state and other institutions (government agencies, the military, medical and cultural industries) and knowledge producers (e.g., scientists, professors) affirm certain ideas and practices as true and delegitimate or silence alternative practices and interpretations.

ritual of discourse society's orderly, routinized ways (e.g., confession) of producing subjects talking about socially repressed secrets and practices.

semiotic code cultural code or meanings inscribed in language and other symbols in a given societal context.

surveillance continuous monitoring and disciplining of bodies by social institutions across private and public domains.

techniques of bio-power exertion of control over the body/bodies through institutional procedures (e.g., classroom schedules, Census categories) and practices (e.g., confession).

RELEVANT NEWSPAPER STORIES

All news stories are from the *New York Times* unless otherwise noted, and can be accessed via www.wiley.com/go/dillon. See NEWS icons in the margins above.

NEWS 11.1   "They stand when called upon, and when not," February 25, 2009.

NEWS 11.2   "Census will not record same-sex marriages," July 18, 2008.

NEWS 11.3   "Quick, do you know your B.M.I.?" December 28, 2006.
"Priced out of weight loss camp," August 16, 2008.

NEWS 11.4   "Behind a meeting that exposed Edwards' affair," August 10, 2008.

NEWS 11.5   "The myth of the victimless crime," March 12, 2008.
"Do as he said," March 13, 2008.
"Really dangerous liaisons," March 12, 2008.

NEWS 11.6   "Charles Moskos, policy adviser, dies at 74," obituary, June 5, 2008.

NEWS 11.7   "Outing the out of touch," June 10, 2007.
"Gay Britons serve in military with little fuss, as predicted discord does not occur," May 21, 2007.

NEWS 11.8   "House backs broad protections for gay workers," November 8, 2007.

NEWS 11.9   "Gay kiss is edited out of yearbook," June 4, 2007.

NEWS 11.10   Gallup poll data can be accessed at: www.gallup.com. In the "search" box, type in "homosexuality." See, for example, the report "Tolerance for gay rights at high-water mark," May 29, 2007.

NEWS 11.11   "An American family," November 26, 2006.
"An extended nuclear family? Gay men, lesbians and the kids they are making and raising, sort of together," November 19, 2006.
"Young gay rites" April 27, 2008.

NEWS 11.12   "Definition of marriage is at heart of California case," March 5, 2008.
"California court overturns a ban on gay marriage," May 16, 2008.

NEWS 11.13   "In the heartland and out of the closet," December 28, 2006.

NEWS 11.14   "Gay and evangelical, seeking paths of acceptance," December 12, 2006.

NEWS 11.15   *Boston Globe*, July 17, 2007; "A lifestyle distinct: The muxe of Mexico," August 7, 2008.

NOTES

1 Kimmel argues that it was "not just 'man' as in generic mankind" that the classical theorists had in mind, "but a particular type of masculinity, a definition of manhood that derives its identity from participation in the market-place, from interaction with other men in that marketplace – in short, a model of masculinity for whom identity is based on homosocial competition" (2005: 27). The American cultural emphasis on "self-made men" evokes and reaffirms an emphasis on an aggressive, competitive, virile masculinity.

2 Seidman (1996: 11) states: "I take as central to Queer theory its challenge to what has been the dominant foundational concept of both homophobic and affirmative heterosexual theory: the assumption of a unified homosexual identity. I interpret Queer theory as contesting this foundation and therefore the very telos of Western homosexual politics."

CHAPTER TWELVE
SOCIOLOGICAL THEORIES OF RACE AND RACISM

KEY CONCEPTS

slavery
colonialism
race-segregation
apartheid
post-colonial theory
Otherness
identity politics
affirmative action
race
racism
whiteness
cultural identity
double-consciousness
black underclass
nihilism
popular culture
politics of conversion
black cultural democracy
political race
culture lines
new racism
crisis of raciology
planetary humanism

CHAPTER MENU

Timeline 12.1	Major events in the historical evolution of black equality (1791–present)
1791	William Wilberforce's motion to dismiss the slave trade approved by British Parliament
1792	Slavery abolished in Dutch colonies
1794	Slavery abolished in French colonies
1808	US federal government prohibits import of slaves into the country
1837	US Congress passes gag law suppressing debate on slavery
1861–1865	American Civil War: fought over individual states' rights to slavery
1863	Emancipatory Proclamation of President Abraham Lincoln
1865	President Lincoln assassinated
1866	US Congress passes Civil Rights Act granting citizenship and equal civil rights for Negro freedmen
1866	US Congress passes Southern Homestead Act, providing public land for sale to freedmen at relatively low prices
1909	Founding of National Association for the Advancement of Colored People (NAACP)
1944	Establishment of United Negro College Fund, with its well-known slogan: "A mind is a terrible thing to waste"
1954	US Supreme Court, in *Brown versus Board of Education of Topeka*, rules that racial segregation in schools violates Fourteenth Amendment to US Constitution
1957	Civil Rights Act passed in US; violence in Little Rock, Arkansas, against school integration
1962	Algeria becomes independent from France
1963	Kenya becomes independent from Great Britain
1964	Race riots in US as result of enforcement of civil rights laws
1965	Britain passes Race Relations Act
1967	US Supreme Court, in *Loving versus Virginia*, rules as unconstitutional state laws banning interracial marriage
1968	Britain passes Commonwealth Immigration Act imposing restrictions on immigrants
1968	Martin Luther King, Jr, leader of civil rights movement in US, assassinated
1986	*Oprah Winfrey Show* goes into national syndication

WEB 12.2

1994	Dr Lonnie Bristow first African-American president of American Medical Association (AMA)
2001–2005	Colin Powell first African-American US secretary of state
2007	African-Americans CEOs/CFOs at several major corporations including American Express, McDonald's USA, Aetna, Time Warner, Sears, Boeing, Xerox, Merrill Lynch
2007	Tony Dungy first African-American to coach winning NFL Super Bowl team (Indianapolis Colts defeated Chicago Bears)
November 4, 2008	Barack Obama elected the forty-fourth president of US, first African-American to hold the office; he won over 50 percent of the popular vote and several states that had voted Republican in the past

RACIAL OTHERNESS

THE COLOR LINE

William Du Bois, a Harvard-trained black sociologist, writer, and political activist, is widely recognized as "the prime inspirer, philosopher, and father of the Negro protest movement," and among the most influential pioneers in black sociology (Marable 1986: 214–215). In 1903, Du Bois wrote:

> The problem of the twentieth century is the problem of the color-line, – the relation of the darker to the lighter races of men in Asia and Africa, in America and the islands of the sea ... the question of Negro slavery was the real cause of the [US Civil War] conflict ... No sooner had Northern armies touched Southern soil than this old question, newly guised, sprung from the earth, – What shall be done with negroes? (Du Bois 1903/1969: 54–55)

🖳 WEB 12.1

Over one hundred years later, the color lines of race and racism still matter in determining social and economic status, political opportunity, and everyday experiences. Colonialism has ended; laws mandating race-segregation in schools, neighborhoods, cafeterias, hotels, and swimming pools have disappeared; the most persistent form of apartheid ended in South Africa in 1994; and currently in the US, for example, black men and women are among those individuals who have achieved the highest levels of success in government, law, business, academia, literature, television, sports, and music (see Timeline 12.1).

What then is the color-line problem? It is the persistence of racism in the everyday lived experiences of non-whites as they go about finding a job, securing a promotion, getting a bank loan, hailing a cab, hanging out with friends on the street, driving on the highway.[1] In the US, for example, being black restricts individuals' life-chances and their life outcomes: whether searching for a nanny or a supermarket, walking the fashion runway, or among football coaches, lawyers, and corporate executives, being black is in many instances an impediment to success. Alternatively, whites belong to the preferred, the privileged, and the protected race, and anyone who is not white, and especially black, can expect harassment, intimidation, and discrimination for no other apparent reason than the perceived color of their skin. This is the "color-coding" society in which we live (Anderson 1990). Its color-coding presuppositions work – as documented by the sociologist Elijah Anderson (1990; 1999a; 2003), a major ethnographer of black urban neighborhoods – to make the "anonymous black male," in particular, the object of police surveillance, associating black and male with criminality (1990: 190). This is an everyday reality illuminated in the movie *Boyz N The Hood*.

BIOGRAPHICAL NOTE

William Edward Burghardt Du Bois was born in Great Barrington, Western Massachusetts, in 1868. Though he was admitted to Harvard University, he could not afford to pay for his education there and, instead, with funding from local white community leaders in Great Barrington, went to Fisk University in Nashville, Tennessee, for his undergraduate education. During the summers at Fisk, he traveled throughout rural Tennessee teaching summer school and getting to know the everyday details of life for rural black southerners. Du Bois subsequently studied at Harvard, where he received a second BA, and an MA and a PhD in history. While at Harvard, he was awarded a fellowship to study in Berlin, Germany, for two years. After completing his PhD, Du Bois spent the bulk of his academic career as professor of sociology at Atlanta University. He was a

prolific book-writer and magazine editor, and, among his many political activities, was a founding member and highly involved in the activities of the National Association for the Advancement of Colored People (NAACP), and in other race-based groups. In 1945, Du Bois was a consultant to the US delegation at the founding of the United Nations. An avowed socialist, Du Bois made frequent visits to the Soviet Union and to other countries. He died in Ghana in 1963, at the age of 95 (Marable 1986: 219–222). Du Bois's biographer, the sociologist Manning Marable, has stated: "Few intellectuals have done more to shape the twentieth century than W. E. B. Du Bois. Only Frederick Douglas and Martin Luther King, Jr., equaled Du Bois's role in the social movement for civil rights in the United States" (1986: viii).

Although there is no one overarching sociological theory of race and racism, the writings of Du Bois and of several contemporary scholars variously employ Marxist-inspired, and to a lesser extent Weberian and other, conceptualizations of societal processes to address the historical, economic, social, and cultural dimensions of race and racism. We have already discussed Patricia Hill Collins's (1990; 2004) analysis of the intersectionality of race and gender (cf. chapter 10). This chapter introduces the key ideas of some additional core scholars writing on race and racism; some of these are sociologists while others have an intellectual background in the humanities, and are associated with post-colonial theory, a term used to refer to the writings of various scholars (e.g., Said 1978; Fanon 1967; Gilroy 1987; Bhabha 1994; Hall 1990) who critique the legacy of western imperialism for previously colonized cultures and countries.

The idea of Otherness, and specifically of racial Otherness, of racial difference, was given prominence by the Palestine-born, American literary and post-colonial theorist Edward Said (pronounced *Sai-eed*). His writings on literature, culture, and imperialism elaborated arguments infused with theoretical strands from Karl Marx and Michel Foucault. In his book *Orientalism* (1978), Said argues that the Orient, the East (e.g., the Middle East, Turkey), is not simply a geographically defined category of place, but an *idea*, a form of representation, of imagining and accentuating cultural difference. Drawing on examples from European literature and art, Said argues that westerners/Europeans imagine the Orient as an exotic and strange place, and describe and relate to it in stereotypical and mythical ways. These ideas/images (imaginings) serve to accentuate and reinforce the Orient's difference from the West, a difference that derives from and legitimates the West's colonization and rule over the East. Thus Said argues, following Foucault (cf. chapter 11), that language, discourse, the categories of the Orient and the Occident, are not innocent words on a page but are produced by and imbued with power. The West represents the Orient not only as different from, but as *inferior* to, the West. In parallel fashion to how sociologists (and the World Bank) distinguish between developed ("first world") and developing ("third world") countries (cf. chapter 6), all distinctions, Said argues, are relative, not absolute; they are entwined with particular relational histories and politics: "As much as the West itself, the Orient is an idea that has a history and a tradition of thought, imagery, and vocabulary that has given it reality and presence in and for the West. The two geographical entities thus support and to an extent reflect each other" (Said 1978: 5).

Said argues that the relationship between the West and the East is a relationship of power and domination. This relationship is rooted in their shared history, and in what Marx (cf. chapter 1) would identify as the lived material realities of the colonizer and the colonized in their relations with one another. As Said emphasizes, the Orient is not just geographically "adjacent to Europe; it is also the place of Europe's greatest and richest and oldest colonies" (1978: 1). This history has political and cultural consequences and means, for example, that "ideas, cultures and histories cannot be seriously understood or studied without ... their configurations of power ... also being studied" (ibid.: 5). Central to this relationship is the West's casting of the East as Other (different, inferior); its invocation and reinforcement of an Otherness that reproduces the cultural superiority of the West and its attendant political power to colonize (literally and metaphorically) the East. Thus the notion of Orientalism is not simply an idea or a geographical place; it is "a cultural and political fact" (1978: 13).

Otherness, therefore, is not simply a benign way to acknowledge difference but a political and cultural representation (1978: 26–28) that reifies and ultimately denigrates differences, such that what is defined as Other can be suppressed by those who are not-Other, i.e., the West vis-à-vis the East, whites vis-à-vis Arabs, whites vis-à-vis blacks, and importantly too, same-race ethnic groups vis-à-vis each other (e.g., English versus Irish; Northern Italians versus Sicilians). In short, all racial (and ethnic) categories and representations make sense only in terms of the political and cultural histories (e.g., colonialism, colonial-type domination, slavery) which have produced particular kinds of Otherness, of difference.

THE PHENOMENOLOGY OF BLACKNESS

The phenomenological reality of Otherness, how the everyday/everynight, here-and-now reality (cf. chapter 9) is different for racially different individuals, is eloquently voiced by **Frantz Fanon**, a Caribbean-born writer and medical doctor. As Fanon phrases it, "the fact of blackness" (1967: 109) overrides all the other attributes of a person (or a neighborhood or a country). The fact of blackness is imbued with Otherness and, as with all who are categorized as Other (Latinos, Jews, Arabs, Muslims, Indians, etc.), the fact of Otherness is invariably experienced as a "battered down" identity (Fanon 1967: 112). In the overarching stigma system that race is, if "the normals" in Goffman's terms are white, then blacks and other non-whites are "less than human" (cf. chapter 8). Their otherness is not simply a matter of difference but of inferiority, an inferiority that is collectively imposed (by whites) and collectively felt (by blacks and other non-whites) in subtle and not so subtle ways everyday.

BIOGRAPHICAL NOTE

Frantz Fanon was born in 1925 in Martinique, a Caribbean island colonized and still controlled by France. During World War II, he left Martinique and enlisted in the army with the Free French Forces (following the fall of France to the Nazis in 1940). After the war, he returned to Martinique, where he received his undergraduate degree, and then moved to France, where he studied medicine and psychiatry. Soon thereafter, he moved to Algeria (a French colony) and was living and working there during the Algerian War of Independence (1956–1962) against France. Fanon traveled extensively in Algeria and through other countries in Africa and, as in Martinique, he observed first-hand the impact of colonialism on subjugated individuals' everyday lives. His writings have had a critical impact in establishing colonialism/post-colonialism as a legitimate area of cultural and social scientific inquiry. Fanon was being treated for leukemia in the US in 1961 when he died; in recognition of his efforts on behalf of the colonized, his body lay in state in Tunisia prior to its burial in Algiers.

Fanon recounts his experience of blackness while working as a medical doctor in the then French-controlled colony of Algeria in the 1940s and 1950s:

The white world, the only honorable one, barred me from all participation. A man was expected to behave like a man. I was expected to behave like a black man – or at least like a nigger. I shouted a greeting to the world and the world slashed away my joy. I was told to stay within bounds, to go back where I belonged ... My blackness was there, dark and unarguable. And it tormented me, pursued me, disturbed me, angered me. Negroes are savages, brutes, illiterates. But in my own case I knew that these statements were false ... We [blacks] had physicians, professors, statesmen. Yes, but something out of the ordinary still clung to such cases ... It was always the Negro teacher, the Negro doctor; brittle as I was becoming, I shivered at the slightest pretext. I knew, for instance, that if the physician made a mistake it would be the end of him and of all those who came after him. What could one expect, after all, from a Negro physician? ... The black physician can never be sure how close he is to disgrace. I tell you, I was walled in: No exception was made for my refined manners, or my knowledge of literature, or my understanding of the quantum theory. I requested, I demanded explanations. Gently, in the tone that one uses with a child, they introduced me to the existence of a certain view that was held by certain people, but I was always told "We must hope that it will very soon disappear." What was it? Color prejudice ... It was hate; I was hated, despised, detested, not by the neighbor across the street ... but by an entire race. (Fanon 1967: 114–115, 117–118)

SOCIAL CHANGE, RACE, AND RACISM

The world has changed much since Fanon's time. A long history of black activism in advancing racial equality (e.g., Gilmore 2008), has helped ensure the increased incorporation of blacks and other minorities into politics, business, academia, the professions (e.g., Anderson 1999b), and other previously discriminatory social institutions (e.g., schools, colleges, mass media). Additionally, since the 1960s, due to the impact of the civil rights movement, blacks have come to affirm and celebrate their group identity. Black identity politics entails blacks' collective recovering and remembering of a shared history (of oppression), and their simultaneous pursuit of policies implementing black equality. This translates into a political agenda that compels white society to institutionalize laws and public policies that affirm blacks' social, political, and economic equality with whites, while simultaneously acknowledging blacks' history of difference. Thus today, blacks are, by and large, no longer the socially invisible "nobodies" eloquently rendered by Ralph Ellison (1947) in *Invisible Man*.

WEB 12.2

WEB 12.3

The tension that exists between a collectively shared (biological) race and racial history, and the shared political goal of racial equality, was highlighted in 2008 by the presidential candidacy of the then Senator Barack Obama. Obama's mixed racial background – a white Kansas mother, a black Kenyan father, and a childhood upbringing in Indonesia – and his elite educational credentials (e.g., Harvard law graduate) and demeanor, prompted some blacks to question whether he is "really" black, even as they welcomed his candidacy as illustrative of the achieved equality of "blacks." In addition to Obama's "racially diluted" genetic-biological inheritance, his biography does not include the narrative of discrimination and oppression that, for many, defines what it means to be (biologically and culturally) black. Nevertheless, Obama's candidacy (and his subsequent historic victory) opened up public debate on race, on the particular color lines we still draw today, and on what it means to be of mixed-race identity – all complex issues.

NEWS 12.3

The various political and cultural tensions that accompany the institutionalization of racial equality point to the sociological complexity entailed in the understanding of race and of racism. Though the color line certainly continues to exist today and to matter in everyday life, there are many nuances and ambiguities in how, and where, that line is drawn, and in how its meanings vary across different contexts. The black legal scholar and civil rights activist Lani Guinier elaborates on the multidimensionality of race. She emphasizes that

> Race is many things, not just a single thing. It can be stigmatizing, but it can also be liberating. If we think in categories, and think about race only as if it were a single category, we conflate many different spheres of racial meaning. We fail to specify if we mean biological race, political race, historical race, or cultural race. (Guinier and Torres 2002: 4)

Because of all of the changes in the status of blacks since World War II (e.g., the civil rights movement in the US; the ending of apartheid in South Africa; the recent movement toward ending affirmative action policies in the US), there is a strong tendency (largely, though not exclusively, among whites) to think that the task of achieving racial equality is no longer pressing. The sociologist Howard Winant notes: "There is a prominent, indeed growing tendency to consider this task as largely accomplished: to operate, in other words, as if racial oppression had already been largely overcome, as if the errors of white supremacy had already been corrected" (2001: 8).

Winant (and many other scholars and activists) argue, however, that in the post-1960s, post-colonial world, race and racism have not disappeared – their meanings have changed (2001: 307). As the influential race theorist and sociologist **Paul Gilroy** (1987: 110), emphasizes, "Racism does not ... move tidily and unchanged through history. It assumes new forms and articulates new antagonisms in different situations." Thus, Robert Blauner (2001: 195), a noted sociologist of race, argues "there are two languages of race in America." What he means by this is that blacks and whites have different interpretations of social change and different understandings of whether and how race matters in everyday social reality.

BIOGRAPHICAL NOTE

Paul Gilroy was born in London, England, in 1956 to a Guyanese father and English mother. He received his BA from Sussex University and his PhD from Birmingham University, where he studied with Stuart Hall at the Centre for Contemporary Cultural Studies. Gilroy spent the early part of his academic career on the faculty at various English universities, and in 2000, he was awarded an endowed professorship at Yale University in sociology and African American studies. He returned to England in 2005 as the first holder of the Anthony Giddens Professorship in Social Theory at the London School of Economics.

What exactly, then, do sociologists mean when they invoke such complex terms as "race" and "racism"? Race, Winant argues, is "a concept that signifies and symbolizes sociopolitical conflicts and interests in reference to different types of human bodies" (2001: 317). When sociologists talk of race, then, they tend to focus on yet another analytically separate but intertwined dimension of the systematic patterning of social inequality, stratification, and conflict. And, although we see the fact of someone's blackness as and through body color, what we do with blackness (and with any body color) – how we use it to differentiate and regulate what particular types of bodies can and cannot do in society – is not a predetermined biological outcome, but the product of particular societies making particular decisions about body color at particular historical moments, decisions that come to encrust themselves upon our culture and social institutions. As such, racial inequality – the fact of blackness, for example (Fanon 1967) – is not just something that is subjectively experienced by any given individual, but something that gets objectively structured into social institutions and everyday culture. Race, therefore, and racial categorization, are an engine of, and mechanism reproducing, inequality, whether we focus, following Marx (cf. chapter 1), on economic relations, or more broadly, following Weber (cf. chapter 3), on economic inequality, social status, and cultural worldviews.

Therefore, although race "appeals to biologically based human [physical] characteristics ... selection of these particular human features for purposes of racial signification is always and necessarily a social and historical process" (Winant 2001: 317). As categories of gender and sexuality are used to impose, legitimate, and reproduce distinctions that appear to be determined by biological characteristics but which are, in fact, distinctions used as a veil for maintaining the power of one group at the expense of another, so too is race. And racism parallels sexism in the multiple and multilayered ways in which a society's institutional practices and everyday language and attitudes signify that one group (blacks, women) is inferior to another (whites, men).

Although the word "racism" only came into public use in the 1960s (Blauner 2001: 196), the "ideas and practices it denotes" have been part of the modern era for centuries. (Winant 2001: 317). Winant acknowledges that what is entailed in racism is complex. Nonetheless, he argues that it can "be provisionally defined as inhering in one or more of the following: 1. signifying practice that essentializes or naturalizes human identities based on racial categories or concepts; 2. social action that produces unjust allocation of socially valued resources, based on such significations; 3. social structure that reproduces such allocations" (2001: 316).

Or, in more specific, everyday cultural terms, Gilroy explains:

The idea that blacks comprise a problem, or more accurately, a series of problems, is today expressed at the core of racist reasoning. It is closely related to a second idea which is equally pernicious, just as popular and again integral to racial meanings. This defines blacks as forever victims, objects rather than subjects, beings that feel yet lack the ability to think, and remain incapable of considered behavior in an active mode. The oscillation between black as problem and black as victim has become today the principal mechanism though which "race" is pushed outside of history and into the realm of natural inevitable events [e.g., blacks' high rates of non-marital births]. This capacity to evacuate any historical dimension to black life remains a fundamental achievement of racist ideologies ... Seeing racism in this way, as something peripheral, marginal to the essential patterns of social and political life can, in its worst manifestations, simply endorse the view of blacks as an external problem, an alien presence visited on Britain [or some other colonizing country] from the outside ... Racism rests on the ability to contain blacks in the present, to repress and to deny the past. (1987: 11–12)

CONSTRUING WHITENESS

Several sociologists argue that any theorizing about race must also include attention to the construal of whiteness. This is because both "white people and people of color live racially structured lives" (Frankenberg 1993: 1); thus scholars engaged in "whiteness studies" remind us that white people are "colored white" (Roediger 2002: 15–16). Accordingly, the sociology of race (and of ethnicity) is not just about the experiences of blacks or other minority racial (or ethnic) groups, but also requires attention to whites and their relation to non-whites. Ruth Frankenberg (1993: 1) explains that "whiteness is [first] a location of structural advantage, of race privilege. Second, it is a 'standpoint,' a place from which white people look at ourselves, at others and society. Third, whiteness refers to a set of cultural practices that are usually unmarked and unnamed." These practices include for example, the taken-for-granted presumption that whites hire black nannies, not the inverse; and that whiteness is what pervades fashion, mass media, and religious images, e.g., representations of Jesus Christ (e.g., Roediger 2002: 27–43).

NEWS 12.1

The task for the sociologist, then, is to problematize the taken-for-grantedness of whiteness, to investigate how its meanings change in different social-historical eras and contexts (e.g., Roediger 1991; 2005; Jacobson 2006), and to probe how whiteness matters in determining white people's everyday lives and their race consciousness (Frankenberg 1993: 18). David Roediger, using a Marxist-inspired and historical analysis, argues that in the US, whiteness became a sought-after identity for *white* working-class European immigrants (e.g., Irish, Italians) in Boston and other northern industrial cities in the nineteenth century (see also Williams 1990). Although considered "non-white" – because they were ethnically, culturally, and economically inferior to the capitalist class of (largely) English, Protestant origin – these low-wage workers affirmed their whiteness as a way to gain social status by differentiating themselves from (and as superior to) blacks. Fearing economic dependence (against the backdrop of a slave-owning society and the relations of black inferiority it created), the white working class constructed blacks (and not the white capitalist class) as Other, as a racially inferior out-group, thus sowing the seeds of the long (and continuing), complex history of racial prejudice among working-class whites (e.g., McDermott 2006).

Although there are many forms of persistent inequality in society, racial inequality carries an intensely symbolic and emotion-laden burden. This is largely because of the specifically racial history of slavery. Its profound and multifaceted legacy – especially for African-Americans – continues to resonate in social relations today, as underscored by the persistence of the noose as a symbol of hatred and violence against blacks. World slavery institutionalized whites and Arabs as masters, and blacks as slaves (e.g., Patterson 1982). And as Winant argues, the modern world-system (elaborated by Wallerstein; cf. chapter 15), the development and expansion of capitalism, cannot be understood without taking full account of the centrality of race "as *both* cause and effect" in its origins and development (Winant 2001: 20). Slavery, Winant argues, the coerced "chattelization" of others, was central to capitalist expansion (ibid.: 294). The trade in slaves, slaves' labor power, and the commodities the slaves produced provided the core resources of a geographically and economically expanding industrial capitalism (ibid.: 25).

NEWS 12.2
WEB 12.1

Slavery's impact in the racial formation of society is thus at the heart of the intermeshing of history, economics, and culture that defines the modern world. Winant forcefully makes the case that any analysis of society must apprehend the historical and continuing significance of race:

> Race has been fundamental in global politics and culture for half a millennium. It continues to signify and structure social life not only experientially and locally, but nationally and globally. Race is present everywhere: it is evident in the distribution of resources and power, and in the desires and fears of individuals from Alberta to Zimbabwe. Race has shaped the modern economy and nation-state. It has permeated all available social identities, cultural forms, and systems of signification. Infinitely incarnated in institutions and personality, etched on the human body, racial phenomena affect the thought, experience, and accomplishments of human individuals and collectivities in many familiar ways, and in a host of unconscious patterns as well ... Race must be grasped as a fundamental condition of individual and collective identity, a permanent, although tremendously flexible, dimension of the modern global social structure. (2001: 1)

CULTURAL HISTORIES AND POST-COLONIAL IDENTITIES

Several scholars emphasize (e.g., Bhabha 1994; Gilroy 1987; Guinier and Torres 2002; Hall 1992, Roediger 2002; Winant 2001) that the construct of race is flexible in that racial categories and their meanings change over time and across different socio-historical contexts. Large-scale social forces, such as colonialism, immigration, post-colonialism, and globalization, invariably impact the societal and cultural context in which race is defined and lived out by particular racial groups vis-à-vis one another, amidst relations and representations of domination and subordination. In this view, racial and ethnic identity (like other forms of identity) is dynamic, and is especially contingent on the varied and multifaceted pre-colonial, colonial, and post-colonial histories of specific racial/ethnic groups. As **Stuart Hall**, a highly influential race and cultural theorist argues:

> Cultural identity ... is a matter of "becoming" as well as of "being." It belongs to the future as much as to the past. It is not something that already exists, transcending place, time, history and culture. Cultural identities come from somewhere, have histories. But, like everything which is historical, they undergo constant transformation. Far from being eternally fixed in some essentialised past, they are subject to the continuous "play" of history, culture and power ... identities are the names we give to the different ways we are positioned by, and position ourselves within, the narratives of the past. (1990: 225)

BIOGRAPHICAL NOTE

Stuart Hall was born in Kingston, Jamaica, in 1932 and moved to England in 1951. He was a Rhodes Scholar at Oxford University, from where he received his MA. He was among the pioneers of cultural studies and in the mid-1960s joined Birmingham University's highly influential Centre for Contemporary Cultural Studies (CCCS), which he subsequently directed. He conducted several analyses of the mass media, his research demonstrating the active interpretive cultural work that audiences do. After many years at the CCCS, Hall was appointed in 1979 as professor of sociology at the Open University in London. Currently retired, he continues to write extensively and is a frequent commentator in the British media on culture and politics.

The "traumatic character" of slavery and of colonialism for black people and black experiences can only begin to be understood, Hall argues, by recognizing how different subordinated groups internalize a particularized identity of themselves. The cultural particularity among blacks emerges out of the ongoing interaction between, on the one hand their varied pre-colonial histories of difference – i.e., slaves came from different villages, different tribal communities, different countries, different cultures, etc., and hence did not have a shared pre-colonial history or cultural background – and, on the other hand and at the same time, the similarity of the context of their colonization and treatment by the colonizers, such as the British (Hall 1990: 225–228).

This interplay between cultural differences and similarities, between discontinuities and continuities, thus underscores the difficulty of talking about *the* colonial experience or about *the* post-colonial experience as if there were just one, or as if there were one that similarly defined the experiences of all subordinated racial-ethnic groups. Hall alerts us that these cultural differences (and similarities) are not simply between blacks of African compared to Caribbean descent; rather, within the Caribbean, for example, Jamaicans differ from Martinicans (1990: 227). Similarly, the post-colonial theorist Homi Bhabha (1994) argues that representations of Orientalism, such as Said's (1978) critique (see p. 375 above), ignore the various ambiguities and contradictions with which western literature imagines the colonial subject (e.g., as both docile and aggressive). In parallel fashion, black feminist scholars (e.g., Collins 1990) make the point that sociological understanding is severely limited when discussion of "women's experience" does not take account of how racial, ethnic, and other intersecting differences complicate any and all generalization about gender (cf. chapter 10).

In any case, the end of colonialism does not mean the end of colonial ties and relationships, as underscored by immigrant population flows especially from the (previously) colonized to the colonizing society. Thus, for example, England since the 1950s has become a visibly multicultural society, one in which whole communities of ethnic Jamaicans, Indians, Egyptians, and other groups have settled (seeking economic opportunity) and in the trans-generational process have become part of the cultural fabric of English society. Today, therefore, "being Black and British," as Hall (1990) argues, is a new cultural identity, one crafted out of the post-colonial diaspora.

Being black and British changes not just what it means to be black, but also what it means to be British. Black is no longer necessarily an identity of "Otherness" – an otherness defined against and marginalized by white British colonial power – but one which is constitutive of the past and the present British societal history and collective identity. In this reading, therefore, British identity can no longer be assumed to signify whiteness. What was previously unthinkable – being black *and* British – is now a de facto post-colonial reality, and one that must be incorporated into the imagining of what it means to be part of the British nation/culture. The difficulty in fully realizing this new identity, however, is highlighted by Paul Gilroy (1987), whose historically grounded reminder that "there ain't no black in the Union Jack" (the title of one of his books), cautions us, like Du Bois, that color lines and symbolic and material histories do not disappear with the formal end of colonialism (or of slavery).

SLAVERY AS SOCIAL DOMINATION, SOCIAL DEATH

While appreciating the diversity that characterizes black experiences and black identities, it is still possible nevertheless to talk in general analytical terms about the social fact of slavery and its generalized impact on black experience(s) broadly defined. Orlando Patterson (1982) has argued that slavery must be understood – in the conceptual language of Karl Marx (cf. chapter 1) – as a relation of domination, and more specifically as an extreme instance of such relations. Based on his comparative-historical analysis of the nature of slavery across many different types of societies (including the US, Europe, Asia, the West Indies, and Arab countries), Patterson underscores the distinct centrality of *coercion* in the master–slave relationship and the heavy social-psychological and cultural costs that slavery imposed on slaves. In Patterson's analysis, slavery, in essence, is a form of "social death." He explains:

> Slavery is one of the most extreme forms of the relation of domination, approaching the limits of total power from the viewpoint of the master, and of total powerlessness from the viewpoint of the slave. Yet, it differs from other forms of extreme domination in very

special ways ... It is unusual ... both in the extremity of power involved ... and in the qualities of coercion that brought the relation into being and sustained it ... In his powerlessness the slave became an extension of his master's power ... Perhaps the most distinctive attribute of the slave's powerlessness is that it always originated ... as a substitute for death, usually violent death ... The condition of slavery did not absolve or erase the prospect of death. Slavery was not a pardon; it was, peculiarly, a conditional commutation. The execution was suspended only as long as the slave acquiesced in his powerlessness. The master was essentially a ransomer. What he bought or acquired was the slave's life, and restraints on the master's capacity wantonly to destroy his slave did not undermine his claim on that life. Because the slave had no socially recognized existence outside of his master, he became a social nonperson. (1982: 1, 2, 4–5)

Additionally, Patterson argues, the slave was denied all ties to his family and blood relatives, and to his cultural ancestry; he was dispossessed of his "community of memory," cut off from any meaningful understanding of his historical, social, and cultural genealogy. As such, the slave's dishonoring, the "absence of any independent social existence" apart from his ties to his owner and master, the fact that "he had no name of his own to defend," also had severe emotional and psychological consequences for slaves. Their social and cultural dishonoring, their loss of a social identity, Patterson argues, contributed to producing the slave's "servile personality," the "crushing and pervasive sense of knowing that one is considered a person without honor and that there simply is nothing that can be done about it" (1982: 10–12).

Patterson acknowledges that slaves had informal social relations with one another – something that Emile Durkheim would likely emphasize (cf. chapter 2) and would likely see as functional to maintaining slaves' shared sense of community notwithstanding the objective conditions of their daily lives. But Patterson, using a Marxist framing, underscores that in terms of the societal power structure, the slaves' social relations were denied legitimacy; the only legitimacy given the slaves' lives was that which they did in servitude for their master. Thus slaves' sexual and parenting relationships were not socially recognized (i.e., not recognized in law as marriages or as families; Patterson 1982: 6). Similarly, Patterson acknowledges that slaves had a past, had a history (1982: 5), but, he maintains, the conditions of their enslavement did not allow them to process and integrate this past as we, for example, would do in telling our family story, the narrative of our family heritage. In all of these ways, therefore, slaves were considered social non-persons and treated as such; "The slave was the ultimate human tool, as imprintable and as disposable as the master wished" (1982: 7).

WILLIAM DU BOIS: SLAVERY AND RACIAL INEQUALITY IN THE US

In the US South, 90–95 percent of the black population at the end of the eighteenth and for much of the nineteenth century (1810–1860) was enslaved (Marable 1986: 483). The legacy of slavery for the collective identity of blacks, therefore, is one whose scars are not easily erased by the signing of legislation affirming the equality of blacks and whites. Rather, as several Marxist-inspired black scholars emphasize (e.g., Marable 1986; Patterson 1982), the experience of slavery produces an alienated consciousness in blacks. Du Bois called this a double-consciousness, meaning that blacks as ex-slaves must invariably see themselves through the eyes of the white master. In *The Souls of Black Folk*, one of his most renowned books, Du Bois elaborated:

> The Negro is ... born with a veil ... [one that] only lets him see himself through the revelation of the other world. It is a peculiar sensation, this double-consciousness, this sense of always looking at one's self through the eyes of others, of measuring one's soul by the tape of a world that looks on in amused contempt and pity. One ever feels his twoness, – an American, a Negro; two souls ... two unreconciled strivings; two warring ideals in one dark body ... The history of the American Negro is the history of this strife, – this longing to attain self-conscious manhood, to merge his double self into a better and truer self. In this merging he wishes neither of the older selves to be lost. He would not Africanize America, for America has too much to teach the world and Africa. He would not bleach his Negro soul in a flood of white Americanism, for he knows that Negro blood has a message for the world. He simply wishes to make it possible for a man to be both a Negro and an American, without being cursed and spit upon by his fellows, without having the doors of Opportunity closed roughly in his face. (1903/1969: 45–46)

Black men, Du Bois argues, were emasculated by slavery, by the violence of the Civil War conflict over its resolution, and by the economic terms and context of their freedom during Reconstruction (Du Bois 1903/1969: 62). As freed ex-slaves *some* blacks were able to take advantage of the relatively cheap parcels of land made available by the US War Department's Freedmen's Bureau (established in 1865) and the Southern Homestead Act (1866), and were thus able to acquire "40 acres and a mule" (e.g., Oubre 1978), early resources considered critical to the long-term economic success of some black families. Overall, however, as Du Bois argues, the legal emancipation of the slaves did not ensure their economic and social emancipation. Emancipation, rather, he argues, though welcomed by some in the South who felt "that the nightmare was at last over" (1934/2007: 549), was essentially followed by the economic and political enslavement of the freed slaves, whose new-found legal freedoms competed with the economic objectives of white landowners, white laborers, and white small farmers.

NEWS 12.4

Du Bois thus gives particular emphasis to the economic sources and consequences of racial inequality and – following a Marxian line of analysis – elaborates on the significance of slavery in the creation of capitalist profit through the exploitation of blacks (1934/2007: 9–11). Du Bois states:

> It must be remembered and never forgotten that the civil war in the South ... was a determined effort to reduce black labor as nearly as possible to a condition of unlimited exploitation and build a new class of capitalists on this foundation. The wage of the Negro worker despite the war amendments, was to be reduced to the level of bare subsistence by

taxation, peonage, caste, and every method of discrimination. This program had to be carried out in open defiance of the clear letter of the law. (Du Bois 1934/2007: 549; see also 1903/1969: 54–78)

Consequently, Du Bois argues, the economic exploitation of the freed slaves underscored the deep racial wedge of division between ex-slaves and their white ex-masters. Further, racial divisions were used by white capitalists to drive a competitive wedge between black and white laborers; white landowners encouraged white laborers to regard black laborers as obstacles impeding their chances for economic advancement – the white workers' "chance to become capitalists" (e.g., 1934/2007: 14–15). White racism, and the mechanisms in place to suppress ex-slaves' economic advancement (e.g., through low, subsistence wages), converged not only to undermine blacks' social and economic progress but, symbolically, to consolidate for whites the idea that blacks are racially inferior (1903/1969: 68).

TRANSFORMING RACIAL-SOCIAL INEQUALITY

President Barack Obama's electoral victory in 2008 was celebrated as a historical marker of racial equality in the US. It symbolized the possibility that being black and American would henceforth constitute a oneness of identity rather than the double-consciousness that Du Bois saw as the burden of African-Americans.

Although preoccupied with the slavery/post-slavery economic and social conditions of blacks, Du Bois's vision of social equality was not confined to the plight of blacks alone. He contended: "The emancipation of man is the emancipation of labor" (1934/2007: 11), and he envisaged a democracy in which "all labor, blacks as well as white, became free" (1934/2007: 9), free of capitalist exploitation. He argued that this vision was best realized through the creation of a socialist society, which, despite its many shortcomings, offered a more just alternative for blacks and for society in general, irrespective of race (Marable 1986). Therefore, while Du Bois was intellectually and emotionally engrossed in the problem of race, the color line, he believed that the inequalities produced by the color line were exacerbated by capitalism, namely, the use of racial differences to divide the working class and to suppress their realization that under capitalism, all wage-workers, regardless of race, are exploited and disposable.

It is interesting to know that Du Bois heard Max Weber lecture when Du Bois was studying in Berlin for two years (1892–1894) before completing his doctorate at Harvard, and actually met Weber during the latter's visit to the US in 1904 (Marable 1986: 63). Nevertheless, Du Bois's writings present a critique of capitalism that is much more closely aligned with Marx's than with Weber's, even though Du Bois too, like Weber, recognized the significance of religion and culture as autonomous engines of social life. Indeed, partly as a result of his appreciation for the ways in which non-economic institutions matter in structuring and anchoring individual life experiences, Du Bois was highly critical of all forms of racism – not just in economic and labor relations but in education, religion, culture, the arts. Nevertheless, he was especially critical of the racism embedded in the labor movement (1935/1996: 434–435), arguing, for example, that the American labor movement's own racism prevented it from recognizing capitalist exploitation of labor as a whole; its racism, Du Bois maintained, made it side with the "captains of industry who spend large sums of money to make laborers think that the most worthless white man is better than any colored man" (1935/1996: 434). In short, emphasizing the conjoint adverse effects of economic and racial inequality, he argued, "To be a poor man is hard, but to be a poor race in a land of dollars is the very bottom of hardships" (1903/1969: 49–50).

GENDER EQUALITY

Prophetic for his time, Du Bois also emphasized the intersectionality of inequality, namely the ways in which social class, race, and gender are intermixed in the reproduction of inequality (see, for example, Collins (1990) on the relevance of intersectionality today; cf. chapter 10). Thus as early as 1915, when the issue of women's suffrage was gaining momentum in the US, Du Bois argued:

> The statement that woman is weaker than men is sheer rot. It is the same sort of thing that we hear about "darker races" and "lower classes." Difference, either physical or spiritual, does not argue weakness or inferiority. That the average woman is spiritually different from the average man is undoubtedly just as true as the fact that the average white man differs from the average Negro; but this is no reason for disenfranchising the Negro or lynching him. It is inconceivable that any person looking upon the accomplishments of women today in every field of endeavor … could for a moment talk about a "weaker" sex … To say that men protect women with their votes is to overlook the testimony of the facts. In the first place, there are millions of women who have no natural men protectors: the unmarried, the widowed, the deserted and those who have married failures. To put this whole army out of court and leave them unprotected is more than unjust, it is a crime. … [Moreover] a woman is just as much a thinking, feeling, acting person after marriage as before. (1915/1996: 378)

Du Bois here expresses what appears as an essentialist view of gender differences, i.e., that there are natural (or innate "spiritual") differences between women and men. He is fully clear, however, that gender differences, whatever their source, are not legitimate grounds for discrimination. In his unequivocal view, women are not a sub-species, dependent on and inferior to men, but are autonomous human beings equal in capacity to men. Further, Du Bois was emphatic that democracy required equality for all discriminated groups, and hence the project of claiming equality for blacks entailed not just equality for black men, but for black and white women too. Thus: "The meaning of the twentieth century is the freeing of the individual soul; the soul longest in slavery and still in the most disgusting and indefensible slavery is the soul of womanhood" (1915/1996: 379).

RACE AND CLASS

THE BLACK MIDDLE CLASS

Increasingly today, sociologists in the US talk about the black middle class (e.g., Pattillo-McCoy 1999; Pattillo 2005). The black middle class, however, is not a new phenomenon. In the mid-1950s, E. Franklin Frazier, a highly influential black sociologist and president of the American Sociological Association (in 1948), wrote about what he termed "the new Negro middle class" (1955/1968: 256–266), comprised primarily of those working in white-collar professional and supervisory occupations. Frazier noted that

> The changes which occurred in the economic and social organization of the United States as the result of two world wars brought into existence a new middle class group among Negroes. The primary cause of this new development was the urbanization of the Negro population on a large scale. Prior to World War I about nine-tenths of the Negro population was in the South, and less than 25 per cent of Southern Negroes lived in cities ... The migration to Northern cities was especially crucial since it created large Negro communities in an area that was relatively free from the legal and customary discriminations under which Negroes live in the South. (Frazier 1955/1968: 258)

The effects of this migration, Frazier argued, were to expand the educational, occupational, and political opportunities for blacks, changes that intertwined to lay the economic and cultural basis of the new black middle class (ibid.).

But despite the emergence of a flourishing black middle class, Frazier was very critical of what he observed to be its anti-intellectualism, its disavowal of its religious and other traditions, and its ostentatious search for social status. Frazier argued that the cultural characteristics of the black middle class he described stemmed from and reflected the racial divide, the chasm that existed between the black and the white middle classes. This divide, Frazier argued, led the black middle class to reject its own history and collective pride in that history, while seeking acceptance from its economic peers in the white middle class, an acceptance that had not been forthcoming. Consequently, the black middle class occupied a nether-land, cut off from their racial roots and with unrealized cultural aspirations. Frazier elaborates:

During its rise to its present position, the [black] middle class has broken with its traditional background and identification with the Negro masses. Rejecting everything that would identify it with the Negro masses and at the same time not being accepted by white American society, the [black] middle class has acquired an inferiority complex that is reflected in every aspect of its life ... The middle-class Negro shows the mark of oppression more than the lower class Negro who finds a shelter from the contempt of the white world in his [traditions] ... and in his freedom from a gnawing desire to be recognized and accepted. Although the middle-class Negro has tried to reject his traditional background and racial identification, he cannot escape from it. Therefore, many middle-class Negroes have developed self-hatred. They hate themselves because they cannot escape from being identified as Negroes. (1955/1968: 263, 265)

THE BLACK CLASS DIVIDE

By contrast with the racial divide that separated the black middle class from their white middle-class peers in the 1950s and 1960s, many sociologists writing today argue that, in the US, race has declined in significance relative to class. William Julius Wilson, the foremost sociologist of race and class inequality, argues that the contemporary black class structure makes it "increasingly difficult to speak of a single or uniform black experience" (1978: 144). In his book *The Declining Significance of Race*, Wilson argues that as a result of economic and policy changes since the 1970s, and of the shifts that have occurred in economic and occupational mobility patterns, "class has become more important than race in determining black life-chances in the modern industrial period" (1978: 150). He elaborates:

The recent mobility patterns of blacks lend strong support to the view that economic class is clearly more important than race in predetermining job placement and occupational mobility. In the economic realm, then, the black experience has moved historically from economic racial oppression experienced by virtually all blacks to economic subordination for the **black underclass** ... a deepening economic schism seems to be developing in the black community, with the black poor falling further and further behind middle- and upper-income blacks. (1978: 152)

Wilson thus draws attention to the ever-growing economic divide among blacks, the economic stratification within the so-called *black community* – a term which suggests unity rather than divisions, and which through its use both essentializes blacks (as if they are a homogeneous group) and papers over the real economic divisions among blacks that Wilson and other sociologists document. Wilson argues, moreover, that racial strife today has more to do with socio-political issues than with economic opportunities per se. Race continues to matter a lot in regard to decisions about the public funding of schools and municipal services, for example, but has significantly less importance in determining access to jobs and economic competition and conflict in general (1978: 152).

Wilson is not arguing that racial problems derive from more fundamental economic class problems (1978: ix) inherent in the capitalist structure, as a

Marxist-derived analysis might claim. He argues, instead, that it is "the inter-section of class with race" that is crucial (1978: ix). Therefore, notwithstanding income differences between blacks and whites in a particular occupation or economic sector, and notwithstanding evidence of barriers against blacks in particular elite occupational settings (e.g., NFL coaches, fashion models, corporate CEOs), in the economic sphere overall, Wilson argues, "class has become more important than race in determining black access to privilege and power" (ibid.: 2).

Further, Wilson maintains that the economic stagnation of the black underclass has more to do with changes in the structure of the economy (e.g., the decline of manufacturing and service jobs in city neighborhoods as a result of globalization) than with racial discrimination per se (1978: 1–2). In other words, the economic barriers encountered by the black underclass today, unlike in the past when there were (race-based) barriers against virtually all blacks, "have racial significance only in their consequences, not in their origins" (ibid.: 2). Of particular consequence, the rising strength of the black middle class means that the gap in income and associated life-chances – of securing a college education, living in a safe neighborhood, having a stable family household, extending one's mortality – between rich and poor blacks is growing, and, by extension, driving a cultural wedge between blacks, just as socio-economic differences have long been a source of cultural division among whites.

At the same time, however, notwithstanding the gains made by the black middle class, their lives still differ from those of white middle-class Americans. Mary Pattillo (2005) underscores the continuing racial divisions in lived experience among the middle class and the continuing need for affirmative action policies that recognize these differences. Using US Census data on race and neighborhood patterns, Pattillo argues that:

> Although more advantaged than poor blacks, middle-class blacks live [in neighborhoods] with more crime, more poverty, more unemployment, fewer college graduates, more vacant housing and more single-parent families than similar whites, and indeed than much poorer whites. Moving to the suburbs makes residential life a little more comfortable, but it does not erase the racial disadvantage. These disparities alone underscore the continuing need for affirmative action, for ignoring the importance of race would have college admissions officers, for example, assume that a middle-class black student has it better than a working-class white student. (2005: 323)

RACE, COMMUNITY, AND DEMOCRACY

The early emphasis of Du Bois on the democratic imperative of equality for all blacks and all disadvantaged groups (see pp. 386–388) continues to characterize the writings of many contemporary black scholars. As Manning Marable points out "The greatest casualty of racism is democracy. Afro-Americans have understood this for many decades, and their leaders have attempted to redefine the American political system for the benefit of all citizens, regardless of race, gender, and social class" (Marable 1986: 1). Cornel West, one of the best-known sociologists and public commentators on race and racism in the US, argues that any discussion of race must begin with an analysis of the structural and cultural conditions which perpetuate racial inequality: "We must begin not with the problems of black people but with the flaws of American society – flaws rooted in historic inequalities and longstanding cultural stereotypes" (1993: 3). Blacks, he maintains, are the "them" in society who must fit in with "us" – with white America. Yet white America, West argues, resists "fully accepting the humanity of blacks" (ibid.).

The price that blacks pay for their marginality in and to white society, West contends, is nihilism. He chooses the word "nihilism" not to denote some abstract, existential, philosophical sense of loss but to underscore "the murky waters of despair and dread that ... flood the streets of black America" (West 1993: 12), the bleakness, fear, and meaninglessness that characterize blacks' everyday lived realities. He argues that the nihilistic threat to the very *existence* of the black community does not just come from economic deprivation and political powerlessness but so penetrates the vision and feelings of blacks that it constitutes a sort of collective psychological angst or depression (ibid.: 12–13). Nihilism, he states, is to be understood as *"the lived experience of coping with a life of horrifying meaninglessness, hopelessness, and (most important) lovelessness"* (ibid.: 14).

West acknowledges that nihilism is not new in black America. What is new is that, unlike in the past when blacks had strong religious and civic institutions that provided strong familial and communal buffers against hopelessness and despair (West 1993: 15) – as Du Bois and other early black sociologists such as E. Franklin Frazier (1949) discussed – in current times, this "cultural armor" has been eroded. It has been eroded, West argues, especially by the ever-greater impingement of market forces on daily life. Echoing a Marx–Weber–Frankfurt School critique, he argues that the economic rationality of the market dominates an ever-widening band of decisions that impact the public good as a whole and the well-being of black communities in particular. As is well documented, black families and communities confront the array of problems attendant on the downsizing and elimination of jobs in their neighborhoods, and the everyday deprivation this causes is further exacerbated by the under-funding of schools, hospitals, and clinics, and even the elimination of supermarkets, in urban neighborhoods.

NEWS 12.5

SCARRING OF BLACK AMERICA

West highlights the social-psychological scarring caused by the economic and cultural battering of blacks and black identity. He states:

> This *angst* resembles a kind of collective clinical depression in significant pockets of black America. The eclipse of hope and collapse of meaning in much of black America is linked to the structural dynamics of corporate market institutions that affect all Americans. Under these circumstances black existential *angst* derives from the lived experience of

ontological wounds [i.e., wounds that rupture the individual's basic sense of self, and his or her trust in people and social institutions] and emotional scars inflicted by white supremacist beliefs and images permeating US society and culture. These beliefs and images attack black intelligence, black ability, black beauty, and black character daily in subtle and not-so-subtle ways ... The accumulated effect of the black wounds and scars suffered in a white-dominated society is a deep-seated anger, a boiling sense of rage, and a passionate pessimism regarding America's will to justice. (1993: 17–18)

Not coincidentally, West, who is also a religion scholar, sounds like many black religious pastors whose theological outlook tends to see the scarring of black America as an intertwined political, economic, and pastoral problem (e.g., McRoberts 2003). It is this sort of language that, in part, drew controversy on President Obama's ex-pastor, Rev. Jeremiah Wright, and his politically engaged

📖 NEWS 12.6 black church in Chicago.

The scarring of black America, or what, following Durkheim (cf. chapter 2), can be referred to as the social disintegration in black communities, is underlined, West (1993: 15) argues, by the high incidence of suicide among young black people. Although for several decades black youth were much less likely than white youth to commit suicide, the gap has narrowed considerably. In 1970, white teenage males were twice as likely as black teenage males to commit suicide, but by 1994, the rates were almost identical (McLoyd and Lozoff 2001: 336).

The disintegration of black communities is further underscored by the fragility of blacks' interpersonal and social relationships, and the attendant violence among blacks: Turning their collective anger against one another, black-on-black homicides and rapes and domestic violence are higher than for other groups in the US (see Box 12.1). The social disintegration in black communities and the pessimism as to blacks' life-chances and life-outcomes is crystallized in the statistic that there are more young black men in prison than there are in college. In 2007, Orlando Patterson wrote: "one in three male African Americans in their 30s now has a prison record, as do nearly two-thirds of all black male high

📖 NEWS 12.7 school dropouts."

Box 12.1 Facts of blackness

Blacks are less likely than whites to:
- Have a college education
- Receive recommended medical screening tests (for breast cancer, diabetes)
- Own their own homes

Blacks are more likely than whites to:
- Live below the poverty line
- Be victims of homicide – by a ratio of 6 to 1
- Be incarcerated – by a ratio of 8 to 1   📖 NEWS 12.7

BLACK POPULAR CULTURE

Much of black popular culture, and especially its rap songs, music videos, and movies, gives voice to racial inequality and to the scarring of and social disintegration in black communities. The appeal and power of pop culture lies precisely in its ability both to comment on the realities of lived experience and simultaneously to fantasize about more extreme and more benign versions of those realities. As Stuart Hall observes: "Popular culture always has its base in the experiences, the pleasures, the memories, the traditions of the people. It has connections with local hopes and local aspirations, local tragedies and local scenarios that are the everyday practices and the everyday experiences of ordinary folks" (1992: 25).

Black popular culture presents a complex mix of images and content. One thing it does is celebrate consumption and commodification. As Marx first alerted us (cf. chapter 1), and as was subsequently elaborated by the Frankfurt School (cf. chapter 5), the material and ideological forces of capitalism produce a highly commodified culture. It is difficult if not impossible to resist the market forces that dominate our society, consumer forces whose impact is accelerated by globalization (cf. chapter 15) and the instantaneous and ceaseless flow of images and commodities. Many of our favorite pop songs celebrate the culture of consumption, the rush of sheer commodification that permeates black and white society. When we hear Kanye West sing "Flashing Lights" or Britney Spears sing "Give Me More," they seem to be singing about affluent consumers in America and globally, irrespective of race.

Nevertheless, consumption and commodification seem especially accentuated in black rap culture, fashion, and jewelry. As I noted in the Introduction, "Louie," sung by Blood Raw featuring Young Jeezy, was Jam of the Week on MTV Jams (the week of June 6, 2008); a song celebrating Louis Vuitton merchandise. Yet notably, it is whites who get to advertise Vuitton in elite magazines, e.g., Andre Agassi and Steffi Graf in the *New Yorker*. In poor neighborhoods with low-quality schools (e.g., MacLeod 1995), it is not surprising that the latest sports shoes and fashion apparel are core sources of symbolic affirmation; consumption can trump achievement (whether in school or on the basketball court). The "code of the street" rewards the one with swagger (e.g., Anderson 1999a), and it is hard to have swagger without Air-Jordan basketball shoes or whatever the latest consumer fashion may be. Not surprisingly, then, black pop culture is in the vanguard of the celebration of consumption.

Reflecting the lived experience of racial and economic inequality, many popular rappers with extensive cross-racial appeal, like Fabolous, celebrate their rise "From Nothin' to Somethin'."

Another theme that black pop culture accentuates is the inequality and oppression among blacks. Both Patricia Hill Collins (2004: 25–42; cf. chapter 10) and Cornel West (1993: 18; 8–91) discuss the degrading ways in which heterosexual black men treat black women and black gays, and they see this denigration as among the most pressing problems confronting black communities. There is emancipatory power in the race and class consciousness elaborated by Dr Dre, Tupac, and EZ-E, to inspire political mobilization. At the same time, however, its political impact in bringing about real social change is compromised by the vivid talk and explicit images of male–female degradation and oppression that characterize the songs and videos of these same artists. Blacks and whites are beholden to images of oppression wherein black men cannot see black women as equals, but see them rather through the exaggerated extremes of idealization (as in appreciation for their heroic mothers, e.g., Tupac's "Dear Mama" or Kanye West's "Hey Mama") and its opposite, contempt (as in the view of women as sex chattels; e.g., Snoop Dogg). Against this reality, black scholars argue that the effort to craft a new racial egalitarian politics is all the more urgent.

NEW RACIAL POLITICS

To fight against market, consumption, and pop cultural forces in any politically meaningful way is a daunting challenge, especially given the accelerated speed of globalizing cultural and economic processes (cf. chapter 15). Nonetheless, while market and cultural conditions structure the circumstances of our lives, they do not, as Cornel West reminds us, dictate or determine our political response to those conditions (1993: 12). Thus West, Patterson and other black scholars – implicitly recognizing the autonomy of political processes and of political power from economic and market forces as elaborated by Max Weber (cf. chapter 3) – highlight the need for visionary black leaders who will confront rather than deny the cultural problems that exist within black communities (e.g., crime, unstable families, and gender inequality).

📖 NEWS 12.7

Politics of conversion

West calls for a transformation in political leadership among blacks, one that promotes a politics of conversion (1993: 18). He argues that black nihilism and despair have to be countered with a vision of hope, a vision that leads blacks to affirm their individual and collective self-worth (1993: 18–19). West explains:

> The politics of conversion proceeds principally on the local level – in those institutions in civil society still vital enough to promote self-worth and self-affirmation. It surfaces on the state and national levels only when grassroots democratic organizations put forward a collective leadership that has earned the love and respect of and, most important, has proved itself *accountable* to, these organizations. (1993: 19)

The politics of conversion, West argues, requires a prophetic commitment to new ways of thinking and reasoning about racial identity – about what it means to be black – and new ways of organizing racial politics, new approaches that move beyond a narrow and ultimately authoritarian-machismo understanding of racial identity and inter-racial competition (1993: 23–32). West calls blacks to form coalitions with non-blacks and to nurture the anti-racist strands that can be found among whites, Jews, Latinos, and Asians (notwithstanding the varied, historically based racist tensions between and among all these groups). And importantly, in addition to building solidarity across races, he argues that conversion must work to produce an authentic solidarity among blacks themselves. In particular, in accord with Du Bois's vision, West stresses the imperative of working toward the achievement of a black cultural democracy, a state of affairs in which blacks would respect each other across their own differences, a point also emphasized by Patricia Hill Collins (cf. chapter 10). "Instead of authoritarian sensibilities that subordinate women or degrade gay men and lesbians, black cultural democracy promotes the equality of black women and men and the humanity of gay men and lesbians. In short, black cultural democracy rejects the pervasive patriarchy and homophobia in black American life" (West 1993: 29).

In a similar vein, Guinier and Torres (2002) argue for the creation of a new racialized politics. They emphasize the need to think about race not in biological or cultural terms but in political terms, and they use the term political race to describe their vision, whereby "racialized identities may be put to service to achieve social change through democratic renewal" (2002: 11). Like West, they envisage this project as being cross-racial and involving critique and transformation of the socio-political system that enables the perpetuation of racial and other forms of inequality. They emphasize that the inequalities most acutely experienced by racial minorities are inequalities signaling "social justice deficiencies in the larger [societal] community"; as such they poison the whole social atmosphere and need to be

---

Topic 12.1   The post-racial politics of President Barack Obama

As a presidential candidate, Barack Obama gave a major public speech in March 2008 on race and race relations in which he articulated what might be seen as a post-racial political agenda. Obama stressed his confidence in Americans' ability to move beyond the racial wounds of the past while simultaneously making progress in committing to social and economic policies that would advance opportunities for all Americans, irrespective of race. In his speech, Obama urged African-Americans to embrace the burdens of their past without becoming victims of their past; and he urged white Americans to recognize America's history of racial discrimination while committing not just to words but to deeds that will help remedy past injustices that excluded blacks from the "ladders of opportunity" available to whites. Obama urged blacks and whites, and all Americans, to realize that: "Your dreams do not come at the expense of my dreams, that investing in the health, welfare and education of black and brown and white children will ultimately help all of America prosper."

NEWS 12.8

redressed – "Racialized communities signal problems with the ways we have structured power and privilege" (2002: 12). While recognizing that racial and other sources of group identity can motivate individuals to join particularized social movements (2002: 80), Guinier and Torres nonetheless emphasize the necessity for a trans-racial commitment to social change. They state: "Political race seeks to construct a new language to discuss race, in order to rebuild a progressive democratic movement led by people of color but joined by others" (2002: 12).

CULTURE AND THE NEW RACISM

RACIAL LINES AS CULTURE LINES

Paul Gilroy also argues for new racial politics, though he takes a somewhat different tack than other scholars (e.g., Collins 2004; West 1993; Guinier and Torres 2002). In his book *Against Race* (2000), Gilroy argues against the idea that the color line matters in modern times. Instead of color lines, he argues, it is culture lines that are critical to the production of conflict and inequality, and to how culture and power get intertwined in ways that divide and subdivide humanity. As an immigrant West Indian growing up in London in the wake of World War II (Gilroy 2000: 2–5), Gilroy became sensitive to the subtle ways in which Nazi and Fascist symbolism (in graffiti, for example, and in the fashion and style adopted by white youth gangs such as Teddy boys and skinheads; e.g., Hall and Jefferson 1976), and ethno-nationalist ideologies in general, use race and racial distinctions for destructive ends.

Gilroy argues that the affirmation of racial differences and the symbolic glorification of the uniqueness of discrete racial cultures seen, for example, on ethnic festive days and at ethnic festivals – the "currently fashionable obligations to celebrate incommensurability [distinctiveness] and cheerlead for absolute identity" (2000: 6–7) – convey the message that every race is beautiful. This, of course, is not quite true in an unequal society where race differentiates life-chances and life-outcomes. This celebration, moreover, simultaneously distracts attention from the routine ways in which racism permeates the state, schools, public housing, and other social institutions (ibid.: 5). Thus when white suburban teenagers emulate black street culture and fashion (e.g., black rap music and style), their "acting black" might be seen as an effort to cross over and transcend racial differences; but it might also effectively reinforce the cultural (and economic) divisions between blacks and whites (Roediger 2002: 212–240). Whites can act black, but, unlike blacks, they invariably do so with the secure knowledge that they can stop acting black whenever they choose, and moreover, that their chances of economic success, of being arrested, etc., will be largely unaffected by acting black. Blacks do not have this security. Moreover, while "acting black" has symbolic value – is a source of status – among white peers, the inverse is not true.

Thus, when black students strive to achieve educational success – recognizing education as a pathway to socio-economic mobility – they are denigrated by their black friends for "acting white," thus dampening black students' motivation to succeed in school (e.g., Ogbu 2003).

More generally, Gilroy is concerned that race has become commercialized such that we are drawn to advertisements which proclaim the glamour of racial differences (e.g., "Black is beautiful"), and that consumer culture increasingly sees all bodies, and especially black bodies, as commodities to be reworked and manipulated (think of Denis Rodman, or Tupac; Gilroy 2000: 22–23; see also Collins 2004). The commercialization and commodification of race detracts from and "do[es] nothing to change the everyday forms of racial hierarchy" (Gilroy 2000: 23). To the contrary, this "actively de-politicized consumer culture … of racialized appearances" (ibid.: 21), one that is propelled by globalization and the new immigrant flows across countries, blurs the boundaries of racial difference. One important consequence of this superficial blurring is the creation of new tensions from the anxiety that takes hold when individuals and groups cannot draw the clear lines of racial difference (of everyone knowing their place in the social-racial order) to which society is historically accustomed (see also Roediger 2002).

Gilroy argues that race as such – race as a persistent source of political and social inequality – becomes secondary to the primary purpose of using black bodies and black popular culture to make cultural statements about consumption, beauty, and adornment, even as this adornment reproduces reminders about the well-established historical inferiority of blacks (e.g., Tupac's "Thug Life" tattoos; Gilroy 2000: 22–23). In sum, Gilroy argues, the biological basis for socially categorizing racial differences on the basis of body color has now been displaced by a cultural colonization, one that racializes bodies in ways that fit market and consumption criteria.

NEW RACISM

The commercialization of race is part of the broader culturation of racial differences, and both are components of what is often called the new racism: the racism that emerges when a dominant racial-cultural group attributes core cultural differences to the worldviews and ways of being of minority racial groups. The new racism rejects the old grounds for racism, i.e., the view that "biology was both destiny and hierarchy" (Gilroy 2000: 32), and instead presumes that "nature, history, and geopolitics dictated that people should cleave to their own kind and be most comfortable in the environments that matched their distinctive cultural and therefore nationalist modes of being in this world" (ibid.).

A racism based on cultural separateness, of keeping people with their "own kind," was the ideological justification for apartheid in South Africa and is a justification similarly used to uphold racial discrimination in other social contexts.

Princeton University, for example, unlike Harvard and Yale, "long had a systematic policy of excluding blacks" (Karabel 2005: 232). In the 1940s, when it was debating whether to admit blacks, leading Princeton faculty "claimed that a concern for the well-being of blacks was the source of their opposition to admitting them" (Karabel 2005: 234–235). And students who opposed change (over half the student body) similarly argued that "blacks would not be happy at Princeton" (2005: 235).

Thus, rather than saying that members of a minority racial or ethnic group are (biologically) inferior to the dominant race, the new racist tendency instead is to emphasize that "these people" are culturally different. The claim is that their ways of being are at odds with the cultural purity of the dominant group and its ways of organizing and ordering society – e.g., "that their criminality is an expression of their distinctive culture" (Gilroy 1987: 69, 109) – and by extension, they would be better off in their own country, neighborhood, country club, or university, among people like themselves. In short, highlighting cultural distinctions between groups, even or especially when those differences are romanticized as in the "celebration" of racial and cultural difference, can be a veil for the denigration of those who are not part of the dominant culture.

NEW RACISM AND GENETIC TECHNOLOGY

The new racism, the accentuation/clarification of racial-cultural separateness and difference, is further abetted by advances in DNA testing technology, a technology that promises to allow us to determine once and for all time an individual's exact racial composition. Many individuals today aspire to claim (and some to negate) a cultural identity that is based on a particular racial genetic inheritance. But, as in the complex relation between technology and societal processes in general (first elaborated by the Frankfurt School theorists; cf. chapter 5), technology in and of itself does not resolve the contradictions and inequalities in society. On the one hand, DNA technology can help people discover their roots and reconstruct racial histories and genealogies that were buried with enslavement (cf. Patterson 1986) or that went undocumented by public officials and by generations of black illiteracy. This is the objective of "The Root," a new website for black genealogy.

NEWS 12.9

At the same time, however, the expectation of scientific clarity on racial composition/identity that technology promises can also exacerbate what Gilroy refers to as the crisis of raciology (2000: 25). The crisis surrounding the boundaries between the races, between what comprises and doesn't comprise a particular racial identity, may be further muddied rather than illuminated by technology. Just as the commercialization of the glamour of black bodies confuses the representation of race and the boundaries between racial categories, technological innovations may have a parallel effect. The medical imaging of DNA, instead of clarifying what exactly race is genetically and what exact racial composition a given individual has, instead presents us with a surprising and confusing finding: "Current wisdom seems to suggest that up to six pairs of genes are implicated in the outcome of skin 'color.' They do not constitute a single switch" (Gilroy 2000: 49).

The scientific complexity involved in DNA decoding and in interpreting its patterns does not, however, put a halt to the historically deep interest that humans have in knowing who they *really* are. As one recent newspaper article noted, although scientists have emphasized the high degree of shared genetic material that exists between any two individuals, there is a lot of interest in decoding the racial basis of the small fraction of genetic differences that do exist. What DNA decoding will eventually reveal about the genetic traits of different racial groups, and what individuals, corporations, policy-makers, and society as a whole decide to do with this information, will have far-reaching implications (e.g., see Corrigan 2009). It will impact efforts toward reducing racial discrimination and race-based inequality – if, for example, some racial groups are shown to be more susceptible than others to certain diseases. It will also impact related efforts encouraging cross-racial and cross-cultural interaction – if, for example, some people choose only to associate with those with whom they share some genetic material.

NEWS 12.10

In short, we continue to be perplexed by both the culturally visible and the biologically invisible dimensions of race, as we seek to understand the elements of a shared racial and cultural heritage, even as we are aware of the differences (of generation, social class, gender, nation, etc.) that characterize any collectivity. As Gilroy observes – and as the debate over Barack Obama's racial identity highlighted – these varied differences "challenge the unanimity of racialized collectivities. Exactly what, in cultural terms, it takes to belong, and more importantly, what it takes to be recognized as belonging, begin to look very uncertain" (2000: 24–25).

RETHINKING RACIAL DIFFERENCE

Gilroy offers a way out of this uncertainty by challenging us to think differently about race. He rejects both the biological and the cultural foundations of (old and new) racist thinking; he rejects "the foundational oscillation between biology and culture" and the closed circuit that it has become (2000: 52). In their place, he counsels a move toward what he calls a non-racial planetary humanism (ibid.: 2). A planetary humanism would require the abandonment of the exclusionary ways in which race and all group differences (based on gender, nationality, etc.) are construed. It would, by extension, also require the abandonment of the militaristic and other aggressive and symbolic means used to affirm and defend group identities and group differences.

This is a rather utopian recommendation (as Gilroy admits). It requires us to abandon the stubbornness with which we cling to notions of race, whatever our various motivations for doing so – whether as "the beneficiaries of racial hierarchies [who] do not want to give up their privileges" or because, as members of subordinated racial groups, we have developed "complex traditions of politics, ethics, identity, and culture" in our efforts to resist the racial categories imposed upon us (Gilroy 2000: 12). Nonetheless, it is a utopian vision worth our consideration if we are to move beyond the inhumane ways we all too often use to evaluate and punish the Other. Gilroy tells us that we have to "refigure humanism" such that we stop using race (and gender and other differences) "to categorize and divide mankind" (ibid.: 17). It is not that we have to renounce the embodied realities of our existence. But in thinking beyond race (and gender, etc.), we are empowered to begin to recognize the humanity we share with people whose bodies are (biologically and culturally) different from ours. As Gilroy notes, with a refigured planetary humanism,

> The constraints of bodily existence (being in the world) are admitted and even welcomed, though there is a strong inducement to see and value them differently as sources of identification and empathy. The recurrence of pain, disease, humiliation and loss of dignity, grief, and care for those one loves can all contribute to an abstract sense of human similarity powerful enough to make solidarities based on cultural particularity appear suddenly trivial. (2000: 17)

SUMMARY

Racial differences, and in particular the long, historically embedded economic, social, and cultural differences between blacks and whites continue to matter in contemporary society. These differences are evident in the US, a country in which slavery institutionalized a core rupture in black–white relations, and in the UK, where colonialism institutionalized the Otherness of all those who were colonized by the British Empire during its reign of domination in India, the West Indies, and Africa. The black/white divide is not the only racial division that exists either historically or today. Tensions between whites and Arabs, whites and Asians, blacks and Asians, and blacks and Hispanics are also evident. Additionally, there are many ethnic tensions currently apparent in Europe, Africa, and the Middle East.

The persistence of racial divisions in the US, a country which emphasizes freedom and equality, and which has one of the most structurally open systems of individual mobility and stratification in the world, has meant that the nature and impact of racial difference garner a great deal of sociological attention. Thus, following Du Bois's lead, sociologists have variously focused on the structural and cultural forces that reproduce as well as transform the significance of race as a social fact in America and in other societal contexts. Race is a complex, multidimensional topic; the meanings attached to racial categories and the implications of racial differences are contingent on the specific historical and societal context under review. Nonetheless, the scholars discussed in this chapter provide us with many insightful ideas that we can use to think about and to begin to disentangle the complexities inherent in any discussion of race and racism.

POINTS TO REMEMBER

- Du Bois was the first sociologist to systematically draw detailed attention to race, specifically the color line dividing blacks and whites
- Colonialism, and the race-segregated structures of Otherness that it created, were the critical economic-political-cultural force subjugating the lives and life chances of colonized peoples
- Scholars emphasize the socio-historical variation in how race and racism are construed
- There is increasing attention to whiteness as a racial identity and its impact on race consciousness
- Slavery was the most extreme form of black subjugation
- The legacy of slavery for the cultural and social-psychological identity of blacks continues to preoccupy scholars of race (e.g., Patterson, West)
- There is greater recognition today than in the past that there is no single or uniform black cultural or black economic experience
- Sociologists studying inequality document the significance of the intersection of race with class
- There is an ever-expanding gap in income and related life-chances between the black middle class and the black underclass
- Pop culture is a crucial arena in which images of black/white and especially of black/black inequality are given powerful representation
- Many scholars emphasize the necessity for a new racial politics of black equality, and for a new trans-racial politics of equality
- Scholars highlight the blurring of racial differences apparent in the commodification of the black body and of black experiences in pop culture
- Technological advances in genetic testing complicate rather than clarify racial composition
- The cultural blurring of racial differences is part of what Gilroy sees as the crisis of raciology
- Gilroy calls for a planetary humanism, whereby the recognition of our shared humanity overrides the parochialism of our particular racial and other differences

GLOSSARY

affirmative action laws and public policies that seek to redress historical discrimination against blacks and other minority groups in access to education, voting, jobs, housing.

apartheid system of laws and public policies that maintain discriminatory practices against blacks (e.g., white settlers in South Africa against indigenous blacks).

black cultural democracy the idea that in black communities, men and women need to create equality in their social relationships with other blacks whom they demean (e.g., women, gays).

black underclass segment of the black community experiencing persistent chronic poverty.

colonialism economic and political domination by an imperial power over a separate and distant geographical area (e.g., Great Britain over India and the Caribbean; Portugal over Brazil; etc.).

crisis of raciology contemporary blurring of racial boundaries and of the economic and political meanings and implications of racial categories.

cultural identity the historically grounded origins of, and ongoing transformation in, a particular group's sense of who they are and their status vis-à-vis other cultural groups.

culture lines accentuation of the symbolic, cultural, and social (as opposed to biological or physical) differences between groups.

double-consciousness the alienation of blacks' everyday identity/consciousness as a result of slavery such that blacks invariably see themselves through the eyes of (superior) whites, the dominant race.

identity politics strategic use of particular cultural and social identities (based on race, gender, sexuality, ethnicity, etc.) to resist discrimination and/or to gain political advantage.

new racism **(1)** symbols and ideas used (in politics and the mass media) to argue that race-based (biological) differences no longer matter even as such arguments reinforce racial-cultural differences and stereotypes. **(2)** the invocation of cultural and symbolic (rather than biological) criteria to legitimate the societal exclusion or marginalization of particular racial/ethnic groups.

nihilism collective despair and hopelessness in black communities as a result of structurally persistent economic and social inequality.

Otherness social construction of racial, ethnic, and/or geographical differences as inferior to a dominant historical and political power (e.g., the West's construction of Orientalism).

planetary humanism idea that society can transcend its racial, cultural, and other group differences to recognize and realize its collectively shared humanity.

political race invocation of race-based experiences of social inequality to mobilize and expand cross-racial alliances toward the achievement of social and institutional change.

politics of conversion local, grassroots activism in black communities that moves beyond nihilism and insists on innovative and accountable black leadership and the creation of equality for and among all blacks.

popular culture the media images and content pervading everyday culture via television, music, videos, movies, street fashion.

post-colonial theory critiques the legacy of western imperialism for the cultural identities of previously colonized peoples.

race symbolization of social differences based on assumed or perceived natural (innate) differences derived from differences in physical body appearance.

race-segregation legal and systematically imposed divisions in everyday life based on racial differences; e.g., existence of separate schools and swimming pools for blacks and whites in the US until the 1950s.

racism implicit or explicit imposition of exclusionary boundaries and discriminatory practices based on racial appearance or racial categories.

slavery historical institutionalization of coercive, discriminatory, and dehumanizing practices against a subordinate group; typically legitimated on grounds of racial difference.

whiteness term used to underscore that all racial categories, including historically dominant ones (e.g., being white), are socially constructed categories of privilege whose meanings and implications change over time.

RELEVANT NEWSPAPER STORIES

All news stories are from the *New York Times* unless otherwise noted, and can be accessed via www.wiley.com/go/dillon. See NEWS icons in the margins above.

NEWS 12.1 "Reporting while black," September 30, 2007.

"Nanny hunt can be a 'slap in the face' for blacks," December 26, 2006.

"Runways fade to white: Few black models are used by designers, signaling a reverse," October 14, 2007.

"Dungy builds coaching tree by going against the grain," November 4, 2007.

"Room at the top? ... Black executives are wondering," November 1, 2007.

"Lawyers debate why blacks lag at major firms," November 29, 2006.

NEWS 12.2 "The geography of hate," November 25, 2007.

NEWS 12.3 "Obama urges U.S. to grapple with race issue," March 19, 2008.

"Mr. Obama's profile in courage," March 19, 2008.

"Obama's color line," November 30, 2007.

"Where whites draw the line," June 8, 2008.

"Who are we? New dialogue on mixed race," March 31, 2008.

"The push to 'Otherize' Obama," September 20, 2008.

NEWS 12.4 "Forty acres and a gap in wealth," July 18, 2007.

NEWS 12.5 "The vanishing supermarket," May 5, 2008.

NEWS 12.6 "Clinton criticizes Obama over his pastor," March 26, 2008.

NEWS 12.7 "Jena, O.J. and the jailing of black America," opinion editorial, September 30, 2007.

Statistics: US Census Bureau and Department of Justice.

NEWS 12.8 "Audacity to hope for what we can achieve," March 19, 2008.

NEWS 12.9 "Washington Post starts an online magazine for blacks," January 28, 2008. See also "A beginner's guide to tracing your roots" on www.theroot.com.

"DNA tests find branches but few roots," November 25, 2007.

NEWS 12.10 "In DNA era, new worries about prejudice," November 11, 2007.

WEB SUPPLEMENTS

All web supplements are available at www.wiley.com/go/dillon. See WEB icons in the margins above.

WEB 12.1 Slavery

WEB 12.2 The National Association for the Advancement of Colored People (NAACP)

WEB 12.3 The Civil rights movement

NOTE

1 "Driving while black" is popularly used to refer to the stronger probability that black motorists will be stopped more frequently than whites simply for driving. Academics attest to their personal experience of being picked on or ignored (e.g., while signaling for a taxi) because they are black (e.g., West, 1993: x).

CHAPTER THIRTEEN

THE SOCIAL REPRODUCTION OF INEQUALITY

PIERRE BOURDIEU'S THEORY OF CLASS AND CULTURE

KEY CONCEPTS

culture
social classes
economic capital
class fractions
cultural capital
cultural competence
social capital
symbolic capital
institutional field
educational capital
taste
habitus
symbolic goods
aesthetic disposition
game of culture
collective misrecognition
economy of practice
structures

CHAPTER MENU

Pierre Bourdieu has been described as "the most influential and original French sociologist since Durkheim … at once a leading theorist and an empirical researcher of extraordinarily broad interests and distinctive style" (Calhoun 2000: 696). Like Durkheim, Bourdieu emphasized the thoroughly social nature of social life and how it is that a certain social order gets maintained. But unlike Durkheim, Bourdieu made social inequality a key focus. In particular, he underscored how the objective structure of social class and class relations conditions the individual's everyday culture and social interaction. His approach to conceptualizing inequality and stratification shows the influence of Marx, but especially that of Weber. Unlike Marx, who regarded economic capital as the basic source of inequality in society, Bourdieu saw economic capital as just one, though a very important, dimension of inequality. Like Weber, he conceptualized inequality as having multiple dimensions; specifically, he identified the inequality stemming from individuals' and classes' differential amounts of what he termed economic capital, social capital, and cultural capital. In his later years, Bourdieu moved beyond the realm of class inequality per se to engage in public debates about globalization, economic inequality, and everyday human suffering (e.g., Bourdieu 1999); these are important contributions, but because they are less central to his theoretical framing of social and institutional inequality, I exclude them from consideration.

BIOGRAPHICAL NOTE

Pierre Bourdieu was born into a lower-middle-class family in a small town in southwestern France in 1930. He excelled academically and made a career at the highly distinguished College de France, Paris (as did Durkheim). In the mid-1950s, Bourdieu completed required military service in Algeria (following the French–Algerian war), and subsequently worked at the University of Algeria; while there he conducted an ethnographic study of social relations in the province of Kabylia. He was a highly productive researcher and writer; notably, across his many publications, he elaborated concepts based on his extensive empirical (qualitative and quantitative) research studies. Bourdieu died in 2002 at age 72 (Calhoun 2000).

SOCIAL STRATIFICATION

Bourdieu argues that we should think of society as being hierarchically organized or stratified as a three-dimensional space: "a space whose three fundamental dimensions are defined by volumes of capital, composition of capital, and change in these two properties over time (manifested by past and potential trajectories in social space)" (1984: 114). Within the social space (any society) there are many different classes and class subcomponents, all of which are primarily distinguished by "their overall volume of capital, understood as the set of actually usable resources and powers – economic capital, cultural capital and also social capital" (ibid.). The distribution of social classes, therefore, is a function of differences in ownership and use of these different capitals, and "thus runs from those who are best provided with both economic and cultural capital to those who are most deprived in both respects" (ibid.).

ECONOMIC CAPITAL

What comprises economic capital is quite straightforward and easy to measure: money in the bank, home-ownership and other property, investment assets, etc. It is relatively easy for most individuals and families to make a tally of the volume or amount of their economic capital. And there are ways that we can readily see how our volume of economic capital compares to others; after graduation you will be eager to compare your starting salary with that of your friends, knowing that your economic capital, though it may vary over time, is going to largely determine your long-term, post-college lifestyle. We are reminded of acute differences in economic capital when newspapers publish details of the earnings and other economic assets of corporate executives, and list the asset differences among the leading millionaires and billionaires.

While we tend to think of the wealthy as a homogeneous group, Bourdieu highlights the differences within economic groups – i.e., among those who occupy a broadly similar social class position. He argues that economic – and cultural and social capital – varies between what he calls class fractions, sub-components of social classes. Thus, for example, there are competitive economic and lifestyle differences between the very rich and the super-rich in Silicon Valley; among super-rich yacht owners; and among Manhattan's elite who use zip codes as markers of distinction.

NEWS 13.1

CULTURAL CAPITAL

Bourdieu's concepts of social capital and cultural capital follow a logic of acquisition, use, and exchange that is parallel to how we think of economic capital, though these concepts are more difficult to define and measure. We can think of cultural capital as having parallels with Weber's conceptualization of social status and lifestyle (cf. chapter 3), and more specifically with how formal education *and* informal everyday cultural experiences enhance an individual's cultural competence. This competence includes the stylistic ease and familiarity with which the individual carries herself or himself – whether at a party, in a fancy delicatessen, in an art museum, or at a football game – and displays a certain detached practical sense of what is cool (or "hot," "sick," "wicked").

Each social class (and class fraction) has its own culture, and individuals regardless of social class have a certain cultural competence. By the same token, different social contexts vary in the value placed on specific cultural competencies (being cool at a car rally requires a different competence than being cool at a golfing event). Nevertheless, in the objectively stratified order in society as a whole, some competencies are more highly valued than others. Specifically, it is upper-class culture that is the most highly valued – it is the *legitimate* culture. This is the case not because the things and dispositions that the upper class value have greater value in themselves. Rather, it is because the upper class uses strategies of exclusion and inclusion made possible by their privileged location in society (e.g., country club or art gallery membership, attendance at elite schools, etc.), and which enable them to institutionalize hierarchical distinctions between their culture and the tastes they don't value (Bourdieu 1984: 23–28).

In any case, unlike the balance sheet we can read detailing our stock of economic capital, it is more difficult to itemize and make a tally of our cultural capital. We can easily count an individual's years of education, but formal education is only one part of what comprises cultural capital. Assessing the extent of our own, or of someone else's, stylistic comfort and the ease with which they make ordinary everyday choices (e.g., chicken wings or caviar?), calls for a subtle system of classification and evaluation. Moreover, any class schema of everyday cultural taste in the US, for example, would need to incorporate the greater ideological emphasis on popular (mass-democratic) than on elite culture, notwithstanding the importance of class distinctions in the US (e.g., Lamont 1992). The anti-elitism in US culture is reflected, for example, in the frequency with which Republican politicians publicly belittle their Democratic rivals as being out of touch with ordinary folk because they allegedly prefer chardonnay to beer, arugula to lettuce, etc.

SOCIAL CAPITAL

Social capital, for Bourdieu, refers to individuals' social connections, the social networks and alliances that link them in all sorts of direct as well as indirect and informal ways to opportunities that can enhance their stock of capital (whether economic, social, or cultural capital, or any combination thereof). Again, compared to the straightforward tallies we can make of economic capital, the measurement of social capital is more nuanced, though not as nuanced as that of cultural capital. We can make a list of all our friends or a list of those who invite us to parties and we can list important acquaintances, but what weight to assign to different individuals on the list presents a more complicated task. In measuring social capital, the volume is contingent not so much on the number of people you know but on how important the people you know are, i.e., how much economic, cultural, and social capital the people you know have (and are willing to use on your behalf).

When someone you know who has a well-connected family invites you to her house for the weekend and you meet several new people, or just one, with whom you establish a connection, that acquaintance can become a conduit for opportunities that directly impact your subsequent lifestyle and life outcomes. These connections can get you a coveted internship which then converts into a permanent job after you graduate (thus enhancing your economic capital); you meet new people through your internship, becoming friends with some, and these connections in turn open up new possibilities – additional circles of friends with more invitations (thus enhancing your social capital) that make you start going to places such as art museums or jazz clubs that you would not have gone to previously (thus enhancing your cultural capital), which in turn may enhance your social capital (museum/jazz aficionados will seek your company because like them, you like art or jazz, etc.) and which may independently also enhance your economic capital if (after many years of attending museums) you are able to draw on your art competence to help close a financial deal at work ..., and so on. As you can see, while economic, social, and cultural capital are distinct types of capital, there are multiple and mutually interpenetrating links among all three.

ECONOMIC AND CULTURAL CAPITAL IN STRATIFYING SOCIETY

Although Bourdieu discusses all three types of capital, he is most attentive to the role played by economic and cultural capital in producing and reproducing social inequality. Importantly, he sees economic and cultural capital as analytically independent (though interrelated) resources. Thus, an individual can have a lot of economic capital and not much objectively valued cultural capital, or can have a lot of cultural capital and relatively little economic capital. Many newly rich Wall Street investment-fund managers have a remarkably large volume of economic capital, but many of them are low on cultural capital – they experience anxiety in their high socio-economic circles because they do not have the cultural competencies to move with ease in the art and cultural worlds that are a core part of the Manhattan social scene.

NEWS 13.2

Because all types of capital are exchangeable, an individual can use one type of capital to gain more of another type. This is exactly what many economically rich New Yorkers do – they pay to acquire cultural capital. Its acquisition, however, is not based automatically on an economic exchange: Money can quickly earn an individual some cultural capital – if, for example, they purchase an expensive piece of art. But the ease of art appreciation which is so intrinsic to cultural competence/cultural capital means that they must also use their money to get immersed in the art world. Thus many hire art consultants who teach them about different types of art, and who guide them in visits to many different galleries so that eventually they will feel more at ease with making their own personal art choices rather than relying completely on the advice of a paid art consultant. And, importantly, the economically rich may be able to convert their (new) increased cultural capital into additional economic capital if they buy and subsequently sell for profit one of their acquired pieces of art.

NEWS 13.3

By the same token, art historians, while they have high cultural capital, are relatively low on economic capital; but they can use their art expertise to advise rich clients and hence increase their economic capital, as well as further consolidating their cultural capital if they are able to enhance their reputation – their symbolic capital (Bourdieu 1984: 291) – in the institutional field of art and culture as competent and accomplished art advisers. Bourdieu thus sees a very dynamic relation between the different types of capital and the conditions for their exchange and accumulation within and across particular institutional fields.

Bourdieu uses the term "institutional field" in much the same way that sociologists generally discuss the range of different, specialized institutions in society (economy, family, law, education, culture, religion, etc). Additionally, for Bourdieu, however, the analysis of institutional fields – of culture, education, religion, etc. – gives him the opportunity to highlight how the particular practices or the logic and competencies within one field may vary from those of other fields; and, how, notwithstanding this variation, all institutional fields work to reproduce inequality within their respective field and within society as a whole.[1]

In summary, for Bourdieu, each type of capital is and has to be usable; thus economic and cultural capital are resources that can be accumulated and/or converted into other forms of capital and/or traded and transmitted to others (as an inheritance or a gift). They are also, of course, resources that can be only partially used or only partially converted into other types of capital. As Bourdieu emphasizes, there is nothing automatic about the relationship between economic capital and cultural capital (1984: 105); there is autonomy or agency in how any particular family or individual choose to use their economic capital. This becomes readily apparent when you see intra-family cultural or economic differences among those who nonetheless have similar family background and social class origins. In any case, an important point emphasized by Bourdieu is that capital is not simply something that an individual or a social class or class fraction *has*, it is also something they *use*, and use to show, establish, or change their positioning in and among the economic-social-cultural hierarchies that comprise society.

FAMILY AND SCHOOL IN THE PRODUCTION OF CULTURAL CAPITAL

Bourdieu underscores the sociological significance of the family of origin in determining an individual's access to capital. Someone from a relatively poor family can, through educational qualifications (what Bourdieu refers to as academic or educational capital), subsequently gain a considerable amount of capital (economic, social, and/or cultural); indeed, many empirical studies document such patterns of upward occupational and social mobility. At the same time, however, there is a close positive relationship between socio-economic background and educational capital. This means that children who grow up in families of high socio-economic status – i.e., families that have relatively large amounts of economic and/or cultural capital – are more likely than children from families of low socio-economic status to go to and succeed in college (i.e., acquire educational capital) and subsequently achieve occupational-economic success.[2]

Consequently, as Bourdieu argues, "the educational capital held at a given moment expresses, among other things, the economic and social level of the family of origin" (1984: 105). In short, academic capital is contingent on (though also somewhat autonomous of) the cultural capital inherited within the family (1984: 22–23). This insight is influential in socio-linguistics, which recognizes that language skills and vocabulary are determined not simply cognitively but also by the family-social context in which children grow and learn. And, as sociologists document, family learning environments are further mediated by varied gender, ethnic, and social class differences (e.g., Lareau 2003).

Therefore, although we might think of the educational system as a social institution whose functioning and effectiveness stand apart from other institutions, including the family and the economy, this is not the case. Bourdieu argues that the cultural disposition required by schools is one that emphasizes the student's familiarity with a general culture that can only be transmitted by families who already have cultural capital. What he means by this is that children who grow up in families with cultural capital are exposed to everyday cultural experiences (reading, travel, visiting art museums, etc.) and habits (e.g., punctuality, task-completion, an emphasis on knowledge appreciation and on the normalcy of reading, visiting museums, etc.) that cultivate in them the "natural" disposition and habits necessary for success at school – success both in the classroom and, importantly too, among one's peers on the playing fields and in other daily activities.

These cultivated habits are the ones that are conducive to success in terms of the formal curriculum and the school's "scholastically recognized knowledge and practices" (Bourdieu 1984: 23). Academic success, in turn, credentials the individual with the (increasingly) necessary academic qualifications that are the gateway to occupational-economic opportunities and success (Bourdieu 1996: 336; and see n. 2 below). These habits are also crucial to developing the individual's more general "cultivated disposition" (1984: 23), his or her ability to be at ease with the everyday cultural requirements of being a member of the upper class to which academic credentials are a conduit.

Both the family and the school are engaged in cultural transmission (Bourdieu 1984: 23), and these institutions entwine to reinforce the dispositions and practices that constitute and facilitate the accumulation of cultural and economic capital. The school is the one institution in society, Bourdieu argues, that reproduces social divisions both objectively, through its impact in credentializing and positioning individuals in the occupational-social class hierarchy, and subjectively, by inculcating individuals with ways of perceiving and evaluating the social world (1996: xix). In particular, "It is largely through the crucial role it plays in individual and collective transactions between employers ... and employees ... that the educational system directly contributes to the reproduction of social classifications" (ibid.: 121).

BOURDIEU'S IMPACT ON THE SOCIOLOGY OF EDUCATION

Bourdieu's insights into the interlinking of family and school culture have been influential in orienting research and debates within the sociology of education.

In the post-World War II era, the expansion of education, especially university education, in the US and Western European countries was a crucial institutional mechanism promoting economic growth and the expansion of the middle class. Education was widely seen by sociologists and policy-makers as a highly effective system for transmitting the knowledge and values required in a high-functioning society, securing individual upward mobility, and advancing societal modernization and social progress (e.g., Smelser 1968; cf. chapter 4).

This Parsons-influenced perspective was well represented in the research of such renowned sociologists of education as James Coleman (1961), whose analysis of the norms and values that characterize effectively functioning school communities (and consensually shared, more or less, by parents, teachers, and adolescent peers) dominated the field until the 1980s. This functionalist approach drew criticism from education scholars using a Marxist-derived framework. Most notably, Bowles and Gintis (1976) argued that the organization and the authority and rewards system (e.g., grades, competition) of the school (as part of the capitalist superstructure; cf. Marx; see chapter 1) basically perpetuate the economic and class inequality of the larger society.

AUTONOMY OF ECONOMIC AND CULTURAL CAPITAL

It was not really until the 1980s, however, that sociologists had a new way of thinking about the place of school in society. Arguing against Parsons's emphasis on the functionality of schools in determining individuals' positioning within the occupational and stratification sub-systems of society, and against the Marxist view of schools as an arm of capitalist structure and ideology, Bourdieu offered a more dynamic and nuanced analysis of how schools work. By highlighting the analytical and empirical independence of different types of capital, i.e., that cultural capital can be autonomous of economic capital, he advanced sociological recognition that schools produce and transmit cultural capital – e.g., academic credentials and a general cultivated disposition – and do so somewhat independent of the family and of social class. At the same time, Bourdieu's emphasis on the linkages between economic and cultural capital, and between family/social class and school, showed that while the school (or education as an institutional field) has some autonomy from the economy and from family, it nonetheless is positioned to reproduce the socio-economic inequalities that antecede, are reflected in, and extend beyond the school. Importantly, however, this reproduction effect is not automatic; the analytical separateness of cultural and economic capital fosters slippage in the reproduction of both privilege and inequality.

Further, because of the autonomy of cultural and economic capital, Bourdieu's analysis also highlights how educational capital itself becomes a force in inter-class competition (rather than simply a mechanism of upward class mobility). Inter-class competition is fueled by the expansion of educational opportunities and the attendant increase in university enrollment of individuals from lower-class families. It is also pushed by the related emphasis on merit and academic credentials in securing access to well-paying jobs. Bourdieu argues:

> When class fractions who previously made little use of the school system enter the race for academic qualifications, the effect is to force the groups whose reproduction was mainly or exclusively achieved through education to step up their investments so as to maintain the relative scarcity of their qualifications and consequently, their position in the class structure. Academic qualifications and the school system which awards them thus become one of the key stakes in an interclass competition which generates a general and continuous growth in the demand for education and an inflation of academic qualifications. (1984: 133)

Bourdieu's analysis of cultural capital and education was based on empirical studies he conducted of schooling in France (Bourdieu and Passeron 1971; Bourdieu 1996), and hence his theorizing about education is very much grounded in a specific socio-cultural context rather than deduced from abstract generalizations. The educational and social class system in France is more highly stratified and more competitive than in the US (see n. 2 below). Nevertheless, recent empirical studies of education in the US (e.g., Karabel 2005; Lareau 2003; Lareau and Weininger 2003) generally affirm the value of Bourdieu's insights concerning the strong influence of family background on educational capital, and on the role of schools in the transmission and reproduction of cultural and economic capital. This is especially true of elite colleges (e.g., Harvard, Yale) that, by continuing to give preferential treatment to the admission of children of alumni, operate a relatively closed system of upper-class status reproduction, notwithstanding their admission also of modest numbers of students from middle- and lower-income families (Karabel 2005: 548–549).

Topic 13.1 College education and economic mobility

A recent study conducted by the Brookings Institute and the Pew Forum documents the positive benefits of a college education for students who come from low-income families. A college education gives them close to a one-in-five chance of joining the top one-fifth of earners in the US, and almost a two-out-of-three chance of joining the middle class or better. These are good odds. Unfortunately, however, individuals from the lowest-income bracket are far less likely than others to go to college: 11 percent, compared to 53 percent of children from families among the country's highest earners. The majority of children from high-earning families who graduate from college maintain their family's high socio-economic status (SES) in adulthood. Moreover, almost one in four of the children who come from the top income bracket are likely to remain within that bracket in adulthood even if they do not graduate from college. Clearly, while college education significantly enhances the economic opportunities of children from low-income families, for those from high-income families, family SES cushions against the absence of a college degree.

NEWS 13.4

From a social policy perspective, Bourdieu's findings raise challenging issues. Although his schema allows for upward (and downward) mobility, his strong emphasis on the significance of family cultural capital in determining an individual's class position, independent of school, puts a bit of a damper on liberal democratic policies that seek to bolster access to education for the economically and socially underprivileged. One implication of his analysis is that access to education, without the attendant cultural competencies that come with a high social class background, will fall short of making a substantial dent in equalizing the economic and cultural differences between the classes (cf. MacLeod 1995; Willis 1977).

For example, a lower-class individual may be the first in his or her family to go to college and is also likely to come from a neighborhood where very few students go to college. Once in college – not only a new educational but also, for working-class students, a new social class environment – this student will not be as *familiar* as middle-class students with the expectations and practices (e.g., punctuality, independence) that characterize college everyday reality. He or she will not already know that certain study habits and certain seminars, majors, and summer internships are "better" than others in positioning a student for college (and post-college success). Equally important, a lower-class student – feeling out of place in a middle- (and upper-) class environment – may be shyer or less entitled about interacting with and getting academic help from professors (and thus achieving a higher grade). In sum, working-class students who graduate from college are likely to have much greater economic success than those who don't go to college (Fischer et al. 1996). But, on average, they may not do as well in college (and post-college) as middle-class students. This is because working-class students are disadvantaged by working-class culture and family/neighborhood experiences that inhibit the "self-assurance of legitimate membership and the ease given by familiarity" (Bourdieu 1984: 81) with the middle-class culture required, affirmed, and rewarded by schools. Nevertheless, school is still *the* one crucial mechanism facilitating upward mobility (see Topic 13.1).

TASTE AND EVERYDAY CULTURE

THE CLASS CONDITIONING OF TASTE

Bourdieu's analysis of education and cultural capital is part of his larger interest in how ordinary, everyday habits reflect and reproduce social class differences. He emphasizes the social class conditioning of taste in all the "ordinary choices of everyday existence" (1984: 77). Therefore, although we think of our taste in clothes and food as uniquely ours, Bourdieu concludes – from empirical surveys in France of individuals' everyday habits – that individual tastes are patterned along social class lines. We like what we like not on the basis of individual sensory or aesthetic taste per se – no matter how natural some of our tastes may seem to us – but as a consequence of what it is we have learned to like or appreciate or to think is cool as a result of the social conditions and class culture in which we live and in which we have been brought up.

These dispositions and tastes are not the result of formal learning, even though at school and college we learn "the linguistic tools and references which enable aesthetic preferences to be expressed and to be constituted by being expressed" (1984: 53), and we can learn to discover and acquire new tastes. Rather, taste is part of our cultural habitus. The habitus, for Bourdieu refers essentially to the everyday tastes and dispositions we actively and literally (though unconsciously) *embody*, the relatively enduring schemes of perception, appreciation, and appropriation of the world that we enact.[3] We acquire our cultural habitus from the repetitive, everyday habits that we experience (and enact or practice) within our family of origin, a socio-cultural context which itself is conditioned by social class and by the particular everyday habits that distinguish each social class (1984: 101).

In emphasizing the habitus as culturally and physically embodied, Bourdieu means that the tastes we have are not just cognitively learned habits, but also deeply grounded in the smells, looks, and sounds that surrounded and infused the habits in our homes and families while we were growing up. Judgments of taste

> impress themselves through bodily experiences which may be as profoundly unconscious as the quiet caress of beige carpets or the thin clamminess of tattered, garish linoleum, the harsh smell of bleach or perfumes as imperceptible as a negative scent. Every interior expresses, in its own language, the present and even the past state of its occupants, bespeaking the elegant self-assurance of inherited wealth, the flashy arrogance of the nouveaux riches, the discreet shabbiness of the poor and the gilded shabbiness of "poor relations" striving to live beyond their means. (1984: 77)

Tastes in food and how we eat

Similarly, Bourdieu argues that we learn – quite readily, almost naturally, as a result of our own family's habits – to *embody* cultural expectations of what "people like us" eat and do – how we live. Writing in highly generalized terms about class differences in France, he states:

> Tastes in food ... depend on the idea each class has of the body and of the effects of food on the body, that is, on its strength, health, and beauty; and on the categories it uses to evaluate these effects, some of which may be important for one class and ignored by another, and which different classes may rank in different ways. Thus, whereas the working classes are more attentive to the strength of the (male) body than its shape, and tend to go for products that are both cheap and nutritious, the professions prefer products that are tasty, health-giving, light and not fattening. (1984: 190).

He further elaborates:

> The whole body schema, in particular the physical approach to the act of eating, governs the selection of certain foods. For example, in the working classes, fish tends to be regarded as

415

an unsuitable food for men, not only because it is a light food, insufficiently "filling," which would only be cooked for health reasons, i.e., for invalids and children, but also because, like fruit (except bananas) it is one of the "fiddly" things which a man's hands cannot cope with and which make him childlike ... but above all, it is because fish has to be eaten in a way which totally contradicts the masculine way of eating, that is, with restraint, in small mouthfuls, chewed gently, with the front of the mouth, on the tips of the teeth (because of the bones). The whole masculine identity – what is called virility – is involved in these two ways of eating, nibbling and picking, as befits a woman. (1984: 190–191)

Thus it is not just the foods chosen, as Bourdieu stresses, but "the treatment of food and the act of eating" itself that reaffirm and reproduce the different class habits and cultures (1984: 197). Hence, the working class, concerned with eating as a functional task – something necessary to nourish and replenish the body – prefer large portions of heavy foods like meat and stews and don't pay much attention to the meal's presentation. By contrast, the upper class deny eating's primary bodily function, thus preferring small portions of light food (e.g., salad, fish) (1984: 197–198), and instead construe the meal as "a social ceremony" (ibid.: 196).

Further, Bourdieu elaborates on the class-mediated gender differences in the disposition toward food and the body, noting: "There is also the principle of the division of foods between the sexes, a division which both sexes recognize in their practices and their language. It behooves a man to drink and eat more, and to eat and drink stronger things" (1984: 190, 192), to eat meat rather than fish, and to have seconds rather than women's single and smaller portion. Thus, talking about the "abundance" of the working-class meal, Bourdieu notes:

Plain speaking, plain eating: the working class meal is characterized by plenty ... and above all by freedom ... "abundant" dishes are brought to the table – soups or sauces, pasta or potatoes ... and served with a ladle or spoon, to avoid too much measuring and counting, in contrast to everything that has to be cut and divided, such as roasts [of meat]. This impression of abundance, which is the norm on special occasions, and always applies, so far as is possible, for the men, whose plates are filled twice (a privilege which marks a boy's accession to manhood), is often balanced, on ordinary occasions, by restrictions which generally apply to the women, who will share one portion between two, or eat left-overs of the previous day; a girl's accession to womanhood is marked by doing without. (1984: 194–195)

And, as we know from the prevalence of women who diet and who are diagnosed with anorexia, women, somewhat independent of class, tend to "do without." This cultural message is further reinforced by fashion models and a fashion model
NEWS 13.5 industry that requires extreme thinness (i.e., below size 0).

In sum, our judgments of taste are conditioned and structured by the intersecting family and social class context in which we are socialized. We internalize and act on these conditionings through a myriad of everyday practices (e.g., what our family eats for dinner and how, who cooks it and washes up, and whether and how we talk about sports, work, and politics over dinner), practices that are explicitly prescribed by "the semi-legitimate legitimizing agencies" (1984: 77), including women's and "ideal home" magazines and neighborhood stores, reminding us that this is what people like me (us) eat, buy, like (see also Smith's discussion of the ruling discourse of femininity; chapter 10). And, it is through these everyday practices that the macro structures of society – stratification, gender, family, religion, for example – get institutionalized in the individual's everyday life.

GENDERED TASTE

Thus, for example, gender divisions get reproduced through the parallel objective divisions between home and work and between women and men (cf. chapter 10), into which the family habitus and its everyday habits socialize us. Decisions of taste and of fashion are, by and large, established as women's domain; it is women, Bourdieu argues, who are responsible for the consumption of symbolic goods – for the buying and displaying and gift-giving of those goods that reproduce the family's taste/status, or what can be called the "production of the signs of distinction" (Bourdieu 2001: 101). In general, the (symbolic) objects people buy and place on display thus objectify their personal taste, i.e., their cultural capital, and position them hierarchically in relation to others (1984: 282). And, because of women's responsibility for the "conversion of economic capital into symbolic capital within the domestic unit," they are the ones in the vanguard of the competitive cultural practices that characterize intra- and inter-class status competition. Women "are predisposed to enter into the permanent dialectic of pretension and distinction for which fashion offers one of the most favourable terrains and

What looks good, smells good, and tastes good is conditioned by our social class and family habits.

which is the motor of cultural life as a perpetual movement of overtaking and outflanking" (2001: 101).

The sociological pairing of women and fashion is not new. At the start of the twentieth century, Georg Simmel (1904/1971: 309, 313) argued that women were fashion's "staunchest adherents," but he also maintained that this was so because it compensated for their lack of professional career and that, in fact, "emancipated women" were indifferent to fashion. Similarly, Charlotte Perkins Gilman (1903/1972) argued that if women could claim economic equality and be released from the home burdens of "domestic art," they would not need to be so subjugated to fashion.

Bourdieu, however, through writing in a socio-historical context in which gender equality is presumed (but not always practiced), and though a product of France, the same country that produced the highly influential feminist treatise *The Second Sex* (De Beauvoir 1949/1953; cf. chapter 10), does not comment on the social structural origins of, or variation within, the gendering of fashion, and nor does he elaborate on its impact on the reproduction of gender inequality. For him, gender is relevant mostly insofar as it mediates class reproduction (notwithstanding his affirmation of the political significance of the women's movement; 2001: 88–90);[4] and similarly too, race, notwithstanding his (e.g., 2001) studies in Kabylia, an Algerian province. For Bourdieu, racial and gendered contexts matter primarily as explanatory variables accounting for symbolic and other capital accumulation processes.[5]

UPPER-CLASS TASTE

Because taste is conditioned by social class conditions, each social class produces its own distinctive class habitus, a set of taste dispositions that can be seen in the choices made (and not made) by class inhabitants. Talking in highly generalizing terms, Bourdieu argues that the upper-class habitus is, for example, marked by an aesthetic disposition that requires the upper class to admire a work of art or music for its stylistic form rather than any practical function it might have; and similarly with regard to clothes, food, furniture, and other everyday objects. The aesthetic disposition signals both economic and cultural capital and their merging as a result of freedom from economic necessity.

> The aesthetic disposition, a generalized capacity to neutralize ordinary urgencies and to bracket off practical ends, a durable inclination and aptitude for practice without a practical function, can only be constituted within an experience of the world freed from urgency and through the practice of activities which are an end in themselves such as ... the contemplation of works of art. (1984: 54)

This engagement in practices that have no practical function is itself produced (and required) by the upper class's economic power, which, as Bourdieu notes,

> is first and foremost a power to keep economic necessity at arm's length. This is why it universally asserts itself by ... conspicuous consumption, squandering, and every form of

gratuitous luxury … Material or symbolic consumption of works of art constitutes one of the supreme manifestations of *ease,* in the sense both of objective leisure and subjective facility [cultural competence]. (1984: 55)

THE CULTURE GAME

The (established) upper class, therefore, play the game of culture with the playful seriousness (Bourdieu 1984: 54), that comes only from familiarity with its rules, the spoken but also, importantly – as in any game – the unspoken rules, the insider's knowledge of and feel for the game. Like accomplished basketball players on the court, the upper class know the right moves, the insider subtleties that are not necessarily written down anywhere – where to seamlessly position themselves, and when to score and how to score with ease and finesse, thus enhancing their reputation (symbolic capital), and likely too, adding to their economic and cultural capital. And like watching accomplished athletes whose game-playing seems so natural to us, so too the upper class show their "natural" claim on the game – even though, as in sports, we know that notwithstanding any natural talent, the best players also not only know the official rules of the game but train and practice a lot.

The different social classes and class fractions play the culture game through their everyday practices of taste and consumption, practices that serve to distinguish the classes from one another (1984: 250). And the culture game – and the hierarchical positioning games played in other institutional fields (e.g., the religious field; Bourdieu 1998) – "like all social stakes, simultaneously presupposes and demands that one take part in the game and be taken in by it" (1984: 250). We misrecognize the *arbitrariness* of the game's structure and rules; to play is to be taken in by the game. All games are symbolic struggles over the appropriation of scarce goods; only the winners (not the also-rans) get trophies (symbolic capital).

Bourdieu argues that collective misrecognition of the arbitrariness of the social hierarchies and evaluative categories that structure everyday practices is the process which necessarily sustains unequal social relations across all institutional fields (culture, education, art, law, religion). As he states, "there is no way out of the game of culture" (1984: 12). Hence we variously engage in practices that we know are arbitrary (e.g., why should visiting an art museum be considered more culturally worthy than visiting a sports museum?), but which, if we were to acknowledge them as arbitrary, would lose their symbolic power, the symbolic power necessary to maintain unequal class and other unequal social relations (e.g., gender hierarchies in the Catholic church through the exclusion of women from ordination).

WORKING-CLASS TASTE

In contrast to the upper-class, the working-class habitus, Bourdieu argues (with a similarly broad sweep), produces a taste and style that are dictated by economic and cultural necessity: "Necessity imposes a taste for necessity which implies a form of adaptation to and consequently acceptance of the necessary, a resignation to the inevitable" conditions of their class and the choices it allows in their ordinary everyday existence (1984: 373). Necessity produces a working-class habitus whereby, for example, manual workers indicate an appreciation for clothes that are "good value for money," that are cheap and long-lasting, practical or functional, and not stylistically risky. Their choices are not determined by their volume of economic capital alone, though this clearly is an important dimension of necessity. Their choices are co-determined by the coincidence of economic and cultural necessity: Among the working class, conformity rather than personal autonomy is valued.

As Bourdieu points out, this functional disposition toward buying clothes (or toward food) is a *reasonable strategy* for the working class given the economic and cultural capital (and time) that buying more fashionable clothes would require. Moreover, the symbolic capital, the gains to their reputation, that might be expected from such an investment would be low for manual workers (at least while at work, given the nature of their work) compared, say, to clerical workers, whose taste in fashion can enhance their reputation among peers and supervisors at work (1984: 377–378).

There is thus what Bourdieu calls an economy of practice in working-class taste, an economy that also characterizes the practices of all social classes. Given what they've got – given the economic and cultural capital they have – each class makes reasonable strategic investments in order to expand and maximize their symbolic capital. Thus, Wal-Mart's consumer categories are not only a good market-control strategy (see chapter 5, Box 5.1); they also make good cultural sense: "Value-price shoppers," "brand aspirationals," and "price-sensitive affluents" are all comprised of class-situated individuals who are making the most

NEWS 13.6   economically and culturally of what they have got (economically and culturally). Bourdieu states:

> The interest the different classes have in self-presentation, the attention they devote to it, their awareness of the profits it gives and the investment of time, effort, sacrifice and care which they actually put into it are proportionate to the chances of material or symbolic profit they can reasonably expect from it. (1984: 202)

WHO WANTS TO BE A MILLIONAIRE?

Furthermore, Bourdieu emphasizes that because taste is produced in and by a class-conditioned habitus and hence is a relatively enduring system of judgments and dispositions, the individual's taste does not change just because he or she suddenly wins the lottery. "Having a million does not in itself make one able to live like a millionaire; and parvenus [the newly arrived rich] generally take a long time to learn that what they see as culpable prodigality [excessive self-indulgent spending] is, in their new [economic] condition, expenditure of basic necessity" (1984: 374). To live like a millionaire, or as an upwardly mobile rich person, requires the acquisition of a new class disposition such that the individual can be at ease in claiming as his or her own that which he or she can afford, and to learn to appreciate that "one man's extravagance is another man's necessity" (1984: 375). For example, there are nuances between extravagance and necessity in the lifestyles of residents of highly affluent communities like Silicon Valley, California.

The cultural competence projected in being at ease with one's new-found wealth, the "self-assurance of legitimate membership and the ease given by familiarity" (1984: 81), require, Bourdieu argues, following Goffman, a certain amount of role distance. One cannot show oneself as being ever so excited to have all this new money (or to be in a museum or an expensive restaurant for the first time), one has to act as if this is what you are used to, as if this is your habitus (1984: 54). Thus,

> to appreciate the "true value" of the purely symbolic services which in many areas (hotels, hairdressing etc.) make the essential difference between luxury establishments and ordinary businesses, one has to feel oneself the legitimate recipient of this bureaucratically personalized care and attention and to display vis-à-vis those who offer it the mixture of distance (including "generous" gratuities) and freedom which the bourgeois have toward their servants. (1984: 374)

TASTE IN THE REPRODUCTION OF SOCIAL INEQUALITY

The different, economically conditioned class cultures of everyday life reinforce the objective distinctions between the classes (i.e., in how they act and where they come from) as well as the boundaries between the classes and the dispositions that class-situated individuals subjectively feel toward the crossing of class boundaries. One structural consequence of this system of distinction is the reinforcement of class inequality. The familiarity and comfort individuals feel in their own class habitus, with their own culture's ways of doing things, means that working-class individuals, for example, feel less attracted, less entitled, to entering and participating in institutional spaces such as universities whose culture – *the* legitimate culture – they perceive to be so at odds with their own everyday culture. This becomes an objectively structured, and subjectively felt, impediment, therefore, to the educational success (as discussed above, p. 414) and upward mobility of children from working-class families. However, once they make this break, then their own children, born into a higher class fraction, can be more at ease with legitimate culture.

In sum, Bourdieu argues, "We distinguish ourselves by the distinctions we make." Our taste reveals who we are. Taste reveals our social class conditioning and at the same time, embodied in our everyday habits, reproduces and extends the social class conditioning and the social class differences that characterize everyday cultural choices. Thus taste unites and separates. Being the product of the conditionings associated with a particular class of conditions of existence, it unites all those who are the product of similar conditions while distinguishing them from all others. And it distinguishes in an essential way, since taste is the basis of all that one has – people and things – and all that one is for others, whereby one classifies oneself and is classified by others ... Aversion to different life-styles is perhaps one of the strongest barriers between the classes; class endogamy is evidence of this ... Objectively and subjectively aesthetic stances adopted in matters like cosmetics, clothing or home decoration are opportunities to experience or assert one's position in social space, as a rank to be upheld or a distance to be kept. (1984: 56–57)

In short, "Taste is what brings together things and people that go together" (1984: 241).

LINKING MICRO ACTION AND MACRO STRUCTURES

Bourdieu's discussion of everyday tastes, something we generally think of as an individual preference, highlights his more general theoretical emphasis that micro-level individual action matters in society, while at the same time recognizing that individual choices are invariably conditioned by and work back on macro-structural processes (e.g., inequality in society, at work, in gender relations). Therefore, while there is a tendency in sociology to counterpoise micro-level with macro-level analytical perspectives, and similarly to contrast approaches that emphasize individual or collective agency with those which focus on explaining social action in terms of structural and institutional processes, Bourdieu's conceptualization of how we should analyze and understand society transcends these polarizing opposites.

Bourdieu's writing demonstrates the agency of individuals in everyday life – the individual makes choices every day about what food to buy, what clothes to wear, what music to listen to, what church to attend, what political party to support, what gift to buy, etc. Yet, at the same time, the individual – no matter how avant-garde or autonomous – does not act alone or in some sort of existential vacuum. Ordinary, everyday existence is saturated by society and we cannot escape from its structural and cultural forces. Individual agency, then, is always constrained, always structured, as Bourdieu states, by formal education, social class, family habits, and the distinctive (and unequal) cultural codes and practices that these contexts teach us and which we reproduce, more or less, through our everyday social relations and behavior. Thus Bourdieu presents us with a portrait of society wherein individuals embody the habits and attitudes, the culture, of those around them, and act back on that culture in everyday social life with a certain degree of individual autonomy (choosing chicken or fish). Yet the cultural options available to the most agential of individuals are themselves constrained by an objective class (and racial and gender) structure wherein the distribution of resources – economic and cultural resources – makes certain options more reasonable, more "natural," than others. It is through such ordinary, everyday actions as food shopping that we as individuals reproduce the objective structural order, even though we have a certain amount of latitude in the choices and distinctions we make.

ENDLESS STRATIFICATION

Some readers may find Bourdieu's emphasis that we cannot escape the game of culture, i.e., that we cannot escape distinguishing ourselves by the (arbitrary but class-conditioned) taste distinctions we make everyday, too much of an exaggeration of the importance of hierarchies in social life – that everything we do, every taste we express, reflects and feeds into a system of stratification. This is an understandable response to his work. Yet, by making us think about taste as a socially conditioned and socially conditioning set of practices that we all engage in, Bourdieu alerts us to the many small (as well as big) ways in which class divisions get reproduced. This is an important contribution. He does not elaborate on gender distinctions and only briefly acknowledges racial and ethnic differences in taste. Nevertheless, his detailed focus on the minutiae of different lifestyles, not as individual lifestyles per se, but as socially conditioned and socially contextualized individual choices and tastes, can be extended to make us aware that social inequality, in all of its many intersecting locales, is found and reproduced not just in the big structures and institutions of society – where we might expect to find inequality: in schools, on Wall Street, in sports – but also in what we might ordinarily think of as relatively benign everyday sites (e.g., the dinner table) and everyday activities (e.g., having a picnic).

Feminists (e.g., Martineau, Gilman, Smith, Collins, Hochschild) have long identified the kitchen and the home as a site for the reproduction of gender inequality – the gender division of labor in who cooks and who cleans and who smiles and who doesn't get to leave the home for the economic-public world (cf. chapter 10); and theorists like Nancy Chodorow highlight the social-psychodynamic forces that reproduce gendered patterns in the taste or desire for mothering. Bourdieu adds to the sociological understanding of how and why structures of inequality are so resilient because his analysis illuminates how individuals, men and women, acting on their own (socially conditioned) personal taste in making everyday choices about apparently mundane things, are really enacting a sophisticated, multilayered cultural script that telescopes the whole interlocking institutional system of social stratification. This does not mean that women and men do not have individual agency, or that they cannot change the structures and cultural practices that reproduce inequality. But it cautions us that change in the social order is a long and slow process. And it is so largely because of the inscription of cultures of domination (e.g., masculinity) in and through the interconnected institutions (between the state, the economy, the university, mass media, advertising, sports, the church) that produce and reproduce the myriad forms of inequality (Bourdieu 2001: viii).

WEB 10.4

SUMMARY

Across his prolific writings, Bourdieu's overarching focus was on social inequality – on stratification in schools, art, clothes, food, etc. – and on how inequality gets reproduced across varied institutional and cultural domains. He outlines the details of individual choices in the micro contexts of everyday life, but his analysis overall is more concerned with macro structures and processes than with micro relations. Of particular note, his conceptualization of the habitus shows how micro practices are conditioned by and reproduce macro structures (e.g., of class inequality), and how objective macro structures (e.g., the educational system, the social class system) get internalized into individuals' everyday habits and dispositions. His approach thus exemplifies how sociologists must necessarily attend to the interplay of micro and macro processes.

Finally, although Bourdieu discusses the strategic choices made by individuals and the fact that, for example, there are economic efficiencies in working-class tastes (dictated by necessity), he does not regard individual choices as motivated by the same individual self-interested, utilitarian motives elaborated by rational choice theorists such as James Coleman (cf. chapter 7). For Bourdieu, individual choices are invariably located within a class-conditioned cultural habitus and thus are structured by a particular social, economic, and cultural context.

POINTS TO REMEMBER

Pierre Bourdieu (France, 1930–2002)
- Focus on the reproduction of inequality in society
- Inequality due to class-conditioned differences in volume of capital (economic, social, cultural capital)
- Special attention to the links between economic and cultural capital
- School is a major transmitter and reproducer of cultural and economic capital
- Everyday taste is socially conditioned by the class habitus
- Different social classes construe the body, food, and eating differently
- Different social classes have a taste for different cultures, different everyday habits
- Taste reproduces social hierarchies; we distinguish ourselves by the distinctions we make
- Different institutional fields (e.g., education, art, etc.) have their own respective logics of symbolic differentiation and inequality

GLOSSARY

aesthetic disposition the class-inculcated attitude that allows and requires the upper class to admire art, clothes, etc., for style rather than practical function.

class fraction differentiated, hierarchical sub-components of broadly defined social classes (e.g., the middle class); the economic and cultural capital of class fractions varies.

collective misrecognition immersion in a particular habitus or set of everyday practices whereby we (necessarily) fail to perceive the arbitrary, though highly determining ways in which those practices reproduce inequality.

cultural capital familiarity and ease with (the legitimate) habits, knowledge, tastes, and style of everyday living; school requires, transmits, produces, and reproduces cultural capital.

cultural competence possessing the appropriate family and social class background, knowledge, and taste to display (and acquire additional) cultural capital.

culture dispositions, tastes, evaluative judgments, and knowledge inculcated in and as a result of class-conditioned experiences (including formal education).

economic capital amount of economic assets an individual/family has; can be converted into social and cultural capital (and additional economic capital).

economy of practice individuals' and social classes' use of the economic and cultural capital they have to make reasonable strategic investments that expand and maximize their economic, cultural, and symbolic capital.

educational capital competencies acquired through school; can be converted into economic and cultural capital.

game of culture participation in the evaluative and taste practices that confer style or distinction as if "naturally" rather than due to class conditioning; reproduces social class differences.

habitus relatively enduring schemes of perception, appreciation, and appropriation of things, embodied through class-conditioned socialization and enacted in everyday choices and taste.

institutional field specific institutional spheres (e.g., education, culture, religion, law) characterized by institution-specific rules and practices reproducing inequality.

social capital individual's ties or connections to others; can be converted into economic and cultural capital and into additional social capital.

social classes broad groups based on objective differences in amounts of economic, social, and cultural capital.

structure objective ways in which society is organized; e.g., the social class structure exists and has objective consequences for individuals independent of individuals' subjective social class feelings and self-categorization.

symbolic capital one's reputation for competence, good taste, integrity, accomplishment, etc.; has exchange-value, convertible to economic, social, and cultural capital.

symbolic goods goods we buy, display, and give to distinguish ourselves from others; signal and reproduce taste, status, social hierarchy, social class inequality.

taste social class- and family-conditioned, ordinary, everyday preferences and habits, socially learned ways of appreciation, style.

RELEVANT NEWSPAPER STORIES

All news stories are from the *New York Times* unless otherwise noted, and can be accessed via www.wiley.com/go/dillon. See NEWS icons in the margins above.

NEWS 13.1   "The millionaires who don't feel rich," August 5, 2007.
"Measuring wealth by the foot," March 16, 2008.
"An elite zip code becomes harder to crack," March 21, 2007.

NEWS 13.2   "The terrible toll of art anxiety," February 28, 2008.

NEWS 13.3   "The art of buying art, with the help of an adviser," May 27, 2007.

NEWS 13.4   "Higher education gap may slow economic mobility," February 20, 2008. See also www.economicmobility.org.
For wide-ranging statistical data on education trends in the US, click on the US Department of Education's National Center for Education Statistics website: http://nces.ed.gov/.

NEWS 13.5   "Where size 0 doesn't make the cut," September 22, 2006.
"When is thin too thin?" September 21, 2006.
"Health guidelines are set for models. But U.S. fashion industry refuses to say how thin is too thin," January 6, 2007.
"Doctors fault designers' stance over thin models," January 9, 2007.

NEWS 13.6   "It's not only about price at Wal-Mart," March 2, 2007.

NOTES

1   In Bourdieu's (1991, 1998) analysis of the religious field, for example, he construes "religious capital" and its reproduction in terms of the differentiated access of lay people and clergy to the unequally distributed symbolic resources within a particular religious institutional field, e.g. Catholicism; see Dillon (2001).

2   Although in France the state finances the costs of university education, schools and universities are more stratified in terms of status and credentials than in the US. In France, the "grandes écoles" are the most prestigious colleges, mostly admitting students from upper professional and executive class families, who upon graduation are employed in these high-paying, high-status occupational sectors; "universités," in contrast, as "mass institutions" are less selective and less tightly connected to occupational opportunities (Bourdieu 1996: xiv; Lamont 1992: 45, 78).

3   The German social theorist Norbert Elias (1897–1990) used the term "habitus" to refer to the socializing/civilizing process, the social prohibitions, whereby certain everyday social habits and manners (e.g., how to hold your knife and fork) are ingrained in the "civilized" individual, such that habits of "self-restraint" (e.g., "Don't stuff your mouth")

become "second nature," i.e., operating against the individual's "conscious wishes" (Elias 1978: 129). Elias elaborates: socially imposed civilized manners "appear to [individuals] as highly personal, something 'inward,' implanted in them by nature ... later it becomes more and more an inner automatism, the imprint of society on the inner self, the superego, that forbids the individual to eat in any other way than with a fork" (1978: 128–129). See Mennell and Goudsblom (1998) for an introduction to Elias's writings.

4   See Adkins and Skeggs (2004) for a feminist critique and extension of Bourdieu's theorizing.

5   For example, Bourdieu observes that in societies where economic assets are scarce, women are used as objects of capital accumulation: "When – as is the case in Kabylia [province in Algeria] – the acquisition of symbolic capital and social capital is more or less the only possible form of accumulation, women are assets which must be protected from offence and suspicion and which, when invested in exchanges, can produce alliances, in other words social capital, and prestigious allies, in other words, symbolic capital" (Bourdieu 2001: 45).

CHAPTER FOURTEEN

POSTMODERNITY

KEY CONCEPTS

postmodern

fluidity

politics of truth

metanarratives

semiology

deconstruction

post-structuralist

remix

aestheticization of reality

sheer commodification

simulacra

hyperreality

implosion

CHAPTER MENU

Something changed in western society in and around the early 1970s. While the political and cultural turmoil of that era (e.g., Gitlin 1987) became highly consequential for advancing social equality and the rights of women, blacks, gays, and other cultural minorities, a major transformation was also occurring in information technology and computer electronics. In particular, the introduction of video technology into everyday life was a milestone. Video capability may not seem too remarkable to you because you have grown up in a time when it and so many other technological devices are a normal part of almost every household. The introduction of video, however, made a tremendous difference to how we began to think about time and space (a time/space disembeddedness that Giddens (1990) highlights; see chapter 15).

For the first time in human society, video enabled us to be in one place, to record a television program that was being broadcast at a particular time in another place, and to subsequently watch this recorded program at a time and place of our choosing. Video thus ruptured the linear constraint of time and the ordered way in which previously we had assumed time and space went together. In some sense, it ruptured what it means to talk about a here-and-now reality, the presumed coincidence of such a reality, when virtual reality changes the now-ness and the here-ness of experience.

It is this time/space split and its implications across all aspects of our lives that allows David Harvey (1990: vii) to comment: "There has been a sea-change in cultural as well as in political-economic practices since around 1972. This sea-change is bound up with the emergence of new dominant ways in which we experience space and time." Harvey (1990) suggests that this sea-change has produced what he refers to as "the condition of postmodernity." Scholars and writers vary in their specific use of the term postmodern to highlight transformations in various aspects of contemporary culture and society. But what they share is the view that a new term, the "postmodern," is needed in order to highlight what they argue is a qualitative shift in the post-1970s era: the decentering of experience and reality compared to the order and progress of the two hundred or so years that preceded it (e.g., see Best and Kellner 1997).

Although the early decades of the twentieth century witnessed many changes and remarkable progress in science (e.g., Einstein's theory of relativity), politics (expansion of democracy), economics (industrialization/automation), and art and literature (Modernism/Cubism), those changes extended the principles of the Enlightenment. The Enlightenment (as we discussed in the Introduction) created or at least demarcated the modern world, a world based on Reason and on the presumption that reason yielded Truth, and that the application of reason to knowledge, politics, the economy, and social organization would move society progressively forward in a cumulative, linear manner. This was the agenda of modernity.

An emphasis on the *post*modern, then, is used by scholars, most of whom tend to be in the humanities (like queer theorists; cf. chapter 11), to imply that art, literature, architecture, politics, society are beyond reason. Accordingly, there is no one Truth, only our imaginings – and, indeed, any interest in trying to understand the order or reason in the human-social condition is itself beyond reason. Postmodern scholars' rejection of reason and coherence, a rejection that frequently translates into their own opaque writing, makes an outsider's writing and reading about postmodernity a daunting task (e.g., this is a difficult chapter for me to write and probably for you to read). In a nod to the questionable status of "truth" that is part of the postmodern condition, and its disruption of our modern way of thinking about, categorizing, and ordering reality, Fredric Jameson suggests that postmodernism theory is an "effort to take the temperature of the age without instruments and a situation in which we are not even sure there is so coherent a thing as an 'age,' or zeitgeist [spirit] or 'system' or 'current situation' any longer" (1991: xi). But, in any event, we must make an effort to make sense of what postmodernity entails, because although you may (or may not) ultimately disagree with the radical conclusions drawn by some postmodern writers, the theory, nonetheless, grapples with very important issues.

CRITIQUE OF THE MODERN

The postmodern rejection of reason is very different to the critique of reason elaborated by the Frankfurt School (*FS*) (cf. chapter 5). Horkheimer, Adorno, and Marcuse critiqued the use of reason and science for instrumental purposes – for social control and manipulation – and the varied ways in which technological rationality is harnessed to manipulating political and consumer culture such that, they argue, what is ultimately produced is deception and illusion rather than illumination. It is not reason, per se, that *FS* theorists denounce. Rather, they value reason, and the human ability to use reason (normatively) to advance social equality; but they despair at what they see as the use of reason and scientific/technological knowledge for strategic rather than liberating purposes. Rather than pessimistically critiquing the distortion of reason in society, Habermas moves beyond his *FS* colleagues. He elaborates the theory of communicative action as a possible way to retrieve the "proper" use of reason, i.e., to use reasoned argumentation to critique rational instrumental domination and to examine the values and assumptions that underlie all social action (Habermas 1984: 386–388; cf. chapter 5). Habermas, therefore, is not a postmodern theorist. Rather, he is very much wedded to the Enlightenment view of reason, i.e., that reason can be used for emancipatory purposes rather than for social control and domination.

MICHEL FOUCAULT: POSTMODERN TRUTH

Someone who can be considered postmodern is **Michel Foucault**. When we discussed Foucault in chapter 11, we primarily concentrated on his analysis of the body and his underscoring of the myriad ways in which the state and various institutions (the Census, schools, hospitals, churches, etc.) track and regulate individual bodies and whole populations and societies. I don't see much that is distinctly postmodern in this particular analysis – it is really in many ways an extension of the rational reach of the bureaucratization and control processes that Weber first highlighted (cf. chapter 3). What is innovative is Foucault's close analytical focus on the body as the object of multiple controlling and disciplinary practices.

BIOGRAPHICAL NOTE

Michel Foucault: See the biographical note on Foucault in chapter 11.

Where we more clearly see that Foucault is a postmodern theorist is in his discussion of the nature of "truth" and knowledge and how it is that different social contexts, and the regulatory and legitimation practices in those contexts, construct and create truth/knowledge.[1] The philosophy of science is a complex field of inquiry. But, for our purposes, it is sufficient to know that Foucault came to prominence at a time when other scholars had already questioned the Enlightenment idea that science and scientific rationality in and of themselves led to the discovery of truth. Most notably, Thomas Kuhn, a philosopher and historian of science, wrote a highly influential book, *The Structure of Scientific Revolutions*, first published in 1962, showing that scientific knowledge did not proceed in the linear, cumulative fashion that the Enlightenment thinkers envisaged. Science's progress or evolution, was, he argued, highly contingent on scientists' various non-rational assumptions. Kuhn thus challenged the traditional idea that there are scientific truths out there in the world simply waiting to be discovered, and instead showed that the social, historical, and political context in which science is conducted is what shapes what counts for scientific knowledge and what kinds of scientific knowledge are deemed worthy of pursuit and affirmation. He illustrated his theory with the transition from the Ptolemaic (earth-centered) to Copernican (sun-centered) astronomy. He argued that the shift had as much to do with empirical evidence (which is always ambiguous) as with the emergence of a new worldview that was no longer driven by theology (see also Feyerabend 1979; cf. Introduction).

Foucault further elaborated this contingent view of all knowledge. He argues that the history of ideas shows that knowledge has many imperfections and uncertainties. Knowledge has an archaeology (Foucault 1972) and a genealogy (Foucault 1984), a history that is built upon various pieces of bedrock, and that contains many discontinuities and shifts in what is accepted as knowledge and as ways of categorizing and formalizing knowledge and its related practices (evident if, for example, we compare eighteenth- and nineteenth-century psychiatry or criminology). For Foucault, knowledge does not constitute some great linear and total unity of Knowledge or Truth. There is fluidity rather than a reasoned coherence to truth. He further underscored that ideas are not inherently self-evident but have a history, and a history that, like everything else in society, is shaped by various political interests. Thus he emphasized that the ideas, the knowledge that gets established as the Truth – the canon – whether in literature, philosophy, psychiatry (Foucault 1965), medicine (Foucault 1975), criminology (Foucault 1979), sexuality (Foucault 1978), or, we can add, sociology – is not intellectually pure, as if somehow human ideas could ever be above everyday conflicts and social practices. Further, and most importantly, even in the natural sciences, views and theories of the world evolve as a result of empirical evidence and extra-scientific background assumptions (e.g., Foucault 1970, 1972).

Foucault's focus on the social and political contamination of knowledge thus debstabilizes all that we have been socialized to accept and respect as Truth. His analysis puts a rupture in why we pursue learning and knowledge, and deflates our belief and hope that we can find "the" truth, and that its pursuit is a worthwhile goal. Foucault tells us that we are deluded into thinking all this. Instead, he argues, truth is caught up in politics and power and is far from pure.

> Truth isn't outside power, or lacking in power: contrary to a myth whose history and functions would repay further study, truth isn't the reward of free spirits, the child of protracted solitude, nor the privilege of those who have succeeded in liberating themselves. Truth is a thing of this world: it is produced only by virtue of multiple forms of constraint ... Each society has its regime of truth, its "general **politics**" **of truth**: that is, the types of discourse which it accepts and makes function as true ... The political question, to sum up, is not error, illusion, alienated consciousness, or ideology; it is truth itself. (1984: 72–73, 75)

Hence, as we see especially in the accounts of war that are produced by the government and the military, the politics of the situation means that only certain accounts are presented as true, while strands that might complicate that truth get marginalized or suppressed, as we saw with General Taguba's report about Abu Ghraib prison abuse (cf. chapter 6).

NEWS 14.1

POSTMODERN TRUTH AND THE SOCIAL CONSTRUCTION OF KNOWLEDGE

Berger and Luckmann (cf. chapter 9), and Dorothy Smith and Patricia Hill Collins (cf. chapter 10), also, to a large extent, destabilize that which we take to be true. Some sociologists might well categorize those theorists as postmodern in the sense that they challenge the notion of a single truth, of a single ruling text. I see them somewhat differently. I see them as engaged in the critique of the (allegedly) objective, taken-for-granted knowledge – the official canons – rather than being suspicious of all knowledge, all realities. They alert us that different knowledges emerge out of different social contexts and from the different everyday experiences that those contexts give rise to. Their writings thus make us aware that the various narratives (and traditions) that we have always accepted as true – e.g., somehow there is some pure reason why women can't serve in military combat or gays cannot legally marry in many states – do not tell the whole story. These theorists remind us that there are alternative stories that sometimes complement but more often contest and oppose these official narratives.

Sociologists are attentive to the social construction of knowledge, therefore, because social, historical, and generational contexts too (Mannheim 1936/1968) always matter in the creation and perception of knowledge/truth. Importantly, however, scholars who embrace this general perspective do not reject the idea that truth is possible; they simply affirm that different truths (knowledges) get produced collectively by different people out of their lived experiences. For these theorists, truths are discoverable; though no one has a monopoly on truth by virtue of their power or gender or age or social status, etc.

THE IMPOSSIBILITY OF TRUTH

Foucault is different. He goes beyond the social construction of knowledge to argue that no truth is possible and that all knowledge, whether produced by academics or by ordinary people in their everyday lives, is infused and distorted by power. A social construction perspective might lead a sociologist to inquire, for example, into the knowledge, the known social reality, of long-term commitment that gay men and lesbians have come to acquire from their everyday experiences in gay marital-like relationships, and to contrast these experiences/truths with the definition of (heterosexual) marriage institutionalized in law and public policy. The implication of Foucault's logic, however, is that sociologists and others should not pursue any of this knowledge; none of it is worthy of inquiry because all of it necessarily is distorted. This is a rather extreme approach because it undermines all the questions we might ever want to ask on any subject and/or of anyone (whether of those at the center of official power or on the margins). In Foucault's view, talk is oppressive; it oppresses us by the very language we use and the categories we use to describe and talk about our experiences (cf. chapter 11).

DECONSTRUCTION

Foucault's compatriot, the influential French intellectual Jean Lyotard, writes that a postmodern sensibility requires "incredulity towards metanarratives" (1984: xxiv). What he means by this is that we should be doubting of any story, of any narrative – of history, religion, capitalism, science, sociological theory – that presumes or makes connections across disparate ideas, that weaves a story of knowledge about something, and which in the process affirms particular interpretations and particular kinds of knowledge (what we try to do in sociological theory and what scientists and theologians and writers in general do). In other words, if we consider social life to be a narrative of some kind (a text about how the world works, about what social institutions do), then what Lyotard is objecting to is any attempt to make comments about this narrative, because this would presume that we are somehow impartial observers or commentators whose pronouncements get at some invariant and all-knowing big Truth, Truth with a capital T. Note here that Lyotard uses the word *incredulity* – not simply suspicion or resistance or opposition or critique, but incredulity. For him, all narratives and the principles on which they are structured are beyond belief, beyond reason. They are all just simply "very different language games" (ibid.: xxv) that make different claims to a particular kind of legitimated knowledge.

DECONSTRUCTING SALT AND PEPPER

Like Lyotard, philosophers and literary theorists at the forefront of postmodern theory are trained in textual analysis. These theorists focus on the structure of language – i.e., the binary structuring system of signs by which we use words to denote things and meanings (e.g., for Durkheim, the binary of the sacred and the profane; cf. chapter 2). The binary structure of language means that things are invariably defined not in and of themselves but by their opposite; e.g., the word man is used to refer to a man, something that is defined in opposition to woman; or salt is salt and not pepper. Postmodern theorists challenge this binary structure, as exemplified in queer theory's rejection of the homosexuality/heterosexuality binary because it arbitrarily assumes an either/or exclusivity rather than fluidity in sexual desires (cf. chapter 11). These theorists take apart or deconstruct the very rules and principles on which language is based, as well as the socio-cultural reference system or the semiology that gives (arbitrary) signs particular meanings, and which pairs signs, images, and things with one another in a culturally meaningful way.

Semiology is the science of signs (Barthes 1972: 111), the textual analysis of what signs or objects go together in a particular sign-making, sign-inference system. We learn to decode the meanings signified in any piece of content – a photo, an advertisement, a movie, or television drama (e.g., Fiske and Hartley 1978: 59–67). And through analyzing signs and their codes we discern patterns in what particular symbols and signs are arbitrarily put together to create particular meanings, and hence, despite their arbitrariness, seem to "naturally" go together in a particular social and cultural reality. Thus, for example, I cannot think of a cheeseburger without also thinking of fries; similarly when many individuals think of their country they simultaneously think (with loyalty and pride) of its national flag. It is this cognitively and culturally inscribed sign system that advertising exploits so well; a good advertisement, and any representation of style, whether on *Sex and the City* or on punk rockers (e.g., Hebdige 1979), communicates to us what "naturally" goes with what (e.g., fish and chips) (cf. Barthes 1972: 62–64, 109–127). But this "naturalness" is culturally defined. Therefore, although we may think that somewhere out there, there is some sort of amorphous reality – the signified – and signs to label and make sense of it, and that there is a pre-given correspondence or basic truth between the sign and the signified, this in not so. The signs and the signified are not natural, but linguistically and culturally determined.

Postmodern writers reject the order imposed by language and other sign-ordering systems. Most famously, **Jacques Derrida,** a French philosopher, engaged in the deconstruction of the foundational rules of language. He pushed his colleagues and others, including poets and artists, toward a post-structuralist view of language. This approach seeks to dismantle the binary structure of language, and by extension, the binary linguistic codes and meanings which embed all knowledge as well as forms of social organization (e.g., gender, sexuality, race).

BIOGRAPHICAL NOTE

Jacques Derrida was born in French-controlled Algeria to Jewish parents in 1930. As a youth, he became interested in philosophy, which he subsequently studied at university at the prestigious Ecole Normal Superieure in Paris, where he met and became friendly with Michel Foucault. A professor of philosophy, first in Paris and later at the University of California, Irvine, Derrida wrote several books and lectured widely in Europe and the US on philosophy; he is widely regarded as the "father of deconstruction." Married, and with three sons, he died of pancreatic cancer in Paris in 2004.

Post-structuralists underscore that meaning, or what is signified by a given symbol or signifier,

> is not immediately *present* in a sign. Since the meaning of a sign is a matter of what the sign is *not*, its meaning is always in some sense absent from it too. Meaning ... cannot be easily nailed down, it is never fully present in one sign alone, but is rather a kind of constant flickering of presence and absence together. Reading a text is more like tracing this process of constant flickering than it is like counting the beads on a necklace ... The implication of all this is that language is a much less stable affair than the classical structuralism had considered ... it strikes a blow at traditional theories of meaning. (Eagleton 1983: 128, 129)

As further explained by the English literary theorist Terry Eagleton, Derrida argued that we must deconstruct the foundational or first principles of meaning. This is because these first principles are part of, rather than external to, a particular system of meaning. Such principles:

> are commonly defined by what they exclude: they are part of the sort of binary opposition beloved of structuralism. Thus for male dominated societies, man is the founding principle and woman the excluded opposite of this; and as long as such a distinction is tightly held in place the whole system can function effectively. Deconstruction is the name given to the critical operation by which such oppositions can be partly undermined, or by which they can be shown partly to undermine each other in the process of textual meaning. Woman is the opposite, the "other" of man; she is non-man, defective man, assigned a

chiefly negative value in relation to the male first principle. But equally man is what he is only by virtue of ceaselessly shutting out this other or opposite, defining himself in antithesis to it, and his whole identity is therefore caught up and at risk in the very gesture by which he seeks to assert his unique, autonomous existence ... Man therefore needs this other even as he spurns it. (Eagleton 1983: 132–133)

Some of what Derrida says here sounds like what feminists have long argued. For example, Simone de Beauvoir's *The Second Sex* elaborated the otherness of women, their secondary status to men (cf. chapter 10, p. 318). And before de Beauvoir, Charlotte Perkins Gilman discussed society's construal of women as a defective sub-species relative to man (cf. chapter 10). And similarly, Said (1978) discusses the otherness institutionalized in racial definition; how we know who we are by whom we are not (white/black; cf. chapter 12).

But while feminists, for example, want to dismantle the gender system that perpetuates inequality, I don't think – unless they are postmodern feminists – they want to dismantle the whole linguistic system that underlies not just gender, but all social relationships and processes. The feminist agenda is a more narrowly focused intellectual and political one. For deconstructionists, all binaries are problematic (not just man/woman, but good/bad, life/death, construction/destruction).

Deconstructionists like Derrida have been accused of taking apart or deconstructing language for its own sake, of destroying meaning and doing so without reconstructing some alternative meaning that has coherence. Derrida would reject this criticism. He argues that it is not necessary to throw away or dismantle the classical texts (of Plato, Aristotle, etc.). Instead, he argues, we should reread them with a view to finding out "how their thinking works or does not work, to find the tensions, the contradictions ... within their own corpus [body of writing]" (1997: 9). We do not have to abandon the classical texts, the canon of knowledge in philosophy, literature, art, music, etc., but we do have to continuously unpack how the canon got established, how it accumulated all these highly regarded texts, and to question the conventional meanings and intellectual or literary or artistic value that we traditionally associate with those texts. Derrida argues for a constant tension, an uncertainty, in what we accept as knowledge; that we keep revisiting and rethinking what counts as illuminating or meaningful categories and texts. Thus, he states, we do not have to choose between the canon and new works, but "we have to analyze the history ... of the breaks which have produced our current [western] world out of Greece, for instance, out of Christianity, out of this origin, and breaking or transforming this origin, at the same time. So there is this tension" (Derrida 1997: 10).

DECONSTRUCTING THE UN

Much of what I have been outlining may seem abstract. But the deconstructionist project might become clearer if we consider a concrete example. Let's take the

UN, the United Nations. The UN was established in 1945, at the end of World War II, to oversee the political regulation of the world and to encourage cooperation among economically, politically, and culturally diverse nation-states. The ideals informing the UN are grounded in the same highly regarded political-philosophical ideals of democracy, equality, and justice that inform the US and other democratic systems, ideas first elaborated in Plato's *Republic*. However, the economic, political, and cultural dilemmas of today's globalizing world (cf. chapter 15) are quite different from those in play when the UN was established. Various geo-political (e.g., ethnic violence in Africa) and humanitarian crises (e.g., starvation in Myanmar) demand intervention by the UN.

Derrida (2003) acknowledges that it is necessary for the UN to intervene in certain countries. But, he argues,

> it can't intervene the way it should because of laws about state sovereignty. That is, international law, which is a good thing, nevertheless is still rooted in its mission, in its action, in its languages, in a Western concept of philosophy, a Western concept of the state and of sovereignty, and this is a limit. We have to deconstruct the foundations of this international law, but not in order to destroy the international organization ... we have to rethink the philosophical foundations of these international organizations. (2003: 13)

In other words, our contemporary world needs to establish some kind of international or global community but, for Derrida, that community cannot rest on some binary and western understanding of what community is or what state sovereignty is or entails; it must somehow incorporate the values and realities of the plurality of different countries that comprise the world, and not simply the world as defined by western eyes and in terms of western (binary) definitions of democracy, freedom, etc.

Thus Derrida (2003) believes in the authority of the UN and of international law, but argues that the UN's structure and charter need to be modified. He argues that we need to move beyond the traditional (binary) understanding whereby the US, for example, is presented as the exemplar of democracy and good government; and China, for example, is presented as the exemplar of the repression of human rights. Derrida maintains that the UN (and other global institutions such as the International Monetary Fund, IMF) needs to have the power to impose sanctions on all countries, including powerful nations such as the US. But this (new) power, he argues, should not be crafted in ways that produce new binaries (or reproduce old ones). He states:

> It is thus necessary to do everything possible (a formidable and imposing task) for the very long term to ensure that these current failings in the present state of these institutions [e.g., the UN, the IMF] are effectively sanctioned and, in truth, discouraged in advance by a new organization ... but not [by a new] superstate or world government. (Derrida 2003: 114, 120)

This is the deconstructionist contribution: to take what is an existing institution, structure, or text and to show its limits, its internal structural shortcomings and contradictions. But once it is deconstructed, we cannot construct in its place something that rests atop another binary; we have to reconstruct something that transcends binaries. Thus, Derrida tells us that the answer to the UN's limitations is not the creation of a super-state, but something else. But what that something else might be is hard to imagine, because we (and the world at large) think in binaries (us/them; the powerful/the powerless). Indeed, the UN's own internal reports indicate that UN personnel are increasingly subject to attack in various countries because the UN "is perceived by some as a tool of powerful members, rather than an unbiased advocate for all nations." But even if we could construct something that transcends binaries, the deconstructionist project would presumably require that we then deconstruct that structure, and so on. With this logic, therefore, we can see why some critics see deconstruction as destructive and not constructive.

NEWS 14.2

In the meantime, the fact that the UN is in need of restructuring was underscored by its inability to intervene in 2008 in Myanmar, where it could not even enforce the delivery of food supplies to thousands of homeless, starving flood victims. The fear of reproducing binaries, e.g., the idea the West knows better than Africa, is also part of the reason why the UN has stood by from 2007 on while ethnic killings occur in Zimbabwe, killings that totally subvert the values of human rights and democracy, etc., that the UN and the West, and many other countries too, uphold.

NEWS 14.3

The problem, therefore, with the wholesale rejection of binaries is that it can lead to paralysis and the triumph of destruction. This is a core limitation of deconstructionism. It sensitizes us to the limits imposed *a priori* on our imagination and on our social and political structures by a binary conceptual and language system that makes us think in either/or terms. But deconstructionism fails to outline what non-binary thinking would look like or accomplish. With the push against binaries, we are left with no alternative structures; and, fearful apparently of reproducing binaries, we collude in the destruction we witness rather than constructively destroy it. (Of course, seeing Zimbabwe in terms of destruction, and wanting intervention/construction, might be seen as itself a product of limited, binary-prone thinking.)

POSTMODERN CULTURE

POSTMODERN LITERATURE: RUPTURED ORDER

The postmodern rejection of reason and truth is also seen in literature. We are accustomed to thinking of a novel (or any book or research report) as a narrative with a beginning, a middle, and an end, and of it having a plot (themes) and interlinked sub-plots and characters (data) that are all part of the story. These parts cohere to suggest a main interpretation, and also perhaps some well-grounded

437

secondary interpretations. A postmodern novel or any postmodern text abandons all of that structure; it abandons the goal of sense-making, of coherence. Pauline Rosenau explains:

> Post-modernists dramatically revise the conventional roles of author, text, and reader. They diminish the importance of the author and amplify the significance of the text and the reader ... No longer is the reader a passive subject to be entertained, instructed, or amused. S/he is given freedom to attribute meaning to the text without consequence or responsibility ... Meaning does not inhere in a text; it resides in the interaction between the text and the reader ... The post-modern author assumes a novel role in an unexplored post-modern world. S/he strives to write an open text and seeks to compose it so ambiguously, with such an equivocal and enigmatic style, as to encourage an infinity of post-modern interpretations. (1992: 25, 34).

Thus postmodern novels and poems tend to be written in jagged and confusing ways. The structure and presentation of chapters, verses, paragraphs, and lines, as well as the content, can be so baffling that we literally don't know where we are in the narrative, and even if we did know, we still would not know what the narrative is about. Indeed, for the reader to even look for a narrative – a coherent story – is itself not cool; it's not the postmodern thing to do. The text can be about anything we might whimsically want it to be about – as I think some of the poetry of Pulitzer Prize winner Paul Muldoon (2006) shows, e.g., his "Horse Latitudes" and "90 Instant Messages to Tom Moore." His poems seem not to be concerned with creating meaning per se, but focused instead on raw words, language, and the use of language in funny, rhythmic, and obscure ways that draw attention to the arbitrariness of all words and of all language. Perhaps Muldoon as a postmodern poet is a "word freak" (McGrath 2006) rather than a poet in the traditional-classical-modern sense.

The postmodern text defies the order of the modern; it plays with order and defies any particular narrative order; it deliberately avoids authoring or presenting a reasonable or sensible story. And with the author absent, i.e., with the author abdicating authority to tell readers the narrative, to weave a relatively ordered and sensible story for us, we are left to our own devices; we have the freedom to do whatever we want with the text, and to see in it whatever we feel like seeing in it.

What this also means is that we cannot hold the author accountable or responsible for whatever content we might read, interpret, or imagine into the text. The demise of the author, therefore, the abdication of authorial responsibility, is also the abdication of moral authority, thus creating a moral vacuum (Rosenau 1992: 33). In the postmodern understanding, I, as author, am not accountable for my words, for what I claim; it is you the reader who are accountable for your interpretation of them. But how can you be held responsible for words you didn't write? And, by the same token, how can legislators, policymakers, and business, military, and religious leaders be held responsible for decisions they authorize when they are not really the authors of policy/decisions (ibid.)? Yet, as we frequently see, especially in times of scandal and crisis, officials disavow authority for their decisions and actions. The abdication of responsibility for what it is we create or claim – whether in academic, scientific, or fiction writing, or in politics, legislation, or military policy – can thus contribute to producing a society in which chaos can reign; the postmodern gives us permission, it seems, to do as we please and without any sense that the consequences of our words and actions (or inaction) may impact other individuals and collectivities. Taken to its wholesale extreme, this would likely lead to societal breakdown.

EVERYDAY CULTURE

While postmodern theory opens up radical and extreme possibilities, much of what we know as the postmodern is not so extreme and is, in fact, quite familiar. This is especially true in everyday culture. Postmodern culture tends to mix together fragments of many different things – the remix splicing of songs, video clips, photos, and images that come from multiple different sources, traditions, and eras. The postmodern remix opens up all kinds of possibilities and give us great freedom to mix and match all kinds of everything in all kinds of ways. Another effect of this, however, is that we no longer know what is real; what is the original and what is simulated – what is artificially created and imposed on the original; what is the remix and what exactly has been mixed. Thus remix, with its blending of incoherent bits and pieces, exemplifies the postmodern emphasis on the decentering and instability of truth and the muddying of coherence; there is fluidity in what gets put together (Bauman 2000).

Beyond music and art, we see mixed fragments in all sorts of places, and especially in the mix of consumer images we encounter every day. They bombard us with multiple possibilities, multiple simultaneous desires and imaginings. The neo-Marxist cultural theorist **Fredric Jameson** elaborates:

Postmodernism is what you have when the modernization process is complete and nature is gone for good. It is a more fully human world than the older one, but one in which "culture" has become a veritable "second nature." Indeed, what happened to culture may well be one of the more important clues for tracking the postmodern: an immense dilation of its sphere (the sphere of commodities), an immense and historically original acculturation of the Real, a quantum leap in ... the "aestheticization" of reality (... a prodigious exhilaration with the new order of things, a commodity rush, our "representations" of things tending to arouse an enthusiasm and a mood swing not necessarily inspired by the things themselves). So, in postmodern culture, "culture" has become a product in its own right; the market has become a substitute for itself and fully as much a commodity as any of the items it includes within itself: modernism was still minimally and tendentially the critique of the commodity and the effort to make it transcend itself. Postmodernism is the consumption of **sheer commodification** as a process. (Jameson 1991: ix–x)

The "aestheticization of reality" is a difficult phrase. But we can understand it as referring essentially to the unabashed packaging and explicit re-presentation of something ordinary and real as something spectacular ("aesthetic" is another word for art/artistic sensibility). It is the culturing or the remaking – the "beautifying" – of some ordinary element of reality (a particular place, a particular idea) into a commodity to be sold for profit and celebrated and consumed in its newly cultured form, as a cultural package. With clear reference to Marx's discussion of commodity fetishism (cf. chapter 1) and the Frankfurt School's focus on the intertwining of culture and economics (cf. chapter 5), Jameson notes that with the aestheticization of reality, the cultural and the economic "collapse back into one another and say the same thing" (Jameson 1991: xxi).[2]

BIOGRAPHICAL NOTE

Fredric Jameson was born in Cleveland, Ohio, in 1934. He was educated at Haverford College, Pennsylvania, and Yale University, where he completed a doctorate in philosophy. He has written extensively on Marxism and postmodernism, and is currently professor of comparative literature and director of the Duke Center for Critical Theory at Duke University.

For Jameson, postmodernism is best thought of in terms of "the cultural logic of late capitalism" (the title of his book). The equation of economic profit with the images and things that comprise ordinary, everyday culture produces a commodity rush: it is the commodification of something that previously we did not think of as a commodity, but as something else; as something that had its own existence independent of our consumption. With postmodernity, sheer commodification takes over – the commodifying, the consumer packaging, of everything we can think of. Postmodern thinking (as we have discussed) entails the rejection of any overarching, coherent narrative; whether of history or of geography (place), of any knowledge canon, and of master works in art, music, and literature. This means instead, therefore, that

Everything can now be a text ... (daily life, the body, political representations), while objects that were formerly "works" can now be reread as immense ensembles or systems of texts of various kinds, superimposed on each other by way of the various intertextualities, successions of fragments, or ... sheer process (henceforth called textual production or textualization). (Jameson 1991: 77)

These texts, moreover, fuse and remix the sacred and the profane (to borrow Durkheim's categories).

POSTMODERN AESTHETICIZATION: LAS VEGAS AND DUBAI

We see this process of textualization or commodification most clearly perhaps in Las Vegas – in the *production* of a "lavish Las Vegas." What is exciting about Las Vegas as a postmodern reality is the seemingly endless possibilities and redefinitions that it offers. We can "Experience Venice in Vegas – Only at the Venetian. Discover the spirit and passion of Venice at the world's largest four-star and four-diamond resort hotel. Enjoy Venezia, our hotel within a hotel … as grand as Venice itself." "Venezia," moreover, is copyrighted as a commodity trademark; ▦ NEWS 14.4 the hotel owns the name; it has bought and paid for Venezia/Venice. Las Vegas has taken the Real, i.e., Venice (and other real places, e.g., the Eiffel Tower), and recreated it lavishly for us to enjoy: to consume in Las Vegas. We do not need to visit and experience the (real?) Venice in Venice. In Las Vegas, the lavishly re-created world tourist sites are more real, i.e., more sumptuous, than the original; they are better than real.

"Yeah, but the one in Vegas has an endless shrimp buffet."

From *The New Yorker*, October 15, 2007, p. 64. Reproduced by permission of *The New Yorker*.

In other words, with postmodernity, as the French sociologist **Jean Baudrillard** argued, the simulacra, the simulated, lavishly imagined consumer realities, are what is real, and what they produce in fact is a hyperreality. In this view, spectacle, and whatever things (kitchens, bodies), places, events (war, political campaigns), or values (e.g., freedom) we choose to make spectacular become the reality. Baudrillard claimed that this was especially apparent in America:

> America is neither dream nor reality. It is hyperreality. It is a hyperreality because it is a utopia which has behaved from the very beginning as though it were already achieved. Everything here [in the US] is real and pragmatic, and yet it is all the stuff of dreams too. (1991: 28)

(Another way of thinking about simulated reality is to consider our use of air conditioning. Every winter in the US, thousands of retirees move to sunny Florida to avoid the cold northern weather. Once in Florida, however, a utopia of sorts, retirees re-create or simulate winter coolness by switching their indoor air conditioners to match the winter temperatures they have journeyed to avoid.)

BIOGRAPHICAL NOTE

Jean Baudrillard was born in Reims in southeast France in 1929. He studied sociology at the University of the Sorbonne in Paris and subsequently held a faculty position at the University of Paris. He was active in the French student protest movements of the 1960s and maintained his neo-Marxist critical disposition throughout his life. He wrote several books and newspaper commentaries analyzing the centrality of consumption as a signifier of wealth and coolness in contemporary western and global society, but especially in America. Baudrillard died in Paris in 2007.

NEWS 14.4

Las Vegas crystallizes the postmodern subversion of order and Truth. It is an action-packed, free-flowing blurring and remixing of odd fragments of the real and the re-created. Las Vegas, the hedonistic "entertainment capital of the world," mixes old-fashioned gambling fruit-machines and high-end craps tables; gambling culture and high culture, including the Guggenheim Heritage Museum (at the Venetian, of course) and public art works by highly renowned artists and designers; and "sumptuous spas" whose "new aesthetic based on Zen philosophies, boasts a variety of distinct treatments from Egyptian, Indonesian, Thai, Indian, Balinese, and native American traditions." The simultaneous co-occurrence of all these diverse fragments in a simulated hyperreality captures the postmodern sensibility.

All of these amenities (commodities) are not simply for sale; they "have become a key offering in the city's lavish new lifestyle." In the postmodern society, it is not just individuals and groups who have lifestyles (cf. Weber, chapter 3; Bourdieu, chapter 13); cities and suburbs do too. Dubai is another good example of the lifestyle city, a city in the desert that has manufactured itself into a spectacular global metropolis, one that has, among other things, indoor ski slopes.

Topic 14.1   Dubai

Dubai, an old, historically rich Muslim town, markets itself today as: "A futuristic city-state with imaginative and unusual landmarks, from man-made islands in the shape of a map of the world, to Dubailand, a massive theme-park development. Yet Dubai's new incarnation as an avant-garde frontier has only made its history all the more intriguing." "Tradition deliberately shines through the innovative designs of the construction boom. The Fairmont Dubai ... is modeled after an Arabic wind tower ... The Raffles Dubai is shaped like a pyramid, one of the earliest desert marvels, now updated as a hotel with a champagne bar."

NEWS 14.5

NEWS 14.6

This is the postmodern aestheticization of history and of culture. We commodify and repackage our historic cities and villages and mills and mosques and cathedrals into something spectacular; we convert the original thing, with its already interesting history, into an even more intriguing, Disney-like theme-park. And in many instances, it seems, the commodified version of the real is (may be) better, more fun, more exhilarating, more dazzling, more sumptuous than the original.

COMMODIFICATION AND SIMULATION

Jean Baudrillard is hypercritical of cultural commodification and of what he sees as the excesses of consumption. He states that it is as if images – signs of consumption – are more real, more glossy, more culturally significant than any given reality. As in the re-creation or simulation of Dubai as a Disney-like Dubailand, the glossy, cinematic atmosphere is what is outside as well as inside movie theaters (Baudrillard 1991: 56). It is the reality; "It is Disneyland that is authentic [in America]" (ibid.: 104), and we seek to make all realities, including the everyday banality of life in the suburbs, a Disney-like paradise (ibid.: 84–87, 98). We see community simulated in the bucolic names given to new housing developments and gated communities that, having tampered with, if not destroyed, an existing rural community (by encroaching on its expanse of land and way of life) to build the developments, then simulate the feelings of pastoral bliss by using signs, literally street signs, whose names are codes invoking a Paradise-like reality – Sycamore Drive, Willow Road, Happy Hollow Way, etc.

All of this simulated, beautified reality, Baudrillard contends, eludes the pursuit of substance, of living a meaningful life that is not so intertwined with and so highly dependent on the "orgy" of lavish consumption and consumer excess (1991: 30–31). Baudrillard argues that the over-valuing of "mind-blowing

443

consumption" for the sheer sake of consumption "is America's problem and, through America, it has become the whole world's problem" (1991: 30–31). Thus, the pursuit of "endless consumption," and not the expansion of economic equality, becomes the high priority shared across the globe (ibid.: 19, 87); this is evident, for example, in India, where surplus wealth and affluent consumption co-exist right alongside abject poverty (see Topic 15.1, p. 466). For Baudrillard, the real realities of poverty get displaced by the hyper-reality of lavish consumption.

📰 NEWS 14.7

Simulated trees in the mall enhance the naturalness of the mall as a cultural experience, as well as conveying the illusion that shopping is as natural as nature itself.

THE ILLUSION OF REALITY

The postmodern blurs the line between what is real and what is illusory; hence the greater consumer appeal of the simulated Venice (Las Vegas) than of the real Venice (Italy), and of Dubailand than Dubai. More generally, the absence of boundaries between illusion and truth is at the core of the postmodern interest in accentuating the instability of all knowledge; postmodern scholars like Lyotard (1984: xxiv) require us to be incredulous of anything that is presented as true (see p. 432 above).

Baudrillard applies this incredulity to everyday reality, to the simulated hyperreality he diagnoses. In doing so, he makes claims about reality that, sociologically and empirically, are disconcerting. In one of his more notorious essays, *The Gulf War Did Not Take Place*, Baudrillard (1995) argues that the Persian Gulf War in 1991 was not a real war but a simulacrum of war; it was a television event, a television spectacle – an anticipated war which was packaged as endless anticipation by CNN in its programming and, once the bombing started, a "delirious spectacle" of an "electronic war" of stealth bombers and smart bombs (1995: 77, 84). He states:

> By virtue of having been anticipated in all its details and exhausted by all the scenarios … [we become] disappointed and overcome by the suspense as we are today by the media blackmail and the illusion of war. It is as though it had taken place ten times already: why

would we want it to take place again? ... This is the problem with anticipation. Is there still a chance that something which has been meticulously programmed will occur? Does a truth which has been meticulously demonstrated still have a chance of being true? When too many things point in the same direction, when the objective reasons pile up, the effect is reversed ... real things become virtual things. (ibid.: 35, 41)

Clearly, while we can well recognize the spectacle-nature of the television coverage of war, and more generally, of politics, especially presidential election campaigns, I would argue that it is also critical to differentiate between spectacle and reality. The Gulf War did happen, and had and continues to have many real, not simulated, consequences for real people living and working in real places, whether in Iraq, Turkey, Washington, DC, or in the rural American communities from which a disproportionate number of soldiers come. The Gulf War is also real in NEWS 14.8 its ongoing implications for geo-political and military decision-making. If Baudrillard can say that the war didn't really happen, then this means that there is no need for any individuals or groups or countries to take responsibility for its consequences. Baudrillard is being intentionally provocative with such claims, but such provocation, in my view, moves beyond critique, and even beyond deconstruction, and into nihilism. This, apparently, is what he intends. He states:

Here lies the task of any philosophical thought: to go to the limit of hypotheses and processes, even if they are catastrophic. The only justification for thinking and writing is that it accelerates these terminal processes. Here, beyond the discourse of truth, resides the poetic and the enigmatic value of thinking. For, facing a world that is unintelligible and unproblematic, our task is clear: we must make that world even more unintelligible, even more enigmatic. (2000: 83)

It is certainly worthwhile to enter the realm of the poetic and the enigmatic. It also seems to me, however, that as humans endowed with reason, and especially as sociologists trained to work at illuminating the realities that often appear unintelligible, we have to find ways to make sense of reality, no matter how complex and problematic. This, to me, is the emancipatory promise (Habermas 1968/1971: 301–317; cf. Introduction) of sociological theory and analysis. In this vein, the sociological task is to be aware of the postmodern impulse, to recognize its various manifestations, and the sometimes liberating, sometimes chaotic consequences of the redefinitions it imposes in everyday culture, politics, art, literature, and philosophy. We can then incorporate this awareness into our understanding of social structures, social processes, and the meaning of things.

SOCIOLOGICAL ILLUSION

Baudrillard (1983) takes a very different view. He argues that the concepts sociology uses to apprehend reality – concepts such as social class, gender, status, power, institutions, social relations, etc. – are essentially futile. In what is for him a simulated, hyperreal world in which all distinctions and their associated meanings implode, these concepts make no sense. In his view, sociology studies a reality in which the social no longer exists as such; the social is now a simulated reality; it has imploded, disappeared into fantasy and into meaningless "useless consumption" (1983: 78). Media critic Marshall McLuhan (1967) long ago argued that *The Medium Is the Message*, i.e., that media technology – such as the video capability of television to produce spectacular events – dictates the content of reality. In accord with McLuhan, Baudrillard diagnoses what he sees as the disappearance of reality. He argues that because

> the social is destroyed by what produces it (the media, information) and reabsorbed by what it produces (the masses), it follows that its definition is empty ... it conceals that it is only abstraction ... or even simply an *effect* of the social, a simulation and an illusion ... In short, *the medium is the message* signifies not only the end of the message, but also the end of the medium ... mediating between one reality and another, between one state of the real and another – neither in content nor in form. (1983: 66, 102)

In the absence of any real social reality, sociology, Baudrillard argues, loses its purpose. Highlighting sociology's positivist origins, he argues that "Sociology can only depict the expansion of the social and its vicissitudes. It survives only on the positive and definite hypothesis of the social. The reabsorption, the implosion [collapse] of the social escapes it. The hypothesis of the death of the social is also that of [sociology's] own death" (1983: 4). For Baudrillard, sociological concepts have "no sociological reality"; they are simply a veneer for obfuscating and preserving a social order in a world that is no longer social, one that is beyond reason and intelligibility. Thus he states: "all those too explicit concepts which are the glory of the legitimate sciences, have also only ever been muddled notions themselves, but those upon which agreement has nevertheless been reached for mysterious ends: those of preserving a certain code of analysis" (ibid.: 4–5). Sociology creates categories that impose a reality even though social reality has long existed prior to and independent of sociology (ibid.: 67); sociology creates its own reality of the social and as such sociology, for Baudrillard (as for Foucault), is "a machine of truth" (Baudrillard 1983: 69). But the truth that it discovers is false.

My view is that we should be skeptical of everything we read and see, but I also firmly believe that we have to make reasonable efforts to arrive at reasonable inferences about all that comprises society, including postmodernity. Clearly, as a professional sociologist and one writing a sociological theory textbook, I have a vested interest in preserving the idea that there is a discernable social reality, and one that can be apprehended and understood and written about with the help of sociological theories and concepts. But even if I were not a sociologist, I would still like to think that deconstruction can be used to arrive at new meanings rather than to abandon meaning altogether. You, however, may disagree.

SUMMARY

We may or may not choose to embrace the language of postmodernism, and its related ideas of deconstruction and post-structuralism, to appreciate that something has changed in western society within the last few decades. You are growing up in a very different society than your parents did. Many of these differences have to do with the decentering of knowledge and experiences, and the disappearance or marginalization of overarching narratives about the world and how it works. While postmodern theorists such as Baudrillard argue that the postmodern spells the death of the social and the death of sociology, I and many other sociologists believe that social reality and the social structures and processes which shape and comprise that reality – for example, occupational-social class (e.g., Weeden and Grusky 2005), gender, sexual, and racial inequality (see chapters 10, 11, and 12), the state (Giddens 2003) – still matter. Mass media certainly matter too and they do indeed create and accentuate spectacular and simulated realities (as Baudrillard argues).

But the simulated does not displace the real, the social. You can learn a lot about contemporary culture by visiting Las Vegas or Dubai. And while in these places you can also catch fragments of the postmodern in action. But for all the talk of decentering and fluidity, most people still live and work and consume and have fun and experience inequality and globalization (as we discuss in the next chapter) in particular ways in particular places and in relation to particular individual and collective others, notwithstanding the global increase in access to multiple virtual realities. Society is undergoing rapid and far-reaching changes. But many of these changes occur within the bounds of what still is, at least for most individuals in the West, a capitalist, democratic, bureaucratic, and unequal society – whether we call that reality modern, postmodern, or late modern.

This chapter highlighted the various ways in which scholars conceptualize the qualitative shifts that have occurred in human-social experience over the last few decades, and in particular, how these shifts suggest a philosophical and cultural move beyond reason and modernity to postmodernity.

POINTS TO REMEMBER

- Postmodernity disrupts the modernist understanding of the centrality of reason to the discovery of knowledge and truth
- Fluidity is one of the defining markers of the postmodern experience/sensibility
- Emphasis on fluidity dramatically shifts the locus of authority and of authorship and destabilizes the order of texts, things, knowledge
- The postmodern disposition is to be incredulous toward all overarching narratives, all large-scale narratives of history, theory, science, etc.

- Postmodern or post-structuralist theorists challenge the binary structure of language and of (linguistically dependent) social categorizations
- Postmodern theorists deconstruct the conceptual limitations that inhere in language, discourse, knowledge
- Postmodernity affirms the multiplicity of possible texts or of possible readings that can comprise or get imagined into any given text
- The postmodern calls for experimentation with the narrative structure and content of art, music, literature, culture, and knowledge
- Postmodern culture celebrates the remix of disparate and contradictory elements; it collapses traditional distinctions between high and low culture
- Postmodern culture affirms the repackaging and commodification of the Real into simulated and hyperreal consumer realities
- Postmodernists blur the lines between illusion and reality
- Postmodern scholars challenge the realness of social reality

GLOSSARY

aestheticization of reality the cultural packaging and re-presentation of something ordinary as a commodified, spectacular thing for sale in the market.

deconstruction an approach seeking to take apart, dismantle, and push against the order and meaning in language structures and in established institutional practices.

fluidity the idea that in postmodernity, power, knowledge, authority, social relationships, and social experience are mobile and free-floating (fluid) rather than anchored in and ordered by reason, history, structures, traditions, etc.

hyperreality a glossy, lavish, cinematic, consumption-driven, utopian reality dominated by spectacle (e.g., Las Vegas).

implosion the collapse of meaningful distinctions, especially between the real and the simulated.

metanarratives narratives about narratives; a metanarrative critiques or illuminates how the established narratives of history, religion, capitalism, sociology, etc. legitimate particular types of, and a particular order to, knowledge.

politics of truth idea emphasizing that truth is not, and can never be, independent of power; that all truths

are produced by particular power-infused social relationships and social contexts.

postmodern the contemporary era as a time of fluid knowledge and authority, and of decentered experiences, of mixed fragments rather than of (modern) structured order.

post-structuralist an approach seeking to dismantle the binary structure of language and the binary linguistic codes and meanings which embed all knowledge.

remix blending and reworking of several original sounds, themes, or ideas into a new reality.

semiology the study of signs, i.e., showing how arbitrary images/symbols and their particular pairing have a specific cultural meaning and significance.

sheer commodification the cultural or lifestyle packaging of everyday things, places, or experiences as images and commodities purely for the purpose of promoting consumption for the sake of consumption.

simulacra things that are glossy, polished representations and commodified imaginings of other things/realities; the simulated product/representation assumes a more real, more beautiful, more intense, more cinematic presence than the original.

RELEVANT NEWSPAPER STORIES

All news stories are from the *New York Times* unless otherwise noted, and can be accessed via www.wiley.com/go/dillon. See NEWS icons in the margins above.

NEWS 14.1 "The general's report," *New Yorker*, June 25, 2007.

NEWS 14.2 "U.N. personnel increasingly under attack, study finds," July 1, 2008.

NEWS 14.3 "Undeterred by criticism, Mugabe joins peers at African Union meeting," July 1, 2008.
"African Union calls for unity government in Zimbabwe," July 2, 2008.

NEWS 14.4 "Venice, Las Vegas/Venice, Italy," special advertising supplement, *New York Times Magazine*, March 25, 2007.
"In the land of glitter and gambling, plans for an oasis of art," March 8, 2008.

NEWS 14.5 Advertisement, *New Yorker*, October 22, 2007

NEWS 14.6 Advertisement, *New Yorker*, May 12, 2008. For a review of how Dubai was faring in the global recession in late 2008, see "Financial paradise becomes a mirage," *Newsweek*, December 15, 2008.

NEWS 14.7 "Exploring the fringes of India's prosperity through the eyes of the invisible men," August 15, 2008.

NEWS 14.8 "Rural soldiers continue to account for a disproportionately high share of U.S. casualties in Iraq and Afghanistan," University of New Hampshire, Carsey Institute, Fact Sheet. www.carseyinstitute.unh.edu.

NOTES

1 For students who want to pursue these arguments in more depth, McCarthy (1991: 43–75) provides an interesting, clear, and helpful discussion of the similarities and contrasts between the Frankfurt School and Foucault.

2 Jameson (1991: xxi) notes that this collapsing of the cultural and the economic into one another constitutes "an eclipse of the distinction between base and superstructure that has itself often struck people as significantly characteristic of postmodernism in the first place, [and] is also to suggest that the base, in the third stage of capitalism [i.e., postmodernism as opposed to capitalism and late capitalism] generates its superstructures with a new kind of dynamic. And this may also be what (rightly) worries the unconverted about the term; it seems to obligate you in advance to talk about cultural phenomena at least in business terms if not in those of political economy."

CHAPTER FIFTEEN
GLOBALIZATION

Timeline 15.1	Major globalizing economic and political events (1450–present)
1450–1640	Emergence of capitalism in Europe
1815–1917	Accelerated expansion of capitalism
1884	Drawing of Africa's colonial boundaries at Berlin conference
1914–1918	World War I, first global war
1939–1945	World War II
1944	International Monetary Fund (IMF) founded, headquartered in Washington, DC
1945	World Bank Group established, headquartered in Washington, DC
1945	United Nations (UN) founded, headquartered in New York City; 185 member countries; 18 specialized agencies; and a number of programs, councils, and commissions
1946–1991	Cold War between US and Soviet Union
1947	General Agreement on Tariffs and Trade (GATT) formed; precursor to World Trade Organization (WTO)
1948	Organization of American States (OAS; USA, South and Central America, Caribbean) founded, headquartered in Washington, DC
1948	UN Economic Commission for Latin America and the Caribbean (ECLAC) established
1948	World Health Organization (WHO; part of the UN) established
1949	North Atlantic Treaty Organization (NATO) formed, headquartered in Brussels, Belgium
1949	Fourth Geneva Conventions ratified, giving protection to prisoners of war
1957	Treaty of Rome agreed, founding European Economic Community (EEC)
1957	International Atomic Energy Agency (IAEA) established, headquartered in Vienna, Austria
1960	International Development Association (IDA) instituted, headquartered in Washington, DC
1960	Organization of Petroleum Exporting Countries (OPEC) created, headquartered in Geneva, Switzerland, then in Vienna, Austria
1961	Organisation for Economic Cooperation and Development (OECD) established, headquartered in Paris, France
1963	Organization of African Unity (OAU) founded, headquartered in Addis Ababa, Ethiopia
1967	Association of Southeast Asian Nations (ASEAN) established, headquartered in Jakarta, Indonesia

1968	Organization of Arab Petroleum Exporting Countries (OAPEC) established, headquartered in Safat, Kuwait
1975	Latin American Economic System (SELA) founded, headquartered in Caracas, Venezuela (27 members; Central and South America, Caribbean)
1976	OPEC Fund for International Development established, headquartered in Vienna, Austria
1981	Cooperation Council for the Arab States of the Gulf, also known as Gulf Cooperation Council (GCC), founded, headquartered in Riyadh, Saudi Arabia
1988	US–Canada Trade Agreement signed
1989	Collapse of Berlin Wall
1989	Asia-Pacific Economic Cooperation (APEC) established, headquartered in Singapore
1991	Persian Gulf War
1992	European Community becomes European Union (EU)
1994	Euro launched as official currency of some EU member states (not including UK and Denmark)
1994	North American Free Trade Agreement (NAFTA) established between US, Canada, and Mexico
1995	World Trade Organization (replacing GATT) established, headquartered in Geneva, Switzerland
2001	Terrorist attacks on World Trade Center Towers, New York City
2003	US invades Iraq
2008	Olympics in Beijing, China
2008	Russia invades Georgia
Winter 2008	Start of US and global economic recession

Social action today is increasingly impervious to geographical-national borders. You get a sense of this from Box 15.1 (see p. 454).

As this box highlights, globalization is not any one thing but is comprised of several interrelated economic, political, social, and cultural processes (e.g., Robertson 1992; Giddens 1990; 1991; Sklair 2002). By the same token, globalization processes are not driven by any one single mechanism, nor do they impact global, national, or local society in any universal or predetermined way. Further, as its name underscores, globalization involves processes that span the whole world, the *globe*, and as such it is qualitatively different to the inter-*national* relationships, trade relations, migration patterns, and political communication that have long existed between particular countries.

Globalization, therefore, requires a shift in sociological perspective from our tendency to think of society as coinciding with, or happening within and between, specific geographical-national territories. Although there is no single sociological theory of globalization, different theoretical strands help us to make analytical sense of what globalization means for social change and societal processes.

Box 15.1   Global flows

- More than one-tenth of all the goods and services produced in New York City, and 1 in every 20 jobs, are supplied by companies controlled by foreign investors
- General Electric (USA) has research centers in Munich (Germany), Shanghai (China), and Bangalore (India)
- Indian companies are outsourcing jobs to workers in Mexico, Brazil, Chile, and Uruguay
- Every year there is an increasing stream of American, Chinese, and Japanese visitors traveling to South Korea, Mexico, India, and Thailand for surgery and medical care
- Snoop Dog raps in a popular Indian movie video
- The Chinese government and Middle Eastern investors have invested substantial sums of money in American-based financial companies such as Citibank
- Wal-Mart is expanding in China and India
- Ukraine, formerly the Soviet Union's largest republic, has joined the World Trade Organization
- American universities are opening branch campuses in Middle Eastern cities such as Doha (Qatar) and in Dubai (United Arab Emirates), and expanding programs with Chinese and Indian universities
- The Louvre, the renowned Paris museum, has sold rights to the use of its name to a museum being built in Abu Dhabi, the capital city of the United Arab Emirates, in a package estimated to be worth $1.3 billion

---

DEFINING GLOBALIZATION

We can define globalization in general terms as "the *process* of integrating nations and peoples – politically, economically, and culturally – into larger communities" (Eckes and Zeiler 2003: 1), and this process is one which is not linear or incremental but "dynamic, transformational, and synergistic" (ibid.). Thus, just as Durkheim emphasized that society is greater than the sum of the individuals who comprise it (cf. chapter 2), we should think of globalization as being more than the cumulative sum of the nations and populations comprising the globe. It has its own reality, and as such creates social processes and dynamics that cannot be reduced to the economic, political, or cultural actions of any one nation or combined alliance of nations. In Durkheimian language, globalization comprises an objective social fact with its own external and constraining force in society (though, of course, this should not be interpreted to mean that globalization is independent of society or driven by some invisible, non-societal force; rather it is produced by society and impacts other processes in society). And, further, globalization spans and impacts both macro and micro processes. (e.g., Robertson 1992: 61–84)

What might be said to be synergistically new about globalization is the simultaneous circulation and flow of people (migration); of things, including illicit things such as drugs; of ideas – e.g., about gender equality; and of information (e.g., via the internet) about all sorts of people and things, between and among all sorts of people. Globalization processes are clearly driven by, among other variables, advances in communication technology, exponentially accelerated most recently by the synergistic blending of internet and telephone technology. Such technologies free us, or disembed us, from the constraints of time and space, and from the physical, geographical, economic, political, cultural, and social boundaries that define and demarcate our local context such that we can outsource our personal chores – even getting homework tutoring.

As elaborated by **Anthony Giddens** (1991), the disembeddedness of time and space is our current social experience. The physical centers of money, power, and knowledge that characterized past times are increasingly complemented by multiple electronic forums and highways that allow for flexibility, rather than requiring us to be anchored in or to a particular space and bound by a particular clock. We (and individuals in places far distant from us) can take online courses, watch online our favorite sports teams, e-shop, e-bank, e-pray, e-date, e-trade, e-mail. Such disembedded practices inhere in globalization. Giddens argues that globalization is: "best understood as expressing fundamental aspects of time-space distanciation. Globalisation concerns the intersection of presence and absence, the interlacing of social events and social relations 'at distance' with local contextualities" (1991: 21). Thus globalization changes the dynamics of social life across all societal spheres. As succinctly defined by Leslie Sklair, globalization is "a particular way of organizing social life across existing state borders," and as such gives rise to distinctively transnational practices – transnational economic, transnational political, and transnational cultural practices (2002: 8).

NEWS 15.1
NEWS 15.2

NEWS 15.3

BIOGRAPHICAL NOTE

Anthony Giddens was born into a lower middle-class family in London in 1935. The first in his family to go to college, he received his PhD from Cambridge University, where he subsequently spent much of his prolific career. In the 1990s, he became an influential advisor to British prime minister Tony Blair, and is widely acknowledged for elaborating the "third way" social-democratic approach that was central to Blair's and the Labour Party's political agenda (and which is often also used to characterize the policies of the Clinton presidency in the US). Giddens has been widely recognized for his academic and policy contributions, and in 2004 was awarded a peerage. He currently sits in the British House of Lords and continues to advocate social democratic policies as the way forward as societies deal with the impact of globalization.

Clearly, globalization should be of much substantive interest to sociologists, because on the surface, at least, globalization is transforming so many of the taken-for-granted ways of doing things in society and the assumptions we make about those things. How does globalization present itself in, and impact, the social organization of economic, political, and cultural practices and relationships, ones that are increasingly defined in transnational terms? What do globalizing shifts mean for core constructs of interest to sociologists – for bureaucratic (corporate) rationality, the division of labor, economic inequality, the gendered division of labor, the role of the state, the homogenization of culture and consumption? And how more generally do globalizing processes impact social integration, as evidenced through the changing dynamics of everyday life in cities and local communities, and in the shifting contours of civic culture/the public sphere, which now must accommodate anti-globalization protest? These are the questions addressed in this chapter; I address them by highlighting the conceptual frames of theoretically diverse sociologists, all of whom have written extensively on this still-emerging issue.

ECONOMIC GLOBALIZATION

Much of what we hear in the news about globalization focuses on its economic aspects. The first time the word apparently was used was in an article discussing the expansion of global economic markets (Eckes and Zeiler 2003: 1) – the expansion of the world economy such that trade in consumer products increasingly extends beyond a particular country's or region's borders. This was precisely the process predicted by Karl Marx when he spoke of the ever-increasing pressure on capitalists to expand profits by finding and conquering new world markets for their products (cf. chapter 1). Therefore, although the term "globalization" came into use to describe economic changes in the early 1980s, some of its economic manifestations have existed in various guises over many past generations.

Economists focus primarily, if not solely, on the economic mechanisms and consequences of expanding globalized trade in commodity, labor, and capital markets, and generally do so without regard to their social and cultural implications (e.g., Bordo et al. 2003a). Economists generally understand capitalism as effectively regulated by natural forces of demand and supply; many see globalization through this same lens. Thus, for example, the deputy editor of the influential weekly magazine *The Economist* states: "Certainly globalization has a powerful economic momentum of its own. Technological progress, left to its own devices, promotes [economic] integration. … [Economic] integration seems in many ways a natural economic process, which can only be reversed, it at all, when policies are deliberately framed to that end" (Cook 2003: 549).

Further, economists see global trends in intra-national (within-country) inequality as a result largely of "the fact that the opening to trade and foreign investment was incomplete," concentrated, for example, in select cities and provinces at the expense of rural and other areas (Lindert and Williamson 2003: 255). More generally, in this view, global inequality is a result of "differential access to the benefits of the new economy" and of particular countries' and regions' failures to participate in globalization (ibid.: 263).

Sociologists, by contrast, apply a different framework to apprehending the economic aspects of globalization. They fully recognize the opening up of new markets that is entailed in globalization, emphasizing in particular, as Giddens notes (1990: 76), the many advances made post-World War II in expanding global relations of economic interdependence, and the opening up of new geographical centers of industrial production, evidenced in the emergence of newly industrializing countries in the third world (ibid.). But, additionally, sociologists highlight the historical, geographical, and structural unevenness of globalizing economic processes (Wallerstein 2004), and their undermining impact on local subsistence economies (e.g., Giddens 2003: 17).

IMMANUEL WALLERSTEIN: THE MODERN WORLD-SYSTEM

Any sociological discussion of economic globalization must necessarily engage the theorizing of the American sociologist **Immanuel Wallerstein**. He argues that the association of globalization with relatively open economic frontiers between countries is part of a much longer "cyclical occurrence throughout the history of the modern world-system," a world-system in which economic logic is the primary driver (Wallerstein 2004: 93). Wallerstein was influential in establishing the idea of a capitalist world-system. In his three-volume historical analysis of "the creation of the modern world" (1974: 3), he detailed the formation of capitalism as a bounded, historically unique, and economically distinctive world-system that emerged in Europe in the sixteenth century.[1] Although Wallerstein's interest anticipates the globalization dominant in contemporary society, his long historical perspective on the development of capitalist processes makes him skeptical of talk of globalization; he "rarely if ever uses the word globalization" (Sklair 2002: 42), and on his Yale University website, refers to it as "so-called globalization."

BIOGRAPHICAL NOTE

Immanuel Wallerstein was born in New York in 1930. He received his undergraduate and graduate education in sociology at Columbia University, and spent most of his career at the State University of New York, Binghamton, where he was also the founding director of the Fernand Braudel Center for the Study of Economies, Historical Systems and Civilization. He is currently a senior research scholar in the sociology department at Yale University. A renowned expert on Europe and Africa, he is a prolific and wide-ranging author (including collaboration with Andre Gunder Frank). Wallerstein was a founding member of the *Journal of World-Systems Research*, and of the American Sociological Association (ASA) section for the Political Economy of the World System. He was president of the International Sociological Association (1994–1998), and in 2003, received the ASA's Career of Distinguished Scholarship Award.

Using language similar to that of Talcott Parsons, who conceptualized society as a social system (cf. chapter 4), Wallerstein states that a "world-system is a social system, one that has boundaries, structures, member groups, rules of legitimation, and coherence" (1974: 347). But unlike Parsons, Wallerstein is a neo-Marxist and, strongly influenced by Marx's analysis of capitalism, affirms the centrality of unequal relations of production to capital accumulation. Substantially extending Marx, Wallerstein's contribution is his lens on the geographical division of labor in the historical emergence of capitalism (Wallerstein 1974: 349). In this view, we cannot understand the contemporary manifestations of (global) capitalism and its various problems and crises without appreciating the geographical dynamics of its historical evolution. Let us explore what this entails.

MODERN WORLD-ECONOMY

Taking the world-system rather than any particular country (e.g., US, Argentina) as the unit of analysis, Wallerstein analyzes how the relations of production and capital accumulation characterize countries vis-à-vis one another in the world-system's capitalist world-economy. According to Wallerstein, world-economies are structurally divided into core states, peripheral areas, and semi-peripheral areas, among which there is an unequal flow of capitalist resources. He specifically talks about peripheral and semi-peripheral *areas* rather than states, precisely because these areas are characterized by indigenous weak states (1974: 349). A world-system, Wallerstein argues, is

> one in which there is extensive division of labor. This division is not merely functional – that is, occupational – but geographical. That is to say, the range of economic tasks is not evenly divided throughout the world-system. In part, this is the consequence of ecological considerations, to be sure. But for the most part, it is a function of the social organization of work, one which magnifies and legitimizes the ability of some groups within the system to exploit the labor of others, that is to receive a larger share of the surplus [wealth/profit]. (1974: 349)

The critically intertwined links between the geographical and the occupational division of labor in the world-economy are decisive, Wallerstein argues, in reproducing inequality:

> The division of a world-economy involves a hierarchy of occupational tasks, in which tasks requiring higher levels of skill and greater capitalization are reserved for higher-ranking areas ... Hence, the ongoing process of a world-economy tends to expand the economic and social gaps among its varying areas in the very process of its development. (1974: 350)

In short, in the world-system, the core tends to dominate the periphery (1974: 129). And the determining force of the unequal geographical distribution of economic production roles (e.g., industrialization in the core, agriculture in the periphery) is such that core and peripheral areas develop "different class structures ... different modes of labor control" (1974: 162), and different state structures, whereby strong states at the core protect their various economic interests against other relatively strong states, and especially against (weak) states in peripheral areas, and do so in ways that effectively maintain the (unequal) world-system (ibid.: 354–355).

Moreover, seeing culture as a servant of economic interests – in a way similar to Marx's conceptualization of base–superstructure relations (cf. chapter 1) – Wallerstein argues that "any complex system of ideas can be manipulated to serve any political or social objective" (1974: 152). Hence, he notes that Protestantism came to dominate in the core and Catholicism in the periphery. He maintains that this geographical religious distribution was a function of world-system economic forces and not, as Weber argues, driven by differences in theological ideas (cf. chapter 3). As part of his historically detailed explanation, Wallerstein argues for example, that the Catholic church

> as a transnational institution was threatened by the emergence of an equally transnational economic system which found its political strength in the creation of strong state machineries of certain (core) states, a development which threatened the [Catholic] Church's position in these states, [such] that it threw itself wholeheartedly into the opposition of modernity. But, paradoxically, it was its very success in the peripheral countries [e.g., Poland] that ensured the long-term success of the European world-economy. (1974: 156)

WORLD-SYSTEMS IN CONTRAST TO WORLD-EMPIRES

Although it may seem that Wallerstein's world-system is simply another way of talking about empires, this is not the case. World-systems are not the same as empires, though they share some features in common; they may each cover a large spatial area and encompass diverse languages, religions, and cultures – e.g., the British Empire at the height of its power included Ireland, Canada, Australia, India, and several African and Caribbean countries. The distinctive feature of the modern world-system is its world-economy. Wallerstein explains: "It is a 'world-system' not because it encompasses the whole world, but because it is larger than any juridically-defined political unit. And it is a 'world-economy' because the basic linkage between the parts of the system is economic" (1974: 15).

Unlike an empire, therefore, which is a political unit ruled by a single ruler from a centralized political location, the world-economy encompasses many states, several of which have different forms of political organization (1974: 15). And whereas an empire relies on a large administrative staff in place in its varied geographical locations to enforce its economic coercion (e.g., tax collection, property rules), world-systems function by virtue of the (unequal) economic relations among the states. Thus,

> Political empires are a primitive means of economic domination. It is the social achievement of the modern world, if you will, to have invented the technology that makes it possible to increase the flow of the surplus [wealth/profit] from the lower strata to the

upper strata, from the periphery to the center, from the majority to the minority, by eliminating the "waste" of too cumbersome a political superstructure. (ibid.: 15–16)

DISTINCTIVE CHARACTERISTICS OF THE MODERN WORLD-SYSTEM

Wallerstein argues that "the modern world-system (or the capitalist world-economy) is merely one system among many" (1996: 294). It does not, for example, refer to the non-capitalistic systems that have existed over time, nor to those system(s) that might replace the existing one (Wallerstein 2004: 76–90). What is particularly distinctive in the capitalist world-system is that it has managed to destroy all of its historically contemporaneous systems, such as long-dominant empires. And, crucially distinctive, Wallerstein argues, no other historical system was based on "the structural pressure for the ceaseless accumulation of capital" (1996: 295). Earlier systems engaged in long-distance trade but, Wallerstein notes, this was primarily trade in luxuries and *between* center and periphery systems, rather than trade in necessities and *within* a given system, specifically within the modern capitalist world-system (1996: 294). Consequently, earlier forms of trade did not have the same structural imperative toward capital accumulation and profit so fundamental to modern capitalism (cf. Marx; see chapter 1).

Thus Wallerstein (1974: 10) argues that modern capitalism originated as a distinctive world-system or world-economy in sixteenth-century Europe; that this system became consolidated between 1640 and 1815; and that it aggressively expanded during the following hundred years (1815–1917). Wallerstein (1974) argues that there was nothing miraculous about this process. Instead he shows that it was contingent on, among other factors, the economic opportunities for exploitation and expansion created by the ebb and flow of industrial cycles of growth, over-production and decline; the financial and political imperatives for competing monarchies (e.g., England, the Netherlands, Spain, and Portugal) to explore distant lands for new goods and revenue sources, and thus to maintain their political-economic hegemony; far-reaching political struggles and alliances between countries; the emergence of stronger and more autonomous states freed from religious influences; timely alliances between church and state at various critical moments; class alliances among varied social strata (e.g., landed gentry, aristocrats, bureaucrats) within countries; and economic, cultural, and political opportunities presented by both the outbreak and resolution of various wars.

THE STATE IN THE EXPANSION OF CAPITALISM

While Wallerstein also highlights the technological accomplishments of capitalism and its ability to progressively produce more goods for more profit, he is nonetheless emphatic that capitalism does not proceed because of any invisible hand of the market acting alone (as free market economists would contend). His analysis shows, rather, that it is bolstered by strong states that "serve the interests of some groups and hurt those of others" (1974: 354). From a detailed review of the history of European capitalism, Wallerstein concludes: "The state's role in capitalist development has been constant throughout modern history" (1974: 127).

Wallerstein's thesis that the modern capitalist world-system is historically specific and of long duration (i.e., dating from sixteenth-century Europe) also leads him to challenge the typical historical narrative of social change wherein we affirm the significance of late eighteenth-century industrialization and that era's political revolutions as marking a significant turn in advancing economic and political freedom (cf. Introduction). To the contrary, Wallerstein concludes:

> None of the great revolutions of the late eighteenth century – the so-called industrial revolution, the French Revolution, the settler independences of the Americas – represented fundamental challenges to the world capitalist system. They represented its further consolidation and entrenchment. The popular [mass democratic] forces were suppressed, and their potential in fact constrained by the political transformations. (1989: 256)

Most sociologists and historians would likely argue that we should still regard the late eighteenth century as a time of critical transformation in society. At the same time, however, we should also recognize – in the spirit of Wallerstein's argument – that history is usually more complicated than an event-oriented calendar can fully capture. In other words, social change, including globalization, does not happen out of the blue; some of its manifestations and dimensions may be unexpected, but once we trace the precursors of any socio-historical shift, we can usually find that even the most unexpected or tumultuous events and processes were preceded by multiple social, cultural, economic, and political tremors.

CHANGING CONTEXT OF THE CORE–PERIPHERY WORLD

Another important characteristic of the world-system perspective is that it recognizes and, indeed, expects change within the system. Although the world-system is a self-contained and coherent system (Wallerstein 1974: 347), it also has its own internally generated tensions and contradictions. The passing of time, population flow and demographic shifts, and (following Marx) the ever-present contradiction that inheres in capitalist production variously result in cyclical shifts as to which internal structures and groups have more power than others (1974: 347). The structure of the capitalist world-system, therefore, Wallerstein argues, is not set once and for all time by some watershed events in history. Geographical boundaries can expand such that areas external to the system can become incorporated into it, typically into new periphery or semi-periphery areas (mostly, historically, due to colonization of peripheral areas; e.g., Williams 1990). By the same token, particular regions may change their role in the system, such that "core states can become semi-peripheral and semi-peripheral ones peripheral" (1974: 350). Although core states have an advantage over others, their status is not assured across a long period of time, and they necessarily encounter challenges from other core states as to which will be "top dog." We may think of this process, Wallerstein suggests, in terms of a structural "circulation of the elites in the sense that the particular country that is dominant at a given time tends to be replaced in this role sooner or later by another country" (ibid.).

Currently, we can think of the US as among the core states, and we can perhaps think of East Timor as on the periphery. But the post-1990s economic transformation in previously "peripheral" countries such as Ireland, India, and China underscores the theoretical and empirical difficulty in assigning countries/regions within Wallerstein's schema. How many years of continuous economic growth, for example, are necessary for a country to be considered core? Would it more readily be seen as semi-peripheral? As Wallerstein notes, the semi-periphery is not an artificial or residual category; like core and periphery, it too "is a necessary structural element in the world-economy" (1974: 349). But it is also a little murky; semi-peripheral areas constitute a sort of middle area, functioning as "collection points of vital skills that are often politically unpopular. These middle areas ... partially deflect the political pressures which groups primarily located in peripheral areas might otherwise direct against core states and the groups which operate within and through their state machineries" (ibid.: 349–350). Further, being on the semi-periphery means that countries/states are "located outside the political arena of the core states, and find it difficult to pursue the ends in political coalitions that might be open to them were they in the same political arena" (ibid.: 350).

This definition thus further complicates who belongs where. A semi-peripheral designation would obscure the core role that India and China are playing in today's global trade markets as well as their increased weight in world politics. Therefore, although Wallerstein emphasizes the world-system's accommodation of change, its conceptual categories, nonetheless, tend to be somewhat limited, weighed down by past history rather than readily adaptable to current developments.

WORLD-ECONOMY CRISIS

Because the capitalist world-system is historically unique and because it has its own internal tensions, this means, according to Wallerstein, that its historical life-cycle, just as it had a beginning, will also come to an end. This view parallels Marx's prediction of capitalism being displaced by an alternative system of economic and social organization (i.e., communism). Wallerstein argues, in fact, that the capitalist world-economy is in crisis (1996: 295; 2004: 76–90). The crisis has multiple causal sources, including the escalation of production costs, market speculation, and environmental pollution. Particularly critical, for Wallerstein, is the expanding gap in economic resources between core and periphery despite the unprecedented economic growth in the system as a whole (2004: 84). This is a "true crisis" such that its difficulties "cannot be resolved within the framework of the system," but can be "overcome only by going outside of and beyond the historical system of which the difficulties are a part" (Wallerstein 2004: 76).[2] The instability resulting from the crisis "may go on another twenty-five to fifty years" (ibid.: 77), Wallerstein states, and its resolution will depend on the collective choices society makes about what future system(s) it wishes to construct.

FROM WORLD-ECONOMIC TO GLOBAL INEQUALITY

Wallerstein's emphasis on the geographical patterns in economic inequality permeates sociologists' and policy-makers' assessments of current globalization trends (e.g., Sklair 2002), even though they do not necessarily embrace Wallerstein's conceptual categories. A recent report from the United Nations Conference on Trade and Development (UNCTAD) affirms the ongoing relevance of geographical nuance regarding the impact of globalization. While documenting the positive ways in which the greater use of technology (e.g., mobile phones) is enhancing economic prosperity in rural communities in Uganda, Senegal, and Kenya, UNCTAD also warns that a big gulf remains between rich and poor countries. It is these inequalities and the larger structural context shaping economic inequality in its various guises that many globalization sociologists focus on.

NEWS 15.4

THE TRANSNATIONAL CORPORATION

As a general analytical principle, sociologists underscore the overarching significance of core organizing structures – as opposed to economic momentum alone – in shaping the global economy and its societal impact. Thus, for example, Giddens, following a Weberian emphasis on the expansion of bureaucracy, argues that "corporations are the dominant agents within the world economy" (1990: 71). Giddens notes, however, that although corporations are powerful, their power does not go unchecked. Transnational or multinational economic corporations must contend with the state, and with the expanding range of non-governmental organizations (NGOs), many of which are global too, such as Greenpeace, Oxfam (Giddens 2003: xxv), and Amnesty International.

Leslie Sklair, a neo-Marxist sociologist, gives greater emphasis than Giddens to the centrality of the capitalist corporation to globalization. Sklair argues, first of all, that although it is common to think of globalization as essentially meaning capitalist globalization, we should in fact recognize that capitalist globalization is simply one form of globalization, one based on a capitalist mode of production. And, he maintains, it is possible to conceive of alternative modes, such as socialist globalization, a system that would require a shift from capitalist corporate ownership toward the creation of local producer–consumer cooperatives (Sklair 2002: 299–321).

BIOGRAPHICAL NOTE

Leslie Sklair is retired from the sociology faculty at the London School of Economics, where he was also associated with the Center for the Study of Human Rights. He has written several books and journal articles on issues of economic development and globalization.

In any event, Sklair (2002: 7) argues for the analytical necessity of a global systems theory. This perspective emphasizes a dialectical synthesis between states and transnational globalizing forces and institutions, and thus transcends what he sees as inadequacies in current approaches – the tendency to adopt either an international, state-centered approach to globalization (most readily seen in political science; cf. Eckes and Zeiler 2003), or a transnational approach that emphasizes globalism with little reference to national states (seen in economics).

Sklair himself, however, tends to give most attention to the primacy of transnational economic corporations in globalization, and to frame the state primarily in terms of its complicity in such processes. He argues that the "major transnational corporations are the most important and most powerful globalizing institutions in the world today" (2002: 7). As he notes, transnational corporations (e.g., IBM, Microsoft, Philip Morris, General Motors, Wal-Mart, Exxon Mobil, Sony) have not only "grown enormously in size in recent decades, but their global reach has expanded dramatically" (2002: 36). Sklair argues, moreover, that although many transnational corporations are legally domiciled and/or headquartered in the US,

Coca-Cola is among the world's largest and most recognizable transnational corporations, with business operations and sales in more than 200 countries.

Europe, or Japan, this should not obscure the fact that their economic interests, both objectively and as described by the corporations themselves (in annual reports etc.), are truly globalizing in scope (2002: 38).

CLASS INEQUALITY

Sociologists also emphasize the persistence of class inequality notwithstanding the economic gains made globally in individuals' standard or quality of life. Giddens highlights the profit logic and attendant class inequalities that inhere in global markets, stating:

> In their trading relations with one another, and with states and consumers, companies (manufacturing corporations, financial firms and banks) depend upon production for profit. Hence the spread of their influence brings in its train a global extension of commodity markets, including money markets. However, even in its beginnings, the capitalist world economy was never just a market for the trading of goods and services. It involved, and involves today, the commodifying of labour power in class relations which separate workers from control of their means of production ... [a] process ... fraught with implications for global inequalities. (1990: 71–72)

The increased global flow in trade and consumer products, whereby, for example, Chinese manufacturers and suppliers – whether of fashion apparel, children's toys, or flowers – have become highly significant players in the global economy, is frequently at the expense of workers laboring under dangerous sweatshop conditions to meet production demands. And these inequalities fester largely because the expansion of the middle class in China (and elsewhere) is based on a labor system that relies on "young migrant workers who often leave small rural villages for two- or three-year stints at factories, where they hope to earn enough money to return home to start families." Economic globalization can thus be viewed as exacerbating on a global level the class-based inequalities found in local economic markets. Giddens (2003: xxix) and other Weber-inspired sociologists (e.g., Held 2004: 164–165), who see the state as an actor which can intervene to ensure a more equitable distribution of market resources, argue for the state's institutionalization of reforms (e.g., labor laws) that would protect workers' rights.

NEWS 1.2

NEWS 15.5

NEWS 15.5

While Sklair acknowledges that the standard of living of millions of people across the globe has been vastly improved by capitalist globalization in ways unimaginable to an earlier generation, he too emphasizes that this achievement has not eliminated class inequality; rather, "capitalist globalization produces class polarization" (2002: 27, 26). For Sklair, however, unlike for Giddens and Held, this polarization is not correctable within the current capitalist globalization system. It is rather a crisis of globalization; "the distinctiveness of the class polarization thesis is that it recognizes both increasing emiseration (poverty) and increasing enrichment, thus in all countries, rich and poor, privileged communities are to be found" (2002: 50). This polarization is evident across several domains – in access to education, health care, the internet, etc. (2002: 48–53) – and is most visibly underscored by the emergence across the globe – whether in Los Angeles, Mexico City, Chicago, or Mumbai – of gated, affluent communities geographically separated from ghettos and factories (2002: 51). And Sklair argues, the transnational capitalist class – comprised of "corporate executives, world leaders, those who run the major international institutions, globalizing professionals, the mainstream mass media" – accepts and colludes in the perpetuation of this inequality (2002: 56). This economically and politically powerful class, from "the material base" provided them by the transnational corporations, "unquestionably dictates economic transnational practices, and is the most important single force in the struggle to dominate political and cultural-ideology transnational practices" (2002: 9).

Topic 15.1   Class polarization in India

Although India has experienced enormous economic growth since the early 1990s and has become a major player in global economic production, it is a country in which class polarization is highly visible. In Guragon, for example, a booming town in the northern part of India, the highly affluent, cosmopolitan professional class who live within gated communities encounter an everyday reality that is far different from that of the many servants, nannies, and chauffeurs who serve them round the clock. The flat-screen televisions, air conditioning, and other modern amenities of the newly rich are not affected by the water and electricity outages that last an average of 12 hours a day in the slums right outside their gates. Immaculately groomed gated communities not only provide residents with their own utilities; they also have their own private schools, health clinics, and cricket clubs. Overall, poverty in India has shown significant decline, but "more than a quarter of all Indians live below the poverty line (subsisting on roughly $1 a day) [and] nearly half of all Indian children are clinically malnourished."

NEWS 15.6

Taking a more differentiated approach to the class inequality produced by globalization, **Saskia Sassen** (2007: 168) argues that globalization produces a new form of stratification, a denationalized class of global workers. This is a heterogeneous class comprised of three class groups whose occupational conditions and lifestyles vary considerably; Sassen's analysis thus follows a more fine-grained, Weberian rather than Marx-derived, polarization thesis. She argues that the cosmopolitanism of a transnational professional and executive class – those who work and move between the global financial centers in London, New York, Tokyo, Frankfurt, etc. – does not apply to the other global classes, such as the class of transnational government officials and experts (a class that includes many mid-level workers, e.g., immigration and police officers); and particularly not to what she spotlights as an emergent class of disadvantaged, resource-poor workers and activists, many of whom live in transnational immigrant communities (2007: 168–169).

We see, therefore, that sociologists, like economists, recognize the "integration" of commodity, labor, and capital markets that economic globalization entails. But sociologists emphasize that market integration is part of a long, though changing, historical-geographical process. This is a process which is neither seamless nor apolitical, and which is characterized by considerable economic disparities between and within countries/regions. Sociologists further underscore that economic globalization proceeds in tandem with the expansion of the power of transnational corporations, and creates new forms of class stratification, characterized by substantial inter-class social and economic inequalities.

POLITICAL GLOBALIZATION: THE NATION-STATE IN THE NEW ORDER

Another analytical focus of globalization scholars is the role of the nation-state in the new global order. You remember that Max Weber underscored the significance of the state as the embodiment of bureaucratic, rational legal authority in modern society (cf. chapter 3). The state and its various bureaucracies regulate society, including the economy (cf. Giddens and Held above) and other social institutions, maintain order and security, and protect state borders. Globalization scholars disagree about the significance and authority of the state in a globalized society wherein national borders are increasingly less salient. Free trade between countries; transnational political, economic, and cultural alliances – highlighted by the ongoing (though politically contested) expansion of the European Union; transnational military alliances (e.g., NATO); and the global flow of internet and satellite information that is (relatively) impervious to national boundaries (remember the internet crackdown in Myanmar) – means that the state may lose its autonomy. Additionally, transnational citizenship (e.g., among member states of the EU) and transnational laws and legal forums (e.g., the European Court) further challenge the discrete political, legal, and cultural power of the nation-state.

NEWS 5.1

467

In Sklair's (2002) Marxist-derived analysis of capitalist globalization, the state has little institutional autonomy. As we saw above, for Sklair the main political actor is the transnational capitalist class, and specifically those who are members of the capitalist class in the most powerful (capitalist) states (2002: 7). Although he concedes that the nation-state cannot be ignored, he nonetheless argues that a state-centered focus obscures the decreased relevance of state territorial borders, the system of global relationships, and the changing power dynamics between states and non-state actors, including transnational corporations (2002: 8). Thus, for example, Sklair argues that the terrorist attacks of 9/11 highlight the importance of a transnational rather than a nation-state approach to understanding within-state/global occurrences (2002: 11). We can readily see that 9/11 was not the result of a war between one state and another (or of one inter-state alliance against another, as in World War II, for example), but of a transnational terror alliance against one location of capitalist globalization.

Unlike Sklair, Giddens (who has long shown the influence of Weber in his writing) identifies the nation-state system as a key player in globalization dynamics. He argues that while there is overlap between the political and economic dimensions of globalization, each sphere has its own institutional autonomy.

> The main centers of power in the world economy are capitalist states ... The domestic and international economic policies of these states involve many forms of regulation of economic activity, but ... their institutional organization maintains an "insulation" of the economic from the political. This allows wide scope for the global activities of business corporations, which always have a home base within a particular state but may develop many other regional involvements elsewhere. (Giddens 1990: 70; see also 2003: xxv)

Giddens (1990: 70) recognizes that many business corporations – e.g., Coca-Cola, Nike, Microsoft – exert enormous economic and political power within their own home countries as well as across the world. But he also makes the important point that corporations lack certain powers that states have, namely, as Weber first noted, "territoriality and control of the means of violence within their own territories. No matter how great their economic power, industrial corporations are not military organizations (as some of them were during the colonial period) and they cannot establish themselves as political/legal entities which rule a given territorial area" (1990: 70–71).

The global geo-political order, however, is also complicated by the global diffusion of military power. Giddens, in fact, sees what he calls the world military order as a discrete analytical dimension of globalization (1990: 74). Again here, Giddens emphasizes that military power often overlaps, but does not always correlate, with a country's positioning within the world capitalist and the nation-state system. As he points out, many economically weak "third world" countries are militarily powerful: "In an important sense there is no 'Third World' in respect of weaponry, only a 'First World,' since most countries maintain stocks of technologically advanced armaments," including, in some cases, nuclear technology (1990: 74–75) – e.g., Pakistan, and North Korea (and hence their importance in the network of US geo-political relations; see chapter 7).

ECONOMICS AND POLITICS: THE NEW IMPERIALISM

The conjoint force of strong economic and strong military power preoccupies David Harvey (2003). His lens on the varied military, political, and economic globalizing forces in play today leads him to argue for what he calls the new imperialism. This view, though arguing for a dynamic tension between state territorial-political interests and capitalist economic interests, ultimately tends to see the triumph of a capitalist economic logic (Harvey 2003: 30, 33). Harvey argues that while the traditional understanding of imperialism tended to see "an easy accord" between territorial and economic interests (e.g., the British Empire), the current global situation, exemplified by the US invasion of Iraq, and its attend-ant move toward creating new allies in the Middle East (e.g., Saudi Arabia), Eastern Europe, and Turkey, is driven more by economic than political-territorial interests (Harvey 2003: 198–199). For Harvey, "The fundamental point is to see the territorial and the capitalist logics of power as distinct from each other" (2003: 29); economic and political interests can be antagonistic and certainly do not always coincide – including the fact that a country's internal politics (2003: 211) are frequently conflicted over global economic (e.g., anti-NAFTA sentiment in the US) and political-territorial policies (e.g., anti-war opinion).

Nevertheless, Harvey argues, the global geo-political agenda of the US is "all about oil" (2003: 18). Its primary economic interests intertwine with military-territorial interests, such that it consolidates a

> vital strategic bridgehead ... on the Eurasian land mass that just happens to be the centre of production of the oil that currently fuels (and will continue to fuel for at least the next fifty years) not only the global economy but also every large military machine that dares to oppose that of the United States. This should ensure the continued global dominance of the US for the next fifty years. (Harvey 2003: 198–199)

THE STATE'S NEGOTIATION OF LOCAL AND GLOBAL FORCES

While Giddens emphasizes the nation-state's territorial and policing-military rights, he does not present the state solely in terms of its strategic economic and security-military interests. Rather, he argues: "The material involvements of nation states are not governed purely by economic considerations ... They do not operate as economic machines but as 'actors' jealous of their territorial rights, concerned with the fostering of national cultures, and having strategic geopoliti-cal involvements with other states or alliances of states" (1990: 72). The state, to be sure, has economic and territorial interests, but, Giddens argues, it also has cultural interests and a commitment to fostering and protecting its own particular cultural identity, a concern that, along with its economic and security interests, will shape its geo-political engagement.

These multiple, autonomous interests of the state show themselves in what Giddens refers to as the dialectical nature of globalization, namely, the push and pull between centralizing, inter-state (or transnational) tendencies and the assertion of state sovereignty (1990: 73). We see many examples of this push–pull among states that are members of the European Union (EU). On the one hand, most EU states share a single financial currency (the Euro) and want taxation and trade policies facilitating the free flow of goods among member countries. This is the push of centralization. But at the same time, individual countries protest against policies that threaten the economic interests of one of their own within-state constituencies (e.g., against EU restrictions on local property development rules in member countries). The assertion of state sovereignty over and against the pull of common European interests was most apparent during the global financial crisis of fall 2008; individual EU member countries quickly and

NEWS 15.7

unilaterally acted to protect their own nation's economic interests. Various push–pull dynamics play out elsewhere. India, for example, strongly embraces the pull toward the international capitalist economy, but it also ignores localized demands to bolster its existing national infrastructure, especially the need to build more schools despite their obvious necessity to Indians' success in the local-

NEWS 15.8

global economy.

Globalization also coincides with the emergence of new nationalist or ethno-nationalist movements (e.g., Scottish nationalism in the political-legal context of the UK; Giddens 2003: 13). Indeed there is irony, or sociological complexity, in the fact that globalization, celebrated in part as the triumph of the irrelevance of borders (e.g., in economic trade, internet communication), coincides with the drawing of new territorial borders that undermine the societal cohesiveness of an established national identity. This is part of a post-colonial legacy whereby previously colonized or subordinated states, regions, or ethnic groups reclaim an identity that is no longer defined in terms of the Other (cf. Said 1978; see chapter 12). This process is most evident in the relatively rapid transformation of Ukraine and Georgia, former Soviet republics, into politically and economically independent countries that have become new members of the World Trade Organization (WTO), and against the objections

NEWS 15.9

of Russia (which itself is not a member despite its increasing economic power). The creation of new nations – e.g., the split of Czechoslovakia into Slovakia

NEWS 15.10

and the Czech Republic; and Kosovo's declaration of independence from Serbia – points to the reclaiming of territory and of a national and cultural identity that can stand alone without being defined (or signified) by its relation to the dominant (signifier) country. We see a similar tendency toward deconstruction occurring in Belgium, a long-established democratic nation-state which is currently in conflict as a result of tensions between French-speaking and Dutch-

NEWS 15.11

speaking Belgians.

Somewhat similarly to Giddens, political scientist James Rosenau argues that globalization as a concept is insufficient to capture the full dynamic complexity of the political alignments and tensions that characterize our current era. He offers the notion of distant proximities as a way of thinking about the intertwining of the global and the local in world affairs. He explains:

> The best way to grasp world affairs today requires viewing them as an endless series of distant proximities in which the forces pressing for greater globalization and those inducing greater localization interactively play themselves out ... Distant proximities encompass the tensions between core and periphery, between national and transnational systems, between communitarianism and cosmopolitanism, between cultures and subcultures, between states and markets, between urban and rural, between coherence and incoherence, between integration and disintegration, between decentralization and centralization, between universalism and particularism, between pace [speed/flow] and space, between the global and the local ... All of these tensions are marked by numerous variants; they take different forms in different parts of the world, in different countries ... in different communities ... in different cyberspaces, with the result that there is enormous diversity in the way people experience the distant proximities of which their lives are composed. Whatever the diversity, however, locating distant proximities ... enables us to avoid the trap of maintaining an analytic separation between foreign and domestic politics. (2003: 4–5)

It is noteworthy that in emphasizing the need to avoid the either/or conceptual binary (local/global) in discussing globalization, Rosenau references the work of the cultural theorist Stuart Hall, who, as we discuss in chapter 12, elaborates the co-occurrence of difference and similarity in racial histories and identities (e.g., being black *and* British). In any event, from the point of view of conducting research on globalization, systematic attentiveness to the intermingling of the local and the global in specific social, political, historical, and cultural contexts offers a fruitful way to begin to apprehend the many varied manifestations and consequences of everyday life in a globalizing society.

THE IMPOTENT POST-NATIONAL STATE?

Zygmunt Bauman (2000) offers a more pessimistic view than Giddens and Rosenau of the place of the state in the globalizing world. In particular, he sees the state as being increasingly limited in its ability to function as a sovereign state on behalf of its own people and its own national interests. Thus for Bauman, with supra-national forces – global trade, global currencies, global military alliances (e.g., NATO), and economic-political alliances (e.g., the EU) – increasingly dominating global society, the nation-state becomes a less autonomous and less powerful political-economic-military actor. He argues that in a global world wherein global processes impact whole societies irrespective of national boundaries, the nation can no longer be considered the core economic, political, or military unit.

BIOGRAPHICAL NOTE

Zygmunt Bauman was born in Poland in 1925 to Jewish parents. He studied philosophy at the University of Warsaw and subsequently received his MA in sociology. He moved to England, to the University of Leeds, in the early 1970s, partly as a result of the anti-Semitism experienced by his family. Bauman has written extensively on various aspects of modernity, among other topics. He is currently a retired professor of sociology at the Universities of Leeds and Warsaw.

Bauman chooses the phrase "liquid modernity" to refer to the fluidity of contemporary globalized societal processes. He highlights in particular how this fluidity impacts the role of the nation-state in an era that we need to think of, he argues, in terms of "after the nation-state." In this new post-national order, we are "orphaned," Bauman claims, unprotected by the state and its institutions, against the powerful forces of globalization and economic and social change. Bauman concludes that if a nation tries to protects its citizens from unemployment and other economic losses (due to globalization), its failure to play by the global economic rules will result in further economic punishment:

> The orphaned individual [can no longer] huddle under the nation's wings ... The freedom of state politics is relentlessly eroded by the new global powers ... Insubordinate governments, guilty of protectionist policies or generous public provisions for the "economically redundant sectors" of their populations and of recoiling from leaving the country at the mercy of "global financial markets" and "global free trade," would be refused loans and are denied reduction of their debts; local currencies would be made global lepers, speculated against and pressed to devalue; local stocks would fall head down on the global exchanges; the country would be cordoned off by economic sanctions and told to be treated by past and future trade partners as a global pariah; global investors would cut their anticipated losses, pack up their belongings and withdraw their assets, leaving local authorities to clean up the debris and bail the victims out of their added misery. (2000: 185–186)

Thus Bauman sees the state as a victim of globalization, whereas Sklair, for example, sees the state – and "the globalizing elements in governments and bureaucracies who are members of the transnational capitalist class" – as being complicit in globalization: "Often governments will go along with globalization not because they cannot resist it but because they perceive it to be in their own interests" (Sklair 2002: 6).

Another post-nationalist consequence is that the relevance of a nation's territoriality itself is called into question. Bauman argues that, whether in the pursuit of economic or military power, the fluidity of force and the accelerated speed at which it can target its object (and achieve its objectives) make for a world in which territoriality is less and less desired; rather than being prized, territory can become a burdensome constraint (2000: 188) – it can literally bog down the invading country (e.g., the US in Vietnam). Thus the *electronic* waging of war allowed by technological advances in "smart bombs" and geographically distant, remotely piloted surveillance airplanes and missile firing systems – an approach increasingly favored by US military leaders – reduces (or suppresses) the on-the-ground consequences of military action for the military aggressor. Responsibility both for the war and for its aftermath gets displaced amidst the fluidity of force and space, notwithstanding the fact that war invariably occurs in some localized on-the-ground setting; in other words, smart bombs generally target people and communities, not other smart bombs.

NEWS 15.12

Bauman comments:

> The cumbersome jobs of ground occupation, local engagements and managerial and administrative responsibilities, [are] quite out of tune with liquid modernity's techniques of power. The might of the global elite rests on its ability to escape local commitments, and globalization is meant precisely to avoid such necessities, to divide tasks and functions in such a way as to burden local authorities, and them only, with the role of guardians of law and (local) order. (2000: 188)

However, as we see in Iraq, the US cannot escape from the local complications of its territorial (and electronically waged) invasion. It cannot avoid the many administrative, civic, and political dilemmas and the attendant financial costs encountered in rebuilding a working society. This state of affairs thus further adds to the perception of the civil-political impotence of the state in contemporary society (notwithstanding its globalizing military power).

NEWS 5.24

THE DENATIONALIZED STATE

Contrary to Sklair and Harvey, who see the state as complicit in globalization; to Giddens, who sees it as adapting more or less to the push and pull of globalization; and to Bauman, who sees its erosion of power as an inevitable consequence of globalization, Sassen argues for a reconceptualization of the state. She argues that sociologists need to think of the denationalized state. In this framing, with globalization, the state loses some aspects of authority within its national territory, due to overriding transnational trade agreements or transnational laws and human rights agreements. But, at the same time, the state can also increase its authority beyond the nation; it does this through, for example, participation in "governing the global economy in a context increasingly dominated by deregulation, privatization, and the growing authority of non-state actors" (2007: 49). Thus the state, Sassen argues, is "one of the strategic institutional domains in which critical work on the development of globalization takes place" (2007: 4).

Sassen, therefore, frames the state as an actively engaged institutional actor that can proactively attempt "to link into the global economy, to claim jurisdiction over the various tasks involved in globalization, thereby securing [its] own power"

NEWS 5.21

(2007: 51). The state, after all, is "the ultimate guarantor of the rights of global capital" (2007: 54). It has, for example, the legal and political authority to approve or reject corporate mergers (e.g., in the US, JP Morgan's acquisition of Bear Stearns, or the potential merger of Microsoft and Yahoo!). The state, moreover, encounters new regulatory opportunities, as evidenced by policy debates over its role in outlining internet access and security standards. Despite the frequently voiced emphasis on the autonomy of digitalized technology and its avoidance of national territorial restrictions, it is still the case that states have the power to enforce a particular kind of internet-digital environment within and beyond their own national territory (e.g., Sassen 2007: 82–96). Cyberspace attacks on one country's internet infrastructure by another, such as Russia's on Georgia in the weeks preceding its military invasion of the country in 2008, or the Chinese government's blocking of foreign journalists' access to Amnesty International's and other politically threatening web pages during the Olympics (August 2008), similar to the blocks it imposes on its own citizens' internet access, further underscore the state-territoriality of internet space.

NEWS 15.13

Sassen argues that while we commonly think of globalization as the growing interdependence of the world and the formation of global institutions (e.g., the WTO) and global processes (global financial markets), it is also necessary to recognize that "the global partly inhabits the national" (2007: 3). Thus, for example, the services that are critical to the globalizing economy (e.g., financial markets and their corporate-professional infrastructure) are invariably located in national-geographical spaces – state-controlled national territory (2007: 49), even as their products, operations, and impact transcend any one nation.

In sum, it is evident that sociologists vary in their appraisal of the role and power of the state in and amidst globalization. The extent to which the state becomes relatively impotent, or instead acquires new institutional significance as a denationalized actor, is an empirical question that remains to be answered over the new few decades. In the meantime, the unprecedented intervention of national governments in the US and in European countries, in rescuing corporations and financial markets from further collapse during the recession of 2008–2009, suggests that the power of the nation-state and its various bureaucracies is not likely to soon diminish.

NEWS 5.19
NEWS 5.21

CULTURAL GLOBALIZATION

The "pooling of knowledge" via internet technology is one of the main engines of cultural globalization (Giddens 1990: 76). One way of thinking about the impact of the global pooling of information – whether stock prices or celebrity gossip – and of the culture it transmits, is the concept of unicity, introduced by Roland Robertson (1992). He argues: "Globalization has to do with the movement of the world as a whole in the direction of unicity – meaning oneness of the world as a single sociocultural place" (2005: 348). Robertson is careful to point out that unicity is not to be confused with global societal integration or unification; and he acknowledges, moreover, that unicity is a fuzzy concept insofar as there are no criteria for deciding when it has been achieved (ibid.). Nevertheless, the concept helps us to think about the multiple interconnectedness of individuals, places, experiences, and institutions that seems to be so distinctive of what it means to live in a globalized society.

CULTURAL HOMOGENIZATION

Oneness of culture has long been demarcated by a community's shared symbols (cf. Durkheim; see chapter 2). That today we experience, however partially, a oneness of global culture is crystallized by the world's shared recognition of the Golden Arches – the McDonald's sign that greets us in Dublin, Paris, Seattle, Austin, or Dubai; McDonald's is a "global icon" (Ritzer 2000: 1–7). The McDonaldization of society, a phrase coined by George Ritzer (2000), captures the convergence and homogenization of culture across the globe, notwithstanding the simultaneous significance of local cultural differences. McDonald's offers the world a standardized cultural experience (Ritzer 2000: 22–26); McDonald's is more or less the same across the globe, though it should be noted that its "commercial opportunism" is such that it adjusts its menu and advertising to enhance its appeal to local consumers in Singapore, Paris, Seoul (Sklair 2002: 185–186). Moreover, the power of cultural traditions – despite the global diffusion of ideas of gender equality – means that in Riyadh, Saudi Arabia, McDonald's has separate sections for men and for completely covered women.

NEWS 15.14

In general, the globalization of culture is especially apparent in consumption. The fact that American brands such as McDonalds and Abercrombie and Fitch are well known beyond American borders might be seen as simply reinforcing and extending American cultural imperialism, resulting from the one-way flow of American ideas and products to the rest of the world; an idea that gained prominence in the post-World War II decades with the surging global popularity of Disney, Coca-Cola, and other American cultural icons and products (Tunstall 1977). Today, however, the one-way flow of American culture overseas is tempered somewhat by the indigenous development of cultural industries in countries such as India, Mexico, and Brazil, even though they largely imitate American movies and soap-operas, etc., and are consumed primarily by their home-country residents rather than by more globally dispersed audiences (Sklair 2002: 176–184). The one-way flow is also tempered by the greater global visibility of non-American shops and brands – Louis Vuitton, Prada, Chanel – and art galleries in affluent world cities, and the general availability of a greater array of everyday "ethnic" foods, changes propelled by global migration patterns.

NEWS 15.15

Global consumer trends are also driven, as Sklair underscores, by transnational advertising agencies (2002: 180), which thoroughly promote the first world (especially Americanized) consumer lifestyle in the third world. Given the extensive promotion of cigarettes and other products considered unhealthy in the West

Cultural globalization often means cultural homogenization. The ideal for many Asian women is a Caucasian face, a standard of beauty promoted by the cosmetics industry globally, as advertised (above) by Chanel in Seoul, South Korea. (Photo courtesy of Chulsoo Kim.)

NEWS 15.16

(2002: 187–204), it is not surprising that a recent World Health Organization (WHO) report documents a soaring increase in cigarette sales in poor and middle-income countries, a trend that coincides with the implementation of smoking bans in public bars and restaurants in Europe and the US. Following a Marxist–Frankfurt School analysis of the media-advertising industry (cf. chapter 5), Sklair notes that the consumer culture promoted in third world countries is greatly at odds with the everyday material existence of the people living there, an existence which for many borders on starvation. He thus suggests that we "pause to distinguish the effects of consumerism in societies where affluence is the norm (though even here some people may be without the necessities of life) and societies where poverty is the norm (though some people may be very affluent)" (2002: 187).

CULTURAL BORDERS

The various trends suggesting an emergent global culture co-exist alongside the creation of new cultural barriers. As Robertson observes, in some places and in some socio-political contexts, "borders are becoming more rather than less salient" (2005: 348). The ongoing controversy in the US over illegal immigration is a case in point – specifically, the building of a steel fence to secure the US–Mexico border. This wall of sheet metal and concrete – 700 miles long, 15 feet high, and guarded by electronic radar surveillance towers – creates a physical and cultural barrier between the US and Mexico, and disrupts the local ties and relationships between American and Mexican neighbors. Similarly, the Israeli government has built a wall to separate Israelis from Palestinians. And, as a result of the response to the ongoing threat of world terrorism that is also part of our globalized experience, public access to landmark buildings and tourist sites is complicated if not denied by the erection of steel and concrete barriers.

Beyond the concrete, we still have many cultural and cognitive barriers reflecting the intersecting differences of religion, race, region, country, gender, sexuality, class, etc., that divide individuals locally and globally. The embrace of economic globalization does not mean the embrace of political-cultural equality, as underscored by the gender walls in McDonalds in economically rich Saudi Arabia, a major actor in economic globalization processes.

NEWS 15.14

Similarly, even before 9/11 exacerbated latent suspicions between westerners and people from Islamic countries, Samuel Huntington (1996), in a controversial book called *The Clash of Civilizations*, argued for the existence of historically deep cultural and ideological differences between various world civilizations (e.g., Japanese, Islamic, North American). In Huntington's view, these differences are not only unbridgeable but are bound to lead to violent conflict. Today, the many ongoing conflicts around the world, often centered on the contestation of vastly different ideas of individual and political authority, freedom, equality, community, etc., suggest that, as Max Weber noted over one hundred years ago, different world cultures produce different worldviews that, in turn, contribute to the institutionalization of different economic and political structures (see chapter 3).

This remains the case at least in regard to the perseverance of vastly different political and gender structures across the globe even as economic globalization pushes toward the convergence of economic markets and consumer culture. China, for example, is a major player in the global economy and a major producer and consumer of globalized consumerism (e.g. Sklair 2002: 244–271). Yet some of its cultural beliefs and their translation into political institutions and procedures (e.g., regarding human rights, freedom of expression, the one-child-per-family rule), are starkly at odds not only with principles of social equality, but with the ideology of deregulation – of individual freedom, and the absence of government control and intervention – that is so strongly affirmed by economists and policy-makers as the preferred route to ensuring the momentum of an integrated global economy and society (e.g., Bordo et al. 2003b).

NEWS 15.17

CITIES AND MIGRATION IN A GLOBALIZING SOCIETY

Throughout history, cities have been the dynamic center of political, economic, and social change (e.g., Athens, Florence, London). Durkheim invested much sociological significance in the copious opportunities that city life provides for social interaction and interdependence (cf. chapter 2). Not surprisingly, globalization processes and the transformations they yield once again re-center attention on the place of the city in society.

GLOBAL CITIES

Saskia Sassen has written extensively about the global cities that underlie the global economy. She explains:

> The global economy needs to be produced, reproduced, serviced, and financed ... [Its operational functions] have become so specialized that they can no longer be contained in the functions of corporate headquarters. Global cities are strategic sites for the production of these specialized functions to run and coordinate the global economy. Inevitably located in national territories, global cities are the organizational and institutional space for the major dynamics of denationalization. (2007: 73; see also Sassen 1991)

Global cities "accumulate immense concentrations of economic power" (2007: 111), and Sassen argues that, unlike world cities (e.g., Paris, Rome), which have existed through time, global cities are distinctively new: "They are the terrain on which multiple globalization processes assume material and localized forms" (2007: 23–24). As such, global cities constitute a new geography, one that is no longer demarcated by a North/South division but in fact incorporates several strategic cities in the Southern hemisphere (ibid.: 24), including Tokyo; Sao Paulo, Brazil; and Mexico City.[3]

Not all world cities are (or will become) global cities – that is to be empirically assessed in terms of the extent to which they are, or become, centers for global economic operations. Today, many cities might be considered global cities even though there are significant differences of scale among them in the amount and the reach of the global operations they oversee (e.g., Dublin compared to New York or Singapore). Sassen's conceptualization of the global city makes a lot of intuitive sense. It is theoretically vague, however, regarding how we should empirically assess, categorize, and differentiate among cities/global cities.

TRANSNATIONAL MIGRATION

Global cities are not just the location for the transnationalization of capital but also, of course, for the transnationalization of the labor that sustains the economic and corporate services and the everyday infrastructure of the global economy. The transnational labor market is a highly stratified one – it includes cosmopolitan professionals as well as mid-level government and low-wage workers (Sassen 2007: 168–169). The last group, in particular, is comprised of many migrants and immigrants. One of the core features of our global age is immigration, and this truly is a worldwide and growing phenomenon. Sociologists and demographers argue that we are currently witnessing unprecedented population flows, with an estimated 200 million people classified as migrants. Among these are "Latvian mushroom workers in Ireland ... Tajik construction workers in Russia, farm-hands from Burkina Faso who pick Ghanian crops, and the Peruvians who take jobs left behind by Ecuadorean workers who have emigrated to Spain."

NEWS 15.18

New trends in the transnationalization of labor, Sassen argues, mean that we need to be attentive to the new processes entailed in social identity formation. She argues that the (old) analytical "language of immigration ... overlooks the trans-nationalization in the formation of identities and loyalties among various popula-tion segments that explicitly reject the imagined community of the nation. With this rejection come new solidarities and notions of membership" (2007: 122–123). In other words, while sociologists have tended, in accord with Durkheim, to emphasize the nation as a unit of collective identity (with a shared culture and common beliefs), or, following Weber, to emphasize shared territoriality, this framing tends to marginalize those within a given nation who have more transi-tory cultural-geographical histories. As Stuart Hall argues, such singular notions of identity do not capture the complexity of colonial identities (cf. chapter 12). Nor do they encapsulate contemporary transnational trends. The nation, in short, for many individuals and groups, is no longer an overarching source of social identity. People move, literally, between nations, and their identities, solidarities, and commitments are not tied exclusively to any one nation – to, in the old lan-guage of immigration, either the host nation or the sender nation. Thus, many migration scholars emphasize that transnational identities are transforming indi-viduals' economic, religious, political, and social commitments and relationships in all sorts of varied and multilayered ways (e.g., Levitt 2007).

Much of this transnational identity formation can be seen in cities. Cities, as Sassen emphasizes, are

> strategic sites for both the transnationalization of labor and the formation of transna-tional identities. In this regard, they form a site for new types of politics, including new types of transnational politics. Cities are the terrain on which people from many countries are most likely to meet and a multiplicity of cultures can come together. The international character of major cities lies not only in their telecommunications infrastructure and international firms; it lies also in the many cultural environments in which their workers exist. (2007: 123)

Consequently, Sassen is optimistic that the very presence in global cities of struc-turally disadvantaged workers, especially "women, immigrants, people of color, groups with a mostly troubled relation to the national state," has the potential to make global cities the sites for political change and increased social equality.

This is because, Sassen argues, the economic, social and political forces in global cities are less bound up with any one nation-state per se (notwithstanding the local nationalized territory in which these cities are located), and hence more autonomous of the state's institutional mechanisms maintaining the status quo. Therefore, in contrast with Bauman, who sees globalization as further marginalizing economically disadvantaged groups who cannot rely on the state to protect them (or itself) from globalization (see above, p. 472), Sassen sees political ferment as possible among transnational, disadvantaged workers who are not politically tied to any one state. Again, the extent to which Bauman's pessimism and Sassen's optimism get realized remains to be empirically assessed by labor and migration scholars.

GLOBALIZATION OF RISK

That globalization processes involve an ongoing interplay between local and global forces is underscored by what theorists see as the increased encounter with risk – so much so that the German theorist Ulrich Beck (1992) refers to contemporary society as risk society. And although risk (like opportunity) is created, in large part, by society – especially by the push toward economic prosperity and progress (Beck 1992: 40) – this does not make it any less threatening. Thus, for example, while we can travel the globe in a relatively efficient manner today, the same efficiency also applies to the travel time for the global circulation of contaminated foods and of disease, with the effect that illness spreads more rapidly, and diseases appear in places where they were thought not to occur or to have disappeared (e.g., TB in the US).

NEWS 15.19

By the same token, as a result of advances in scientific technology, we have more apparatuses creating increased risk (e.g., military-nuclear armament technology) and ways of treating various risks (e.g., nuclear medicine). We also have more information and greater access to information (e.g., genetic profiling, WebMD) making us aware of the risks that surround us (e.g., of getting cancer, living in a polluted city, etc.). But all of this technology and information does not resolve – as Weber (cf. chapter 3) and Frankfurt School theorists (cf. chapter 5) underscored – how we should deal with and negotiate among the risks and the risk information we encounter. For example, individuals who discover from newly developed medical prognostication tests that they have an elevated risk of cancer still have to decide which course of action (surgery, radiation) prior to the onset of symptoms might ensure a better outcome; and to decide, moreover, among transnational, geographically diverse medical venues where to receive (buy) treatment, whether at a distant medical-tourist resort in Mexico or at a more locally situated clinic.

NEWS 15.20

Risk is not new; all societies through time have encountered it. But Beck (1992) and Giddens (2003) emphasize that, today, our detailed knowledge of risk and its possible outcomes is unprecedented. Yet we cannot control or eliminate the uncertainties surrounding the probable outcome of a particular risk for us individually; hence, we are afflicted by risk and its uncertainties (Beck 1992: 23–24). Thus, while we "are creating something that has never existed before, a global cosmopolitan society," at the same time, globalization "is shaking up our existing ways of life, no matter where we happen to be … It is not settled or secure, but fraught with anxieties" (Giddens 2003: 19).

Risk, moreover, is a fate universal in scope, Beck argues, rather than unevenly distributed along economic class lines. Although toxic industrial accidents may initially have a more immediate impact on particular economically and socially disadvantaged communities – because of the geographical concentration of factories and power plants, etc., in poorer neighborhoods and in poorer global regions – in the risk society everyone is at risk, including the rich. Risk's inclusivity is further crystallized by global changes in the environment, and by the terrorist targeting of centers of high finance and power. Beck elaborates:

> Risk positions are not class positions. With the globalization of risks a social dynamic is set in motion, which can no longer be composed of and understood in class categories. Ownership implies non-ownership and thus a social relationship of tension and conflict, in which reciprocal social identities can continually evolve and solidify – "them up there, us down here." The situation is quite different for risk positions. Anyone affected by them is badly off, but deprives the others, the non-affected, of nothing. Expressed in an analogy: the "class" of the "affected" does not confront a "class" that is not affected. It confronts at most a "class" of not-yet-affected people. The escalating scarcity of health will drive even those still well off today (in health and well-being) into the ranks of the "soup kitchens" provided by insurance companies tomorrow, and the day after tomorrow into the pariah community of the invalid and the wounded. (1992: 39–40)

In short, "freedom from risk can turn overnight into irreversible affliction" (1992: 40). And this is a fate that, for all the achievements of modernity, cannot be overcome by individual achievement. Beck states: "Now there exists a kind of *risk fate in developed civilization*, into which one is born, which one cannot escape with any amount of achievement … we are *all* confronted similarly by that fate" (1992: 41).

What then are individuals and society to do? Clearly, many individuals and collectivities are quite planful and creative in trying to minimize risk. For example, the US Olympic delegation to Beijing, worried about drug and pesticide contaminants in Chinese products and the increased risk not only of disease but of yielding an illegal positive drug presence in individual athletes, planned to have 25,000 pounds of lean protein shipped from the US to China in advance of the 2008 Olympic games – even though, as we know, US products too (beef, spinach, tomatoes, peanut butter paste) are not risk-free.

NEWS 15.21

Beyond specific instances, Giddens calls for a macro-societal response: the "deepening of democracy" at local and transnational levels. This is necessary, he states, because: "The old mechanisms of government don't work in a society where citizens live in the same information environment as those in power over them" (2003: 75). Giddens argues that, whether in advanced democratic or socialist/communist societies, the varying degrees of secrecy and the backstage political alignments of the past can no longer withstand the onslaught of what he sees as a currently resurging citizen involvement in politics and in policy-making and the desire to build strong democratic institutions (2003: 75–82). He is optimistic that these changes can be used to control what might appear as, or is in fact for him, a "runaway world" propelled by unprecedented, globalized social change (2003: xxxi).

Although it is true that globalization is changing the texture of everyday life, Giddens's invocation of a "runaway world" is at odds, by and large, with the relatively orderly way in which globalization is occurring. While we can identify various economic (e.g., recession) and political (e.g., ethnic violence in Kenya) crises, the disorder caused by these events is not historically unprecedented, and is hardly indicative of a runaway world or the result of globalization. The problems that became obvious in the economy in 2008, for example, whether the sub-prime mortgage investing of Citibank and other large banks, or the trading losses of the French bank Societe Generale, have not been created by globalization per se, though what happens in the US (or France or Thailand, etc.) quickly reverberates in domestic and global markets as a result of the computerization of money markets and electronic trading (cf. Zaloom 2006). Further, many economic disruptions, such as the US and global financial crises of 2008–2009 – often due to a lack of oversight and competent decision-making – are exacerbated by political deregulation, a force that is part of, but not created by, globalization per se. Similarly, while the availability of cheap labor in Mexico and in China clearly contributes to the heightened risk of loss in manufacturing jobs in the US, job loss is not a new phenomenon accompanying globalization; unemployment has challenged American (and other) societies in previous eras (e.g., the Great Depression, 1920s/1930s).

NEWS 15.22

DILEMMAS OF THE SELF IN A GLOBAL SOCIETY

Giddens (1990; 1991) also highlights the varied dilemmas of self-identity that become accentuated for individuals in a globalizing society. For many, globalization, and the internet in particular, brings an expansion of possibilities for the self. These new opportunities are liberating in many ways, but they can also make us feel insecure. What gives us self-security – the feeling of being at home/on one's own stomping ground and knowing what's what – is neither tied to nor necessarily produced in our local space and time. This is all part of the lack of grounding, the disembeddedness, of global society that Giddens argues may weaken our sense of ontological security, i.e., our trust in the world and the people with whom we interact. Thus, he argues, each of us must negotiate some middle ground in carving out a flexible but coherent self amidst the polarizing dilemmas of the self we necessarily encounter.

We have to negotiate (a) between a *unified* and a *fragmentary* self; (b) between the *powerlessness* one might feel against the juggernaut of global forces, on the one hand, and on the other the knowledge that you too are free to *appropriate* the latest technology and, for example, post your own YouTube video; (c) between the *authority* the internet gives you to directly access and read commentaries on Marxism, or on a new Italian restaurant, and the *uncertainty* you experience when you see that there are several contradictory views on any topic – how can you know what to think, do, or believe amidst these conflicting perspectives? And, finally, there is the dilemma of negotiating between what is truly an authentic *personalized* experience for you, and what you embrace because it is marketed or *commodified* as the latest fad. (Do you need to be in therapy because of persisting interpersonal conflicts in your life, or because Nicole Richie, Paris Hilton, and friends are in therapy?)

How we resolve such self-dilemmas has implications for our individual, everyday, social-psychological functioning, and will also contribute to shaping the kind of politics we engage in and the sort of society we try to foster. If globalization, as Sassen (2007) argues, creates new political opportunities toward building a more egalitarian society, and, as Giddens (2003) argues, demands a deepening of democracy, then it seems important that individuals develop a sense of self that is not fragmented and diffuse, but can authoritatively commit to specific values or general policy proposals, a commitment which itself is buoyed by an appropriate sense of empowerment, one that is aware of but not intimidated by social forces (such as thinking of globalization as a juggernaut against which one is helpless). In this framing, then, globalization requires the active participation of individuals in the public sphere – in local, national, and transnational forums – wherein they debate the individual and societal opportunities and risks presented by globalization.

POLITICAL MOBILIZATION IN THE GLOBALIZING SOCIETY

Some scholars argue that the internet-electronic age makes opportunities for political engagement more accessible. **Manuel Castells**, a neo-Marxist scholar, suggests that the network society is more conducive to challenging the hierarchies

BIOGRAPHICAL NOTE

Manuel Castells was born in Barcelona, Spain, in 1942. He received his PhD in sociology from the University of Paris, where he was subsequently a professor. He spent most of his career as professor of sociology and city and regional planning at the University of California, Berkeley, and in 2003, accepted a distinguished chair at the University of Southern California. Castells is widely recognized for his academic and policy expertise on the information society, and has received numerous international awards. He continues to lecture widely and to write on the challenges posed by the network society.

institutionalized into social life. In *The Information Society*, a three-volume, empirically detailed study, Castells (1997) argues that the network society emerged during the last quarter of the twentieth century as a result of the convergence of the information technology revolution; the restructuring of capitalism and of nation-states; and the political and cultural effectiveness of the social movements of the 1960s and 1970s. These changes influenced the emergence of more decentralized forms of social organization, political and religious movements, and social relationships. We see such decentralization, for example, in Silicon Valley: The dot.com workplace favors a relatively egalitarian, informal, and open-plan system (with software engineers working on their laptops in coffee shops, etc) – a model that starkly contrasts with the bureaucratized structures in government, finance, and many other work sectors. These workplaces, we should note, like those of Google and Microsoft, also provide extensive leisure and dining activities for their employees. This strategy maintains employees on *campus* (as these sprawling workplaces are called) amidst blurred work–leisure boundaries that likely keep them not only at work (on campus) but also working, despite the relaxed and egalitarian atmosphere.

In any event, in the network society, Castells argues:

> For the first time in history, the basic unit of economic organization is not a subject, be it individual (such as the entrepreneur) ... or collective (such as the capitalist class, the corporation, the state) ... *the unit is the network*, made up of a variety of subjects and organizations relentlessly modified as networks adapt to supportive environments and market structures. (1997: 198)

Castells (2000: 695) argues that new, digitalized information technology enhances networks' decentralized flexibility and the efficient performance of complex and wide-ranging tasks. As in the pre-internet era, it is largely an economic logic which influences network composition. Thus,

> all regions in the world may be linked into the global economy, but only to the point where they add value to the value-making function of this economy, by their contribution in human resources, markets, raw materials, or other components of production and distribution. If a region is not valuable to such a network, it will not be linked up; or if it ceases to be valuable, it will be switched off, without the network as a whole suffering major inconvenience. (2000: 695)

Nonetheless, Castells argues, non-economic values and goals can also, in principle, be programmed into the network. Just as the social movements of the 1960s and 1970s used the public square (public streets and parks) to mobilize and protest against the established institutional powers, so too, but with much greater efficiency, flexibility, and reach, the social change movements of today can set emancipatory goals and mobilize global support for particular causes through the creation of global communication networks (e.g., Castells 2000: 695; 1997: 470). As such the internet can be seen as a crucial resource facilitating the deepening of democracy envisaged by Giddens (2003: 75). One example of this perhaps was the transformation in the funding of Barack Obama's 2008 presidential campaign, whereby ordinary individuals (many of whom apparently were politically inactive previously) used the internet to donate small amounts of money to his campaign, thus expanding the political citizen-donor base and the amounts gathered as well as perhaps making him a candidate less dependent on and beholden to large donors.

THE ANTI-GLOBALIZATION MOVEMENT

Today, the anti-globalization movement, a broadly defined and relatively loose association of various groups and initiatives, is at the forefront of efforts to redefine societal values about economic growth, socio-economic equality, and the relations of individuals to one another and to their natural environment. Sklair argues that the success to date of the movement lies in its strategic ability to have been able to make connections between what he sees as the twin crises of capitalist globalization: class polarization and ecological sustainability/environmental issues (2002: 278). The anti-globalization movement challenges the globalization practices of transnational corporations, the activities of the state and the transnational capitalist class, and the culture and ideology of consumerism (ibid.). Many of the anti-globalization efforts we see are highly localized (e.g., opposition to Wal-Mart in New York). But as Sklair contends, "Precisely because capitalist globalization works mainly through transnational practices, in order to challenge these practices politically, the movements that challenge them have to work transnationally too" (2002: 280). This entails political confrontation with local, national, and transnational politicians and officials as well as political activism centered on strategic national and inter-national symbolic sites (e.g., the WTO; World Bank meetings; annual World Economic Forum meetings at Davos, Switzerland). One such transnational activist channel is the ("anti-globalization") World Social Forum (WSF), in which Wallerstein, concerned about the globalization crisis (see above, pp. 462–463), is active. The WSF counterpoises itself against the "pro-globalization" World Economic Forum of leading corporate and political figures. Wallerstein argues for the systemic need to expand social equality such that the rights of all individuals and groups, those of majorities and of minorities, are recognized, even though, as he acknowledges, the question of whose rights should be given precedence in any given sphere is not easily settled (2004: 88–90).

NEWS 15.24

ALTERNATIVE VISIONS OF GLOBALIZATION

The anti-globalization movement, with the help of Irish-born world celebrities Bob Geldof and Bono, has had some success in getting several issues of human rights and social justice – poverty, AIDS, women's rights, environmental sustainability – on the agenda of global financiers and politicians (e.g., Evans 2005; Sachs

2005). In view of feminist theorists' emphasis on the importance of women's standpoint to the crafting of new institutional realities against the ruling powers in society (e.g., Smith; Collins; cf. chapter 10), it is especially noteworthy that women have been at the forefront of anti-globalization activism. They have a strong presence in local grassroots movements and community organizations as well as in transnational forums on women's equality (e.g., Naples and Desai 2002).

Some sociologists warn that transnational activism and the transnational "exchange" of ideas and scholarship should not be a one-sided reproduction of the dominance of American/European ideas and experiences as the only valid or best framework (e.g., Ray 2006: 463). This bias informed Parsons's modernization theory (cf. chapter 4) and, Gunder Frank argues, is also present in Wallerstein's Eurocentric world-system perspective – as if European capitalism is the only valid historical model of economic development (Gunder Frank and Gills 1996b: 4). The importance of attentiveness to non-US/non-European ideas and practices is particularly timely today given the emphasis on globalizing processes and transnational relations. It may, however, be difficult to realize; one of the products of globalization is the expansion of "global universities," i.e., branches of American universities in non-western societies (e.g., the Middle East), teaching American-based curricula.

NEWS 15.25

Demonstrating, however, that globalization processes and outcomes contain much variation, Manisha Desai reports that among activist women forging "transnational feminist solidarities" in local sites and via networks and world conferences, "At these sites, the flow of ideas and activism is no longer unidirectional, from the North to the South, but multidirectional" (2002: 15). Desai argues, moreover, that notwithstanding the contradictions that globalization represents for women – indicated, for example, by selective increases in women's work (e.g., in Ghana), women's decreased participation in the labor force (e.g., in post-Soviet countries) (Desai 2002: 16–18), and their overrepresentation in low-paying manual work (Sassen 2007: 112) – women are successful in resisting globalization and creating counter-hegemonic structures:

> Many activist women's efforts focus, to varying degrees and in various ways, on developing concrete economic alternatives based on sustainable development, social equality, and participatory processes, though such economic initiatives have not been as successful at the transnational level … These counterhegemonies have succeeded in transforming the daily lives of many women at the local level. (Desai 2002: 33)

It may seem odd to talk about the "success" of anti-globalization protests and initiatives, or of the critiques of globalization occasionally voiced by leading globalizers (e.g., Microsoft's Bill Gates), amidst the ever-increasing reach of globalizing forces in everyday life. Yet, Sklair maintains:

> The significance of these public demonstrations of divisions over globalization is that they send messages of confusion to the public at large, and the anti-globalization movement can use them to great advantage … [to co-opt and maybe even] … actually convert some influential members of the transnational capitalist class to their views on important issues. (2002: 282, 283)

Sklair himself believes that capitalist globalization cannot resolve its ecological and class polarization crises; hence his suggestion that a possible alternative lies in socialist globalization (see above p. 463).

In a somewhat similar vein, though less economically radical, David Held (2004) argues for a global social democracy to underpin the new global economy. This project, he explains:

> is a basis for promoting the rule of international law; greater transparency, accountability and democracy in global governance; a deeper commitment to social justice; the protection and reinvention of community at diverse levels; and the transformation of the global economy into a free and fair rule-based economic order. The politics of global social democracy contains clear possibilities of dialogue between different segments of the "pro-globalization/anti-globalization" political spectrum, although it will, of course, be contested by opinion at the extreme ends of the spectrum. (2004: 163)

Held thus envisages the regulation and taming of global markets (2004: 164–167), rather than, as Sklair does, the restructuring of their ownership. Both agree, however, that the systematic, global implementation of the ethics of human rights and social justice is imperative.

SUMMARY

Although globalization is currently of much interest to sociologists and non-sociologists alike, the larger historical-geographical context for the emergence of economic globalizing processes has long been of interest to sociological theorist Immanuel Wallerstein. In this chapter, therefore, we first discussed his modern world-system perspective, and then proceeded to explore how several other sociologists conceptualize globalization. By contrast with economists, who tend to affirm the autonomy of economic momentum as the main driver of globalization, sociologists focus on the structures and particular forms of social organization that shape and result from globalization. Thus sociologists are attentive to the expansion of economic corporations, the impact of the globalizing division of labor on geographical-regional inequality and class polarization, and the role of the nation-state in the new transnational society. Sociologists also explore the core relevance of consumer culture and ideology, for example, and assess how globalizing forces impact cities, migration, social identities, risk, and political opportunities and activism.

As in other areas of sociology, there is a divergence in emphasis among globalization theorists. Thus, for example, Sklair, using a Marxist-derived perspective, underscores the primacy of economic profit, transnational corporations, and the transnational capitalist class in driving globalization, and also the class polarization and ecological crises that globalization exacerbates. Giddens, by contrast, tends to apply a more Weber-derived perspective, emphasizing the continuing significance of the state and of its relations with other bureaucratic actors, including economic corporations. Sassen too leans toward a Weberian approach, especially in highlighting the class socio-economic differentiation that characterizes transnational workers, and in envisaging an active role for the state in regulating and influencing globalization processes. Her focus on global cities and their impact on shifting the contours of social and political interdependence has echoes of Durkheim, though with a more activist political focus.

POINTS TO REMEMBER

Wallerstein's world-system perspective emphasizes:

- Globalization yet another cyclical occurrence in the history of the modern world-system
- Capitalism emerged as a world-system in sixteenth-century Europe and subsequently expanded
- Capitalist world-system distinguished by its capitalist world-economy
- World-system characterized by a geographical division of labor in the production of capitalist profit
- Capitalist world-economy comprises core, peripheral, and semi-peripheral areas
- World-system is currently in a state of systemic crisis
- Crisis exacerbated by increasing economic core–periphery inequality, and by systemic failures to institutionalize social equality

Sociologists who study globalization emphasize:

- Interrelated economic, political, social, and cultural dimensions of globalizing processes
- Impact of the globalizing expansion of the division of labor on increasing living standards/quality of life *and* economic inequality
- Expansion of transnational corporations
- Expansion of class polarization within both highly advanced and newly industrializing countries and regions
- Emergence of transnational workers whose life-chances and experiences vary widely, especially those between the cosmopolitan professionals/executives and low-wage, resource-poor workers
- Continuing, though changed – and disputed – relevance of the nation-state in transnational economic, political, and cultural processes
- Emergence of new political and economic alignments
- Expansion of cultural homogenization across the globe, largely consumer-centered and American-driven
- Emergence of global cities as part of the corporate infrastructure of globalization
- Emergence of transnational social identities
- Expansion of risk and its universal character
- Conflicting dilemmas of the self that emerge as a result of the impact of information technology and other global forces on everyday life

- In a globalized network society, electronic networks can be programmed to reproduce existing inequality and/or to accomplish alternative goals
- Political emergence of the anti-globalization movement and its articulation of alternative forms of globalization
- Vanguard role of women in forging transnational feminist solidarities and new forms of economic and social organization

GLOSSARY: WALLERSTEIN

capitalist world-system the historical emergence of the modern capitalist economy in sixteenth-century Europe.

core states those at the center of world economic production (e.g., the US).

crisis idea that the current problems of the capitalist world-economy cannot be resolved within the framework of the capitalist world-system.

geographical division of labor the idea that specific countries/world regions emerged as core drivers of the

historical emergence of capitalist trade and economic expansion.

peripheral areas those areas marginal but necessary to world economic production.

semi-peripheral areas those structurally necessary to the world-economy but outside its core political and economic coalitions.

world-economy capitalist world-system economy; divided into core, peripheral, and semi-peripheral geographical areas among which there is an imposed, unequal flow of resources.

GLOSSARY: OTHER THEORISTS

anti-globalization movement broad array of local and transnational social movement organizations, community groups, and political activists opposing various aspects of globalization.

capitalist globalization emphasis that the current era of globalization represents one specific, historically dominant type or mode of production; i.e., capitalist, not socialist, globalization.

class polarization result of the increase in both extreme poverty and extreme affluence in all globalizing countries.

cultural imperialism the idea that the global distribution and sale of American-produced cultural content (e.g., movies, television shows, pop music, advertising, consumer ideology) constitutes a form of political-cultural control of other countries.

denationalized class global workers (professionals/executives, government bureaucrats, and low-skilled

service workers) necessary to the coordination and maintenance of the globalized financial and service infrastructure.

denationalized state a state that wields authority within and beyond its own national geographical territory and on globalization issues that implicate it and other nation-states.

dialectical nature of globalization push and pull between local and global interests; e.g., between centralizing, transnational interests (e.g., the EU) and the assertion of state sovereignty.

dilemmas of the self challenges encountered in negotiating a flexible yet coherent self amidst the many insecurities and opportunities confronting the individual in a globalizing, disembedded world.

disembeddedness unmooring of individuals and of institutional practices from specific locales, traditions, and time/space constraints.

distant proximities local and globalizing tendencies that forcefully interact across contemporary society.

geo-political axis along which a country's (or group of countries') political-economic and geographical or regional interests coincide.

global cities cities in which the core organizational structures and workers necessary to the functioning of the global economy are located.

globalization interrelated transformation in economic, political, social, and cultural practices and processes toward increased global integration.

global social democracy vision of globalized society underpinned by principles of fair play, participatory democracy, and social justice.

global systems theory analytical approach emphasizing the dialectic between states/international alliances and transnational globalizing forces and institutions.

McDonaldization the thesis that cultural icons, products, and standards are increasingly similar across the world.

network society one in which information technology networks are the dominant shapers of new, decentralized, economic and social organizations and relationships.

new imperialism the idea that a country's geo-political and military strategies today are driven primarily by capitalist economic interests.

post-national the current era of transnational political organizations (e.g., the EU) and other globalizing forces, with the nation-state no longer considered the core or most powerful political unit.

risk society the global expansion, awareness, and impact of risk and of the insecurities and anxieties it produces in society.

socialist globalization form of globalization that would gradually eliminate privately owned big business, establish local producer–consumer cooperatives, and implement social equality/human rights.

transnational capitalist class comprised of corporate executives/professionals and political, institutional, and media leaders who play a dominant role along with transnational corporations in advancing capitalist globalization and inequality.

transnational practices the idea that (capitalist) globalizing processes require and are characterized by specific transnational economic, political, and cultural-ideological practices or ways of being.

unicity the idea that as a result of globalization processes, the world as a whole is moving toward socio-cultural oneness.

RELEVANT NEWSPAPER STORIES

All news stories are from the *New York Times* unless otherwise noted, and can be accessed via www.wiley.com/go/dillon. See NEWS icons in the margins above.

NEWS 15.1   "Drug trade, once passing by, takes root and toll, in Mexico," October 3, 2007.
"[US] D.E.A. exposes a steroid web with China tie," September 25, 2007.

NEWS 15.2   "Saudis rethink taboo on women behind the wheel," September 28, 2007.
"Beyond skimpy skirts, a rare debate on identity [in Dubai]," October 19, 2006.

NEWS 15.3   "Hello, India? I need help with my math," October 31, 2007.

NEWS 15.4   "Mobiles narrow digital divisions," *BBC News* online, February 7, 2008.

NEWS 15.5   "In Chinese factories, lost fingers and low pay," January 5, 2008.

NEWS 15.6   "Inside gate, India's good life; outside, the servants' slums," June 9, 2008.

"Exploring the fringes of India's prosperity through the eyes of the invisible men," August 15, 2008.

"Royal care for some of India's patients, neglect for others," June 1, 2008.

NEWS 15.7   "European disunion: Facing a financial crisis, nations put self-interest first," October 8, 2008.

"State defends 'local needs' planning rules to avert EU action," *Irish Times*, October 15, 2007.

NEWS 15.8   "India, a stirring giant, is the new place to see and be seen," December 13, 2007.

"India's school shortage means glut of parental stress," February 6, 2008.

NEWS 15.9   "Ukraine joins the W.T.O." February 6, 2008.

NEWS 15.10   "Kosovo struggles to forge an identity," December 17, 2007.

"Independence daze: Who deserves to be free?" January 6, 2008.

"In a showdown, Kosovo declares its independence," February 18, 2008.

NEWS 15.11   "A surreal state," November 17, 2007.

"Bickering Belgians find a point of unity in toughening borders," October 10, 2007.

NEWS 15.12   "Sharpened tone in debate over culture of military," April 23, 2008.

NEWS 15.13   "Before the gunfire, cyberattacks," August 13, 2008.

"Russian forces capture military base in Georgia," August 12, 2008.

"China to limit web access during Olympic Games," July 31, 2008.

NEWS 15.14   "Cultural collisions [in Riyadh] in the slow lane to modernity," May 9, 2007.

NEWS 15.15   "As the Poles get richer, fewer seek British jobs," October 19, 2007.

NEWS 15.16   "W.H.O. and Bloomberg open global antismoking project," February 8, 2008.

"Billionaires back antismoking effort," July 24, 2008.

NEWS 15.17   "Keeping an eye on China's security," January 31, 2008.

"Dissident's arrest hints at Olympic crackdown," January 30, 2008.

"Sex, lies and family planning," *Newsweek*, January 28, 2008.

NEWS 15.18   "A tiny staff, tracking people across the globe," February 4, 2008.

NEWS 15.19   "China not sole source of dubious food," July 12, 2007.

"Drug tied to China had contaminant, FDA says," March 6, 2008.

NEWS 15.20   "$300 to learn risk of cancer of the prostate," January 17, 2008.

"Despite doubts, cancer therapy draws patients," January 18, 2008.

"Do my breast implants have a warranty?" January 17, 2008.

"Have surgery. Go sightseeing," March 24, 2007.

NEWS 15.21 "Wary U.S. Olympians will bring food to China," February 9, 2008.

NEWS 15.22 "[EU] Regulators warn France against protecting bank," February 1, 2008.

NEWS 15.23 "Wish you were here … having a great detox," March 29, 2007.

NEWS 15.24 "A stand against Wal-Mart and, for now, a victory," March 12, 2008.

NEWS 15.25 "Universities rush to set up outposts abroad," February 10, 2008.

NOTES

1 Although Gunder Frank sets his analysis of the development of underdevelopment within the contemporary capitalist world system (cf. chapter 6), for him the use of the term "world system" (without a hyphen) simply connotes the world – the existence of the same world system that has been in existence for 5,000 years (Gunder Frank and Gills 1996b: 3; see also Amin et al. 1990). Rather than identifying a unique *capitalist* world-system, Gunder Frank sees capitalism and socialism as part of the one *same* world system (Gunder Frank and Gills 1996a: xvii). For Gunder Frank, contemporary capitalism is not so different from earlier forms of economic organization and domination reaching far further back than sixteenth-century Europe – the context that for Wallerstein marks the emergence of a distinctive capitalist world-system or world-economy.

2 Wallerstein's definition of crisis is similar to that of Habermas (cf. chapter 5). See Wallerstein (1980) for an elaborated assessment of the "crises" that have characterized the development of capitalism.

3 Sassen lists New York, London, Tokyo, Paris, Frankfurt, Zurich, Amsterdam, Los Angeles, Toronto, Sydney, Hong Kong, Bangkok, Taipei, Sao Paulo, and Mexico City as geographical spaces that "bind the major international financial and business centers" in the network of global cities (2007: 111).

GLOSSARY

accomplishment of social reality the idea that social reality does not have a pre-given objective order, but needs to be achieved on an ongoing basis by societal members.

accounts how individuals categorize events, experiences, and everyday reality such that their accounts produce an ordered reality that makes sense and is credible in a given societal context.

achievement versus ascription one of Parsons's five patterned value-orientations whereby modern society emphasizes achievement rather than ascriptive (e.g. inherited status) criteria.

action-reward/punishment orientation behavior as motivated by the individual's perception of its likely rewards and punishments.

activist knowledge knowledge generated from within oppressed groups' lived experiences; empowers individuals to resist and take action against their oppression.

actors (1) general – any individual, collective, or institutional (e.g., the state) social unit engaged in social action. **(2)** dramaturgical – individuals performing roles.

adaptation economic function (or institutional subsystem) necessary in all societies and societal sub-units.

administered world bureaucratic-state regulation and control diminishing the political autonomy of individuals and the public sphere.

aesthetic disposition the class-inculcated attitude that allows and requires the upper class to admire art, clothes, etc., for style rather than practical function.

aestheticization of reality the cultural packaging and re-presentation of something ordinary as a commodified, spectacular thing for sale in the market.

affirmative action laws and public policies that seek to redress historical discrimination against blacks and other minority groups in access to education, voting, jobs, housing.

agency individuals, groups, and other collectivities exerting autonomy in the face of social institutions, social structures, and cultural expectations.

alienated labor the objective result of the economic and social organization of capitalist production (e.g., division of labor); takes four forms: **(a) alienation from products produced**: Wage-workers are alienated from the product of their labor; a worker's labor power is owned by the capitalist, and consequently the products of the worker's labor belong not to the worker but to the capitalist who profits from them. **(b) alienation within the production process**: Wage-workers are actively alienated by the production process; labor is not for the worker an end in itself, freely chosen, but coerced by and performed for the capitalist; the worker is an object in the production process. **(c) alienation of workers from their species being**: By being reduced to their use-value (capitalist profit), workers are estranged from the creativity and higher consciousness that distinguish humans from animals. **(d) alienation of individuals**

from one another: The competitive production process and workplace demands alienate individuals from others.

alternative sociology starts from the lived experiences and the standpoint of women and other minority groups rather than claiming an objectivity that largely cloaks male-centered knowledge; leads to the empowerment of women and men.

altruistic suicide results from tightly regulated social conditions in which the loss of comrades, or an individual's loss of honor in the community, makes suicide obligatory.

analytical Marxism use of social scientific methods to highlight how the interest maximization strategies of individual and collective rational actors impact class formation, exploitation, and class alliances.

androcentric culture institutional practices and ideology whereby maleness defines humanity and the social reality of men and women.

anomic suicide results when society experiences a major disruption that uproots the established norms.

anti-globalization movement broad array of local and transnational social movement organizations, community groups, and political activists opposing various aspects of globalization.

apartheid system of laws and public policies that maintain discriminatory practices against blacks (e.g., white settlers in South Africa against indigenous blacks).

appearance signals indicating the individual's social statuses and "temporary ritual state" (e.g., a nurse dressed for work).

asceticism avoidance of emotion and spontaneous enjoyment as demonstrated by the disciplined, methodical frugality and sobriety of the early Calvinists.

audience individuals who witness our role performance and for whom we perform.

authority structures varied sources of legitimation, authority, or power in modern society; possible sources of ongoing normal conflict.

background knowledge an individual's stock of previous experiences and knowledge of reality; impacts how they categorize and evaluate current experiences.

back-stage staging area for front-region behavior, where actors do the preparatory work to ensure a successful performance.

behavior conditioning human behavior as determined (conditioned) as a function of previous experience of, and/or perceived future, rewards and punishments.

behaviorism strand in psychology emphasizing that humans behave in predictable ways in particular situations.

bifurcation of consciousness knowledge that emerges from the contradictory realities women experience due to the split between objectified knowledge and women's everyday, localized experiences.

bio-power the institutional use of bodies and body practices for purposes of political, administrative, and economic control.

black cultural democracy the idea that in black communities, men and women need to create equality in their social relationships with other blacks whom they demean (e.g., women, gays).

black feminist thought knowledge voiced by black women from within their lived experiences and across the different sites of their everyday reality.

black underclass segment of the black community experiencing persistent chronic poverty.

black women's standpoint the common experiences that all African-American women share as a result of being black women in a society that denigrates women of African descent.

body idiom information conveyed through body language/display.

bourgeoisie the capitalist class; owners of the means of production, who stand in a position of domination over the proletariat (the wage-workers).

breaching experiments designed to disrupt a particular micro-social reality in order to illustrate the fragility that underlies the order and routines of everyday reality.

bureaucracy formal organizational structure characterized by rational, legal authority, hierarchy, expertise, and impersonal rules and procedures.

calling intrinsically felt obligation toward work; work valued as its own reward, an opportunity to glorify God.

Calvinism theology derived from John Calvin; emphasis on the lone individual whose after-life is predestined by God.

canon established body of core knowledge/ideas in a given field of study.

capital money and other resources invested in the production of commodities whose sale accumulates profit for the capitalist.

capitalism a historically specific way of organizing commodity production; produces profit for the owners of the means of production (e.g., factories, land, oil wells); based on structured inequality between capitalists and wage-laborers whose exploited labor power produces capitalist profit.

capitalist globalization emphasis that the current era of globalization represents one specific, historically dominant type or mode of production; i.e., capitalist, not socialist, globalization.

capitalist world-system the historical emergence of the modern capitalist economy in sixteenth-century Europe.

celebrity mass media celebration of the public legitimacy and influence of actors and other media personalities irrespective of their credentials.

center–satellite the idea that some states/regions are dominant in (core to) world economic production whereas others are marginal or peripheral (e.g., the North–South divide).

charisma non-rational authority held by an individual who is perceived by others to have a special personal gift for leadership.

charismatic community group of individuals (disciples) who follow and defer to a charismatic individual's authority.

Christianizing of secular society the thesis that Christian-derived values (e.g., Protestant individualism, the Golden Rule) would penetrate the everyday culture and non-religious institutional spheres of modern secular society.

church any moral community unified by sacred beliefs and practices.

civil religion the civic-political symbols, ceremonies, and rituals (e.g., presidential inaugurations) that characterize society's public life and reaffirm its shared values.

civil society sphere of society mediating between individuals and the state; e.g., informal groups, social movements, mass media.

class individuals who share an objectively similar economic situation determined by property, income, and occupational resources.

class consciousness the group consciousness necessary for wage-workers (the proletariat) to recognize that their individual exploitation is part and parcel of capitalism, which requires the exploitation of the labor power of all wage-workers (as a class) by the capitalist class in the production of profit.

class fraction differentiated, hierarchical sub-components of broadly defined social classes (e.g., the middle class); the economic and cultural capital of class fractions varies.

classical theory the ideas, concepts, and intellectual framework outlined by the founders of sociology (Marx, Durkheim, Weber, Martineau).

class polarization result of the increase in both extreme poverty and extreme affluence in all globalizing countries.

class relations unequal relations of capitalists and wage-workers to capital. Capitalists (who own the means of production used to produce capital/profit) are in a position of domination over wage-workers, who, in order to live, must sell their labor power to the capitalists.

collective conscience a society's collectively shared beliefs and sentiments; regulates social life.

collective misrecognition immersion in a particular habitus or set of everyday practices whereby we (necessarily) fail to perceive the arbitrary, though highly determining ways in which those practices reproduce inequality.

collective representation the symbols and categories a society uses to denote its commonly shared, collective beliefs, values, interpretations, and meanings.

colonialism economic and political domination by an imperial power over a separate and distant geographical

495

area (e.g., Great Britain over India and the Caribbean; Portugal over Brazil; etc.).

colonization of the lifeworld the idea that the state and economic corporations (including mass media) increasingly penetrate and dominate all aspects of everyday life.

commercialization of feeling the training, production, and control of human emotions for economic profit.

commodification of labor the process by which, like manufactured commodities, wage-workers' labor power is exchanged and traded on the market for a price (wages).

common-sense knowledge knowledge derived from individuals' everyday practices; what seems "natural" or obvious in their social environment.

communicative action the idea that social action should be determined by a rationally argued consensus driven by rationally argued ethical norms rather than strategic partisan interests.

communicative rationality back-and-forth reasoned examination of the claims and counter-claims made by communication partners in a communicative exchange. The reasonableness of the arguments expressed rather than the power or social status of the communication partners determines the communicative outcome.

communism envisaged by Marx as the final phase in the evolution of history, whereby capitalism would be overthrown by proletarian class revolution, resulting in a society wherein the division of labor and private profit would not exist.

concepts specifically defined ideas about the social world elaborated by a given theorist/school of thought.

conceptual framework the relatively coherent set of ideas or concepts that a given theorist or a given school of thought uses to elaborate a particular perspective on things; a particular way of looking at, theorizing about, social life.

confession production of discourse as a result of the interrogation of the self (by the self or others, real and imagined), typically with regard to body practices.

conflict groups competing interest groups in society.

conformist individual who accepts cultural goals and institutionalized means toward their achievement.

constructionist view of sexuality the idea that homosexuality and what it means to be gay has varied across history and social context; contrasts with an essentialist view.

contemporary theory the successor theories/ideas elaborated to extend and engage with the classical theorizing of Marx, Durkheim, Weber, and Martineau.

contract society's legal regulation of the obligations it expects of individuals in their relations with one another; its regulatory force comes from society.

contradictory class locations employees, such as professionals, managers, and bureaucrats, whose objective location in the class-occupational structure as members neither of the capitalist nor of the proletarian class means that their economic interests are not *a priori* allied with any one particular class.

controlled rationality strategic use of instrumental reason to attain a particular (controlled) end.

controlling images demeaning images and representations of, for example, black women circulated by the largely white-controlled mass media and other social institutions.

conversation analysis detailed analysis of the specific, pragmatic steps in how language and speech are used in everyday conversation to create order.

conversation of gestures process by which our signals bring forth a meaningful response in another.

core states those at the center of world economic production (e.g., the US).

crisis (1) when the state or other social institutions are perceived as being structurally unable to respond to a particular societal problem due to limitations in how the structures themselves are constituted (Habermas). **(2)** idea that the current problems of the capitalist world-economy cannot be resolved within the framework of the capitalist world-system (Wallerstein).

crisis of raciology contemporary blurring of racial boundaries and of the economic and political meanings and implications of racial categories.

critical theory Frankfurt School critique of the one-sided, strategic use of reason in democratic capitalist societies to advance economic, political, and cultural power, and suppress critique of social institutions and social processes, rather than to increase freedom, social equality, and democratic participation.

cues verbal and non-verbal signs, signals, messages.

cultural capital familiarity and ease with (the legitimate) habits, knowledge, tastes, and style of everyday living; school requires, transmits, produces, and reproduces cultural capital.

cultural competence possessing the appropriate family and social class background, knowledge, and taste to display (and acquire additional) cultural capital.

cultural goals objectives and values affirmed in a given society; e.g., economic success.

cultural identity the historically grounded origins of, and ongoing transformation in, a particular group's sense of who they are and their status vis-à-vis other cultural groups.

cultural imperialism the idea that the global distribution and sale of American-produced cultural content (e.g., movies, television shows, pop music, advertising, consumer ideology) constitutes a form of political-cultural control of other countries.

cultural lag when societies that experience economic and social modernization experience a delay in adjusting their (traditional) values to accommodate change.

cultural system institutionalized norms, values, motivations, symbols, and beliefs (cultural resources).

cultural totalitarianism the repression of diversity in the expression of individual needs and opinions; accomplished by the restricted sameness of content and choices available in the economic, political, and cultural marketplace.

culture (1) beliefs, rituals, ideas, worldviews, and ways of doing things. Culture is socially structured, i.e., individuals are socialized into a given culture and how to use it in everyday social action. **(2)** dispositions, tastes, evaluative judgments, and knowledge inculcated in and as a result of class-conditioned experiences (including formal education) (Bourdieu).

culture industry corporate economic control of the mass media and its emphasis on advertising and business rather than providing cultural content (e.g., ideas, story plots) that would challenge rather than bolster the status quo.

culture lines accentuation of the symbolic, cultural, and social (as opposed to biological or physical) differences between groups.

deconstruction an approach seeking to take apart, dismantle, and push against the order and meaning in language structures and in established institutional practices.

definition of the situation socialization of individuals into a society's generalized expectations of behavior across an array of social settings (Thomas); crucial to how actors interpret and perform in a particular role-performance setting (Goffman).

democracy political structure derived from the ethos that because all individuals are endowed with reason and created equal they are entitled (and required) to participate in the political governance of their collective life in society.

democratization of conflict establishment of formally organized interest groups and of institutional mechanisms (e.g., labor courts, mediation panels) to regulate group conflicts.

denationalized class global workers (professionals/executives, government bureaucrats, and low-skilled service workers) necessary to the coordination and maintenance of the globalized financial and service infrastructure.

denationalized state a state that wields authority within and beyond its own national geographical territory and on globalization issues that implicate it and other nation-states.

dependence an underdeveloped or peripheral country's relation to a developed country due to the historical economic and structural inequalities between them.

development economic growth and related societal changes in previously undeveloped countries.

deviance the result of discrepancies between society's culturally approved goals and the institutional means toward their realization.

dialectic of Enlightenment the thesis that the ideas affirmed by the Enlightenment (e.g., the use of reason in the advancement of freedom, knowledge, and democracy) have been turned into their opposite (reason in the service of control, inequality, political passivity) by the instrumentally rational domination exerted by capitalist institutions (e.g., the state, economic and media corporations).

dialectic of power and resistance ongoing conflicts (and changes) in society produced by group power inequalities and group resistance to those inequalities.

dialectical materialism the idea that historical change (i.e., material/economic change) is the result of conscious human activity emerging from and acting on the socially experienced inequalities (and contradictions) in historically conditioned (i.e., human-made) economic forces and relations.

dialectical nature of globalization push and pull between local and global interests; e.g., between centralizing, transnational interests (e.g., the EU) and the assertion of state sovereignty.

diffuseness of expectations unspecified expectations characterize non-economic and non-contractual social relationships (e.g., friendships).

dilemmas of the self challenges encountered in negotiating a flexible yet coherent self amidst the many insecurities and opportunities confronting the individual in a globalizing, disembedded world.

disciplinary practices institutional practices (through schools, churches, clinics, prisons, etc.) used to control, regulate, and subjugate individuals, groups, and society as a whole.

discourse categorizations, talk, and silences pertaining to social practices.

discourse of femininity images, ideas, and talk in society informing how women should present themselves and behave vis-à-vis men and society as a whole.

disembeddedness unmooring of individuals and of institutional practices from specific locales, traditions, and time/space constraints.

distant proximities local and globalizing tendencies that forcefully interact across contemporary society.

distorted communication ways in which current economic and political arrangements and cultural assumptions (e.g., free markets; individual self-reliance) impede communicative rationality.

division of labor the separation of occupational sectors and workers into specialized spheres of activity; produces for Marx, alienated labor, and for Durkheim, social interdependence.

docile bodies produced as a result of the various institutional techniques and procedures used to discipline, subjugate, use, and improve individual (and population) bodies.

domestic world home–neighborhood sphere of women's activity in a man-made world; deemed inferior to the public world in which men work, rule, and play.

domination authority/legitimacy; the probability that individuals will be persuaded/obliged to comply with a given command.

double-consciousness the alienation of blacks' everyday identity/consciousness as a result of slavery such that blacks invariably see themselves through the eyes of (superior) whites, the dominant race.

dramaturgical perspective using the metaphor of drama to describe social life.

economic base the economic structure or the mode of production of material life in capitalist society. Economic relations (relations of production) are determined by ownership of the means of production and rest on inequality between private-property-owning capitalists (bourgeoisie) and property-less wage-workers. Economic relations determine social relations, and social institutional practices (i.e., the superstructure).

economic capital amount of economic assets an individual/family has; can be converted into social and cultural capital (and additional economic capital).

economic efficiency purposive utility and resource rationality of a given course of action.

economy of practice individuals' and social classes' use of the economic and cultural capital they have to make reasonable strategic investments that expand and maximize their economic, cultural, and symbolic capital.

educational capital competencies acquired through school; can be converted into economic and cultural capital.

egoistic suicide results from modern societal conditions in which individuals are excessively self-oriented and insufficiently integrated into social groups/society.

emancipated society when previously marginalized individuals and groups are free to fully participate across all spheres of society; one in which freedom rather than domination is evident in institutional practices.

emancipatory knowledge the use of sociological knowledge to advance social equality.

emotional action subjectively meaningful, non-rational social action motivated by feelings.

emotional display socially learned and regulated presentation of emotional expression.

emotional labor emotion work individuals do at and as work, for pay; has exchange-value.

emotion work control or management of feelings in accordance with socially and culturally defined feeling rules.

empiricism use of evidence or data in describing and analyzing society.

encapsulated interest in exchange relations of mutual dependence, we trust individual and other social actors, believing that they sincerely appreciate our interests and merge (encapsulate) our interests with theirs.

encounter acts and gestures comprising communication about communicating (e.g., how we initially respond when someone steps into an elevator we are riding; or when we encounter an acquaintance on the street).

Enlightenment eighteenth-century philosophical movement emphasizing the centrality of individual reason and scientific rationality over against non-rational beliefs and forms of social organization (e.g., monarchy).

essentialist view of sexuality the idea that being gay, and the social characteristics associated with being gay, are a natural and essential part of the gay individual's biology.

ethnomethodology shared methods ordinary people (societal members) use to make sense of everyday experiences across different settings.

everyday/everynight world continuous reality of women's lives as they negotiate the gendered responsibilities of motherhood, marriage, work, etc.

exchange network sets of actors linked together directly or indirectly through exchange relations.

exchange-value the price (wages) wage-workers get on the market for the (coerced) sale of their labor power to the capitalist; determined by how much the capitalist needs to pay the wage-workers in order to maintain their labor power, so that the workers can subsist and maintain their use-value in producing profit for the capitalist. The workers' exchange-value is of less value to the worker than their use-value is to the capitalist.

exploitation the capitalist class caring about wage-workers only to the extent that wage-workers have "use-value," i.e., can be used to produce surplus value/profit.

externalization an aspect of the dynamic process by which individuals maintain social reality, whereby they act on and in regard to the already existing (human-created and externalized) objective reality (e.g., institutions, everyday practices in society).

false consciousness the embrace of the illusionary promises of capitalism.

false needs the fabrication or imposition of consumer wants (needs) as determined by mass media, advertising, and economic corporations in the promotion of particular consumer lifestyles; and which consumers (falsely) feel as authentically theirs.

feeling rules socially defined, patterned ways of what to feel and how to express emotion in social interaction and in responding to and anticipating social events.

femininity (man-made) societal ideals and expectations informing how women should think and act in a society which rewards masculinity and male control of women.

feminist revolution transformation of knowledge and of social and institutional practices such that women are considered fully equal to men.

feminist theory focuses on women's inequality in society, and how that inequality is structured and experienced at macro and micro levels.

fetishism of commodities the mystification of commodities whereby we inject them with special properties beyond what they really are (e.g., elevating an Abercrombie and Fitch shirt to something other than what is really is, i.e., cotton converted into a commodity), while remaining ignorant of the exploited labor and unequal class relations that determine its production and consumption.

fluidity the idea that in postmodernity, power, knowledge, authority, social relationships, and social experience are mobile and free-floating (fluid) rather than anchored in and ordered by reason, history, structures, traditions, etc.

frame simplifying reality by selectively interpreting, categorizing (and prioritizing) simultaneously occurring activities.

front the self-presentation maintained by the individual to project an intended definition of the situation in executing a particular role performance.

front-stage area where role performances are given.

functional analysis the combination of theory, method, and data to provide a detailed account of a given social phenomenon such that the description illuminates the phenomenon's particular social functions.

functionalism term used (often interchangeably with "structural functionalism") to refer to the theorizing of Durkheim (and successor sociologists, e.g., Parsons) because of a focus on how social structures determine and are effective in, or functional to, maintaining social cohesion/ the social order.

functions necessary tasks accomplished by specific social institutions (e.g., family, economy, occupational structure) ensuring the smooth functioning of society.

functions of social conflict social integration due to the interdependent coexistence of conflict groups, and social change resulting from institutional resolution of group conflict.

game of culture participation in the evaluative and taste practices that confer style or distinction as if "naturally" rather than due to class conditioning; reproduces social class differences.

game theory a scientific experimental method used mostly by economists to predict interest maximization decisions.

gender ideology a society's dominant beliefs elaborating different conceptualizations of women and men and of their self-presentation, behavior, and place in society.

genealogy (of knowledge/power) interconnected social, political, and historical antecedents to, and context for, the emergence of particular ideas/social categories.

generalized other community or society as a whole.

geographical division of labor the idea that specific countries/world regions emerged as core drivers of the historical emergence of capitalist trade and economic expansion.

geo-political axis along which a country's (or group of countries') political-economic and geographical or regional interests coincide.

global cities cities in which the core organizational structures and workers necessary to the functioning of the global economy are located.

globalization interrelated transformation in economic, political, social, and cultural practices and processes toward increased global integration.

global social democracy vision of globalized society underpinned by principles of fair play, participatory democracy, and social justice.

global systems theory analytical approach emphasizing the dialectic between states/international alliances and transnational globalizing forces and institutions.

glossing practices shorthand ways in which language and speech utterances are used to communicate in particular social contexts.

goal attainment political function (or institutional subsystem) necessary in all societies and societal sub-units.

grand theory elaborate, highly abstract theory which seeks to have universal application.

group conflict emerges when the manifest interests of one group conflict with those of another.

habitus relatively enduring schemes of perception, appreciation, and appropriation of things, embodied through class-conditioned socialization and enacted in everyday choices and taste.

hegemony process by which the institutions (e.g., mass media) and culture in capitalist society are orchestrated to produce consent by the masses to the status quo.

here-and-now reality immediate pragmatic salience of individuals' everyday reality.

heterosexist presumption that heterosexuality is normative (and normal) and that other sexual feelings and practices are socially deviant.

historical materialism history as the progressive expansion in the economic-material-productive forces in society.

homogenization standardization of products and choices in consumption and politics driven by the mass orientation (sameness) most profitable to the culture industry.

honest bodies rejection of sexual exploitation and degradation (e.g., of women and gays), and the affirmation of sexual images, desires, and practices that recognize the emotional-relational context of sexual expression.

human capital skills, education, health, and other competences/resources that individuals possess; influences their future economic and social-psychological functioning.

hyperreality a glossy, lavish, cinematic, consumption-driven, utopian reality dominated by spectacle (e.g., Las Vegas).

"I" part of the self; the "I" is the (subjective) acting self, and is only able to act because it internalizes the attitudes toward the "Me" (as an object) received from others' behavior/responses toward the acting "I."

ideal speech situation when communication partners use reason (communicative rationality) to seek a common understanding of a question at issue, and to embark on rationally justified, mutually agreed, future action.

ideal type an exhaustive description of the characteristics expected of a given phenomenon.

identity politics strategic use of particular cultural and social identities (based on race, gender, sexuality, ethnicity, etc.) to resist discrimination and/or to gain political advantage.

ideology ideas in everyday circulation; determined by the ruling economic class such that they make our current social existence seem normal and desirable.

implosion the collapse of meaningful distinctions, especially between the real and the simulated.

impression management symbolic and strategic communicative work toward orchestrating a particular definition of the situation and a successful role performance.

inalienable rights Enlightenment belief that all individuals by virtue of their humanity and their naturally endowed reason are entitled to fully participate in society in ways that reflect and enrich their humanity (e.g., freedom of speech, of assembly, to vote, etc.).

individualism cultural ethos of individual independence, responsibility, and self-reliance.

inequality structured into the profit objectives and organization of capitalism whereby the exploited labor power of wage-workers produces surplus value (profit) for the capitalist class.

information economy dominance of information or service commodities, produced and exchanged for profit.

in-group particular community (or group/society) in which we are immersed, whose habits we have inherited, and with which we are "at home."

innovator individual who accepts cultural goals but substitutes new means toward their attainment.

institutional ethnography an investigation that starts with individual experiences as a way to discover how institutions work, and how they might work better for people.

institutional field specific institutional spheres (e.g., education, culture, religion, law) characterized by institution-specific rules and practices reproducing inequality.

institutionalized means approved practices in society toward the achievement of specific goals (e.g., a college education as the means toward achieving a good career or economic success).

instrumental domination strategic use of reason (knowledge, science, technology) to control others.

instrumental rational action behavioral decisions or action based on calculating, strategic, cost–benefit analysis of goals and means.

integration regulatory function (or institutional sub-system) necessary in all societies (and societal sub-units).

interaction rituals routinized ways of self-presenting/behaving in the co-presence of others (e.g., greeting rituals).

interdependence ties among individuals; for Durkheim, the individualism required by the specialized division of labor creates functional and social interdependence.

interest group any group whose members consciously share and express similar interests.

internalization an aspect of the dynamic process by which individuals create social reality such that, in experiencing an external, objective reality (e.g., institutional practices, social inequality), they translate (internalize) it into their own particular, subjectively experienced reality.

interpretive process interpretation of the meaning of individuals' verbal and non-verbal communication and of the meanings of other things in the social environment is an ongoing activity.

interpretive understanding *Verstehen*; task of the sociologist in making sense of the varied motivations that underlie meaningful action; because sociology studies human lived experience (as opposed to physical phenomena), sociologists need a methodology enabling them to empathically understand human-social behavior.

intersectionality multiple crisscrossing ways in which different histories and diverse structural locations (based on race, gender, class, etc.) situate individuals' experiences and life-chances.

knowing from within the idea that sociological knowledge must start from within the lived realities of the individuals and groups studied.

language a socially shared meaning system.

latent functions unanticipated and unrecognized (functional or dysfunctional) consequences of an intended course of action.

latent interests unspoken, tacit interests of one group vis-à-vis another.

legal authority based on rational, impersonal norms and rules; imposed by the state and other bureaucracies; dominant in modern societies.

legitimation crisis when national or other collectivities lose trust in the ability of the state (or other institutions) to adequately respond to major systemic disruptions in the execution of institutional tasks (e.g., the effective functioning of the banking system).

lifeworld from the German word *Lebenswelt*; the world of everyday life and its taken-for-granted routines, customs, habits, and knowledge.

looking-glass self self-perception and behavior contingent on our knowing (or imagining) how others (would) respond toward us.

macro analytical focus on large-scale social structures (e.g., capitalism) and processes (e.g., class inequality).

management of feeling control of emotion via the creation of a publicly observable and convincing bodily display.

manifest functions intended and recognized consequences of a particular course of action.

manifest interests explicitly stated objectives.

manner signals which function to indicate the tone in the interaction role a performer expects to play in an oncoming situation (e.g., the sympathetic grief counselor).

marginal utility extent to which one course of action rather than another proportionally increases an individual's resources or advances their interests.

masculinity societal expectations governing the self-presentation and behavior of men; accentuates characteristics and traits that are the opposite of femininity.

mass culture advertising and other mass mediated content delivered by a technologically sophisticated, profit driven, corporate culture industry.

mass society thesis idea that individuals in society are passive, unaware of and uninvolved in, politics.

maximization of utility behavior motivated by principles advancing self-interest.

McDonaldization the thesis that cultural icons, products, and standards are increasingly similar across the world.

"Me" part of the self; the self as object ("Me"); the internalization of the expectations and attitudes of others toward "Me" and to which "I" (as the acting subject) respond.

meaning significance given to particular symbols and things in our environment.

means of production resources (e.g., land, oil wells, factories, corporations) owned by the bourgeoisie and used for the production of commodities/profit as a result of the labor power of wage-workers.

mechanical solidarity social bonds and cohesion resulting from the overlapping social ties that characterize traditional societies/communities.

members individuals who comprise society and accomplish social reality.

metanarratives narratives about narratives; a metanarrative critiques or illuminates how the established narratives of history, religion, capitalism, sociology, etc. legitimate particular types of, and a particular order to, knowledge.

micro analytical focus on small-scale, individual, face-to-face, and small group interaction.

micro-economic model presumes that individuals act to maximize their own self-interests and self-satisfaction.

middle-range theory generates theoretical explanations grounded in and extending beyond specific empirical realities.

mode of production how a society organizes its material-social existence (e.g., capitalism).

modernization theory the thesis that all societies will inevitably and invariably follow the same linear path of economic (e.g., industrialization), social (e.g., urbanization, education), and cultural (e.g., democracy; self-orientation) progress achieved by American society.

moral community any group or collectivity unified by awareness of their shared social interdependence.

moral density social ties created as a result of interaction with the multiplicity of diverse others encountered in modern society.

moral individualism individuals (as social beings) interacting with others for purposes other than simply serving their own selfish or material interests.

morality social life; the social ties that regulate individual appetites; sociology's subject matter; can be studied with scientific objectivity.

nation-state rational, legal, bureaucratic actor; has specific territorial interests; entitled to use physical force to protect and defend its internal and external security.

natural attitude the individual's orientation toward his or her social environment, a reality which seems natural because it is the everyday reality which he or she knows.

neofunctionalism refers to the approach of contemporary sociologists who embrace Parsons's theoretical perspective but who amend some of its claims.

neo-Marxist ideas derived from Marx's theory of capitalism but reworked in new ways and/or with new applications to take account of the transformations in capitalism.

net gain when the benefits of a course of action outweigh its costs.

network society one in which information technology networks are the dominant shapers of new, decentralized, economic and social organizations and relationships.

neutrality versus affectivity one of Parsons's five patterned value-orientations whereby modern societies differentiate between institutional spheres and relationships based on impersonality (e.g., work) rather than emotion (e.g., family).

new imperialism the idea that a country's geo-political and military strategies today are driven primarily by capitalist economic interests.

new middle class the expanding sector of educated (but politically indifferent) salaried managers, professionals, and sales and office workers that resulted from the post-World War II expansion of bureaucracy and the consumer economy.

new racism (1) symbols and ideas used (in politics and the mass media) to argue that race-based (biological) differences no longer matter even as such arguments reinforce racial-cultural differences and stereotypes.

(2) the invocation of cultural and symbolic (rather than biological) criteria to legitimate the societal exclusion or marginalization of particular racial/ethnic groups.

nihilism collective despair and hopelessness in black communities as a result of structurally persistent economic and social inequality.

non-rational action behavior motivated by emotion and/or tradition rather than by reasoned judgment.

normative rationality evaluative use of reason to advance values (or prescriptive norms) of equality and freedom.

objectification the dehumanization of wage-workers as machine-like objects, whose maintenance (with subsistence wages) is necessary to the production of commodities (objects) necessary to capital accumulation/profit. The term is interchangeable with "alienation."

objective reality the social reality, including objectively existing social institutions (economic, legal, etc.), language, and social processes (e.g., gender/race inequalities), into which individuals are socialized.

objectivity (1) positivist idea (elaborated by Comte) that sociology can provide an unbiased (objective) analysis of a directly observable and measurable, objective social reality. This approach presumes that facts stand alone and have an objective reality independent of social and historical context and independent of any theories/ideas informing how we frame, look at, and interpret facts. **(2)** term used by Weber to highlight the professional obligation of scientists, researchers, and teachers to report and discuss "inconvenient facts," i.e., facts that disagree with or contradict their personal feelings and opinions.

one-dimensionality sameness; lack of meaningful alternatives in mass culture and politics.

on-the-ground observation data gathering in the everyday social context or setting in which individuals interact; ethnography.

organic solidarity social ties and cohesion produced by the functional interdependence of individuals and groups in modern society.

organization assets specific skills and resources controlled by the class of professionals/bureaucrats/managers who have technical knowledge and expertise.

Otherness social construction of racial, ethnic, and/or geographical differences as inferior to a dominant historical and political power (e.g., the West's construction of Orientalism).

other-worldly non-material motivations; e.g., after-death salvation; the opposite of this-worldly.

out-group everyday reality of those who have different everyday habits to us, and which to us seem "strange."

Panopticon model (invoked by Foucault) to highlight how disciplinary power works by keeping the individual a constant object of unceasing surveillance/control.

part aspect of a social role.

parties political groups or associations which seek to influence the distribution of power in society.

passing the impression management and self-presentation symbolic work an individual must do in order to cover up or secretly maintain a stigmatized identity.

patriarchal society one in which white men have a privileged position by virtue of the historically grounded, man-made construction of social institutions, texts, and practices.

pattern maintenance (latency); socialization function (or institutional subsystem) necessary in all societies and societal sub-units.

pattern variables Parsons's schema of five separate, dichotomously opposed value-orientations determining social action.

performance the idea that social life, society, is based on the socially structured, acting out (performance) of particular social roles.

peripheral areas those areas marginal but necessary to world economic production.

personality system the individual's inculcation of the values and habits necessary to effective functioning in a given society (e.g., ambitious, hardworking, and conscientious personality types favored in the US).

phenomenology focuses on the reality of everyday life and how individuals make sense of their everyday experiences.

physical density the number of people encountered in the conduct of everyday life.

planetary humanism idea that society can transcend its racial, cultural, and other group differences to recognize and realize its collectively shared humanity.

plausibility structure group and institutional settings (e.g., churches) and laws that affirm (make plausible) the objective reality of individuals' subjectively experienced realities.

pluralistic simultaneous co-existence of many diverse strands (of thought, of research, of people).

political dependency dependence of citizens on the state to resolve problems and crises created, by and large, by the state and economic institutions.

political race invocation of race-based experiences of social inequality to mobilize and expand cross-racial alliances toward the achievement of social and institutional change.

politics of conversion local, grassroots activism in black communities that moves beyond nihilism and insists on innovative and accountable black leadership and the creation of equality for and among all blacks.

politics of sexuality focus on the various ways in which ideas about sex and sexuality are used to create and contest divisions between and within particular social groups based on gender and sexual orientation differences.

politics of truth idea emphasizing that truth is not, and can never be, independent of power; that all truths are produced by particular power-infused social relationships and social contexts.

popular culture the media images and content pervading everyday culture via television, music, videos, movies, street fashion.

positivist the idea that sociology as a science is able to employ the same scientific method of explanation used in the natural sciences, focusing only on observable data and studying society with the same objectivity used to study physical/biological phenomena.

post-capitalist society the result of transformations in the economy and in the occupational and class structures since the mid-twentieth century that make capitalist society structurally different from its late nineteenth-century incarnation.

post-colonial theory critiques the legacy of western imperialism for the cultural identities of previously colonized peoples.

postmodern the contemporary era as a time of fluid knowledge and authority, and of decentered experiences, of mixed fragments rather than of (modern) structured order.

post-national the current era of transnational political organizations (e.g., the EU) and other globalizing forces, with the nation-state no longer considered the core or most powerful political unit.

post-structuralist an approach seeking to dismantle the binary structure of language and the binary linguistic codes and meanings which embed all knowledge.

power (1) the probability that a social actor (e.g., the state, an individual) can impose its will despite resistance (Weber). **(2)** an unequally divided, perpetual source of conflict and resistance (Dahrendorf). **(3)** an ongoing circulatory process with no fixed location or fixed points of origin and resistance (Foucault).

power dependence basis of power in an exchange relation; the power of actor A over actor B in the A–B relation is a function of B's dependence on A.

power elite upper echelon in the interlocking network of economic, political, and military decision-makers; holders of power and wealth in society.

power imbalances in any social exchange relation, interaction is contingent on differentiation between and among the actors in terms of who gets more out of the relationship.

practical knowledge knowledge needed to accomplish routine everyday tasks in the individual's environment.

pragmatism strand in American philosophy emphasizing the practicalities that characterize, and the practical consequences of, social action and interaction.

predestination Calvinist doctrine that an individual's salvation is already determined at birth by God.

presentation of self ongoing symbolic work the role-performing actor does to project an intended definition of a situation.

primary group has a critically formative and enduring significance in child socialization (e.g., family).

private property accumulated by capitalists from profits produced by wage-workers' labor; both a source and consequence of the inequality between capitalists and workers.

profane ordinary, mundane, non-sacred things in society.

profit accumulation of capital as a result of the gap between commodity production costs (e.g., raw materials, production facilities, wages) and their market price.

proletariat wage-workers who, in order to live, must sell their labor power to the capitalist class, which uses them to produce commodities creating capitalist surplus value/profit.

promotional culture constant stream of consumer advertising dominating mass media content and public space (e.g., highways).

props things in a setting that bolster (prop up) the actor's intended definition of the situation.

public sphere public, relatively informal spaces (e.g., coffee shops, public squares) and non-state-controlled institutional settings (e.g., mass media, voluntary and non-profit organizations) where individuals and groups freely assemble and discuss political and social issues; produces "public opinion." *See also* civil society.

public world the non-domestic arena; domains of work, politics, sports, etc., the sphere given greater legitimacy in society.

Puritan ethic emphasis on methodical work, sober frugality, and the avoidance of spontaneous emotion.

queer theory rejects the heterosexual/homosexual binary in intellectual thought, culture, and institutional practices; shifts attention from the unequal status of gays and lesbians in (heterosexist) society to instead focus intellectual and political agendas on the fluidity of all sexuality.

race symbolization of social differences based on assumed or perceived natural (innate) differences derived from differences in physical body appearance.

race-segregation legal and systematically imposed divisions in everyday life based on racial differences; e.g., existence of separate schools and swimming pools for blacks and whites in the US until the 1950s.

racism implicit or explicit imposition of exclusionary boundaries and discriminatory practices based on racial appearance or racial categories.

rational action a reason-based, logical, methodical, deliberate, and planful approach to social behavior.

rationality emphasis on the authority of reason in deliberating about, and evaluating explanations of, the nature of reality/social phenomena.

reason human ability to think about things; to create, apply, and evaluate knowledge; and as a consequence, to be able to evaluate one's own and others' lived experiences and the socio-historical context which shapes those experiences.

rebel individual who rejects cultural goals and institutionalized means, and who substitutes alternative goals and alternative means toward attaining those goals.

recipe knowledge particular ways of doing things in a particular social environment.

regime of truth institutional system whereby the state and other institutions (government agencies, the military, medical and cultural industries) and knowledge producers (e.g., scientists, professors) affirm certain ideas and practices as true and delegitimate or silence alternative practices and interpretations.

region any role-performance setting bounded to some extent by barriers to perception (e.g., walls divide a restaurant's kitchen from its dining area).

reification from the Latin word *res*, "thing"; process whereby we think of social structures (e.g., capitalism), social institutions, and other socially created things (e.g., language, technology, "Wall Street") as things independent of human construction rather than as social creations that can be modified and changed to meet a society's changing needs and interests and to accomplish particular normative or strategic goals.

relations of ruling institutional and cultural routines which govern and maintain the unequal position of women in relation to men within and across all societal domains.

religion a social phenomenon, collectively defined by the things, ideas, beliefs, and practices a society or community holds sacred; socially integrating.

remix blending and reworking of several original sounds, themes, or ideas into a new reality.

retreatist individual who rejects cultural goals and institutionalized means, and who, by and large, withdraws from active participation in society.

risk society the global expansion, awareness, and impact of risk and of the insecurities and anxieties it produces in society.

ritual of discourse society's orderly, routinized ways (e.g., confession) of producing subjects talking about socially repressed secrets and practices.

ritualist individual who rejects cultural goals but who accepts and goes along with the institutional means toward their achievement.

rituals (1) collectively shared, sacred rites and practices that affirm and strengthen social ties, and maintain social order (Durkheim). **(2)** routinized ways of acting and interacting that reflect status differences and maintain social order (Goffman).

rituals of subordination symbolic signals in self-presentation (e.g., body posture of one actor vis-à-vis another) indicating status differences or social inequality.

routines socially prescribed, ordered ways of accomplishing particular things or establishing particular situational definitions and meanings in executing a role performance.

routinization of charisma the rational translation of individual charisma into organizational goals and procedures.

ruling class the class which is the ruling material force in society (capitalists/bourgeoisie) being also the ruling intellectual/ideological force, ensuring the protection and expansion of capitalist economic interests.

ruling ideas ideas disseminated by the ruling (capitalist) class, invariably bolstering capitalist economic interests.

ruling practices array of institutional and cultural practices which maintain unequal gender relations in and across society.

ruling texts core man-made texts (e.g., Bible, Constitution, laws, advertising) which define gender and other power relations in society.

sacred all things a society collectively sets apart as special, requiring reverence.

scarcity value determines power imbalances in any exchange relationship; a function of the relation between the supply of, and demand for, rewards.

scheme of reference stock of accumulated knowledge and experiences we use to interpret and make sense of new experiences.

scientific management industrial method introduced in the early twentieth century by Frederick Taylor to increase worker efficiency and productivity by controlling workers' physical movements.

scientific rationality use of scientific information to advance planful precision in task execution.

scientific reasoning emphasis on the discovery of explanatory knowledge through the use of empirical data and their systematic analysis rather than relying on philosophical assumptions and faith/religious beliefs.

secularization the thesis that religious institutions and religious authority decline with the increased modernization of, and institutional differentiation in, society.

segregated audiences when role-performing actors are able to keep the audiences to their different roles separate from one another; facilitates the impression management required in a particular setting.

self reflexively active interpreter of symbols and meanings in the individual's environment; comprised of the "I" and the "Me."

self- versus collectivity orientation one of Parsons's five patterned value-orientations whereby modern society emphasizes individual over communal interests.

self-alienation produced as a result of emotional laborers' splitting of internal feelings and external emotion management.

semiology the study of signs, i.e., showing how arbitrary images/symbols and their particular pairing have a specific cultural meaning and significance.

semiotic code cultural code or meanings inscribed in language and other symbols in a given societal context.

semi-peripheral areas those structurally necessary to the world-economy but outside its core political and economic coalitions.

setting the bounded social context in which a social role is performed.

sheer commodification the cultural or lifestyle packaging of everyday things, places, or experiences as images and commodities purely for the purpose of promoting consumption for the sake of consumption.

simulacra things that are glossy, polished representations and commodified imaginings of other things/realities; the simulated product/representation assumes a more real, more beautiful, more intense, more cinematic presence than the original.

situations of dependency term used to highlight the social, historical, and economic variation that exists among developing economies.

slavery historical institutionalization of coercive, discriminatory, and dehumanizing practices against a subordinate group; typically legitimated on grounds of racial difference.

social capital individuals' ties or connections to others; can be converted into economic capital.

social classes broad groups based on objective differences in amounts of economic, social, and cultural capital.

social construction of reality social reality as the product of humans acting intersubjectively and collectively. Social reality exists as an objective (human-social) reality to which individuals respond and which can be changed by individuals acting collectively.

social control methodical regulation curtailing the freedom of individuals, groups, and society as a whole.

social exchange all forms of social behavior wherein individuals exchange resources with others in order to attain desired ends.

social facts external and collective social things (structures, practices, norms) regulating and constraining individual and social behavior.

social integration degree to which individuals and groups are attached to society. Individuals are interlinked and constrained by their ties to others.

socialist globalization form of globalization that would gradually eliminate privately owned big business, establish local producer–consumer cooperatives, and implement social equality/human rights.

socialization process by which individuals learn how to be social – how to participate in society – and thus how to use and interpret symbols and language, and interact with others.

social roles socially scripted role-performance behavior required of a person occupying a particular status and/or in a particular setting.

social structures forms of social organization (e.g., capitalism, democracy, bureaucracy, education, gender) in a given society which structure or constrain social behavior across all spheres of social life, including the cultural expectations and norms (e.g., individualism) which underpin and legitimate social institutional arrangements.

social system(s) interconnected networks of institutional subsystems and relationships that comprise society and all of its sub-units.

sociological theory the body of concepts and conceptual frameworks used to make sense of the multilayered, empirical patterns and underlying processes in society.

sociology of knowledge demonstrates how the organization and content of knowledge is a social activity contingent on the particular socio-historical circumstances in which it is produced.

solidarity social cohesion resulting from shared social ties/bonds.

species being what is distinctive of the human species (e.g., mindful creativity).

specificity versus diffuseness one of Parsons's five patterned value-orientations whereby modern society emphasizes role specialization rather than general competence.

stage specific setting or place where the role-performing actor performs a particular social role.

standardization imposition of sameness or homogenization in culture and politics.

standpoint a group's positioning within the unequal power structure and the everyday lived knowledge that emerges from that position.

standpoint of the proletariat the positioning of the proletariat vis-à-vis the production process, from within which they perceive the dehumanization and self-alienation structured into capitalism, unlike the bourgeoisie, who experience capitalism (erroneously) as self-affirming.

status social esteem or prestige associated with style of life, education, and hereditary or occupational prestige.

status differentials comprise social inequality (stratification); gap in achievement and rewards based on differences in individuals' achieved competence (doctor/patient) and ascribed social roles (male/female).

steering problems emerge when economic and political institutions do not work as functionally intended and as ideologically assumed (e.g., the market's "invisible hand" working to produce economic growth and social integration), thus causing problems (e.g., recession) whose resolution demands state intervention in the system (e.g., shift in federal monetary policy).

stigma society's categorization or differentiation of its members as inferior based on the social evaluation and labeling of various criteria of undesired difference.

stock of preconstituted knowledge cumulative body of everyday knowledge and experiences that individuals have from living in a particular social environment.

stratification inequality between groups (strata) in society based on differences in economic resources, social status and prestige, and political power.

strong ties exist when people are closely bonded to others (e.g., cliques); close off interaction or sharing of information with individuals or groups outside the group; source of community fragmentation.

structural-functionalism term used to refer to the theorizing of Durkheim and Parsons because of their focus on how social structures determine, and are effective in (functional to) maintaining, the social order, society (social equilibrium).

structure objective ways in which society is organized; e.g., the social class structure exists and has objective consequences for individuals independent of individuals' subjective social class feelings and self-categorization.

subjectively meaningful action wherein the individual attaches subjective meaning to his or her behavior and takes account of, and is oriented to, the behavior of others.

subjective reality the individual's subjective experience and interpretation of the external, objective reality.

subsistence wage minimum needed to sustain workers' existence (livelihood) so that their labor power is maintained and reproduced for the capitalist.

subsystems spheres of social (or institutional) action required for the functioning and maintenance of the social system (society) and its sub-units (institutions, small groups, etc.).

subuniverses of meaning collectivities that share and objectify individuals' similarly meaningful interpretations of reality.

***sui generis* reality** the idea that society has its own nature or reality – its own collective characteristics or properties, which emerge and exist independent of the characteristics of the individuals in society.

superstructure non-economic social institutions (legal, political, educational, cultural, religious, family) whose routine institutional practices and activities promote the beliefs, ideas, and practices that are necessary to maintaining and reproducing capitalism.

surplus value capitalist profit from the difference between a worker's exchange-value (wages) and use-value; the extra value over and above the costs of commodity production (i.e., raw materials, infrastructure, workers' wages) created by the labor of wage-workers.

surveillance continuous monitoring and disciplining of bodies by social institutions across private and public domains.

symbol any sign whose interpretation and meaning are socially shared.

symbolic capital one's reputation for competence, good taste, integrity, accomplishment, etc.; has exchange-value, convertible to economic, social, and cultural capital.

symbolic goods goods we buy, display, and give to distinguish ourselves from others; signal and reproduce taste, status, social hierarchy, social class inequality.

symbolic interactionism sociological perspective emphasizing society/social life as an ongoing process wherein individuals continuously exchange and interpret symbols.

symbolic universes overarching meaning systems (e.g., religion, science) that integrate and order individuals' everyday realities.

systems of domination penetration of the regulatory control of the state and other bureaucratic and corporate entities into everyday life.

systems of trust establishment of organizations and groups to mediate transactions between social actors. These systems influence the decisions of self-interested actors to place trust and to be trustworthy in order to maximize gains.

taste social class- and family-conditioned, ordinary, everyday preferences and habits, socially learned ways of appreciation, style.

team when role-performers co-operate to stage a single routine or performance and project a shared definition of the situation.

technical rationality calculated procedures and techniques used in the strategic implementation of instrumental goals.

techniques of bio-power exertion of control over the body/bodies through institutional procedures (e.g., classroom schedules, Census categories) and practices (e.g., confession).

technological determinism the assumption that the use of a particular technology is determined by features of the technology itself rather than by the dominant economic, political, and cultural interests in society.

technological rationality proliferation of technological devices and procedures in strategically managing and controlling everyday corporate and individual activities.

this-worldly the material reality of the everyday world in which we live and work.

total institutions highly regimented establishments (e.g., prisons) in which the barriers that customarily divide individuals' everyday functions (sleeping, eating, and working) are removed.

traditional action non-rational, subjectively meaningful social action motivated by custom and habit.

traditional authority derived from long-established traditions or customs; dominant in traditional societies but co-exists in modern society with legal-bureaucratic and charismatic authority.

transnational capitalist class comprised of corporate executives/professionals and political, institutional, and media leaders who play a dominant role along with transnational corporations in advancing capitalist globalization and inequality.

transnational practices the idea that (capitalist) globalizing processes require and are characterized by specific transnational economic, political, and cultural-ideological practices or ways of being.

triangle of power the intersection of economic, political, and military institutions.

trust confidence in the reciprocity and sincerity of economic, professional, and other social relationships.

typifications customary (typical) ways in which an individual's intersubjective social environment is organized; how things and individuals (as role/status types) are presumed to work/behave.

underdevelopment economies in the third world whose development is hindered by their relational dependence on, and exploitation by, the economically developed first world.

uneven modernization when societies experience modernization more quickly in one sphere of society (e.g., the economy) than in another (e.g., education; developing the educated workforce necessary to the changed economy).

unicity the idea that as a result of globalization processes, the world as a whole is moving toward socio-cultural oneness.

unit act analytically, the core of social action; comprised of a social actor, a goal, specific circumstances, and a normative or value orientation.

universalistic versus particularistic one of Parsons's five patterned value-orientations whereby modern society emphasizes impersonal rules and general principles rather than personal relationships.

use-value the usefulness of wage-workers' labor in the production of profit.

utilitarianism idea from classical economics that individuals are rational, self-interested actors who evaluate alternative courses of action on the basis of their usefulness (utility) or resource value to them.

value neutrality the idea that scientists and researchers do not inject their personal beliefs and values into the conduct, evaluation, and presentation of their research.

value-rational action rational, purposeful behavior motivated by commitment to a particular value (e.g., loyalty) and independent of its outcome or success probability.

values questions concerning the goals or ends that individuals, organizations, institutions, and societies should purposefully embrace or pursue.

value system shared value-orientation (culture) that functions to maintain societal cohesion/integration.

Verstehen German for "understanding"; refers to the process by which sociologists seek interpretive understanding of the subjective meanings that individuals and collectivities give to their behavior/social action.

voluntaristic action the thesis that social actors are free to choose among culturally constrained goals and the means to accomplish those goals.

weak ties when people have loose ties to acquaintances across several different social contexts. Weak ties expand individuals' access to information and opportunities, and can facilitate community cohesion.

whiteness term used to underscore that all racial categories, including historically dominant ones (e.g., being white), are socially constructed categories of privilege whose meanings and implications change over time.

wide-awakeness the practical consciousness and attentiveness required in attending to the "here and now" tasks and realities of everyday life.

world-economy capitalist world-system economy; divided into core, peripheral, and semi-peripheral geographical areas among which there is an imposed, unequal flow of resources.

world system the world as a relational system comprised of structurally unequal, developed and underdeveloped economies.

REFERENCES

Adkins, Lisa, and Beverley Skeggs, eds. 2004. *Feminism after Bourdieu*. Oxford: Blackwell.

Adorno, Theodor, E. Frenkel-Brunswik, D. J. Levinson, and R. N. Sanford. 1950. *The Authoritarian Personality*. New York: Harper and Row.

Alexander, Jeffrey, ed. 1985. *Neofunctionalism*. Beverly Hills, CA: Sage.

Althusser, Louis. 1969. *For Marx*. New York: Pantheon.

Amin, Samir, Giovanni Arrighi, Andre Gunder Frank, and Immanuel Wallerstein. 1990. *Transforming the Revolution: Social Movements and the World-System*. New York: Monthly Review Press.

Andersen, Margaret, and Patricia Hill Collins. 1995. *Race, Class, and Gender: An Anthology*. Belmont, CA: Wadsworth.

Anderson, Elijah. 1990. *Streetwise*. Chicago: University of Chicago Press.

Anderson, Elijah. 1999a. *Code of the Street*. New York: Norton.

Anderson, Elijah. 1999b. "The Social Situation of the Black Executive." Pp. 3–29 in Michele Lamont, ed. *The Cultural Territories of Race: Black and White Boundaries*. Chicago: University of Chicago Press.

Anderson, Elijah. 2003. *A Place on the Corner*. Chicago: University of Chicago Press. 2nd edition.

Anderson, Elijah, and Douglas Massey. 2001. "The Sociology of Race in the United States." Pp. 3–12 in Elijah Anderson and Douglas Massey, eds. *Problem of the Century: Racial Stratification in the United States*. New York: Russell Sage Foundation.

Ang, Ien. 1985. *Watching Dallas: Soap Opera and the Melodramatic Imagination*. New York: Routledge.

Appadurai, Arjun. 1996. *Modernity at Large: Cultural Dimensions of Globalization*. Minneapolis: University of Minneapolis Press.

Audi, Robert, ed. 1999. *The Cambridge Dictionary of Philosophy*. New York: Cambridge University Press. 2nd edition.

Barthes, Roland. 1972. *Mythologies*. London: Paladin.

Bartky, Sandra Lee. 1998. "Foucault, Femininity, and the Modernization of Patriarchal Power." Pp. 25–45 in Rose Weitz, ed. *The Politics of Women's Bodies*. New York: Oxford University Press.

Bartunek, Jean, Mary Ann Hinsdale, and James Keenan, eds. 2006. *Church Ethics and Organizational Context: Learning from the Sex Abuse Scandal in the Catholic Church*. New York: Rowman and Littlefield.

Baudrillard, Jean. 1983. *In the Shadow of the Silent Majorities, or the End of the Social and Other Essays*. Columbia University, NY: Semiotext(e).

Baudrillard, Jean. 1991. *America*. London: Verso. 4th edition.

Baudrillard, Jean. 1995. *The Gulf War Did Not Take Place*. Bloomington, IN: Indiana University Press. Introduction by Paul Patton.

Baudrillard, Jean. 2000. *The Vital Illusion*. New York: Columbia University Press.

Bauman, Zygmunt. 2000. *Liquid Modernity*. Cambridge: Polity.

Beck, Ulrich. 1992. *Risk Society: Towards a New Modernity*. London: Sage.

Becker, Gary. 1964. *Human Capital*. New York: Columbia University Press.

Becker, Gary. 1976. *The Economic Approach to Human Behavior*. Chicago: University of Chicago Press.

Becker, Gary. 1996. *Accounting for Tastes*. Cambridge, MA: Harvard University Press.

Bellah, Robert. 1967. "Civil Religion in America." *Daedalus* 96: 1–21.

Bellah, Robert. 1973. "Introduction." Pp. ix–lv in Robert Bellah, ed. *Emile Durkheim: On Morality and Society*. Chicago: University of Chicago Press.

Bellah, Robert. 2005. "Response to 'Religion in the Public Sphere' by Jurgen Habermas." Kyoto Laureate Symposium, University of San Diego. Unpublished paper.

Bellah, Robert, Richard Madsen, William Sullivan, Ann Swidler, and Steven Tipton. 1985. *Habits of the Heart: Individualism and Commitment in American Life*. Berkeley: University of California Press.

Berger, Peter, 1967. *The Sacred Canopy: Elements of a Sociological Theory of Religion*. Garden City, NY: Doubleday.

Berger, Peter, and Thomas Luckmann. 1966. *The Social Construction of Reality: A Treatise in the Sociology of Knowledge*. New York: Anchor Books. 1967 edition.

Bernard, Jessie. 1972. *The Future of Marriage*. New York: Bantam.

Bernard, Jessie. 1998. "My Four Revolutions: An Autobiographical History of the ASA." Pp. 3–20 in Kristin Myers, Cynthia Anderson, and Barbara Risman, eds. *Feminist Foundations: Toward Transforming Sociology*. Thousand Oaks, CA: Sage.

Berube, Allan. 1990. *Coming Out Under Fire*. New York: Free Press.

Best, Steven, and Douglas Kellner. 1997. *The Postmodern Turn*. New York: Guilford.

Bhabha, Homi. 1994. *The Location of Culture*. London: Routledge.

Bianchi, Suzanne, John Robinson, and Melissa Milkie. 2006. *Changing Rhythms of American Family Life*. New York: Russell Sage Foundation.

Bittman, Michael, Paula England, Liana Sayer, Nancy Folbre, and George Matheson. 2003. "When Does Gender Trump Money? Bargaining and Time in Household Work." *American Journal of Sociology* 109: 186–214.

Black, C. E. 1966. *The Dynamics of Modernization: A Study in Comparative History*. New York: Harper and Row.

Black, Donald. 1976. *The Behavior of Law*. New York: Academic Press.

Blau, Peter. 1964. *Exchange and Power in Social Life*. New York: John Wiley & Sons.

Blau, Peter. 1974. *On the Nature of Organizations*. New York: John Wiley & Sons.

Blauner, Robert. 2001. *Still the Big News: Racial Oppression in America*. Philadelphia: Temple University Press.

Block, Fred. 1987. *Revising State Theory: Essays in Politics and Postindustrialism*. Philadelphia: Temple University Press.

Blumberg, Abraham. 1974. "Introduction." Pp. i–xi in *Auguste Comte: The Positive Philosophy*. Translated and condensed by Harriet Martineau. New York: Calvin Blanchard.

Blumer, Herbert. 1969. *Symbolic Interactionism: Perspective and Method*. Englewood Cliffs, NJ: Prentice Hall.

Bordo, Michael, Alan Taylor, and Jeffrey Williamson, 2003a. "Introduction." Pp. 1–10 in Michael Bordo, Alan Taylor, and Jeffrey Williamson, eds. *Globalization in Historical Perspective*. Chicago: University of Chicago Press.

Bordo, Michael, Alan Taylor, and Jeffrey Williamson, eds. 2003b. *Globalization in Historical Perspective*. Chicago: University of Chicago Press.

Bourdieu, Pierre. 1984. *Distinction: A Social Critique of the Judgment of Taste*. Cambridge, MA: Harvard University Press.

Bourdieu, Pierre, 1991. "Genesis and Structure of the Religious Field." *Comparative Social Research* 13: 1–44.

Bourdieu, Pierre. 1996. *The State Nobility: Elite Schools in the Field of Power*. Stanford: Stanford University Press.

Bourdieu, Pierre. 1998. *Practical Reason: On the Theory of Action*. Stanford: Stanford University Press.

Bourdieu, Pierre. 1999. *The Weight of the World: Social Suffering in Contemporary Society*. Stanford: Stanford University Press.

Bourdieu, Pierre. 2001. *Masculine Domination*. Stanford: Stanford University Press.

Bourdieu, Pierre, and Jean-Paul Passeron. 1971. *Reproduction: In Education, Culture, and Society*. Beverly Hills, CA: Sage.

Bowles, Samuel, and Herbert Gintis. 1976. *Schooling in Capitalist America*. New York: Basic Books.

Burawoy, Michael. 1979. *Manufacturing Consent*. Chicago: University of Chicago Press.

Burgess, Jean, and Joshua Green. 2009. *YouTube: Online Video and the Politics of Participatory Culture*. Oxford: John Wiley & Sons/Polity.

Buss, David. 2003. *The Evolution of Desire: Strategies of Human Mating.* New York: Basic Books.

Butler, Judith. 1990. *Gender Trouble: Feminism and the Subversion of Identity.* New York: Routledge.

Calhoun, Craig. 1995. *Critical Social Theory: Culture, History, and the Challenge of Difference.* Cambridge, MA: Blackwell.

Calhoun, Craig. 2000. "Pierre Bourdieu." Pp. 696–730 in George Ritzer, ed. *The Blackwell Companion to Major Social Theorists.* Malden, MA: Blackwell.

Cannon, Katie. 1985. "The Emergence of a Black Feminist Consciousness." Pp. 30–40 in Letty Russell, ed. *Feminist Interpretations of the Bible.* Philadelphia: Westminster Press.

Cardoso, Fernando, and Enzo Faletto. 1979. *Dependency and Development in Latin America.* Berkeley: University of California Press.

Castells, Manuel. 1997. *The Rise of the Network Society.* Volume One. Malden, MA: Blackwell. 2nd edition.

Castells, Manuel. 2000. "Toward a Sociology of the Network Society." *Contemporary Sociology* 29: 693–699.

Chevan, Albert, and Randall Stokes. 2000. "Growth in Family Income Inequality, 1970–1990: Industrial Restructuring and Demographic Change." *Demography* 37: 365–380.

Chodorow, Nancy. 1978. *The Reproduction of Mothering: Psychoanalysis and the Sociology of Gender.* Berkeley: University of California Press.

Coleman, James. 1961. *The Adolescent Society.* Glencoe, IL: Free Press.

Coleman, James. 1990. *Foundations of Social Theory.* Cambridge, MA: Harvard University Press.

Coleman, James, with E. Campbell, C. Hobson, J. McPartland, A. Mood, F. Weinfeld, and R. York. 1966. *Equality of Educational Opportunity.* Washington, DC: U.S. Government Printing Office.

Collins, Patricia Hill. 1990. *Black Feminist Thought: Knowledge, Consciousness, and the Politics of Empowerment.* New York: Routledge. 2nd edition 2000.

Collins, Patricia Hill. 2004. *Black Sexual Politics.* New York: Routledge.

Collins, Randall. 1986. "The Passing of Intellectual Generations: Reflections on the Death of Erving Goffman." *Sociological Theory* 4: 106–113.

Comte, Auguste. 1855/1974. *The Positive Philosophy.* New York: Calvin Blanchard. Translated and condensed by Harriet Martineau. Introduction by Abraham Blumberg.

Comte, Auguste. 1891/1973. *The Catechism of Positive Religion.* Clifton, NJ: Augustus M. Kelley. Translated by Richard Congreve. 3rd edition.

Conboy, Katie, Nadia Medina, and Sarah Stanbury, eds. 1997. *Writing on the Body: Female Embodiment and Feminist Theory.* New York: Columbia University Press.

Connell, R. W. 1987. *Gender and Power: Society, the Person and Sexual Politics.* New York: Cambridge University Press.

Connell, R. W. 1995. *Masculinities.* New York: Cambridge University Press.

Cook, Clive. 2003. "Globalization in Interdisciplinary Perspective." Pp. 549–552 in Michael Bordo, Alan Taylor, and Jeffrey Williamson, eds. *Globalization in Historical Perspective*. Chicago: University of Chicago Press.

Cook, Karen, and Joseph Whitmeyer. 2000. "Richard Emerson." Pp. 486–512 in George Ritzer, ed. *The Blackwell Companion to Modern Social Theory*. Malden, MA: Blackwell.

Cook, Karen, Russell Hardin, and Margaret Levi. 2005. *Cooperation Without Trust?* New York: Russell Sage Foundation.

Cooley, Charles Horton. 1902/1998. *On Self and Social Organization*. Chicago: University of Chicago Press. Edited and with an introduction by Hans-Joachim Schubert.

Cooley, Charles Horton. 1909. *Social Organization: A Study of the Larger Mind*. New York: Charles Scribner's Sons.

Cornwell, Benjamin, Edward Laumann, and L. Philip Schumm. 2008. "The Social Connectedness of Older Adults: A National Profile." *American Sociological Review* 73: 185–203.

Corrigan, Oonagh. 2009. "Genetics and Social Theory." Pp. 343–359 in Bryan Turner, ed. *The New Blackwell Companion to Social Theory*. Malden, MA: Blackwell.

Coser, Lewis. 1956. *The Functions of Social Conflict*. Glencoe, IL: Free Press.

Cott, Nancy. 1987. *The Grounding of Modern Feminism*. New Haven, CT: Yale University Press.

Dahrendorf, Ralf. 1959. *Class and Class Conflict in Industrial Society*. Stanford: Stanford University Press.

Dahrendorf, Ralf. 1968. *Essays in the Theory of Society*. Stanford: Stanford University Press.

Davis, Kingsley, and Wilbert Moore. 1945. "Some Principles of Stratification." *American Sociological Review* 10: 242–249.

De Beauvoir, Simone. 1949/1953. *The Second Sex*. Harmondsworth: Penguin.

Denzin, Norman. 1990. "Harold and Agnes: A Feminist Narrative Unfolding." *Sociological Theory* 9: 198–216.

Denzin, Norman. 1991. "Back to Harold and Agnes." *Sociological Theory* 9: 280–285.

Derrida, Jacques. 1997. *Deconstruction in a Nutshell: A Conversation with Jacques Derrida*. New York: Fordham University Press. Edited and with a commentary by John Caputo.

Derrida, Jacques. 2003. "Autoimmunity: Real and Symbolic Suicides. A Dialogue with Jacques Derrida." Pp. 85–136 in Giovanna Borradori, ed. *Philosophy in a Time of Terror*. Chicago University of Chicago Press.

Desai, Manisha. 2002. "Transnational Solidarity: Women's Agency, Structural Adjustment, and Globalization." Pp. 15–33 in Nancy Naples and Manisha Desai, eds. *Women's Activism and Globalization: Linking Local Struggles and Transnational Politics*. New York: Routledge.

De Tocqueville, Alexis. 1835–1840/2004. *Democracy in America*. Volumes One and Two. New York: Library of America. Translated by Arthur Goldhammer.

De Vault, Marjorie. 1991. *Feeding the Family: The Social Construction of Caring as Gendered Work*. Chicago: University of Chicago Press.

Dillon, Michele. 1993. *Debating Divorce: Moral Conflict in Ireland*. Lexington, KY: University Press of Kentucky.

Dillon, Michele. 1999. "The Authority of the Holy Revisited: Habermas, Religion, and Emancipatory Possibilities." *Sociological Theory* 17: 290–306.

Dillon, Michele. 2001. "Pierre Bourdieu, Religion, and Cultural Production." *Cultural Studies: Critical Methodologies* 1: 411–429.

Dillon, Michele, and Paul Wink. 2007. *In the Course of a Lifetime: Tracing Religious Belief, Practice, and Change*. Berkeley: University of California Press.

Domhoff, G. William. 2006a. *Who Rules America? Power, Politics and Social Change*. New York: McGraw-Hill.

Domhoff, G. William. 2006b. "Mills's *The Power Elite* 50 Years Later." *Contemporary Sociology* 35: 547–550.

Dreyfus, Herbert, and Paul Rabinow. 1983. *Michel Foucault: Beyond Structuralism and Hermeneutics*. Chicago: University of Chicago Press.

Du Bois, W. E. B. 1903/1969. *The Souls of Black Folk*. New York: New American Library. Introductions by Nathan Hare and Alvin Poussaint.

Du Bois, W. E. B. 1915/1996. "Woman Suffrage." Pp. 377–379 in Eric Sundquist, ed. *The Oxford W. E. B. Du Bois Reader*. New York: Oxford University Press.

Du Bois, W. E. B. 1934/2007. *Black Reconstruction in America*. New York: Oxford University Press.

Du Bois, W. E. B. 1935/1996. "A Negro Nation Within the Nation." Pp. 431–438 in Eric Sundquist, ed. *The Oxford W. E. B. Du Bois Reader*. New York: Oxford University Press.

Duneier, Mitchell. 1992. *Slim's Table*. Chicago: University of Chicago Press.

Durkheim, Emile. 1893/1984. *The Division of Labour in Society*. New York: Free Press. Introduction by Lewis Coser. Translated by W. D. Halls.

Durkheim, Emile. 1895/1982 *The Rules of Sociological Method*. New York: Free Press. Edited and with an introduction by Steven Lukes. Translated by W. D. Halls.

Durkheim, Emile. 1897/1951. *Suicide: A Study in Sociology*. New York: Free Press. Introduction by George Simpson. Translated by John Spaulding and George Simpson.

Durkheim, Emile. 1912/2001. *The Elementary Forms of Religious Life*. Oxford: Oxford University Press. Translated by Carol Cosman.

Durkheim, Emile. 1914. "The Dualism of Human Nature and its Social Conditions." Pp. 149–163 in Robert Bellah, ed. *Emile Durkheim: On Morality and Society*. Chicago: University of Chicago Press.

Eagleton, Terry. 1983. *Literary Theory: An Introduction*. Minneapolis: University of Minnesota Press.

Eckes, Alfred, and Thomas Zeiler. 2003. *Globalization and the American Century*. New York: Cambridge University Press.

Ehrenreich, Barbara, and Arlie Russell Hochschild, eds. 2002. *Global Woman: Nannies, Maids, and Sex Workers in the New Economy*. New York: Holt.

Elias, Norbert. 1978. *The Civilizing Process: The History of Manners*. New York: Urizen Books. Translated by Edmund Jephcott.

Ellison. Ralph. 1947. *Invisible Man*. New York: Vintage International. 2nd edition 1995.

Emerson, Richard. 1962. "Power Dependence Relations." *American Sociological Review* 27: 31–41.

Emerson, Richard. 1972. "Exchange Theory, Part I. A Psychological Basis for Social Exchange. Exchange Theory, Part II. Exchange Relations and Network Structures." Pp. 38–87 in Joseph Berger, Morris Zelditch, and Bo Anderson, eds. *Sociological Theories in Progress*. Volume 2. Boston: Houghton Mifflin.

Engels, Friedrich. 1844. "The Origin of the Family, Private Property, and the State." Pp. 734–759 in Robert Tucker, ed. *The Marx–Engels Reader*. New York: Norton. 2nd edition.

Engels, Friedrich. 1878. "Socialism: Utopian and Scientific." Pp. 683–717 in Robert Tucker, ed. *The Marx–Engels Reader*. New York: Norton. 2nd edition.

England, Paula. 2005a. "Gender Inequality in Labor Markets: The Role of Motherhood and Segregation." *Social Politics* 12: 264–288.

England, Paula. 2005b. "Emerging Theories of Care Work." *Annual Review of Sociology* 31: 381–399.

England, Paula. 2006. "Devaluation and the Pay of Comparable Male and Female Occupations." Pp. 352–356 in David Grusky and Szonja Szelenyi, eds. *The Inequality Reader: Contemporary and Foundational Readings in Race, Class, and Gender*. Boulder, CO: Westview Press.

England, Paula, and George Farkas. 1986. *Households, Employment, and Gender*. New York: Aldine.

Epstein, Cynthia Fuchs, Bonnie Oglensky, Robert Saute, and Carroll Seron. 1999. *The Part Time Paradox: Time Norms, Professional Lives, Family and Gender*. New York: Routledge.

Epstein, Steven. 1987. "Gay Politics, Ethnic Identity: The Limits of Social Constructionism." *Socialist Review* 93–94: 9–54.

Eribon, Didier. 1991. *Michel Foucault*. Cambridge, MA: Harvard University Press.

Evans, Peter. 2005. "Counterhegemonic Globalization: Transnational Social Movements in the Contemporary Political Economy." Pp. 655–670 in Thomas Janoski, Robert Alford, Alexander Hicks, and Mildred Schwartz, eds. *Handbook of Political Sociology*. New York: Cambridge University Press.

Faludi, Susan. 1991. *Backlash*. New York: Crown.

Fanon, Frantz. 1967. *Black Skin, White Masks*. New York: Grove Press. Translated by Charles Lam Markmann.

Fenstermaker, Sarah, and Candace West, eds. 2002. *Doing Gender, Doing Difference: Inequality, Power, and Institutional Change*. New York: Routledge.

Feyerabend, Paul. 1979. *Against Method*. London: Verso.

Fine, Gary Alan, and Philip Manning. 2000. "Erving Goffman." Pp. 457–485 in George Ritzer, ed. *The Blackwell Companion to Major Social Theorists*. Malden, MA: Blackwell.

Finke, Roger, and Rodney Stark. 1992. *The Churching of America, 1776–1990: Winners and Losers in Our Religious Economy*. New Brunswick, NJ: Rutgers University Press.

Fischer, Claude, and Michael Hout. 2006. *Century of Difference: How America Changed in the Last One Hundred Years*. New York: Russell Sage Foundation.

Fischer, Claude, Michael Hout, Martin Sanchez Jankowski, Samuel Lucas, Ann Swidler, and Kim Voss. 1996. *Inequality by Design: Cracking the Bell Curve Myth*. Princeton: Princeton University Press.

Fiske, John, and John Hartley. 1978. *Reading Television*. London: Methuen.

Foucault, Michel. 1965. *Madness and Civilization: A History of Insanity in the Age of Reason*. New York: Random House.

Foucault, Michel. 1970. *The Order of Things: An Archaeology of the Human Sciences*. London: Tavistock.

Foucault, Michel. 1972. *The Archaeology of Knowledge*. London: Tavistock.

Foucault, Michel. 1975. *The Birth of the Clinic: An Archaeology of Medical Perception*. New York: Pantheon.

Foucault, Michel. 1978. *The History of Sexuality*. Volume One. New York: Random House.

Foucault, Michel. 1979. *Discipline and Punish: The Birth of the Prison*. New York: Penguin.

Foucault, Michel. 1984. "Truth and Power." Pp. 51–75 in Paul Rabinow, ed. *The Foucault Reader*. New York: Pantheon.

Foucault, Michel. 1984/1994. "Sex, Power, and The Politics of Identity." Pp. 163–173 in Paul Rabinow, ed. *Michel Foucault: Ethics, Subjectivity and Truth*. New York: New Press.

Frankenberg, Ruth. 1993. *White Women, Race Matters: The Social Construction of Whiteness*. Minneapolis: University of Minnesota Press.

Frazer, Elizabeth, and Nicola Lacey. 1993. *The Politics of Community: A Feminist Critique of the Liberal-Communitarian Debate*. Toronto: University of Toronto Press.

Frazier, E. Franklin. 1949. *The Negro in the United States*. New York: Macmillan.

Frazier, E. Franklin. 1955/1968. "The Negro Middle Class." Pp. 239–279 in E. Franklin Frazier, *On Race Relations: Selected Writings*. Chicago: University of Chicago Press. Edited and with an introduction by G. Franklin Edwards.

Friedan, Betty. 1963. *The Feminine Mystique*. New York: Norton

Frisby, David, ed. 1994. *Georg Simmel: Critical Assessments*. Volume 1. London: Routledge.

Gamson, William. 1992. *Talking Politics*. New York: Cambridge University Press.

Garfinkel, Harold. 1967. *Studies in Ethnomethodology*. Englewood Cliffs, NJ: Prentice Hall.

Garfinkel, Harold, and Harvey Sacks. 1986. "On Formal Structures of Practical Actions." Pp. 160–192 in Harold Garfinkel, ed. *Ethnomethodological Studies of Work*. London: Routledge and Kegan Paul.

Gerschenkron, Alexander. 1962. *Economic Backwardness in Historical Perspective*. Cambridge, MA: Harvard University Press.

Gerth, H. H., and C. Wright Mills. 1946. "Introduction: A Biographical View." Pp. 1–31 in Max Weber, *From Max Weber: Essays in Sociology*. New York: Oxford University Press. Translated, edited, and with an introduction by H. H. Gerth and C. Wright Mills.

Giddens, Anthony. 1976. "Introduction." Pp. 1–12b in Max Weber, 1904–1905/1958. *The Protestant Ethic and the Spirit of Capitalism*. New York: Scribner's and Sons. Translated by Talcott Parsons.

Giddens, Anthony. 1990. *The Consequences of Modernity*. Stanford: Stanford University Press.

Giddens, Anthony. 1991. *Modernity and Self-Identity: Self and Society in the Late Modern Age*. Stanford: Stanford University Press.

Giddens, Anthony. 2003. *Runaway World: How Globalization is Reshaping our Lives*. New York: Routledge.

Gilligan, Carol. 1982. *In a Different Voice*. Cambridge, MA: Harvard University Press.

Gilman, Charlotte Perkins. 1903/1972. *The Home: Its Work and Influence*. Urbana, IL: University of Chicago Press. Introduction by William O'Neill.

Gilman, Charlotte Perkins. 1911. *Man-Made World or Our Androcentric Culture*. New York: Charlton.

Gilmore, Glenda. 2008. *Defying Dixie: The Radical Roots of Civil Rights, 1919–1950*. New York: Norton.

Gilroy, Paul. 1987. *"There Ain't No Black in the Union Jack": The Cultural Politics of Race and Nation*. London: Hutchinson.

Gilroy, Paul. 2000. *Against Race: Imagining Political Culture Beyond the Color Line*. Cambridge, MA: Harvard University Press.

Gitlin, Todd. 1980. *The Whole World is Watching: Mass Media in the Making and Unmaking of the New Left*. Berkeley: University of California Press.

Gitlin, Todd. 1987. *The Sixties: Years of Hope, Days of Rage*. New York: Bantam Books.

Glassmeir, Amy. 2005. *An Atlas of Poverty in America: One Nation, Falling Apart, 1960–2003*. University Park, PA: Pennsylvania State University, Department of Geography.

Glendon, Mary Ann. 1987. *Abortion and Divorce in Western Law*. Cambridge, MA: Harvard University Press.

Goffman, Erving. 1959. *The Presentation of Self in Everyday Life*. New York: Doubleday.

Goffman, Erving. 1961. *Asylums: Essays on the Social Situation of Mental Patients and Other Inmates*. Chicago: Aldine.

Goffman, Erving. 1963a. *Stigma: Notes on the Management of Spoiled Identity*. New York: Simon & Schuster.

Goffman, Erving. 1963b. *Behavior in Public Places: Notes on the Social Organization of Gatherings*. Glencoe, IL: Free Press.

Goffman, Erving. 1967. *Interaction Ritual: Essays in Face-to-Face Behavior*. Chicago: Aldine.

Goffman, Erving. 1969. *Strategic Interaction*. Philadelphia: University of Pennsylvania Press.

Goffman, Erving. 1971. *Relations in Public*. New York: Basic Books.

Goffman, Erving. 1974. *Frame Analysis: An Essay on the Organization of Experience*. Cambridge, MA: Harvard University Press.

Goffman, Erving. 1979. *Gender Advertisements*. Cambridge, MA: Harvard University Press.

Gramsci, Antonio. 1929/1971. *Selections from the Prison Notebooks*. London: Lawrence and Wishart. Edited and translated by Quentin Hoare and Geoffrey Nowell Smith.

Granovetter, Mark. 1973. "The Strength of Weak Ties." *American Journal of Sociology* 78: 1360–1380.

Granovetter, Mark. 1974. *Getting a Job: A Study of Contacts and Careers*. New York: Cambridge University Press.

Granovetter, Mark. 1985. "Economic Action and Social Structure: The Problem of Embeddedness." *American Journal of Sociology* 91: 481–510.

Guinier, Lani, and Gerald Torres. 2002. *The Miner's Canary: Enlisting Race, Resisting Power, Transforming Democracy*. Cambridge, MA: Harvard University Press.

Gunder Frank, Andre. 1967. *Capitalism and Underdevelopment in Latin America*. New York: Monthly Review Press.

Gunder Frank, Andre, and Barry Gills. 1996a. "Preface." Pp. xv–xxii in Andre Gunder Frank and Barry Gills, eds. *The World System: Five Hundred Years or Five Thousand?* New York: Routledge.

Gunder Frank, Andre, and Barry Gills. 1996b. "The 5,000-Year World System." Pp. 3–55 in Andre Gunder Frank and Barry Gills, eds. *The World System: Five Hundred Years or Five Thousand?* New York: Routledge.

Gutman, Herbert. 1976. *The Black Family in Slavery and Freedom, 1750–1925*. New York: Pantheon.

Habermas, Jurgen. 1968/1971. *Knowledge and Human Interests*. Boston: Beacon Press.

Habermas, Jurgen. 1975. *Legitimation Crisis*. Boston: Beacon Press.

Habermas, Jurgen. 1984. *The Theory of Communicative Action*. Volume One. Boston: Beacon Press.

Habermas, Jurgen. 1987. *The Theory of Communicative Action*. Volume Two. Boston: Beacon Press.

Habermas, Jurgen. 1989. *The Structural Transformation of the Public Sphere*. Cambridge, MA: MIT Press.

Habermas, Jurgen. 1996. *Between Facts and Norms: Contributions to a Discourse Theory of Law and Democracy*. Cambridge, MA: MIT Press.

Habermas, Jurgen. 2008. "Notes on a Post-Secular Society." *New Perspectives Quarterly* 25: 4.

Halberstam, David. 1993. *The Fifties*. New York: Ballantine Books.

Hall, Stuart. 1990. "Cultural Identity and Diaspora." Pp. 222–237 in Jonathan Rutherford, ed. *Identity: Community, Culture, Difference*. London: Lawrence & Wishart.

Hall, Stuart, 1992. "What is this Black in Black Popular Culture?" Pp. 21–32 in Gina Dent, ed. *Black Popular Culture*. Seattle: Bay Press.

Hall, Stuart, and Tony Jefferson, eds. 1976. *Resistance through Rituals: Youth Subcultures in Post-War Britain*. London: Hutchinson.

Halle, David, and L. Frank Weyher. 2005. "New Developments in Class and Culture." Pp. 207–219 in Mark Jacobs and Nancy Hanrahan, eds. *The Blackwell Companion to the Sociology of Culture*. Malden, MA: Blackwell.

Ham, J. 1999. "Social Contract." Pp. 855–856 in Robert Audi, ed. *Cambridge Dictionary of Philosophy*. 2nd edition. New York: Cambridge University Press.

Harding, Sandra, ed. 1987. *Feminism and Methodology*. Bloomington, IN: Indiana University Press.

Harding, Sandra. 1991. *Whose Science? Whose Knowledge? Thinking from Women's Lives*. Ithaca, NY: Cornell University Press.

Hartsock, Nancy. 1998. *The Feminist Standpoint Revisited and Other Essays*. Boulder, CO: Westview Press.

Harvey, David. 1990. *The Condition of Postmodernity*. Oxford: Blackwell.

Harvey, David. 2003. *The New Imperialism*. Oxford: Oxford University Press.

Hays, Sharon. 2003. *Flat Broke with Children: Women in the Age of Welfare Reform*. New York: Oxford University Press.

Hebdige, Dick. 1979. *Subculture: The Meaning of Style*. London: Methuen.

Hekman, Susan, ed. 1996. *Feminist Interpretations of Foucault*. University Park, PA: Pennsylvania State University Press.

Held, David. 2004. *Global Covenant: The Social Democratic Alternative to the Washington Consensus*. Cambridge: Polity.

Heritage, John. 2009. "Conversation Analysis as Social Theory." Pp. 300–320 in Bryan Turner, ed. *The New Blackwell Companion to Social Theory*. Malden, MA: Blackwell.

Hilbert, Richard. 1990. "Ethnomethodology and the Micro-Macro Order." *American Sociological Review* 6: 794–808.

Hilbert, Richard. 1991. "Norman and Sigmund: Comment on Denzin's Harold and Agnes." *Sociological Theory* 9: 264–268.

Hochschild, Arlie. 1979. "Emotion Work, Feeling Rules, and Social Structure." *American Journal of Sociology* 85: 551–575.

Hochschild, Arlie. 1983. *The Managed Heart: Commercialization of Human Feeling*. Berkeley: University of California Press.

Hochschild, Arlie. 2003. *The Commercialization of Intimate Life: Notes from Home and Work*. Berkeley: University of California Press.

Hochschild, Arlie, with Anne Machung. 1990. *The Second Shift*. New York: Avon Books.

Hoecker-Drysdale, Susan. 1992. *Harriet Martineau: First Woman Sociologist*. Oxford: Berg

Homans, George Caspar. 1950. *The Human Group*. New York: Harcourt, Brace.

Homans, George Caspar. 1961/1974. *Social Behavior: Its Elementary Forms*. New York: Harcourt Brace Jovanovich.

Homans, George Caspar. 1967. "Fundamental Social Processes." Pp. 27–78 in Neil Smelser, ed. *Sociology: An Introduction*. New York: John Wiley & Sons.

Horkheimer Max, and Theodor Adorno. 1972/2002. *The Dialectic of Enlightenment*. Stanford: Stanford University Press. Edited by Gunzelin Schmid Noerr. Translated by Edmund Jephcott.

Hout, Michael. 1989. *Following in Father's Footsteps: Social Mobility in Ireland*. Cambridge, MA: Harvard University Press.

Huntington, Samuel. 1996. *The Clash of Civilizations and the Remaking of World Order*. New York: Simon and Schuster.

Inkeles, Alex, and David Smith. 1974. *Becoming Modern: Individual Change in Six Developing Countries*. Cambridge, MA: Harvard University Press.

Jacobs, Jerry, and Kathleen Gerson. 2004. *The Time Divide: Work, Family, and Gender Inequality*. Cambridge, MA: Harvard University Press.

Jacobson, Matthew Frye. 2006. *Roots, Too: White Ethnic Revival in Post-Civil Rights America*. Cambridge, MA: Harvard University Press.

Jameson, Fredric. 1991. *Postmodernism or, the Cultural Logic of Late Capitalism*. Durham, NC: Duke University Press.

Jay, Martin. 1973. *The Dialectical Imagination: A History of the Frankfurt School and the Institute of Social Research 1923–1950*. London: Heinemann.

Kanter, Rosabeth Moss. 1977. *Men and Women of the Corporation*. New York: Basic Books.

Karabel, Jerome. 2005. *The Chosen: The Hidden History of Admission and Exclusion at Harvard, Yale, and Princeton*. Boston: Houghton Mifflin.

Kessler, Ronald, Sandro Galea, Russell Jones, and Holly Parker. 2006. "Mental Illness and Suicidality after Hurricane Katrina." *Bulletin of the World Health Organization*. www.who.int/bulletin/volumes/84/10/06-03319.pdf

Kimmel, Michael. 2005. *The Gender of Desire: Essays on Male Sexuality*. Albany, NY: SUNY Press.

Kimmel, Michael. 2007. *Classical Sociological Theory*. New York: Oxford University Press.

Kuhn, Thomas. 1962/1970. *The Structure of Scientific Revolutions*. Chicago: University of Chicago Press. 2nd edition.

Lakoff, Robin. 1990. *Talking Power: The Politics of Language in Our Lives*. New York: Basic Books.

Lamont, Michele. 1992. *Money, Morals, and Manners: The Culture of the French and the American Upper-Middle Class*. Chicago: University of Chicago Press.

Lareau, Annette. 2003. *Unequal Childhoods*. Berkeley: University of California Press.

Lareau, Annette, and Elliot Weininger. 2003. "Cultural Capital in Educational Research: A Critical Assessment." *Theory and Society* 32: 567–606.

Laslett, Barbara, and Barrie Thorne, eds. 1997. *Feminist Sociology: Life Histories of a Movement*. New Brunswick, NJ: Rutgers University Press.

Levitt, Peggy. 2007. *God Needs No Passport*. New York: New Press.

Lidz, Victor. 2000. "Talcott Parsons." Pp. 388–431 in George Ritzer, ed. *The Blackwell Companion to Major Social Theorists*. Malden, MA: Blackwell.

Lindert, Peter, and Jeffrey Williamson. 2003. "Does Globalization Make the World More Unequal?" Pp. 227–271 in Michael Bordo, Alan Taylor, and Jeffrey Williamson, eds. *Globalization in Historical Perspective*. Chicago: University of Chicago Press.

Lipset, Seymour Martin. 1981. "Harriet Martineau's America." Pp. 5–42 in Harriet Martineau. 1837/1981. *Society in America*. New Brunswick, NJ: Transaction Books. Edited, abridged, and with an introduction by Seymour Martin Lipset.

Lorber, Judith, and Lisa Jean Moore, eds. 2006. *Gendered Bodies: Feminist Perspectives*. New York: Oxford University Press.

Luckmann, Thomas. 1978. "Preface." Pp. 7–13 in Thomas Luckmann, ed. *Phenomenology and Sociology*. New York: Penguin.

Luhmann, Niklas. 2002. *Theories of Distinction: Redescribing the Descriptions of Modernity*. Stanford: Stanford University Press.

Lukacs, Georg. 1968. *History and Class Consciousness: Studies in Marxist Dialectics*. Cambridge, MA: MIT Press.

Luker, Kristin. 1984. *Abortion and the Politics of Motherhood*. Berkeley: University of California Press.

Lukes, Steven. 1973. *Emile Durkheim: His Life and Work*. New York: Penguin.

Lyotard, Jean-Francois. 1984. *The Postmodern Condition: A Report on Knowledge*. Minneapolis: University of Minnesota Press.

MacLeod, Jay. 1995. *Ain't No Makin' It: Aspirations and Attainment in a Low-Income Neighborhood*. Boulder, CO: Westview Press.

Malacrida, Claudia, and Jacqueline Low, eds. 2008. *Sociology of the Body: A Reader*. New York: Oxford University Press.

Mannheim, Karl. 1936/1968. *Ideology and Utopia: An Introduction to the Sociology of Knowledge*. New York: Harcourt, Brace, and World.

Marable, Manning. 1986. *W. E. B. Du Bois: Black Radical Democrat*. Boston: Twayne.

Marchand Roland, 1985. *Advertising the American Dream*. Berkeley: University of California Press.

Marcuse, Herbert. 1964. *One-Dimensional Man: Studies in the Ideology of Advanced Industrial Society*. Boston: Beacon Press.

Marsden, Peter. 2005. "The Sociology of James Coleman." *Annual Review of Sociology* 31: 1–24.

Martineau, Harriet. 1837/1981. *Society in America*. New Brunswick, NJ: Transaction Books. Edited, abridged, and with an introduction by Seymour Martin Lipset.

Martineau, Harriet. 1838. *How to Observe Morals and Manners*. London: Charles Knight.

Martineau, Harriet. 1855/1974. *The Positive Philosophy of Auguste Comte*. Freely translated and condensed. New York: AMS Press. New introduction by Abraham Blumberg.

Marx, Karl. 1844/1978. "Alienation and Social Classes." Pp. 133–135 in Robert Tucker, ed. *The Marx–Engels Reader*. New York: Norton. 2nd edition.

Marx, Karl. 1844/1988. *Economic and Philosophical Manuscripts*. Amherst, NY: Prometheus Books.

Marx, Karl. 1847/1978. *Wage Labour and Capital*. Peking: Foreign Language Press.

Marx, Karl. 1858/1973. *Grundrisse. Foundations of the Critique of Political Economy*. New York: Random House.

Marx, Karl. 1859/1978. "Preface to 'A Contribution to the Critique of Political Economy.'" Pp. 3–6 in Robert Tucker, ed. *The Marx–Engels Reader*. New York: Norton. 2nd edition.

Marx, Karl. 1852. "The Eighteenth Brumaire of Napoleon Bonaparte." Pp. 594–617 in Robert Tucker, ed. *The Marx–Engels Reader*. New York: Norton. 2nd edition.

Marx, Karl. 1867/1906. *Capital: A Critique of Political Economy*. New York: Modern Library.

Marx, Karl, and Friedrich Engels. 1846/1947. *The German Ideology*. New York: International Publishers.

Marx, Karl, and Friedrich Engels. 1848/1967. *The Communist Manifesto*. London: Penguin. Introduction by A. J. P. Taylor.

Mauss, Marcel. 1967. *The Gift: Forms and Functions of Exchange in Archaic Societies*. New York: Norton.

McCarthy, Thomas. 1984. "Translator's Introduction." Pp. v–xlii in Jurgen Habermas, *The Theory of Communicative Action*. Volume One. Boston: Beacon Press.

McCarthy, Thomas. 1991. *Ideals and Illusions: On Reconstruction and Deconstruction in Contemporary Critical Theory*. Cambridge, MA: MIT Press.

McClellan, Scott. 2008. *What Happened: Inside the Bush White House and Washington's Culture of Deception*. New York: Public Affairs.

McCloskey, Deirdre. 1999. *Crossing: A Memoir*. Chicago: University of Chicago Press.

McDermott, Monica. 2006. *Working Class White: The Making and Unmaking of Race Relations*. Berkeley: University of California Press.

McGrath, Charles. 2006. "Word Freak." *New York Times Magazine* (November 19).

McLoyd, Vonnie, and Betsy Lozoff. 2001. "Racial and Ethnic Trends in Children's and Adolescents' Behavior and Development." Pp. 311–350 in Neil Smelser, William Julius Wilson, and Faith Mitchell, eds. *America Becoming: Racial Trends and Their Consequences*. Volume II. Washington, DC: National Academy Press.

McLuhan, Marshall. 1967. *The Medium Is the Message*. New York: Bantam Books.

McRobbie, Angela. 1991. *Feminism and Youth Culture: From Jackie to Just Seventeen.* Boston: Unwin Hyman.

McRoberts, Omar. 2003. "Worldly or Otherworldly? 'Activism' in an Urban Religious District." Pp. 412–422 in Michele Dillon, ed. *Handbook of the Sociology of Religion.* New York: Cambridge University Press.

Mead, George Herbert. 1934. *Mind, Self, and Society.* Chicago: University of Chicago Press.

Mennell, Stephen, and Johan Goudsblom. 1998. "Introduction." Pp. 1–45 in Norbert Elias, *On Civilization, Power, and Knowledge: Selected Writings.* Chicago: University of Chicago Press. Edited and with an introduction by Stephen Mennell and Johan Goudsblom.

Merton, Robert K. 1949. *Social Theory and Social Structure: Toward the Codification of Theory and Research.* Glencoe, IL: Free Press.

Merton, Robert K. 1968. *Social Theory and Social Structure.* New York: Free Press. Enlarged edition.

Mills, C. Wright. 1948. *The New Men of Power: America's Labor Leaders.* New York: Harcourt, Brace.

Mills, C. Wright. 1951. *White Collar: The American Middle Classes.* New York: Oxford University Press.

Mills, C. Wright. 1956. *The Power Elite.* New York: Oxford University Press.

Mills, C. Wright. 1959. *The Sociological Imagination.* New York: Oxford University Press.

Moss, Laurence, and Andrew Savchenko. 2006. *Talcott Parsons: Economic Sociologist of the Twentieth Century.* Malden, MA: Blackwell.

Muldoon, Paul. 2006. *Horse Latitudes.* New York: Farrar, Straus, and Giroux.

Myers, Kristin, Cynthia Anderson, and Barbara Risman, eds. 1998. *Feminist Foundations: Toward Transforming Sociology.* Thousand Oaks, CA: Sage.

Naples, Nancy, and Manisha Desai, eds. 2002. *Women's Activism and Globalization: Linking Local Struggles and Transnational Politics.* New York: Routledge.

Nemoianu, Virgil. 2006. "The Church and the Secular Establishment: A Philosophical Dialog between Joseph Ratzinger and Jurgen Habermas." *Logos* 9: 17–42.

Ogbu. John. 2003. *Black American Students in an Affluent Suburb: A Study of American Disengagement.* Mahwah, NJ: Lawrence Erlbaum.

O'Neill, William. 1972. "Introduction to this Edition." Pp. vii–xviii in Charlotte Perkins Gilman. 1903/1972. *The Home: Its Work and Influence.* Urbana, IL: University of Illinois Press.

Oubre, Claude. 1978. *Forty Acres and a Mule: The Freedmen's Bureau and Black Land Ownership.* Baton Rouge, LA: Louisiana State University Press.

Outhwaite, William. 1975. *Understanding Social Life: The Method Called Verstehen.* London: Allen & Unwin.

Outhwaite, William. 2000. "Jurgen Habermas." Pp. 651–669 in George Ritzer, ed. *The Blackwell Companion to Major Social Theorists.* Malden, MA: Blackwell.

Parsons, Talcott. 1937. *The Structure of Social Action*. New York: Free Press.

Parsons, Talcott. 1949/1954. *Essays in Sociological Theory*. Glencoe, IL: Free Press.

Parsons, Talcott. 1951. *The Social System*. Glencoe, IL. Free Press.

Parsons, Talcott. 1967. "Christianity and Modern Industrial Society." Pp. 385–421 in Talcott Parsons. *Sociological Theory and Modern Society*. New York: Free Press.

Parsons, Talcott. 1971. *The System of Modern Societies*. Englewood Cliffs, NJ: Prentice Hall.

Parsons, Talcott, and Robert Bales. 1955. *Family Socialization and Interaction Process*. New York: Free Press.

Patterson, Orlando. 1982. *Slavery and Social Death: A Comparative Study*. Cambridge, MA: Harvard University Press.

Pattillo, Mary. 2005. "Black Middle Class Neighborhoods." *Annual Review of Sociology* 21: 305–329.

Pattillo-McCoy, Mary. 1999. *Black Picket Fences: Privilege and Peril among the Black Middle Class*. Chicago: University of Chicago Press.

Pavlov, Ivan. 1927. *Conditioned Reflexes*. New York: Oxford University Press.

Pence, Ellen, and Michael Paymar. 1993. *Education Groups for Men who Batter: The Duluth Model*. New York: Springer.

Pew Forum on Religion and Public Life. 2006. *Pragmatic Americans Liberal and Conservative in Social Issues*. Washington, DC: Pew Research Center.

Pew Forum on Religion and Public Life. 2008. *The U.S. Religious Landscape Survey: Religious Beliefs*. Washington, DC: Pew Research Center.

Pew Research Center for the People and the Press. 2004. *Voters Liked Campaign 2004, But Too Much "Mud-Slinging."* Washington, DC: Pew Research Center.

Pierce, Jennifer. 1995. *Gender Trials: Emotional Lives in Contemporary Law Firms*. Berkeley: University of California Press.

Polletta, Francesca. 2006. *It Was Like a Fever: Storytelling in Protest and Politics*. Chicago: University of Chicago Press.

Przeworski, Adam. 1985. *Capitalism and Social Democracy*. New York: Cambridge University Press.

Rawls, Anne. 2000. "Harold Garfinkel." Pp. 545–576 in George Ritzer, ed., *The Blackwell Companion to Major Social Theorists*. Malden, MA: Blackwell.

Ray, Raka. 2006. "Is the Revolution Missing or Are We Looking in the Wrong Places?" *Social Problems* 53: 459–465.

Ritzer, George. 2000. *The McDonaldization of Society*. Thousand Oaks, CA: Pine Forge Press.

Robertson, Roland. 1992. *Globalization: Social Theory and Global Culture*. London: Sage.

Robertson, Roland. 2005. "Globalization: Sociology and Cross-Disciplinarity." Pp. 345–366 in Craig Calhoun, Chris Rojek, and Bryan Turner, eds. *The Sage Handbook of Sociology*. Thousand Oaks, CA: Sage.

Rocher, Guy. 1974. *Talcott Parsons and American Sociology*. London: Nelson.

Roediger, David. 1991. *The Wages of Whiteness: Race and the Making of the American Working Class*. London: Verso.

Roediger, David. 2002. *Colored White: Transcending the Racial Past*. Berkeley: University of California Press.

Roediger, David. 2005. *Working Toward Whiteness: How America's Immigrants Became White: The Strange Journey from Ellis Island to the Suburbs*. New York: Basic Books.

Roemer, John. 1982. "New Directions in the Marxian Theory of Exploitation and Class." *Politics and Society* 11: 253–287.

Roemer, John. 1994. "Introduction." Pp. ix–xvi in John Roemer, ed. *Foundations of Analytical Marxism*. Volume 1. Brookfield, VT: Edward Elgar.

Romero, Mary. 1992. *Maid in the U.S.A.* New York: Routledge.

Rosenau, James. 2003. *Distant Proximities: Dynamics beyond Globalization*. Princeton: Princeton University Press.

Rosenau, Pauline. 1992. *Post-Modernism and the Social Sciences: Insights, Inroads, and Intrusions*. Princeton: Princeton University Press.

Roth, Louise Marie. 2006. *Selling Women Short: Gender and Money on Wall Street*. Princeton: Princeton University Press.

Ryan, Alan. 1993. "Foucault's Life and Hard Times." *New York Review of Books* (April 8): 12–17.

Sachs, Jeffrey. 2005. *The End of Poverty: Economic Possibilities for our Times*. New York: Penguin.

Said, Edward. 1978. *Orientalism*. New York: Random House.

Saint-Simon, Henri. 1807–1813/1975. *Selected Writings on Science, Industry and Social Organisation*. London: Croom Helm. Translated and edited by Keith Taylor.

Sassen, Saskia. 1991. *The Global City*. Princeton: Princeton University Press.

Sassen, Saskia. 2007. *A Sociology of Globalization*. New York: Norton.

Schraepler, Hans-Albrecht. 1997. *Directory of International Economic Organizations*. Washington, DC: Georgetown University Press.

Schubert, Hans-Joachim. 1998. "Introduction." Pp. 1–31 in Charles Horton Cooley. 1902/1998. *On Self and Social Organization*. Chicago: University of Chicago Press. Edited and with an introduction by Hans-Joachim Schubert.

Schudson, Michael. 1984. *Advertising: The Uneasy Persuasion*. Berkeley: University of California Press.

Schutz, Alfred. 1962. *Collected Papers*. The Hague: M. Nijhoff. Edited and with an introduction by Maurice Natanson.

Schutz, Alfred. 1970. *On Phenomenology and Social Relations: Selected Writings*. Chicago: University of Chicago Press. Edited and with an introduction by Helmut Wagner.

Seidman, Steven, ed. 1996. *Queer Theory/Sociology*. Malden, MA: Blackwell.

Seidman, Steven. 1997. *Difference Troubles: Queering Social Theory and Sexual Politics*. New York: Cambridge University Press.

Seidman, Steven. 2004. "Are We All in the Closet? Notes Toward a Sociological and Cultural Turn in Queer Theory." Pp. 255–269 in Roger Friedland and

John Mohr, eds. *Matters of Culture*. New York: Cambridge University Press.

Shalin, Dmitri. 2000. "George Herbert Mead." Pp. 302–344 in George Ritzer, ed. *The Blackwell Companion to Major Social Theorists*. Malden, MA: Blackwell.

Sherman, Rachel. 2007. *Class Acts: Service and Inequality in Luxury Hotels*. Berkeley: University of California Press.

Simmel, Georg. 1903, 1908, 1917/1950. *The Sociology of Georg Simmel*. Glencoe, IL: Free Press. Translated, edited, and with an introduction by Kurt Wolff.

Simmel, Georg. 1904, 1907, 1921/1971. *On Individuality and Social Forms*. Chicago: University of Chicago Press. Edited and with an introduction by Donald Levine.

Skinner, B. F. 1938. *The Behavior of Organisms*. New York: Appleton Century.

Sklair, Leslie. 2002. *Globalization: Capitalism and its Alternatives*. Oxford: Oxford University Press.

Smelser, Neil. 1959. *Social Change in the Industrial Revolution*. Chicago: University of Chicago Press.

Smelser, Neil. 1962. *Theory of Collective Behavior*. Glencoe, IL: Free Press.

Smelser, Neil. 1968. *Essays in Sociological Explanation*. Englewood Cliffs, NJ: Prentice Hall.

Smelser, Neil, and Richard Swedberg, eds. 2005. *The Handbook of Economic Sociology*. New York: Russell Sage Foundation.

Smith, Adam. 1759/1976. *The Theory of Moral Sentiments*. Indianapolis, IN: Liberty Classics. Introduction by E. G. West.

Smith, Adam. 1776/1925. *An Inquiry into the Nature and Causes of the Wealth of Nations*. London: Methuen. 4th edition. Edited and with an introduction by Edwin Cannan.

Smith, Dorothy. 1987. *The Everyday World as Problematic: A Feminist Sociology*. Boston: Northeastern University Press.

Smith, Dorothy. 1990a. *The Conceptual Practices of Power: A Feminist Sociology of Knowledge*. Boston: Northeastern University Press.

Smith, Dorothy. 1990b. *Texts, Facts, and Femininity: Exploring the Relations of Ruling*. New York: Routledge.

Smith, Dorothy. 2005. *Institutional Ethnography: A Sociology for People*. Lanham, MD: AltaMira/Rowman & Littlefield.

Snow, David, and Leon Anderson. 1993. *Down on their Luck: A Study of Homeless Street People*. Berkeley: University of California Press.

Starr, Paul. 1982. *The Social Transformation of American Medicine*. New York: Basic Books.

Stein, Arlene. 1997. *Sex and Sensibility: Stories of a Lesbian Generation*. Berkeley: University of California Press.

Stein, Arlene, and Kenneth Plummer. 1996. "'I Can't Even Think Straight': Queer Theory and the Missing Sexual Revolution in Sociology." Pp. 129–144 in Steven Seidman, ed. *Queer Theory/Sociology*. Cambridge, MA: Blackwell.

Stets, Jan, and Jonathan Turner. 2006. *Handbook of the Sociology of Emotions*. New York: Springer.

Swidler, Ann. 2001. *Talk of Love: How Culture Matters*. Chicago: University of Chicago Press.

Tallichet, Suzanne. 2006. *Daughters of the Mountains: Women Coal Miners in Central Appalachia*. University Park, PA: Pennsylvania State University Press.

Taylor, Dianna, and Karen Vintges, eds. 2004. *Feminism and the Final Foucault*. Urbana: University of Illinois Press.

Taylor, Frederick. 1911. *The Principles of Scientific Management*. New York: Harper.

Taylor, Keith, ed. 1975. *Henri Saint-Simon: Selected Writings on Science, Industry and Social Organisation*. London: Croom Helm.

Thomas, William I. 1923. *The Unadjusted Girl*. Boston: Little, Brown.

Thompson, John. 1981. "Editor's Introduction." Pp. 1–26 in Paul Ricoeur, *Hermeneutics and the Human Sciences*. Cambridge: Cambridge University Press. Edited and translated by John Thompson.

Tucker, Robert, ed. (1978) *The Marx–Engels Reader*. New York: Norton. 2nd edition.

Tunstall, Jeremy. 1977. *The Media are American*. New York: Columbia University Press.

Turner, Bryan S. 1996. *The Body and Society*. London: Sage. 2nd edition.

Turner, Bryan S. 2009. "The Sociology of the Body." Pp. 513–532 in Bryan Turner, ed. *The New Blackwell Companion to Social Theory*. Malden, MA: Blackwell.

Van Gundy, Karen. 2006. *Substance Abuse in Rural and Small Town America*. University of New Hampshire, Durham: Carsey Institute.

Voss, Kim, and Rachel Sherman. 2000. "Breaking the Iron Law of Oligarchy: Tactical Innovation and the Revitalization of the American Labor Movement." *American Journal of Sociology* 106: 303–349.

Wacquant, Loic. 2004. *Body and Soul: Notebooks of an Apprentice Boxer*. New York: Oxford University Press.

Wallace, Ruth. 1989. "Introduction." Pp. 7–19 in Ruth Wallace, ed. *Feminism and Sociological Theory*. Newbury Park, CA: Sage.

Wallerstein, Immanuel. 1974. *The Modern World-System I: Capitalist Agriculture and the Origins of the European World-Economy in the Sixteenth Century*. New York: Academic Press.

Wallerstein, Immanuel. 1980. *The Modern World-System II: Mercantilism and the Consolidation of the European World-Economy, 1600–1750*. New York: Academic Press.

Wallerstein, Immanuel. 1989. *The Modern World-System III: The Second Era of Great Expansion of the Capitalist World-Economy, 1730–1840s*. New York: Academic Press.

Wallerstein, Immanuel. 1996. "World System Versus World-Systems: A Critique." Pp. 292–296 in Andre Gunder Frank and Barry Gills, eds. *The World System: Five Hundred Years or Five Thousand?* New York: Routledge.

Wallerstein, Immanuel. 2004. *World-Systems Analysis: An Introduction*. Durham, NC: Duke University Press.

Watson, John B. 1930. *Behaviorism*. Chicago: University of Chicago Press.

Weber, Marianne. 1926/1975. *Max Weber: A Biography*. New York: John Wiley & Sons. Translated and edited by Harry Zohn.

Weber, Max. 1904–1905/1958. *The Protestant Ethic and the Spirit of Capitalism*. New York: Scribner's and Sons. Translated by Talcott Parsons. Introduction by Anthony Giddens [1976].

Weber, Max. 1946. *From Max Weber: Essays in Sociology*. New York: Oxford University Press. Translated, edited, and with an introduction by H. H. Gerth and C. Wright Mills.

Weber, Max. 1949. *The Methodology of the Social Sciences*. New York: Free Press. Translated and edited by Edward A. Shils and Henry A. Finch.

Weber, Max. 1978. *Economy and Society*. Volume One. Berkeley: University of California Press. Edited by Guenther Roth and Claus Wittich.

Weeden, Kim, and David Grusky. 2005. "The Case for a New Class Map." *American Journal of Sociology* 111: 141–212.

Weitz, Rose, ed. 1998. *The Politics of Women's Bodies: Sexuality, Appearance, and Behavior*. New York: Oxford University Press.

West, Candace. 1984. *Routine Complications: Trouble with Talk between Doctors and Patients*. Bloomington, IN: Indiana University Press.

West, Candace, and Don Zimmerman. 1983. "Small Insults: A Study of Interruptions in Conversations Between Unacquainted Persons." Pp. 102–117 in Barrie Thorne, C. Kramarae, and N. Nelney, eds. *Language, Gender and Society*. Rowley, MA: Newbury House.

West, Candace, and Don Zimmerman. 1987. "Doing Gender." *Gender and Society* 2: 125–151.

West, Cornel. 1993. *Race Matters*. Boston: Beacon Press.

Williams, Christine. 1993a. *Doing "Women's Work": Men in Nontraditional Occupations*. Newbury Park, CA: Sage.

Williams, Christine. 1993b. "Psychoanalytic Theory and the Sociology of Gender." Pp. 131–149 in Paula England, ed. *Theory on Gender, Feminism on Theory*. New York: Aldine de Gruyter.

Williams, Richard. 1990. *Hierarchical Structures and Social Value: The Creation of Black and Irish Identities in the United States*. New York: Cambridge University Press.

Willis, Paul. 1977. *Learning to Labour: How Working Class Kids Get Working Class Jobs*. Farnborough: Saxon House.

Wilson, William Julius. 1978. *The Declining Significance of Race*. Chicago: University of Chicago Press.

Winant, Howard. 2001. *The World is a Ghetto: Race and Democracy Since World War II*. New York: Basic Books.

Wright, Erik Olin. 1984. "A General Framework for the Analysis of Class Structure." *Politics and Society* 13: 383–424.

Wright, Erik Olin. 1997. *Class Counts: Comparative Studies in Class Analysis.* New York: Cambridge University Press.

Young, Iris Marion. 1990. *Justice and the Politics of Difference.* Princeton: Princeton University Press.

Zaloom, Caitlin. 2006. *Out of the Pits: Traders and Technology from Chicago to London.* Chicago: University of Illinois Press.

INDEX

SECOND EDITION

The Landscape of Qualitative Research

INTERNATIONAL ADVISORY BOARD

SECOND EDITION

The Landscape of Qualitative Research

Theories and Issues

editors

NORMAN K. DENZIN
University of Illinois at Urbana-Champaign

YVONNA S. LINCOLN
Texas A&M University

SAGE Publications
International Educational and Professional Publisher
Thousand Oaks ■ London ■ New Delhi

For information:

Sage Publications, Inc.
2455 Teller Road
Thousand Oaks, California 91320
E-mail: order@sagepub.com

Sage Publications Ltd.
6 Bonhill Street
London EC2A 4PU
United Kingdom

Sage Publications India Pvt. Ltd.
B-42 Panchsheel Enclave
Post Box 4109
New Delhi 110-017 India

Printed in the United States of America

Library of Congress Cataloging-in-Publication Data

The landscape of qualitative research: Theories and issues / Norman K. Denzin, Yvonna S. Lincoln, editors.— 2nd ed.
    p. cm.
Includes bibliographical references and index.
ISBN 0-7619-2694-1 (Pbk.)
1. Social sciences-Research. 2. Qualitative research. 3. Qualitative reasoning. I. Denzin, Norman K. II. Lincoln, Yvonna S.
H62.L274 2003
300'.7'2—dc21   2002156651

Printed on acid-free paper

03 04 05 06 07 08 09 10 9 8 7 6 5 4 3 2 1

Acquiring Editor:	Margaret H. Seawell
Production Editor:	Claudia A. Hoffman
Typesetter:	Christina Hill
Indexer:	Molly Hall
Cover Designer:	Michelle Lee and Ravi Balasuriya
Cover Photograph:	C. A. Hoffman